Revit Architecture 2014 Basics: From the Ground Up

Elise Moss

ISBN: 978-1-58503-812-1

Publications

SDC Publications
P.O. Box 1334
Mission KS 66222
(913) 262-2664
www.**SDCpublications**.com

Publisher: Stephen Schroff

Printed in the United States of America

Class Files

To download the files that are required for this book, type the following in the address bar of your web browser:

SDCpublications.com/downloads/978-1-58503-812-1

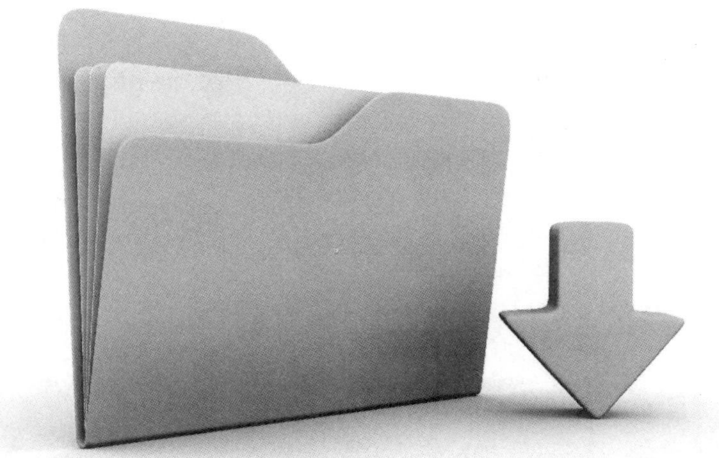

Preface

Revit is a parametric 3D modeling software, used primarily for architectural work. Traditionally, architects have been very happy working in 2D, first on paper, and then in 2D CAD, usually in AutoCAD.

The advantages of working in 3D are not initially apparent to most architectural users. The benefits come when you start creating your documentation and you realize that your views are automatically defined for you with your 3D model. Your schedules and views automatically update when you change features. You can explore your conceptual designs faster and in more depth.

As more architects see and grasp the advantages of creating their building models in 3D, Revit will gain more loyal users.

Revit will not make you a better architect. However, it will allow you to communicate your ideas and designs faster, easier, and more beautifully.

The book is geared towards users who have no experience in 3D modeling and very little or no experience with AutoCAD. Some experience with a computer and using the Internet is assumed.

I have endeavored to make this text as easy to understand and as error-free as possible…however, errors may be present. Please feel free to email me if you have any problems with any of the exercises or questions about Revit in general.

Acknowledgements

A special thanks to James Cowan, Tobias Hathorn, Rick Rundell, Christie Landry, and Steve Burri, Autodesk employees who are tasked with supporting and promoting Revit. Additional thanks to Carl Bass for his support and encouragement.

Additional thanks to Scott Davis, James Balding, Rob Starz, and all the other Revit users out there who provided me with valuable insights into the way they use Revit.

Thanks to Stephen Schroff and Mary Schmidt, who work tirelessly to bring these manuscripts to you, the user, and provide the important moral support authors need.

My eternal gratitude to my life partner, Ari, my biggest cheerleader throughout our years together.

Elise Moss
Elise_moss@mossdesigns.com

TABLE OF CONTENTS

Lesson 3

Floor Plans

Lesson 1
The Revit Interface

When you install Revit, you can select which templates are installed with the software.

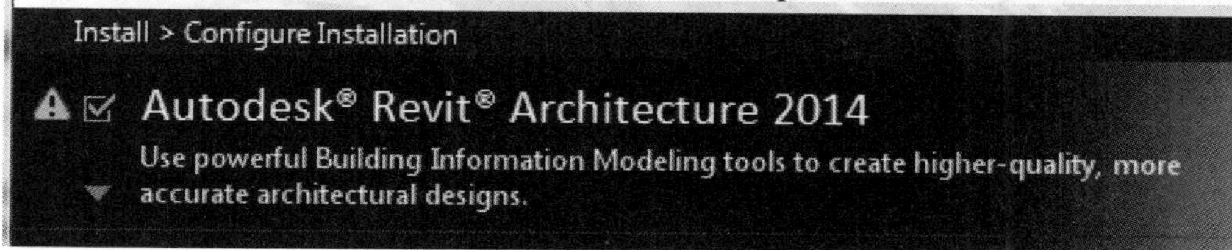

Select the down arrow beneath the software name.

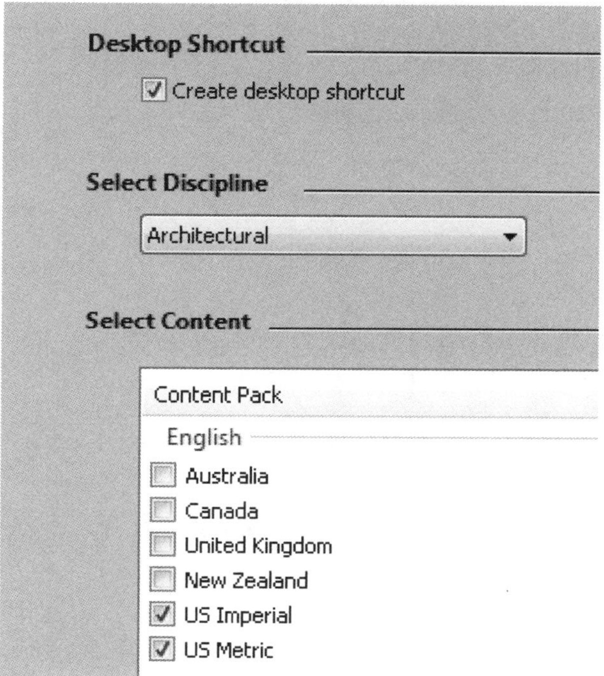

Select the default discipline you will be working in. This will set your default template. Place a check mark next to the templates you would like installed with the software. Use the scroll bar to select which content packs you want to have installed. Select the up arrow to return to the installation, then press Install.

Revit can be started from your Start menu or the desktop icon.

Go to Start→Programs→Autodesk →Revit Architecture 2014→Revit Architecture 2014.
You can also type Revit in the search field under Programs and it will be listed.

When you first start Revit, you will see this screen.

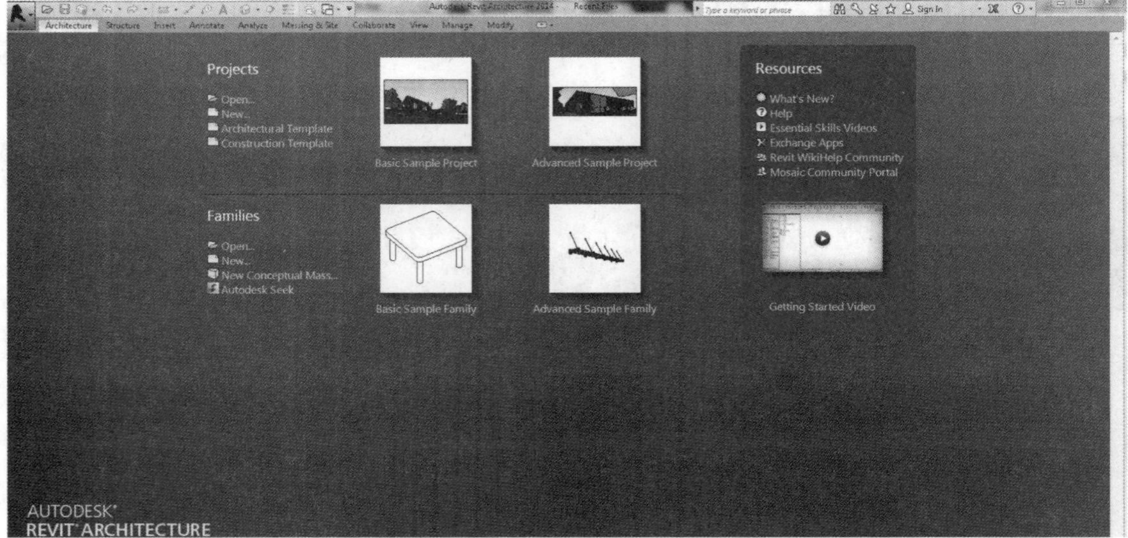

It is divided into three sections:

The top section is to Open or Start a new project. Revit calls the 3D building model a project. Some students find this confusing.

The second section is used to open, create, or manage Revit families. Revit buildings are created using Revit families. Doors, windows, walls, floors, etc., are all families.

The third section, Resources, contains help, tutorials, and videos to help new users learn how to work in Revit.

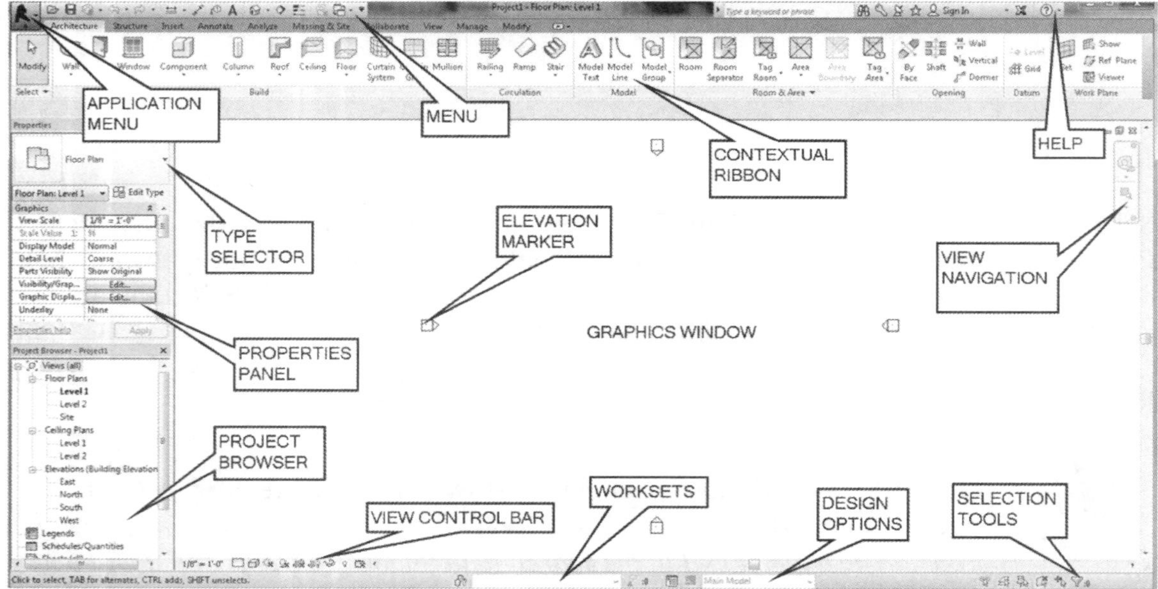

The Revit Ribbon

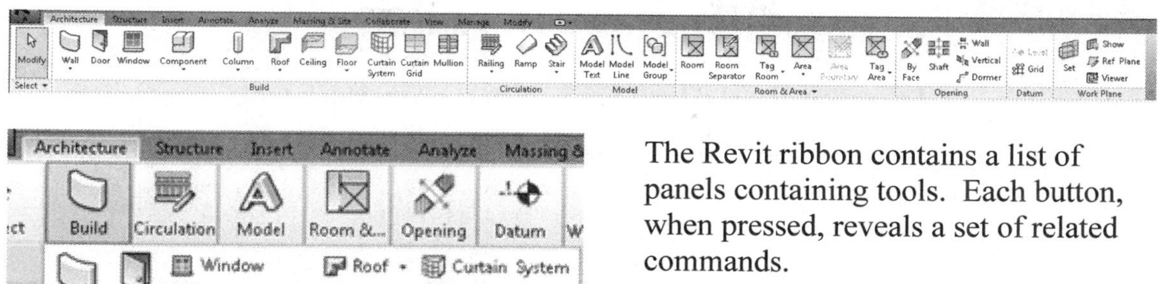

The Revit ribbon contains a list of panels containing tools. Each button, when pressed, reveals a set of related commands.

The Quick Access Toolbar (QAT)

Most Windows users are familiar with the standard tools: New, Open, Save, Undo, and Redo.

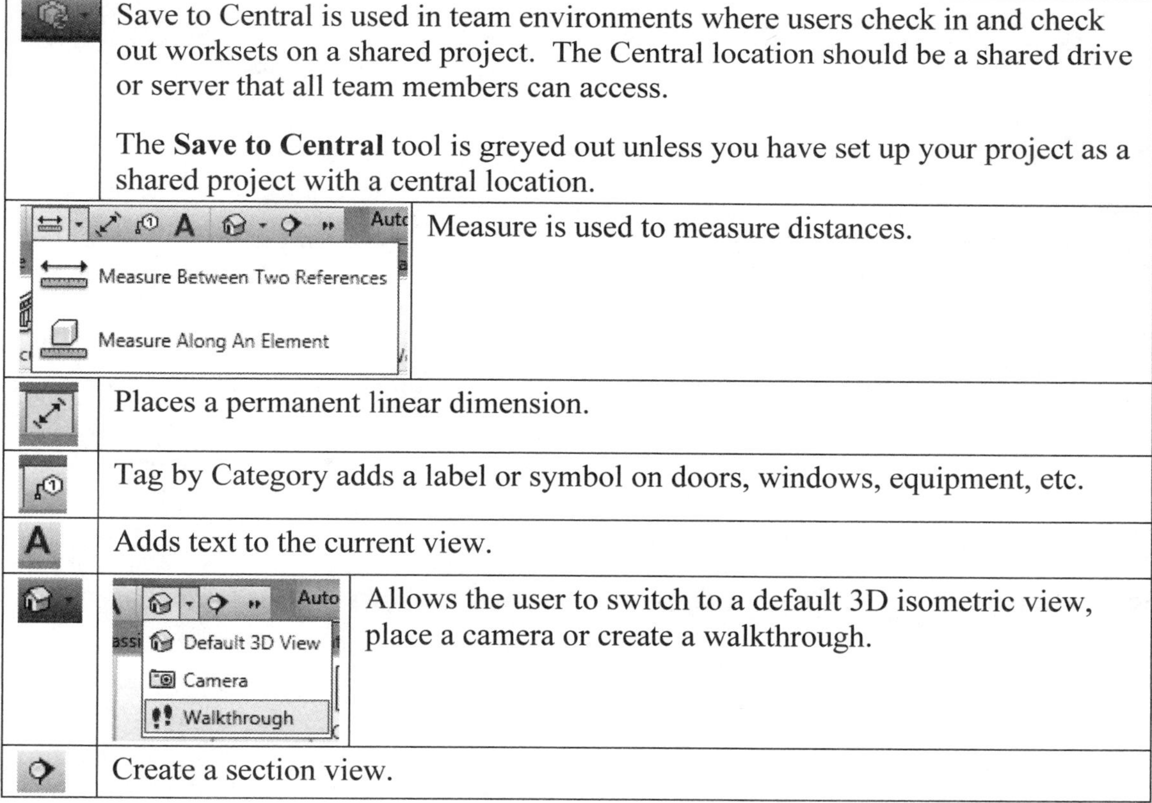

	Save to Central is used in team environments where users check in and check out worksets on a shared project. The Central location should be a shared drive or server that all team members can access. The **Save to Central** tool is greyed out unless you have set up your project as a shared project with a central location.
Measure Between Two References Measure Along An Element	Measure is used to measure distances.
	Places a permanent linear dimension.
	Tag by Category adds a label or symbol on doors, windows, equipment, etc.
	Adds text to the current view.
Default 3D View Camera Walkthrough	Allows the user to switch to a default 3D isometric view, place a camera or create a walkthrough.
	Create a section view.

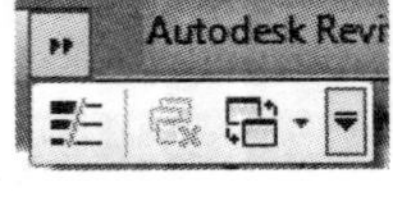	Additional tools are available on the flyout section. The first tool allows users to set lineweight. The second tool closes non-active windows. The third tool allows the user to select/switch to a different window. The down arrow allows users to customize which tools appear on the Quick Access toolbar.

Printing

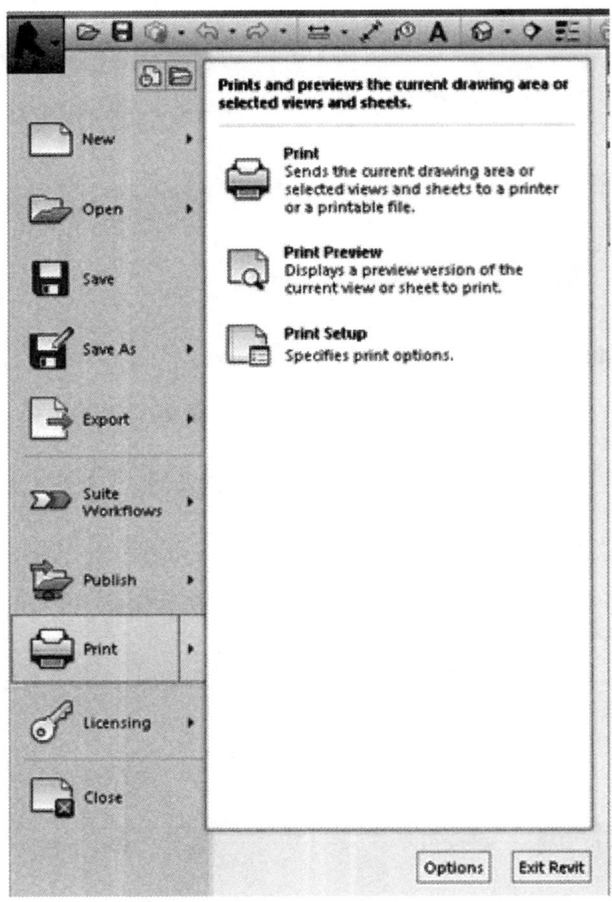

Print is located in the Application Menu.

The Print dialog is fairly straightforward.

Select the desired printer from the drop-down list, which shows installed printers.

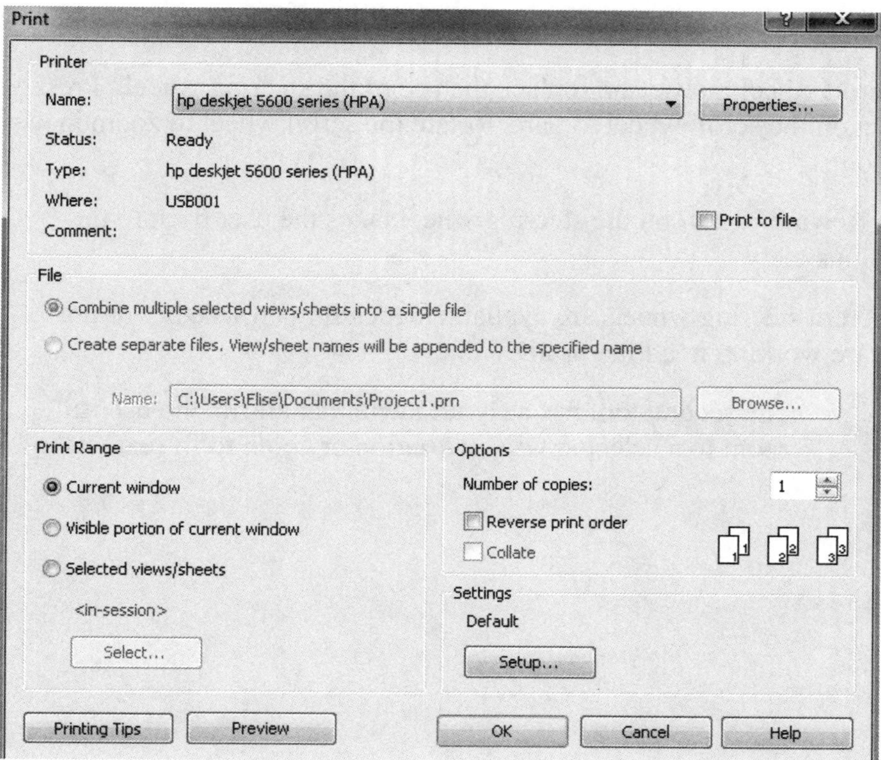

You can set to 'Print to File' by enabling the check box next to Print to File.

The Print Range area of the dialog allows you to print the current window, a zoomed in portion of the window, and selected views/ sheets.

Undo

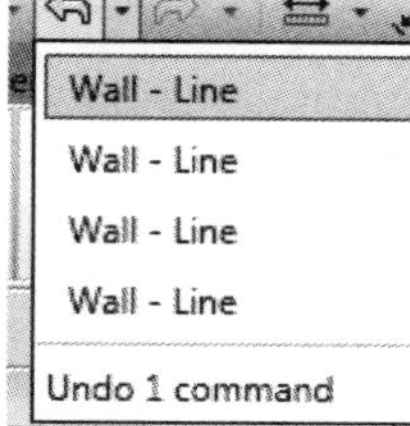

The Undo tool allows the user to select multiple actions to undo. To do this, use the drop down arrow next to the Undo button, you can select which recent action you want to undo. You cannot skip over actions (for example, you can't undo 'Note' without undoing the two walls on top of it.)

Ctl-Z also acts as UNDO.

Redo

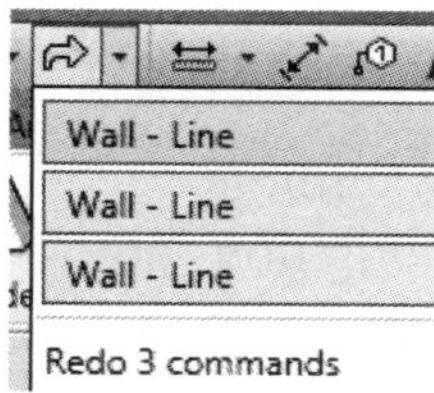

The Redo button also gives you a list of actions, which have recently been undone. Redo is only available immediately after an UNDO. For example, if you perform UNDO, then WALL, REDO will not be active.

Ctl-Y is the shortcut for REDO.

Viewing Tools

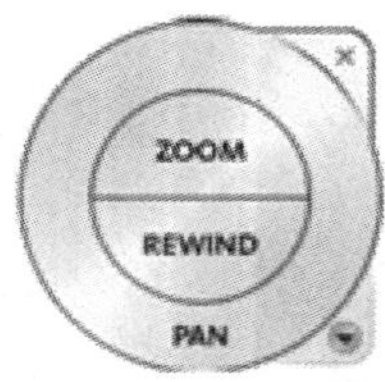

A scroll wheel mouse can replace the use of the steering wheel. Press down on the scroll wheel to pan. Rotate the scroll wheel to zoom in and out.

The Rewind button on the steering wheel takes the user back to the previous view.

Different steering wheels are available depending on whether or not you are working in a Plan or 3D view.

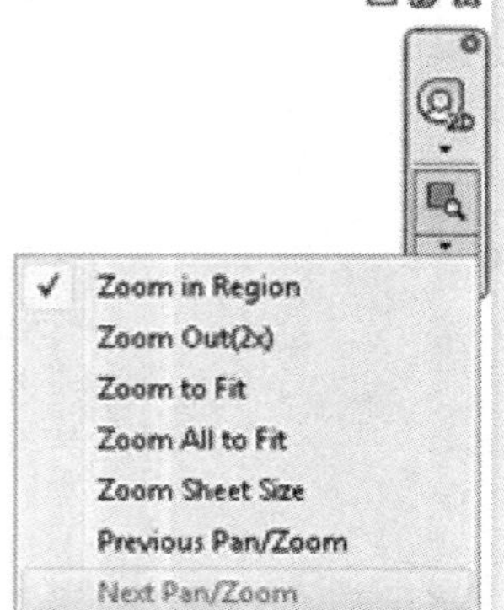

The second tool has a flyout menu that allows the user to zoom to a selected window/region or zoom to fit (extents).

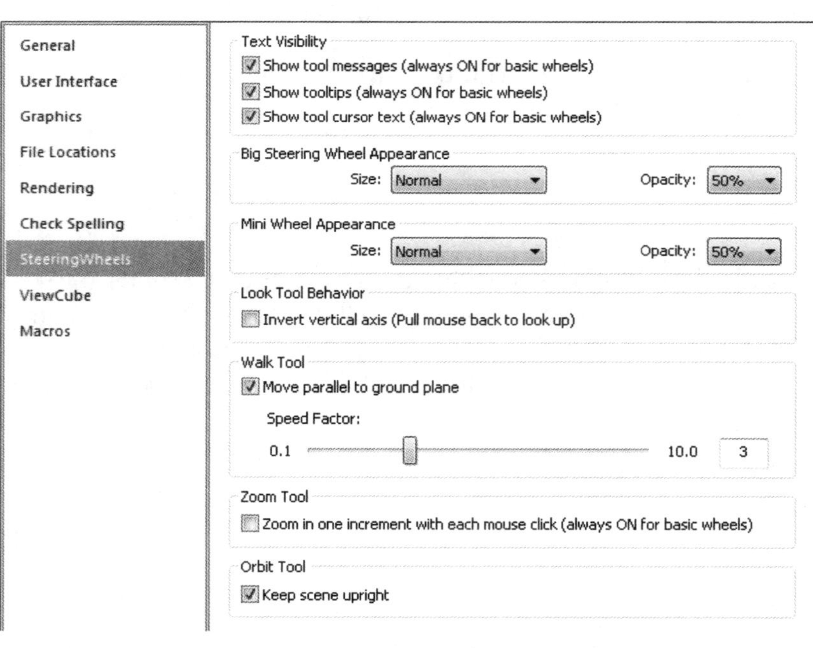

You can control the appearance of the steering wheels by right clicking on the steering wheel and selecting Options.

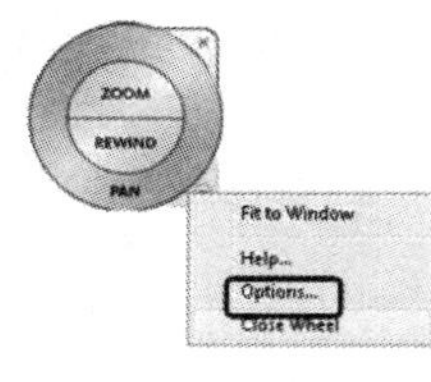

Orient to a view allows one to render an elevation straight on without perspective. Orient to a plane allows user to create sweeps along non-orthogonal paths.

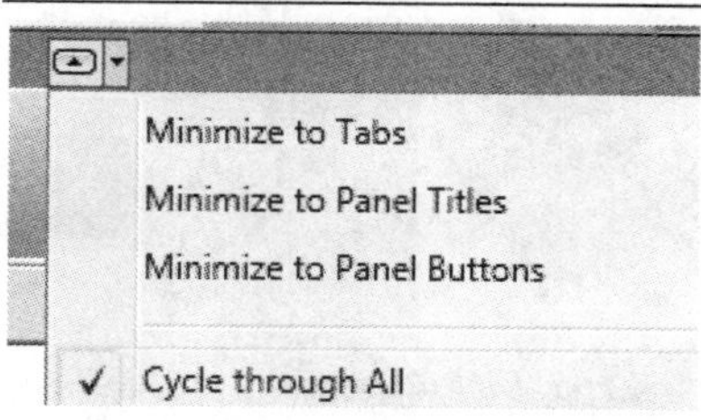

➢ If you right click on the Revit Ribbon, you can minimize the ribbon to gain a larger display window.

Exercise 1-1:

Using the Steering Wheel & ViewCube

Drawing Name: *basic_project.rvt*
Estimated Time: 30 minutes

This exercise reinforces the following skills:

- ViewCube
- 2D Steering Wheel
- 3D Steering Wheel
- Project Browser
- Shortcut Menus
- Mouse

1.

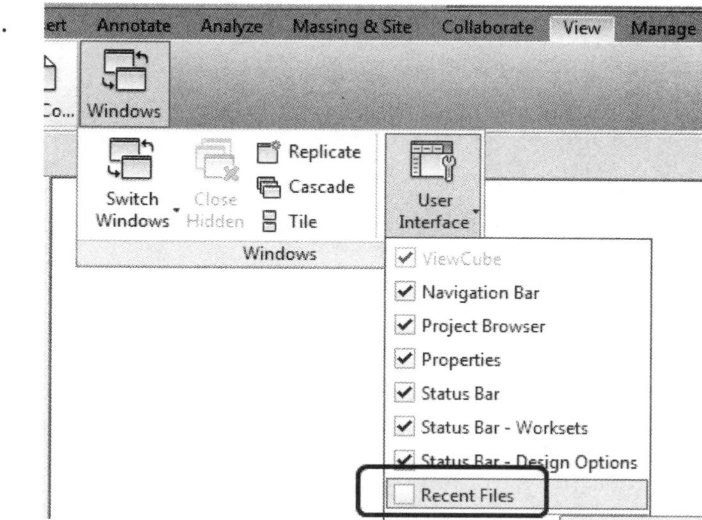

Go the View tab on the ribbon.

Select **Windows→User Interface→Recent Files**.

2. The Recent Files screen launches.

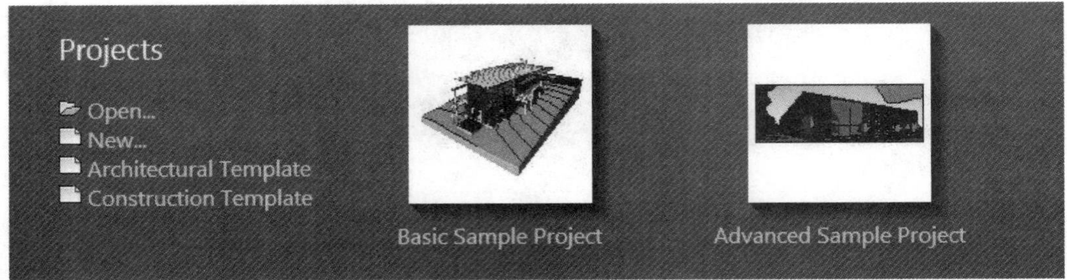

3. Select the Basic Sample Project file. The file name is *rac_basic_sample_project.rvt*.

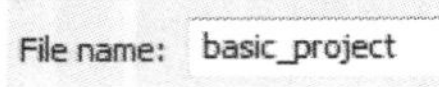

If you do not see the Basic Sample Project listed, you can use the file basic_project located on the publisher's website.

4. In the Project Browser:

   Expand the 3D Views.

   Double left click on the {3D} view.

   This activates the view.

   The active view is already in BOLD.

5. If you have a mouse with a scroll wheel:
   Experiment with the following motions.

   If you roll the wheel up and down, you can zoom in and out.

   Hold down the SHIFT key and press down the scroll wheel at the same time. This will rotate or orbit the model.

   Press down the scroll wheel. This will pan the model.

6. When you are in a 3D view, a tool called the ViewCube is visible in the upper right corner of the screen.

7. 

   Click on the top of the cube as shown.

8. 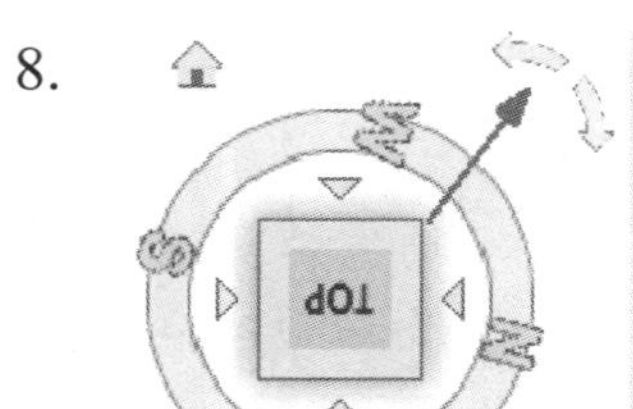

   The display changes to a plan view.

   Use the rotate arrows to rotate the view.

9. 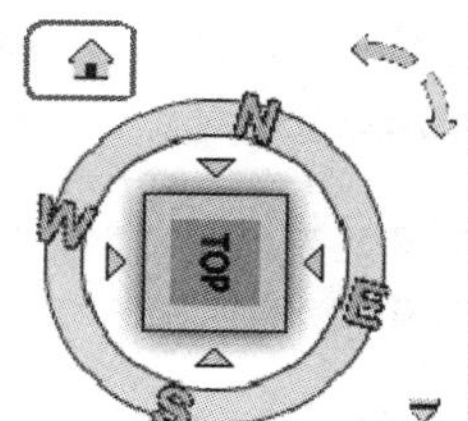

Click on the little house (home tool) to return to the default view.

10. 

Select the Steering Wheel tool located on the View toolbar.

11. A steering wheel pops up.

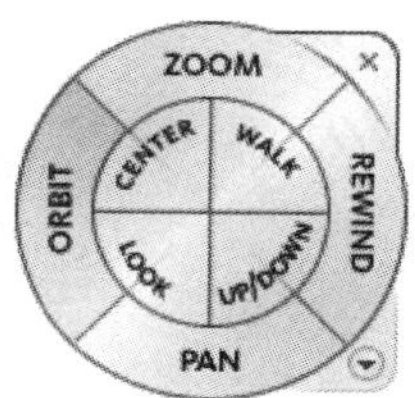

Notice that as you mouse over sections of the steering wheel they highlight.

Mouse over the Zoom section and hold down the left mouse button. The display should zoom in and out.

Mouse over the Orbit section and hold down the left mouse button. The display should orbit.

Mouse over the Pan section and hold down the left mouse button. The display should pan.

12. 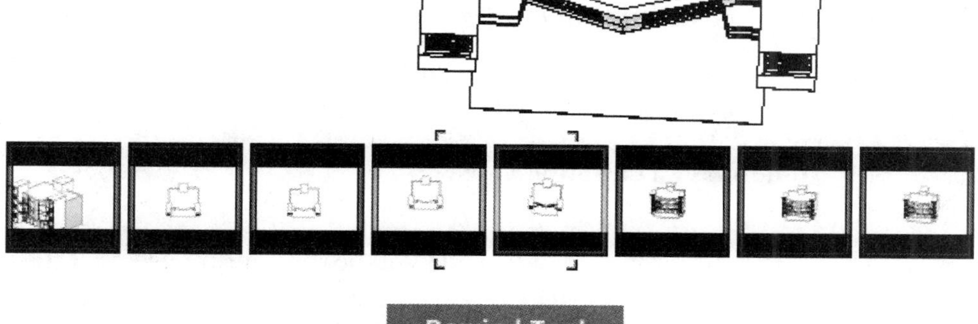

Select the Rewind tool.
A selection of previous views is displayed.
You no longer have to back through previous views. You can skip to the previous view you want.
Select a previous view to activate.

13. 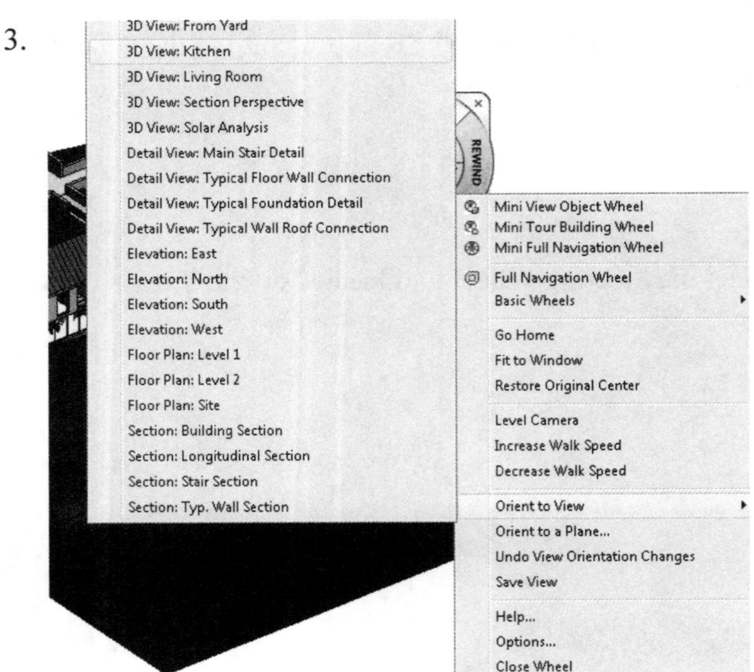

Place the mouse cursor over the steering wheel.

Right click and a shortcut menu appears.

Select **Orient to View→ 3D View: Kitchen**.

14. 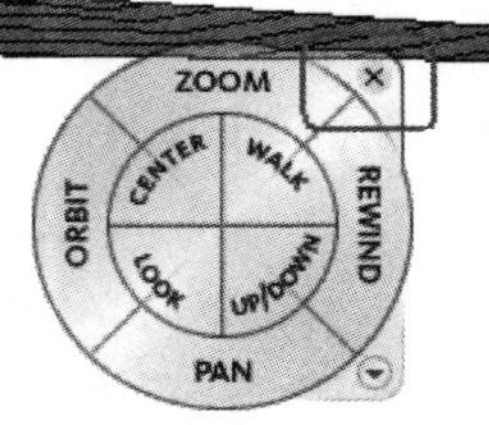

Click on the **x** to close the steering wheel.

15. 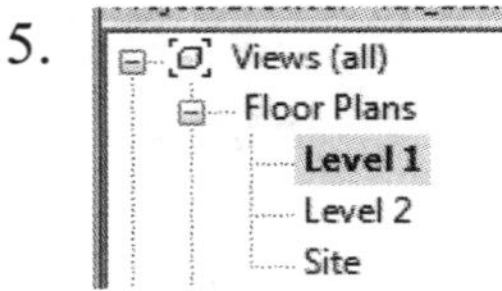

Double click on **Level 1** in the Project Browser.

This will open the Level 1 floor plan view.

Be careful not to select the ceiling plan instead of the floor plan.

16. 

This is an elevation marker.

It defines an elevation view.

17. 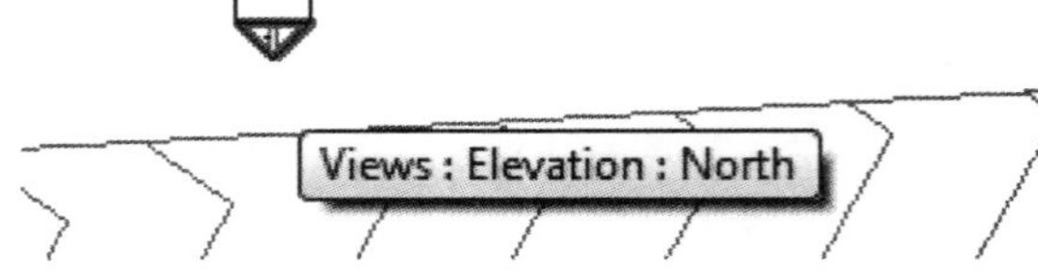

If you hover your mouse over the triangle, you will see the name of the associated elevation view.

18. 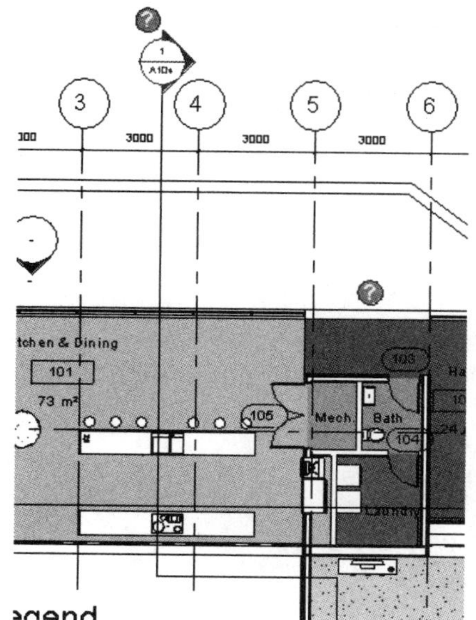

Locate the section line on Level 1 labeled A104.

Double left click on the arrow portion of the section line.

19. This view has a callout.

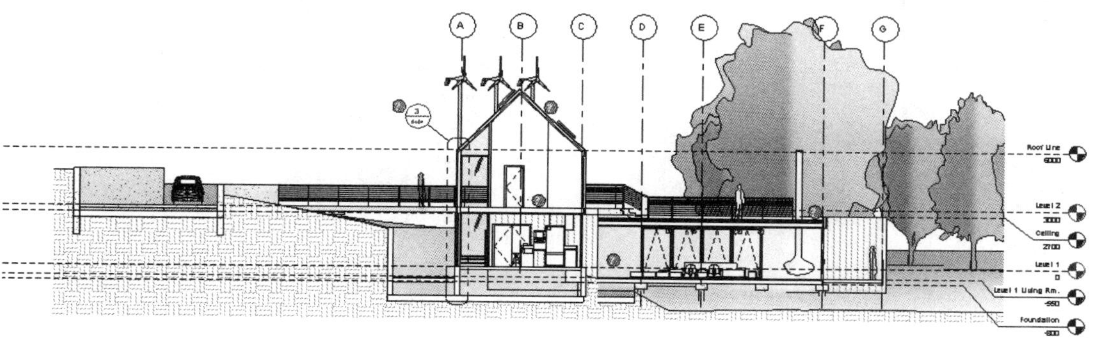

Double left click on the callout bubble.

The bubble is located on the left.

20. The callout view has three more callouts.

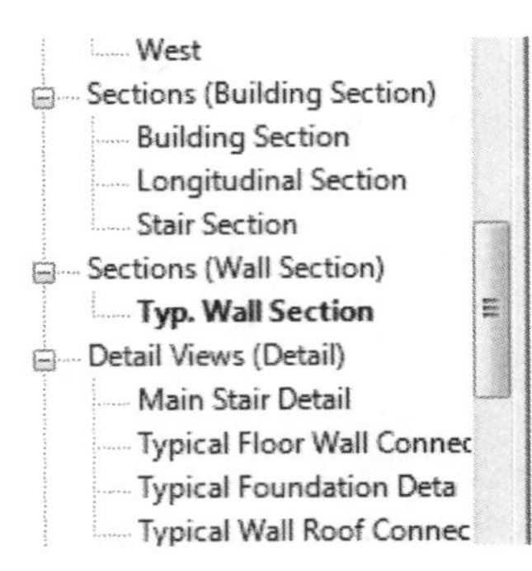

Scroll down the Project Browser.

Can you identify the name of the active view?

Hint: The active view is always bold.

21.

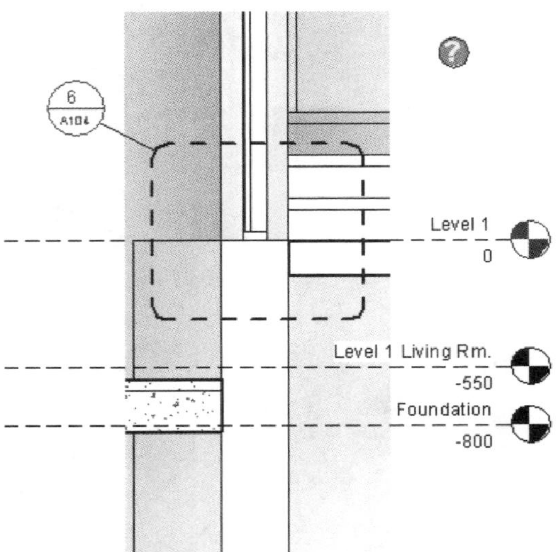

To the right of the view, there are levels.

Some of the levels are blue and some of them are black.

The blue levels are story levels - they have views associated with them.

The black levels are reference levels - they do not have views associated with them.

Double left click on the Level 1 bubble.

22. The Level 1 floor plan is opened.

Level 1 is also in BOLD in the project browser.

23.

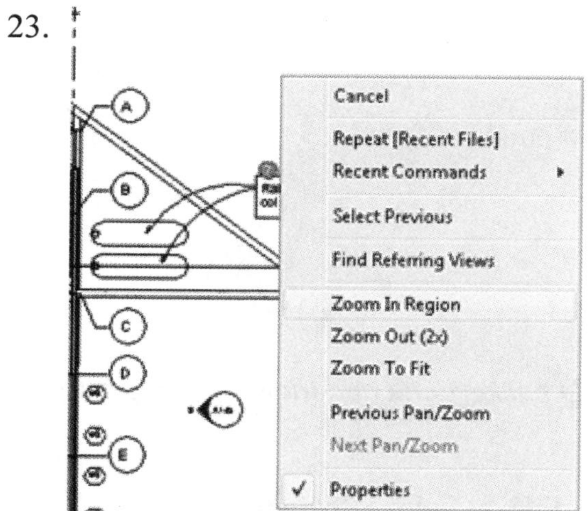

Right click in the window.

On the shortcut menu:
Select **Zoom In Region**.

This is the same as the Zoom Window tool in AutoCAD.

24.

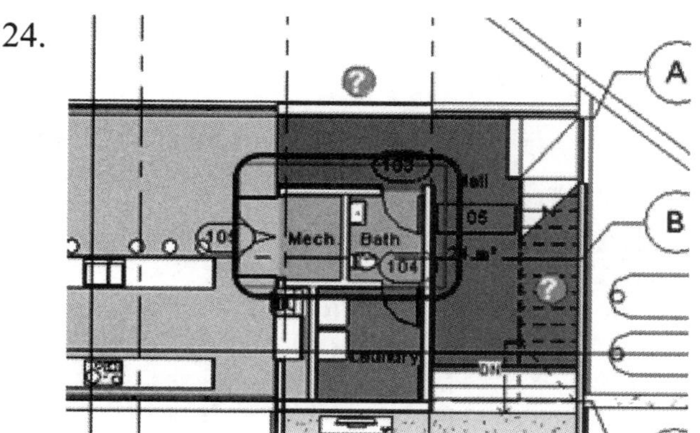

Place a rectangle with your mouse to zoom into the bathroom area.

25. 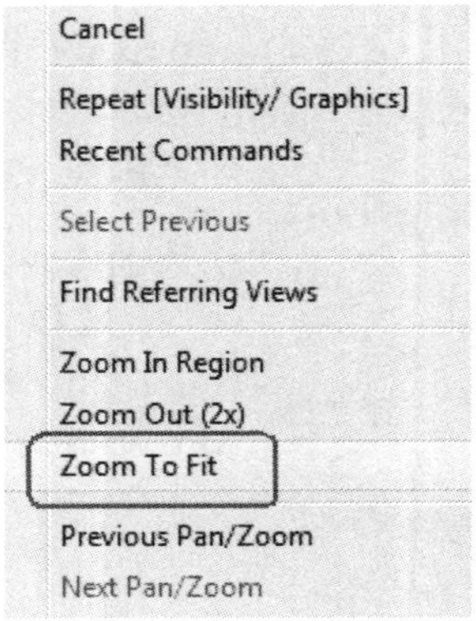 Right click in the window.

On the shortcut menu:
Select **Zoom To Fit**.

This is the same as the Zoom Extents tool in AutoCAD.

26. Close the file without saving.

Exercise 1-2:
Changing the View Background

Drawing Name: *basic_project.rvt*
Estimated Time: 5 minutes

This exercise reinforces the following skills:

- Graphics mode
- Options

Many of my students come from an AutoCAD background and they want to change their background display to black.

1. 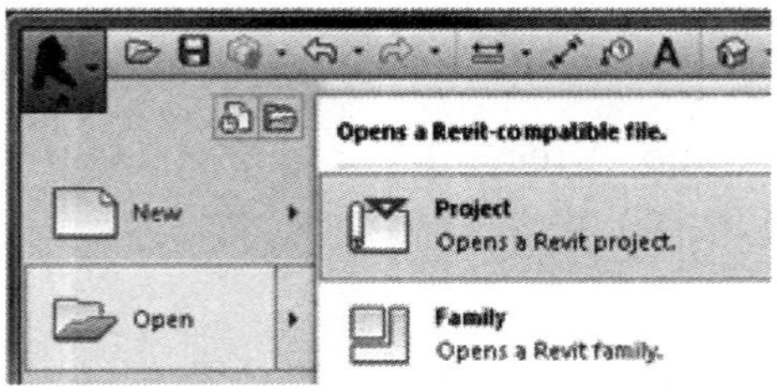 Go to **File→Open→Project**.

2. 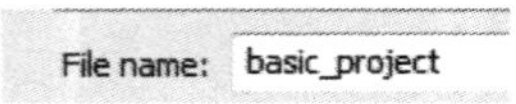 Locate the file called *basic_project.rvt*.

This is located on the publisher's website.

3. 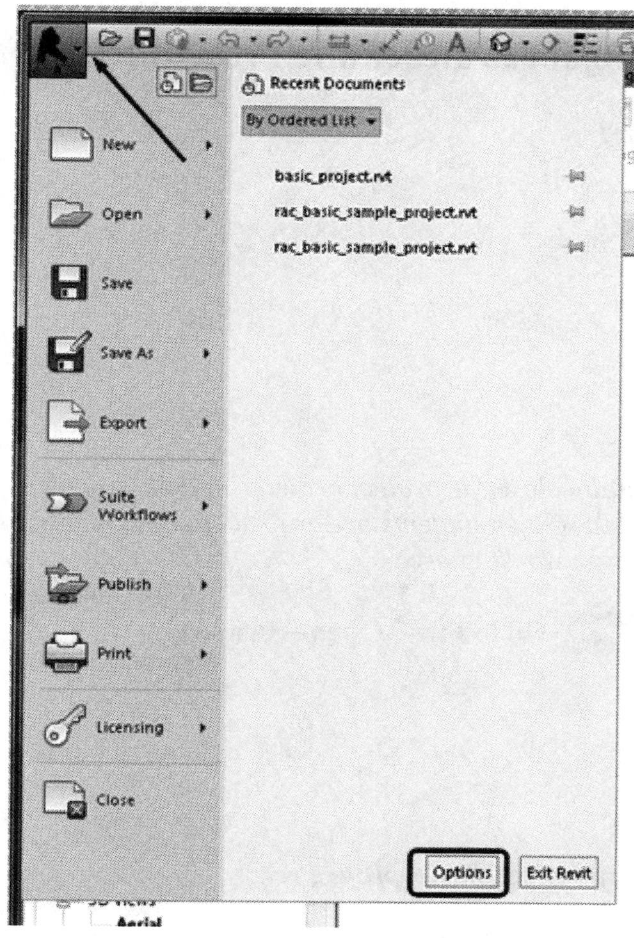

Select the drop-down on the Application Menu.

Select **Options**.

4. General
User Interface
Graphics
File Locations
Rendering
Check Spelling
SteeringWheels
ViewCube
Macros

Unknown video card

The installed video card 'NVIDIA GeForce 7800 GTX' has not been tested with Revit.
You may continue to use Hardware Acceleration.
If you experience graphics display issues, you should:
- Turn off Hardware Acceleration

Get information on supported hardware

Graphics Mode
Use Hardware Acceleration (Direct3D®)
Use Optimized View Navigation
Use Anti-Aliasing

Colors
Invert background
Selection: RGB 000-059-189 Semi-transparent
Pre-selection: RGB 000-059-189
Alert: RGB 255-128-000

Select **Graphics**.

Enable **Invert background** to set the background to black.

Press **OK**.

5. Close the file without saving.

Exercise 1-3:

Closing and Opening the Project Browser and Properties Palette

Drawing Name: *basic_project.rvt*
Estimated Time: 5 minutes

This exercise reinforces the following skills:

- User Interface
- Ribbon
- Project Browser
- Properties panel

Many of my students will accidentally close the project browser and/or the properties palette and want to bring them back. Other students prefer to keep these items closed most of the time so they have a larger working area.

1. 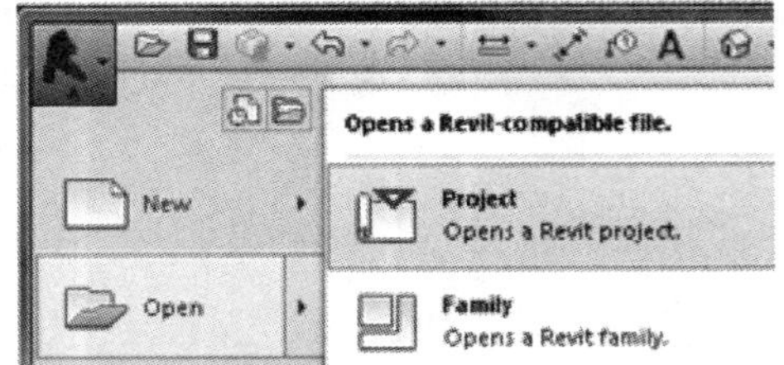

Go to **File→Open→Project**.

2. Locate the file called *basic_project.rvt*.

   This is located on the publisher's website.

3. Close the Properties palette by clicking on the x in the corner.

4. Close the Project Browser by clicking on the x in the corner.

5. 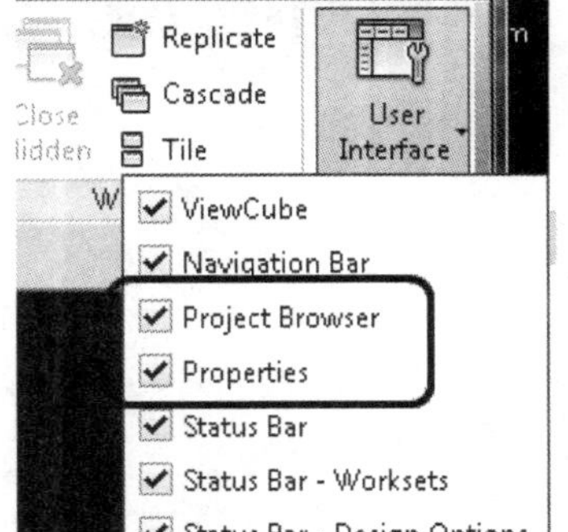

Activate the View ribbon.

   Go to the User Interface dropdown at the far right.

   Place a check next to the Project Browser and Properties to make them visible.

6. Close without saving.

Exercise 1-4:
Changing the Ribbon Display

Drawing Name: *basic_project.rvt*
Estimated Time: 15 minutes

This exercise reinforces the following skills:

- User Interface
- Ribbon

Many of my students will accidentally collapse the ribbon and want to bring it back. Other students prefer to keep the ribbon collapsed most of the time so they have a larger working area.

1. Go to **File→Open→Project**.

2. Locate the file called *basic_project.rvt*.

   This is located on the publisher's website.

3. On the ribbon: Locate the two small up and down arrows.

4. Left click on the white button.

5. The ribbon collapses to tabs.

6. 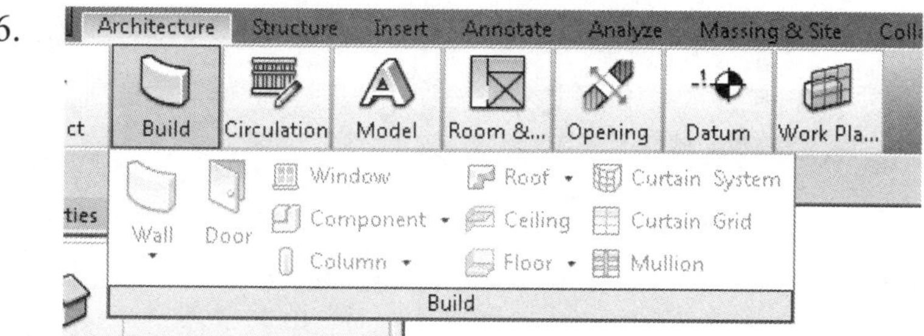

   Left click on the word **Architecture**.
   Hover the mouse over the word **Build** and the Build tools panel will appear.

   The build tools will be grayed out in a 3D view.

7. Click on the white button until the ribbon is restored.

8. The ribbon is full-size again.

9. Click on the black arrow.

10. Click on **Minimize to Panel Buttons**.

11. 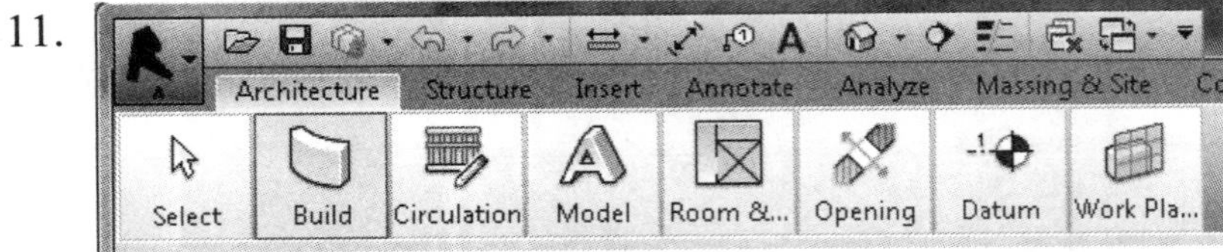

The ribbon changes to panel buttons.

12. 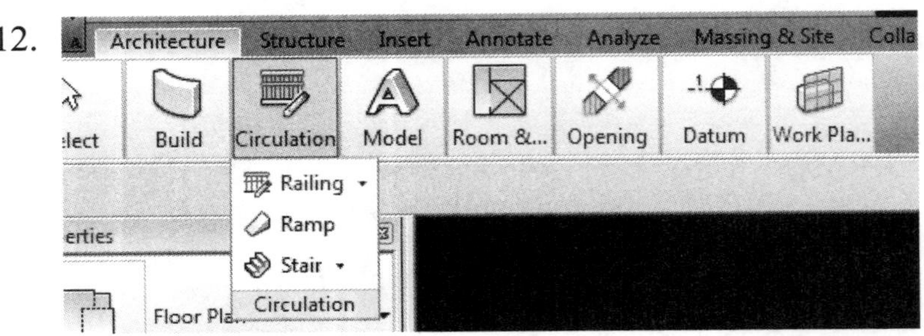

Hover the mouse over a button and the tools for the button will display.

13. Click on the white button to display the full ribbon.

14. Close without saving.

The Modify Ribbon

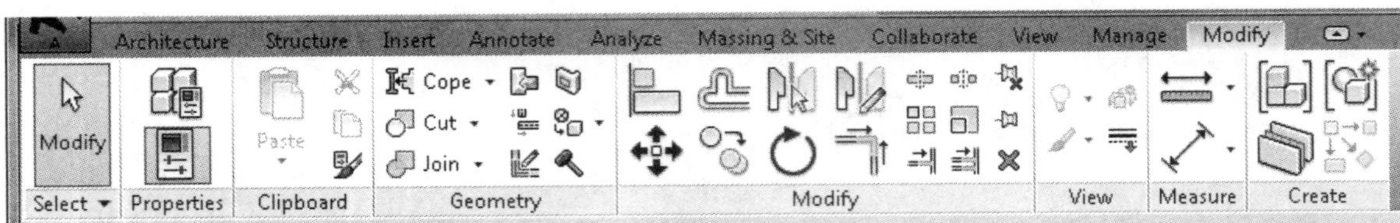

When you select an entity, you automatically switch to Modify mode. A Modify ribbon will appear with different options.

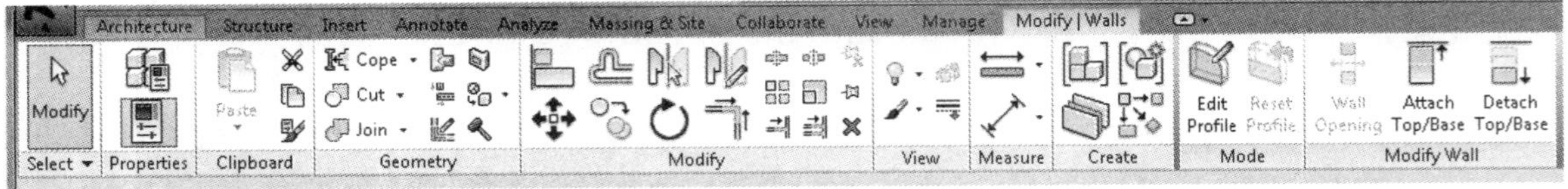

Revit uses three types of dimensions: Listening, Temporary, and Permanent. Dimensions are placed using the relative positions of elements to each other. Permanent dimensions are driven by the value of the temporary dimension. Listening dimensions are displayed as you draw or place an element.

Exercise 1-5

Temporary, Permanent and Listening Dimensions

Drawing Name: dimensions.rvt
Estimated Time: 30 minutes

This exercise reinforces the following skills:

- Project Browser
- Scale
- Graphical Scale
- Numerical Scale
- Temporary Dimensions
- Permanent Dimensions
- Listening Dimensions
- Type Selector

1. Browse to *dimensions.rvt* on the publisher's website.
   Save the file to a folder.
   Open the file.

   The file has four walls.

   The horizontal walls are 80′ in length.

   The vertical walls are 52′ in length.

   We want to change the vertical walls so that they are 60′ in length.

2. Select the House icon on the Quick Access toolbar.

3. 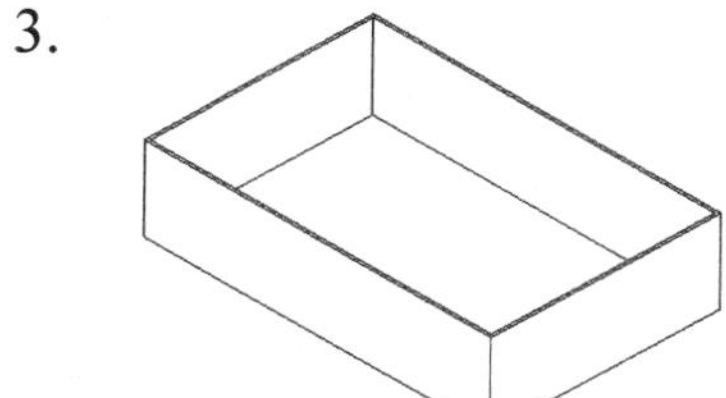

   This switches the display to a default 3D view.

   You see that the displayed elements are walls.

4. Floor Plans
   Level 1
   Level 2
   Site

   Double left click on Level 1 under Floor Plans in the Project Browser.

   The view display changes to the Level 1 floor plan.

5. 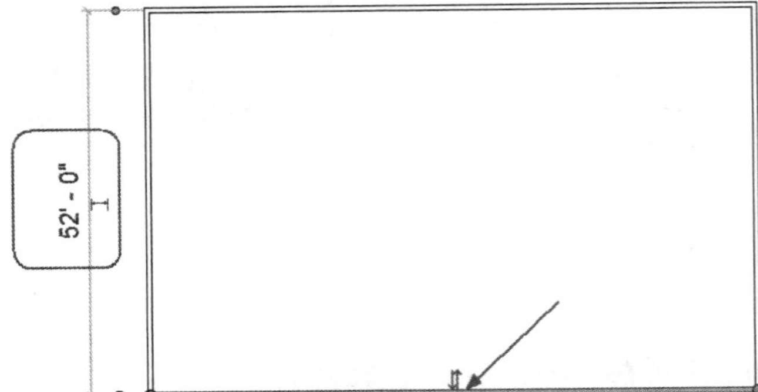

Select the bottom horizontal wall.

A temporary dimension appears showing the vertical distance between the selected wall and the wall above it.

6. 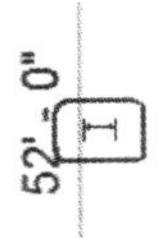

A small dimension icon is next to the temporary dimension.

Left click on this icon to place a permanent dimension.

Left click anywhere in the window to release the selection.

7. Select the permanent dimension extension line, not the text.

A lock appears. If you left click on the lock, it would prevent you from modifying the dimension.

If you select the permanent dimension, you can not edit the dimension value only the dimension style.

8. 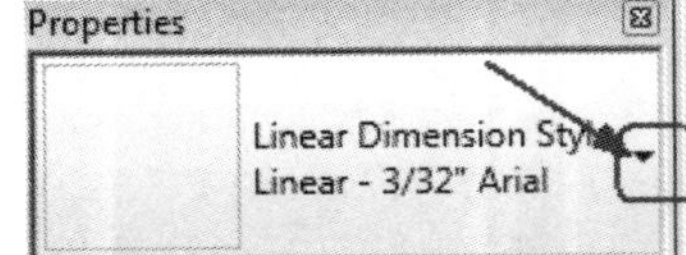

The Properties palette shows the dimension style for the dimension selected.

Select the small down arrow.
This is the Type Selector.

The Type Selector shows the dimension styles available in the project.

9. 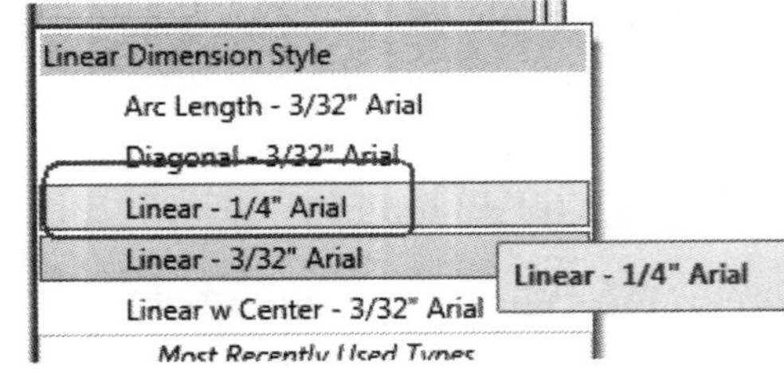

Left click on the Linear- 1/4″ Arial dimension style to select this dimension style.

Left click anywhere in the drawing area to release the selection and change the dimension style.

10. 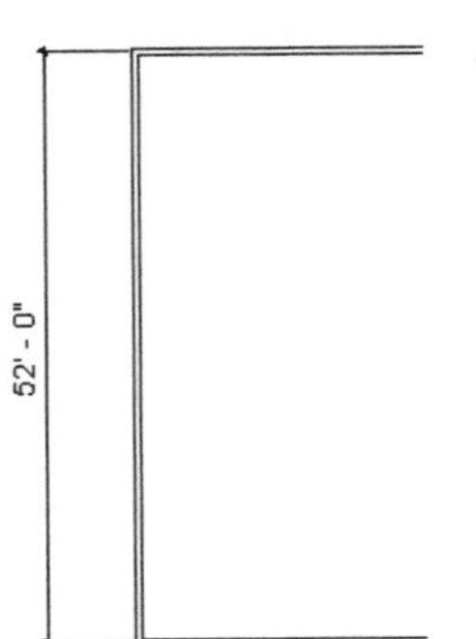

The dimension updates to the new dimension style.

11. Select the right vertical wall.

12. A temporary dimension appears showing the distance between the selected wall and the closest vertical wall.

Left click on the permanent dimension icon to place a permanent dimension.

13. 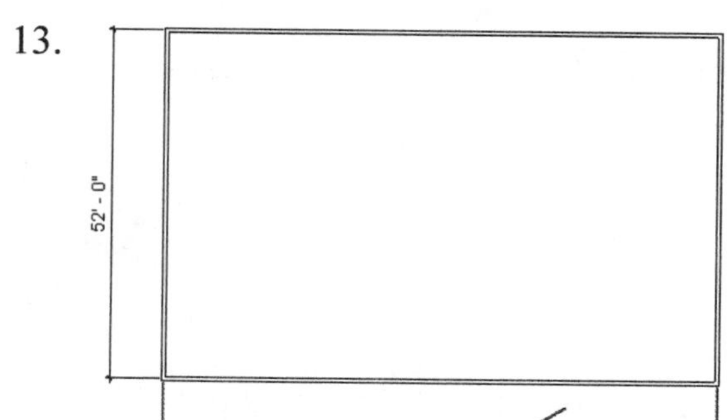

A permanent dimension is placed.

Select the horizontal permanent dimension extension line, not the text.

14. 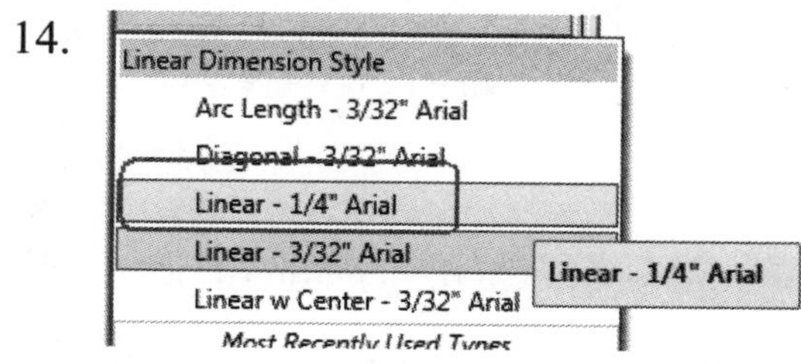

Use the Type Selector to change the dimension style of the horizontal dimension to the Linear- 1/4″ Arial dimension style.

Left click anywhere in the drawing area to release the selection and change the dimension style.

15. 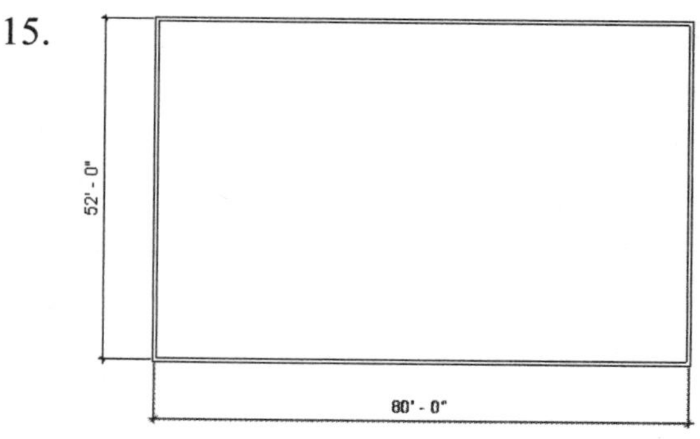

You have placed two *permanent* dimensions and assigned them a new dimension type.

16. Hold down the Control key and select both **horizontal** (top and bottom side) walls so that they highlight.

    NOTE: *We select the horizontal walls to change the vertical wall length and we select the vertical walls to change the horizontal wall length.*

17. 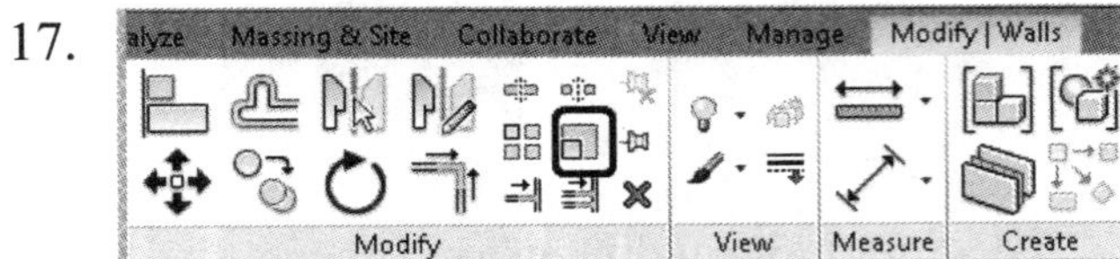

    Select the **Scale** tool located on the Modify Walls ribbon.

    In the Options bar, you may select Graphical or Numerical methods for resizing the selected objects.

18. 

    Enable **Graphical**.

    The Graphical option requires three inputs.

    Input 1: Origin or Base Point
    Input 2: Original or Reference Length
    Input 3: Desired Length

19. Select the left lower endpoint for the first input – the origin.

20. 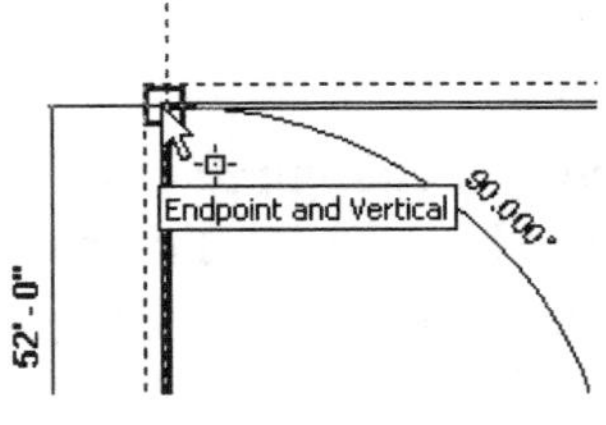

    Select the left upper endpoint for the second input – the reference length.

21. 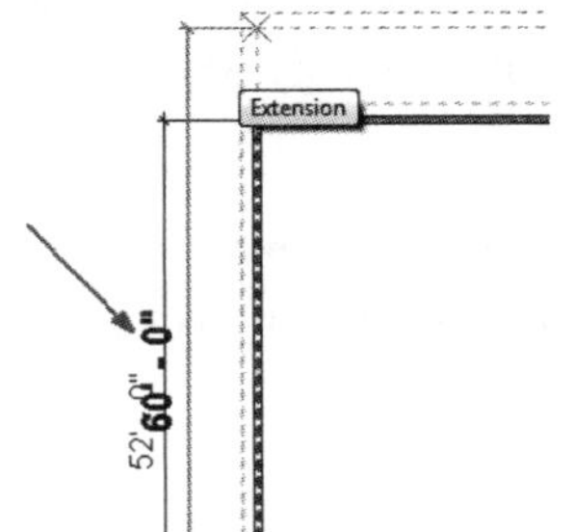

    Extend your cursor until you see a dimension of 60′.

    The dimension you see as you move the cursor is a *listening dimension.*

22. Left click for the third input – the desired length.

Left click anywhere in the window to release the selection and exit the scale command.

Note that the permanent dimension updates.

23. Select the bottom horizontal wall to display the temporary dimension.

24. Left click on the vertical temporary dimension. An edit box will open. Type **50 0**.

Revit does not require you to enter units.

Left click to enter and release the selection.

25. 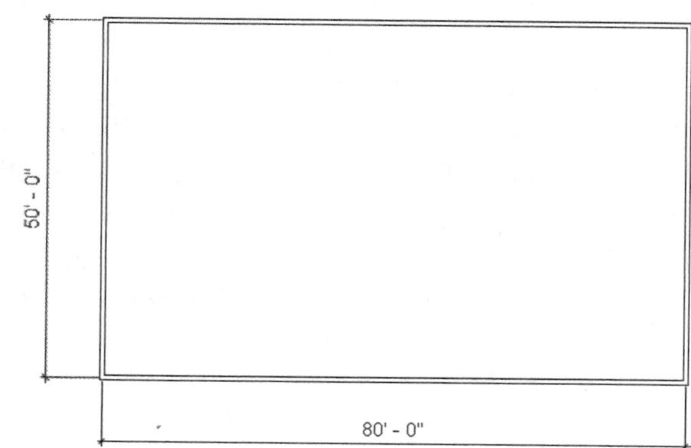

The permanent dimension updates.

Note if you select the permanent dimension, you can not edit the dimension value only the dimension style.

26. Now, we will change the horizontal walls using the Numerical option of the Resize tool.

Hold down the Control key and select the left and right vertical walls.

27. 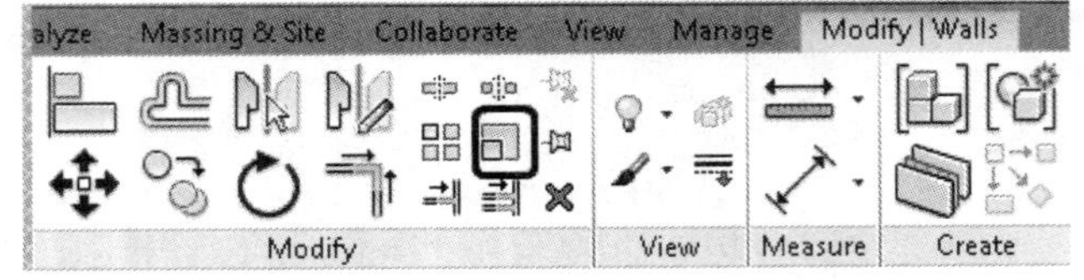

Select the **Scale** tool.

28. Modify | Walls Graphical Numerical Scale: 0.5

Enable **Numerical**.
Set the Scale to **0.5**.

This will change the wall length from **80′** to **40′**.

The Numerical option requires only one input for the Origin or Base Point.

29. Endpoint — Select the left lower endpoint for the first input – the origin.

30. The walls immediately adjust. Left click in the drawing area to release the selection.

Note that the permanent dimension automatically updates.

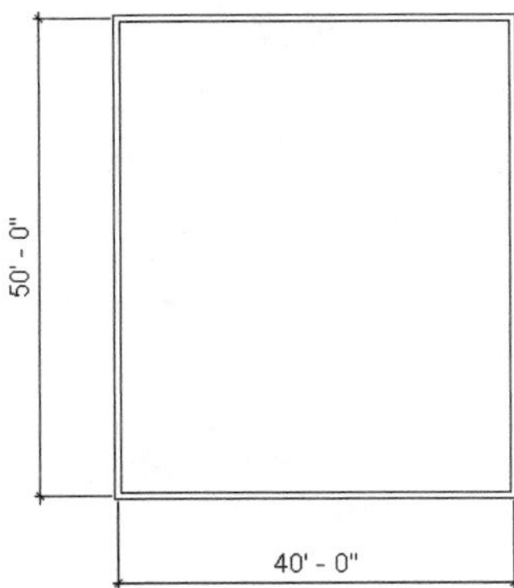

31. Close without saving.

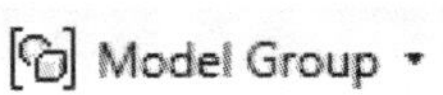

The Group tool works in a similar way as the AutoCAD GROUP. Basically, you are creating a selection set of similar or dissimilar objects, which can then be selected as a single unit. Once selected, you can move, copy, rotate, mirror, or delete them. Once you create a Group, you can add or remove members of that group. Existing groups are listed in your browser panel and can be dragged and dropped into views as required. Typical details, office layouts, bathroom layouts, etc. can be grouped, and then saved out of the project for use on other projects.

If you hold down the Control key as you drag a selected object or group, Revit will automatically create a copy of the selected object or group.

The Collaborate Ribbon

Collaborate tools are used if more than one user is working on the same project. The tools can also be used to check data sets coming in from other sources.

Revit's Menu

When you want to start a new project/building, you go to File→New→Project or use the hot key by pressing Control and 'N' at the same time.

When you start a new project, you use a default template (default.rte). This template creates two Levels (default floor heights) and sets the View Window to the Floor Plan view of Level 1.

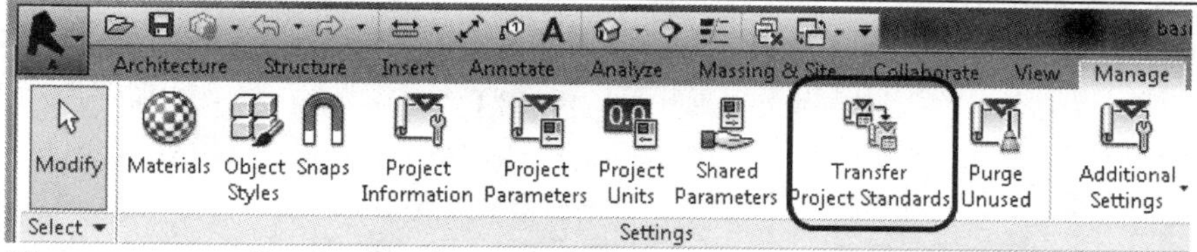

You can transfer the Project settings of an old project to a new one by opening both projects in one session of Revit, then with your new project active, select **Manage→Settings→Transfer Project Standards**.

Check the items you wish to transfer, then click 'OK'.

Transfer Project Settings is useful if you have created a custom system family, such as a wall, floor, or ceiling, and want to use it in a different project.

- If you plan to export to .dwg or import existing .dwg details, it is important to set your import/export setting. This allows you to control the layers that Revit will export to and the appearance of imported .dwg files.
- Pressing the ESC Key twice will always take you to the Modify command.
- As you get more proficient with Revit, you may want to create your own templates based on your favorite settings. A custom template based on your office standards (including line styles, rendering materials, common details, door, window and room schedules, commonly used wall types, door types and window types and typical sheets) will increase project production.

The View Ribbon

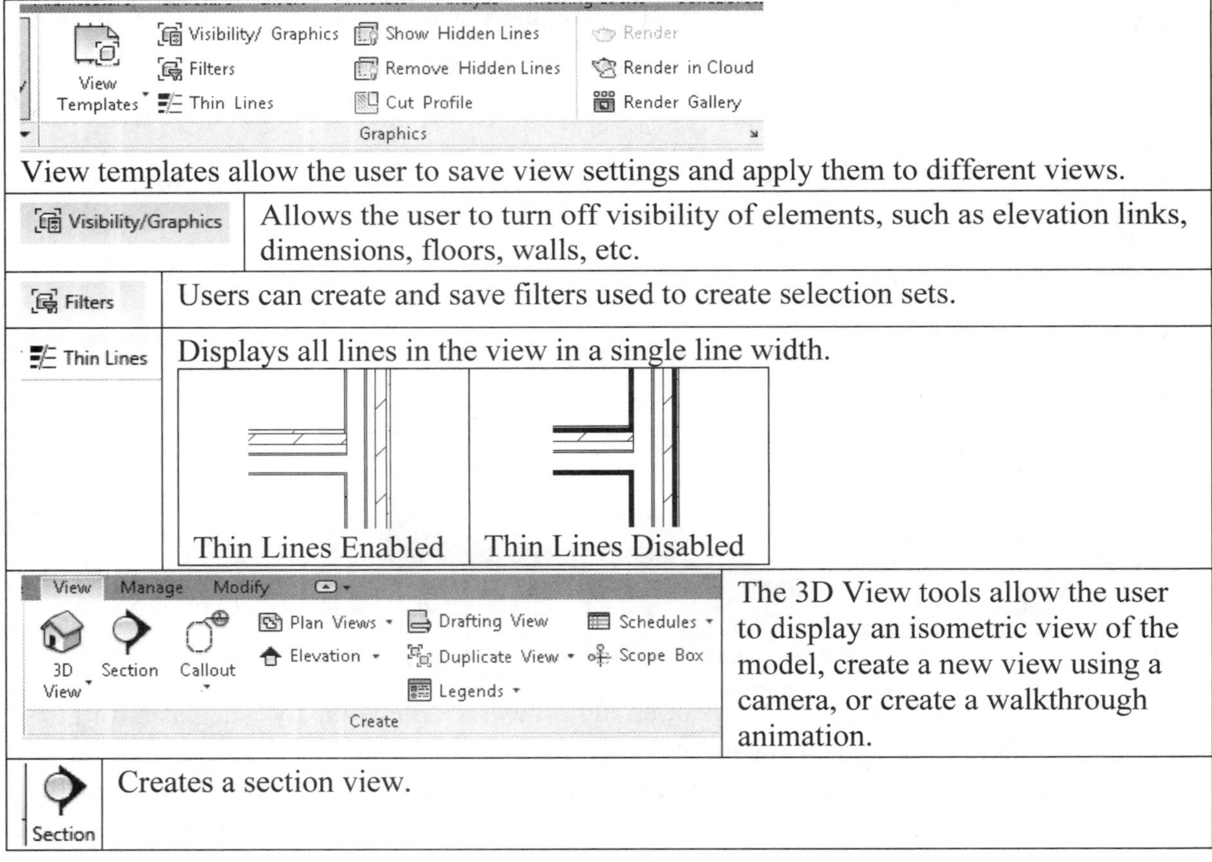

View Templates	View templates allow the user to save view settings and apply them to different views.
Visibility/Graphics	Allows the user to turn off visibility of elements, such as elevation links, dimensions, floors, walls, etc.
Filters	Users can create and save filters used to create selection sets.
Thin Lines	Displays all lines in the view in a single line width. Thin Lines Enabled / Thin Lines Disabled
3D View, Section, Callout (Create panel)	The 3D View tools allow the user to display an isometric view of the model, create a new view using a camera, or create a walkthrough animation.
Section	Creates a section view.

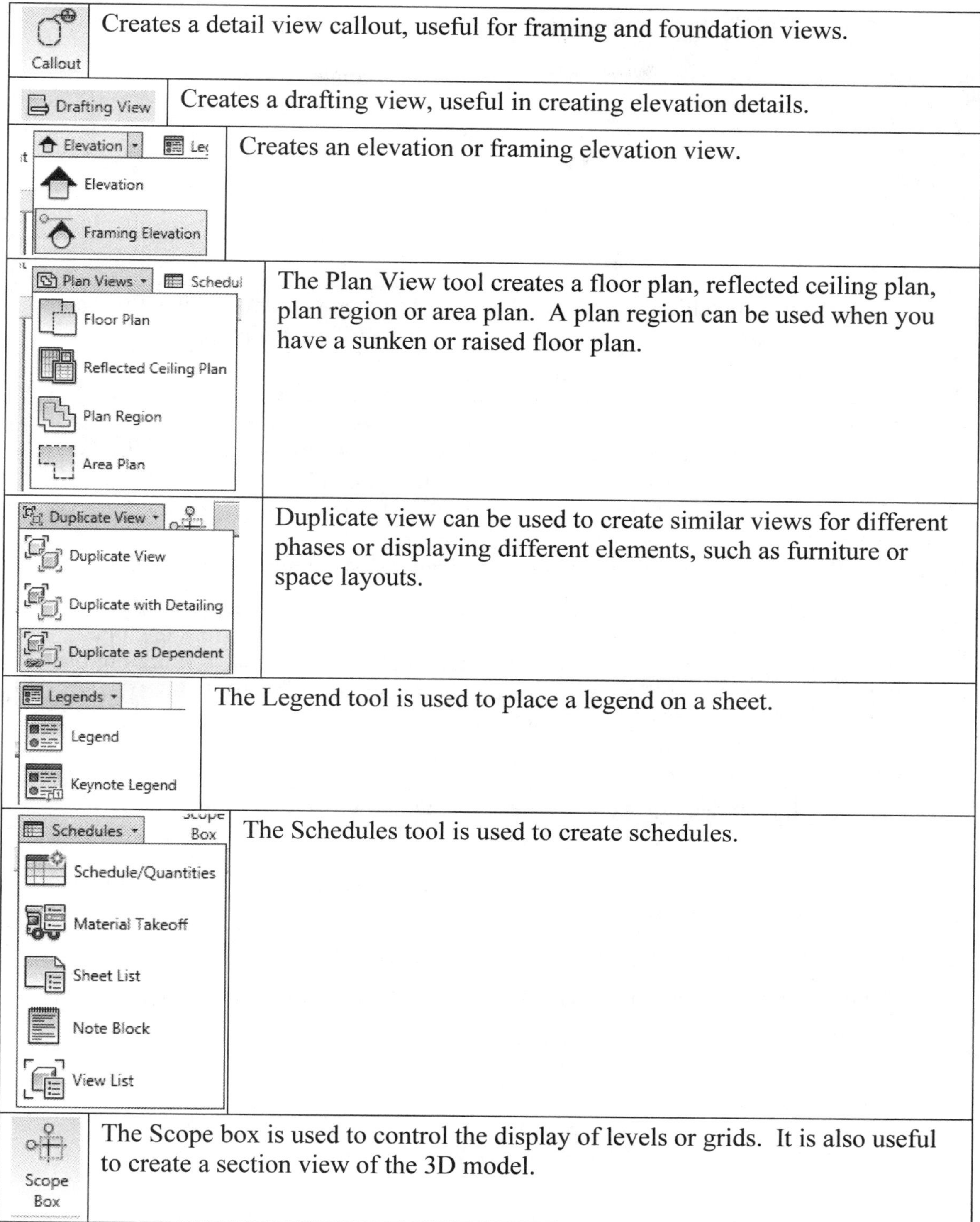

Tool	Description
Callout	Creates a detail view callout, useful for framing and foundation views.
Drafting View	Creates a drafting view, useful in creating elevation details.
Elevation: Elevation, Framing Elevation	Creates an elevation or framing elevation view.
Plan Views: Floor Plan, Reflected Ceiling Plan, Plan Region, Area Plan	The Plan View tool creates a floor plan, reflected ceiling plan, plan region or area plan. A plan region can be used when you have a sunken or raised floor plan.
Duplicate View: Duplicate View, Duplicate with Detailing, Duplicate as Dependent	Duplicate view can be used to create similar views for different phases or displaying different elements, such as furniture or space layouts.
Legends: Legend, Keynote Legend	The Legend tool is used to place a legend on a sheet.
Schedules: Schedule/Quantities, Material Takeoff, Sheet List, Note Block, View List	The Schedules tool is used to create schedules.
Scope Box	The Scope box is used to control the display of levels or grids. It is also useful to create a section view of the 3D model.

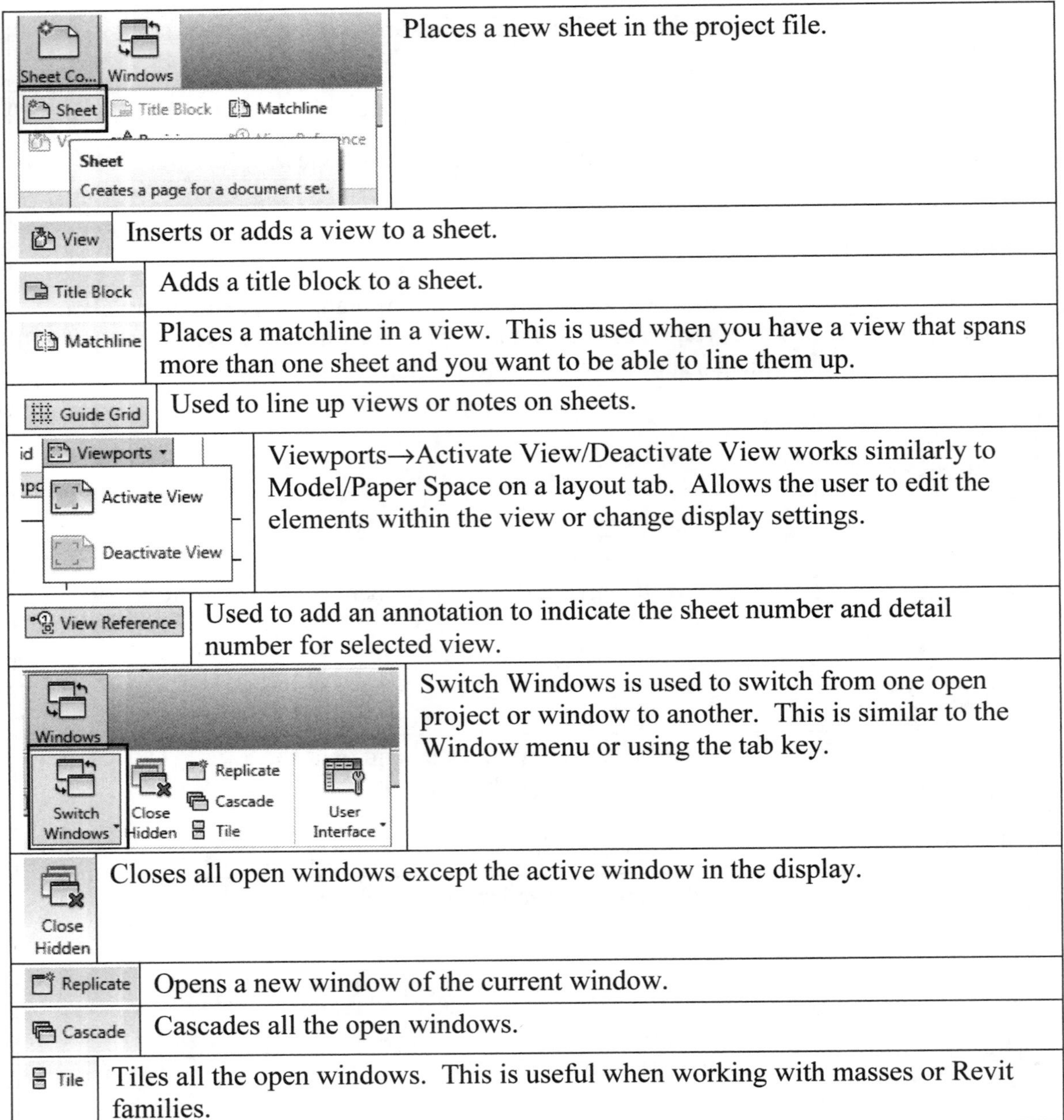

Tool	Description
Sheet	Places a new sheet in the project file.
View	Inserts or adds a view to a sheet.
Title Block	Adds a title block to a sheet.
Matchline	Places a matchline in a view. This is used when you have a view that spans more than one sheet and you want to be able to line them up.
Guide Grid	Used to line up views or notes on sheets.
Viewports: Activate View / Deactivate View	Viewports→Activate View/Deactivate View works similarly to Model/Paper Space on a layout tab. Allows the user to edit the elements within the view or change display settings.
View Reference	Used to add an annotation to indicate the sheet number and detail number for selected view.
Switch Windows	Switch Windows is used to switch from one open project or window to another. This is similar to the Window menu or using the tab key.
Close Hidden	Closes all open windows except the active window in the display.
Replicate	Opens a new window of the current window.
Cascade	Cascades all the open windows.
Tile	Tiles all the open windows. This is useful when working with masses or Revit families.

<table>
<tr>
<td>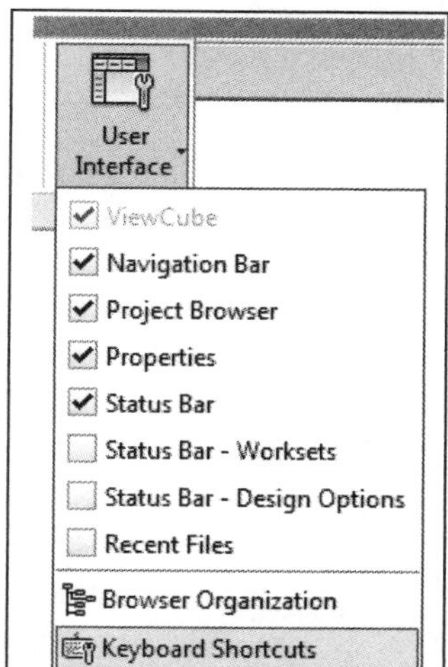
</td>
<td>Controls the visibility of different user navigation systems.

Browser Organization allows the user to customize how views appear in the Project Browser.

We do not use Worksets or Design Options in this text, so both those status bars can be disabled.</td>
</tr>
</table>

Creating standard view templates (exterior elevations, enlarged floor plans, etc) in your project template or at the beginning of a project will save lots of time down the road.

The Manage Ribbon

<table>
<tr>
<td>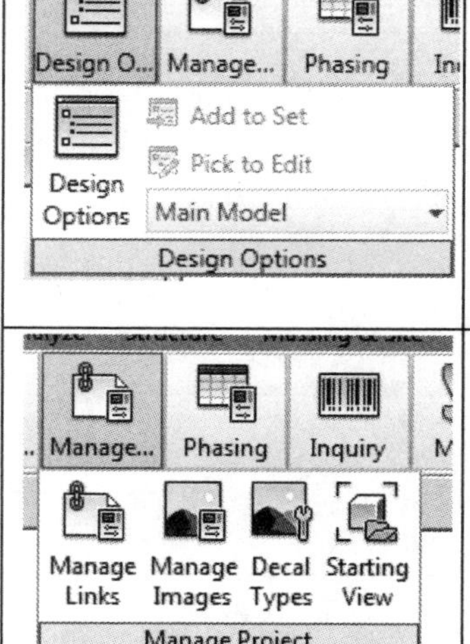
</td>
<td>Design Options are used to design different options for a building model. This allows the user to create different versions of the same building to present to a client.

Elements may be added to different option sets and then displayed.

This is similar to a Configuration Manager.</td>
</tr>
<tr>
<td></td>
<td>This is similar to the External Reference Manager in AutoCAD. This is used when you have inserted external cad files, such as topo files to be used in the model.</td>
</tr>
</table>

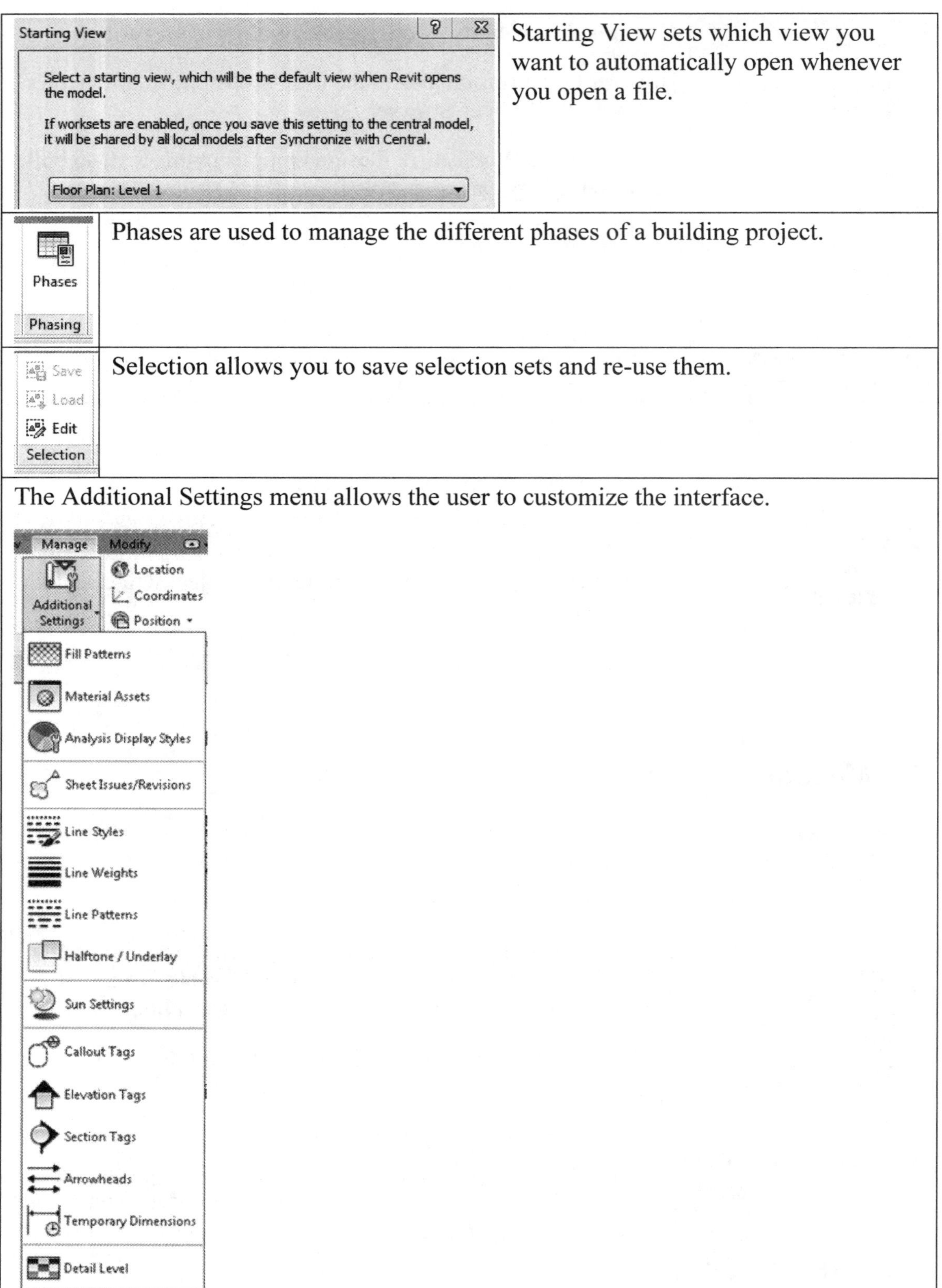

Starting View sets which view you want to automatically open whenever you open a file.

Phases are used to manage the different phases of a building project.

Selection allows you to save selection sets and re-use them.

The Additional Settings menu allows the user to customize the interface.

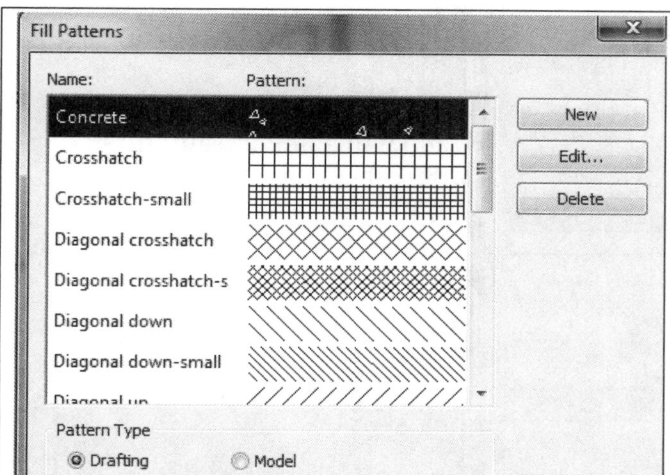

Hatch Patterns or Fill Patterns are controlled under Additional Settings.

These are hatch patterns. Revit comes with a library of standard fill patterns, but you can also edit and create your own custom patterns.

You can import patterns from any *.*pat* file.

Materials

Revit comes with a library of materials, which can be applied to walls, windows, doors, etc. You can also edit and create your own custom materials.

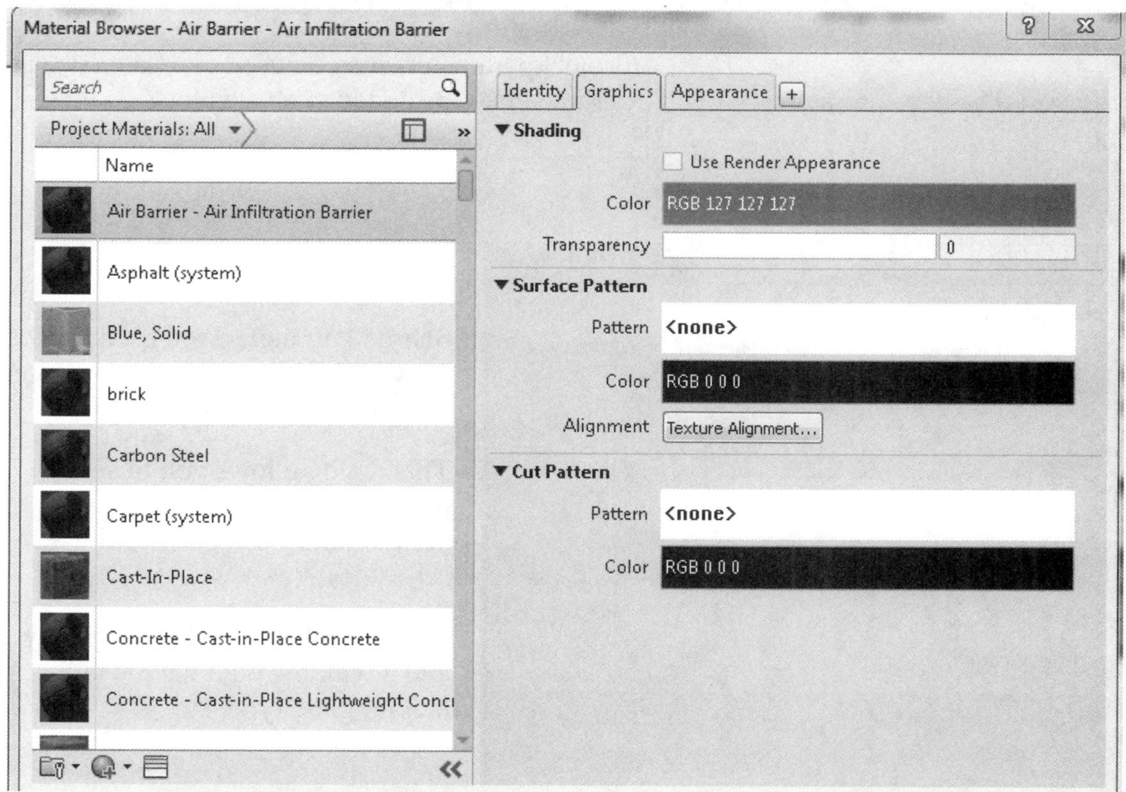

Any image file can be used to create a material.

My favorite sources for materials are fabric and paint websites.

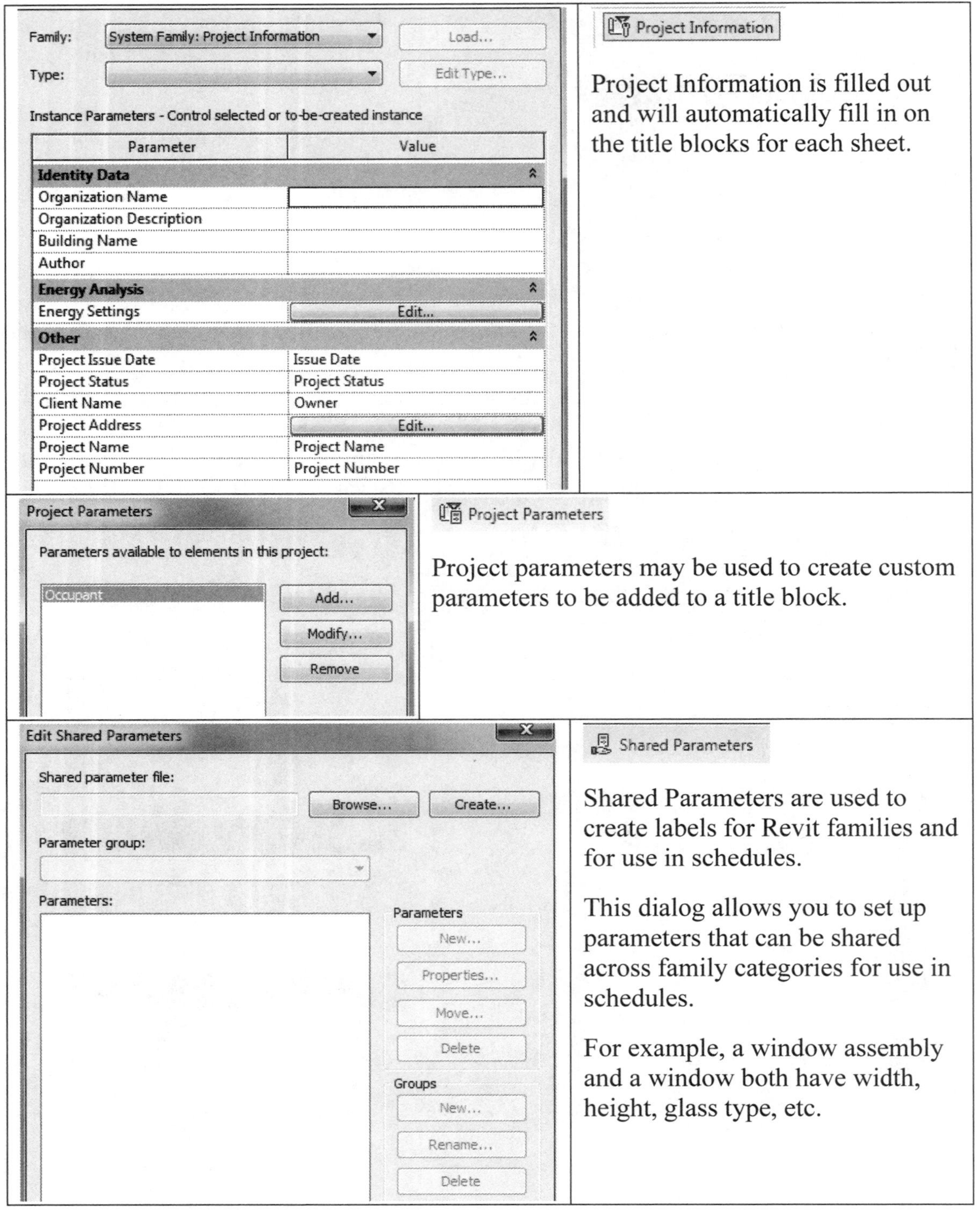

Project Information is filled out and will automatically fill in on the title blocks for each sheet.

Project parameters may be used to create custom parameters to be added to a title block.

Shared Parameters are used to create labels for Revit families and for use in schedules.

This dialog allows you to set up parameters that can be shared across family categories for use in schedules.

For example, a window assembly and a window both have width, height, glass type, etc.

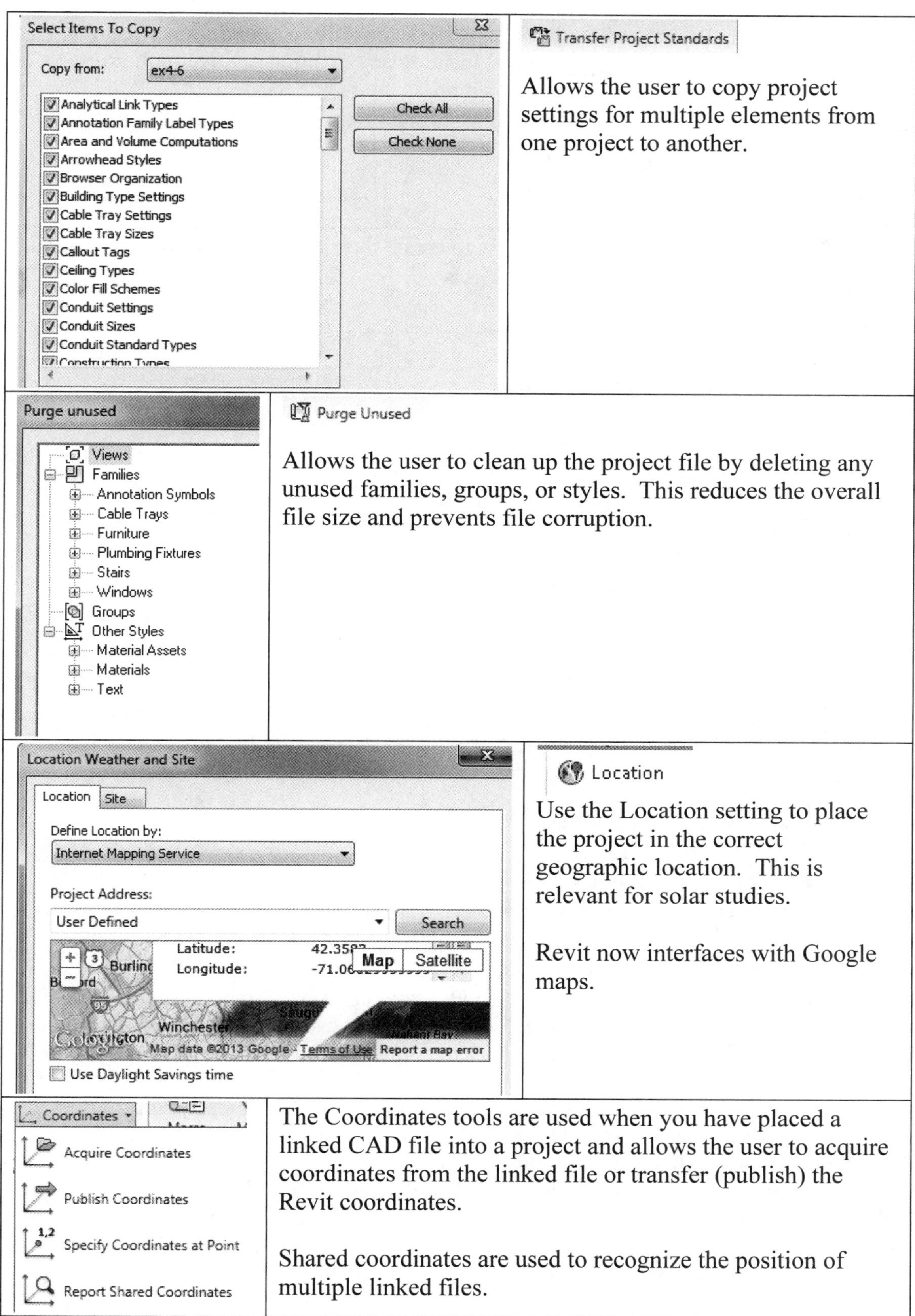

Transfer Project Standards: Allows the user to copy project settings for multiple elements from one project to another.

Purge Unused: Allows the user to clean up the project file by deleting any unused families, groups, or styles. This reduces the overall file size and prevents file corruption.

Location: Use the Location setting to place the project in the correct geographic location. This is relevant for solar studies.

Revit now interfaces with Google maps.

Coordinates: The Coordinates tools are used when you have placed a linked CAD file into a project and allows the user to acquire coordinates from the linked file or transfer (publish) the Revit coordinates.

Shared coordinates are used to recognize the position of multiple linked files.

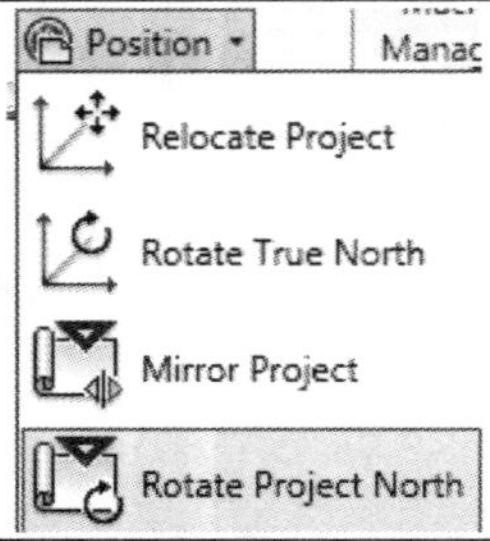

Position: Relocate Project, Rotate True North, Mirror Project, Rotate Project North	The position tools are used to position the model to reflect the correct geographical location and position relative to the sun.
 Macro Manager	The Macro Manager allows users to create their own customization routines using a Visual Studio-style interface.
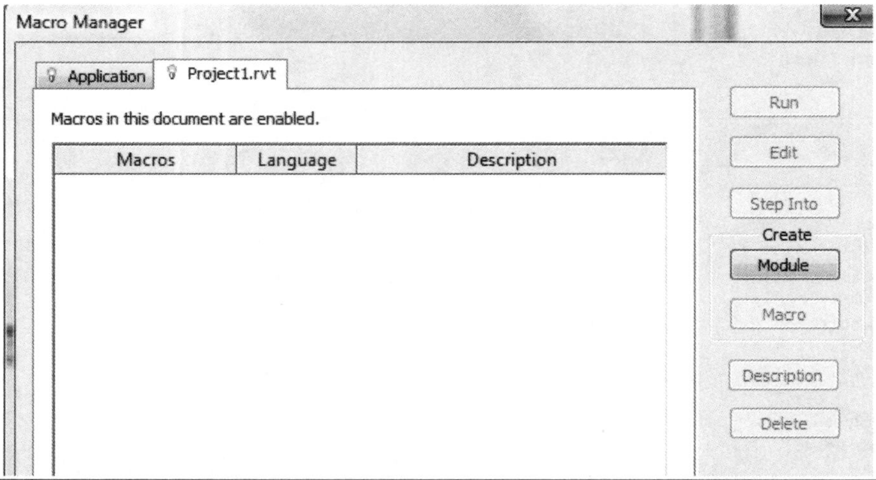 Macro Security	Macros may be embedded in a Revit drawing. Since a macro can also contain a computer virus or spyware, Revit provides the ability for users to determine what security level they want to maintain with drawings.

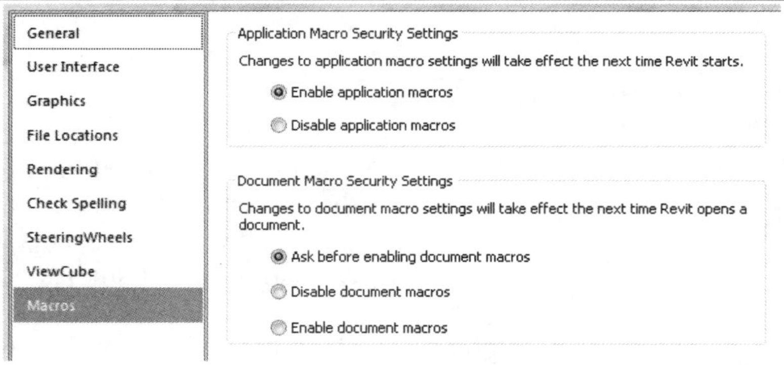

- By default, the Browser lists all sheets and all views.
- If you have multiple users of Revit in your office, place your family libraries and rendering libraries on a server and designate the path under the File Locations tab under Options, this allows multiple users to access the same libraries and materials.

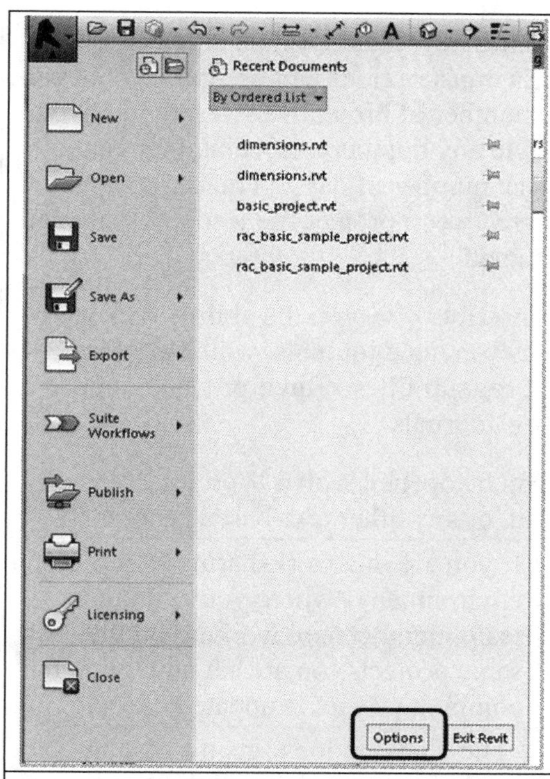

To access the System Options:

Go to the Revit menu and select the Options button located at the bottom of the dialog.

Save Reminder interval:

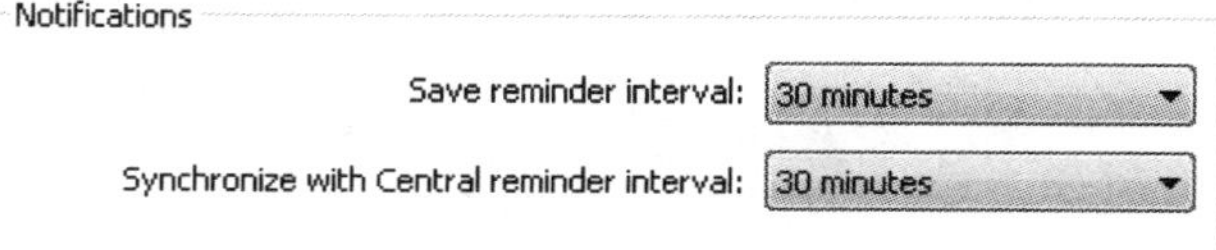

Notifications

You can select any option from the drop-down. This is not an auto-save feature. Your file will not be saved unless you select the 'Save' button. All this does is bring up a reminder dialog at the selected interval.

User Name Username Elise	This indicates the user name that checks in and checks out documents. You can only change the user name when there are no open projects. The username can also be used as a property for sheets.

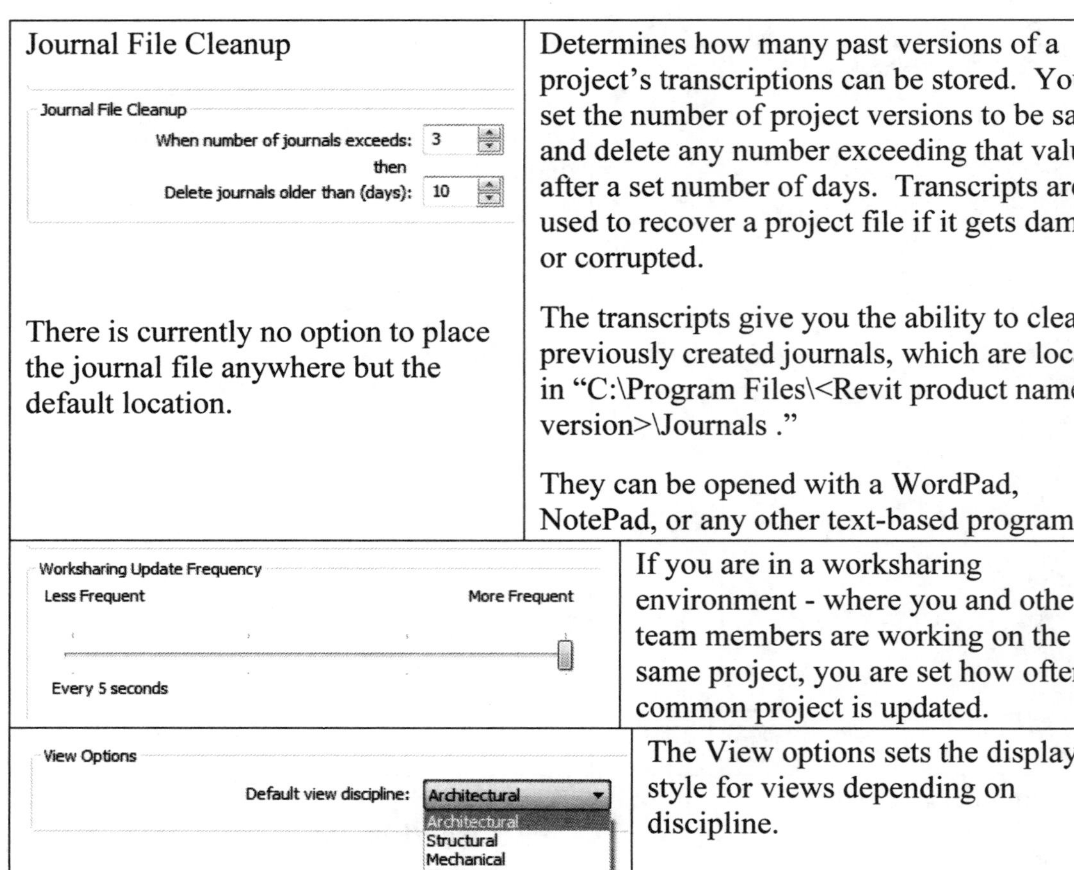

Journal File Cleanup There is currently no option to place the journal file anywhere but the default location.	Determines how many past versions of a project's transcriptions can be stored. You can set the number of project versions to be saved and delete any number exceeding that value after a set number of days. Transcripts are used to recover a project file if it gets damaged or corrupted. The transcripts give you the ability to clean up previously created journals, which are located in "C:\Program Files\<Revit product name and version>\Journals ." They can be opened with a WordPad, NotePad, or any other text-based program.
	If you are in a worksharing environment - where you and other team members are working on the same project, you are set how often the common project is updated.
	The View options sets the display style for views depending on discipline.

The User Interface Options

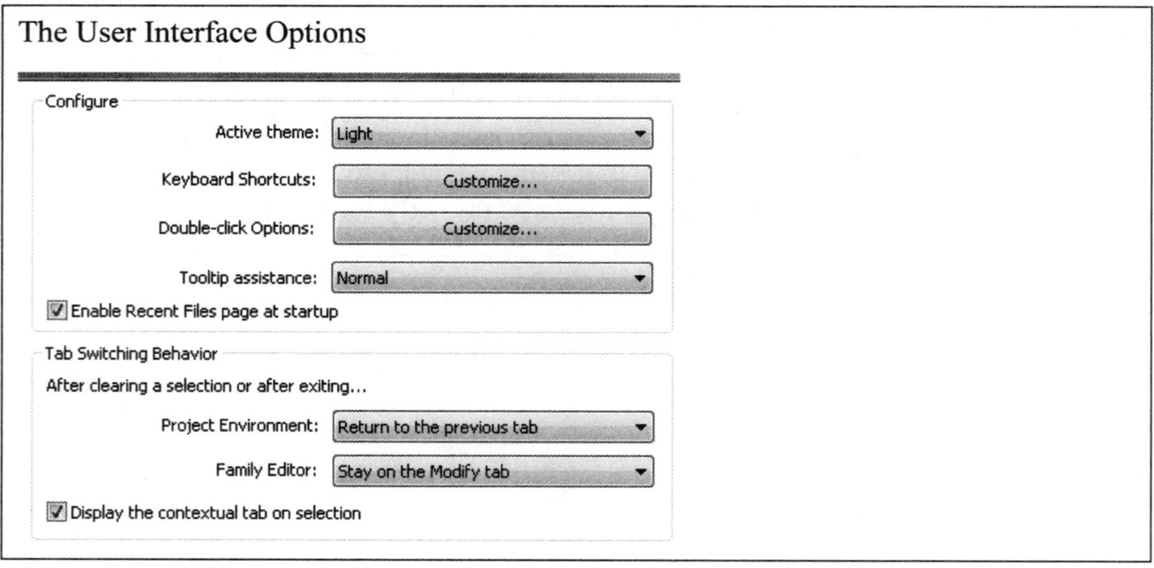

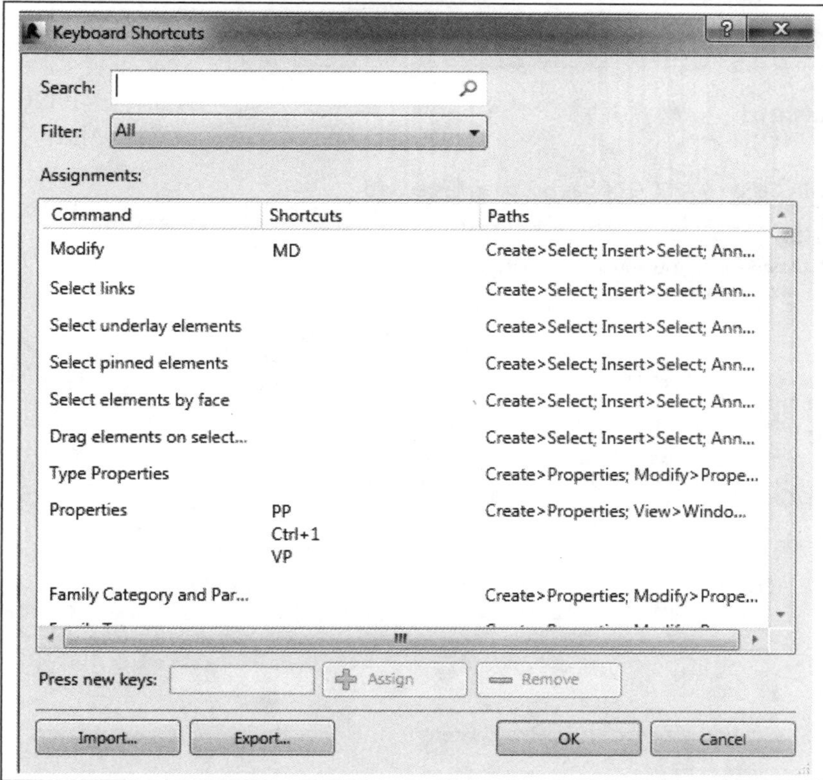

Keyboard Shortcuts (also located under User Interface on the View ribbon) allows you to assign keyboard shortcuts to your favorite commands.

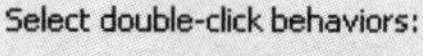

Element Type:	Double-click action:
Family	Edit Family
Sketched Element	Edit Element
Views / Schedules on Sheets	Activate View
Assemblies	Edit Element
Groups	Edit Element
Component Stairs	Edit Element

Double-click Options allows you to determine what happens when you double-left mouse click on different types of elements.

Tooltip Assistance

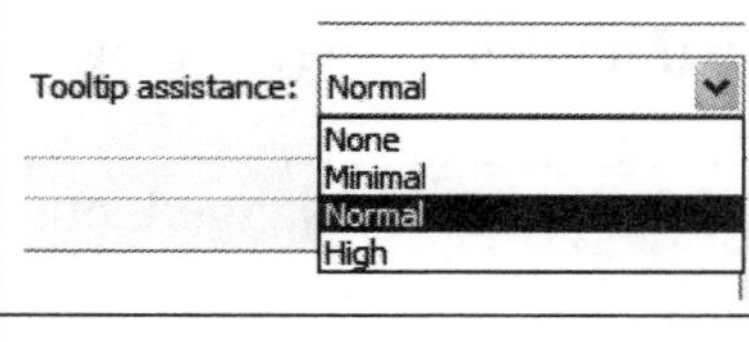

This setting controls the number of help messages you will see as you work.

Tab Switching Behavior

After clearing a selection or after exiting...

Project Environment: Return to the previous tab

Family Editor: Stay on the Modify tab

☑ Display the contextual tab on selection

Users can also control what happens when they tab from one window to another.

The Graphics tab

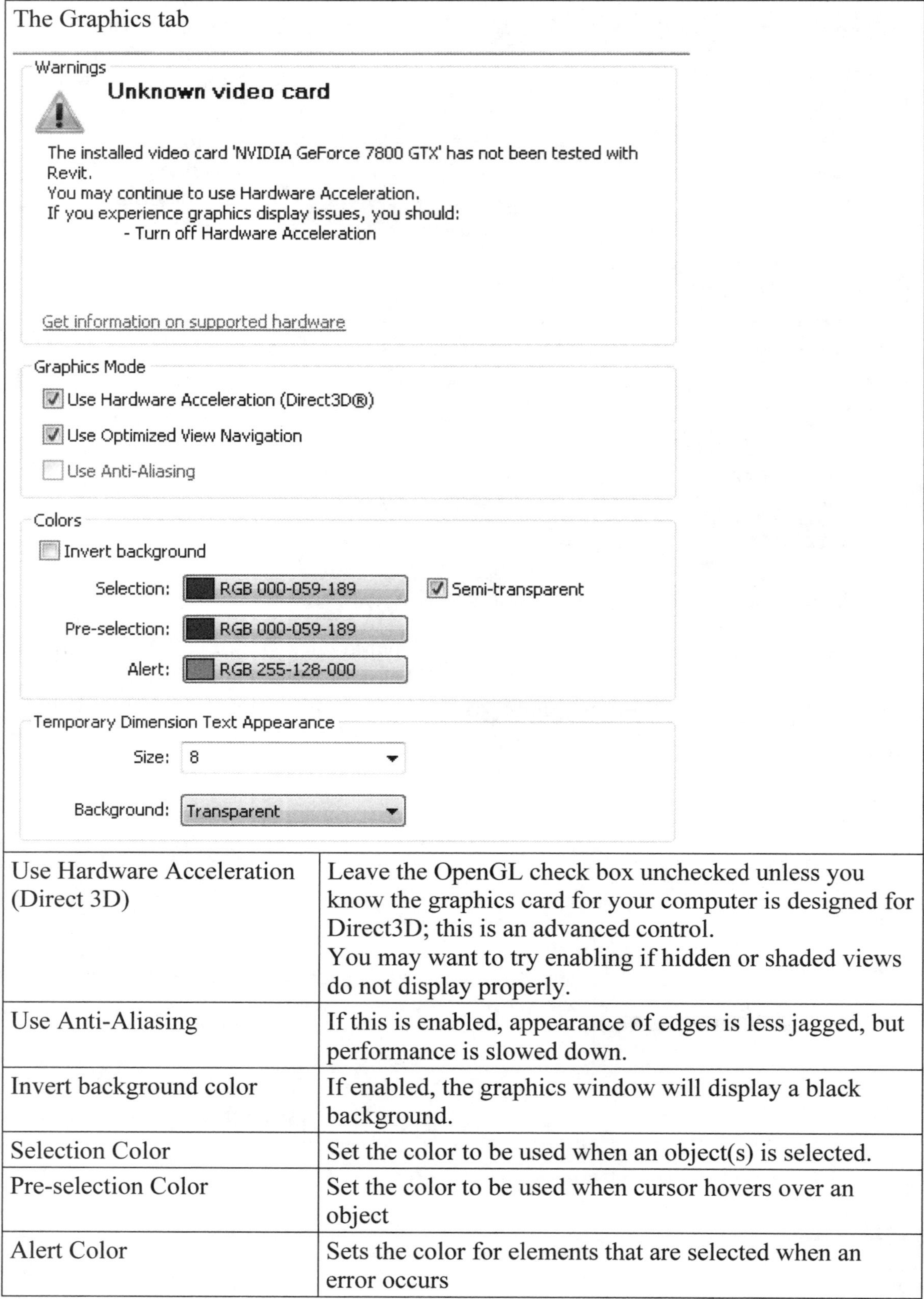

Use Hardware Acceleration (Direct 3D)	Leave the OpenGL check box unchecked unless you know the graphics card for your computer is designed for Direct3D; this is an advanced control. You may want to try enabling if hidden or shaded views do not display properly.
Use Anti-Aliasing	If this is enabled, appearance of edges is less jagged, but performance is slowed down.
Invert background color	If enabled, the graphics window will display a black background.
Selection Color	Set the color to be used when an object(s) is selected.
Pre-selection Color	Set the color to be used when cursor hovers over an object
Alert Color	Sets the color for elements that are selected when an error occurs

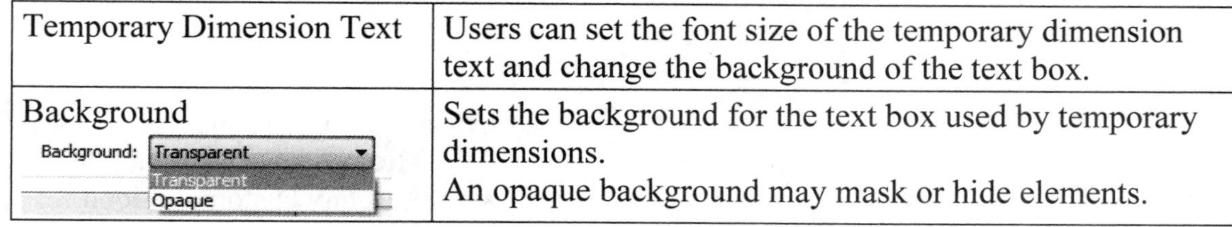

Temporary Dimension Text	Users can set the font size of the temporary dimension text and change the background of the text box.
Background Background: Transparent / Transparent / Opaque	Sets the background for the text box used by temporary dimensions. An opaque background may mask or hide elements.

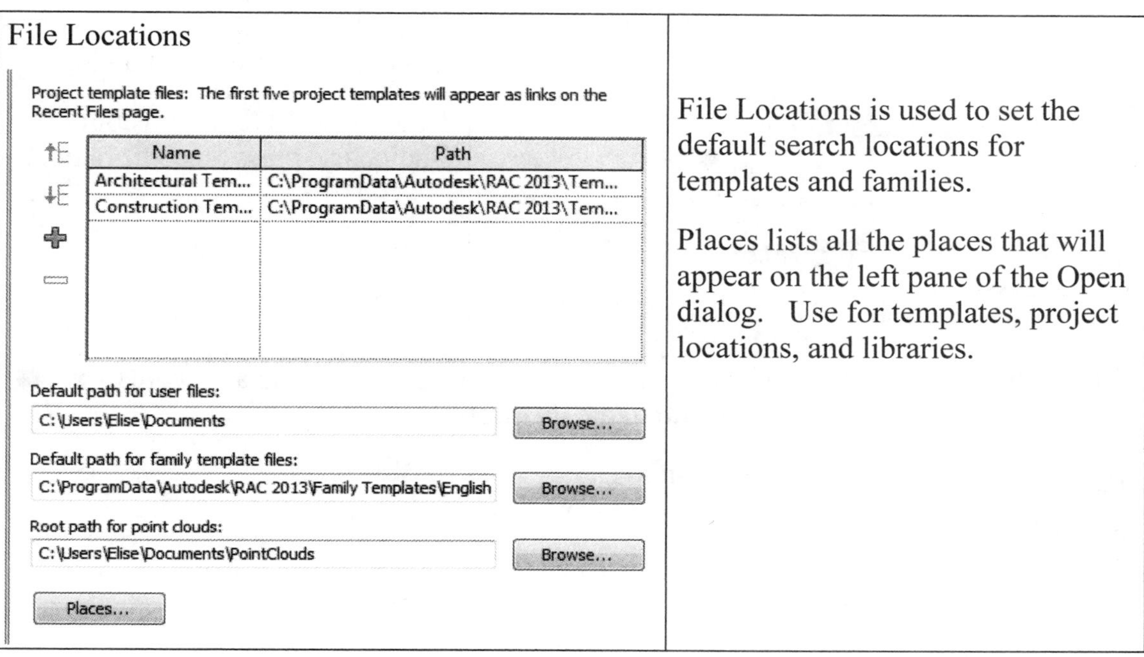

File Locations	File Locations is used to set the default search locations for templates and families. Places lists all the places that will appear on the left pane of the Open dialog. Use for templates, project locations, and libraries.

Rendering	Rendering controls where you are storing your AccuRender files and directories where you are storing your materials. This allows you to set your paths so Revit can locate materials and files easily. If you press the Get More RPC button, your browser will launch to the Archvision website. You must download and install a plug-in to manage your RPC downloads. There is a free exchange service for content, but you have to create a login account.

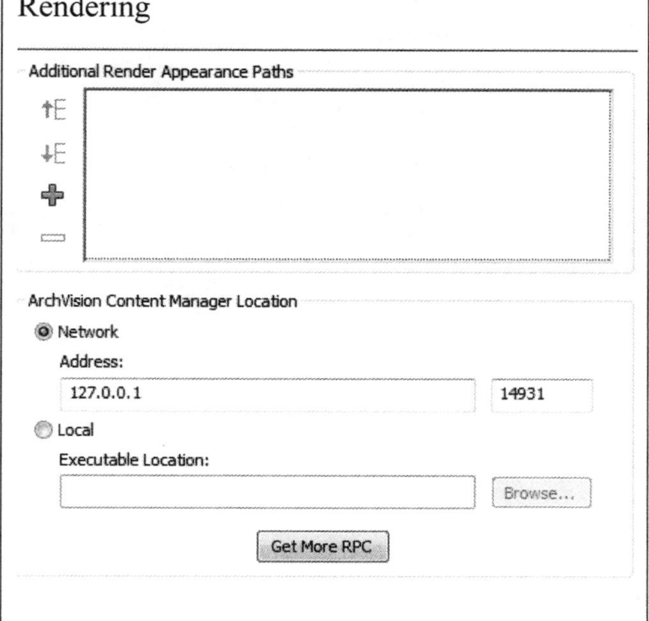

Check Spelling

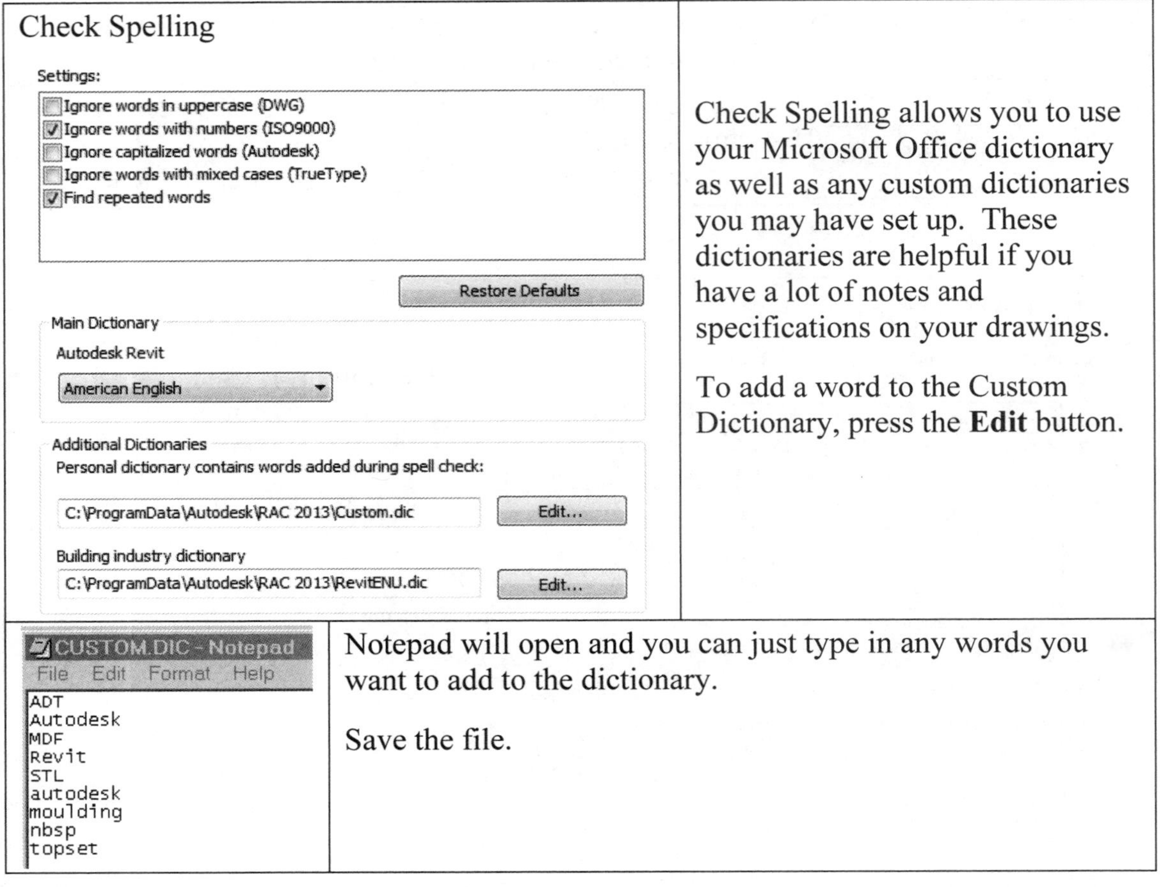

Check Spelling allows you to use your Microsoft Office dictionary as well as any custom dictionaries you may have set up. These dictionaries are helpful if you have a lot of notes and specifications on your drawings.

To add a word to the Custom Dictionary, press the **Edit** button.

Notepad will open and you can just type in any words you want to add to the dictionary.

Save the file.

SteeringWheels

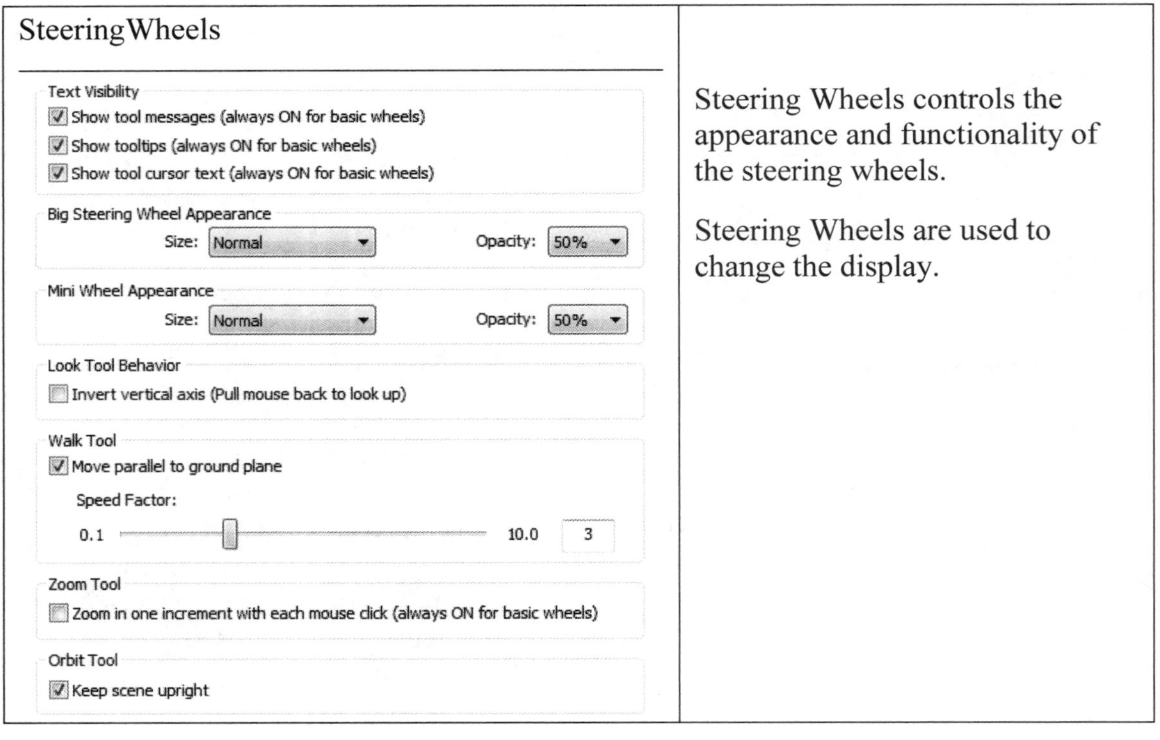

Steering Wheels controls the appearance and functionality of the steering wheels.

Steering Wheels are used to change the display.

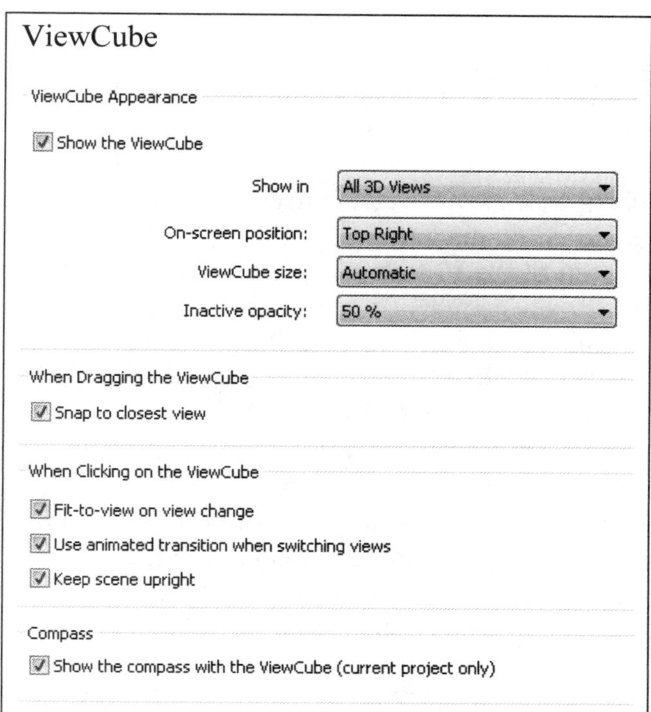

ViewCube controls the appearance and location of the ViewCube.

The user can also determine how the display changes when the ViewCube is selected.

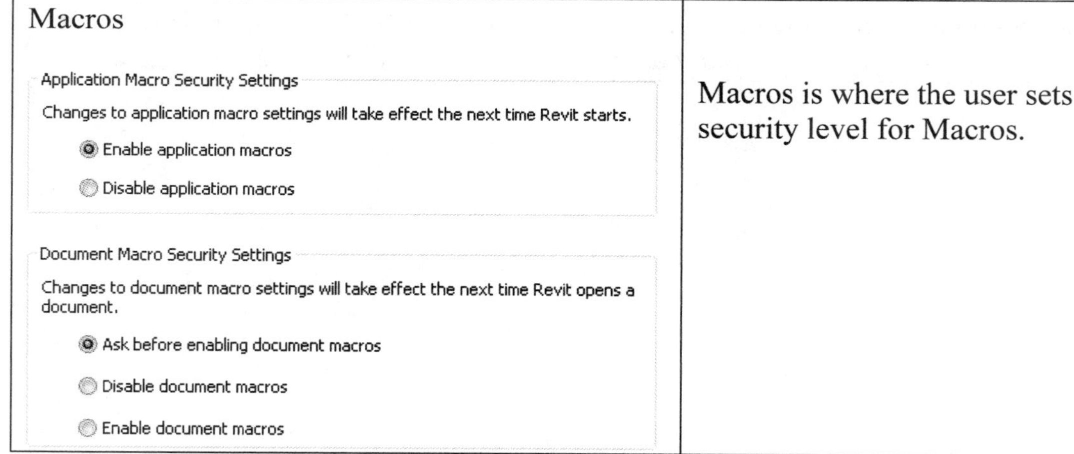

Macros is where the user sets the security level for Macros.

To boost productivity, store all your custom templates on the network for easy access and set the pointer to the correct folder.

The Help Menu

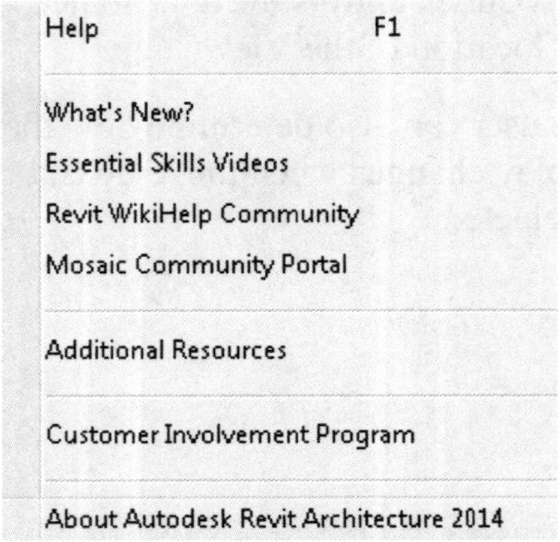

Help F1

What's New?
Essential Skills Videos
Revit WikiHelp Community
Mosaic Community Portal

Additional Resources

Customer Involvement Program

About Autodesk Revit Architecture 2014

Revit Help (also reached by function key F1) brings up the Help dialog.

What's New allows veteran users to quickly come up to speed on the latest release.
Essential Skills Videos is a small set of videos to help get you started. They are worth watching especially if your computer skills are rusty.
Revit WikiHelp Community is a set of searchable help documents created by users.
Mosaic Community Portal is an internet based website with tutorials and videos.
Additional Resources launches your browser and opens to a link on Autodesk's site. The Revit Web Content library takes you to Autodesk Seek, where you can download content from manufacturers.

The **Customer Involvement Program** is used by Autodesk to track your usage of their software remotely using your internet connection.
About Revit Architecture 2014 reaches a splash screen with information about the version and build of the copy of Revit you are working with. If you are unsure about which Service Pack you have installed, this is where you will find that information.

Exercise 1-6
Setting File Locations

Drawing Name: Close all open files
Estimated Time: 5 minutes

This exercise reinforces the following skills:

- ❑ Options
- ❑ File Locations

1. Close all open files or projects.

2. 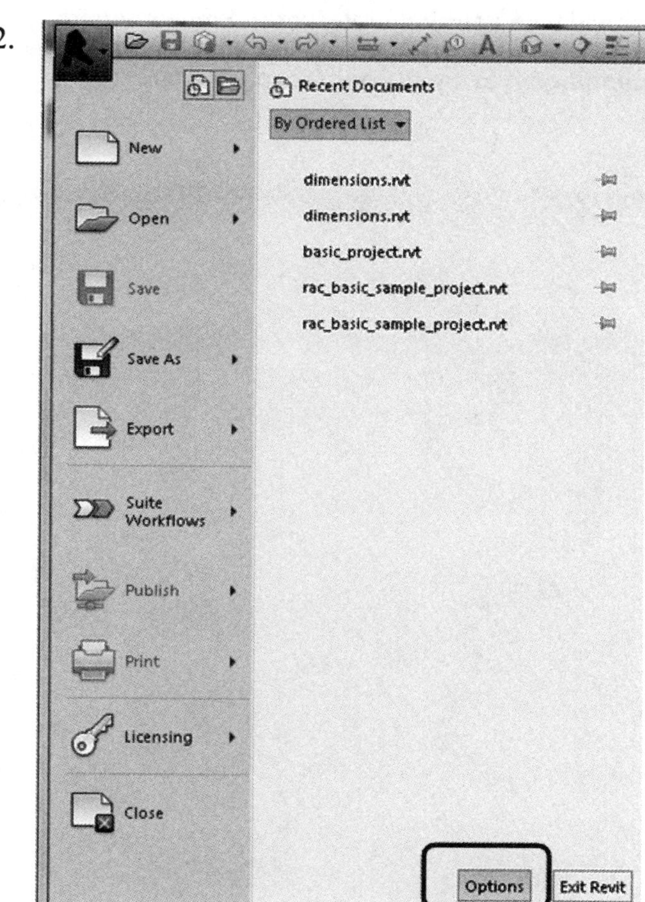

Go to **Applications Menu**.

Select the **Options** button at the bottom of the window.

3. File Locations Select the **File Locations** tab.

4. 

In the **Default path for users** section, pick the **Browse** button.

5. Default path for user files:

C:\Users\Elise\Dropbox\Revit 2014 Basics\exercise files\ Browse...

Navigate to the local or network folder where you will save your files. When the correct folder is highlighted, pick **Open**. Your instructor or CAD manager can provide you with this file information.

I recommend to my students to bring a flash drive to class and back up each day's work onto the flash drive. That way you never will lose your valuable work. Some students forget their flash drive. For those students, make a habit of uploading your file to Google Documents, Dropbox, or use www.yousendit.com to email your file to yourself.

Lesson 1 Quiz

True or False

1. Revit Warnings do not interrupt commands, so they can be ignored and later reviewed.
2. Deactivate View on the View menu is used to remove Views from Sheets
3. The Visibility\Graphics dialog is used to control what elements are visible in a view.

Multiple Choice [Select the Best Answer]

4. Temporary dimensions:

   A. drive the values that appear in the permanent dimensions.
   B. display the relative position of the selected element.
   C. display the size of the selected element.
   D. display only when an element is selected.

5. When you select an object, you can access the element properties by:

   A. Right click and select Element Properties.
   B. Select Element Properties→Instance Properties on the Ribbon Bar.
   C. Go to File→Properties.
   D. Using the Properties pane located on the left of the screen.

6. The interface item that changes appearance constantly depending on entity selections and command status is ____________________.

   A. Ribbon
   B. Project Browser
   C. Menu Bar
   D. Status Bar

7. View Styles available in Revit are ____________________.

   A. Wireframe
   B. Hidden Line
   C. Shaded
   D. Consistent Colors
   E. All of the Above

8. The shortcut key to bring up the steering wheel is _________.

   A. F2
   B. F3
   C. VV
   D. F8

9. To add elements to a selection set, hold down the ____ key.

   A. CONTROL
   B. SHIFT
   C. ESCAPE
   D. TAB

10. The color blue on a level bubble indicates that the level:

   A. has an associated view
   B. is a reference level
   C. is a non-story level
   D. was created using the line tool

ANSWERS:

1) T; 2) F; 3) T; 4) A, B, & D 5) D; 6) A; 7) E; 8) D; 9) A; 10) A

Lesson 2
Mass Elements

Mass Elements are used to give you a conceptual idea of the space and shape of a building without having to take the time to put in a lot of detail. It allows you to create alternative designs quickly and easily and get approval before you put in a lot of effort.

Massing Tools

In-Place Mass	Creates a solid shape.
Show Mass	Controls the visibility of mass objects.
Place Mass	Inserts a mass group into the active project.
Curtain System Roof Wall Floor Model by Face	Model by Face: Converts a face into a Roof, Curtain Wall System, Wall, or Floor.

When creating a conceptual mass to be used in a project, follow these steps:

1. Create a sketch of the desired shape(s).
2. Create levels to control the height of the shapes.
3. Create reference planes to control the width and depth of the shapes.
4. Draw a sketch of the profile of the shape.
5. Use the Massing tools to create the shape.

Masses can be used to create a component that will be used in a project - such as a column, casework, or lighting fixture - or they can be used to create a conceptual building.

Exercise 2-1
Shapes

Drawing Name: shapes.rfa
Estimated Time: 5 minutes

This exercise reinforces the following skills:

- Creating the basic shapes using massing tools
- Create an extrude
- Modify the Extrude height
- Create a revolve
- Create a sweep
- Create a blend
- Modify a blend

1. 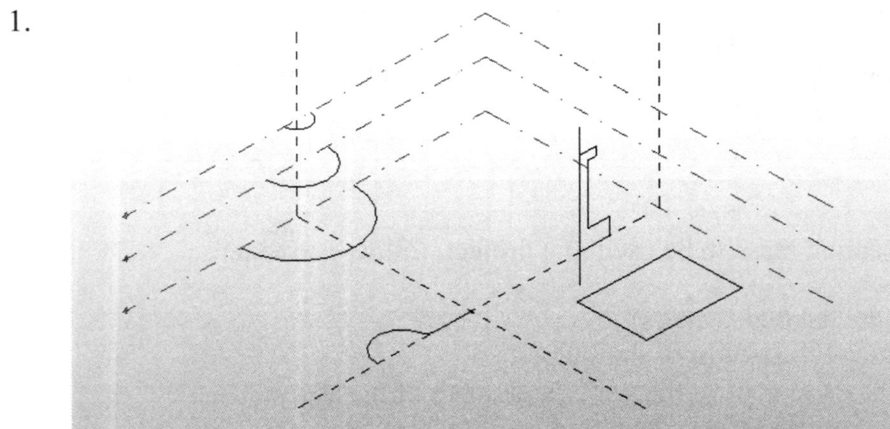

There are several sketches in the file.

Each set of sketches will be used to create a specific type of mass form.

2. 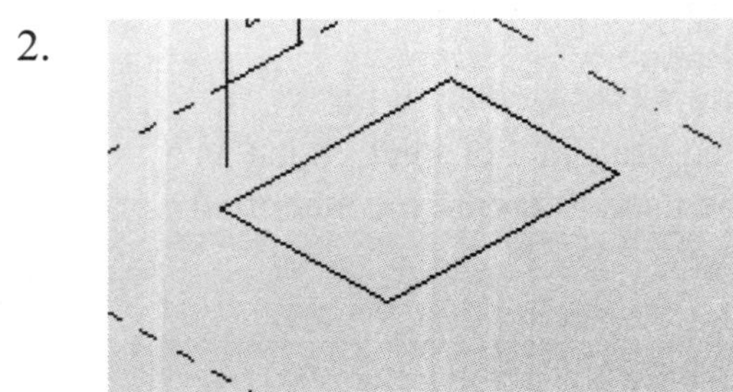

The most basic mass form is an Extrude. This mass form requires a single closed polygonal sketch.

The sketch should have no gaps or self-intersecting lines.

Select the rectangle so it highlights.

3. 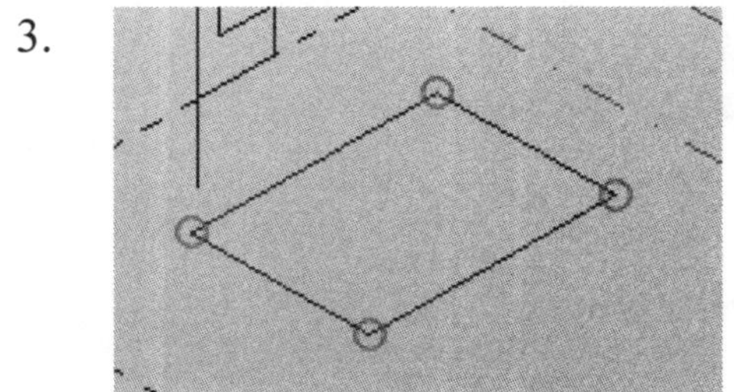

When the sketch is selected, you will see grips activated at the vertices.

4. 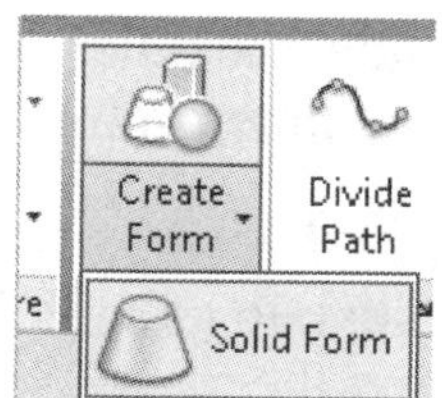

Select **Create Form→Solid Form** to create the extrude.

5. A preview of the extrude is displayed.

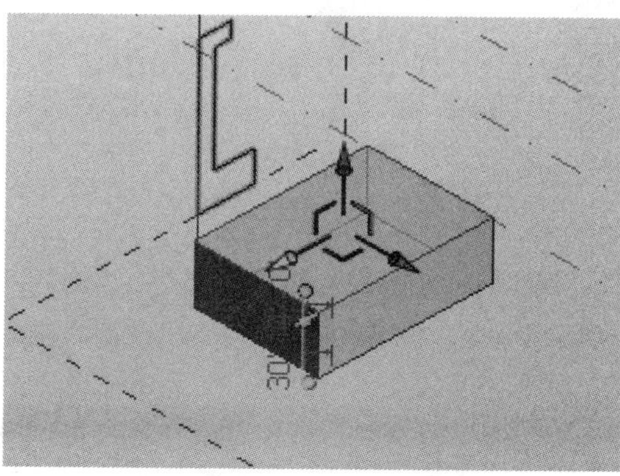

You can use the triad on the top of the extrude to extend the shape in any of the three directions.

There are two dimensions:

The bottom dimension controls the height of the extrude.
The top dimension controls the distance from top face of the extrude and the next level.

6. Activate the **East Elevation**.

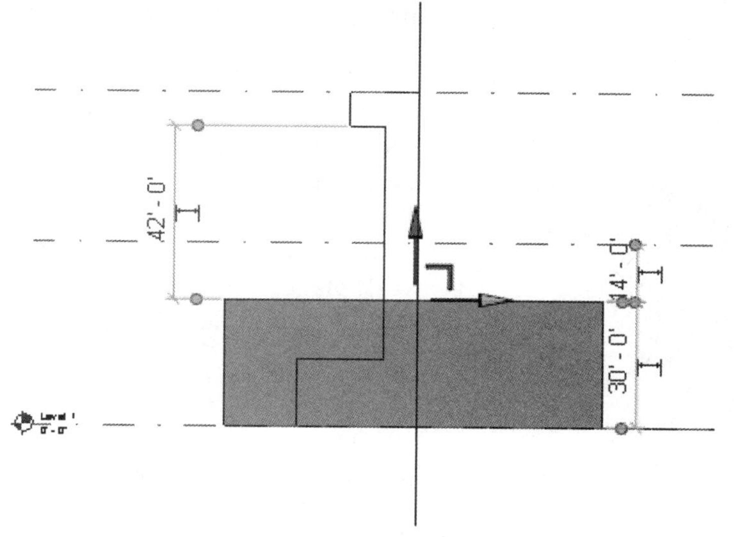

You can see how the dimensions are indicating the relative distances between the top face and the upper level, the bottom face, and another sketch.

7. 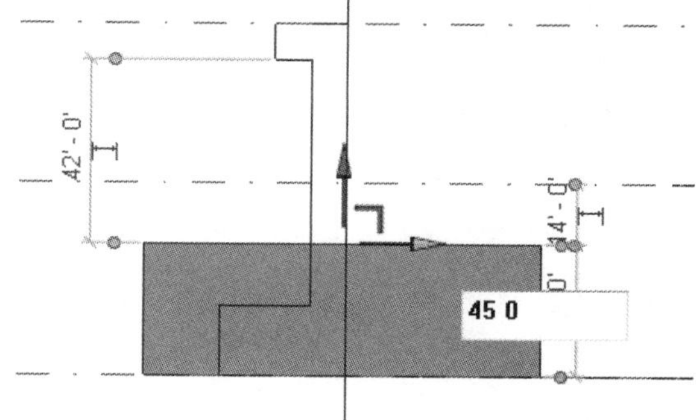

Change the 30′-0″ dimension to **45′-0″**.
To change the dimension, left click on the 30' 0" dimension text.

Press Enter.

8. 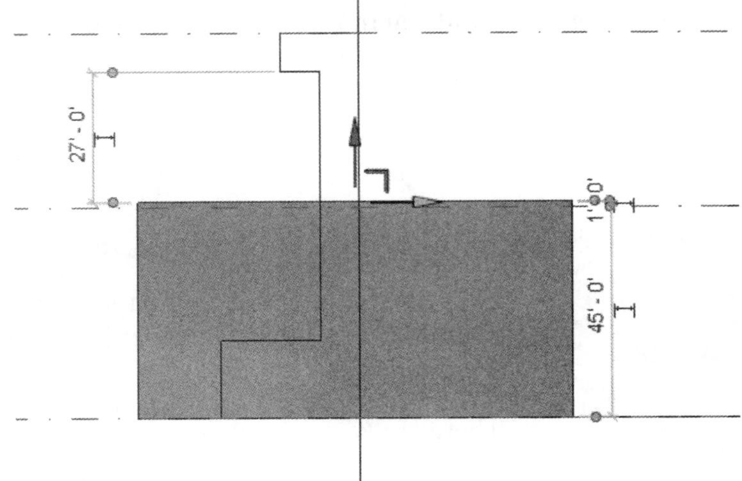

Note how the other relative dimensions update.

Left Click to exit defining the mass.

If you press Enter, you will create a second mass.

9. Switch to a 3D view.

10. 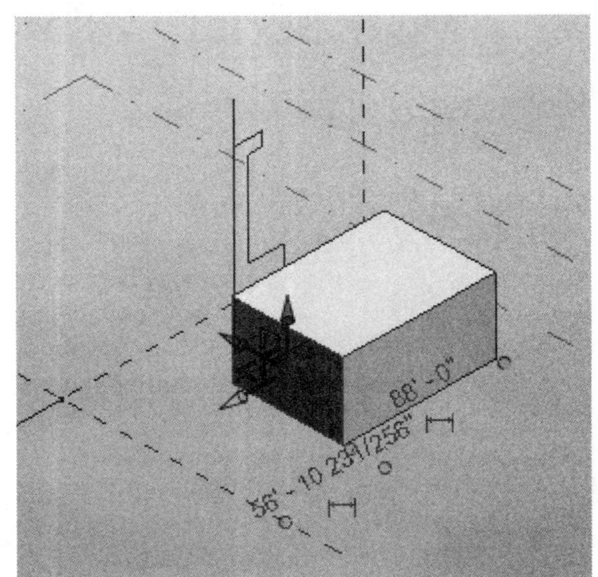

Select the Front/North face of the block.

This activates the triad and also displays the temporary dimensions.

You will see two temporary dimensions. One dimension indicates the distance of the face to the opposite face (the length of the block). One dimension indicates the distance of the face to the closest work plane.

11. 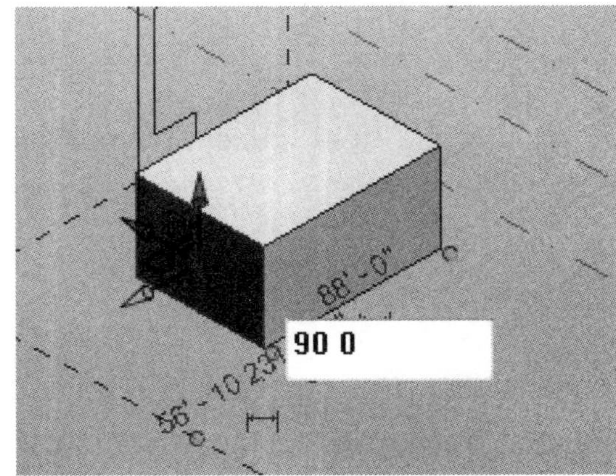

Change the 88′ 0″ dimension to **90′-0″**.

Left click in the window to release the selection and complete the change.

If you press Enter, you will create a second mass.

12. 

Use the View Cube to re-orient the view so you can clearly see the next sketch.

This sketch will be used to create a Revolve.

A Revolve requires a closed polygonal shape PLUS a reference line which can be used as the axis of revolution.

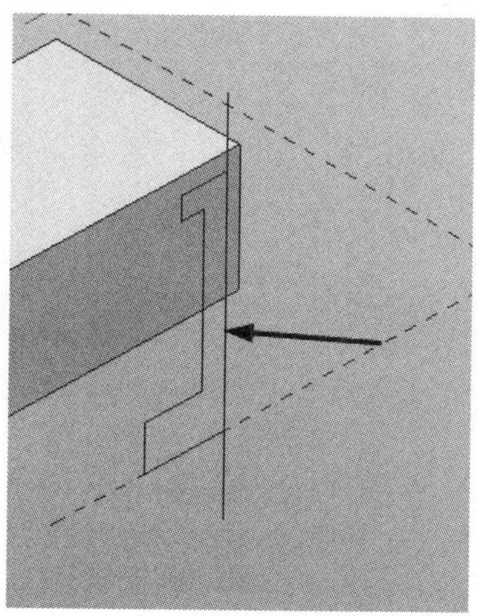

13. 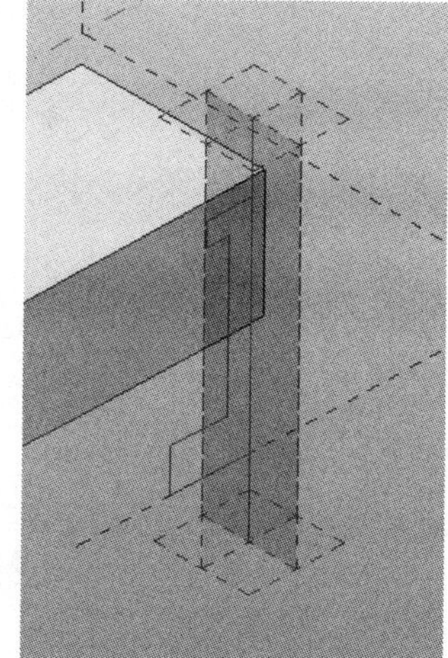

Hold down the CONTROL key and select the Axis Line (this is a reference line) and the sketch.

Note that a reference line automatically defines four reference planes. These reference planes can used to place sketches.

14. 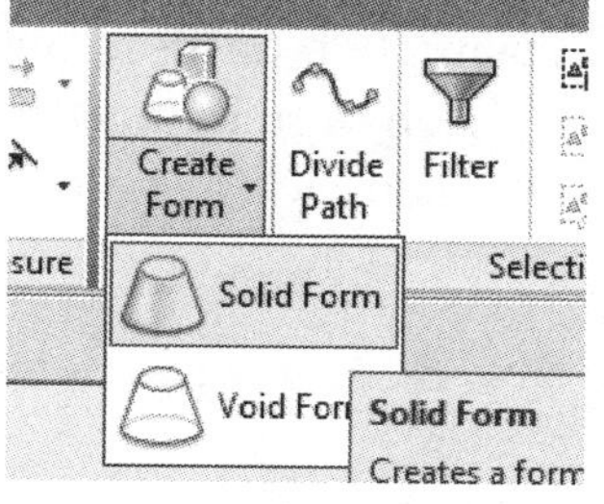

Select **Create Form→Solid Form**.

15. 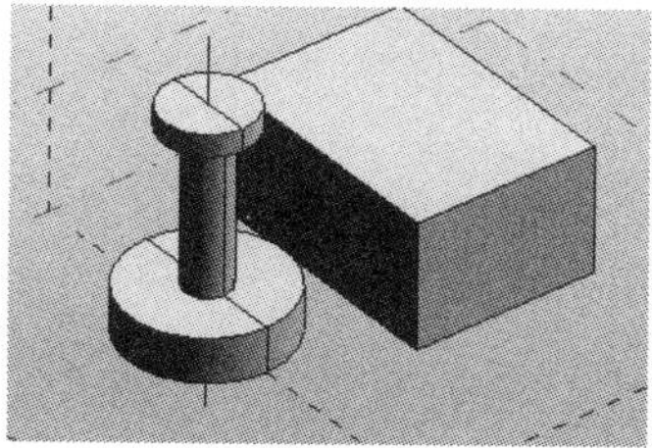

A Revolve will be created.

Our next mass form will be a SWEEP.

A sweep requires two sketches. One sketch must be a closed polygonal shape. This sketch is called the profile. The second sketch can be open or closed and is called the path. The profile travels along the path to create the sweep.

16. 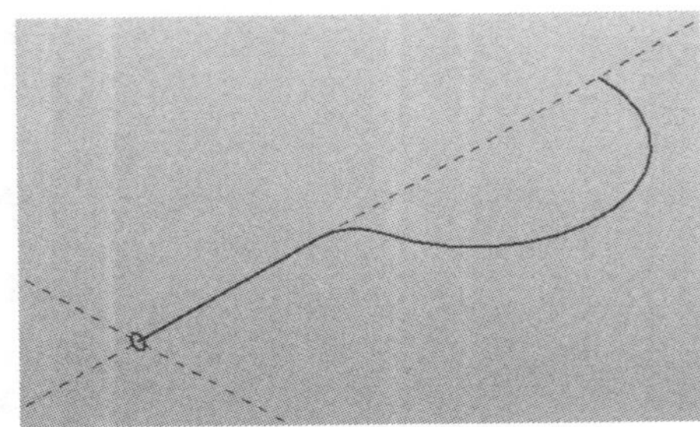

Hold down the CONTROL key and select the small circle and the sketch that looks like a question mark.

The two sketches will highlight.

17. 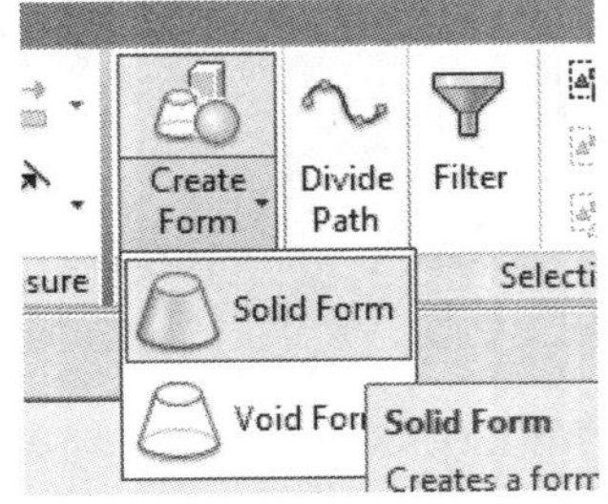

Select **Create Form→Solid Form**.

18. 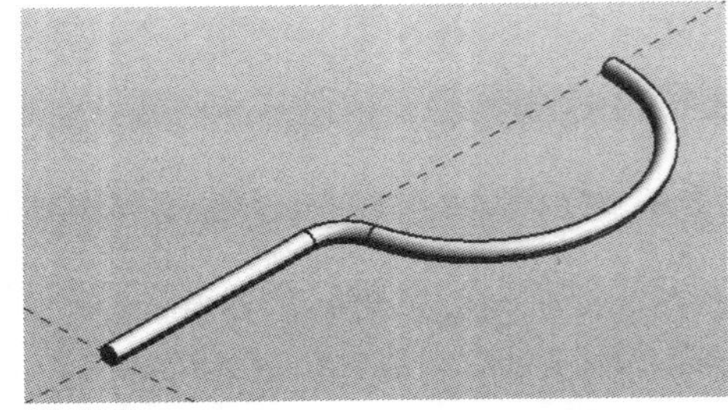

The sweep will be created.

The most common error when creating a sweep is to make the profile too big for the path. If the profile self-intersects as it travels along the path, you will get an error message. Try making the profile smaller to create a successful sweep.

19. 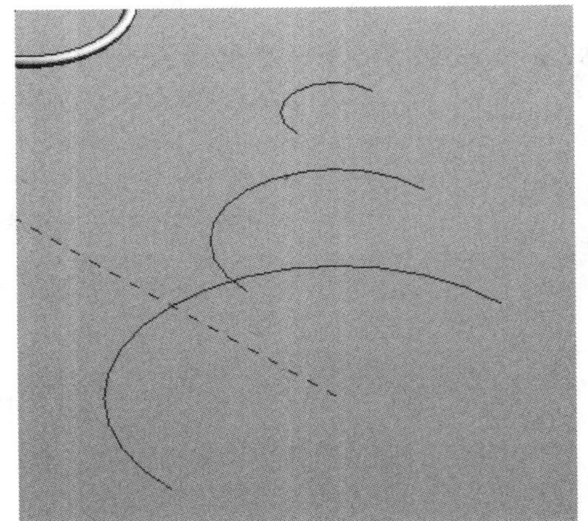

Our final shape will be a BLEND or LOFT. A blend is created using two or more open or closed sketches. Each sketch must be placed on a different reference plane or level.

Hold down the CONTROL key and select the three arcs.

20. 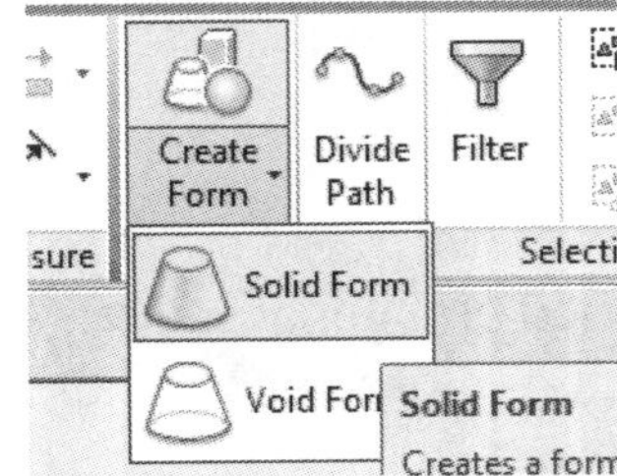

Select **Create Form→Solid Form**.

21.

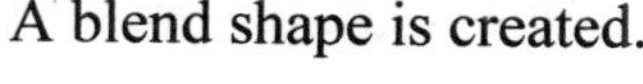

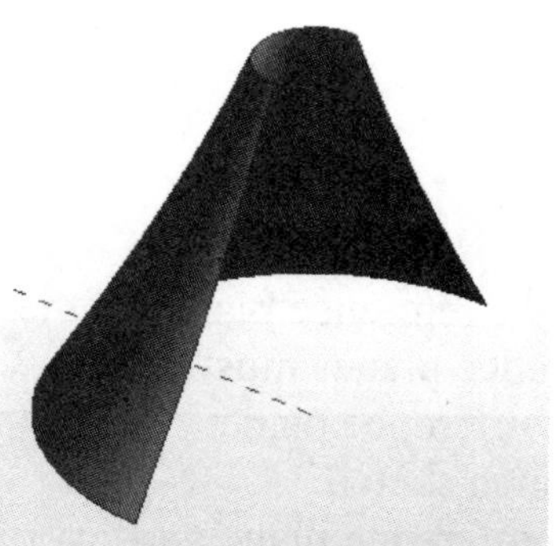

A blend shape is created.

Close without saving.

Challenge Task:

Can you create the four basic shapes from scratch?

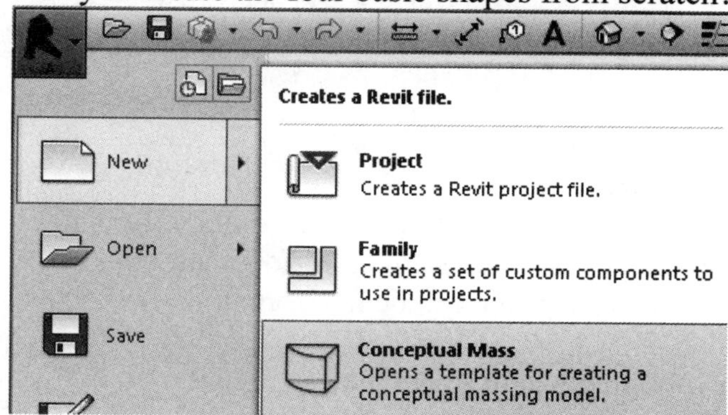

Create an extrude, revolve, sweep and blend using New→Conceptual Mass from the Applications menu.

Steps to make an Extrude:

1. Set your active plane using the Set Work Plane tool.
2. Create a single polygonal sketch – no gaps or self-intersecting lines.
3. Select the sketch.
4. Create Form→Solid Form.
5. Green Check to finish the mass.

Steps to make a Revolve:

1. Set your active plane using the Set Work Plane tool.
2. Switch to a 3D view.
3. Draw a reference line to be used as the axis of revolution.
4. Pick one the planes defined by the reference line as the active plane to place your sketch.
5. Create a single polygonal sketch – no gaps, overlapping or self-intersecting lines – for the revolve shape.

6. Hold down the CONTROL key and select BOTH the sketch and reference line. *If the reference line is not selected, you will get an extrude.*
7. Create Form→Solid Form.
8. Green Check to finish the mass.

Steps to make a Sweep:

1. Activate Level 1 floor plan view. You need to select one reference plane for the profile and one reference plane for the path. The reference planes must be perpendicular to each other. Set Level 1 for the path's reference plane.
2. Draw a path on Level 1. The path can be a closed or open sketch.
3. Create a reference plane to use for the profile. Draw a reference plane on Level 1 – name it profile plane. Make this the active plane for the profile sketch.
4. Switch to a 3D view. Create a single polygonal sketch – no gaps, overlapping or self-intersecting lines. The profile sketch should be close to the path or intersect it so it can follow the path easily. If it is too far away from the path, it will not sweep properly or you will get an error.
5. Hold down the CONTROL key and select BOTH the path and the profile. *If only one object is selected, you will get an extrude.*
6. Create Form→Solid Form.
7. Green Check to finish the mass.

Steps to make a Blend:

1. Blends require two or more sketches. Each sketch should be on a parallel reference plane. You can add levels or reference planes for each sketch. If you want your blend to be vertical, use levels. If you want your blend to be horizontal, use reference planes.
    a. To add levels, switch to an elevation view and select the Level tool.
    b. To add reference planes, switch to a floor plan view and select the Reference Plane tool. Name the reference planes to make them easy to select.
2. Set the active reference plane using the Option Bar or the Set Reference Plane tool.
3. Create a single polygonal sketch – no gaps, overlapping or self-intersecting lines.
4. Select at least one more reference plane to create a second sketch. Make this the active plane.
5. Create a single polygonal sketch – no gaps, overlapping or self-intersecting lines.
6. Hold down the CONTROL key and select all the sketches created. *If only one object is selected, you will get an extrude.*
7. Create Form→Solid Form.
8. Green Check to finish the mass.

Exercise 2-2

Create a Conceptual Model

Drawing Name: default.rte [metric default.rte]
Estimated Time: 5 minutes

This exercise reinforces the following skills:

- Switching Elevation Views
- Setting Project Units
- Add a Level

This tutorial uses metric or Imperial units. Metric units will be designated in brackets.

Revit uses a level to define another floor or story in a building.

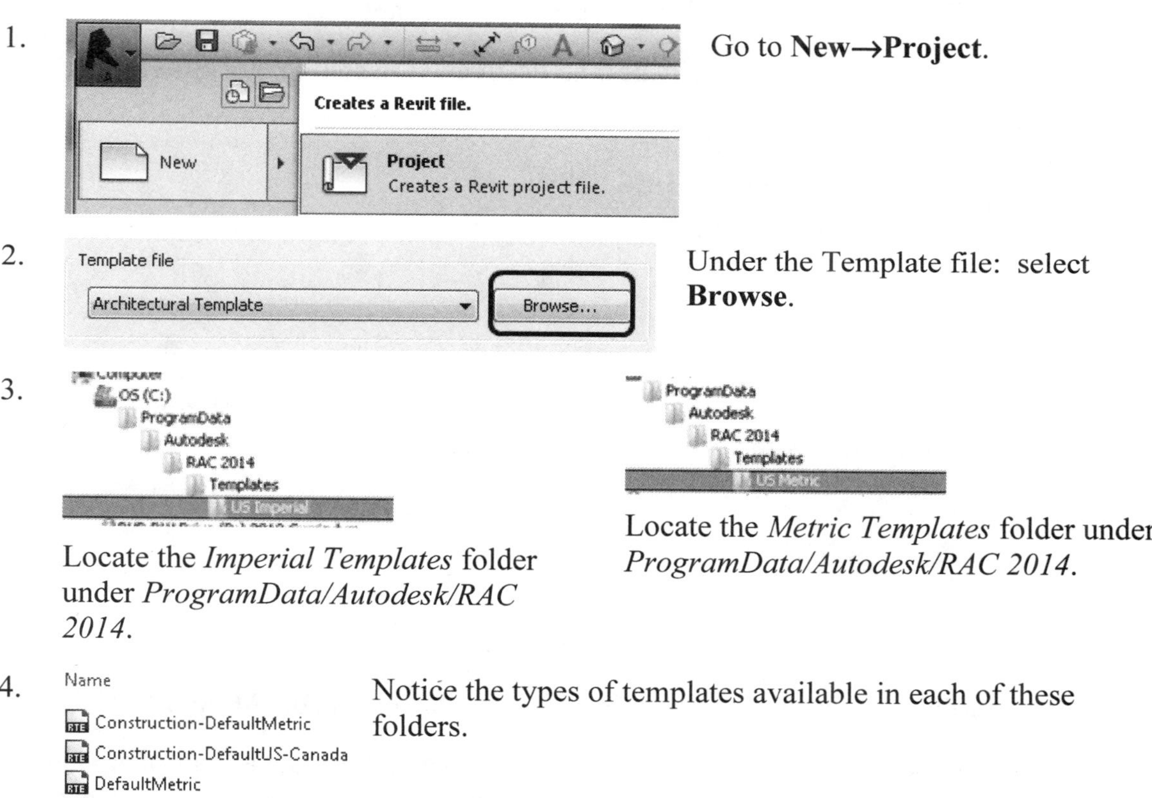

1. Go to **New→Project**.

2. Under the Template file: select **Browse**.

3. Locate the *Imperial Templates* folder under *ProgramData/Autodesk/RAC 2014*.

   Locate the *Metric Templates* folder under *ProgramData/Autodesk/RAC 2014*.

4. Notice the types of templates available in each of these folders.

5. Select the *default.rte [DefaultMetric.rte]* template.

   Brackets indicate metric can be selected as an alternative.

   Press **OK**.

If you accidentally picked Metric when you wanted Imperial or vice versa, you can change the units at any time. Revit will automatically switch any dimensions over to the active units.

To change Project Units, go to the **Manage** Ribbon.

Select **Settings→Project Units.**

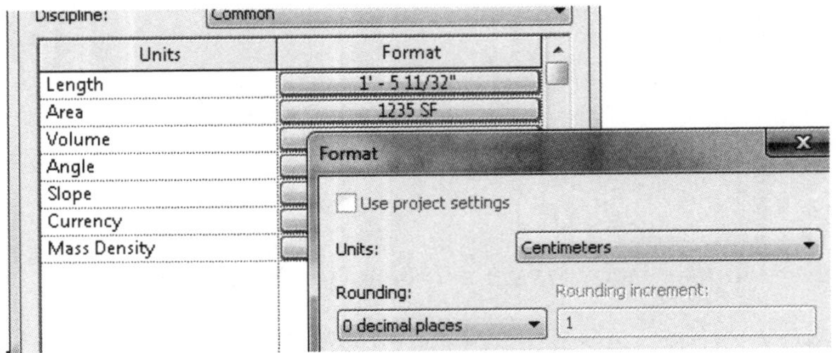

Left click the Length button, then select the desired units from the drop-down list.

6. Double click **East** under Elevations.

   This activates the East view orientation.

7. Select the **Architecture** ribbon.

8. Select the **Level** tool under Datum. (This adds a floor elevation.)

9. Move your mouse to set an elevation of **12′ [3650 mm]**. Pick to start the elevation line.

10. 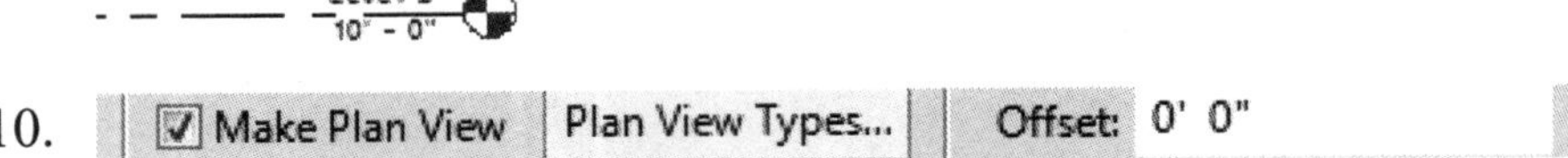

    In the Options bar located on the lower left of the screen, enable **Make Plan View**.

    This should be enabled if you want Revit to automatically create a floor plan view of this level. If you forget to check this box, you can create the floor plan view later using the **View** Ribbon.

Double click on the blue elevation symbol to automatically switch to the floor plan view for that elevation.

---

11. 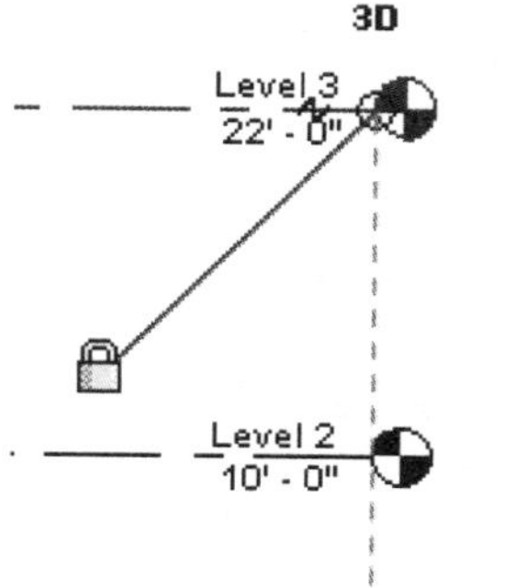

☑ Pick to place the end point to position the level indicator above the other indicators.

12. Basically, you place a new level by picking two points at the desired height.

    Right click and select **Cancel** twice to exit the Level command.

    Revit is always looking for references even among annotations, you will notice that your level tags snap and lock together so when you move one to the right or left, all those in line with it will follow.

    The jogged line allows the user to create a jog if desired.

    If you need to adjust the position of the tag, just click on the line, 3 blue grips will appear. These can be clicked and dragged as needed. You can also right click on a level tag and select 'Hide annotation in view' and the tag and level line will disappear in that view only.

    Hide Annotation in View is only enabled if an object is selected first.

13. Save the file as a project as *ex2-1.rvt.*

Exercise 2-3
Adding an In-Place Mass

Drawing Name: ex2-1.rvt
Estimated Time: 10 minutes

This exercise reinforces the following skills:

- Switching Elevation Views
- Add Mass

1. Open or continue working in the file *ex2-1.rvt*.

2. 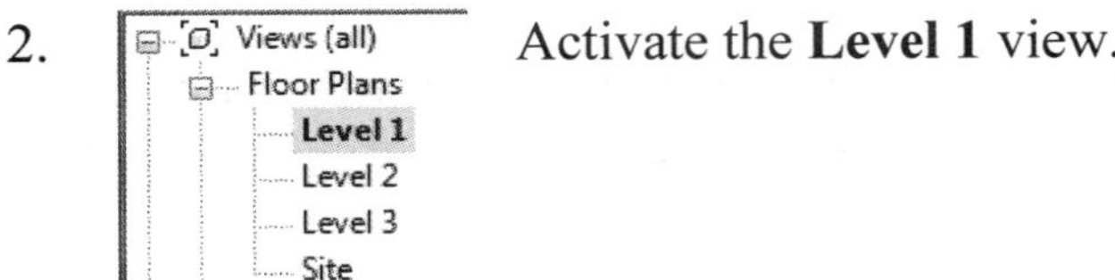

Activate the **Level 1** view.

3. Massing & Site — Select the **Site & Massing** ribbon.

4. In-Place Mass — Select the **In-Place Mass** tool.

Revit uses three different family categories. System families are families which are defined inside the project, such as floors, walls, and ceilings. Model families are external files which can be loaded into the project, such as doors, windows, and furniture. The third family category is in-place masses, which are families created on-the-fly.

5. 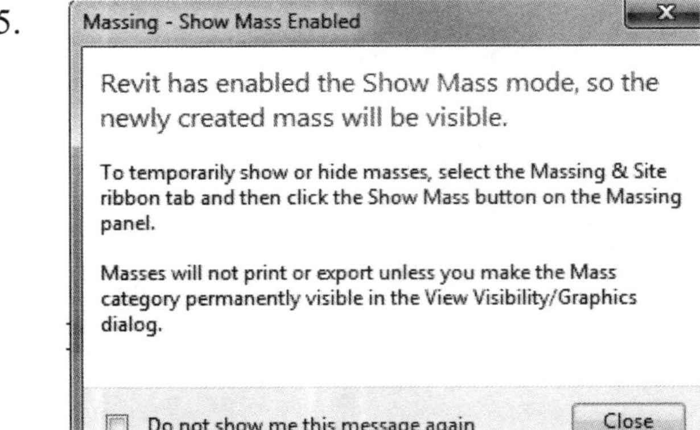

Masses, by default, are invisible. However, in order to create and edit masses you need to see what you are doing. Revit brings up a dialog to let you know that the software is switching the visibility of masses to ON, so you can work.

Press **Close**.

*If you don't want to bugged by this dialog, enable the **Don't show me this message again** option.*

6. 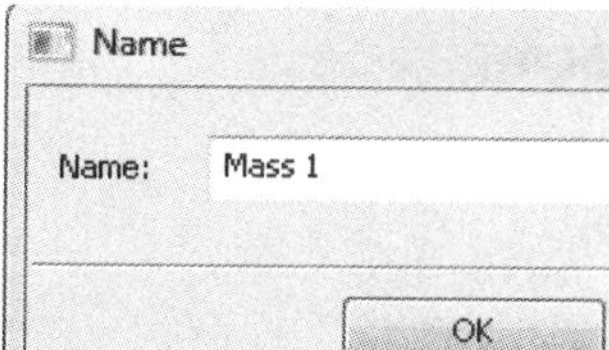

Enter **Mass 1** in the Name field.

Press **OK**.

Next, we create the boundary sketch to define our mass. This is the footprint for the conceptual building.

7. Select the **Line** tool located under the Draw panel.

8. 

Enable **Chain** in the Options bar located on the bottom of the screen.
This allows you to draw lines without always having to pick the start point.
If you hold down the SHIFT key while you draw, this puts you in orthogonal mode.

9. Create the shape shown.
The left figure shows the units in Imperial units (feet and inches).
The right figure shows the units in millimeters.

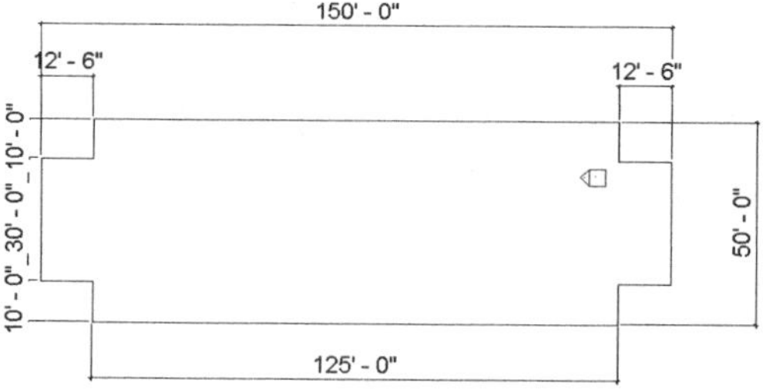

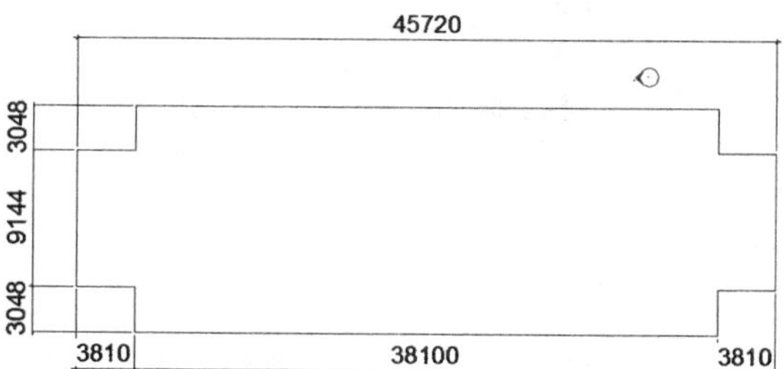

You can draw using listening dimensions or enter the dimension values as you draw.

10. Exit out of drawing mode by right click and select Cancel twice, selecting ESC on the keyboard or by selecting the Modify button on the ribbon.

11. Switch to a 3D view.
Activate the **View** ribbon and select **3D View**.

You can also switch to a 3D view from the Quick Access toolbar by selecting the house icon.

12. Window around the entire sketch so it is highlighted.

13. 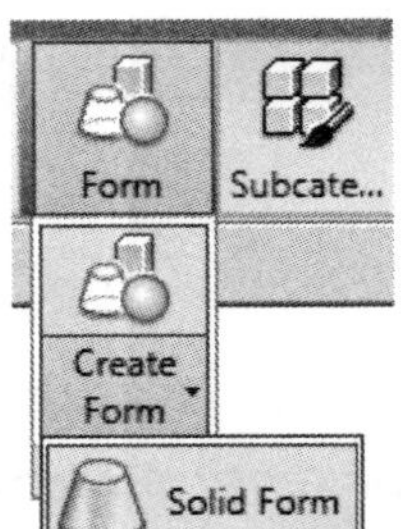

Select **Form→Create Form→Solid Form**.

You must select the sketch to create the form.

If the sketch has any gaps, overlapping lines, or self-intersecting lines, you will get an error. Exit the command and inspect the sketch to make sure it is a cleanly closed polygon.

14. 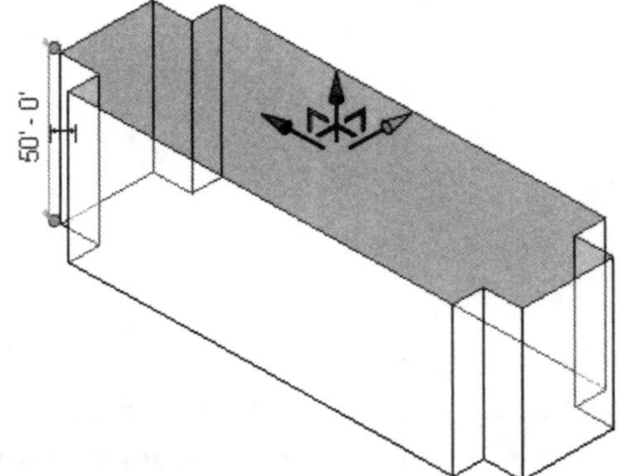

An extrusion distance is displayed. This can be edited, if desired.

15. 

Select the green check box to **Finish Mass**.

The Mass is created.

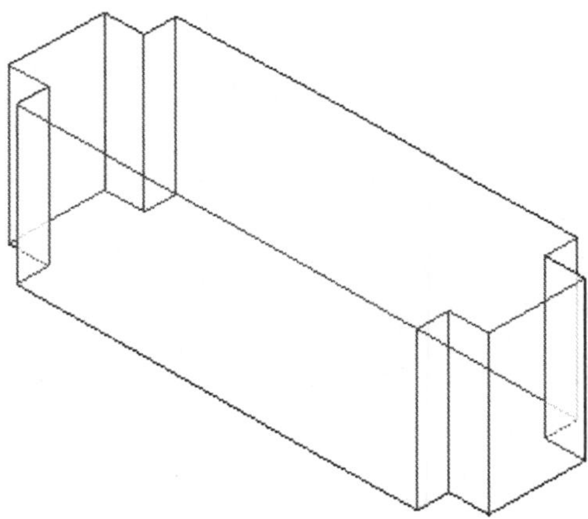

16. Save the file as *ex2-2.rvt*.

Object tracking will only work if the sketch objects are active and available in the current sketch. You can use Pick to copy entities into the current sketch.

Exercise 2-4

Modifying Mass Elements

Drawing Name: ex2-2.rvt
Estimated Time: 30 minutes

This exercise reinforces the following skills:

- Show Mass
- Align
- Modify Mass
- Mirror
- Create Form
- Save View

A short video of this exercise is available on my website to help users with this exercise. Access at *www.mossdesigns.com/documents/ex2-3-revit.avi.*

1. Open *ex2-2.rvt.*

2. Show Mass Form and Floors

   If you don't see the mass, **Show Mass** on the Massing & Site ribbon to turn mass visibility ON.

   Some students may experience this issue if they close the file and then re-open it for a later class.

3. Elevations (Building Elevation)
   East
   North
   South
   West

   Activate the **East** Elevation.

4. We see that top of the building does not align with Level 3.

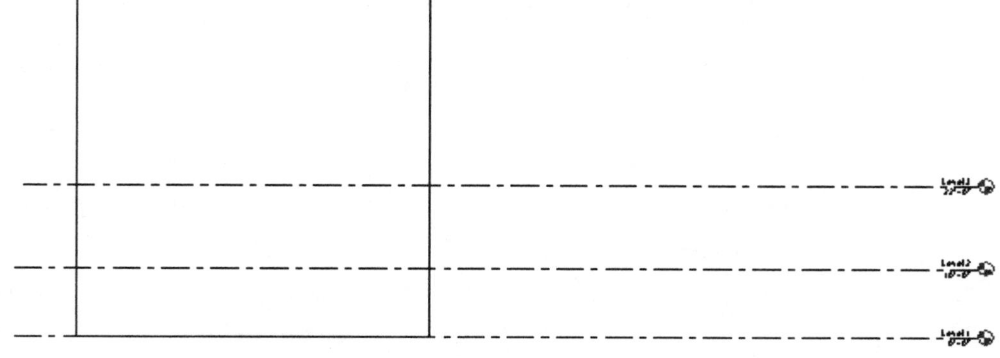

To adjust the horizontal position of the level lines, simply select the line and use the grip to extend or shorten it.

5. Modify Select the **Modify** Ribbon.

6. 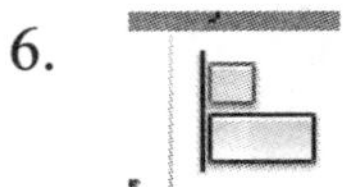 Select the **Align** tool.

When using Align, the first element selected acts as the source, the second element selected shifts position to align with the first element.

7. 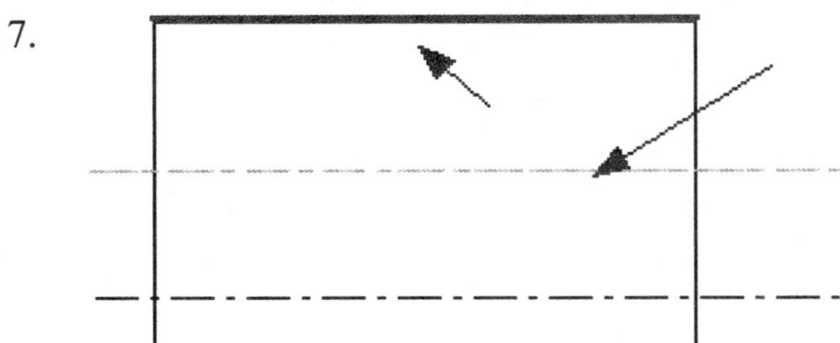

Select the top level line (Level 3) then select the top of the extrusion.

Right click and select **Cancel** twice to exit the Align command.

8. The top of the extrusion now aligns to Level 3.

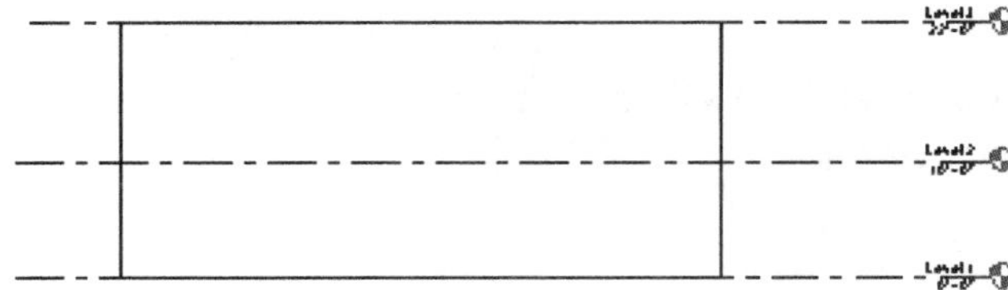

The lock would constrain or lock the top of the extrusion to the level. If the level elevation changes, then the extrusion will automatically update.

9. 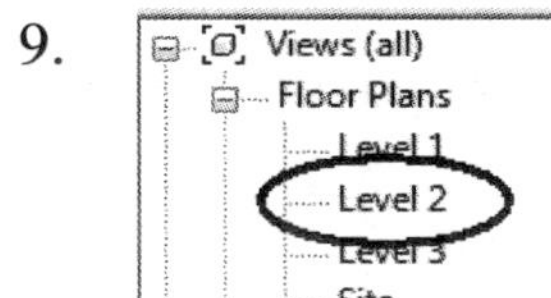

Activate **Level 2** under Floor Plans.

10. In-Place Mass

Select **In-Place Mass** from the Massing & Site ribbon.

11. 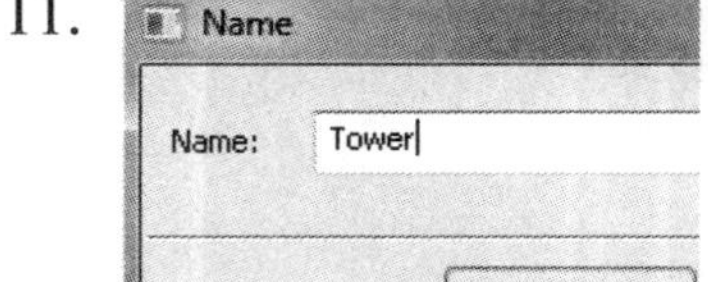

Name the new mass **Tower**.

Press **OK**.

12. 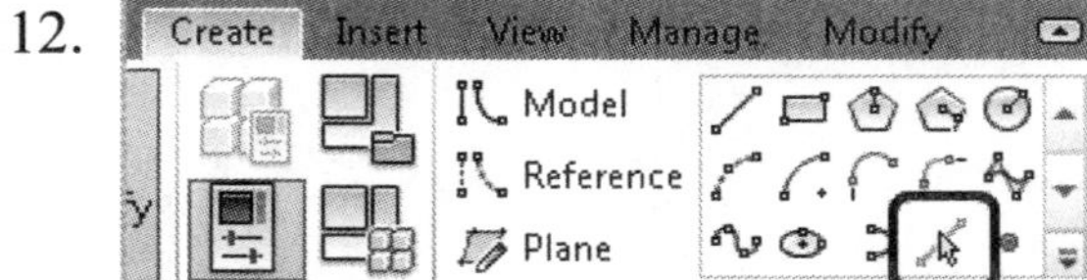

You can use object tracking to locate the intersection between the two corners.

To activate object tracking, enable the **Pick Lines** tool located under Draw. Then select the two lines you want to align with.

13. 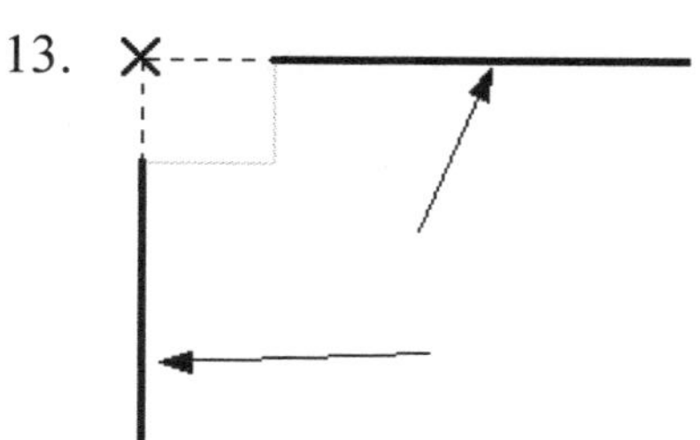

Select the two lines indicated to be used for object tracking to locate the center of the circle.

14. Select the **Circle** tool under Draw.

15. Uncheck Make surface from closed loops on the Options bar. Enable Chain.

16. When you see the large X and the tooltip says Intersection, you will have located the intersection.

Pick to locate the center of the circle at the intersection.

17. Enter a radius of **16′-0″** [**4880**].

When you used the Pick Line tool, you copied those lines into the current sketch. Once the lines were part of the current sketch, they could be used for object tracking.

18. Select the circle sketch so it is highlighted.

19. Select the **Draw Mirror Axis** tool on the Modify panel.

20. Locate the midpoint of the small horizontal line and pick.

21. 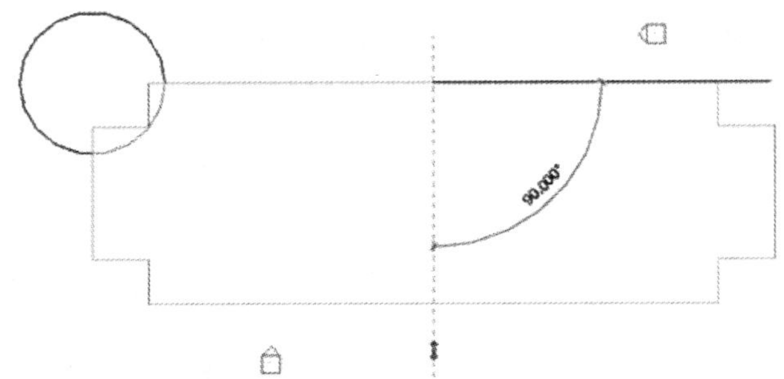

Bring your mouse down in the Vertical direction and pick for the second point of the mirror axis.

22. 

The circle sketch is mirrored.

Left click to release the selection.

23. Switch to a 3D view using the Project Browser.

24. Select **one** of the circles so it is highlighted.
Remember you can only extrude one closed polygon at a time.

Select **Form→Create Form→Solid Form**.

25. 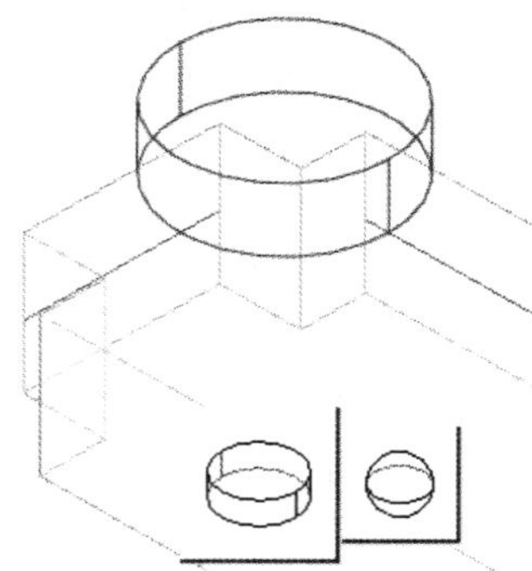

A small toolbar will appear with two options for extruding the circle.

Select the option that looks like a cylinder.

26. 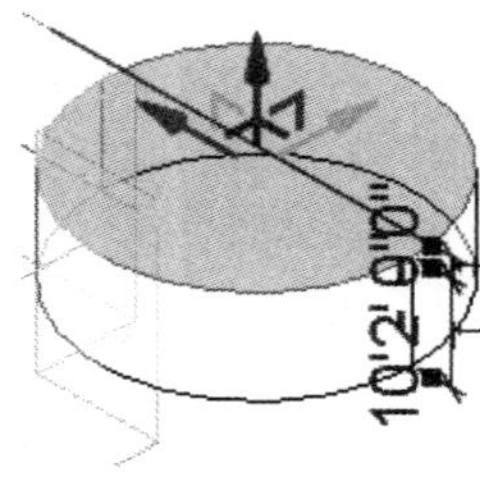

A preview of the extrusion will appear with the temporary dimension. You can edit the temporary dimension to modify the height of the extrusion.

Press ENTER or left click to accept the default height.

27. 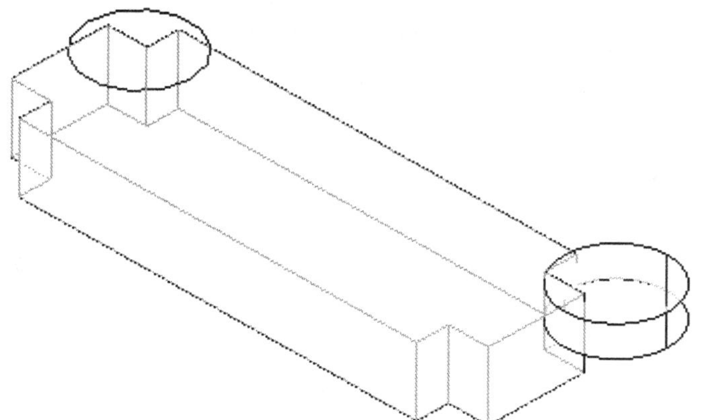

If you press ENTER more than once, additional cylinders will be placed.

The circle is extruded.

28. 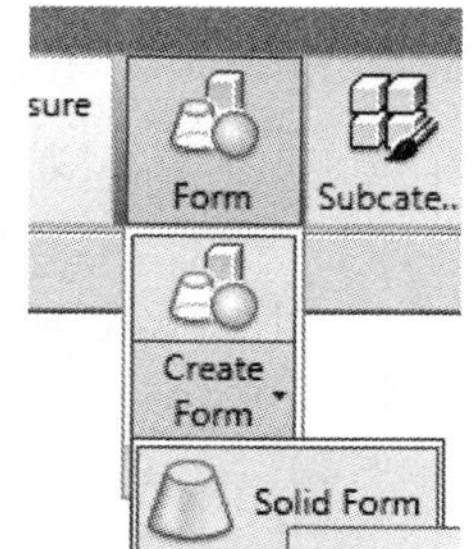

Select the remaining circle so it is highlighted.

Select **Form→Create Form→Solid Form**.

29. 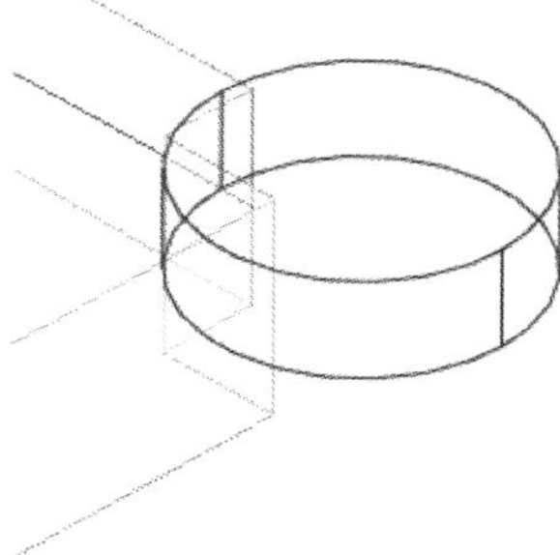

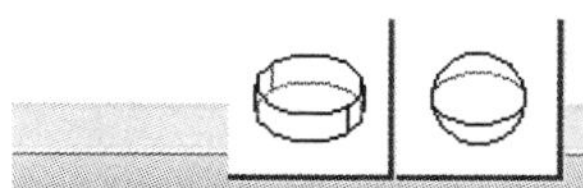

A small toolbar will appear with two options for extruding the circle.

Select the option that looks like a cylinder.

30. 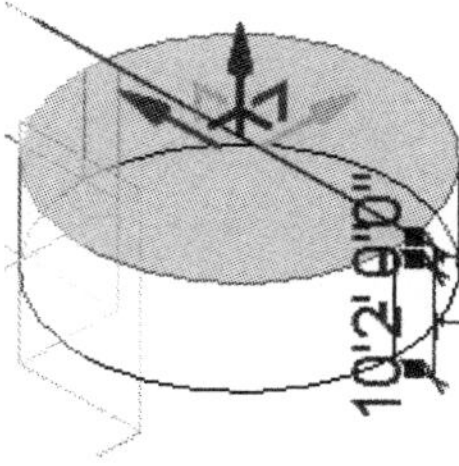

A preview of the extrusion will appear with the temporary dimension. You can edit the temporary dimension to modify the height of the extrusion.

Press ENTER or left click to accept the default height.

31. 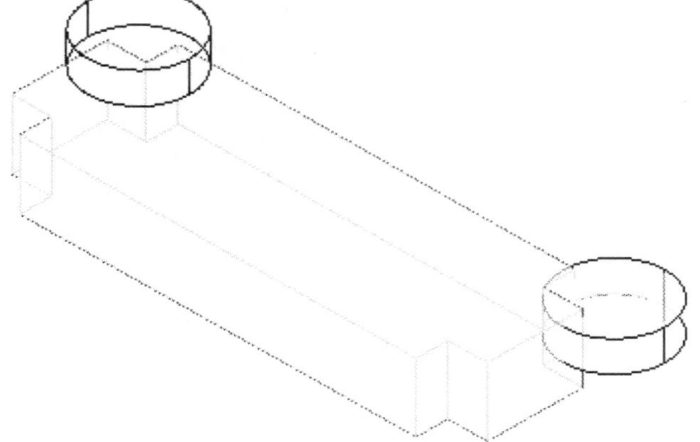

Both circles are now extruded.

32. 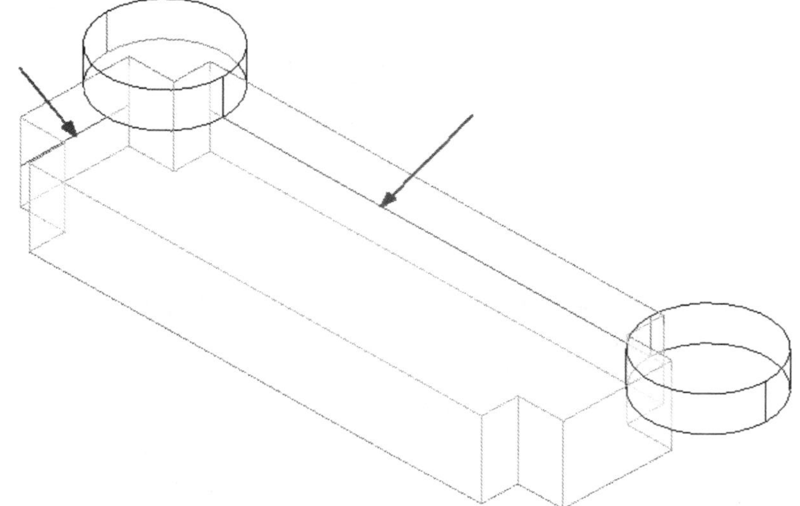

Select the two lines used to locate the circle sketch.

Right click and select **Delete** from the shortcut menu to delete the lines.

You can also press the Delete key on the keyboard or use the Delete tool on the Modify panel.

33. 

Select **Finish Mass**.

If you do not delete the lines before you finish the mass, you will get an error message.

34. 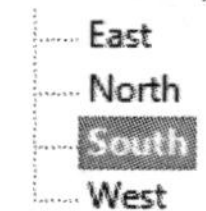

Activate the **South** Elevation.

35. Select each level line.

Right click and select **Maximize 3D Extents**.
This will extend each level line so it covers the entire model.

36. Activate the Modify ribbon.

Select the **Align** tool from the Modify Panel.

37. Multiple Alignment Prefer: Wall faces

On the Options bar, enable **Multiple Alignment**.

38. Select the Level 3 line as the source object.

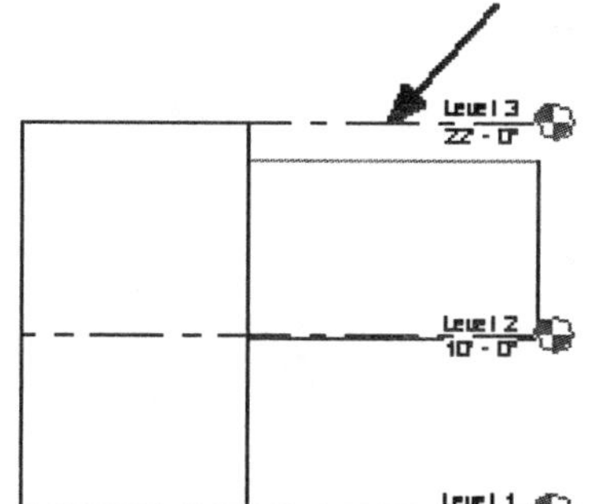

39. Select the top of the two towers as the edges to be shifted.

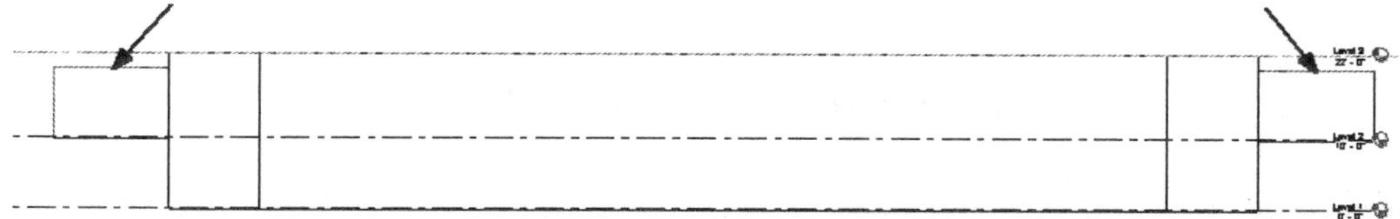

40. 3D Views {3D} Switch to a 3D view using the Project Browser.

41. Use the ViewCube located in the upper right of the screen to orbit the model.

42. To save the new orientation, right click on the ViewCube and select **Save View**.

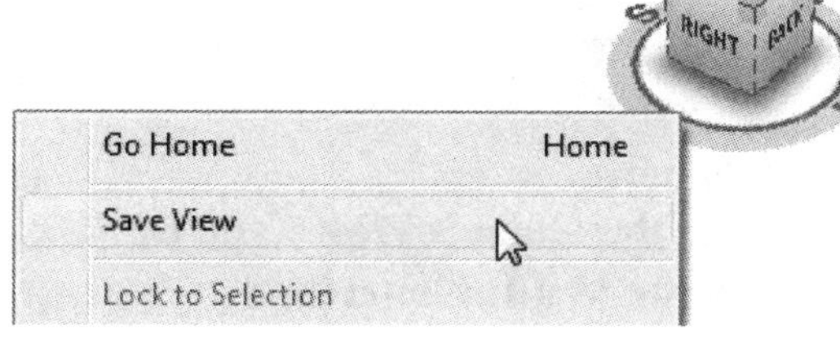

43. Name: 3D Ortho OK

Enter **3D Ortho** for the name of the view.

Press **OK**.

44. 3D Views 3D Ortho {3D} The **Saved** view is now listed in the Project browser under 3D Views.

45. Save the file as *ex2-3.rvt.*

- Pick on a mass element to activate the element's grips. You can use the grips to change the element's shape, size, and location.
- You can only use the **View→Orient** menu to activate 3D views when you are already in 3D view mode.

Exercise 2-5
Create Wall by Face

Drawing Name: ex2-3.rvt
Estimated Time: 15 minutes

This exercise reinforces the following skills:

- Wall by Face
- Trim
- Show Mass

You can add doors and windows to your conceptual model to make it easier to visualize.

1. Open *ex2-3.rvt.*
2.  Activate the **3D Ortho** view under 3D Views.
3.  Activate the **Massing & Site** ribbon.
4. 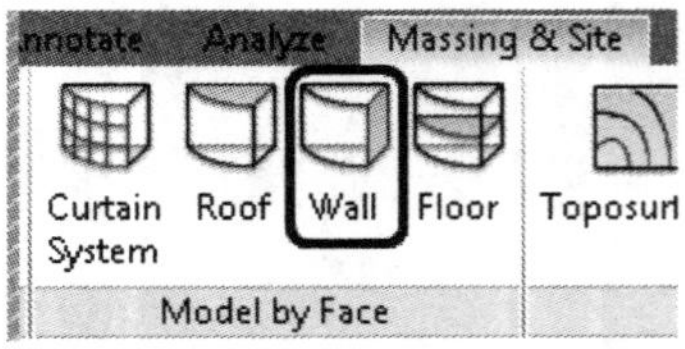 Select **Model by Face→Wall.**
5. 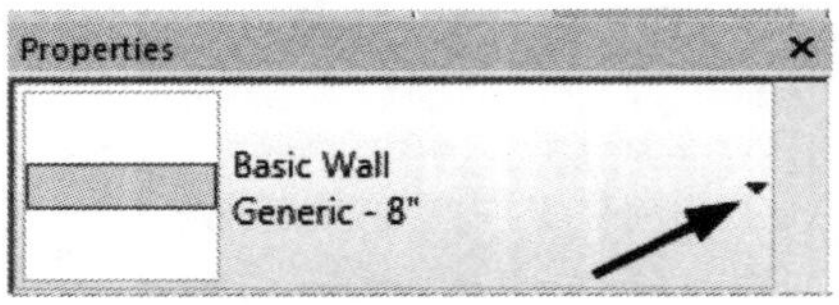 Note the wall type currently enabled in the Properties pane. A different wall type can be selected from the drop-down list available using the small down arrow.

   Imperial:
   Set the Default Wall Type to:
   Basic Wall: Generic- 8″.

   Metric:
   Set the Default Wall Type to:
   Basic Wall: Generic- 200 mm.
6. 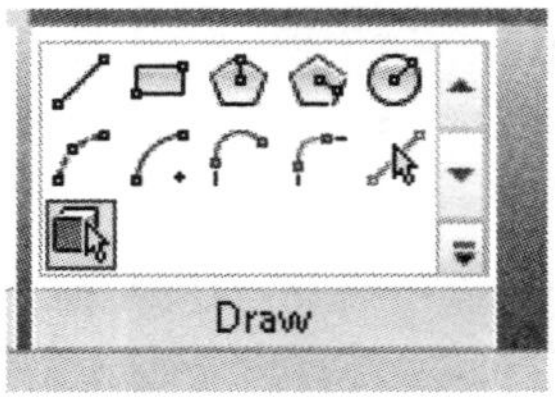 Enable **Pick Faces** from the Draw Panel on the ribbon.

7. 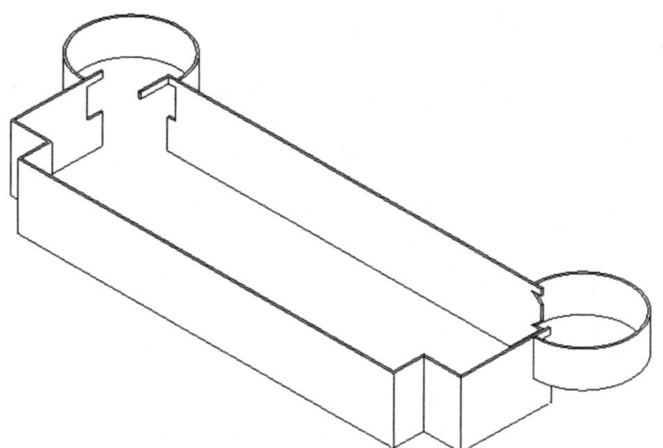

Select each wall and cylinder. The cylinder will be halved by the walls, so you will have to select each half.

You will have to do some cleanup work on the corners where the towers are.

Some students will accidentally pick the same face more than once. You will see an error message that you have overlapping/duplicate walls. Simply delete the extra walls.

8. 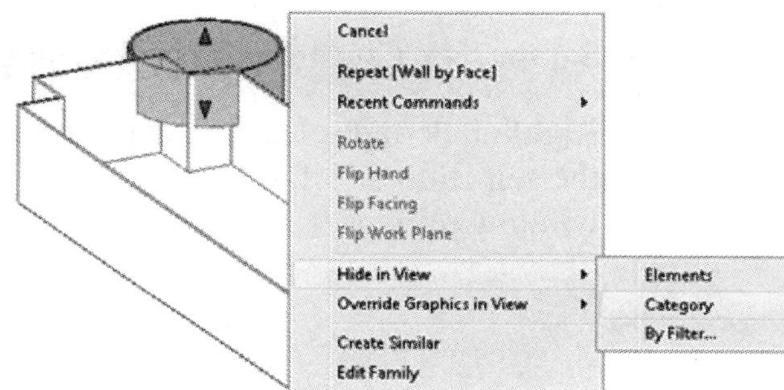

Select any visible mass.
Right click and select **Hide in View→ Category**.

This will turn off the visibility of masses.

9. 

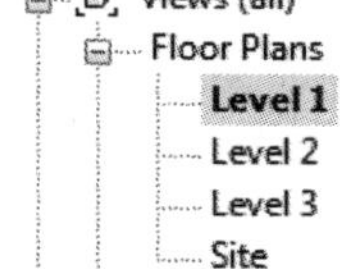

Activate **Level 1** floor plan.

10. 

Window around all the walls to select.

11. 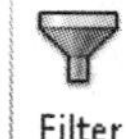

Select the **Filter** tool from the ribbon.

12. 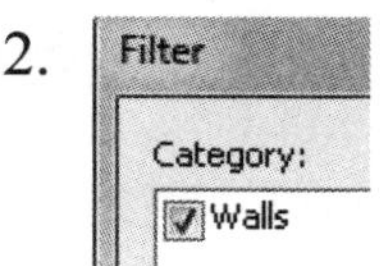

Uncheck all the boxes EXCEPT walls.
Press **OK**.

There are some duplicate walls in this selection.

13. 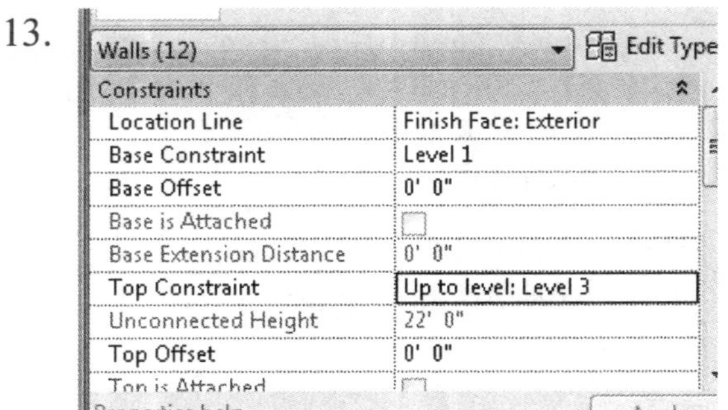

In the Properties pane:

Set the Top Constrain to **up to Level 3**.

Right click and select Cancel to release the selection or left click in the display window to release the selection.

14. 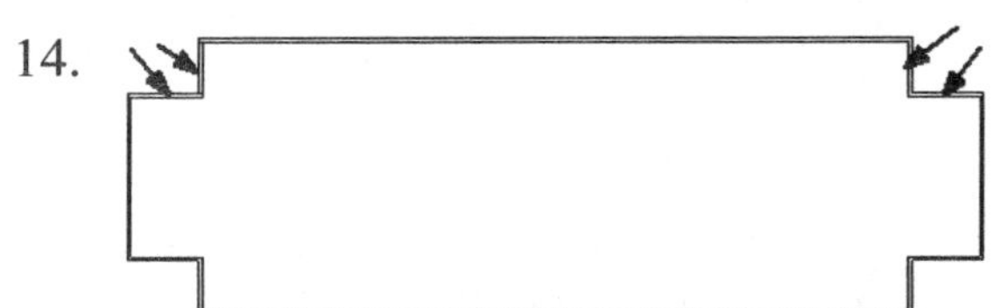

Hold down the Ctrl Key.
Select the four walls indicated.

15. 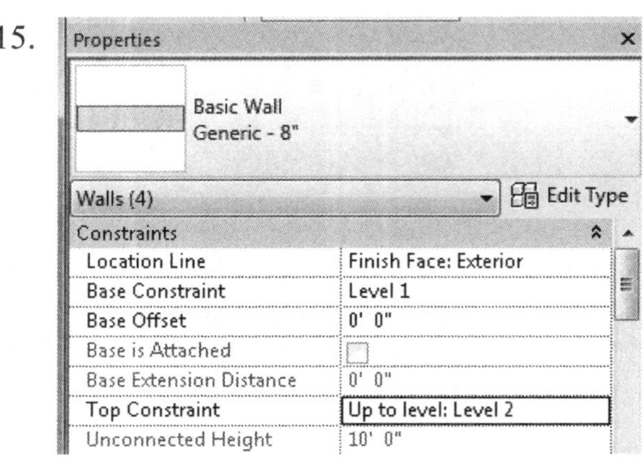

In the Properties pane:

Set the Top Constraint to **up to Level 2**.

Right click and select Cancel to release the selection or left click in the display window to release the selection.

16. 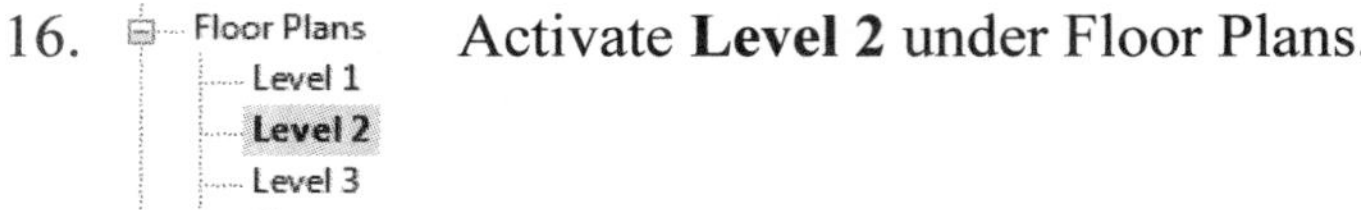

Activate **Level 2** under Floor Plans.

17. 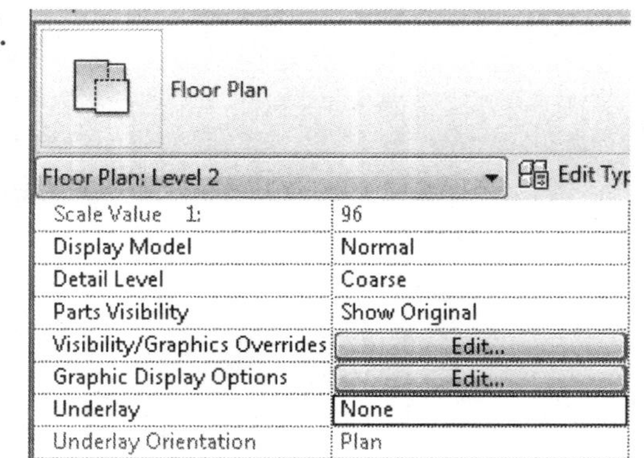

In the Properties Pane:

Set the Underlay to **None**.

This will turn off the visibility of all entities located below Level 2.

Each view has its own settings. We turned off the visibility of masses on Level 1, but we also need to turn off the visibility of masses on the Level 2 view.

18.  On the ribbon: Toggle the Show Mass by View Settings tool to turn the visibility of masses OFF.

19.  The view should look like this with the visibility of masses turned off.

20. 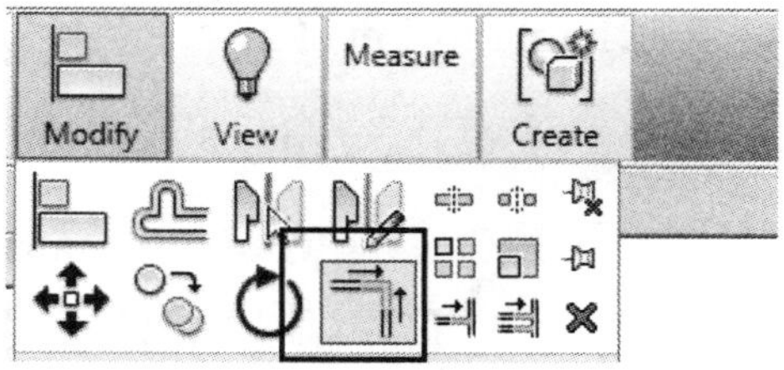 Activate the Modify ribbon.

Select the **Trim** tool from the Modify ribbon to clean up where the tower joins with the walls.

21. When you select to trim, be sure to select the section you want to keep.

22. 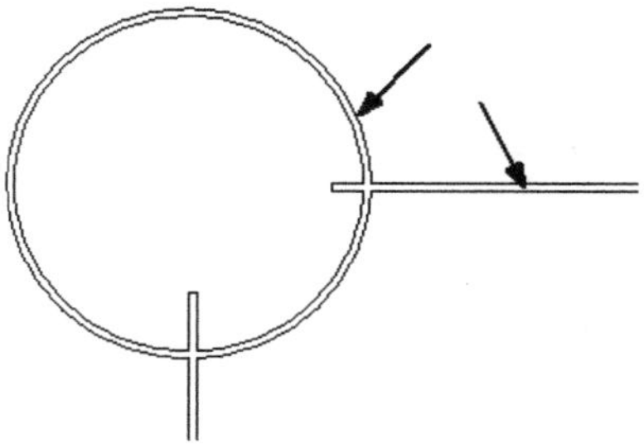 Select the arc and wall indicated.

23. 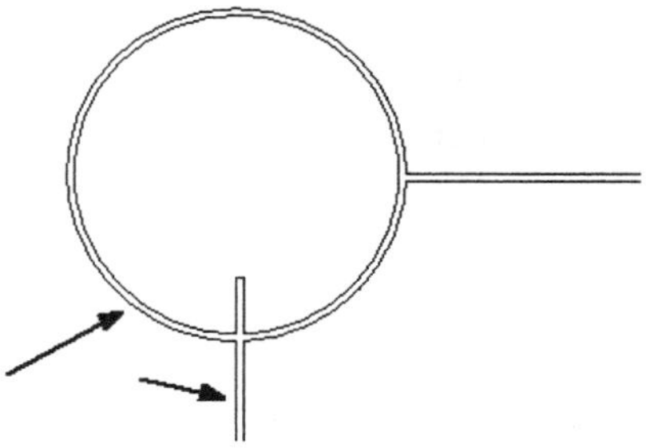 Select the arc and wall indicated.

Select the first line or wall to trim/extend. (Click on the part you want to keep)

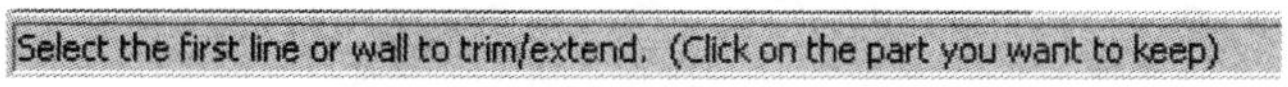

Note that you have some instructions in the lower left of the screen to assist you.

24. 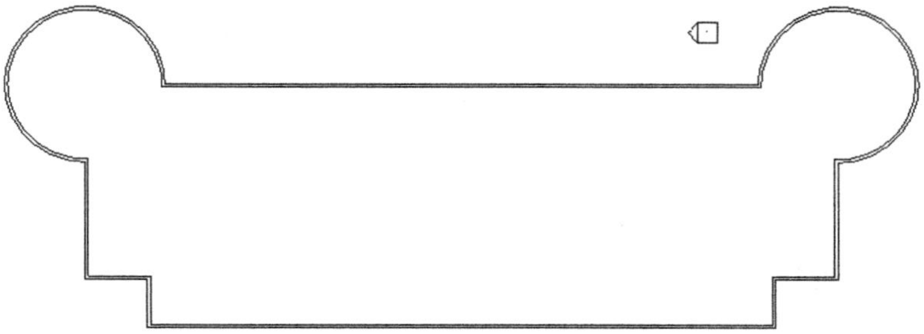 Trim the walls as shown on Level 2.

25. 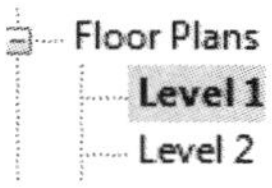 Activate Level 1.

26. 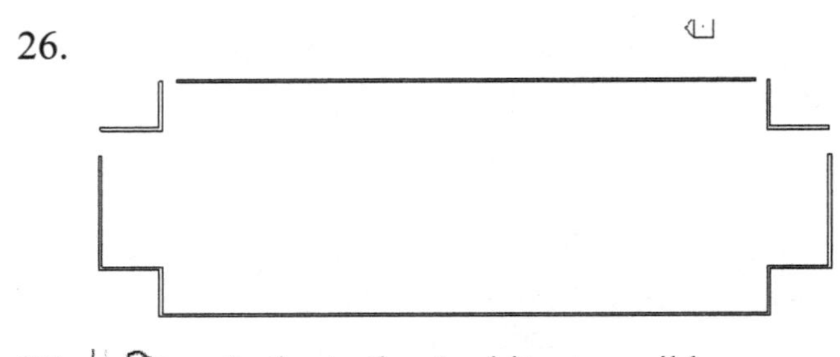

On Level 1, you should only see the walls with no towers.

There are some small gaps where the towers overlap.

27. Activate the Architecture ribbon.

Select the **Wall** tool on the Build Pane.

28. 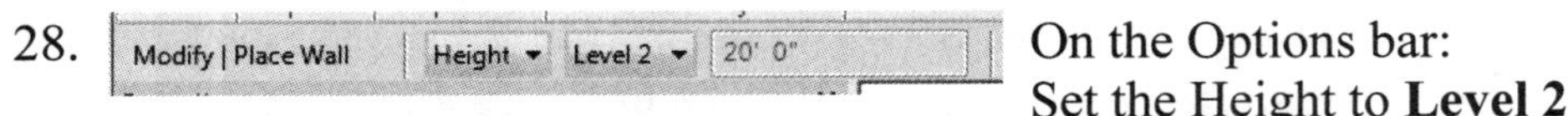

On the Options bar:
Set the Height to **Level 2**.

29. 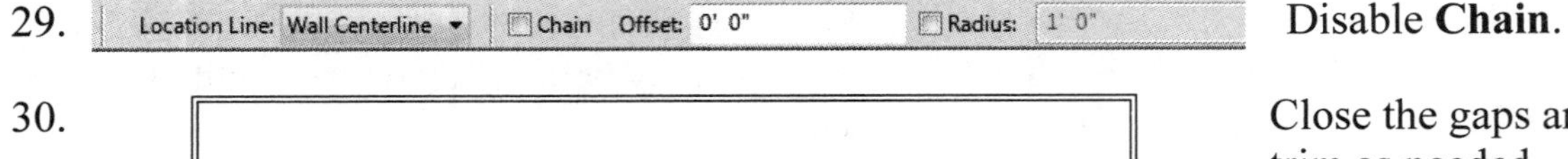

Disable **Chain**.

30. 

Close the gaps and trim as needed.

31. Switch to a 3D view and orbit your model.

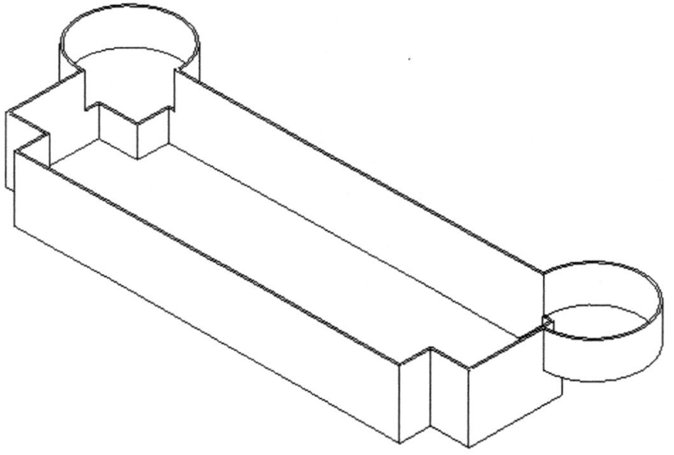

Check to make sure the walls and towers are adjusted to the correct levels.

32. Save as *ex2-4.rvt*.

Exercise 2-6
Adding Doors and Windows

Drawing Name: ex2-4.rvt
Estimated Time: 30 minutes

This exercise reinforces the following skills:

- Basics
- Door
- Load from Library
- Window
- Array
- Mirror
- Shading

You can add doors and windows to your conceptual model to make it easier to visualize.

1. Open *ex2-4.rvt.*

2. Activate **Level 1** under Floor Plans.

3. Level 1 should appear like this.

4. Activate the **Architecture ribbon**.

5. Select the **Door** tool under the Build panel.

6. Select **Load Family** under the Mode panel.

   Doors are model families.

7. 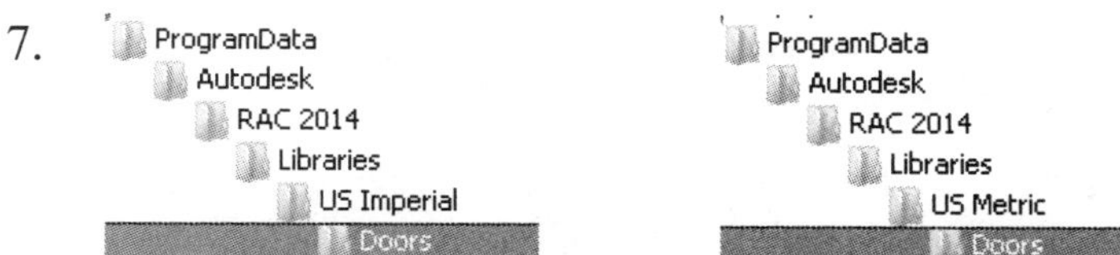

   Browse to the **Doors** folder under the Imperial or Metric library – use Imperial if you are using Imperial units or use Metric if you are using Metric units.

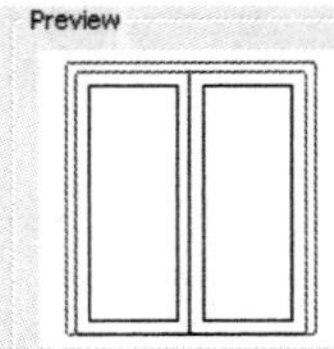

As you highlight each file in the folder, you can see a preview of the family.

Note that the files are in alphabetical order.

8. File name: Double-Panel 2.rfa
Files of type: Family Files (*.rfa)

For Imperial Units:
Locate the *Double-Panel2.rfa* file.

File name: M_Double-Panel 2.rfa
Files of type: Family Files (*.rfa)

For Metric Units:
Locate the *M_Double-Panel 2.rfa* file.

Press **Open**.

9. 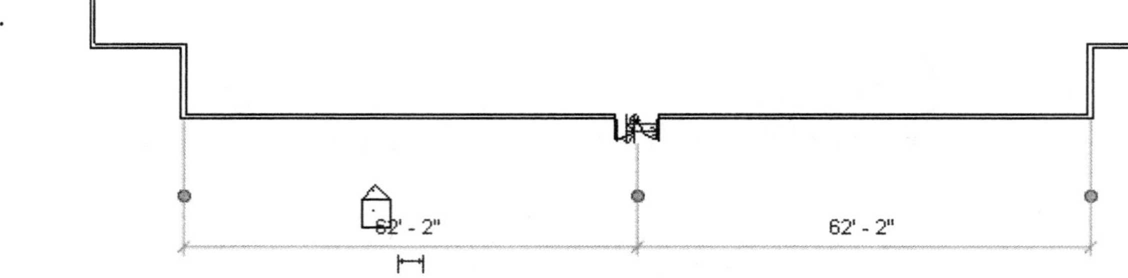

Place the door so it is centered on the wall as shown.
Doors are wall-hosted. So, you will only see a door preview when you place your cursor over a wall.

10. 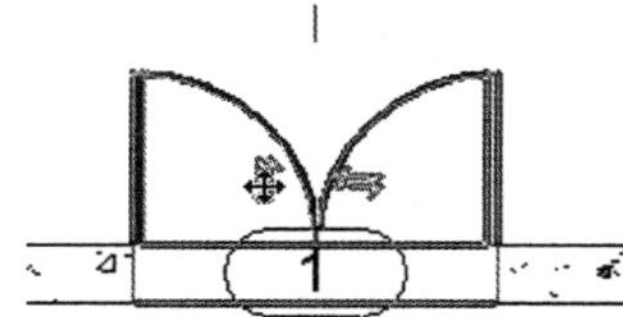

If you press the space bar before you pick to place, you can control the orientation of the door.

After you have placed the door, you can flip the door by picking on it then pick on the vertical or horizontal arrows.

11. 

Pick the **Window** tool from the Build panel.

Windows are model families.

12. Load Family

Select **Load Family** from the Mode panel.

13. 

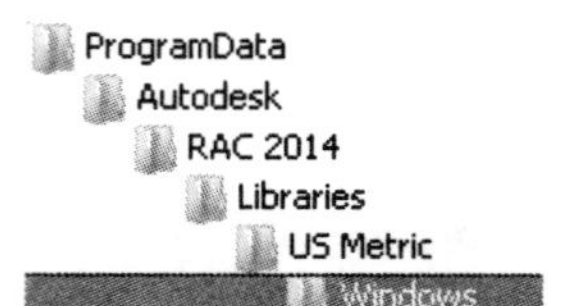

Browse to the **Windows** folder under the Imperial or Metric library – use Imperial if you are using Imperial units or use Metric if you are using Metric units.

14. 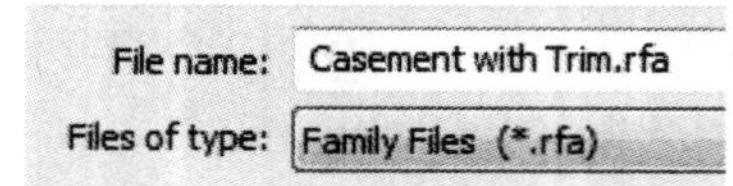

For Imperial Units:
Locate the *Casement with Trim.rfa* file.

For Metric Units:
Locate the *M_Casement with Trim.rfa* file.

Press **Open**.

15. 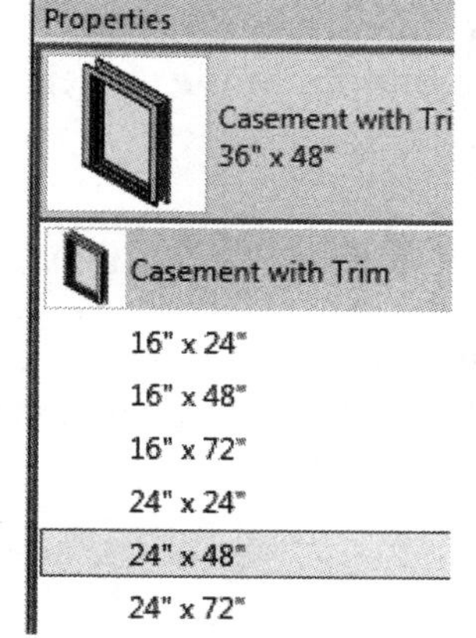

For Imperial Units:

From the drop-down list, select the 24″ x 48″ size for the Casement with Trim window.

Access the list of available sizes using the small down arrow indicated.

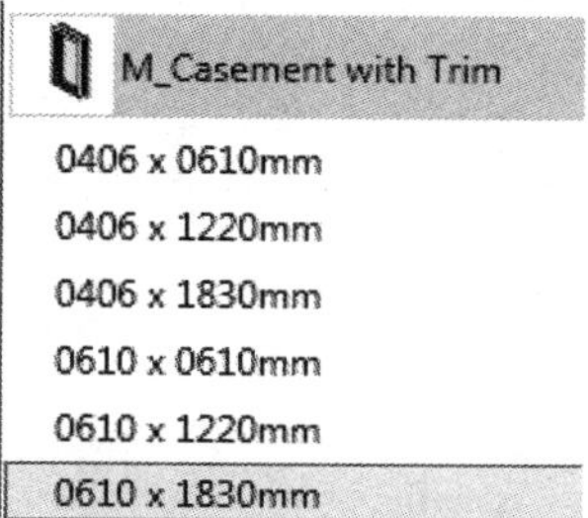

For Metric Units:

From the drop-down list, select the 0610 x 1830 mm size for the M_Casement with Trim window.

16. 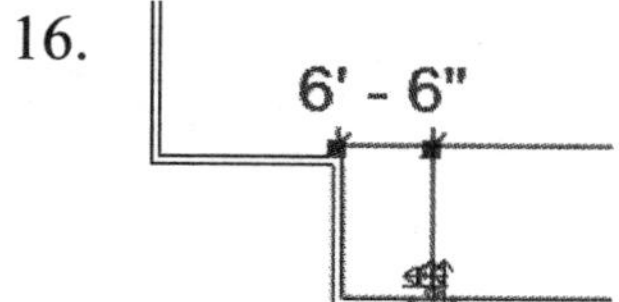

Place the window **6′-6″** [**3000 mm**] from the inner left wall.

Right click and select **Cancel** to exit the command.

17. 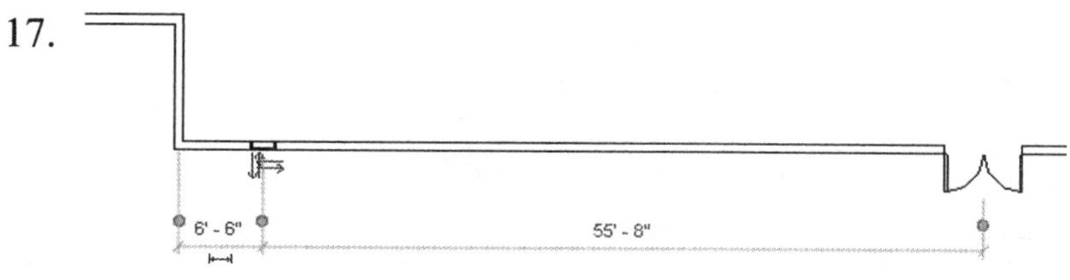

The arrows appear on the exterior side of the window. If the window is not placed correctly, left click on the arrows to flip the orientation.

18. Select the window so it highlights.

19. Select the **Array** tool under the Modify panel.

20. 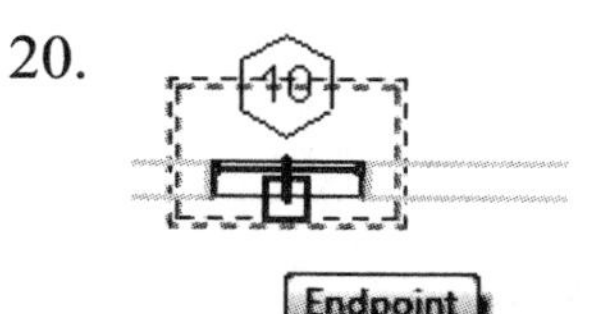

Select the midpoint of the window as the basepoint for the array.

21. Group and Associate Number: 5 Move To: 2nd Last Constrain

Enable Group and Associate. This assigns the windows placed to a group and allows you to edit the array.

Set the array quantity to **5** on the options bar located on the bottom of the screen. Enable **Last**.

If you enable Constrain, this ensures that your elements are placed orthogonally.

Array has two options. One option allows you to place elements at a set distance apart. The second option allows you to fill a distance with equally spaced elements. We will fill a specified distance with five elements equally spaced.

22.

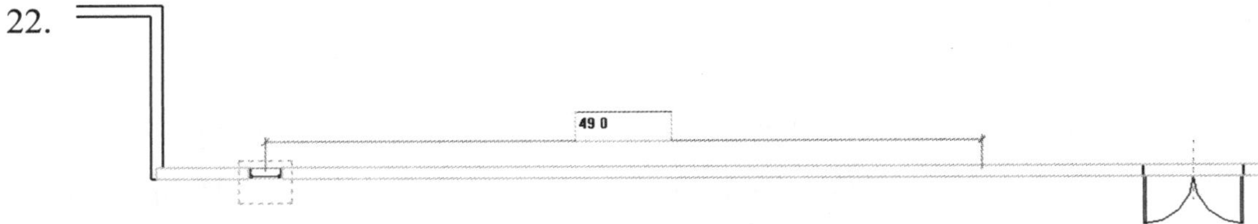

Pick a point **49′-0″** [**14,935.20**] from the first selected point to the right.

23.

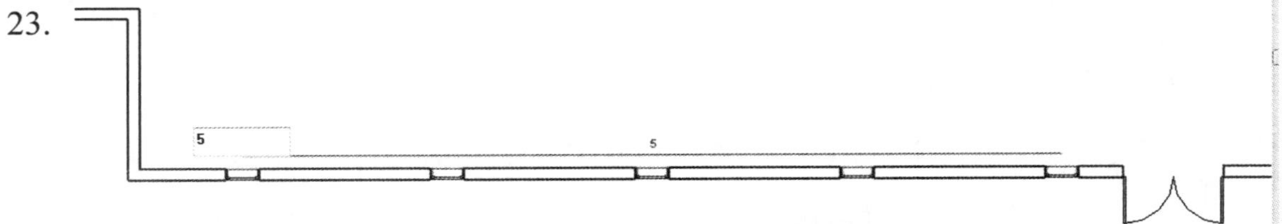

You will see a preview of how the windows will fill the space.

Press **ENTER** to accept.

24. Select the **Measure** tool on the Quick Access toolbar.

25. Check the distance between the windows and you will see that they are all spaced equally.

26.

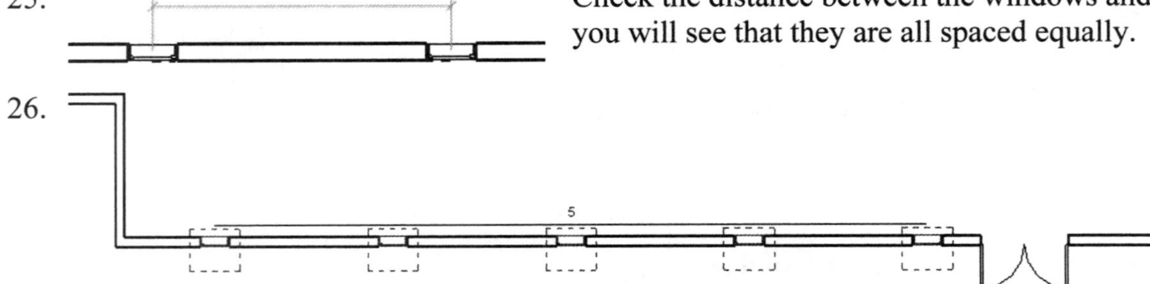

Window around the entire array to select all the windows.

The array count will display.

27. Use the **Mirror→Draw Mirror Axis** tool to mirror the windows to the other side of the wall opposite the door.

28. 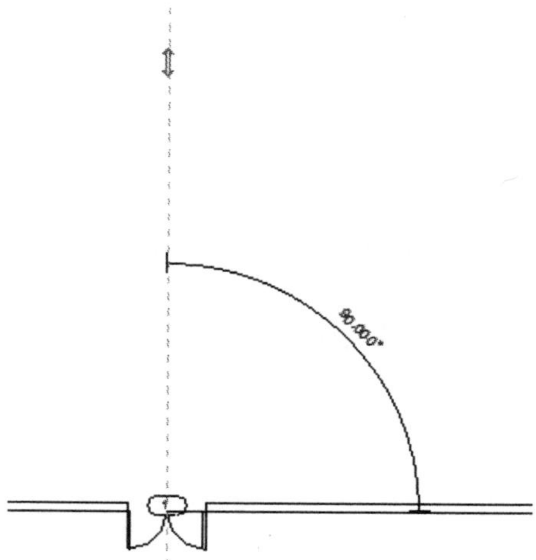

Select the center of the door as the start point of the mirror axis.

Move the cursor upwards at a 90 degree angle and pick a point above the door.

29. Left pick anywhere in the graphics window to complete the command.

You will get an error message and the windows will not array properly if you do not have the angle set to 90 degrees or your walls are different lengths.

30. 3D Views
3D Ortho 2
{3D}

Switch to a **3D** View.

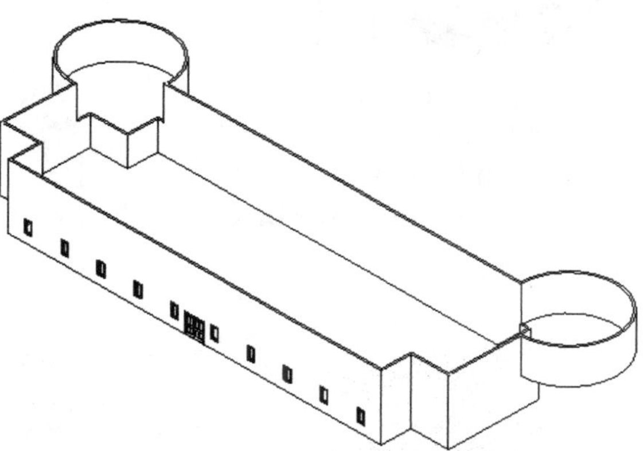

31. 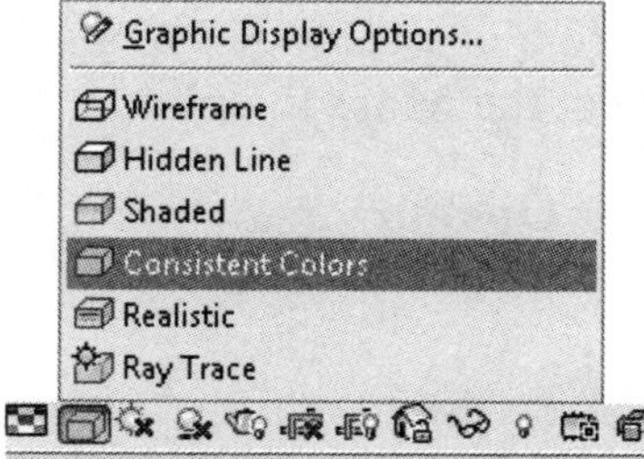

Set the Model Graphics Style to **Consistent Colors**.

We have created a conceptual model to show a client.

32. Save the file as *ex2-5.rvt.*

Exercise 2-7
Creating a Conceptual Mass

Drawing Name: New Conceptual Mass
Estimated Time: 60 minutes

This exercise reinforces the following skills:

- Masses
- Levels
- Load from Library
- Aligned Dimension
- Flip Orientation

1. Close any open files.

2. On the Recent Files pane:

   Select **New Conceptual Mass**.

   If the Recent Files pane is not available, use the Application Menu and go to **New→Conceptual Mass**.

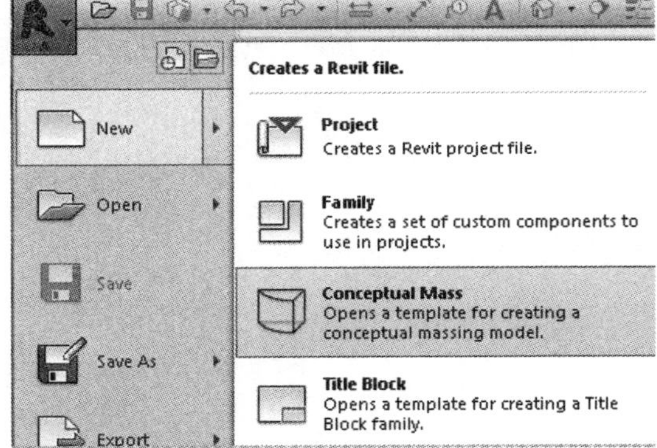

3. Select the **Mass** template.

   Press **Open**.

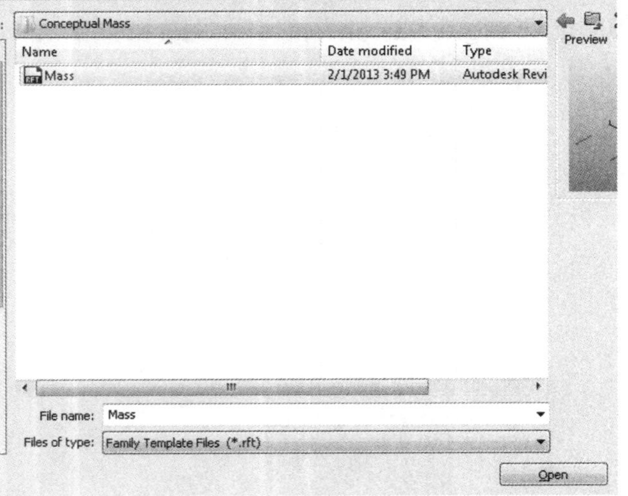

4. Elevations (Elevation 1) / East / North / South / West — Activate the **South Elevation**.

5. Level / Datum — On the Create ribbon, select the **Level** tool.

6. Level 2 50' - 0" — Place a Level 2 at **50′ 0″**.

7. Floor Plans / Level 1 / Level 2 — Activate the **Level 1** floor plan.

8. Plane — Activate the Create ribbon.

   Select the **Plane** tool from the Draw panel.

9. Draw a vertical plane and a horizontal plane to form a box.

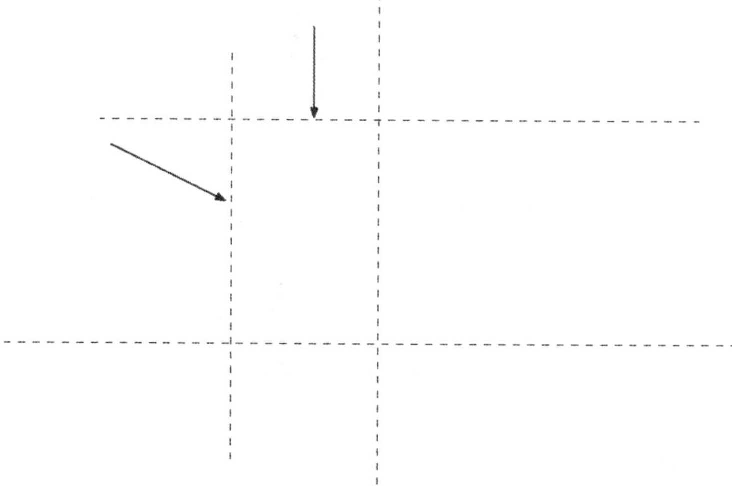

10. 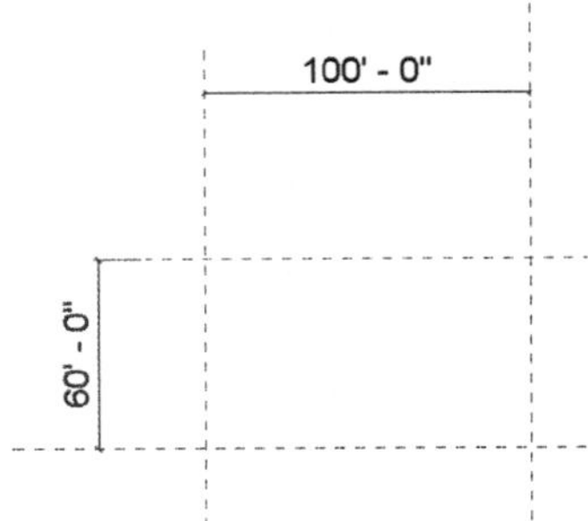

Use the ALIGNED DIMENSION tool to add dimensions to the reference planes.

Set the horizontal dimension to 100′ 0″ overall.

Set the vertical dimension to 60′ 0″ overall.

Remember the permanent dimensions are driven by the values of the temporary dimensions. To set the temporary dimension values, select the reference planes.

11. Activate the Insert ribbon.

Select Load Family from **Library→Load Family**.

12. Browse to the **Mass** folder.

13. 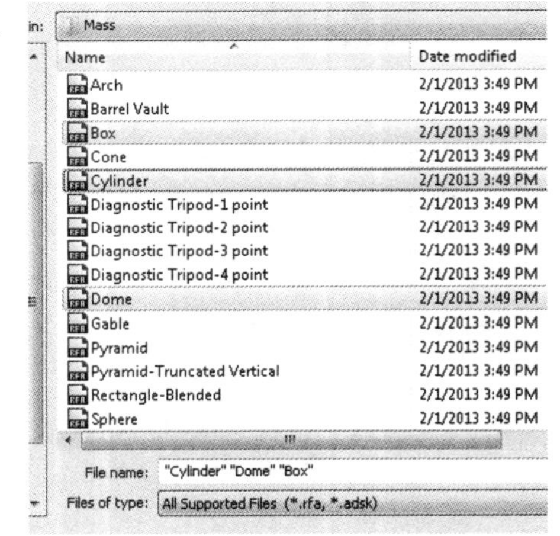

Hold down the CTRL Key and select the *Dome*, *Box*, and *Cylinder* files.
Press **Open**.

14. 

Activate the Create ribbon.

Select the **Component** tool on the Model panel.

15. 

Select the **Box** component using the Type Selector.

16. 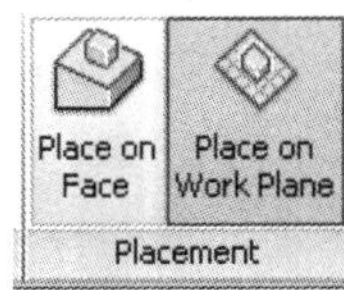

Select **Place on Work Plane** on the Placement panel.

17.  Placement Plane: Level : Level 1 — Set the Placement Plane to **Level 1**.

18. 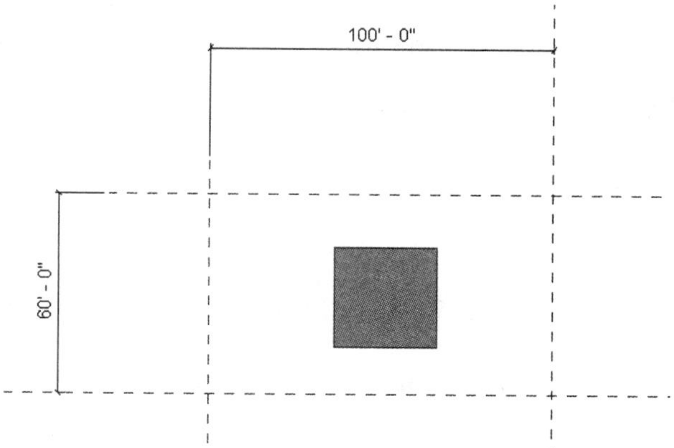 Place the box in the view.

Right click and select **Cancel** twice to escape the command.

19. 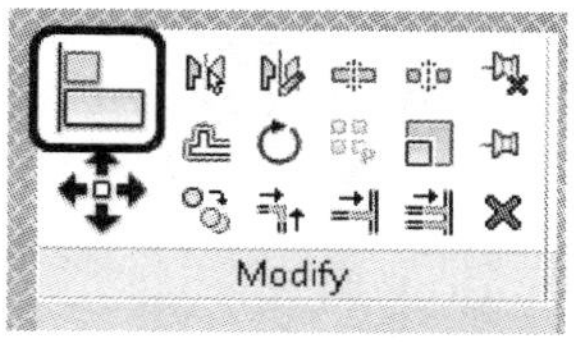 Select the **ALIGN** tool from the Modify panel.

20. 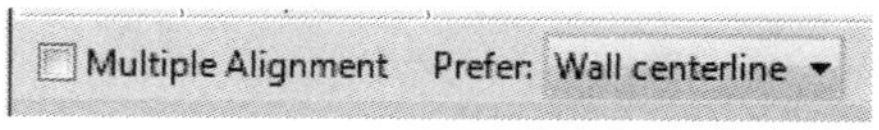 Multiple Alignment Prefer: Wall centerline — Disable Multiple Alignment on the Options bar.

21. 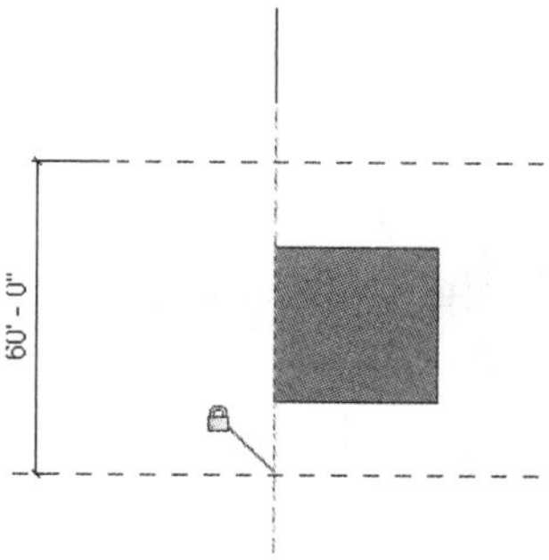 Select the reference plane on the left.

Select the left side of the box.

Left click on the lock to fix the alignment.

22. 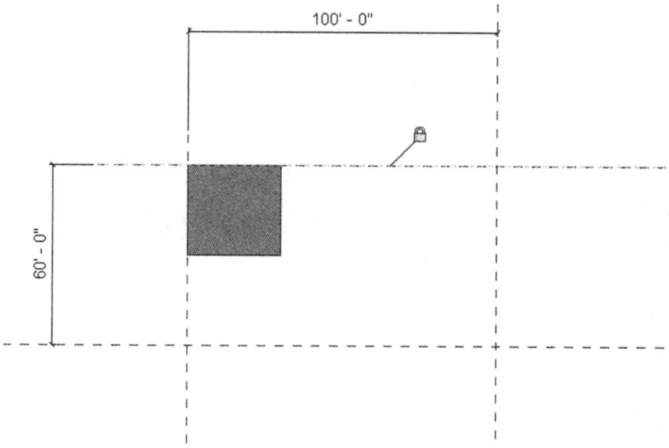 Select the reference plane on the top.

Select the top side of the box.

Left click on the lock to fix the alignment.

Right click and select Cancel to exit the ALIGN command.

23. Left click on the box to select it.

Use the right grip to drag the right side of the box to the right reference plane.

Left click on the lock to fix the alignment.

24. 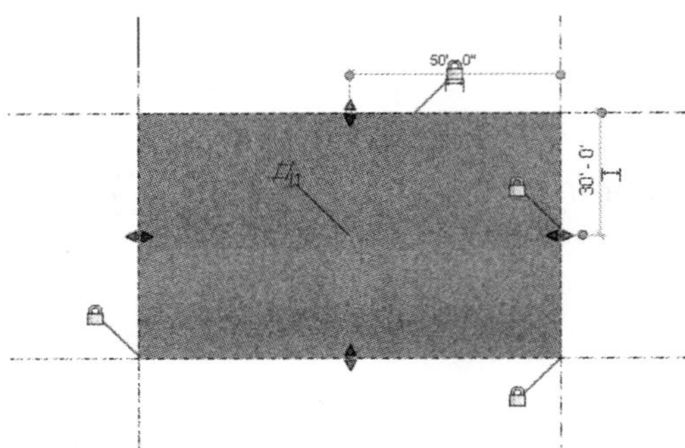

Use the bottom grip to drag the bottom side of the box to the right reference plane.

Left click on the lock to fix the alignment.

Left click in the window to release the selection.

25. Activate the South Elevation.

26. 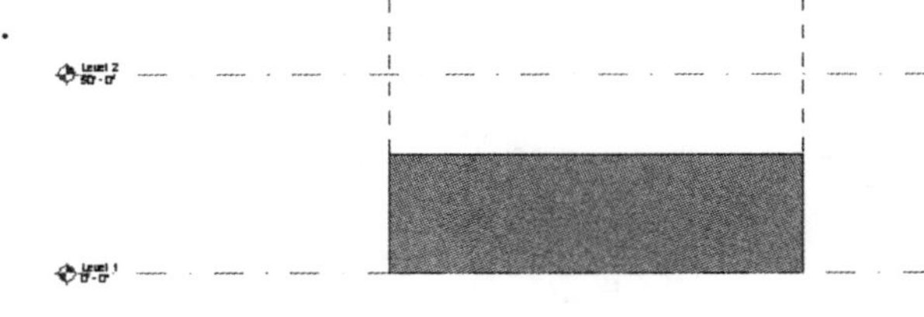

The box height is not aligned to Level 2.

Select the box.

27. 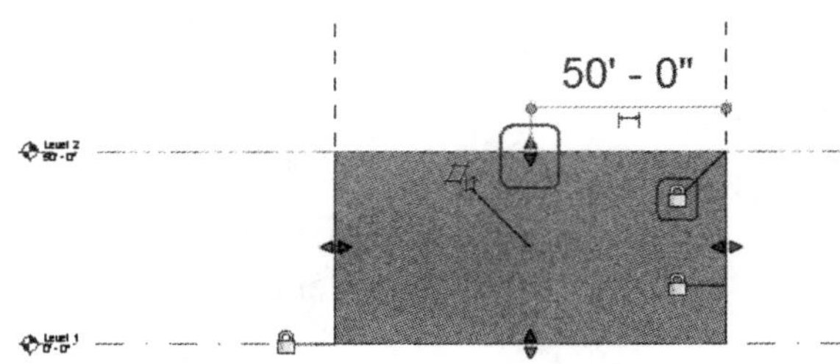

Use the top grip to drag the top of the box even with Level 2.
Left click on the lock to fix the alignment.

Left click in the window to release the selection.

28. 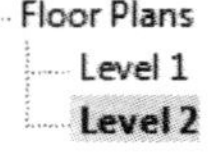

Activate the **Level 2** floor plan.

29. 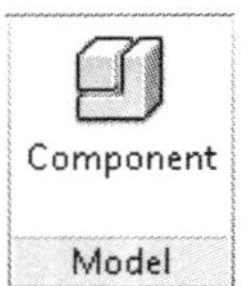

Activate the Create ribbon.

Select the **Component** tool on the Model panel.

30. Properties
Cylinder

Select the **Cylinder** component using the Type Selector.

31.

Dimensions	
Radius	25' 0"
Height	5' 0"

In the Properties Pane:

Set the Radius to **25′ 0″**.
Set the Height to **5′ 0″**.

If you need to adjust the position of the cylinder: Set the Offset to -5′ 0″.

This aligns the top of the cylinder with the top of the box.

32. Place on Face | Place on Work Plane
Placement

Select **Place on Work Plane** on the Placement panel.

33. Placement Plane: Level : Level 2

Set the Placement Plane to **Level 2**.

34. 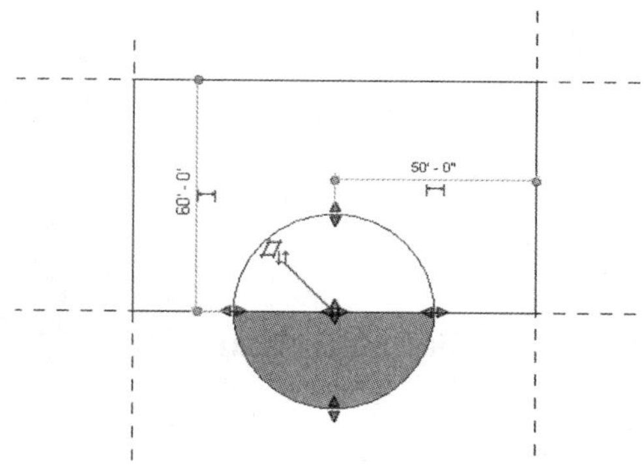

Place a cylinder at the midpoint of the bottom edge of the box.

Right click and select **Cancel** twice to escape the command.

35. Level 5
3D Views
3D View 1
{3D}

Switch to a 3D View.

36. 

You should see the box as well as the cylinder.

37. Floor Plans
Level 1
Level 2

Activate **Level 2**.

38. Component
Model

Activate the Create ribbon.

Select the **Component** tool on the Model panel.

39. 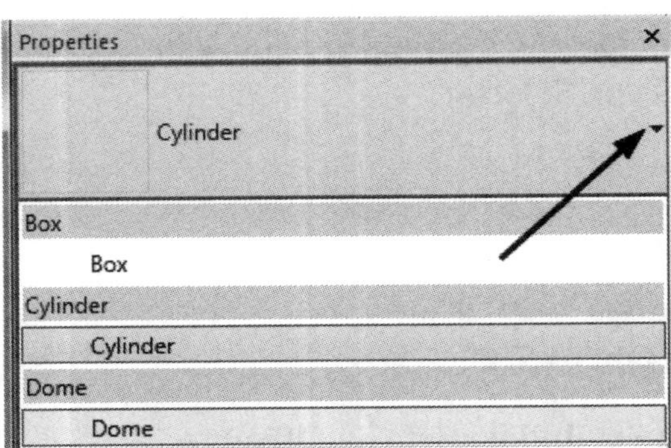

Select the **Dome** component using the Type Selector.

40. In the Properties Pane:

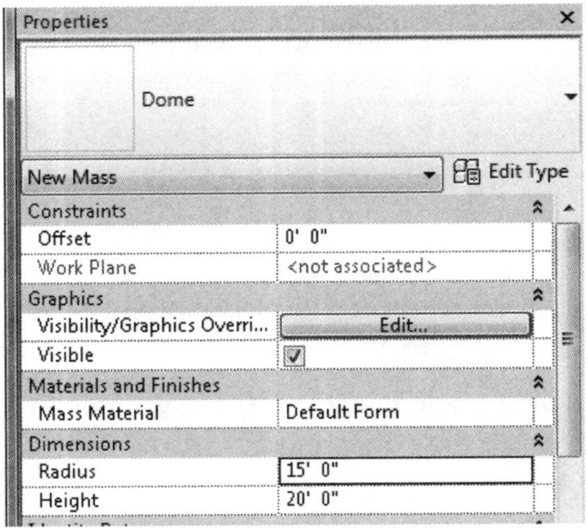

Set the Radius to **15′ 0″**.
Set the Height to **20′ 0″**.

41. 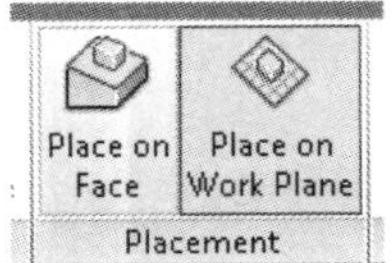

Select **Place on Work Plane** on the Placement panel.

42. 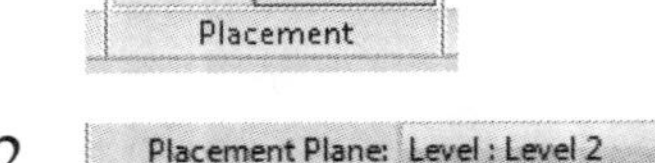

Set the Placement Plane to **Level 2**.

43. 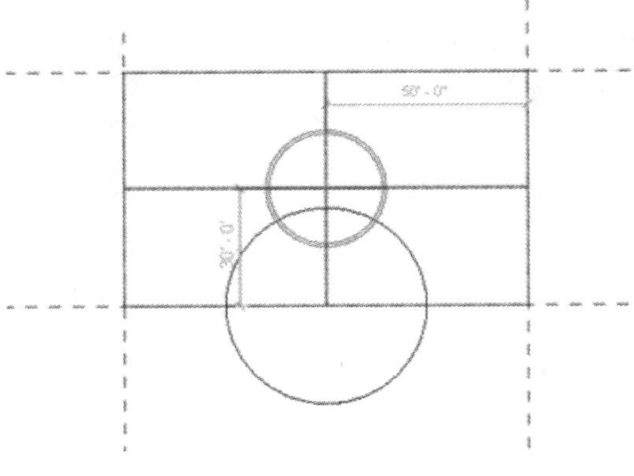

Place the dome so it is centered on the box.

Right click and select Cancel twice to exit the command.

44.

Switch to a 3D View.

45. Switch to a **Wireframe** display.

- Graphic Display Options...
- Wireframe
- Hidden Line
- Shaded
- Consistent Colors
- Realistic
- Ray Trace

46. The dome is upside down.

Select the dome.

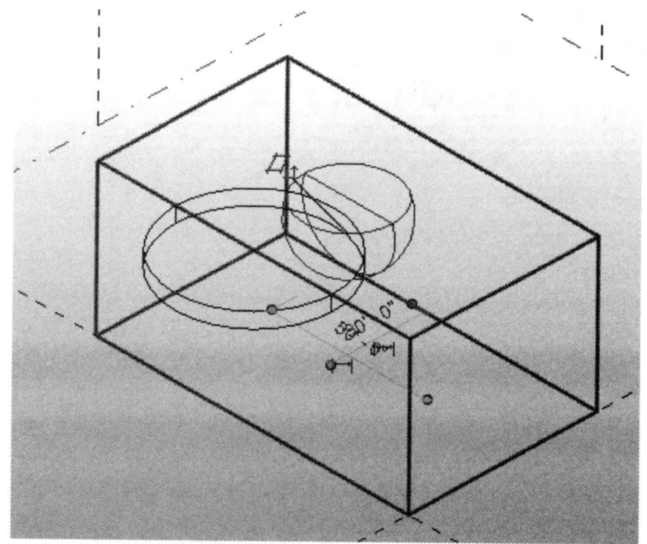

47. Left click on the orientation arrows to flip the dome.

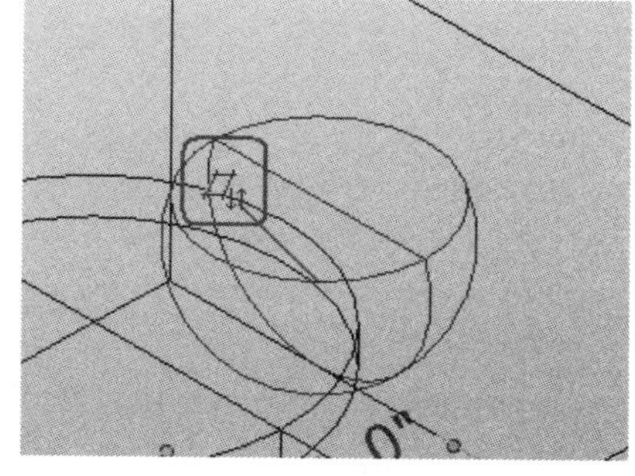

48. In the Properties pane:

Dimensions	
Radius	30' 0"
Height	15' 0"

Change the Radius to **30′ 0″**.
Change the Height to **15′ 0″**.
Press **Apply**.

49. Change the display back to **Shaded**.

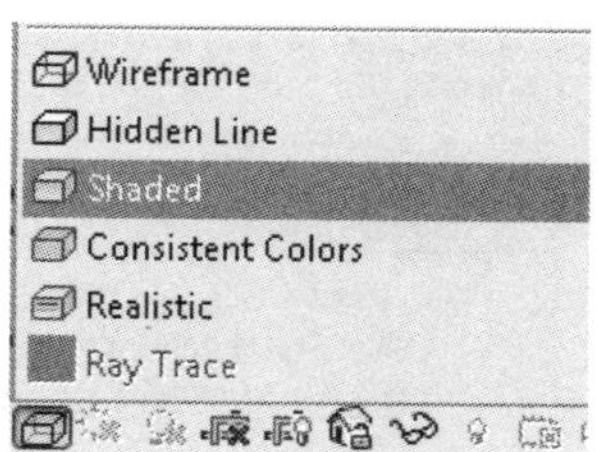

50. Save as *ex2-7.rfa*.

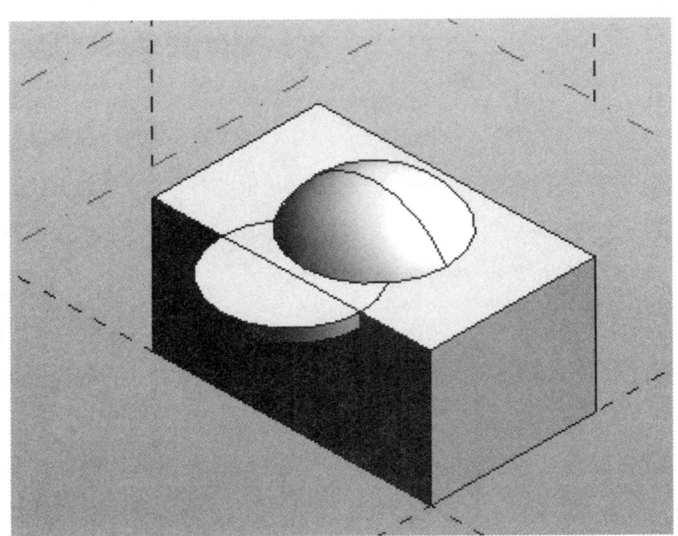

Exercise 2-8

Using a Conceptual Mass in a Project

Drawing Name: New
Estimated Time: 20 minutes

This exercise reinforces the following skills:

- Masses
- Load from Library
- Visibility/Graphics

1. Close any open files.

2. On the Recent Files pane:

   Select **New Project**.

   If the Recent Files pane is not available, use the Application Menu and go to **New→Project**.

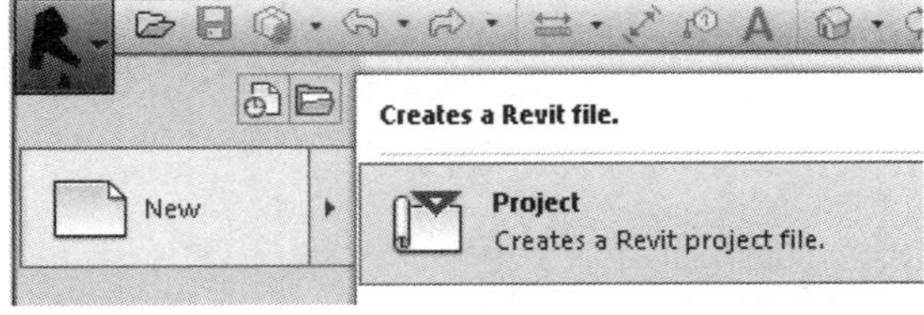

   Press **OK** to accept the Architectural Template.

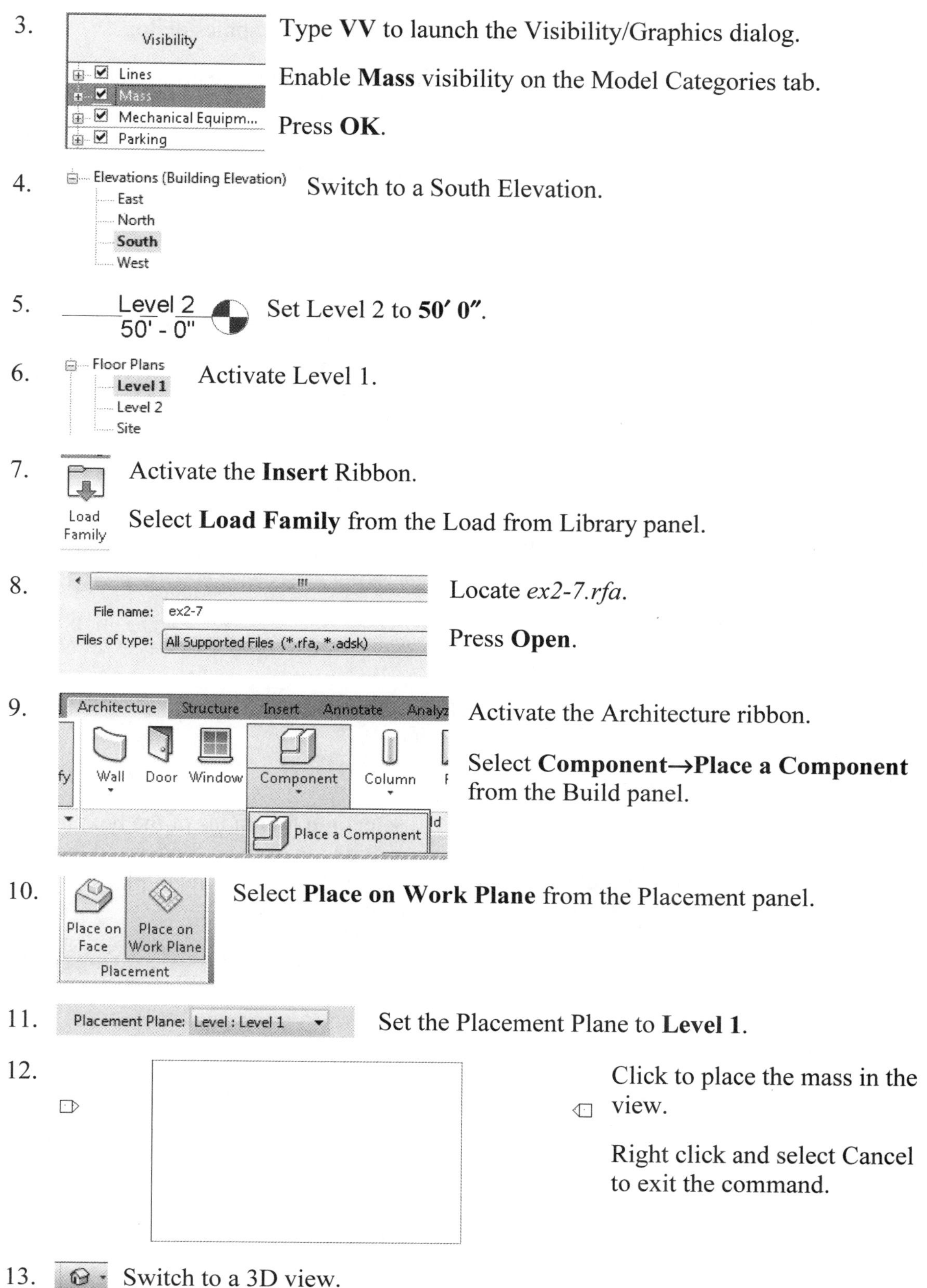

3. Type **VV** to launch the Visibility/Graphics dialog.

   Enable **Mass** visibility on the Model Categories tab.

   Press **OK**.

4. Switch to a South Elevation.

5. Set Level 2 to **50′ 0″**.

6. Activate Level 1.

7. Activate the **Insert** Ribbon.

   Select **Load Family** from the Load from Library panel.

8. Locate *ex2-7.rfa*.

   Press **Open**.

9. Activate the Architecture ribbon.

   Select **Component→Place a Component** from the Build panel.

10. Select **Place on Work Plane** from the Placement panel.

11. Set the Placement Plane to **Level 1**.

12. Click to place the mass in the view.

    Right click and select Cancel to exit the command.

13. Switch to a 3D view.

14. 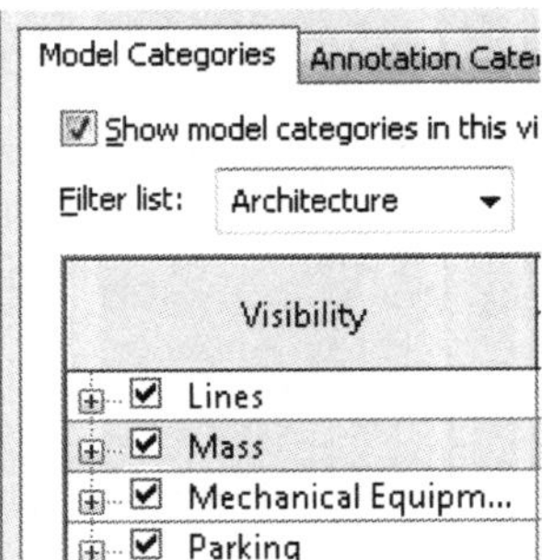

Type **VV** to launch the Visibility/Graphics dialog.

Enable **Mass** visibility on the Model Categories tab.

Press **OK**.

Right click and select **Zoom to Fit** to see the placed mass family.

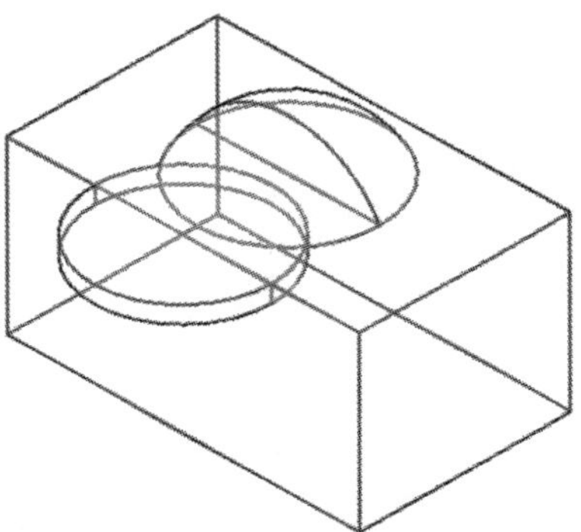

15. 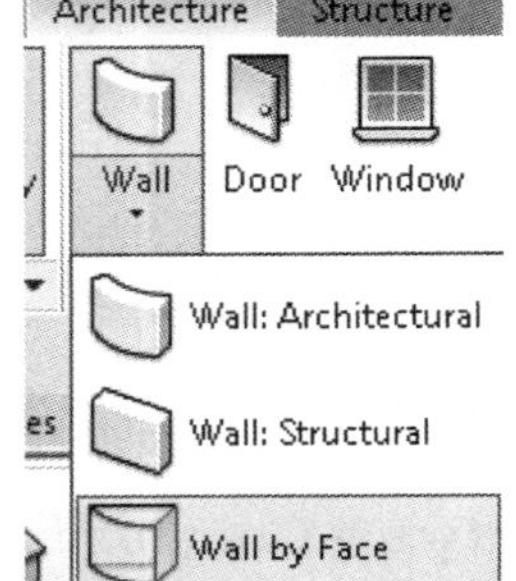

Select the **Wall by Face** tool from the Architecture ribbon.

16. 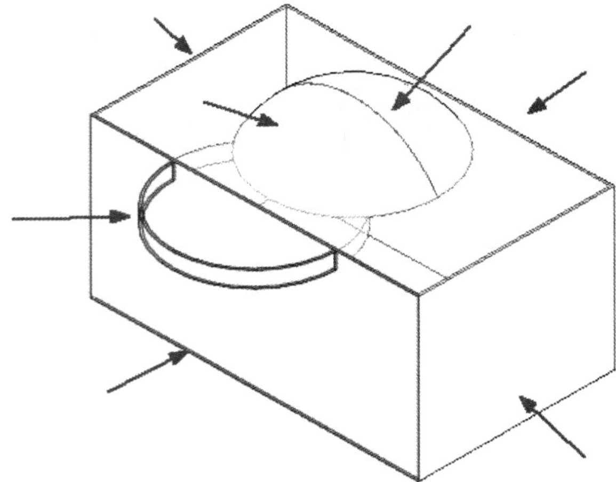

Select the four sides of the box, the outside arc of the cylinder and the two sides of the dome to place walls.

17. 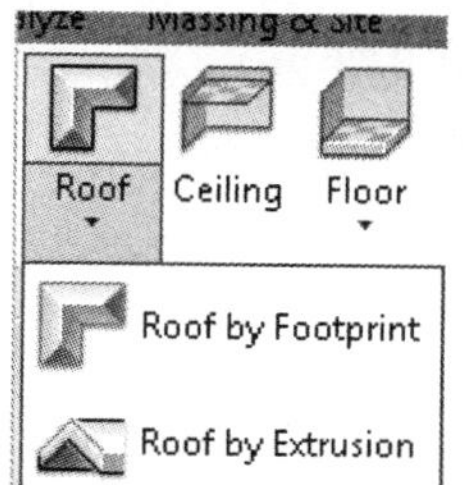

Select the **Roof by Face** tool on the Build panel on the Architecture ribbon.

18. 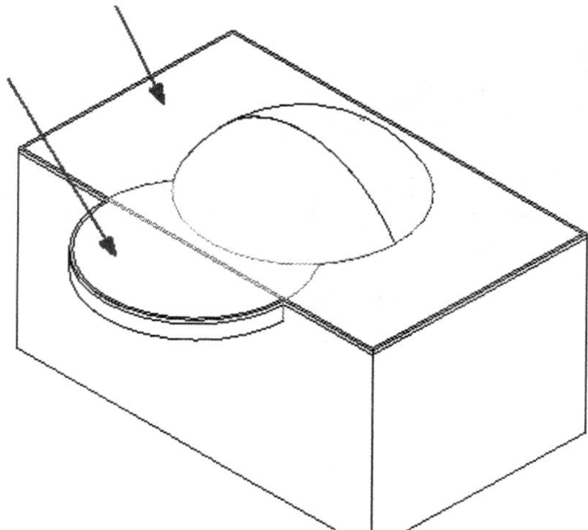

Select the top face of the box and the top half of the cylinder.

19. 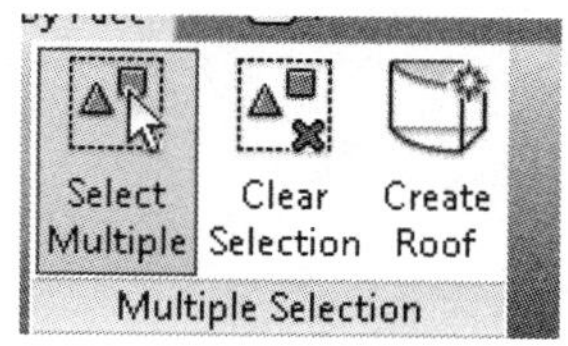

Select **Create Roof** on the ribbon.

20. The roof is placed. Right click and select **Cancel**.

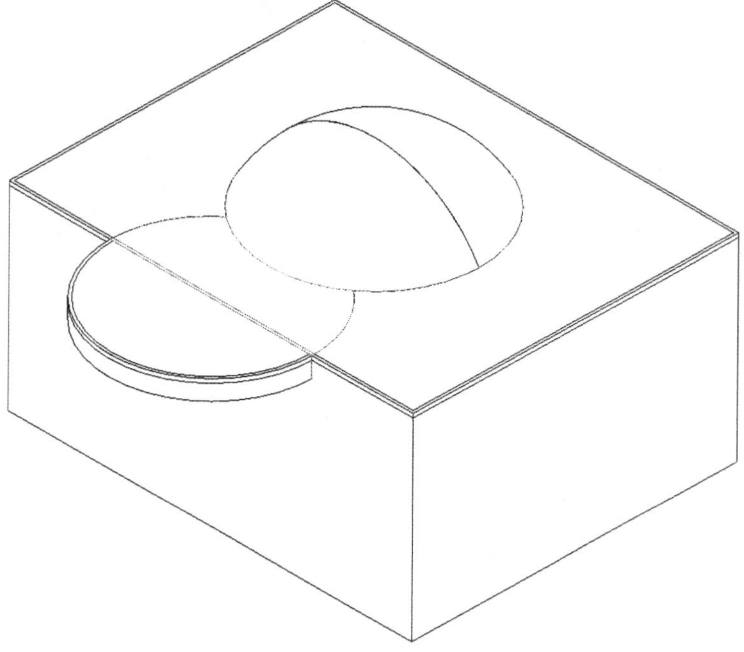

21. 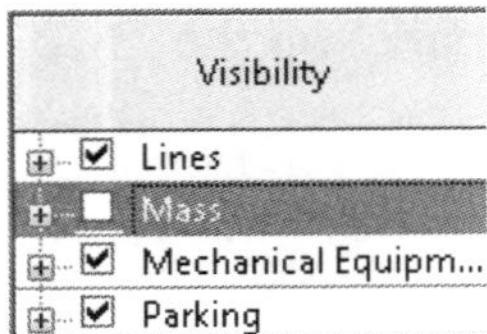

Type **VV** to launch the Visibility/Graphics dialog.

Disable **Mass** visibility on the Model Categories tab.

Press **OK**.

22. 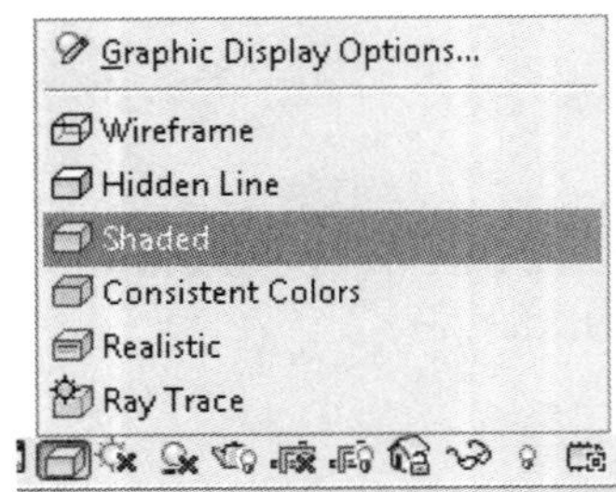

Change the Display to **Shaded**.

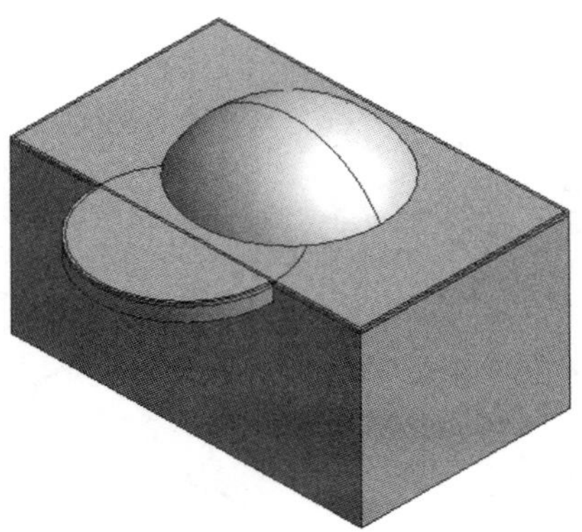

23. Save as *ex2-8.rvt.*

Additional Projects

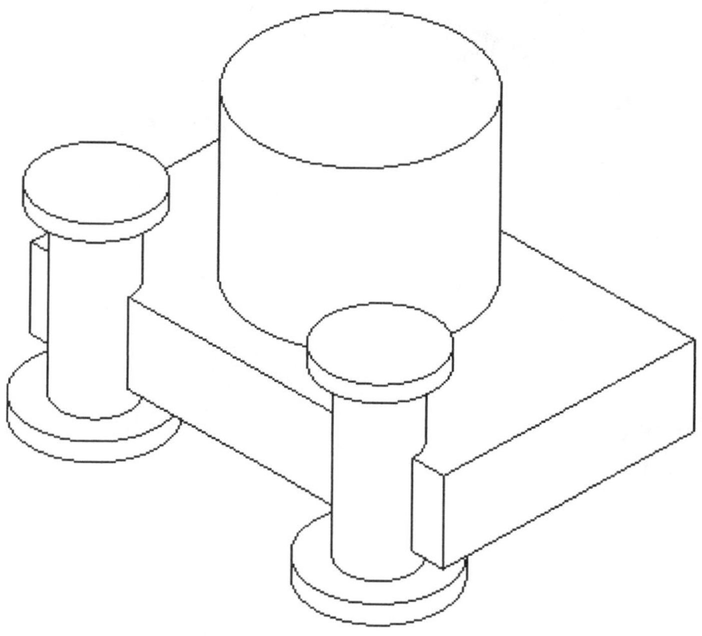

1) Create a conceptual mass family like the one shown.

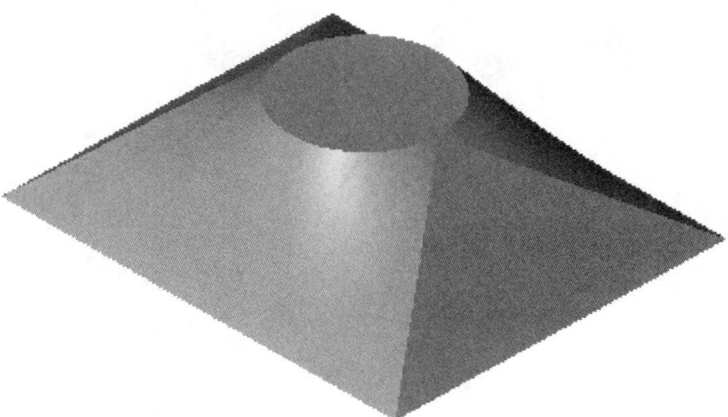

2) Make the shape shown using a Blend. The base is a rectangle and the top is a circle located at the center of the rectangle.

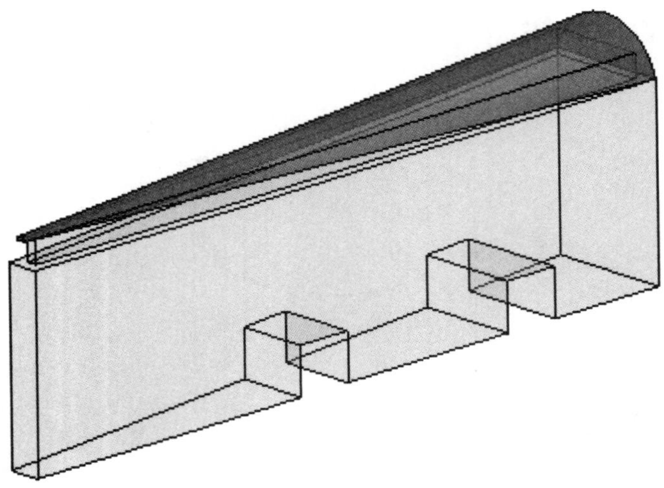

3) Make a conceptual mass family as shown.
   Use Solid Void to create the two openings.

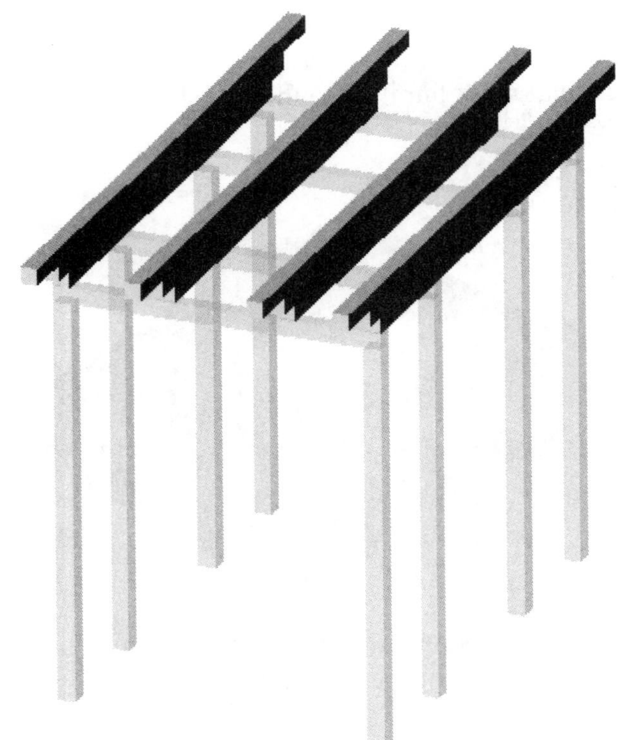

4) Design a pergola using 4″ x 4″ posts and beams.

Lesson 2 Quiz

True or False

1. Masses can be created inside Projects or as a Conceptual Mass file.
2. Forms are always created by drawing a sketch, selecting the sketch, and clicking Create Form.
3. In order to see masses, Show Mass must be enabled.
4. Masses are level-based.
5. You can modify the dimensions of conceptual masses.

Multiple Choice ***[Select the Best Answer]***

6. Faces on masses can be converted to the following:

   A. Walls
   B. Ceilings
   C. Floors
   D. Doors
   E. A, B, and C, but NOT D

7. You can adjust the distance a mass is extruded by:

   A. Editing the temporary dimension that appears before a solid form is created
   B. Use the ALIGN tool.
   C. Use the 3D drag tool
   D. Using the Properties pane located on the left of the screen.
   E. All of the above

8. To insert a conceptual mass family in a project:

   A. Use the INSERT tool.
   B. Use the PLACE COMPONENT tool.
   C. Use the BLOCK tool.
   D. Use the MASS tool.

9. Masses are hosted by:

   A. Projects
   B. Work Planes
   C. Families
   D. Files

10. Mass Visibility can be controlled using:

    A. The SHOW MASS tool.
    B. Display Settings
    C. Object Settings
    D. View Properties

11. Each mass is defined by _____________.

    A. A single profile sketch
    B. Multiple profile sketches
    C. Properties
    D. Materials

12. Revit comes with many pre-made mass shapes. Select the mass shape NOT available in the Revit mass library:

    A. BOX
    B. ARC
    C. CONE
    D. TRIANGLE

ANSWERS:

1) T; 2) T; 3) T; 4) T; 5) T; 6) E; 7) E; 8) B; 9) B; 10) A; 11) A; 12) B

Lesson 3
Floor Plans

- Put a semi-colon between snap increments, not a comma.
- If you edit the first grid number to 'A' before you array, Revit will automatically increment them alphabetically for you; A, B, C, etc.
- You will need to 'Ungroup' an element in an array before you can modify any of the properties.
- To keep elements from accidentally moving, you can select the element and use **Pin Objects** or highlight the dimension string and lock the dimensions.
- You can purge the unused families and components in your project file in order to reduce the file space. Go to **File→Purge Unused.**
- Revit creates stairs from the center of the run, so it may be helpful to place some reference planes or detail lines defining the location of the starting points for the runs of any stairs.
- Floor plans should be oriented so that North is pointing up or to the right.
- The direction you draw your walls (clockwise or counterclockwise) controls the initial location of the exterior face of the wall. Drawing a wall from left to right places the exterior on the top. Drawing a wall from right to left places the exterior on the bottom. When you highlight a wall, the blue flip orientation arrows are always adjacent to the exterior side of the wall.

Throughout the rest of the text, we will be creating new types of families. Here are the basic steps to creating a new family.

1. Select the element you want to define (wall, window, floor, stairs, etc.).
2. Select **Edit Type** from the Properties pane.
3. Select **Duplicate**.
4. Rename: Enter a new name for your family type.
5. Redefine: Edit the structure, assign new materials, change the dimensions.
6. Reload or Reassign: Assign the new type to the element.

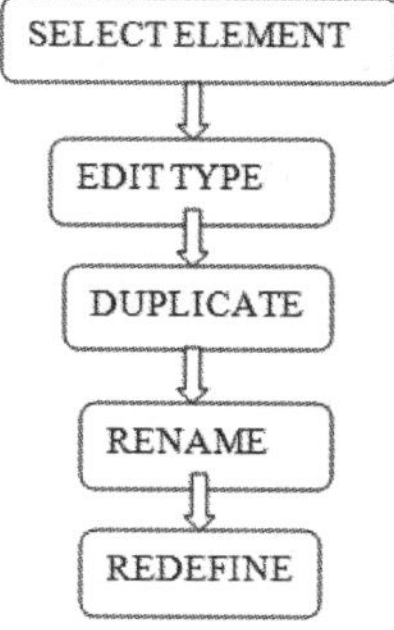

Exercise 3-1
Placing a Grid

Drawing Name: Architectural Template.rte [DefaultMetric.rte]
Estimated Time: 30 minutes

This exercise reinforces the following skills:

- Units
- Snap Increments
- Grid
- Array
- Ungroup
- Dimension
- Dimension Settings

1. Start a new project.

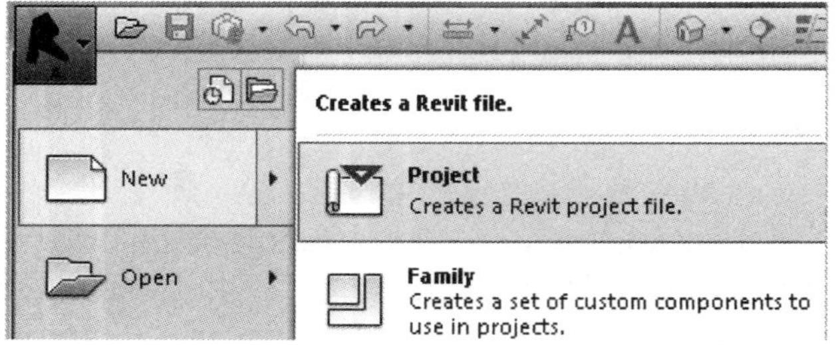

Go to New→Project.

2. 

Select the Architectural Template from the drop-down list.
Press **OK**.

3. Activate **Level 1**.

4. Activate the **Manage** ribbon.

Under **Settings**, select **Snaps**.

5. Set the snap increments for length to **40′; 25′; 5′** [**1500;7620;1220**].

Press **OK**.

Use a semi-colon between the distance values.

6. Activate the **Architecture** ribbon.

7. Select **Grid** under the Datum panel.

8. Click to enter grid start point Pick on the left side of the graphics window to start the grid line.

9. Pick a point above the first point.

Right mouse click and select Cancel twice to exit the Grid mode.

Your first grid line is placed.

10. Select the Grid text to edit it.

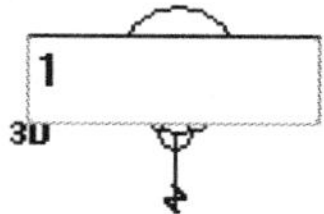

11. Change the text to **A**.

Left click in the graphics window to exit edit mode.

If you edit the first grid letter before you array, Revit will automatically increment the arrayed grid elements.

12. 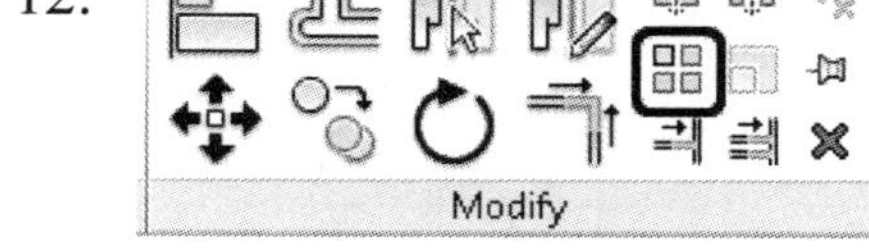

Select the grid line so it is highlighted.

Select the **Array** tool under the Modify panel.

13. 

Disable **Group and Associate**. This keeps each grid as an independent element.
Set the Number to **8**.
Enable Move To: **2nd**.
Enable **Constrain**. This keeps the array constrained orthogonally.

14. 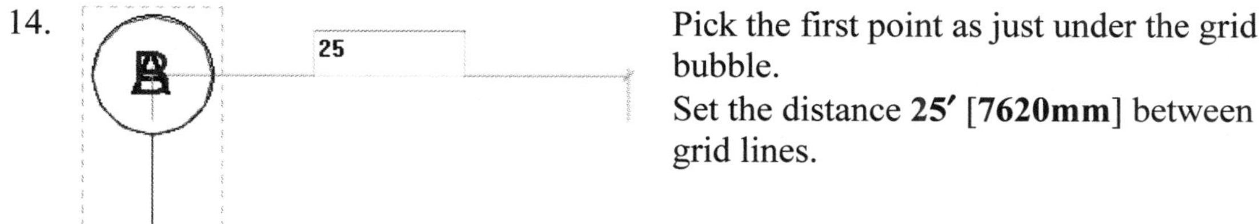

Pick the first point as just under the grid bubble.
Set the distance **25′** [**7620mm**] between grid lines.

15. The array is placed.

Note that the bubbles auto-incremented.

16. Activate the **Architecture** ribbon.

Select the **Grid** tool under the Datum panel.

17. Draw a horizontal line near the bottom of the grid.

Right click and select Cancel to exit the command.

18. Edit the horizontal bubble text. Change it to **1**.

19. The square boxes that appear at the end of the grid lines control the appearance of the grid bubbles. Place a check in both ends of the horizontal grid line.

20. 

Select the horizontal grid line so it is highlighted.

Select the **Array** tool under the Modify panel.

21. 

Disable **Group and Associate**.
Set the Number to **3**.
Enable Move To: **2nd**.
Enable **Constrain**.

22. 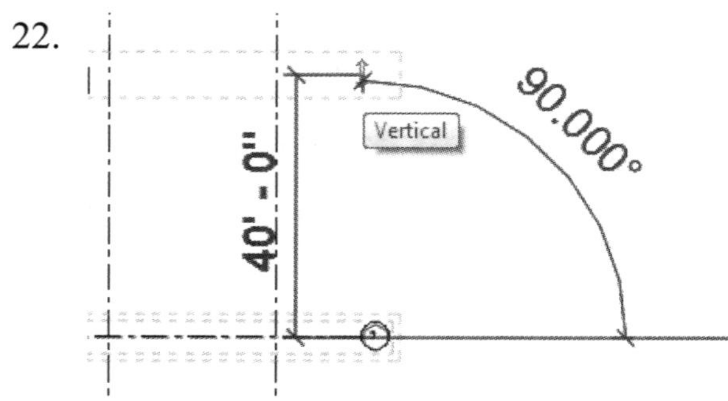

Pick the first point as just under the grid bubble.

Set a distance of **40′** [**12200**] between grid lines.

23. Window around the gridlines so they are all selected.
Use the FILTER tool, if necessary, to only select gridlines.

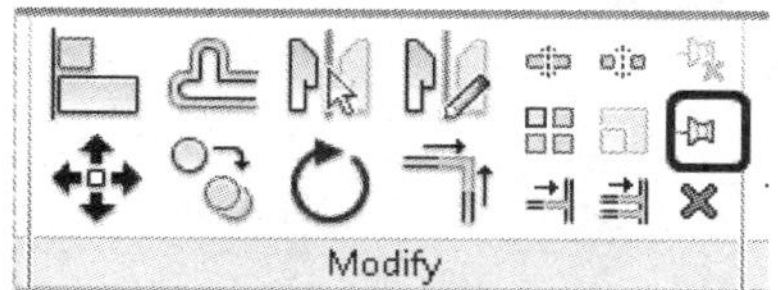

Select the PIN tool on the Modify panel. This will fix the gridlines in place so they can't accidentally be moved or deleted.

24. Save the file as *ex3-1.rvt.*

Exercise 3-2
Placing Walls

Drawing Name: ex3-1.rvt
Estimated Time: 20 minutes

This exercise reinforces the following skills:

- Walls
- Mirror
- Filter
- Move

1. Open or continue working in *ex3-1.rvt.*

2. Architecture Activate the **Architecture** ribbon.

3. Type **VG** to launch the Visibility/Graphics dialog.
Select the **Annotations Categories** tab.

4. 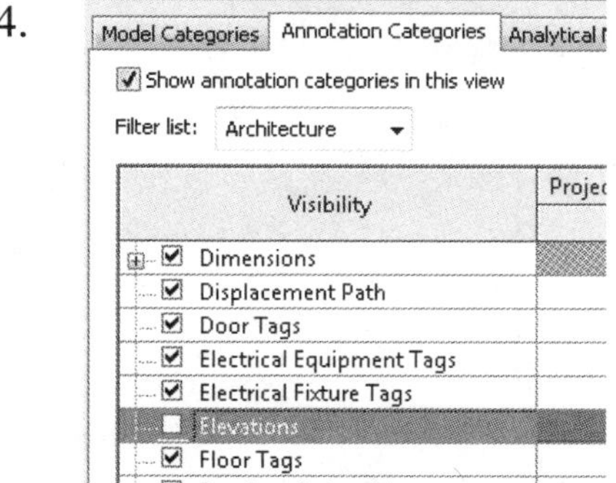

Turn off the Visibility of Elevations in the Visibility/Graphics dialog by unchecking the box.

Press **OK**.

This turns off the visibility of the elevation tags in the display window. This does not DELETE the elevation tags or elevations.

Many users find the tags distracting.

5. 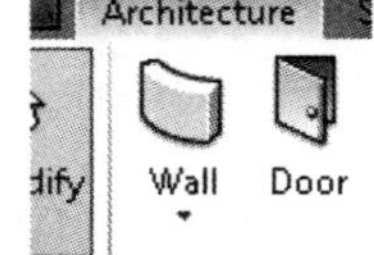

Select the **Wall** tool from the Build panel on the Architecture ribbon.

6. 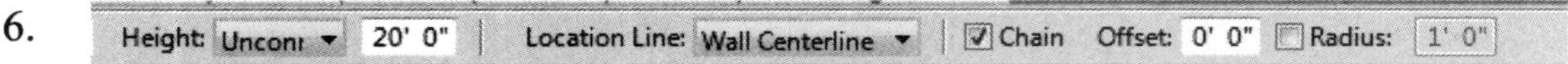

Enable **Chain**.

This eliminates the need to pick a start and end point.

7. Place walls as shown.

To enable the grid bubbles on the bottom, select the grid and place a check in the small square.

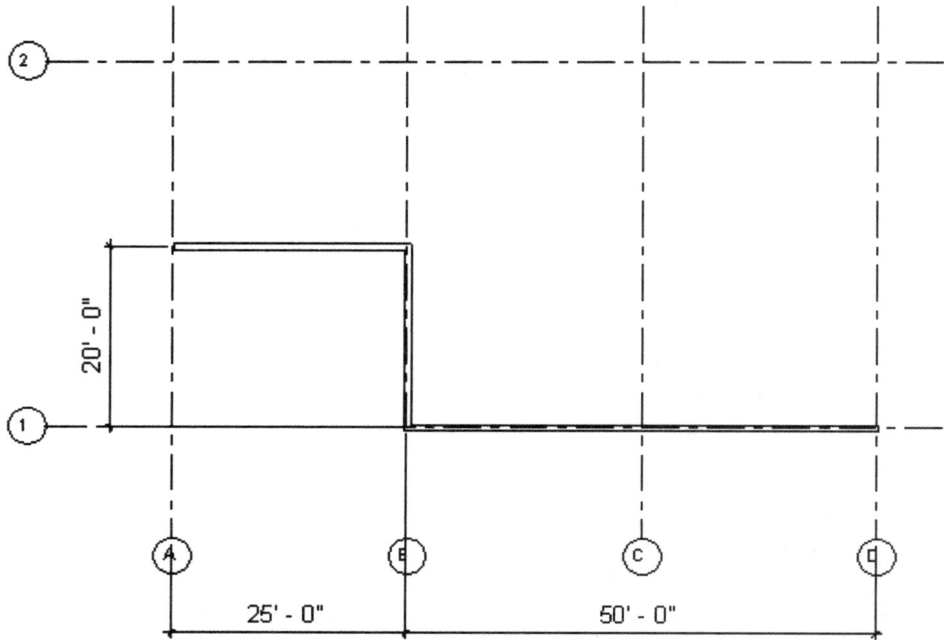

Dimensions are for reference only. Do not place dimensions.

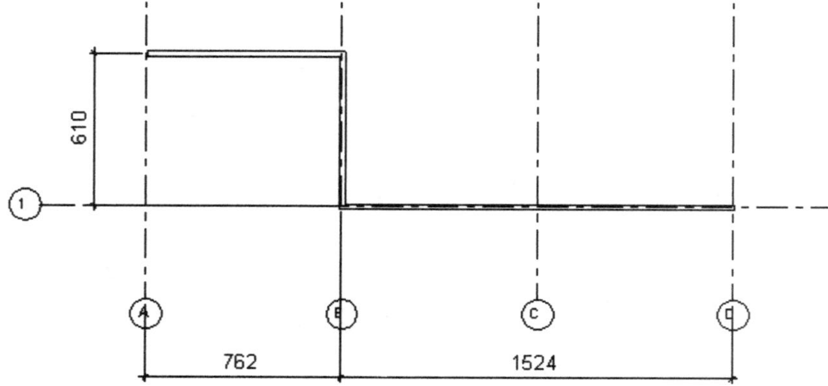

This layout shows units in centimeters.

8. Window about the walls you just placed.

9. Select the **Filter** tool.

10. 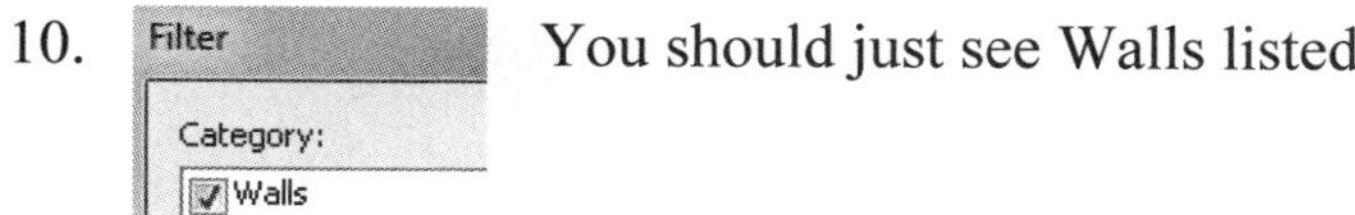

You should just see Walls listed.

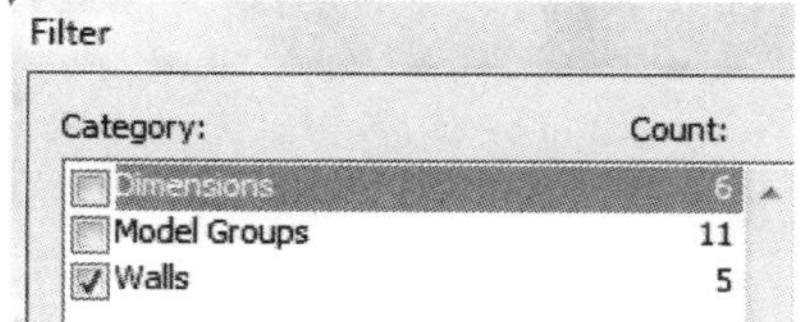

If you see other elements listed, uncheck them and this will select only the walls.

Press **OK**.

Many of my students use a crossing instead of a window or have difficulty selecting just the walls, so use the Filter tool to control your selections and that can save a lot of time.

11. Select the **Mirror→Pick Axis** tool under the Modify Panel.

The Modify Walls ribbon will only be available if walls are selected.

12. Verify that **Copy** is enabled on the Options bar.

13. Select the grid line labeled 2 as the mirror axis.

The walls should mirror over.

14. Select the **Wall** tool from the Build panel on the Architecture ribbon.

15. Draw a vertical wall to close the west side of the building.

16. 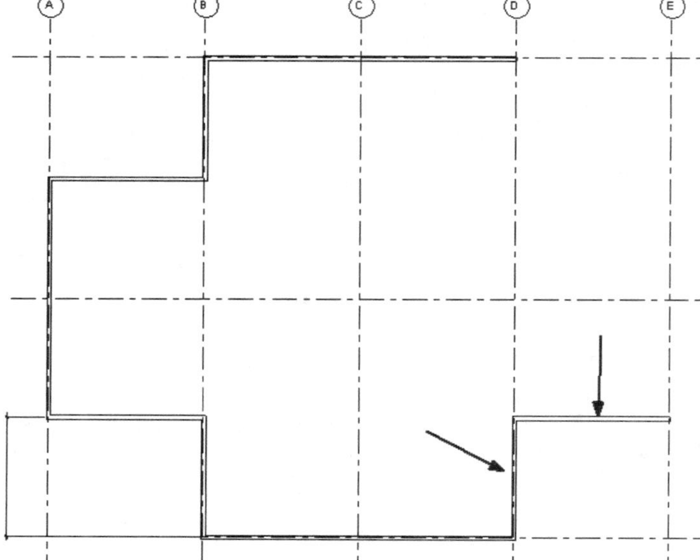

Draw two more walls.

Draw a small vertical wall.
Place a horizontal wall between D and E in the center of the bay.

17. 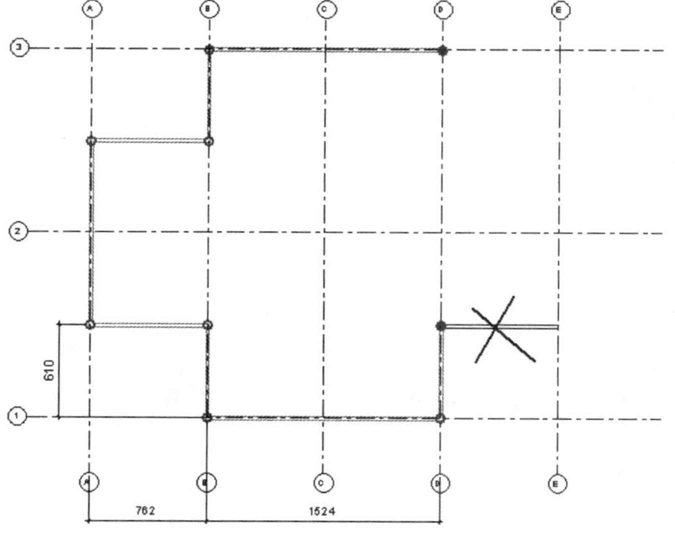

Select all the walls except for the horizontal wall located between D and E grids.

18. Select **Mirror→Draw Axis** from the Modify panel.

19. 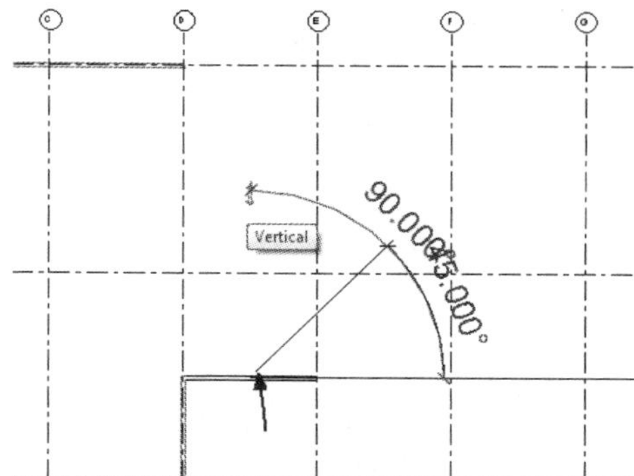

Select the midpoint of the small horizontal wall as the start point for the mirror axis.

Make sure you hold that axis at 90 degrees.

Left click to complete drawing the axis.

20. 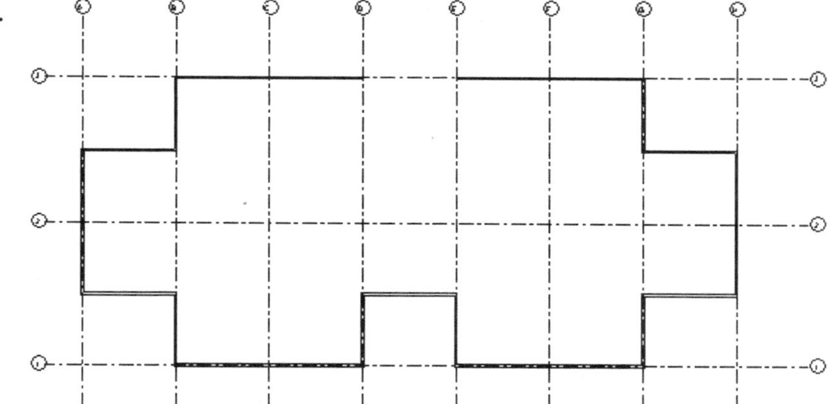

Your building should look like this.

21. 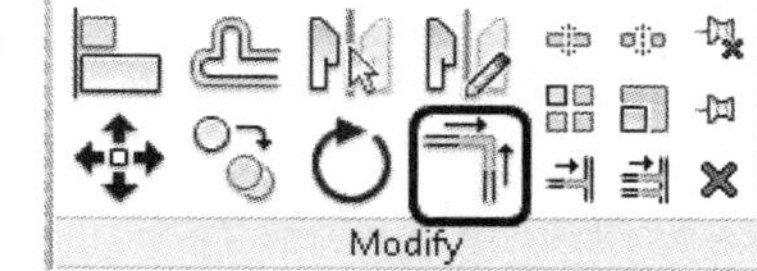

Select the **Trim** tool from the Modify Panel on the Modify ribbon.

22. Select the two upper horizontal walls. The trim tool will join them together.

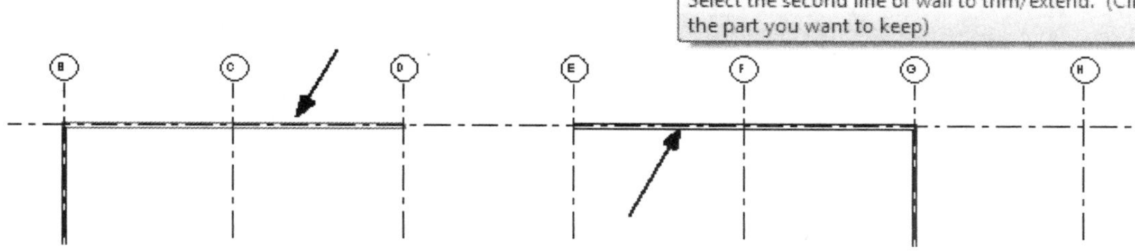

23. 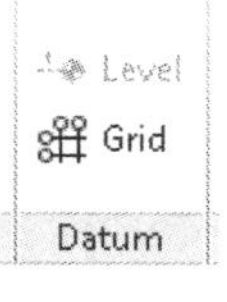

Activate the **Architecture** ribbon.

Select the **Grid** tool from the Datum panel on the Architecture ribbon.

24. Add a grid line along the center line of the walls between Grids 1 and 2.

Label the grid **1.5**.

25.

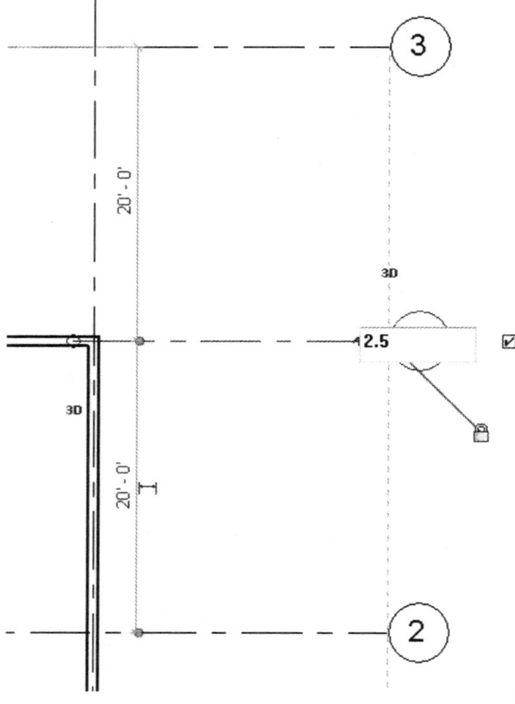

Add a grid line along the center line of the walls between Grids 2 and 3.

Label the grid **2.5**.

26.

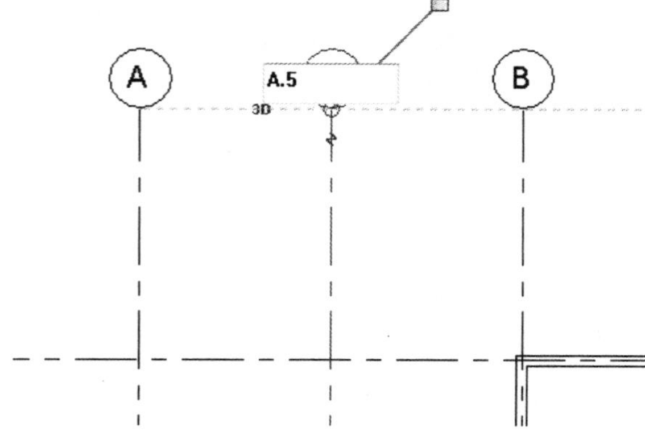

Add a vertical grid line centered between Grids A and B.

You can enter a listening distance of 12' 6" [3810] to place.

Label the grid **A.5**.

27. 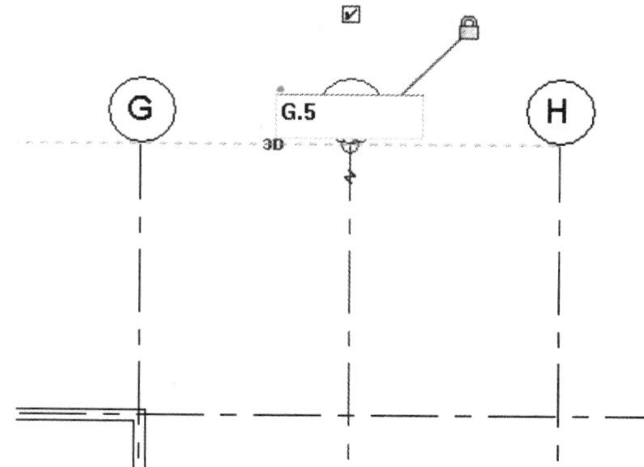

Add a vertical grid line centered between Grids G and H.

You can enter a listening distance of 12' 6" [3810] to place.

Label the grid **G.5**.

28. 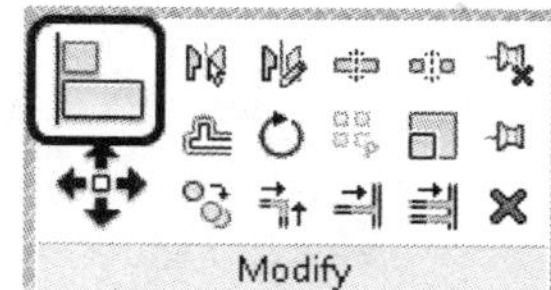

Activate the Modify Ribbon.
Select the **Align** tool on the Modify Panel.

29. Multiple Alignment Prefer: Wall centerline

Enable **Multiple Alignment**.

Set **Wall centerline** as the preference in the Options bar.

30. 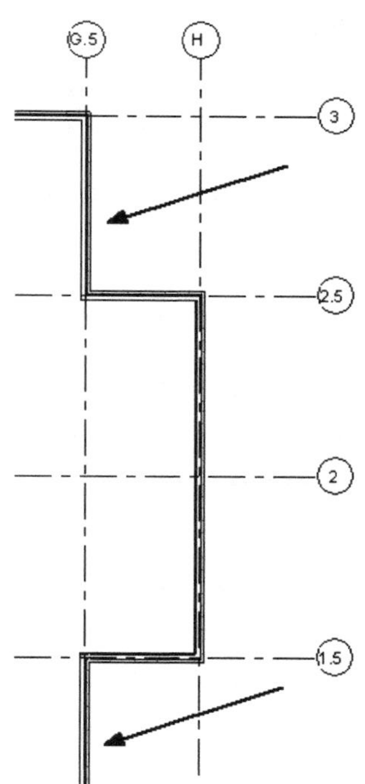

Shift the walls located on the G grid to the G.5 grid using ALIGN.

Select the G.5 grid first, then select the walls.

Right click and select CANCEL.

31. Shift the walls located on the B grid to the B.5 grid using ALIGN.

Select the A.5 grid first, then select the walls.

Right click and select CANCEL twice to exit the command.

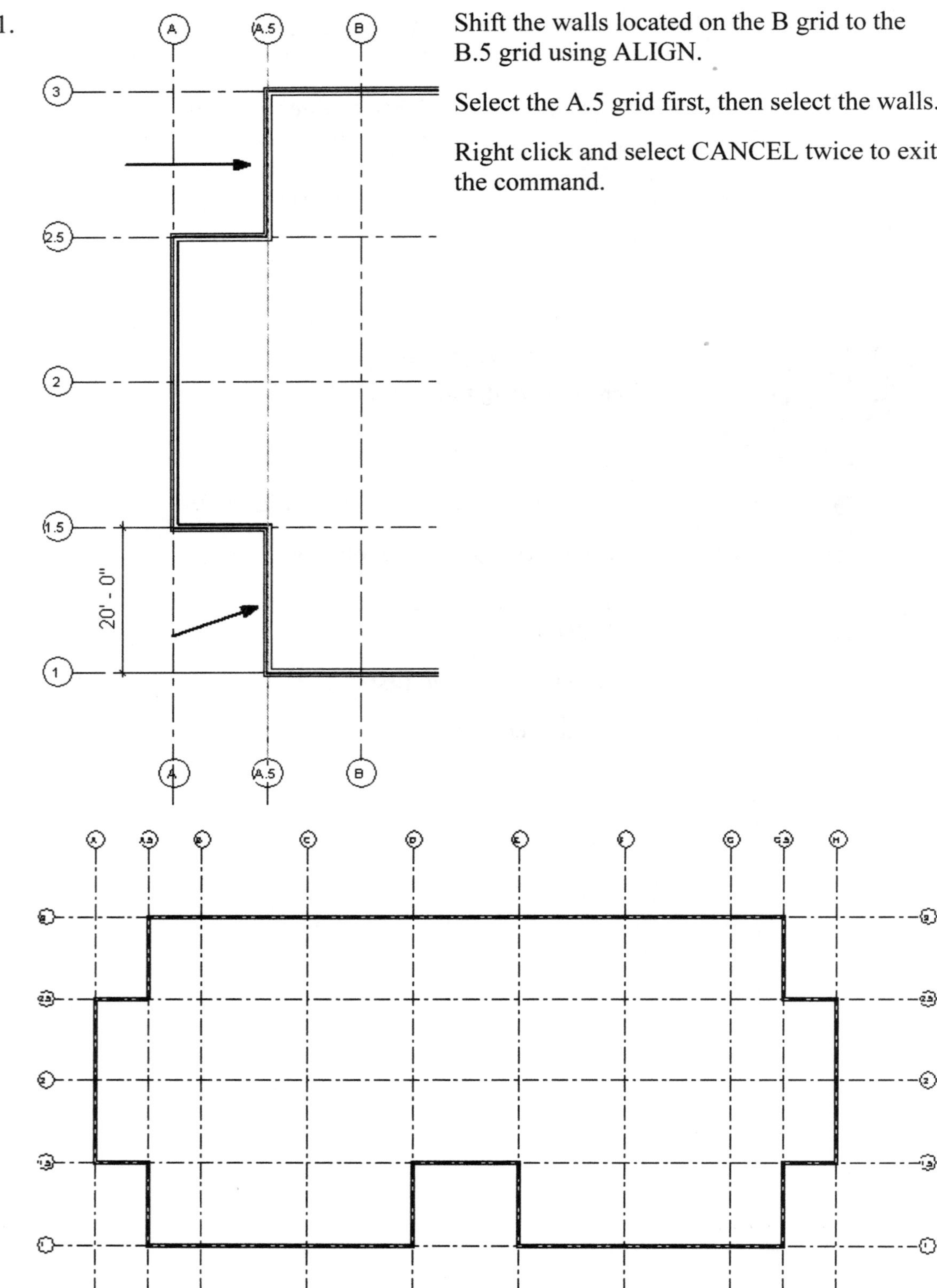

32. Save as *ex3-2.rvt*.

When drawing walls, it is important to understand the ***location line***. This is the layer from which the wall is drawn and controlled from. The location line controls the position of the wall for flipping. It also sets the wall's position when wall thickness is modified. If you change the wall type, say from brick to wood stud, the stud location will be maintained. You can always select the walls and use 'Element Properties' to change the location line. The new user should experiment with this function to fully understand it.

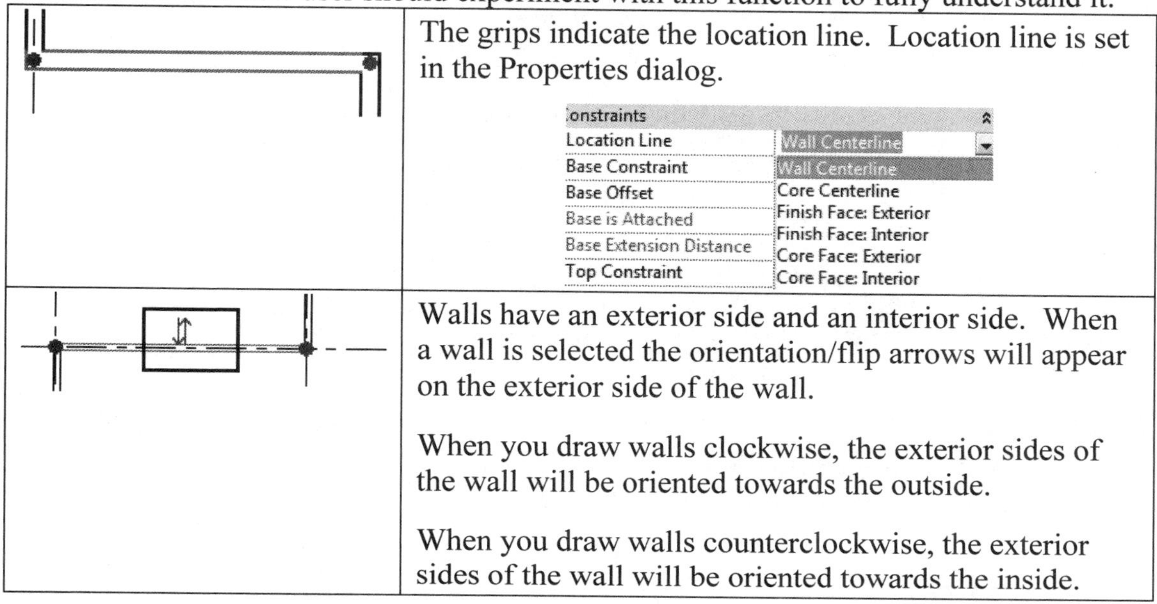

	The grips indicate the location line. Location line is set in the Properties dialog.
	Walls have an exterior side and an interior side. When a wall is selected the orientation/flip arrows will appear on the exterior side of the wall. When you draw walls clockwise, the exterior sides of the wall will be oriented towards the outside. When you draw walls counterclockwise, the exterior sides of the wall will be oriented towards the inside.

Exercise 3-3

Converting an AutoCAD Floor plan

Drawing Name: autocad_floorplan.dwg
Estimated Time: 30 minutes

This exercise reinforces the following skills:

- Import CAD
- Duplicate Wall Type
- Wall Properties
- Trim
- Orbit

Metric units and designations are indicated in brackets [].
There is a video for this lesson on my website at http://www.mossdesigns.com/Pages/Tutorials.aspx

1. 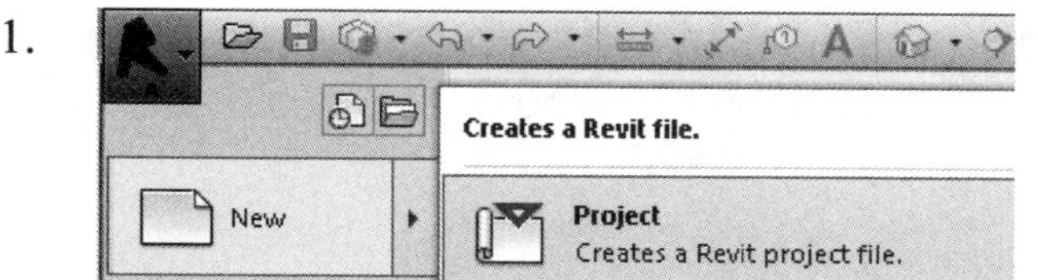

Go to **New→Project**.

2. Press **OK** to use the default template.

3. Activate the **Insert** ribbon.

4. Select the **Import CAD** tool from the Import Panel.

5. Locate the *autocad_floor_plan.dwg*.
This file is located on the publisher's website.

6. 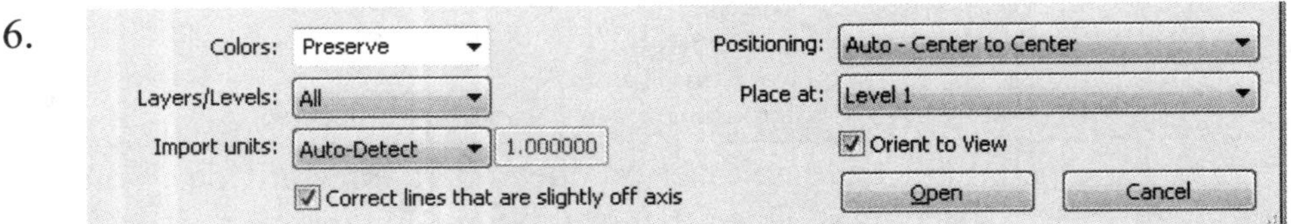

Set Colors to **Preserve**.
Set Layers to **All**.
Set Import Units to **Auto-Detect**.
Set Positioning to: **Auto- Center to Center**.
Press **Open**.

7. 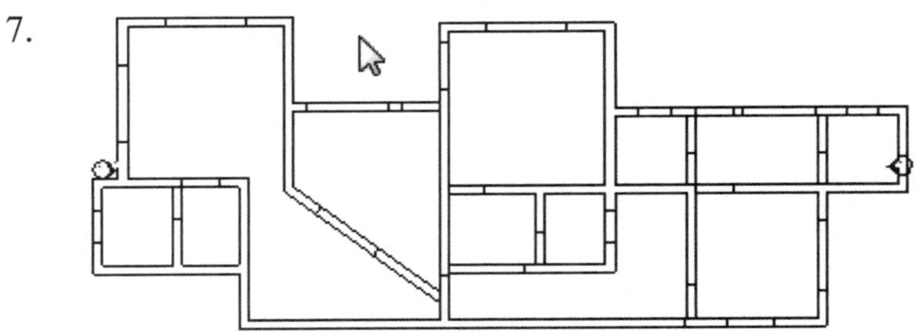

Pick the imported CAD data so it highlights.

8. 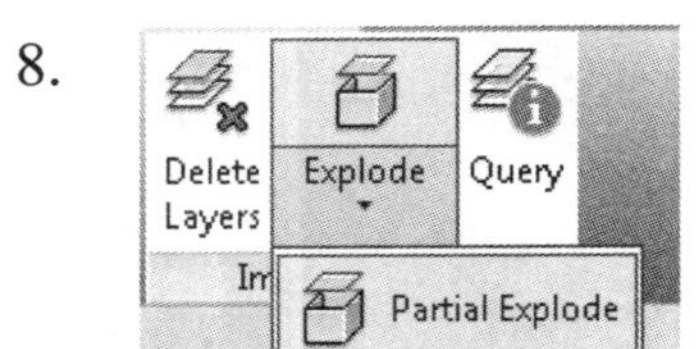

Select the **Partial Explode** tool under the Import Instance panel.

9. 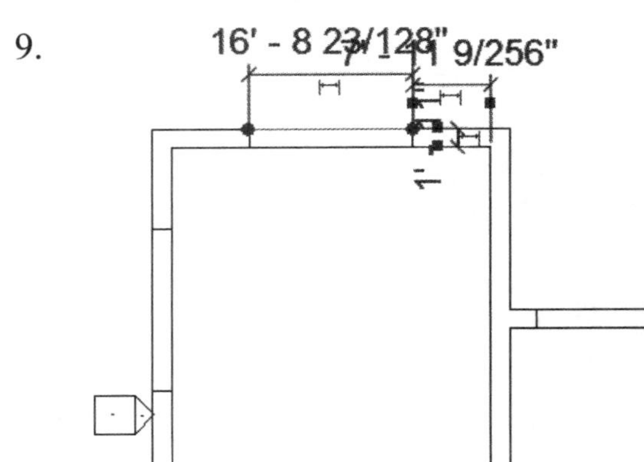

Select a line so it is highlighted.

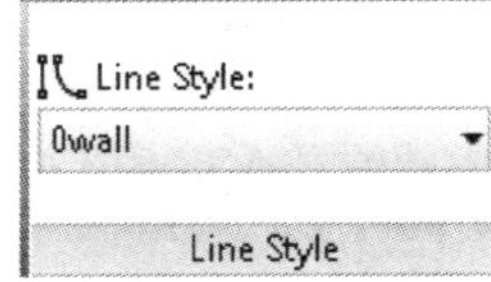

Note the Line Style listed in the Properties pane and on the ribbon.

10. 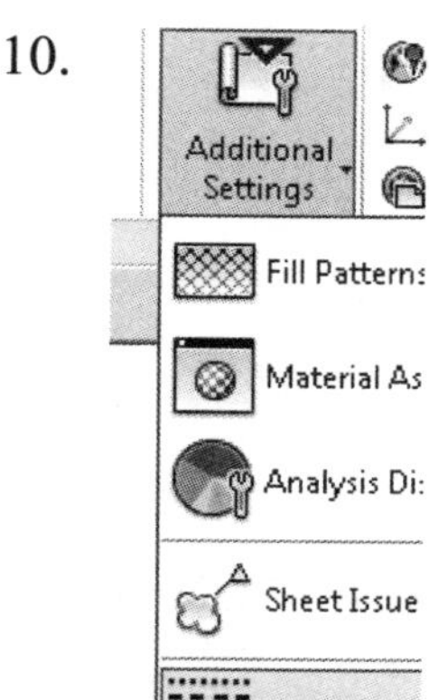

Activate the **Manage** ribbon.

Under Settings→Additional Settings:

Select **Line Styles**.

11.

Category	Line Weight Projection	Line Color	Line Pat
Lines	1	RGB 000-166-000	Solid
0	1	Black	Solid
0wall	1	Black	Solid
0wallthick	4	Black	Solid
<Area Boundary>	6	RGB 128-000-255	Solid

Left click on the + symbol next to Lines to expand the list.
Locate the Line Styles named **0**, **0wall**, and **0wallthick**.

12.

Category	Projection	Line Color	Line Pattern
Lines	1	RGB 000-166-000	Solid
0	1	Cyan	Solid
0wall	1	Cyan	Solid
0wallthick	4	Cyan	Solid

Change the color of **0**, **0wall**, and **0wallthick** line styles to **Cyan**.

Click on the color and then select Cyan from the dialog box.
Press **OK**.

13. 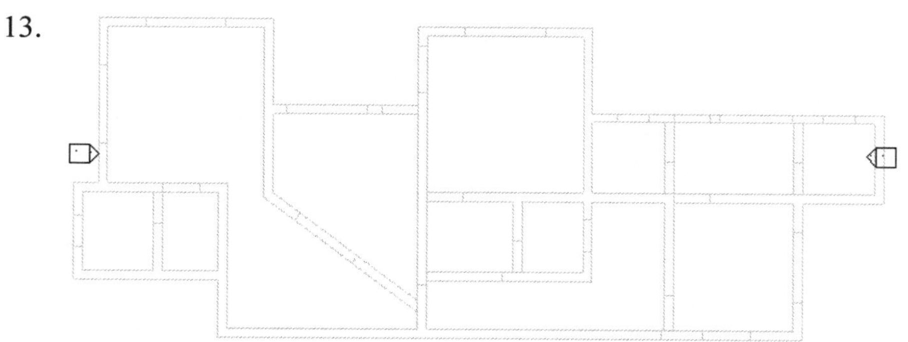

The imported lines will change color to Cyan.

14. Select the **Measure** tool from the Quick Access toolbar.

15. Measure the wall thickness.

1' - 11"

16. Activate the **Architecture** ribbon.

17. 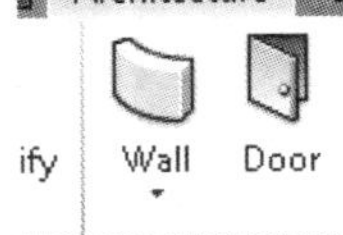

Select the **Wall** tool under the Build panel.

18. Select **Edit Type** from the Properties pane.

19. Select **Duplicate**.

20. Change the Name to **Generic – 1′ 11″ [Generic – 584.2mm]**.

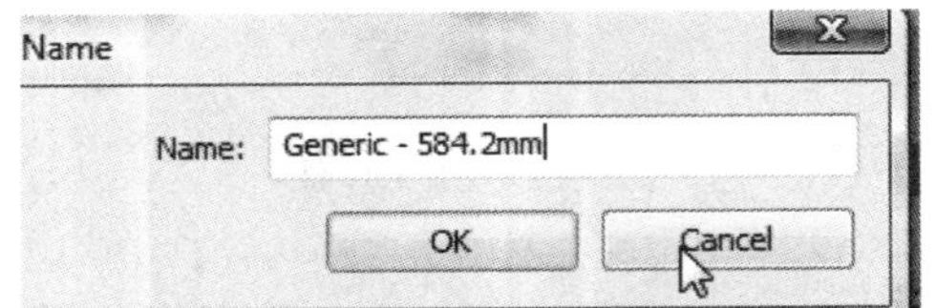

Press **OK**.

21. Select **Edit** next to Structure.

22. 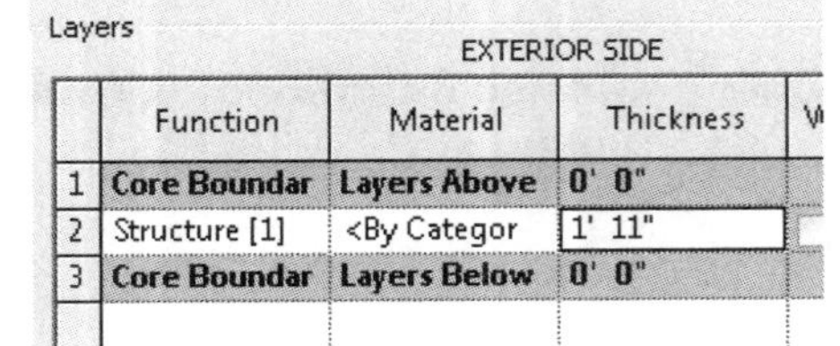

Layers

EXTERIOR SIDE

	Function	Material	Thickness
1	Core Boundar	Layers Above	0' 0"
2	Structure [1]	<By Categor	1' 11"
3	Core Boundar	Layers Below	0' 0"

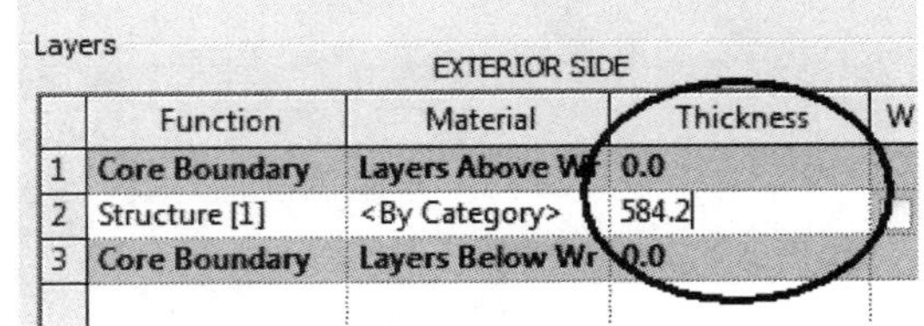

Layers

EXTERIOR SIDE

	Function	Material	Thickness
1	Core Boundary	Layers Above W	0.0
2	Structure [1]	<By Category>	584.2
3	Core Boundary	Layers Below Wr	0.0

Change the thickness to **1′ 11″** [**584.2**].

Press **OK**.

23. Press **OK** to exit the Properties dialog.

24. 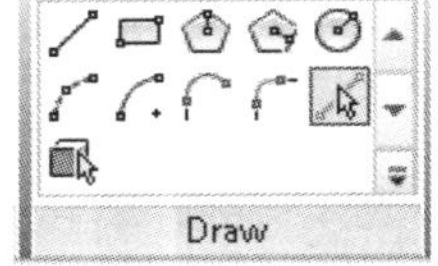

Select the **Pick Lines** tool under the Draw panel.

25. On the Options bar, select **Finish Face: Exterior** for the Location Line.

This means you should select on the exterior side of the wall to place the wall correctly.

26. When you select the line, a preview will appear to indicate the wall orientation. To switch the wall orientation, press the SPACE bar or move the cursor to make a different selection. Select so the dashed line appears inside the wall.

27. Move around the model and select a section of each wall. Do not try to select the entire section of wall or you will get an error message about overlapping walls.

Warning

Highlighted walls overlap. One of them may be ignored when Revit finds room boundaries. Use Cut Geometry to embed one wall within the other.

Delete any overlapping walls.

28\.

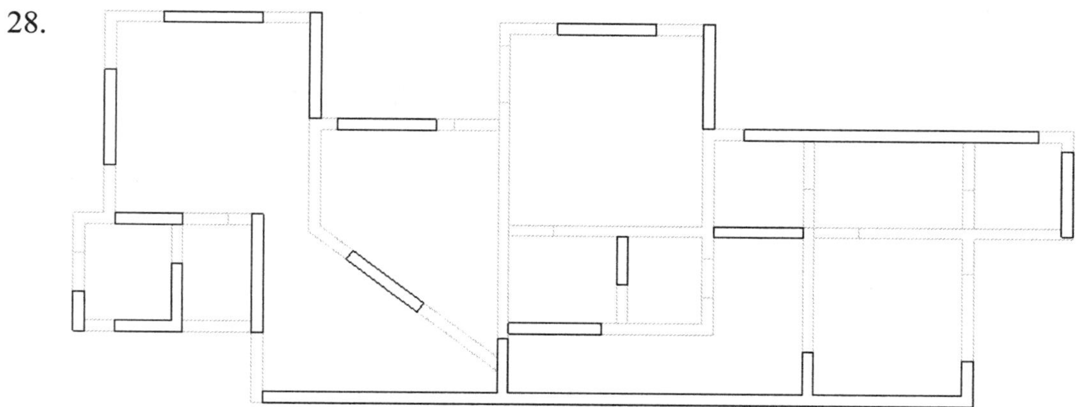

Your model should look similar to this. Note only partial walls have been placed on many of the sections.

29\. Activate the View ribbon.

Select **3D View** from the Create panel.

30\. The model shows the walls placed.

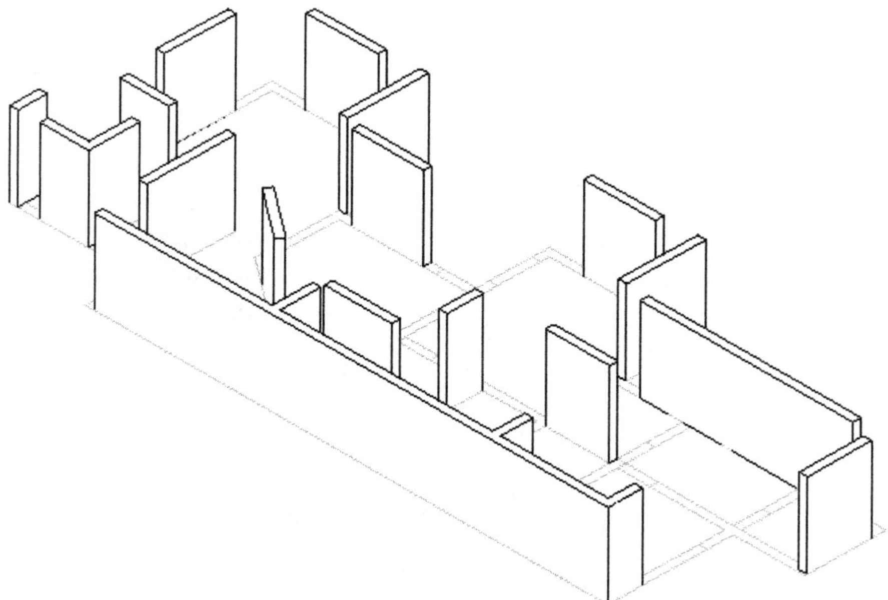

31\. Use the Trim tool to extend and trim the walls to create the floor model.

32.

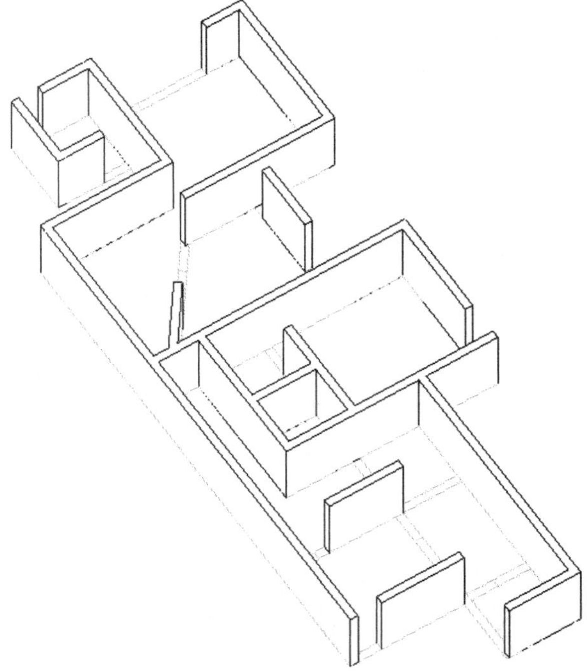

Not all walls can be connected using TRIM.

Some will require use of the EXTEND tool.

33. Select the **Extend Single Element** tool from the Modify panel.

To use this tool, select the face of the wall you want to extend TO first, then the wall you want to extend.

34. Orbit the model so you can see where to trim and extend walls.

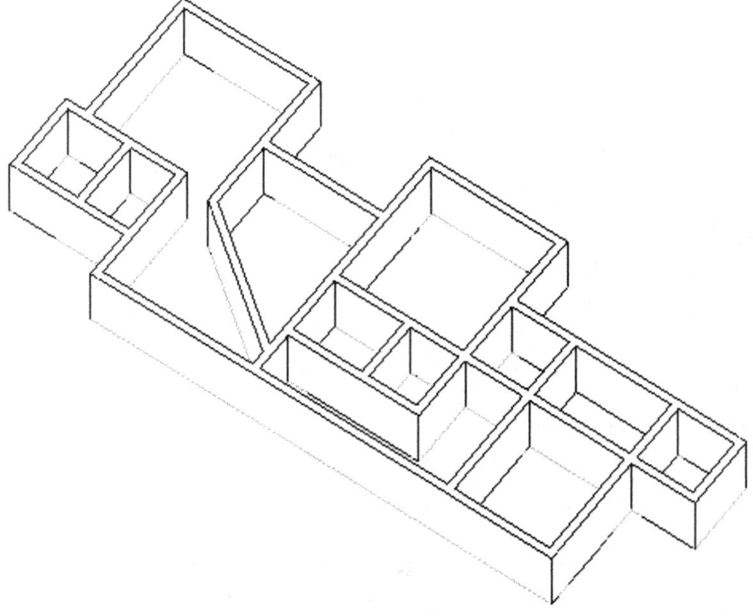

You will still see the colored lines from the original AutoCAD file. They are there to help you check that you placed the walls correctly.

35. Save as *ex3-3.rvt*.

Exercise 3-4

Wall Properties

Drawing Name: ex3-2.rvt
Estimated Time: 40 minutes

This exercise reinforces the following skills:

- Walls
- Filter
- Wall Properties
- Flip Orientation
- Join

[ ] brackets are used to indicate metric units or designations.

1. Open or continue working in *ex3-2.rvt*.
2. Select the exterior walls using **Filter**.
   Use crossing to select the floor plan.
3.  Filter — Select the **Filter** tool.
4. 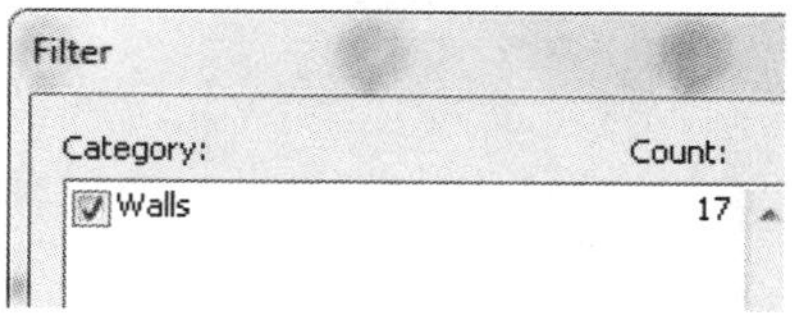 Filter — Category: Walls — Count: 17
   Uncheck all the objects except for Walls.
   Press **OK**.
   This way, only walls are selected.
5.  Edit Type — Select **Edit Type** in the Properties panel.
6. 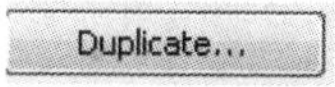 Duplicate... — Select **Generic – 8″** [**Generic – 200 mm**] under Type.
   Select **Duplicate**.
7.  Name: Exterior - 3-5/8" Brick - 5/8" Gypsum — Name: Exterior - 92 mm Brick - 16 mm Gyps
   For the name, enter:
   Exterior - 3-5/8″ Brick — 5/8″ Gypsum [**Exterior- 92mm Brick -16mm Gypsum**].
   Press **OK**.
8. 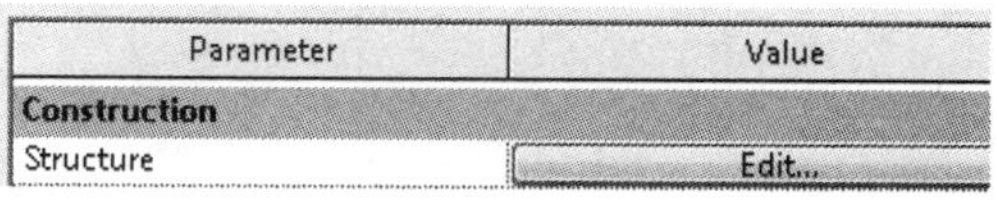 Parameter | Value — Construction — Structure | Edit...
   Select **Edit** for Structure.
9.  << Preview — Enable the Preview button to expand the dialog so you can see the preview of the wall structure.
10. 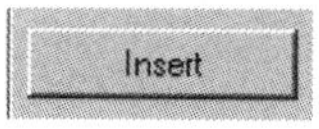 Insert — Select the **Insert** Button.

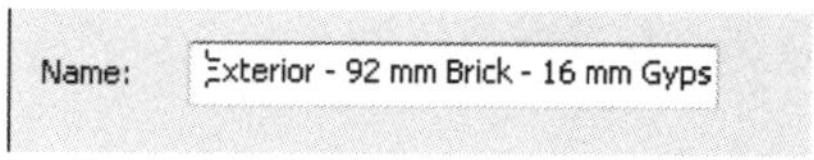

In the dialog, notice that the bottom of the list indicates toward the interior side and the top of the list indicates toward the exterior side of the wall.

11. Select the second line in the Function column.

    Select **Finish 1 [4]** from the drop-down list.

12. Press the **Insert** button until you have seven layers total.

    Arrange the layers as shown.

    Assign the Functions as shown:

    Layer 1: Finish 1 [4]
    Layer 2: Thermal/Air Layer
    Layer 3: Substrate [2]
    Layer 4: Core Boundary
    Layer 5: Structure [1]
    Layer 6: Core Boundary
    Layer 7: Finish 2 [5]

13. Select the **Material** column for Layer 1.

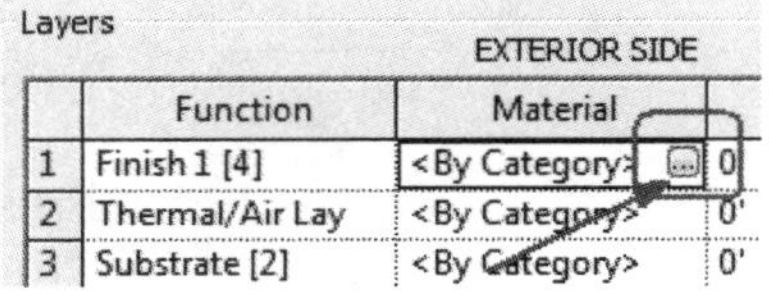

14. In the Materials search box, type **bri**.

15. Any materials with 'bri' as part of the name or description will be listed.

    Highlight **Brick, Common** from the Name list.

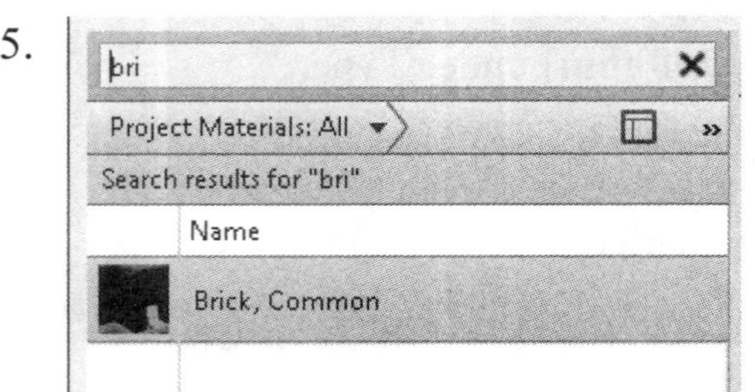

16. Note that we can set how we want this material to appear when we render and shade our model.

    Place a check in the **Use Render Appearance for Shading**.

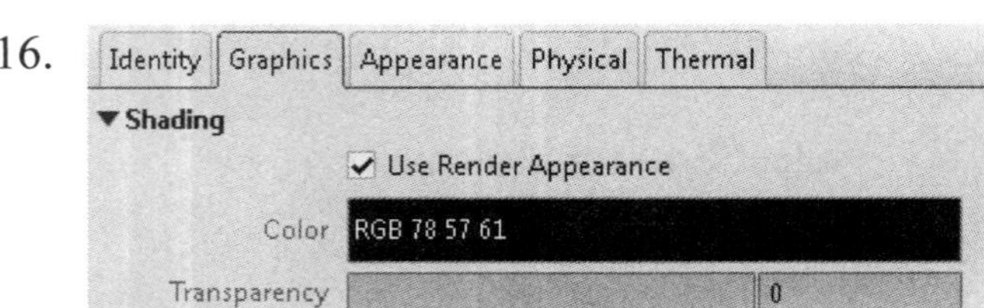

17.

Left mouse click on the fill pattern in the Surface Pattern field.

18.

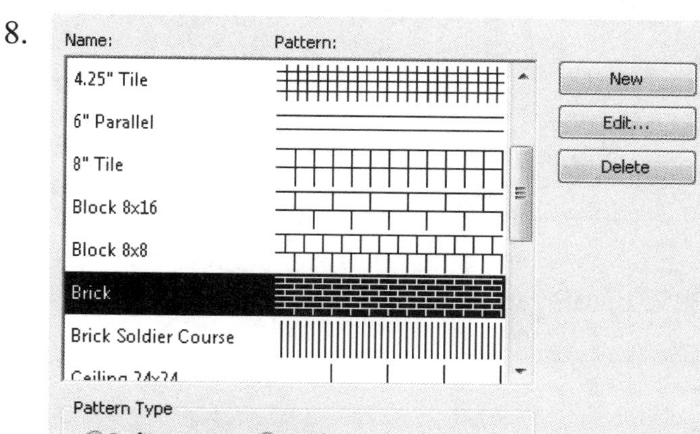

Note you can set how the surface pattern appears in drafting or model mode.

Highlight **Brick [Brick 72x225]**.

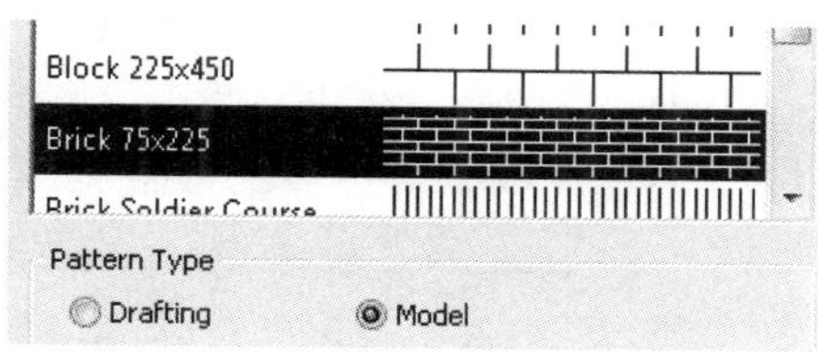

Press **OK**.

19. Select the **Appearance** tab.

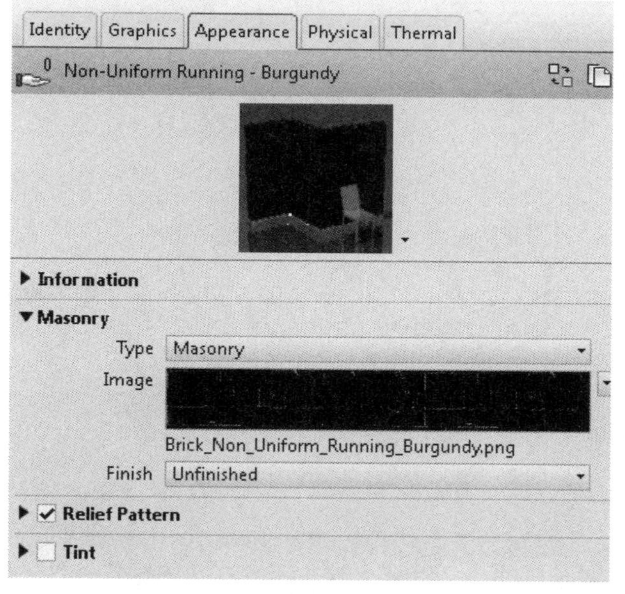

Note the image of how the brick will appear when the wall is rendered.

Press **OK**.

20.

1	Finish 1 [4	Brick, Common	0' 3 5/8"

Change the Thickness to **3 5/8″** [**92mm**].

	Function	Material	Thickness
1	Finish 1 [4]	Brick, Common	92.0

21.

	Function
1	Finish 1 [4]
2	Thermal/Air Layer [3]

Locate Layer 2 and verify that it is set to Thermal/Air Layer. Select the **Material** column.

22. On the Materials tab:

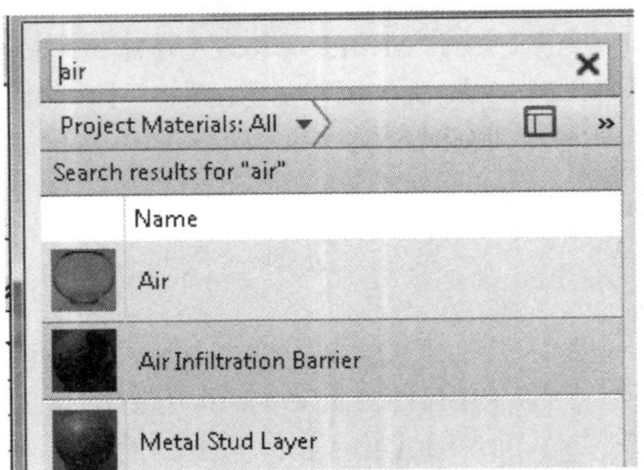

Type **air** in the search field.

Select **Air Infiltration Barrier**.

Press **OK**.

23. Set the Thickness of **Layer 2** to **1″** [**25.4**].

	Function	Material	Thickness
1	Finish 1 [4]	Brick, Common	0' 3 5/8"
2	Thermal/Air Layer [3]	Air Infiltration Barrier	0' 1"

EXTERIOR SIDE

	Function	Material	Thickness
1	Finish 1 [4]	Brick, Common	92.0
2	Thermal/Air Layer [3]	Air Infiltration Barrier	25.4

24. Set Layer 3 to Substrate [2], **Plywood, Sheathing**; Thickness to **½″** [**17.2**].

	Function	Material	Thickness
1	Finish 1 [4]	Brick, Common	0' 3 5/8"
2	Thermal/Air Layer [3]	Air Infiltration Barrier	0' 1"
3	Substrate [2]	Plywood, Sheathing	0' 0 1/2"

	Function	Material	Thickness
1	Finish 1 [4]	Brick, Common	92.0
2	Thermal/Air Layer [3]	Air Infiltration Barrier	25.4
3	Substrate [2]	Plywood, Sheathing	17.2

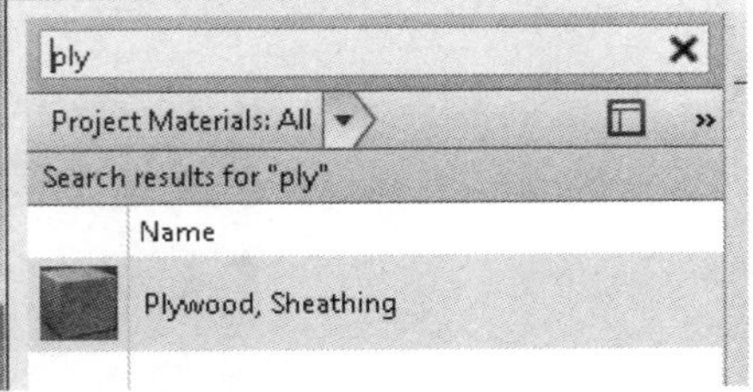

25. Set the Material for Structure [1] to **Metal Stud Layer**.

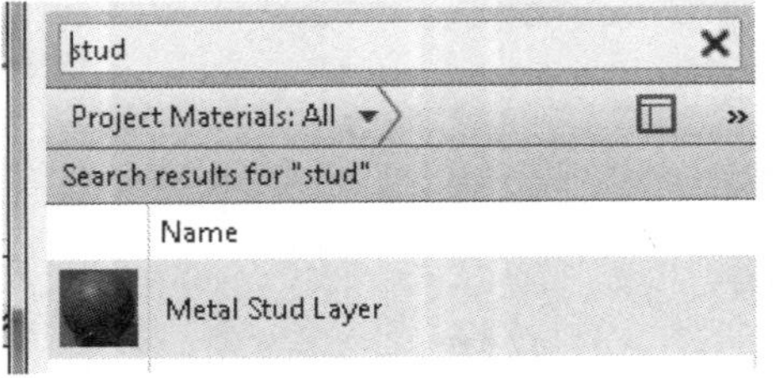

Press **OK**.

26. Set the Thickness for Layer 4 Structure [1] to **6″** [**152.4**].

	Function	Material	Thickness
1	Finish 1 [4]	Brick, Common	0' 3 5/8"
2	Thermal/Air Layer [3]	Air Infiltration Barrier	0' 1"
3	Substrate [2]	Plywood, Sheathing	0' 0 1/2"
4	**Core Boundary**	**Layers Above Wrap**	**0' 0"**
5	Structure [1]	Metal Stud Layer	0' 6"

	Function	Material	Thickness
1	Finish 1 [4]	Brick, Common	92.0
2	Thermal/Air Layer [3]	Air Infiltration Barrier	25.4
3	Substrate [2]	Plywood, Sheathing	17.2
4	**Core Boundary**	**Layers Above Wrap**	**0.0**
5	Structure [1]	Metal Stud Layer	152.4

The Core Boundary Layers may not be modified or deleted.

These layers control the location of the wrap when walls intersect.

27.

	Function
1	Finish 1 [4]
2	Thermal/Air Layer [3]
3	Substrate [2]
4	**Core Boundary**
5	Structure [1]
6	**Core Boundary**
7	Finish 2 [5]

Select the Material column for Layer 7: Finish 2 [5].

28.

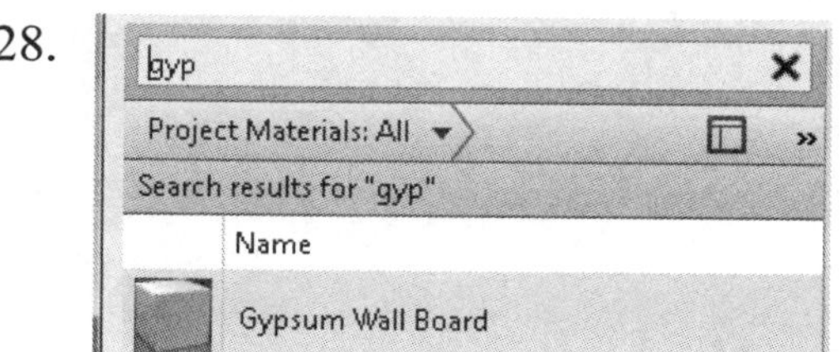

Select **Gypsum Wall Board**.

Press **OK**.

Plasterboard

29.

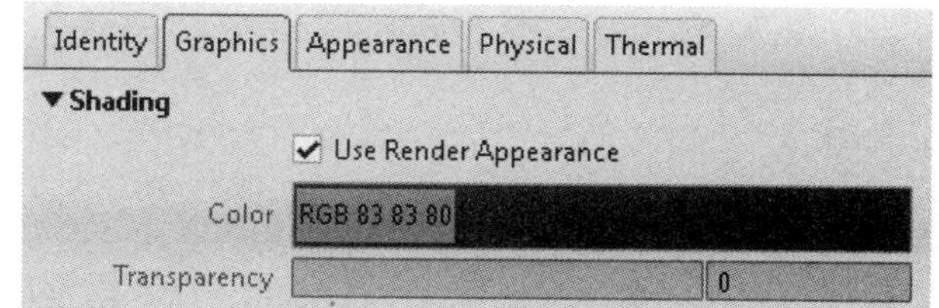

Select the Graphics tab.

Place a check in the **Use Render Appearance** for Shading.

30.

	Function	Material	Thickness
1	Finish 1 [4]	Brick, Common	0' 3 5/8"
2	Thermal/Air Layer [3]	Air Infiltration Barrier	0' 1"
3	Substrate [2]	Plywood, Sheathing	0' 0 1/2"
4	**Core Boundary**	**Layers Above Wrap**	**0' 0"**
5	Structure [1]	Metal Stud Layer	0' 6"
6	**Core Boundary**	**Layers Below Wrap**	**0' 0"**
7	Finish 2 [5]	Metal Stud Layer	0' 0 5/8"

Set Layer 7 to **Finish 2 [5], Gypsum Wall Board**; Thickness to **5/8″** [**16mm**].

Press **OK**.

	Function	Material	Thickness
1	Finish 1 [4]	Brick, Common	92.0
2	Thermal/Air Layer [3]	Air Infiltration Barrier	25.4
3	Substrate [2]	Plywood, Sheathing	17.2
4	**Core Boundary**	**Layers Above Wrap**	**0.0**
5	Structure [1]	Metal Stud Layer	152.4
6	**Core Boundary**	**Layers Below Wrap**	**0.0**
7	Finish 2 [5]	Gypsum Wall Board	16

31. 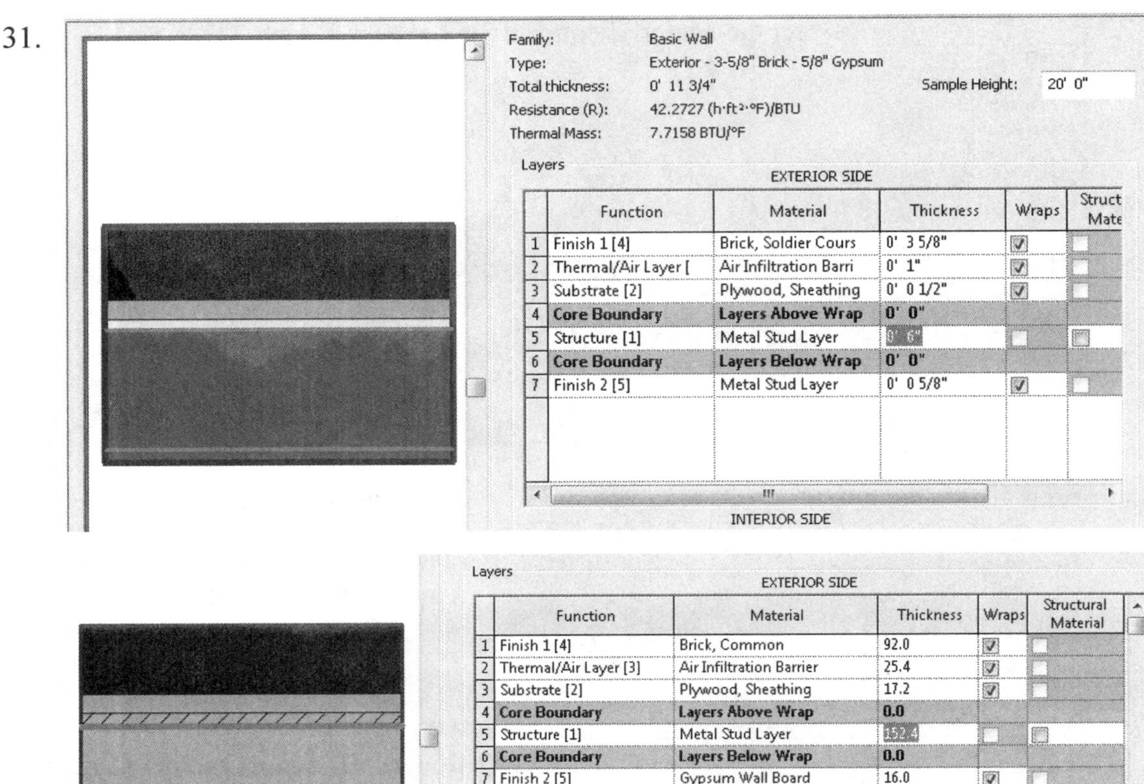

Set Layer 1 to Finish 1 [4], Brick, Common, Thickness: **3-5/8″** [**92**].
Set Layer 2 to Thermal/Air Layer [3], Air Infiltration Barrier,Thickness: **1″** [**25.4**].
Set Layer 3 to Substrate [2], Plywood, Sheathing, Thickness to **½″** [**17.2**].
Set Layer 4 to Core Boundary, Layers Above Wrap, Thickness to **0″**.
Set Layer 5 to Structure [1], Metal Stud Layer, Thickness to **6″** [**152.4**].
Set Layer 6 to Core Boundary, Layers Below Wrap, Thickness to **0″**.
Set Layer 7 to Finish 2 [5], Gypsum Wall Board, Thickness to **5/8″** [**16**].
Press **OK** to exit the Edit Assembly dialog.

32. 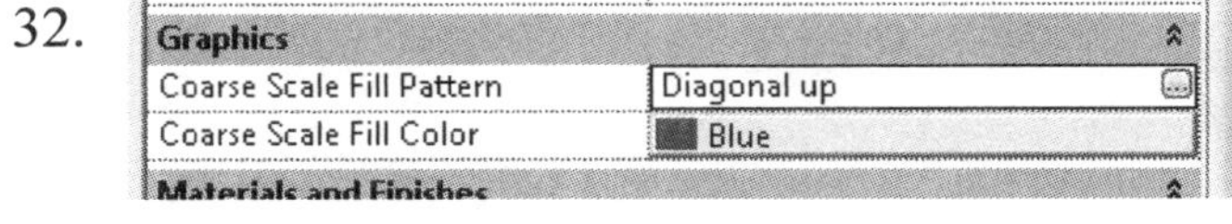

Set the Coarse Scale Fill Pattern to **Diagonal up**.

Set the Coarse Fill Color to **Blue**.

33. Press **OK** to exit the Properties dialog.
Because your walls were selected when you started defining the new wall style, your walls now appear with the new wall style.

34. If you zoom in, you will see that the coarse fill pattern is Diagonal Up and is Color Blue.

35. 

Set the Detail Level to **Medium**.

You will not see the hatching or any change in line width unless the Detail Level is set to Medium or Fine.

36. We now see the wall details, but the brick side is toward the interior and the gypsum board is towards the exterior for some walls. In other words, the walls need to be reversed or flipped.

How do we know the walls need to be flipped?

37. When we pick the walls, the orientation arrows are located adjacent to the exterior side of the wall.

The orientation arrows are the blue arrows that are activated when an object is selected.

38. Select the wall, right click and select **Change wall's orientation** or just click the blue arrows.

39. Go around the building and flip the orientation of the walls so that the brick is on the outside.

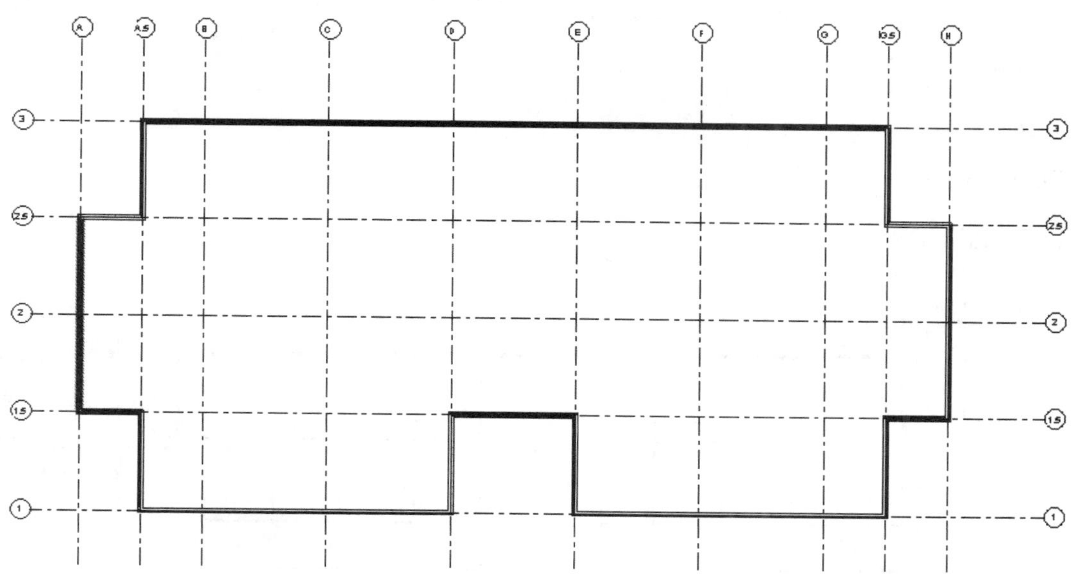

If you have problems selecting a wall instead of a grid line, use the TAB key to cycle through the selection.

40. Save the file *ex3-4.rvt.*

Exercise 3-5
Add Level 1 Interior Walls

Drawing Name: ex3-4.rvt
Estimated Time: 10 minutes

This exercise reinforces the following skills:
A video is available at http://www.mossdesigns.com/Pages/Tutorials.aspx for this exercise.

- ❑ Wall
- ❑ 3D View
- ❑ Visibility
- ❑ Wall Properties

1. Open or continue working in *ex3-4.rvt.*

2.  Floor Plans / **Level 1** / Level 2 / Site — Activate **Level 1**.

3.  Wall — Select the **Wall** tool on the Build panel under the Architecture ribbon.

4. 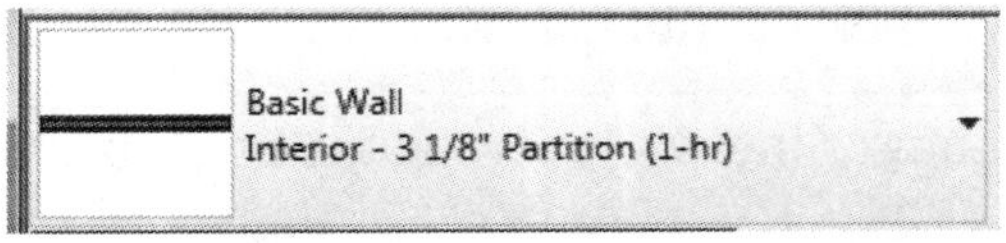 Basic Wall Interior - 3 1/8" Partition (1-hr) / Basic Wall Interior - 138mm Partition (1-hr)

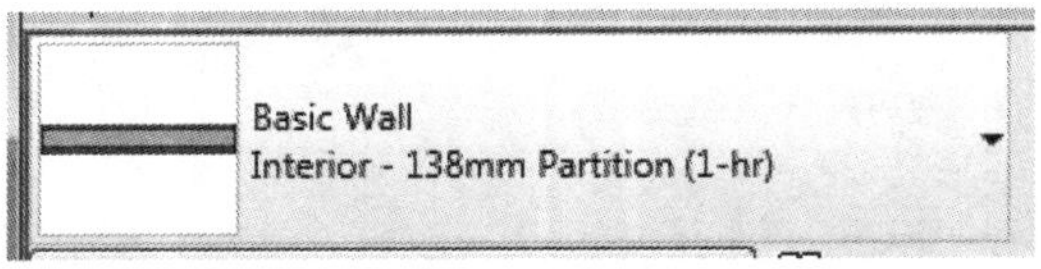

   In the Properties panel, select **Interior: 3 1/8″ Partition (1-hr)** [**Basic Wall: Interior - 138mm Partition (1-hr)**].

5. Place interior walls as shown.

   Imperial Units

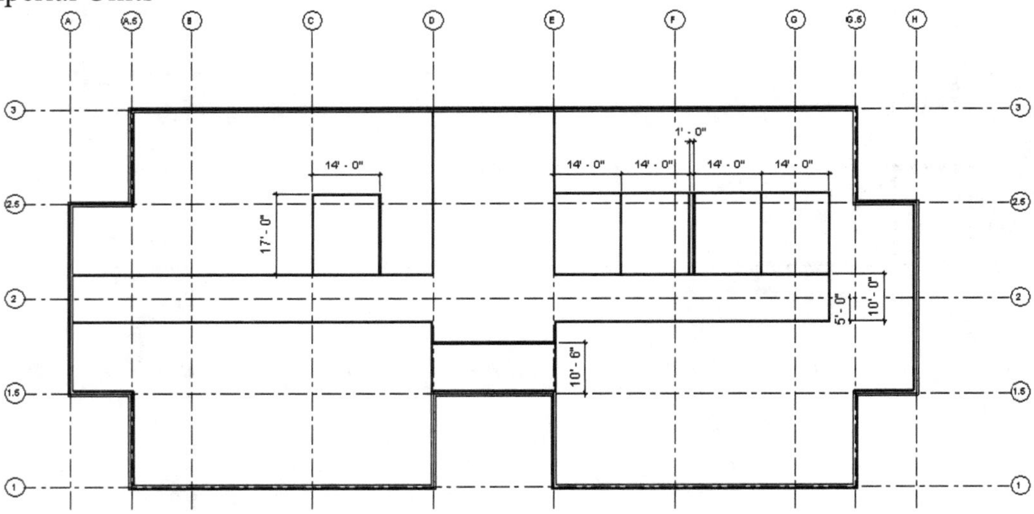

Metric Units (using centimeters)

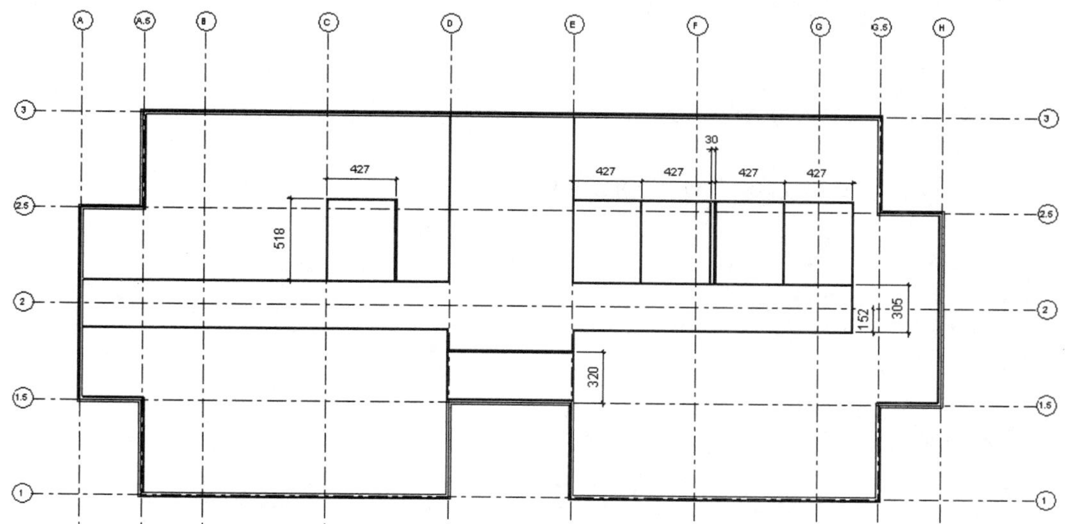

6. Activate the View ribbon.
   Select the **3D View** tool.

   We see our first floor interior walls.

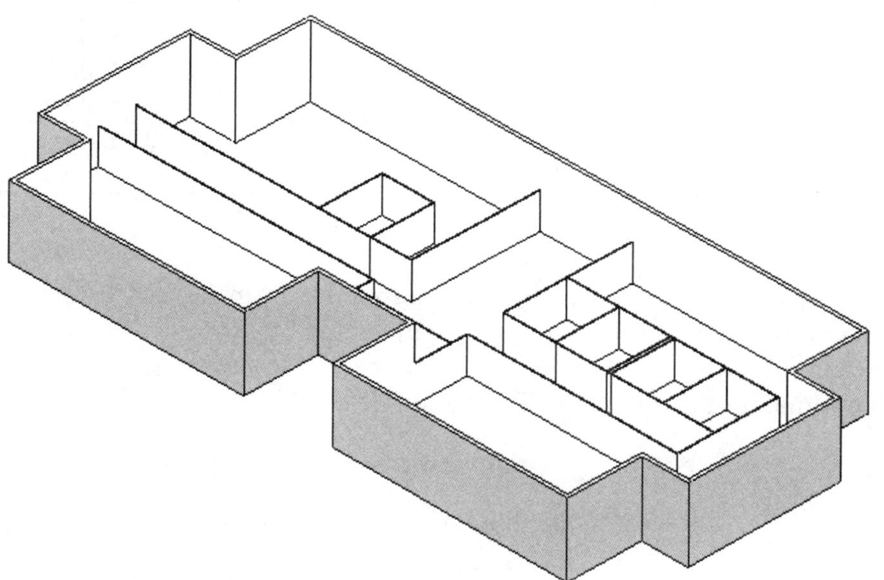

7. Save the file as *ex3-5.rvt*.

Exercise 3-6
Add Level 2 Interior Walls

Drawing Name: ex3-5.rvt
Estimated Time: 20 minutes

This exercise reinforces the following skills:

- View Properties
- Wall
- Wall Properties
- 3D View

1. Open *ex3-5.rvt.*

2.  Activate **3D View**.

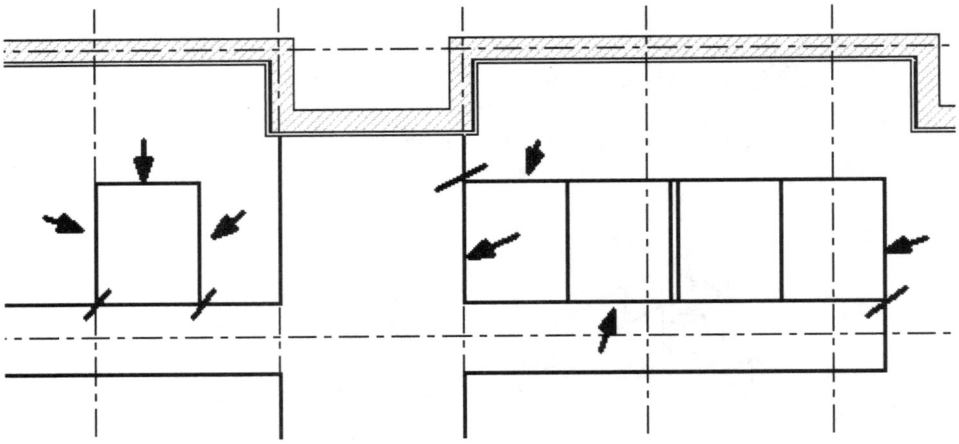

Some of our interior walls will be continuous from Level 1 to Level 2. The walls that will be extended are indicated by arrows. A diagonal line indicates where the walls need to be split or divided as a portion of the wall will be continuous and a portion will be a single story.

3. 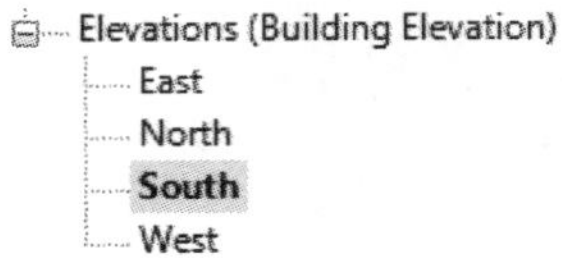 Switch view to a **South Elevation** view.

Double left click in the browser window on the South Elevation view

4. 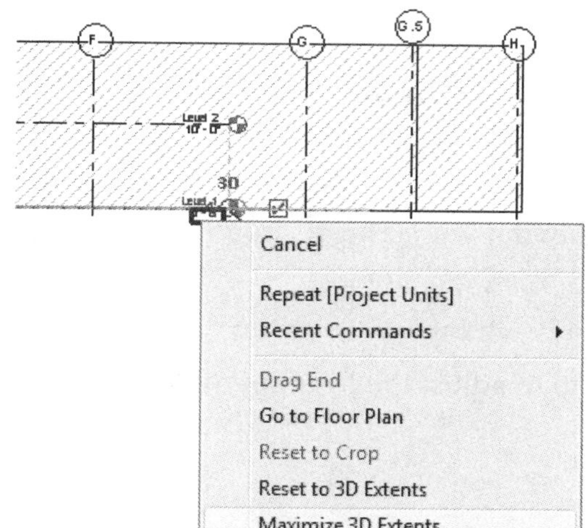

Select the level line.

Right click and select **Maximize 3D Extents**.

This will stretch the level to cover the entire building.

Repeat for the other level.

5. 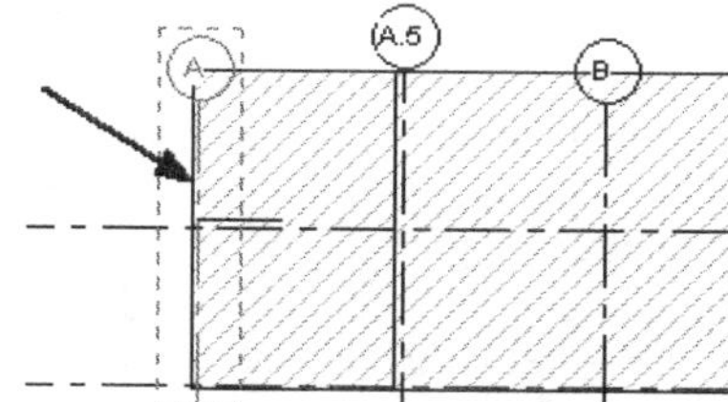

Select the first grid line labeled **A**.

6. 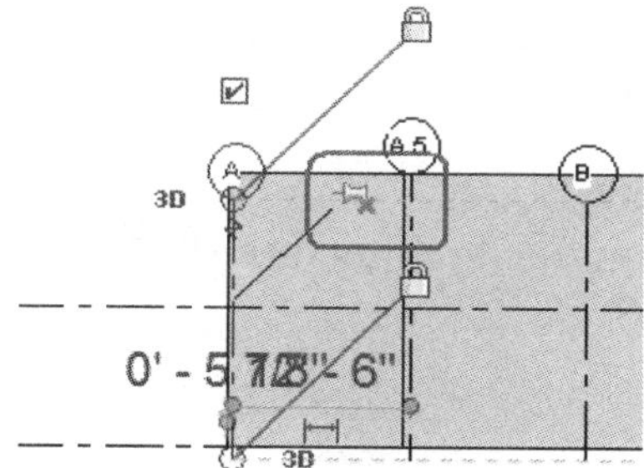

Lift click on the pin to unpin the gridline.

You have to unpin the element before it can be modified.

7. 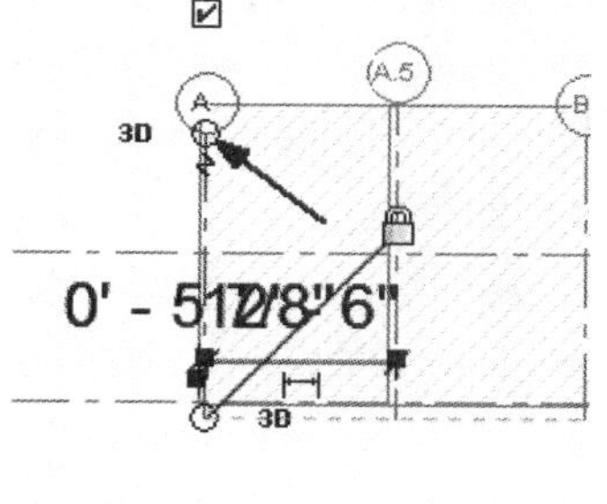

Use the grip indicated to drag the grid line above the building.

8. All the grid lines which were created as part of the array adjust. If you forgot to uncheck Group and Associate when you created the array, you will not be able to adjust the grids without either UNGROUPING or editing the group.

Ungroup

To ungroup, simply select one of the gridlines and select Ungroup from the ribbon.

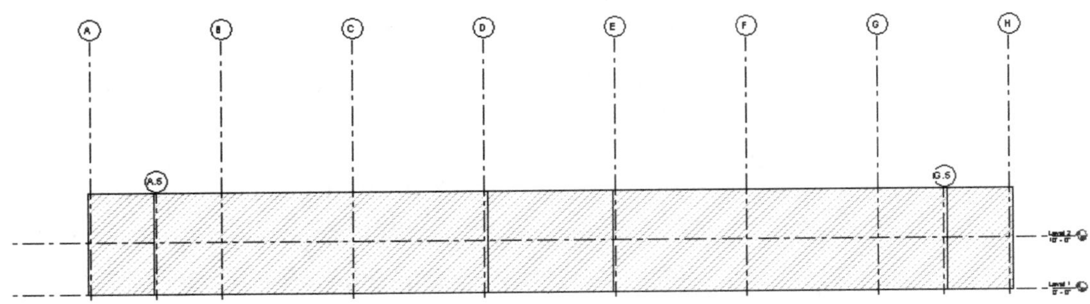

9. Use the grip to adjust the location of the remaining grid lines.

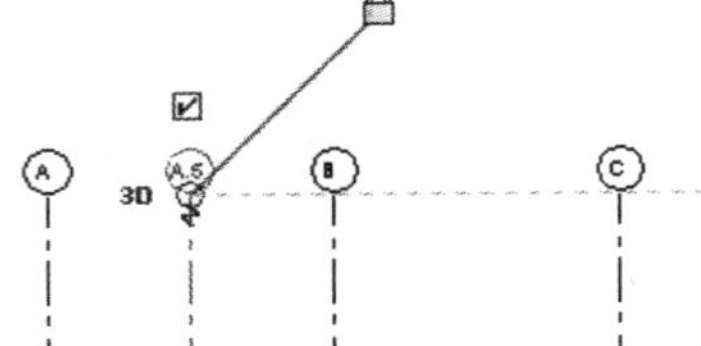

10.

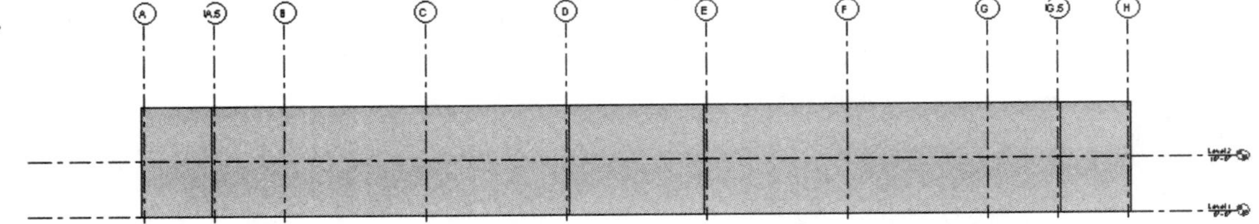

The current model has level lines for the ground plane and second floor, but not for the roof. We will add a level line for the roof to constrain the building's second level and establish a roof line.

11. Select the **Level** tool on the Datum panel on the Architecture ribbon.

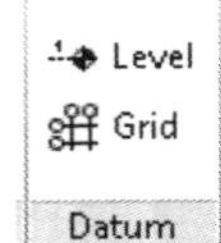

12. Draw a level line **10′** [**4000** mm] above Level 2.

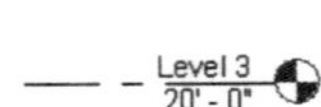

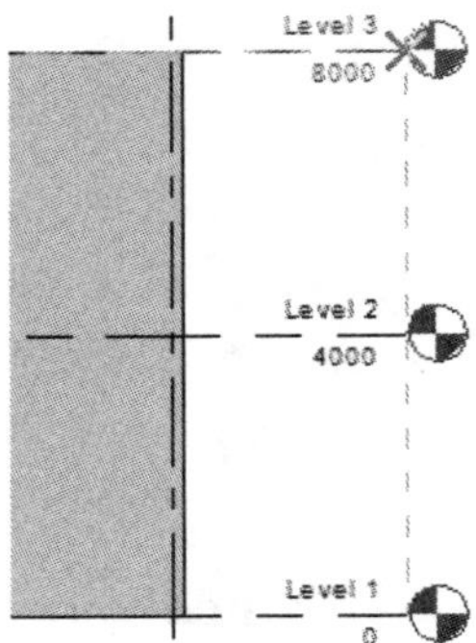

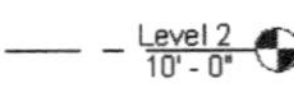

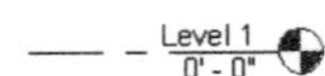

13. Rename Level 3 by double left clicking on the level name. Rename to **Roof Line**.

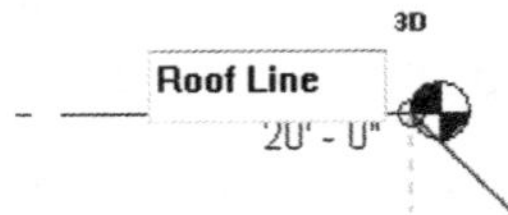

14. Would you like to rename corresponding views?

Press **Yes**.

This renames the views in the Project Browser to Roof Line.

15. Switch back to the Level 1 Floor plan view.

16. Modify

Activate the **Modify** ribbon.

Select the **Split** tool.

17. Delete Inner Segment

Uncheck **Delete Inner Segment** on the Options bar.

18. Split the walls where portions will remain only on level 1 and portions will be continuous up to the roof line.

19. Split the walls at the intersections indicated.

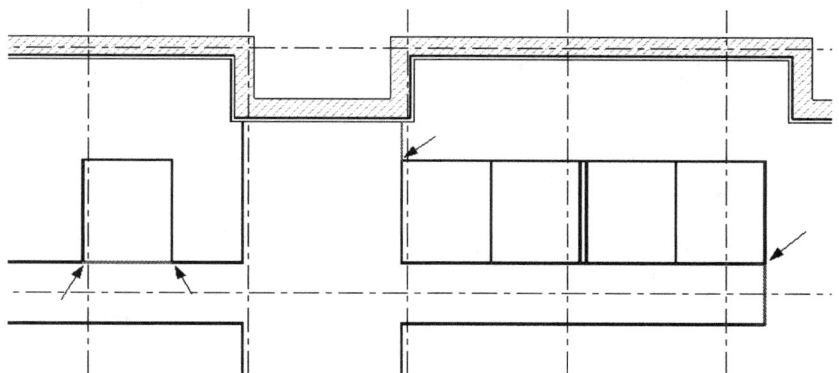

20. Holding down the Control key, pick the walls indicated.

21. 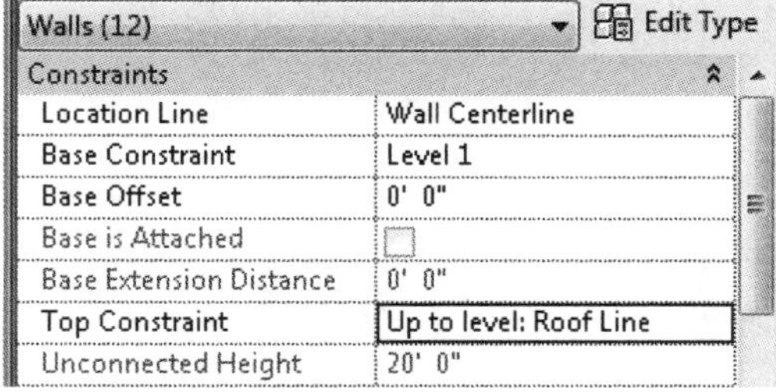

On the Properties pane:

Set the Top Constraint to **Up to Level: Roof line**.

Press **OK**.

By constraining walls to levels, it is easier to control their heights. Simply change the level dimension and all the walls constrained to that level will automatically update.

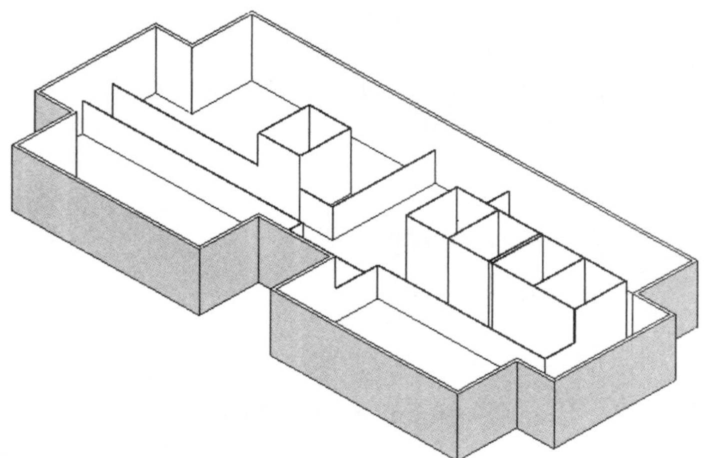

Walls that extend through multiple levels should be created out of just one wall, not walls stacked on top of each other. This improves model performance and minimizes mistakes from floor to floor. For a stair tower, create the wall on the first floor and set its top constraint to the highest level.

22. 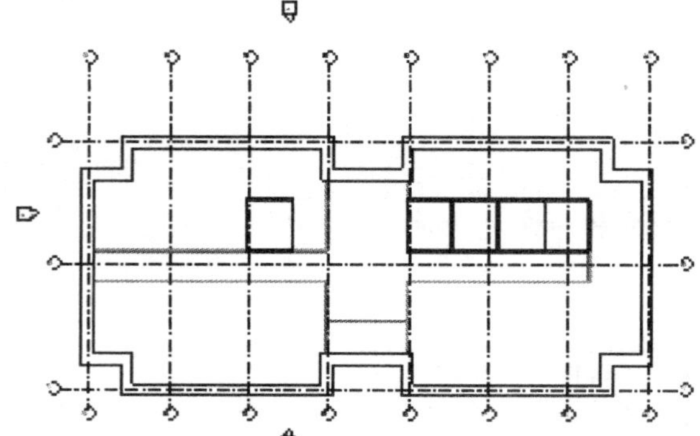

Activate the **Level 2** view.

It can be disconcerting to try to create elements on the second level (Level 2) when you can see the interior walls in the first level (Level 1).

23.

Underlay	None
Underlay Orientation	Plan

On the Properties Pane:
Locate the Underlay parameter and select **None**.

This means that the user will only see what is visible on Level 2.

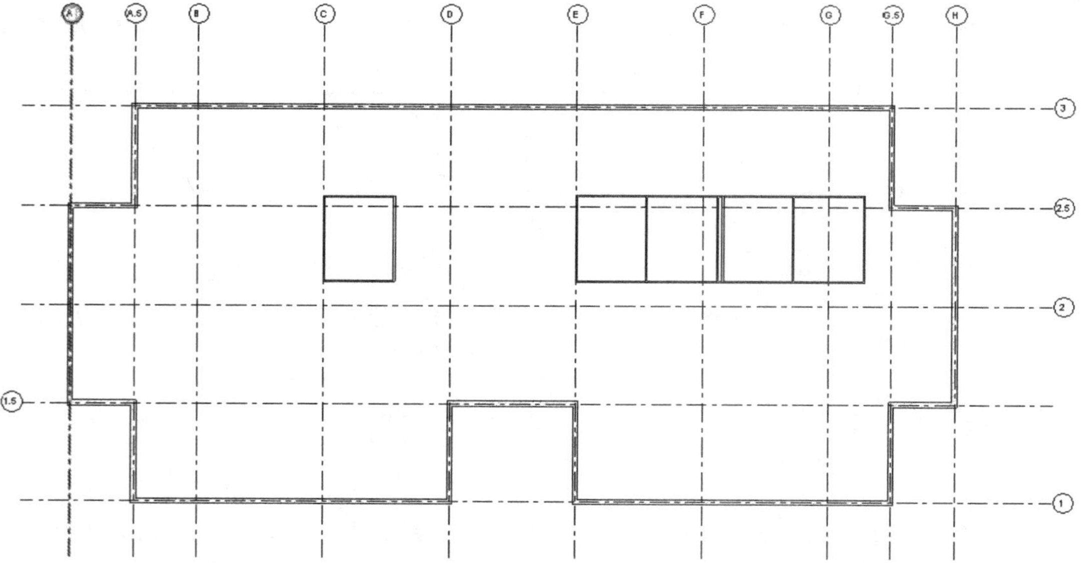

24. Save the file as *ex3-6.rvt*.

Exercise 3-7
Add Doors

Drawing Name: ex3-6.rvt
Estimated Time: 10 minutes

This exercise reinforces the following skills:

- Door
- Load From Library

1. Open or continue working in *ex3-6.rvt.*
2. Activate the **Level 1** view.
3. Home Activate the **Architecture** ribbon.
4. Door Select the **Door** tool from the Build panel.
5. Select **Single-Flush 36″ x 84″** [**M_Single-Flush: 0915 × 2134mm**] from the drop-down.

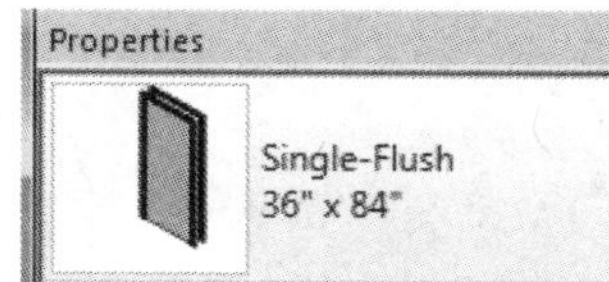

6. Place the doors as shown.

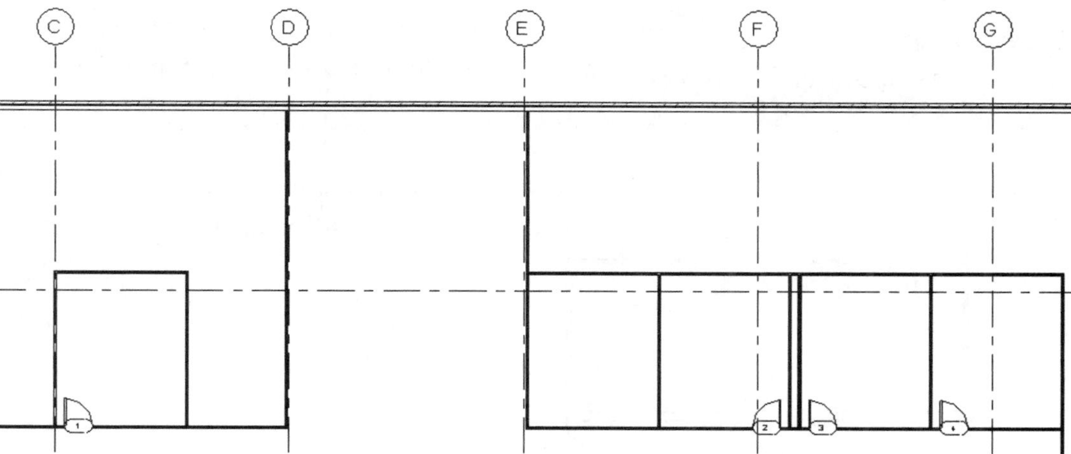

Use the arrows on the doors to flip their orientation.
Place the doors 2′-6″ from the nearest wall.
To position a door, pick on it to activate the dimensions. Then, pick the dimension and enter the desired value.

7. 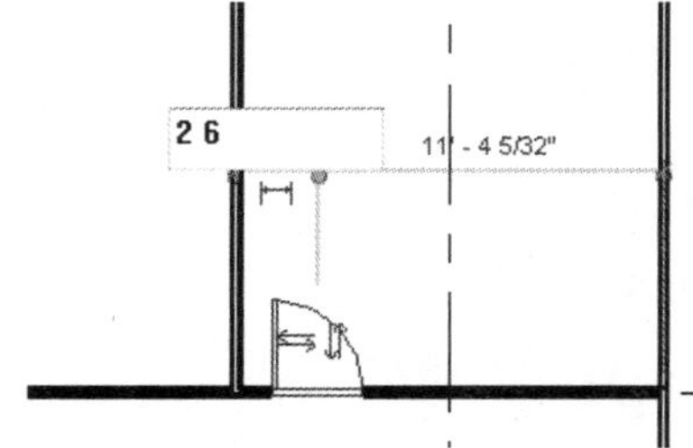

When you pick on a door, it will highlight. You will see a vertical set of arrows and a horizontal set of arrows. To flip a door along the Y-axis, select the vertical arrows. To flip a door orientation along the X-axis, select the horizontal arrows. To modify a door's placement, pick a temporary dimension and edit. The second dimension will automatically adjust accordingly.

Door numbers are often keyed to room numbers – 101A, etc. To edit the door tag, just click on the number and it will change to blue and you can renumber it. You can also change the door number from the Properties dialog box of the door or from the door schedule. A change in any of those locations will update automatically on all other views.

---

8. Select the **Door** tool.

Door

9. 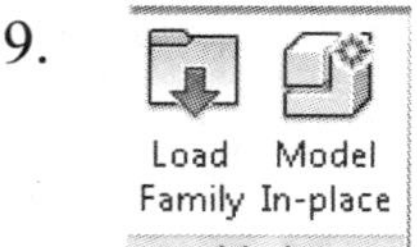

Select **Load Family** from the Mode panel.

10. Browse to the *Doors* folder.

11. 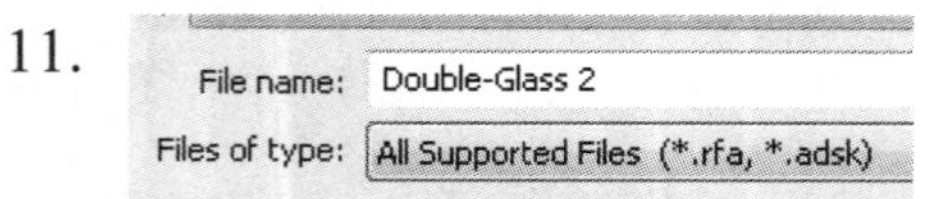

Locate the *Double-Glass 2. Rfa [M_Double-Glass 2.rfa]* file under the *Doors* folder and **Open**.

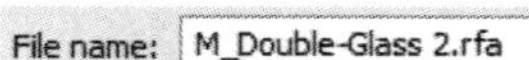

12. 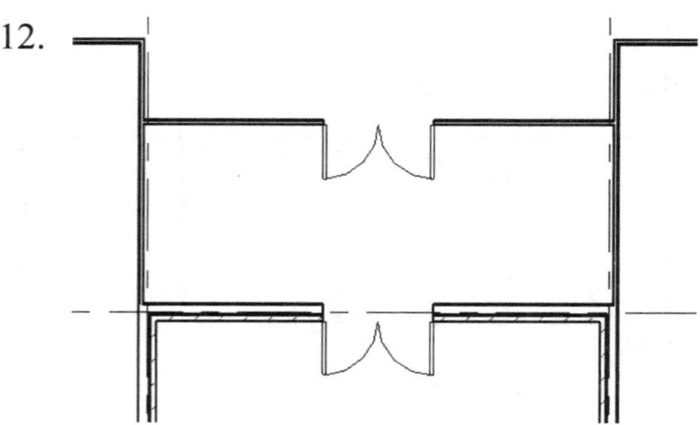

Place two double glass entry doors at the middle position of the entry walls.

The double doors should swing out in the path of egress for accuracy. The interior doors should typically swing into the room space not the hall.

13. Activate **Level 2**.

14. Home Activate the **Architecture** ribbon.

15. Door Select the **Door** tool from the Build panel.

16. Select **Single-Flush 36″ x 84″** [**M_Single-Flush: 0915 × 2134mm**] from the drop-down.

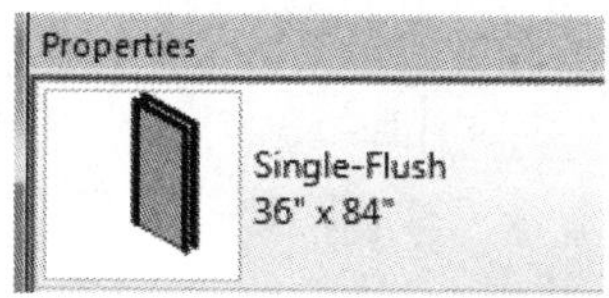

17. Place the doors as shown.

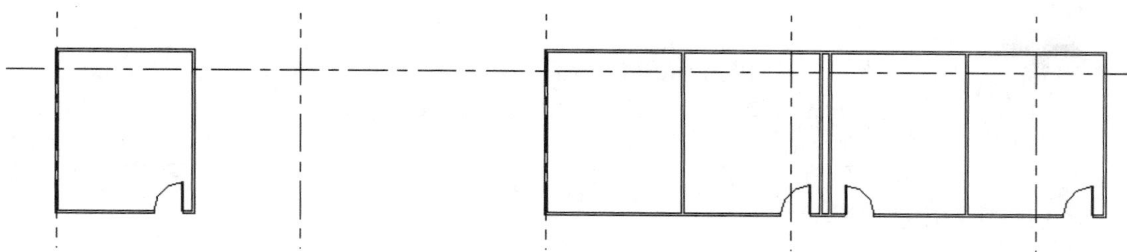

18. Save the file as *ex3-7.rvt*.

Exercise 3-8
Adding Stairs

Drawing Name: ex3-7.rvt
Estimated Time: 40 minutes

This exercise reinforces the following skills:
A video for this exercise is available at http://www.mossdesigns.com/Pages/Tutorials.aspx.

- Stairs
- Edit Sketch
- Activate Dimensions
- Stair Properties

1. Open *ex3-7.rvt*.

2. 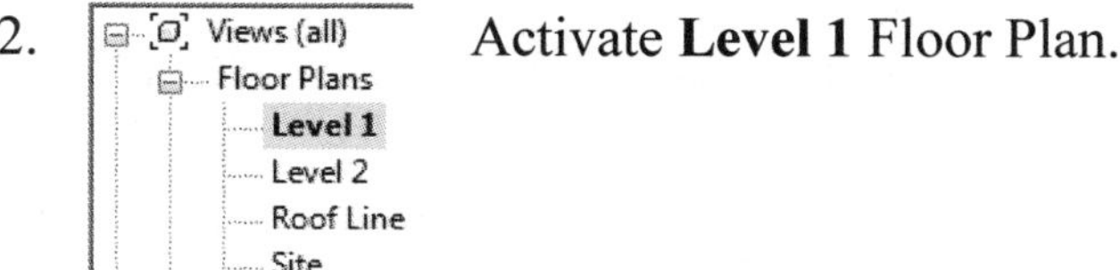

Activate **Level 1** Floor Plan.

3. Select the **Stair by Sketch** tool under the Circulation panel on the Architecture ribbon.

When you are creating a stair, you need to define two boundary lines or curved arcs and the correct number of risers. Revit will automatically calculate the number of risers for you.

You can also pick the railing on the stair and select 'Edit sketch'. Then, add a line, this will make a continuous railing without adding a second piece.

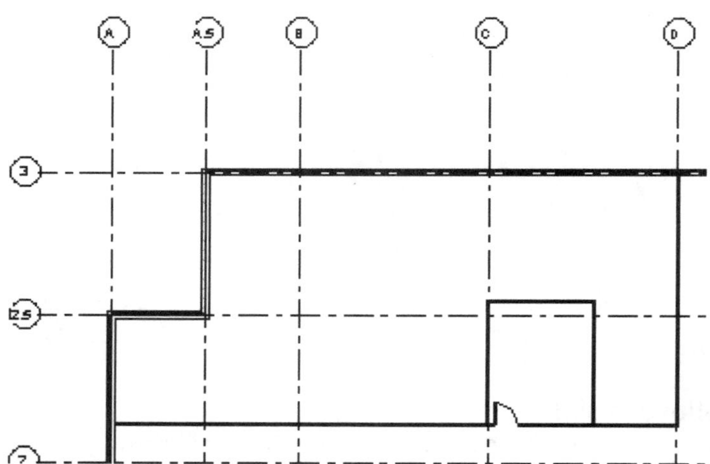

Our first set of stairs will be located in the room at Grids C-2.5.

4. Select the **Boundary** tool.
   This tool allows you to sketch the left and right sides of a stairs.

5. Select the **Pick Lines** tool.

6. 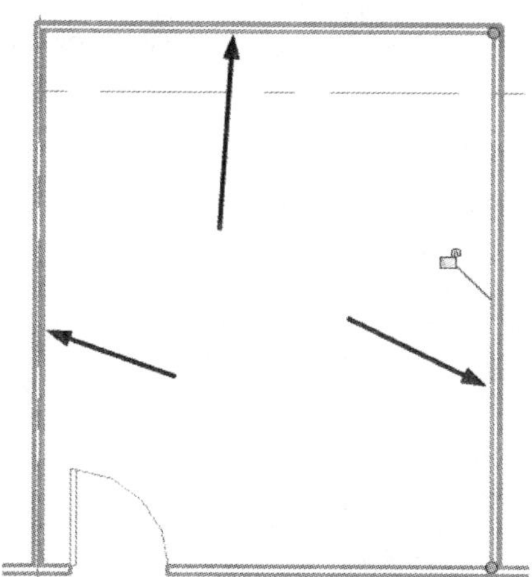

Pick the three interior walls.

7. Set the Offset to **3′ [1060 mm]** on the Options bar.

8. 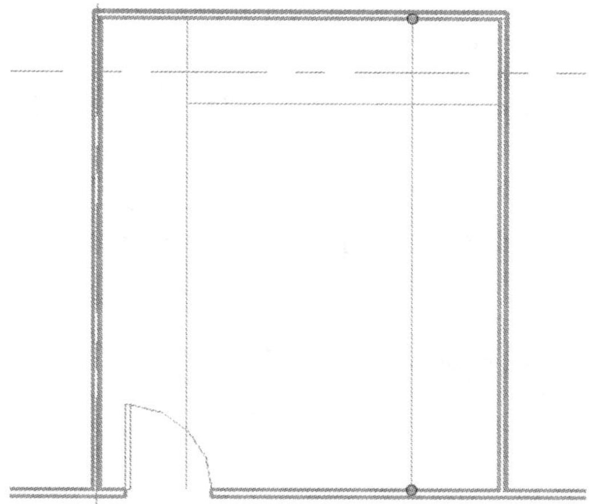

Offset the three lines you just placed.

9. Select the **Trim** tool.

10. 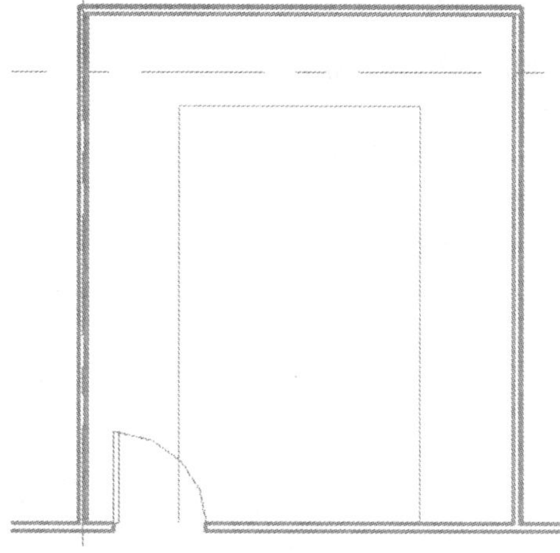

Trim the inner lines as shown.

Select the line sections you want to keep when using the Trim tool.

The lines should form an upside down U.

11. Select each vertical line to activate the grips.

Adjust the end point of each vertical line to bring it into the room.

12. 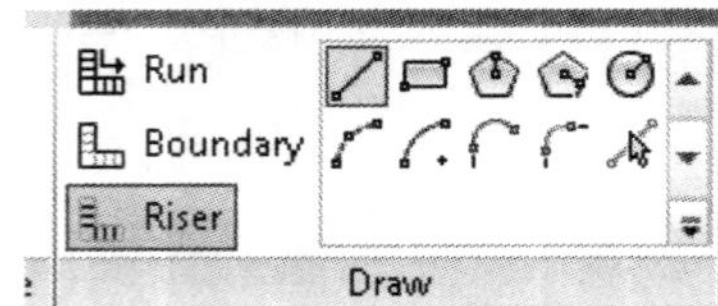

Select the **Riser** tool.

13. 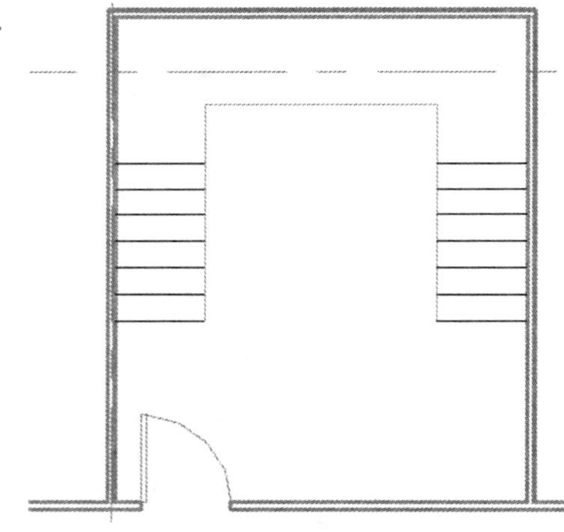

Draw horizontal lines across the boundary lines.

Set the distance between the lines at **11″ [300mm]**.

Risers can not be arrayed. Each riser must be placed independently.

14. 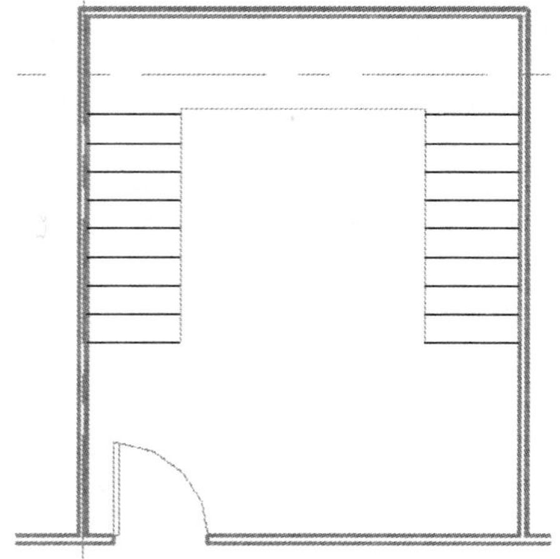

Continue placing the risers until there are 9 risers on each side – 18 total.

15. 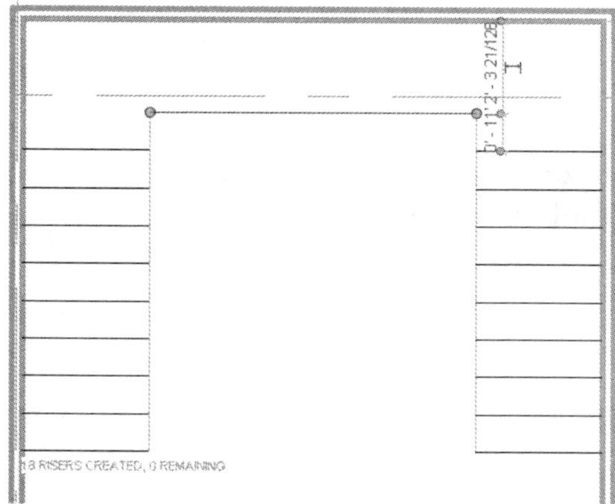

Adjust the inner horizontal boundary line so it is 11″ above the top risers.

Note the riser count is displayed at the lower left. It indicates that no more risers need to be placed.

16. 

Under Mode:
Select the **Green Check** on the ribbon to finish the stairs.

17. An error dialog may appear.

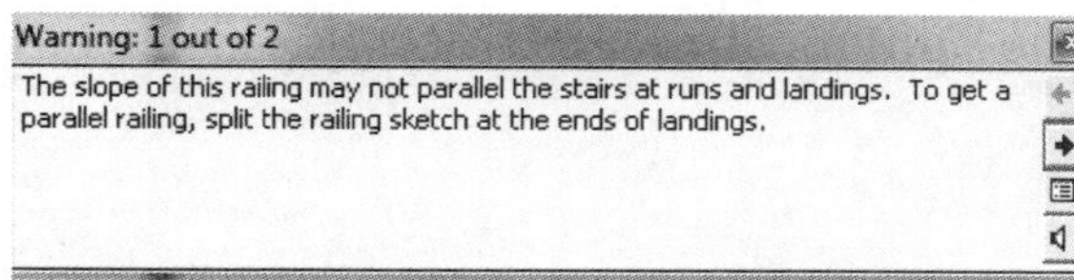

This is because the outer boundary needs to be split to allow the railing to slope properly.

Close the dialog.

18. The stairs are completed.

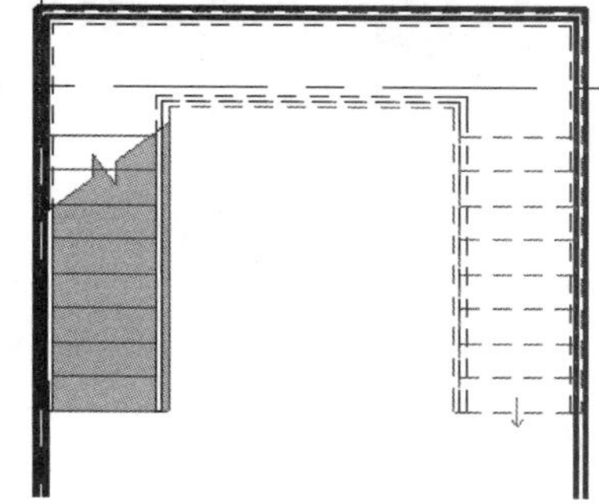

19. Activate the **3D View**.

In the 3D View, we see that the railing does not align properly with the landing.

We will correct this.

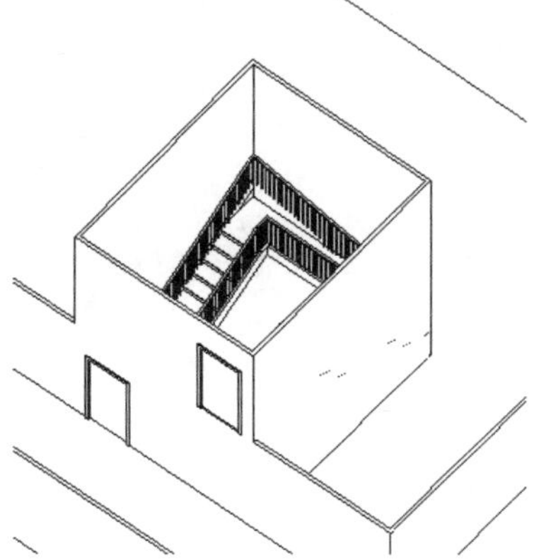

20. 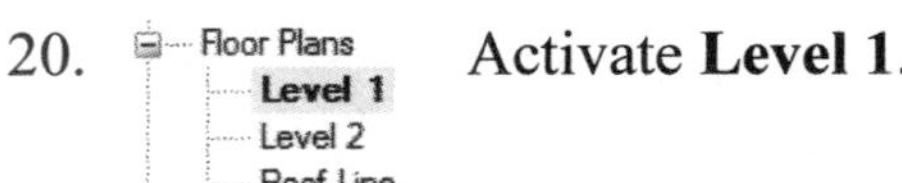

Activate **Level 1**.

21. 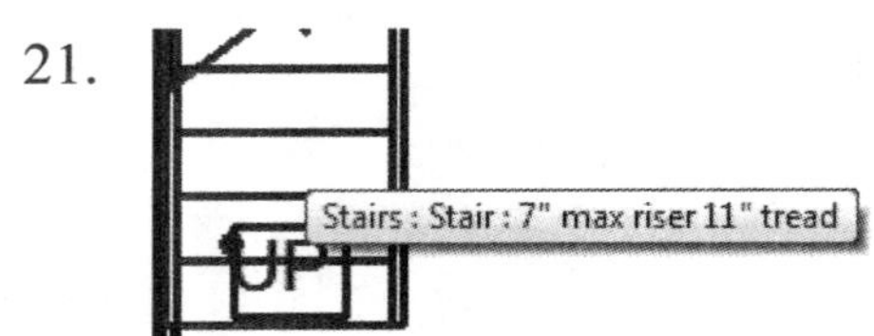

Hover your mouse over the stairs. You should see a tool tip indicating the stairs.

Left click to select the stairs.

22. A small warning tool is displayed on the ribbon.

Select the **Edit Sketch** tool under Mode.

23. Select the **Split** tool under the Modify panel.

24. 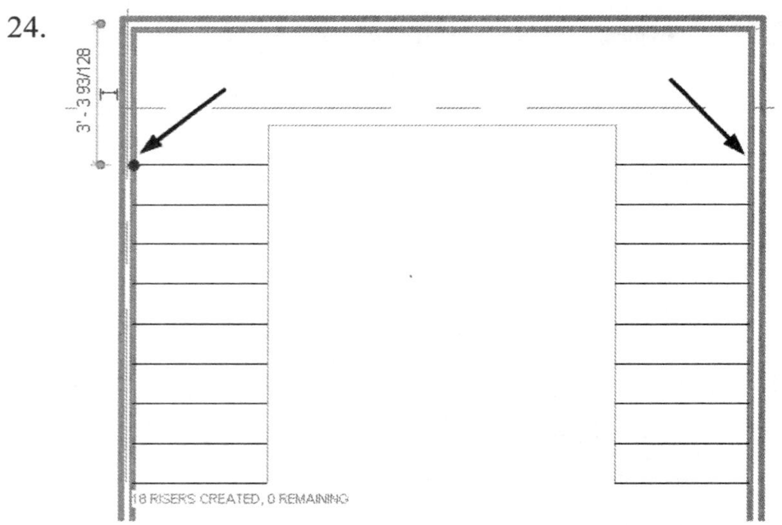

Place a split at the two locations indicated.

25. Under Mode:
Select the **Green Check** to finish the stairs.

26. Activate **3D View**.

27. Press F8 to access the orbit tool.

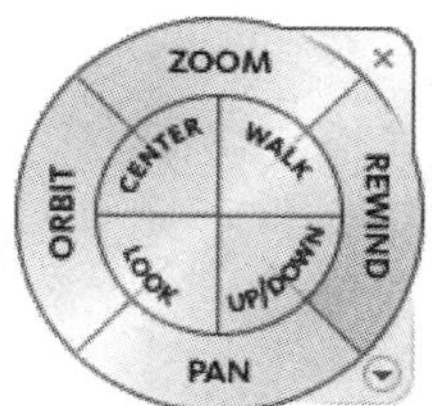

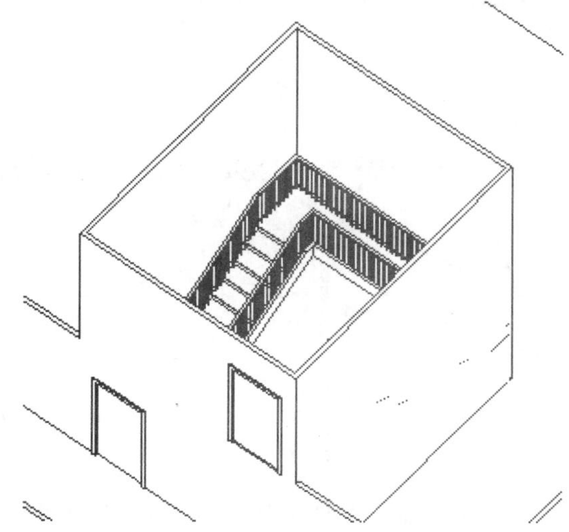

28. Save as *ex3-8.rvt.*

Exercise 3-9

Creating a Handrail on a Wall

Drawing Name: ex3-8.rvt
Estimated Time: 20 minutes

This exercise reinforces the following skills:

- Railings
- Railing Types

1. Open *ex3-8.rvt.*

2. 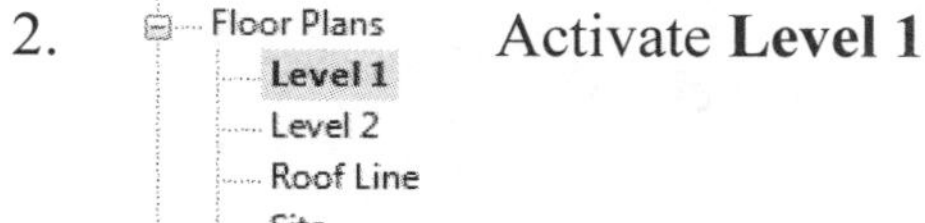

Activate **Level 1**.

3. 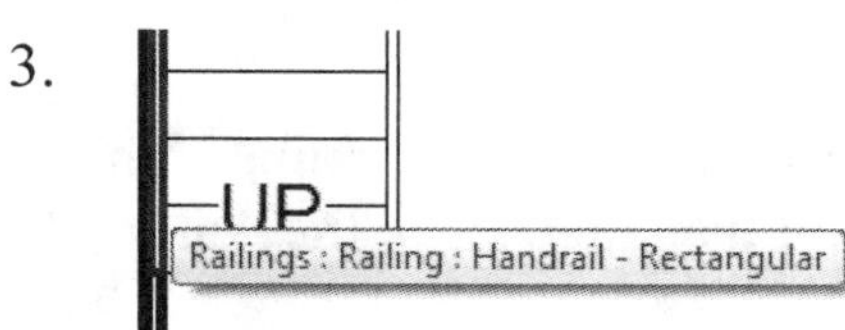

Hover your mouse over the Railing on the left side of the stairs.

Left click to select the railing.

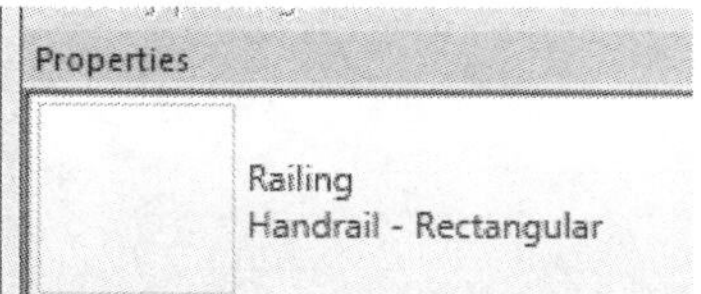

If you have difficulty selecting the railing, use the TAB key to cycle the selection or use the FILTER tool. You can check that you have selected the railing because it will be listed in the Properties pane.

4. 

Select **Edit Path** under the Mode panel.

5. 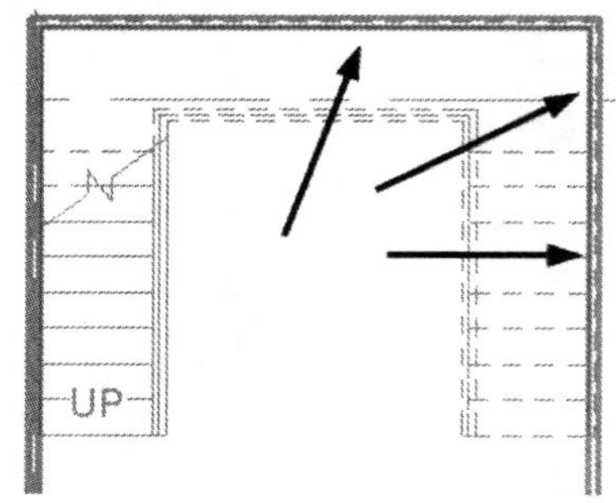

Delete the lines indicated.

6. Move the two remaining lines six inches [152.4 mm] away from the wall.

7. Adjust the top vertical line so it is 1′ 6″ [457.2 mm] above the top riser.

8. Select the **LINE** tool from the Draw panel.

9. Add a short horizontal line at the top of the railing. This is the bar that of the handrail that attaches to the wall.

10. Add a vertical line extending below the bottom riser a distance of 1′ 6″ [457.2 mm].

11. Add another horizontal line that attaches to the wall at the bottom of the railing.

12. Select **Edit Type** from the Properties pane.

13. Select **Duplicate**.

14. Name it **Handrail - Wall.**

Press **OK**.

15. Press **Edit** next to Baluster Placement.

Type Parameters

Parameter	Value
Construction	
Railing Height	3' 0"
Rail Structure (Non-Continuous)	Edit...
Baluster Placement	Edit...
Baluster Offset	0' 0"

16. 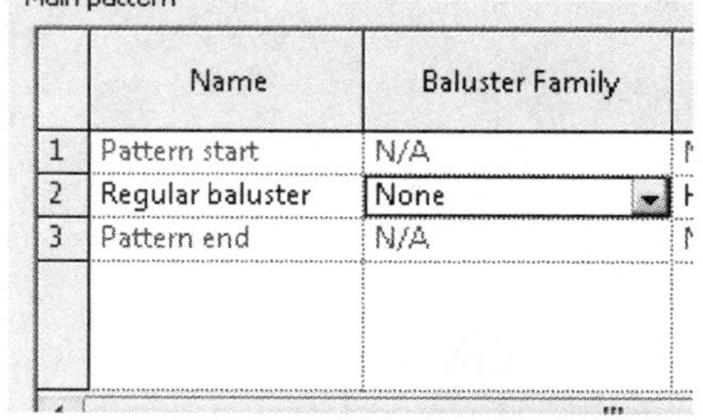

Main pattern

	Name	Baluster Family
1	Pattern start	N/A
2	Regular baluster	None
3	Pattern end	N/A

On Row 2 of the **Main Pattern** table, set the Regular baluster to **None**.

17. 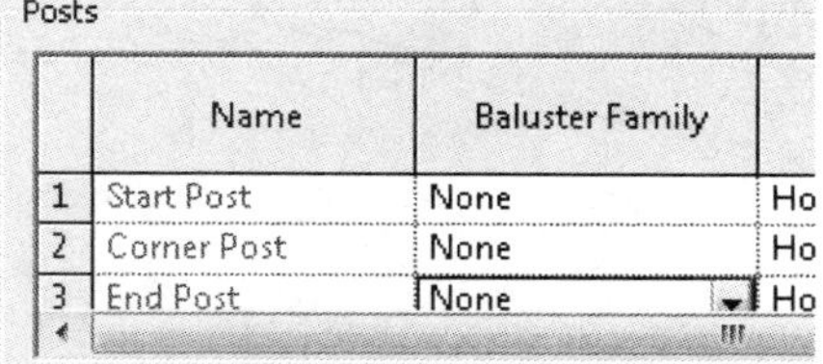

Posts

	Name	Baluster Family
1	Start Post	None
2	Corner Post	None
3	End Post	None

In the **Posts** table, set all the posts to **None**.

18.

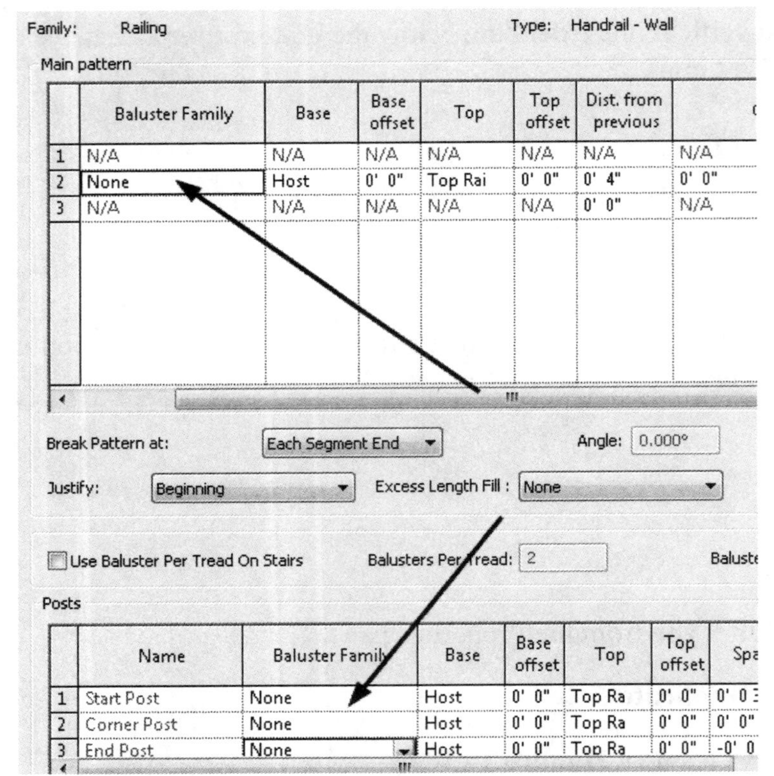

Verify that you have set the balusters to **None** in both areas.

Many of my students will set it to None in one area and not the other.

Press **OK** twice to exit all dialogs.

19. Select the **Green Check** under Mode to exit Edit Mode.

If you get an error message, check the sketch. It must be a single open path. All line segments must be connected with no gaps and no intersecting lines or overlying lines.

20. Switch to a 3D view.

21. Inspect the railing.

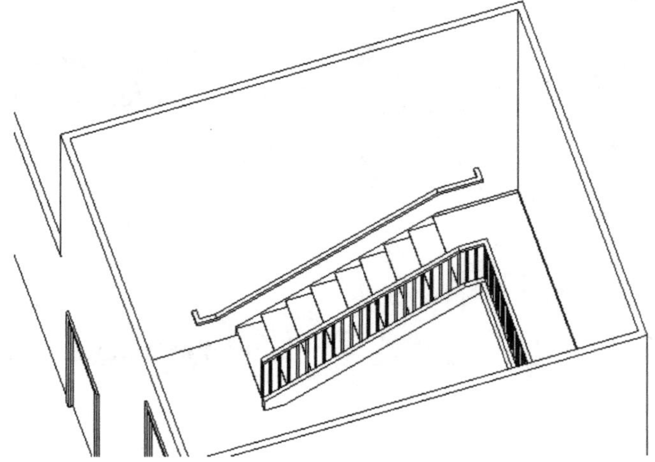

22. Activate **Level 1**.

23. Select the handrail you just created.

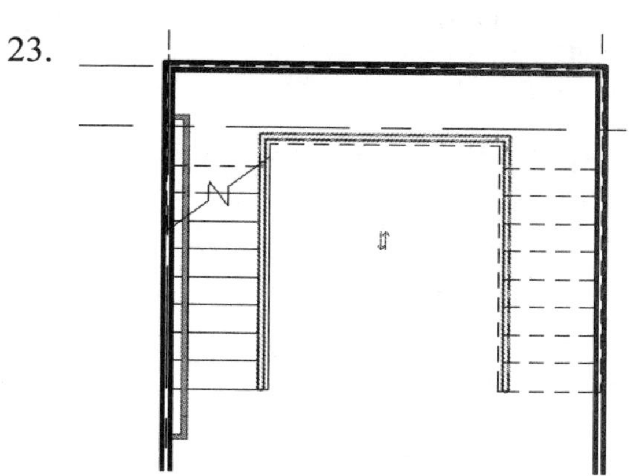

24. Select **Mirror→Draw Axis** from the Modify panel.

Modify

25. Locate the midpoint on the landing and left click as the start of the axis.

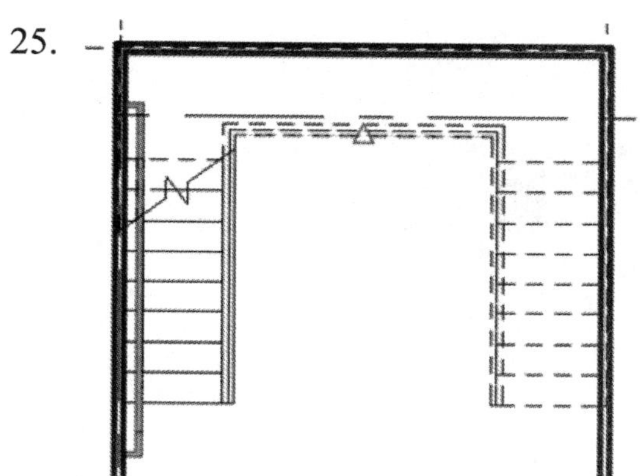

26. Select a point directly below the midpoint to end the axis definition.

You don't see anything – that's because the handrail was placed on the second level.

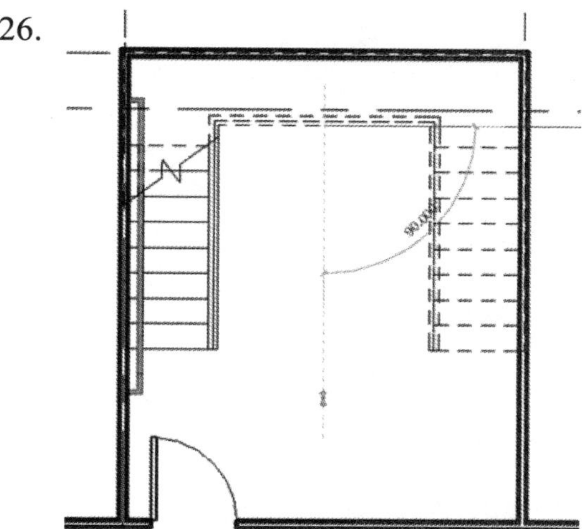

27. Activate **Level 2**.

Floor Plans
Level 1
Level 2
Roof Line
Site

28. 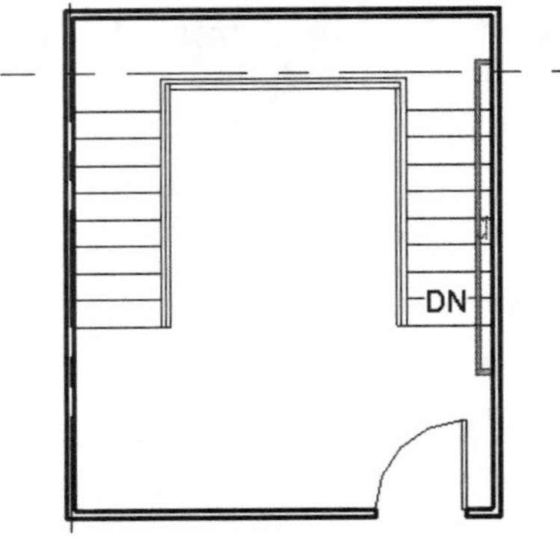

You see the handrail.

29. Switch to a 3D view.

30. Inspect the railing.

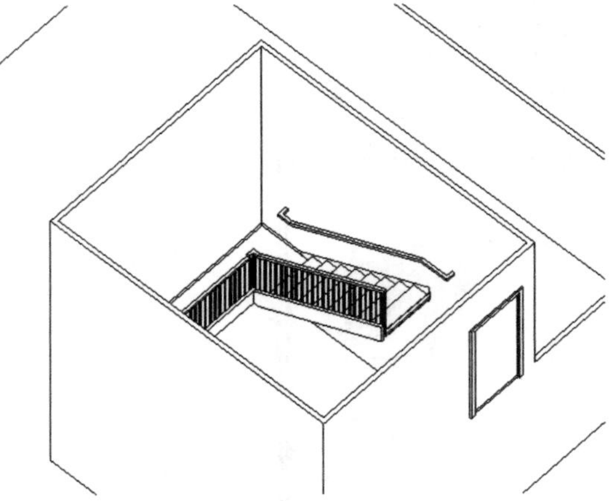

31. Save as *ex3-9.rvt.*

Exercise 3-10
Creating a Stairs Type

Drawing Name: ex3-9.rvt
Estimated Time: 20 minutes

This exercise reinforces the following skills:

- Floor
- Floor Properties

1. Open *ex3-9.rvt.*

2. Floor Plans / Level 1 / Level 2 — Activate **Level 1**.

3. Edit Type — Select the stairs.

   Select **Edit Type** on the Properties pane.

4. Select **Duplicate**.

5. 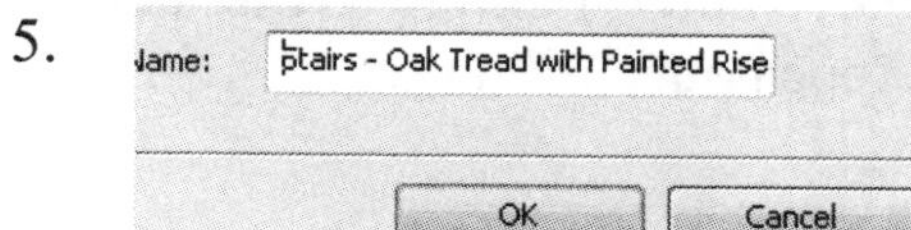

Type **Stairs - Oak Tread with Painted Riser**.

Press **OK**.

6. 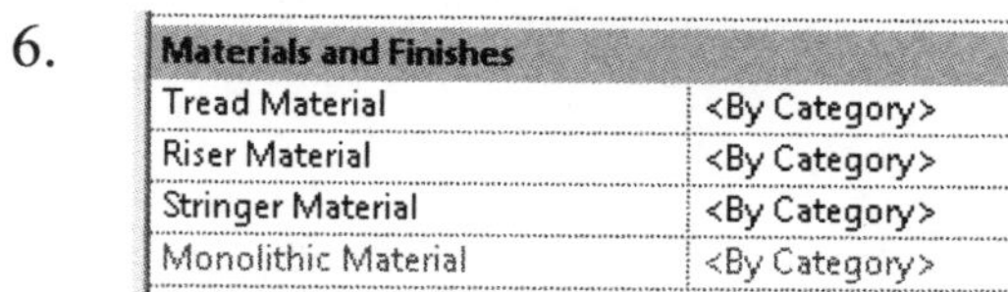

Scroll down to the Materials and Finishes category.

Select the **Tread Material** column.

7. 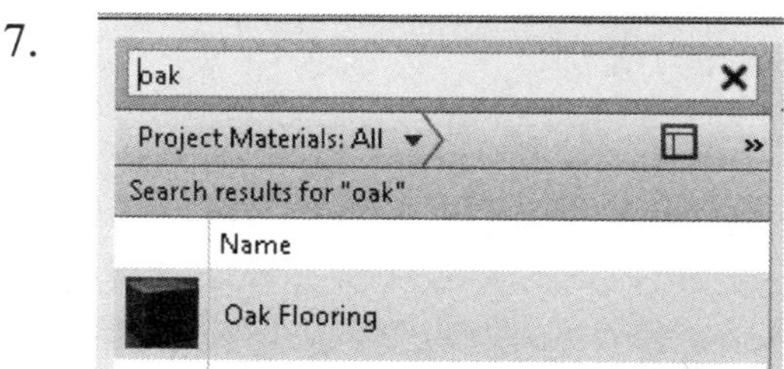

Type **oak** in the search field.
Select the **Oak Flooring** material.

8. 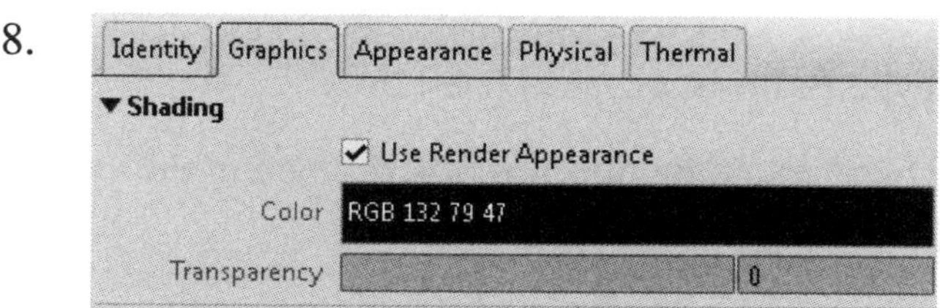

On the Graphics tab:
Enable **Use Render Appearance**.
Press **OK**.

9. Select the **Riser Material** column.

10. Enable the **Asset Browser** on the bottom of the Material Browser dialog.

11. 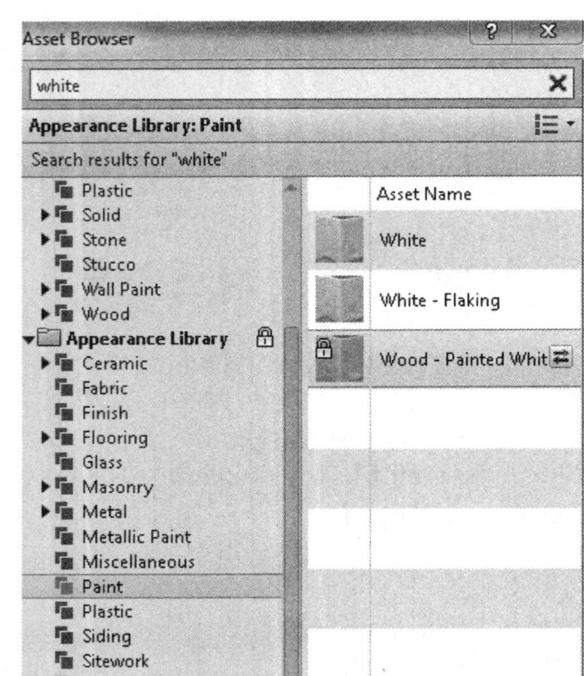

Type **white** in the search field.

Locate **Wood – Painted White** under the Appearance Library.

12. 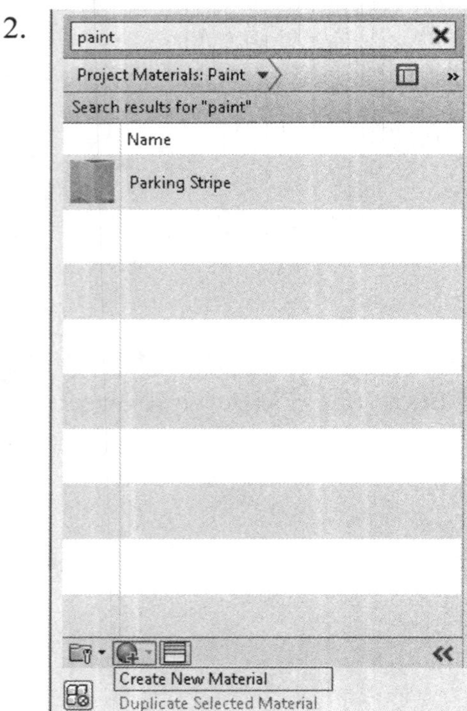

Type **Paint** in the search text box.

There are no paints currently defined in the project.

Select the Create **New Material** tool at the bottom of the dialog.

13. 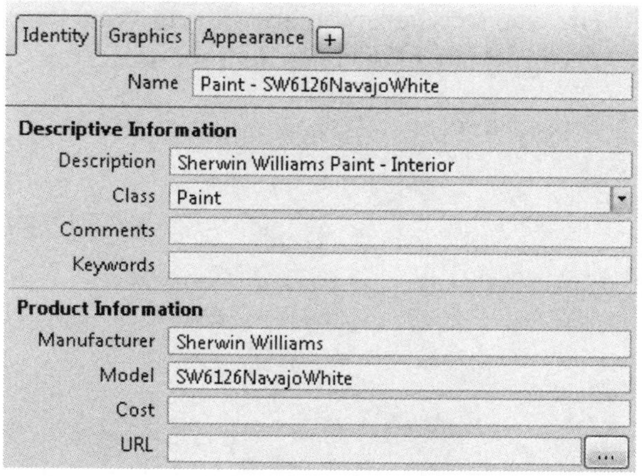 Activate the **Identity** tab.
Type **Paint - SW6126NavajoWhite** in the Name field.
In the Description field, type **Sherwin Williams Paint – Interior**.
Select **Paint** for the Class under the drop-down list.
In the Manufacturer field, type **Sherwin Williams**.
In the Model field, type **SW6126NavajoWhite**.

14. 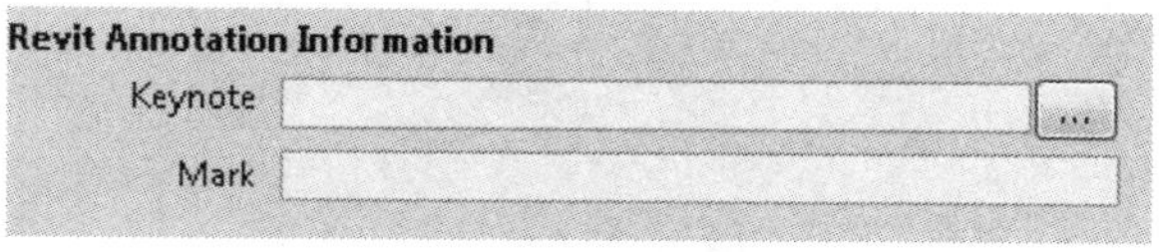 Select the **... browse** button next to Keynote.

15. 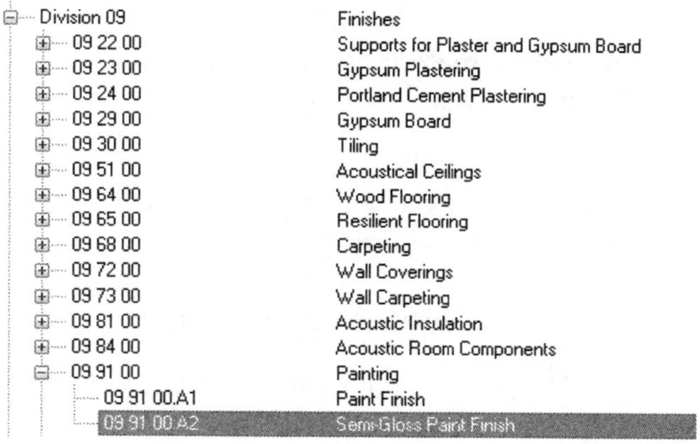 Select the **09 91 00.A2 Semi-Gloss Paint Finish** in the list.

Press **OK**.

16. 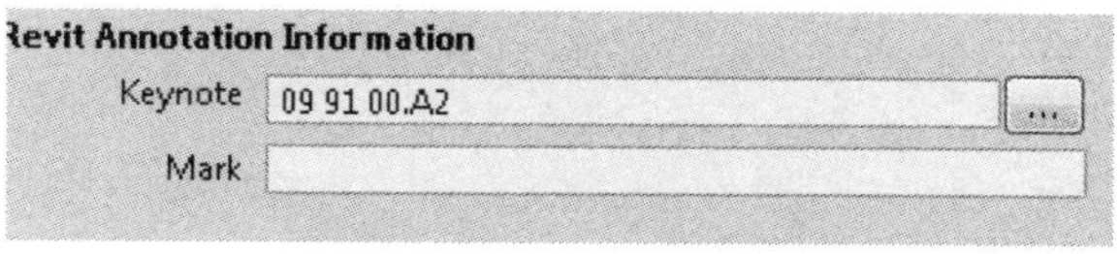 Note the keynote information auto-fills based on the selection.

17. 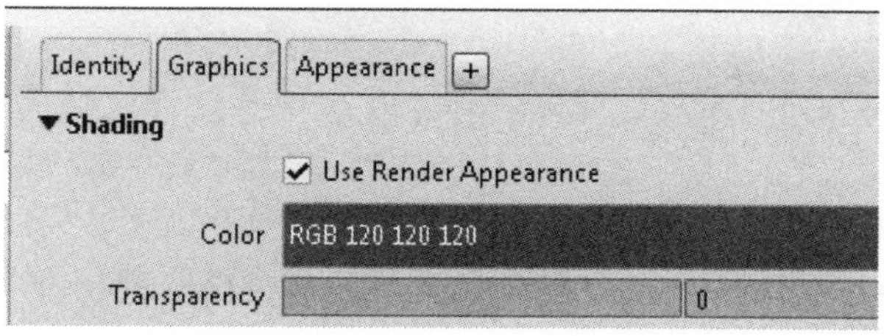 Activate the Graphics tab.

Place a check on **Use Render Appearance for Shading**.

18.  At the bottom of the dialog:

Select **Create New Library**.

19. Browse to where you are storing your work. Assign your materials file a name.

Press **Save**.

20. 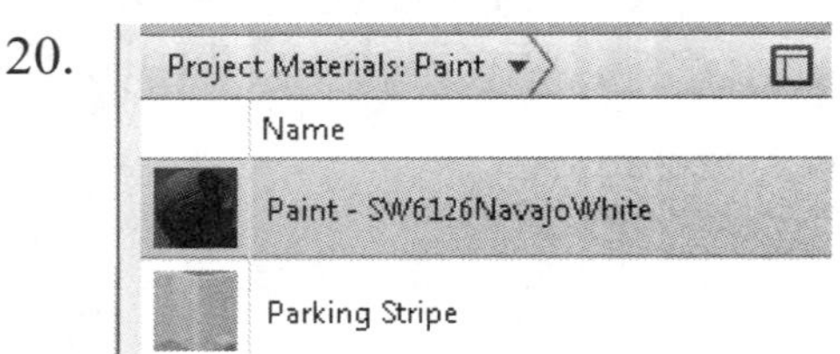

The custom material is now displayed in the Material browser.

This is because the Autodesk Material library is "read-only". You can only create new materials in custom material libraries.

21. 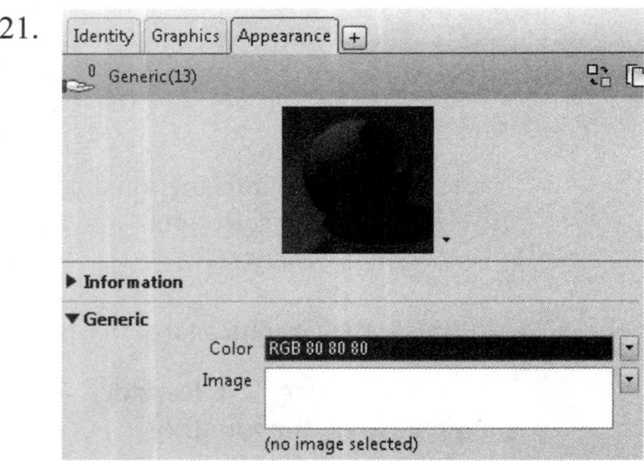

Select the Appearance tab.

Left click on the Color button.

22. 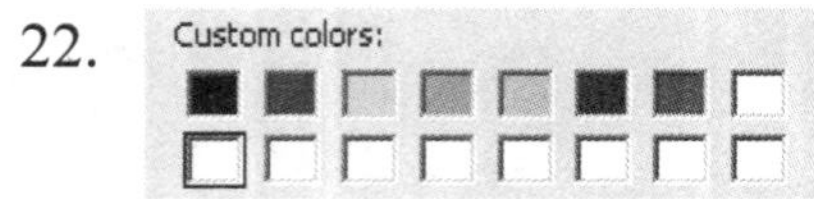

Select an empty color swatch under Custom colors.

23. In the Red field, enter **234**.
In the Green field, enter **223**.
In the Blue field, enter **203**.

Press **Add**.

This matches Sherwin William's Navajo White, SW6126.

24. 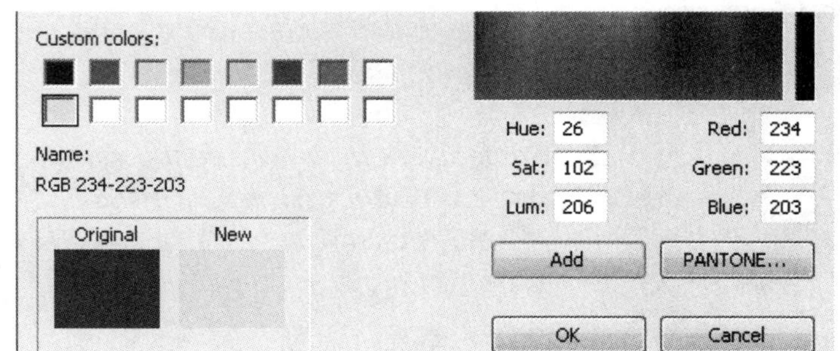

Select the color swatch.

Press **OK**.

25. 

The preview will update to display the new color.

Press **OK**.

26. 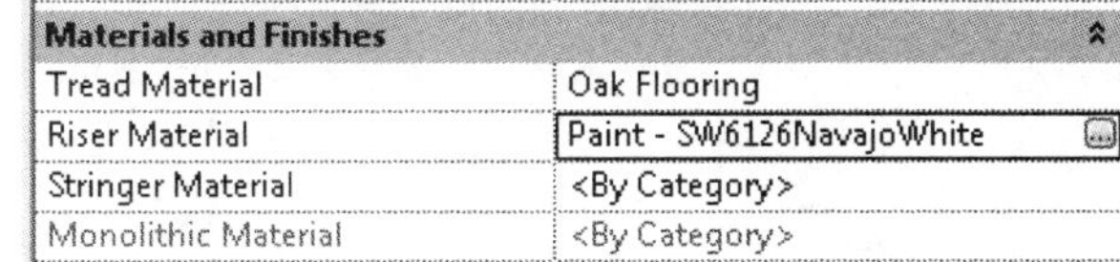

Select the **Stringer Material** column.

27. 

Select the **Oak Flooring** material.

Press **OK**.

28. Press **OK** to close the dialog.

29. Switch to a **3D** view.

30. 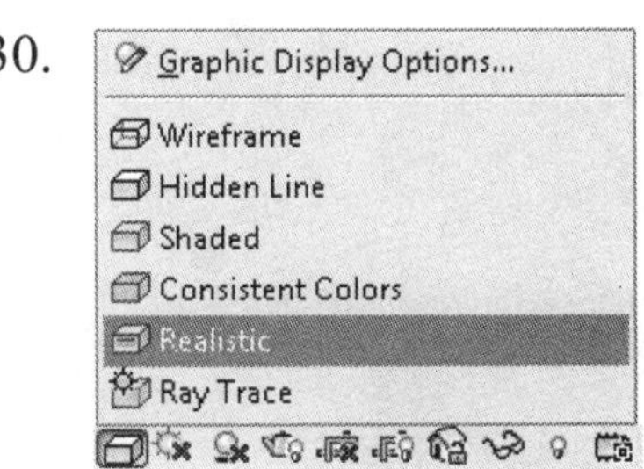

Change the display to **Realistic**.

Orbit around the model to inspect the stairs.

31. 

Observe how the assigned materials affect the stairs' appearance.

Some users may not see the wood pattern on their stairs. This is a graphics card issue. I use a high-end graphics card.

32. If you want the boards to be oriented horizontally instead of vertically on the treads:

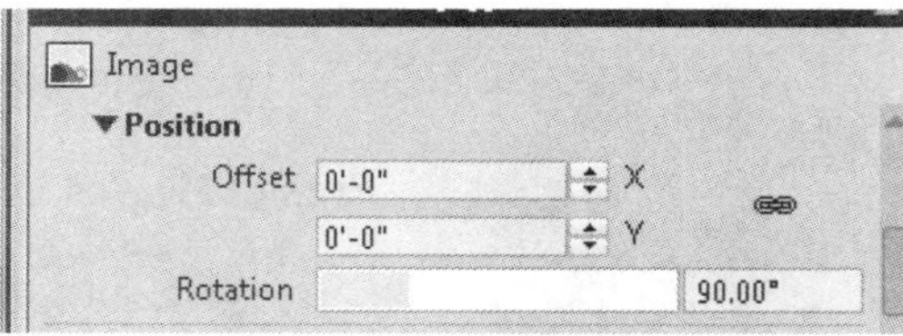

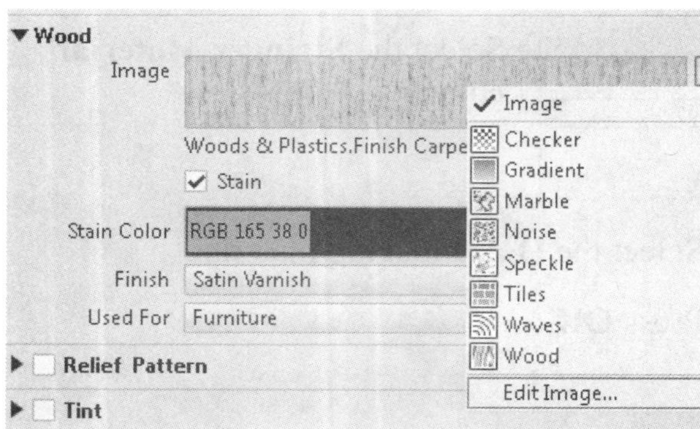

Select the stairs.
Edit Type.
Select the Tread Material.
Select the Appearance tab.

Next to the image picture, select Edit Image from the drop down list.
Expand the Transform area.
Set the Rotation to 90 degree.
Press Done.

33. Save as *ex3-10.rvt*.

Some students have expressed concern about the railing joins at the corners. This is due to the change in elevation at those joins. If you adjust the riser position, you can clean up those areas.

With the riser position adjusted.

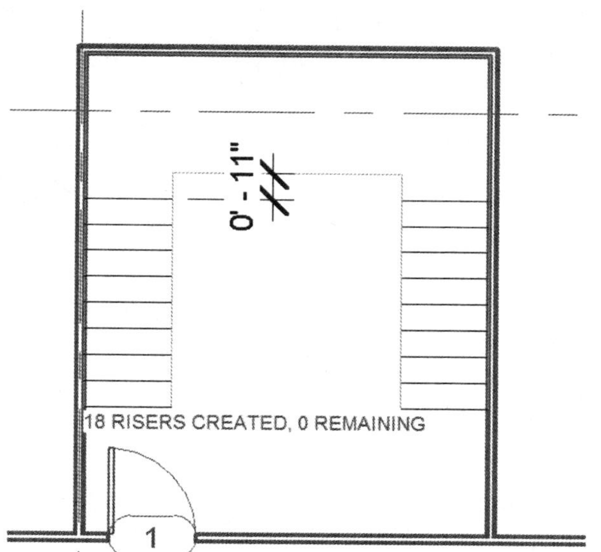

Verify that you have offset the riser a minimum of a tread-width to allow for the railing adjustment.

Exercise 3-11

Modifying the Floor Plan – Skills Review

Drawing Name: ex3-10.rvt
Estimated Time: 30 minutes

This exercise reinforces the following skills:

- 3D View
- Copy
- Align
- Floor
- Railing

1. Open *ex3-10.rvt.*

2. Elevations (Building Elevation)
   East
   North
   South
   West

   Activate the **North** Elevation.

3. 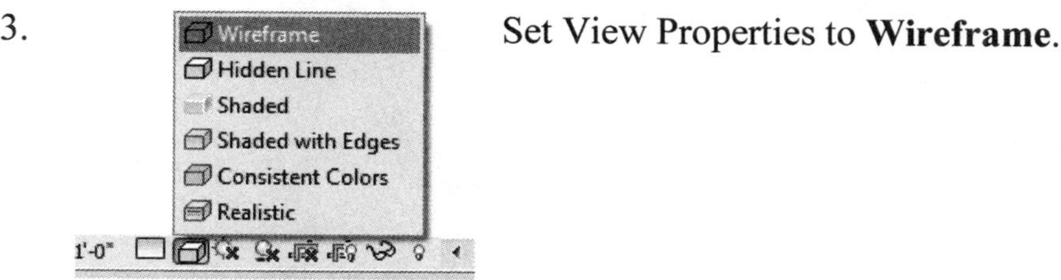

   Set View Properties to **Wireframe**.

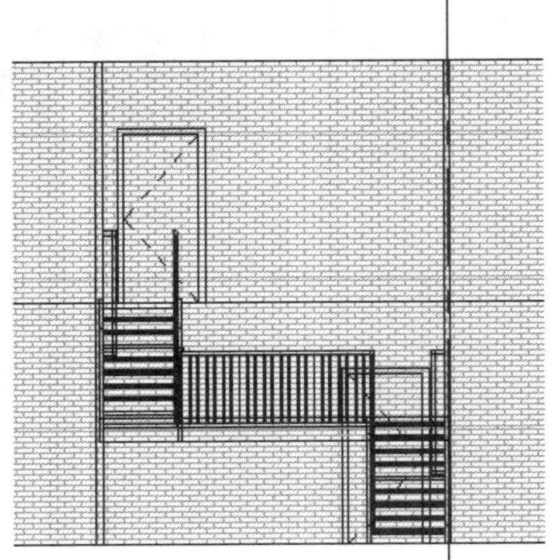

We see that our stairs in elevation look pretty good.

4. Activate **Level 2**.

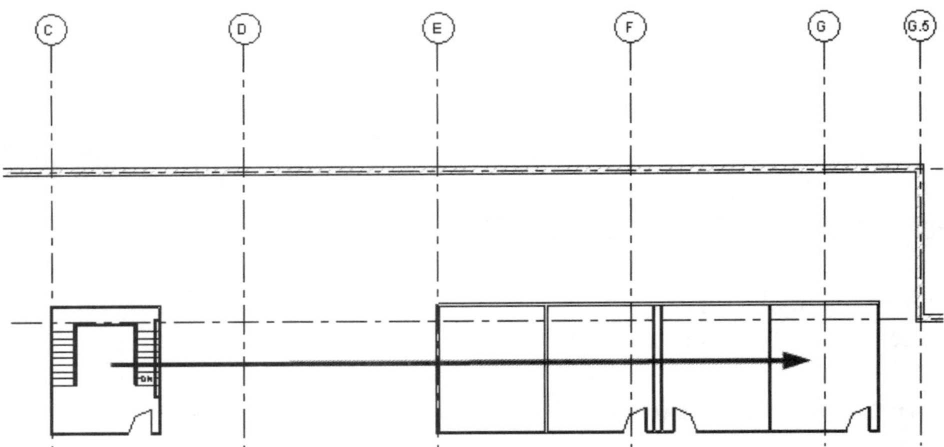

We want to copy the stairs, railings, and landing to the stairwell indicated.

5. Window around the walls, stair and railings.

6. Select the **Filter** tool.

Filter

7. 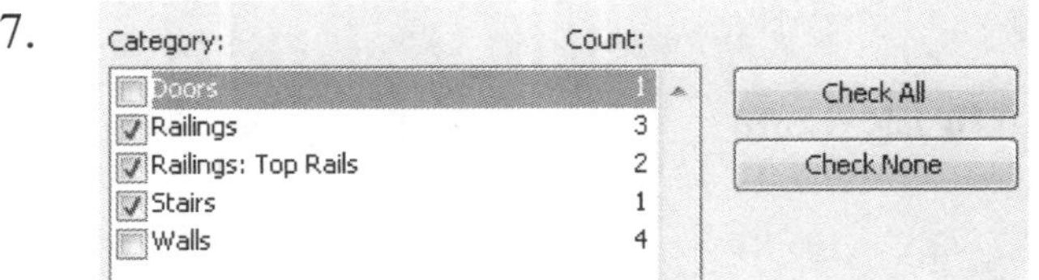

Use **Filter** to ensure that only the Stairs and Railings are selected.

Press **OK**.

8. 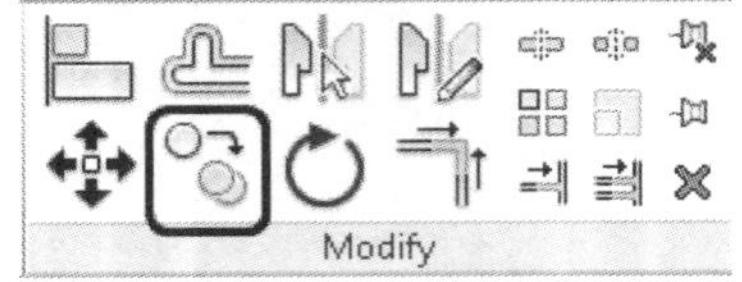

Select **Copy** from the Modify panel.

The Modify→Copy can be used to copy on the same work plane/level only.

9.

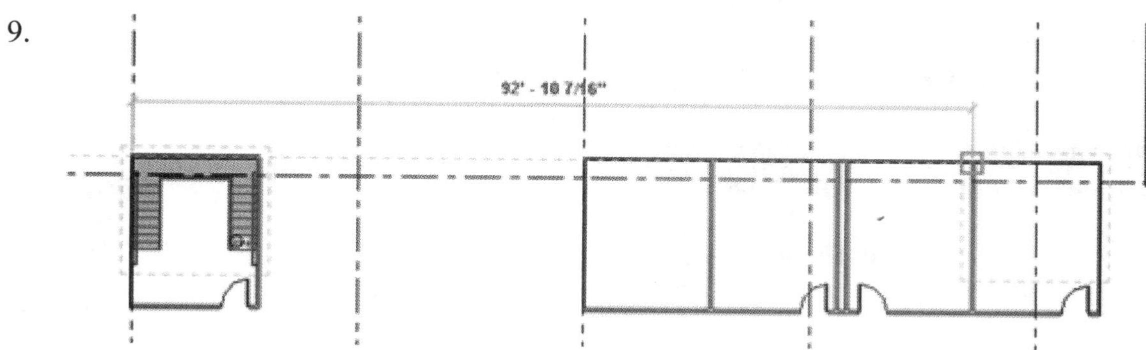

Select the top left corner of the existing stairwell as the basepoint.

Select the top left corner of the target stairwell as the target location.
Left click to release.

(Instead of copying the stair, you can also repeat the process we used before to create a stair from scratch.)

10. 3D Views {3D} Activate **3D View**.

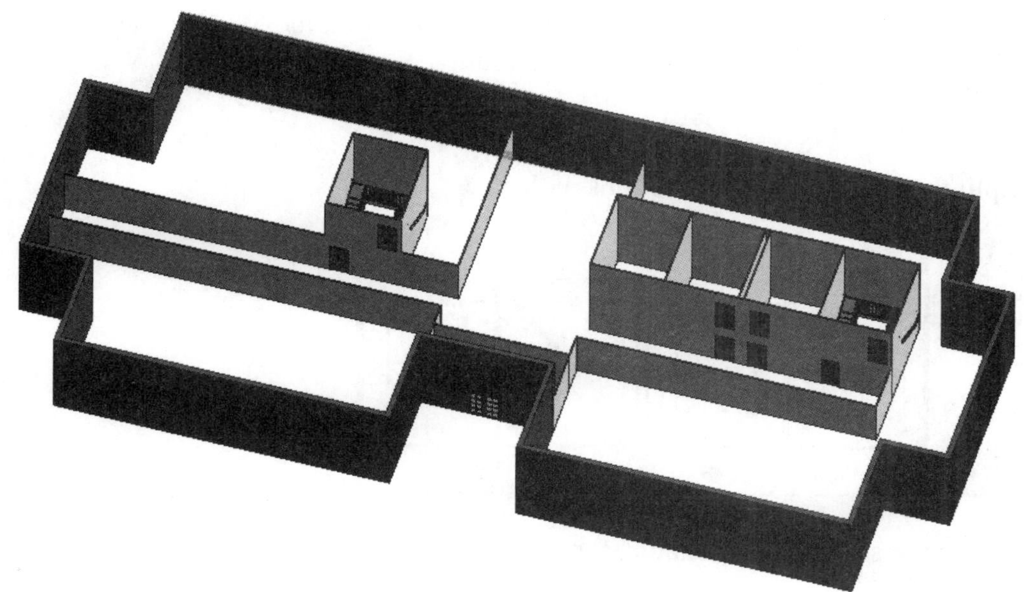

You should see a complete stairs with landing and railing in both stairwells.

11. Save as *ex3-11.rvt*.

Exercise 3-12
Defining a 2-hr Wall

Drawing Name: ex3-11.rvt
Estimated Time: 10 minutes

This exercise reinforces the following skills:

- Split
- Wall Properties

Stairwell walls are usually 2-hour walls. The walls, as currently defined, are 1-hour walls.

1. Open *ex3-11.rvt.*

2. 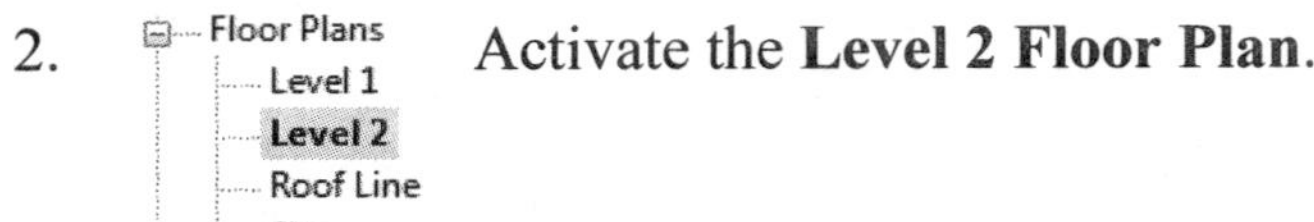

Activate the **Level 2 Floor Plan**.

3. Select the **Split** tool from the Modify panel on the Modify ribbon.

Modify

4. Split the walls at the intersections indicated.

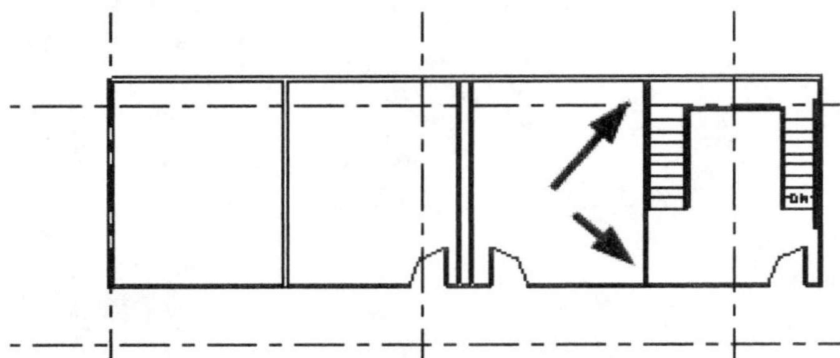

5. Select the stairwell walls indicated.

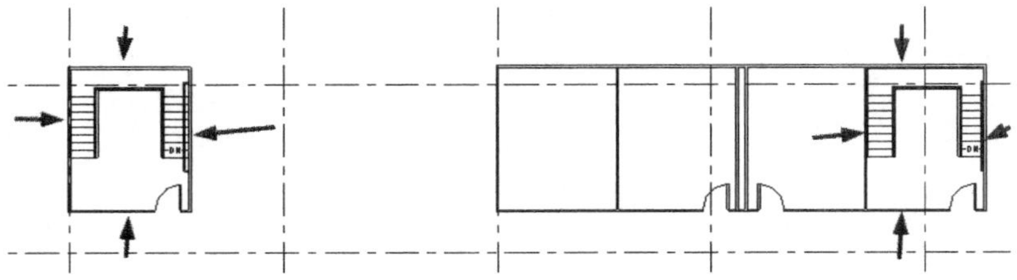

These walls will be defined as 2-hr walls.

6. Filter — You can window around both areas while holding down the CTRL key. Then select the Filter tool from the ribbon.

7. 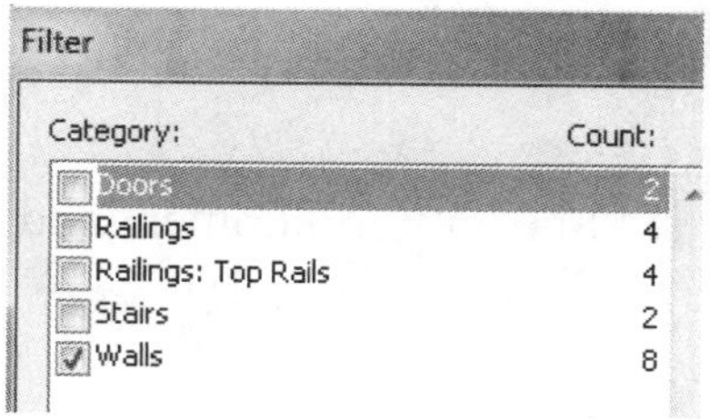 Uncheck all the elements EXCEPT walls.

   Press **OK**.

8. 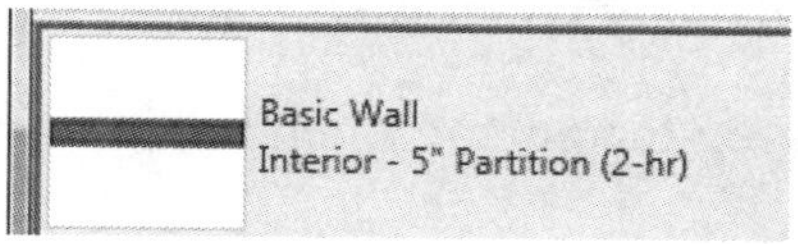 On the Properties pane, select the **Interior - 5″ Partition (2-hr)** [**Basic Wall: Interior - 135mm Partition (2-hr)**] from the Type Selector drop down list.

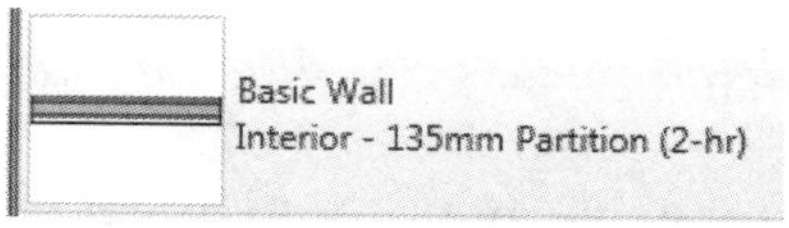

   Left click in the window to clear the selection.

9. Save the file as *ex3-12.rvt*.

Exercise 3-13

Adding an Elevator

Drawing Name: ex3-12.rvt
Estimated Time: 40 minutes

This exercise reinforces the following skills:

- 3D View
- Delete
- Wall Properties
- Families

1. Open *ex3-12.rvt.*

2.  Activate the **Level 1 Floor Plan**.

3.  Activate the **Insert** ribbon.

   Select **Load Family** from the Load from Library panel.

4.  Locate the *Elevator* and the *Door-Elevator* on the publisher's website.

   Press **Open**.

5. Specialty Equipment
Elevator
6' 10" x 5' 2"

The elevator is now available in the Project browser for your current project.

To locate it, look for the folder called Specialty Equipment and expand that folder.

6. Select the *6' 10" x 5' 2" family.*
Hold down the left mouse button and drag into the display window.

7. 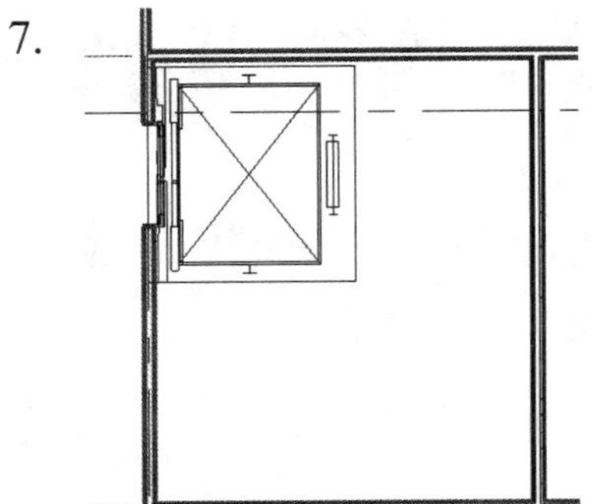

The elevator will appear on the cursor when you hover over a wall.

The elevator is wall-hosted, so needs a wall to be placed.

Press the SPACE bar to rotate the elevator to orient it properly.

Left pick to place.

8. Place two elevators.

Right click and select CANCEL to exit the command.

9. 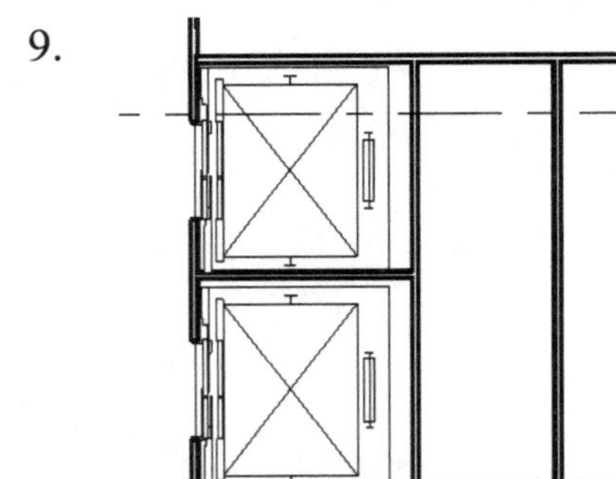

Add a wall behind and to the right of the two elevators as shown.

Add a wall between the two elevator shafts. **Use the midpoint of the wall behind the elevators to locate the horizontal wall.**

Constrain both walls to the Roof Line level.

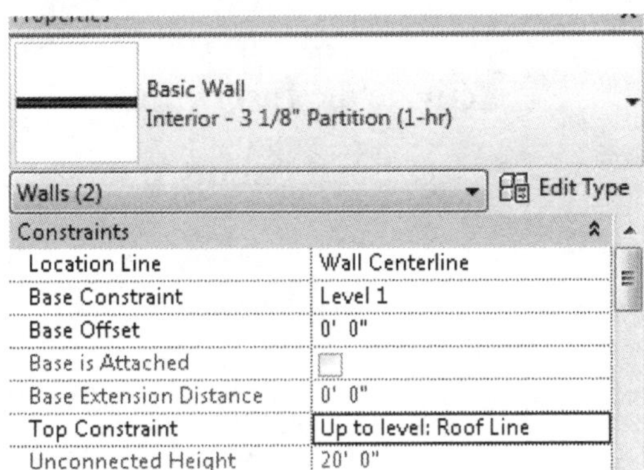

10. Activate the **Manage** ribbon.

11. 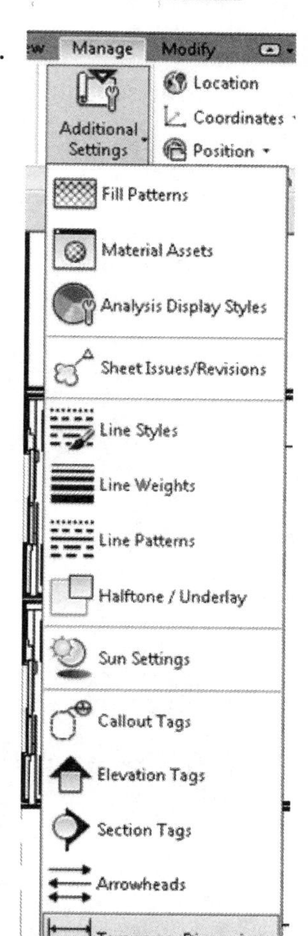

Go to **Settings→Additional Settings→Temporary Dimensions**.

12. Enable **Centerlines** for Walls.

Enable **Centerlines** for Doors and Windows.

Press **OK**.

13. Activate the **Annotate** ribbon.

14. 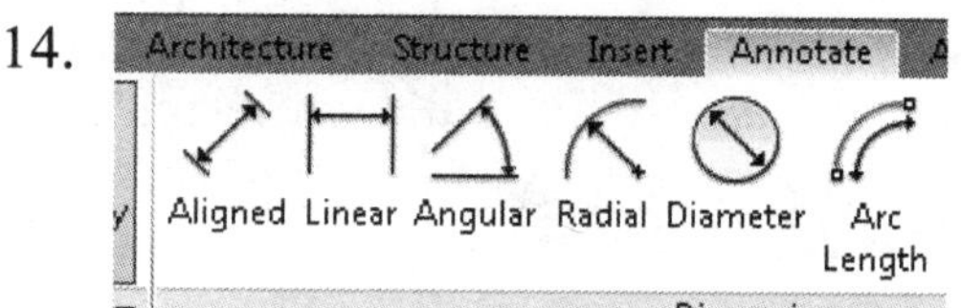

Select the **Aligned** tool under Dimension.

Make sure visibility of dimensions is turned on in the Visibility/Graphics dialog.

15. Select the center of the wall.
Select the center line of the elevator.
Select the center line of the wall.
Left pick to place the continuous dimension.

Repeat for the other elevator.

16. Left click on the EQ symbol to set the dimensions equal and position the elevator centered in the space.

17. The dimension display changes to show EQ symbols.

18. To display dimensions:
Select the extension line of the dimension.

Uncheck the EQ Display to show dimensions.

19.

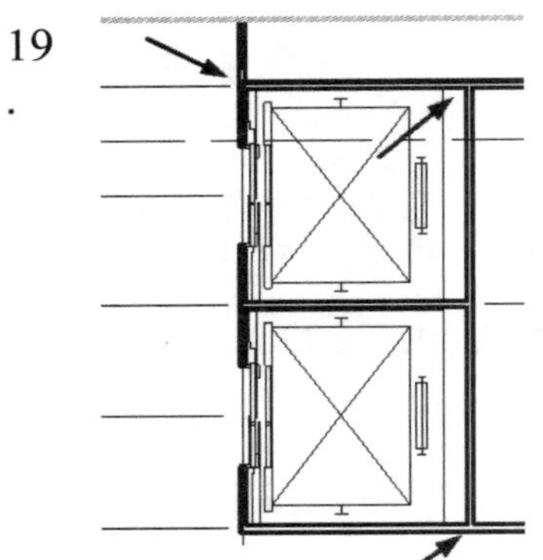

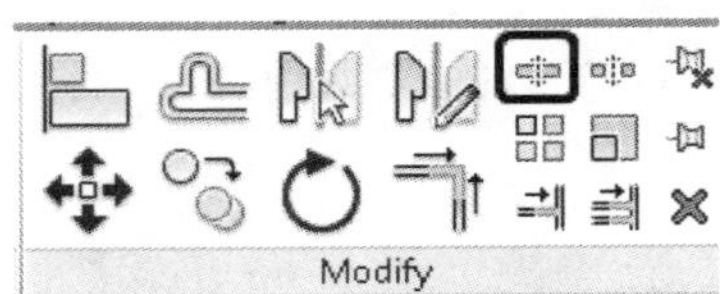

Activate the **Modify** ribbon.
Use the **SPLIT** tool and split the walls at the intersections shown.

20. Elevator shaft walls are 2-hour, usually CMU.

Select the elevator shaft walls.

Filter Use the **Filter** tool to ensure only the walls are selected.

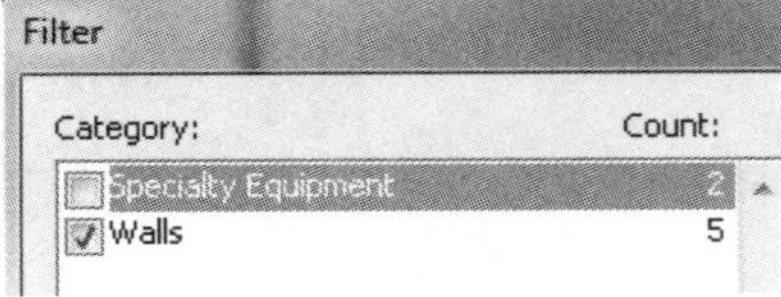

21. Select **Edit Type** from the Properties pane.

22. Select the **Duplicate** button.

23. Name the new wall style **Interior - 4 3/8″ CMU (2-hr) [Interior - 100 mm CMU (2-hr)]**.

Press **OK**.

24. Select **Edit** next to Structure.

25. 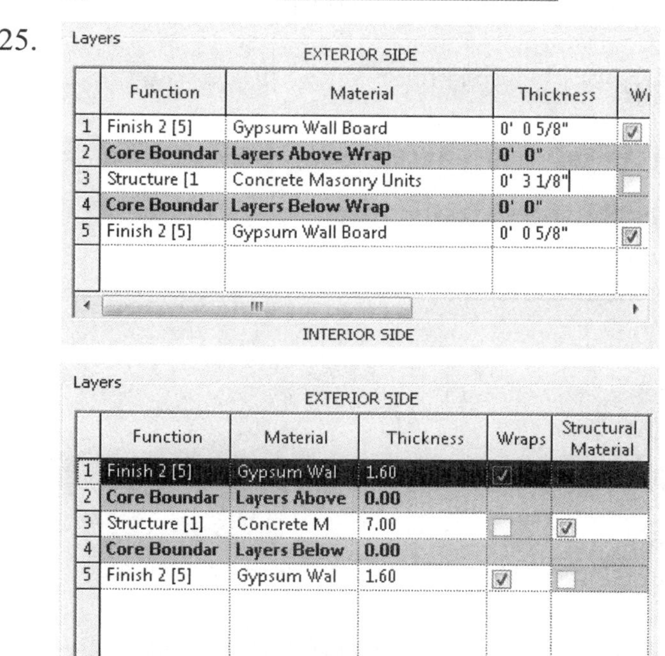
Layers

EXTERIOR SIDE

	Function	Material	Thickness	Wr
1	Finish 2 [5]	Gypsum Wall Board	0' 0 5/8"	☑
2	Core Boundar	Layers Above Wrap	0' 0"	
3	Structure [1	Concrete Masonry Units	0' 3 1/8"	☐
4	Core Boundar	Layers Below Wrap	0' 0"	
5	Finish 2 [5]	Gypsum Wall Board	0' 0 5/8"	☑

INTERIOR SIDE

Layers

EXTERIOR SIDE

	Function	Material	Thickness	Wraps	Structural Material
1	Finish 2 [5]	Gypsum Wal	1.60	☑	
2	Core Boundar	Layers Above	0.00		
3	Structure [1]	Concrete M	7.00	☐	☑
4	Core Boundar	Layers Below	0.00		
5	Finish 2 [5]	Gypsum Wal	1.60	☑	☐

INTERIOR SIDE

Set Layer 1 to Finish 2 [5], **Gypsum Wall Board, 5/8″ [1.6 mm]**.
Set Layer 2 to Core Boundary.
Set Layer 3 to Structure [1], **Concrete Masonry Units, 3 1/8″ [7 mm]**.
Set Layer 4 to Core Boundary.
Set Layer 5 to Finish 2 [5], **Gypsum Wall Board, 5/8″ [1.6 mm]**.

Press **OK**.

26. Set the Coarse Scale Fill Pattern to **Gypsum-Plaster**.

Press **OK**.

27. Set the properties of the elevator shaft walls to the new style: **Interior - 4 3/8″ CMU [Interior-100 mm CMU]**.

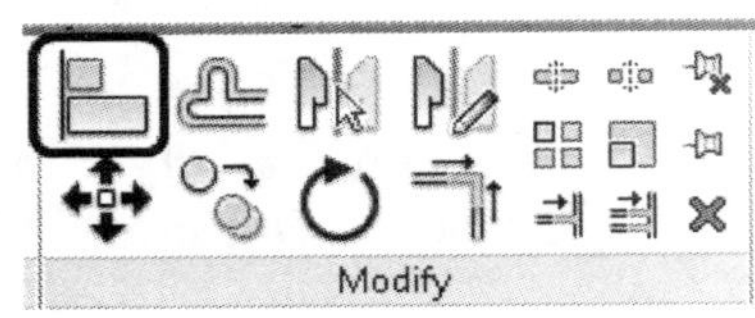

Use **Modify→ALIGN** to adjust the walls.

28. 

Set the Option bar to **Prefer Wall faces**.

29. 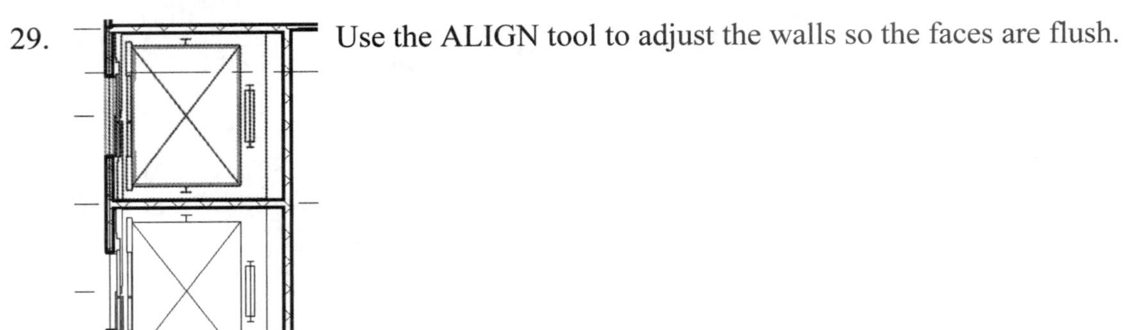

Use the ALIGN tool to adjust the walls so the faces are flush.

30. 3D Views {3D} Switch to a 3D view.

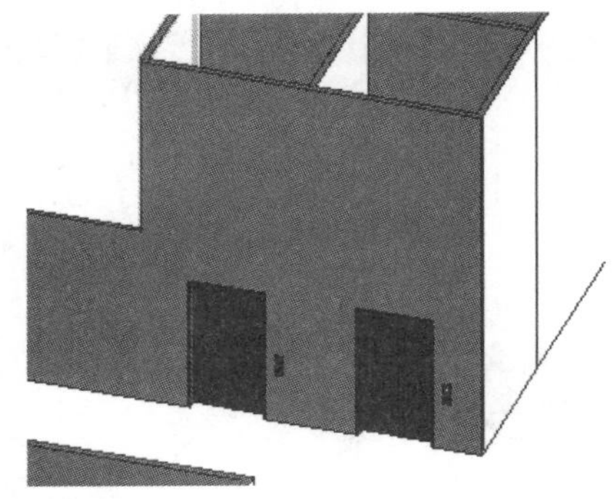

Verify that all the walls appear properly, with walls for the second floor constrained as needed.

Next we add the elevator doors for the second floor.

31. 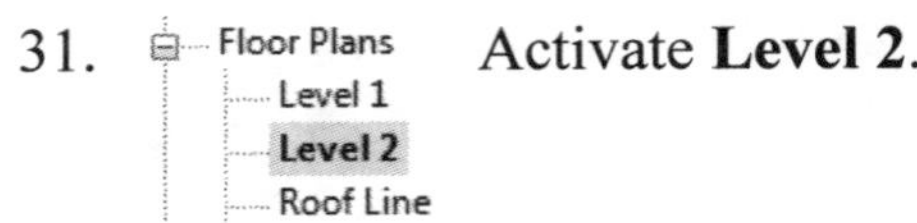

Activate **Level 2**.

32. Door

Activate the **Architecture** ribbon.

Select the **Door** tool.

33. Door-Elevator 12000 x 2290 Opening

Verify that the Door-Elevator is selected on the Properties palette.

34. 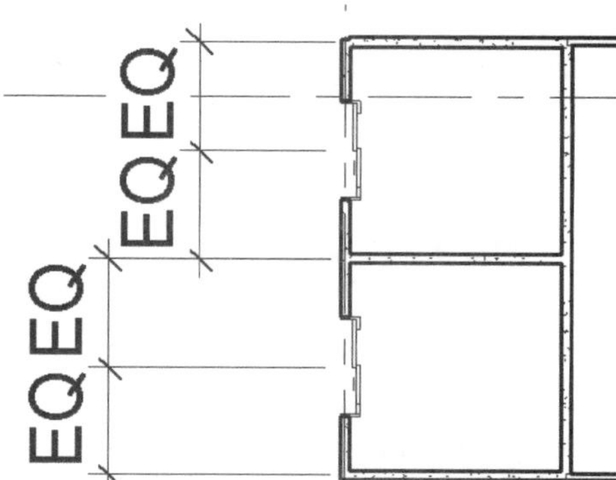

Place the doors so they are centered in each shaft.

35. 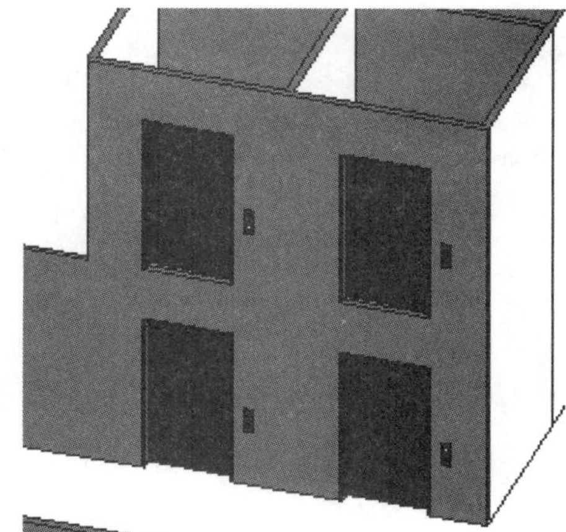

Switch to a 3D view to verify the placement of the elevator doors.

If the doors don't look proper, return to the Level 2 view.

36. 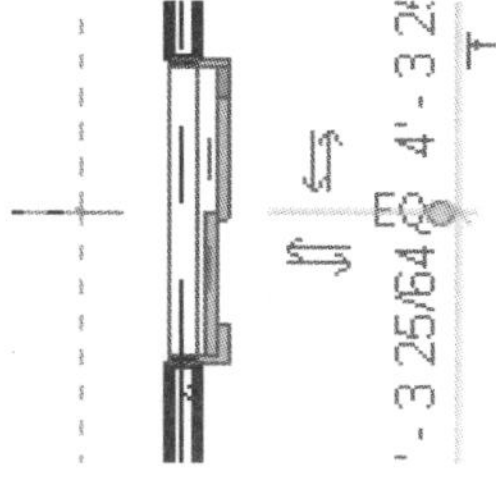

You can use the orientation/flip arrows to re-orient the door or flip the side location for the elevator buttons.

37. Save the file as *ex3-13.rvt.*

- You must have access to the Internet in order to download files from Autodesk Seek (seek.autodesk.com)
- The Snap Settings you use are based on your Zoom factor. In order to use the smaller increment snap distances, zoom in. To use the larger increment snap distances, zoom out.
- When placing a component, use the spacebar to rotate the component before placing.
- You can purge any unused families from your project by using Manage→ Settings→Purge Unused.

Exercise 3-14
Load Family

Drawing Name: ex3-13.rvt
Estimated Time: 15 minutes

This exercise reinforces the following skills:

- Load Family
- Space Planning

All of the content required is on the publisher's website.

1. Open or continue working in *ex3-13.rvt.*
2. Activate **Level 1**.
3. Select the **Component→Place a Component** tool from the Build panel on the Architecture ribbon.
4. Select **Load Family** from the Mode panel.
5. 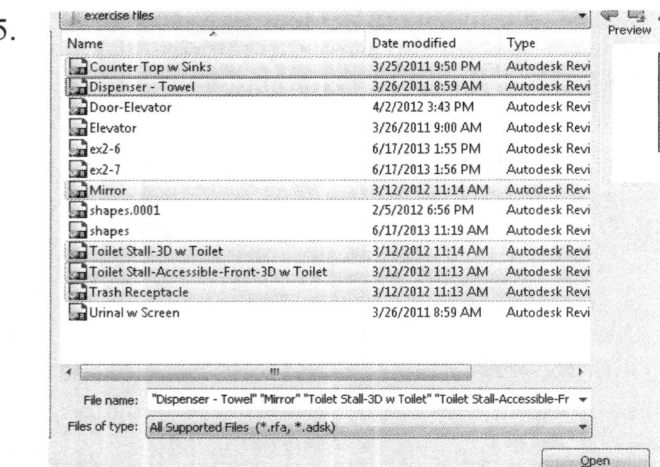

Locate the following files on the publisher's website.

- Urinal w Screen
- Counter Top w Sinks
- Dispenser - Paper Towel
- Toilet Stall - 3D w Toilet
- Toilet Stall - Accessible - Front - 3D w Toilet
- Mirror
- Trash Receptacle

You can select more than one file by holding down the CNTRL key.
Press **Open**.

6. 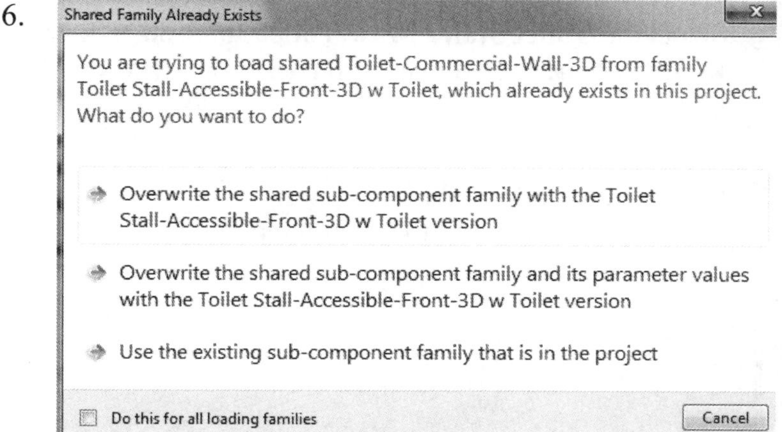

Shared Family Already Exists

You are trying to load shared Toilet-Commercial-Wall-3D from family Toilet Stall-Accessible-Front-3D w Toilet, which already exists in this project. What do you want to do?

- Overwrite the shared sub-component family with the Toilet Stall-Accessible-Front-3D w Toilet version
- Overwrite the shared sub-component family and its parameter values with the Toilet Stall-Accessible-Front-3D w Toilet version
- Use the existing sub-component family that is in the project

Do this for all loading families — Cancel

The toilet stall families share sub-components, so you will see this message.

Select the top option.

7. Under the Properties Pane:

Change Element Type:

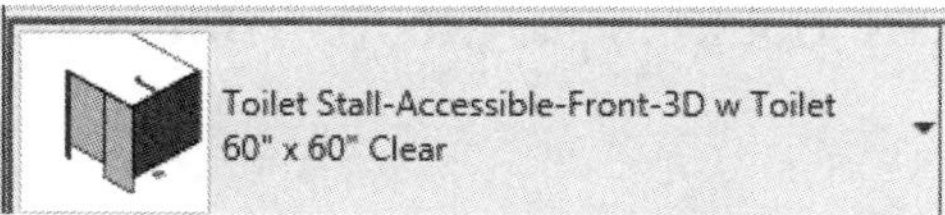

Select the **Toilet Stall-Accessible-Front- 3D w Toilet.**

You need to select the 60" x 60" Clear family.

8. 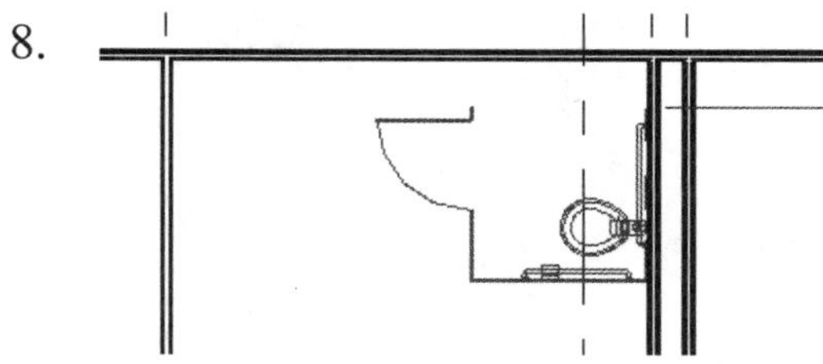

The toilet will be visible when the cursor is over a wall.
Click to place. Do not try to place it exactly.
Simply place it on the wall.

Use the SPACE bar to orient the family.

9. 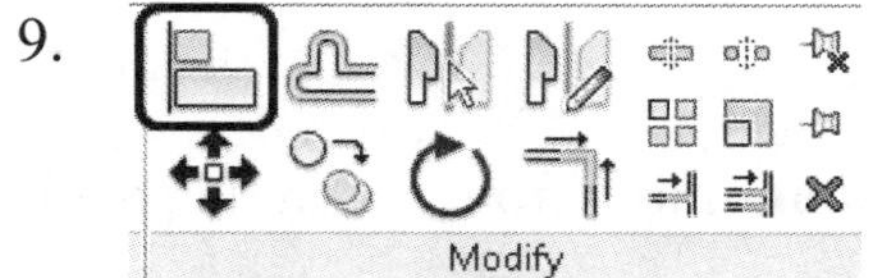

Use the ALIGN tool from the Modify **ribbon** to align the cubicle with the wall.

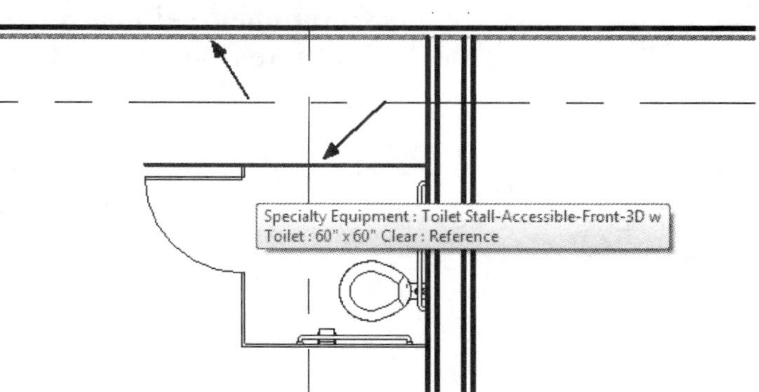

10. Component

Select the **Component→Place a Component** tool from the Build panel on the Architecture ribbon.

11. Properties

Toilet Stall-3D w Toilet 36" x 60" Clear

Select the **Toilet Stall - 3D w Toilet 36″ x 60″ Clear** from the Type drop down list on the Properties pane.

12. 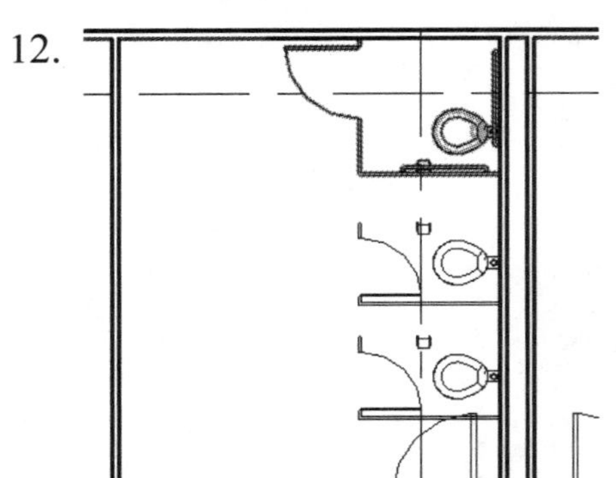

Place two toilet stalls.
Use the SPACE bar to orient the family.

13. 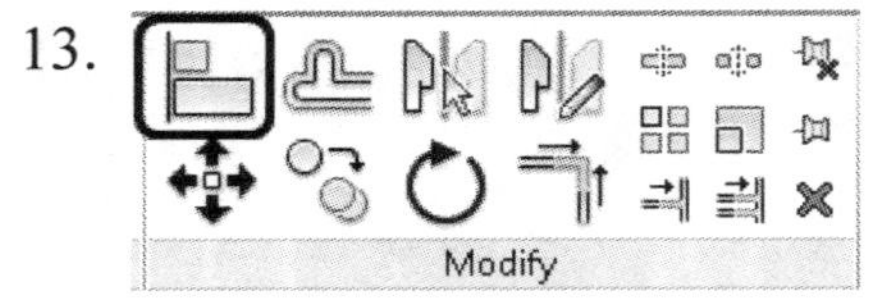

Use the ALIGN tool from the Modify **ribbon** to align the cubicles.

14. 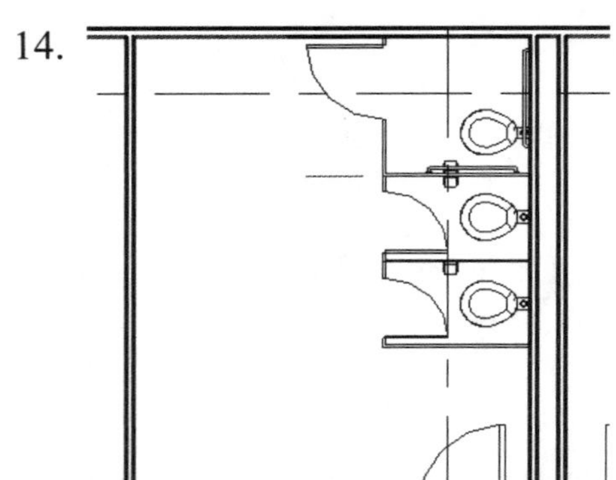

The toilet stalls should all be nestled against each other.

15. 

Select the **Component→Place a Component** tool from the Build panel on the Architecture ribbon.

16. 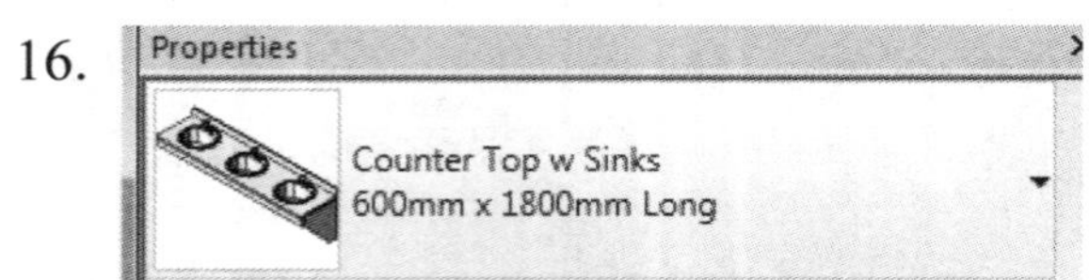

Select the **Counter Top w Sinks 600 mm x 1800 mm Long** from the Type drop down list on the Properties pane.

17. 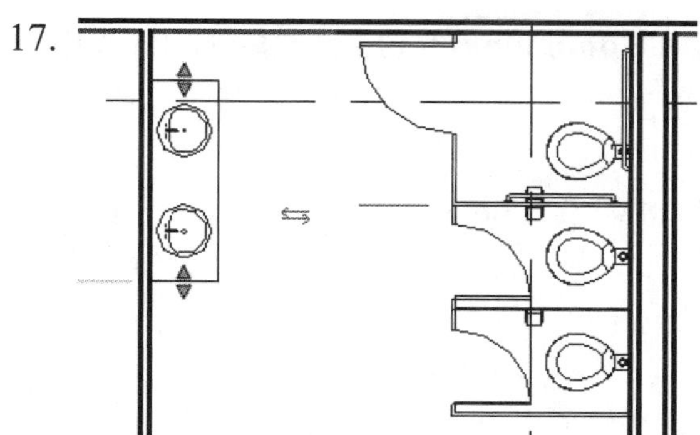

Place the **Counter Top w Sinks 600 mm x 1800 mm Long** in the lavatory.

Notice if you pull the grips on this family you can add additional sinks.

18. Select the **Component→Place a Component** tool from the Build panel on the Architecture ribbon.

19. Select the **Dispenser - Towel** from the Type drop down list on the Properties pane.

20. 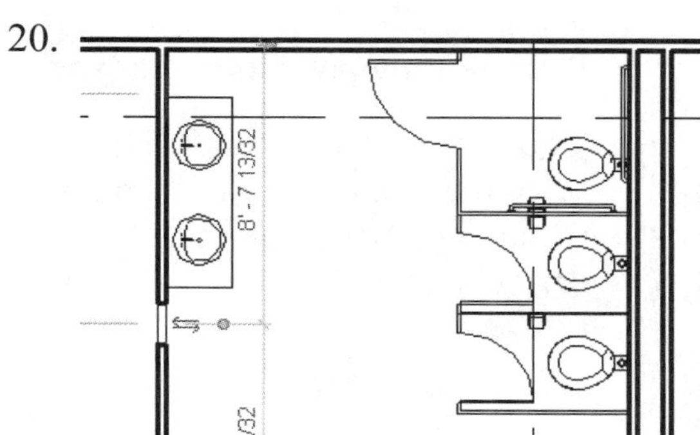

Place the **Dispenser - Towel** next to the sink.

21. Select the **Component→Place a Component** tool from the Build panel on the Architecture ribbon.

22. Select the **Trash Receptacle** from the Type drop down list on the Properties pane.

23. 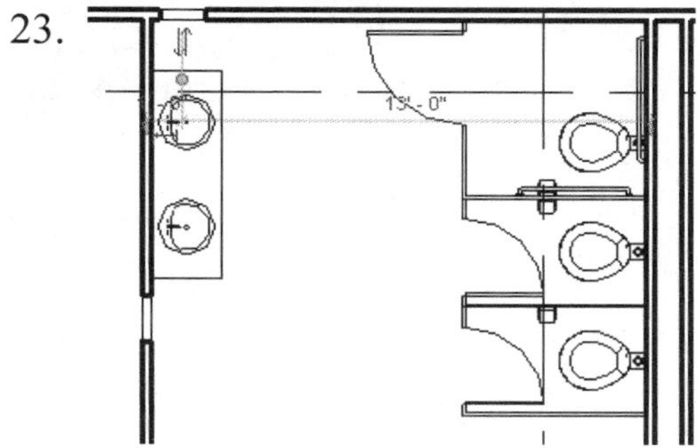

Place the **Trash Receptacle above the sink**.

24. Select the **Component→Place a Component** tool from the Build panel on the Architecture ribbon.

25. Select the **Mirror: 72″ x 48″** from the Type drop down list on the Properties pane.

26. Place the mirror above the sink.

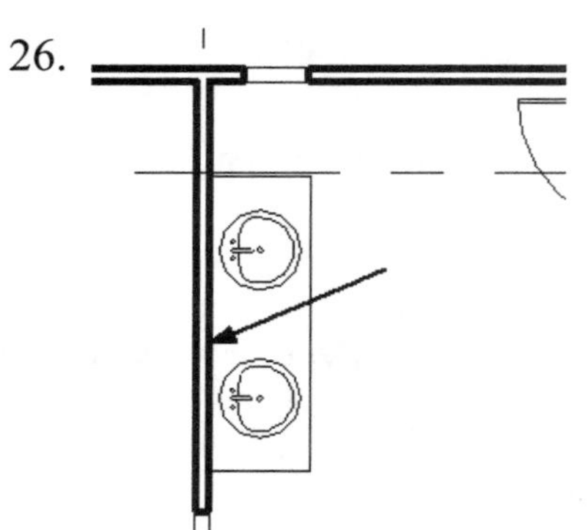

27. Place the components as shown.

You can place components by selecting them from the drop down list on the Option bar or by dragging and dropping from the browser.

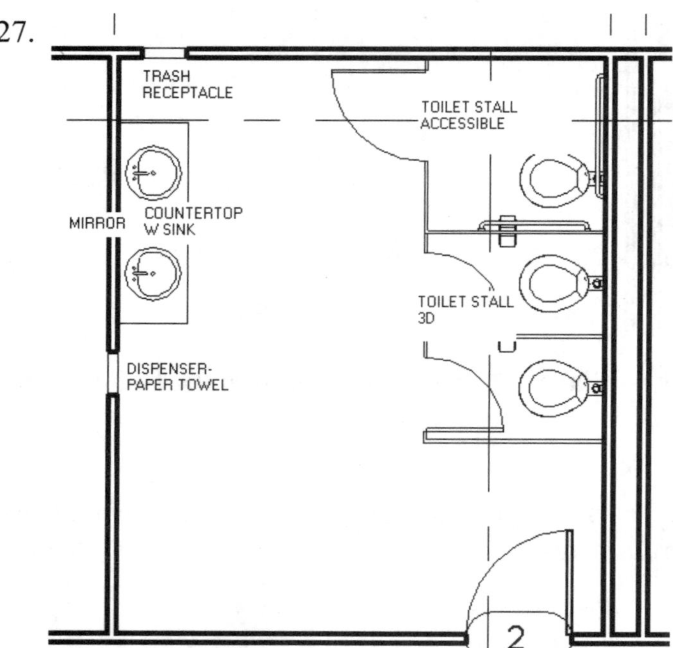

You can flip the orientation of the component by pressing the SPACE bar before you pick to place it.

28. Save the file as *ex3-14.rvt.*

Exercise 3-15
Mirror Components

Drawing Name: ex3-14.rvt
Estimated Time: 15 minutes

This exercise reinforces the following skills:

- Mirror
- Align
- Filter
- Wall Properties

In order for the Mirror to work properly, the rooms need to be identical sizes. This is a challenging exercise for many students. It takes practice to draw a mirror axis six inches from the end point of the wall. If you have difficulty, draw a detail line six inches between the 1′ gap used for plumbing and use the Pick Axis method for Mirror.

1. Open or continue working in *ex3-14.rvt.*
2. Activate **Level 1**.
3. 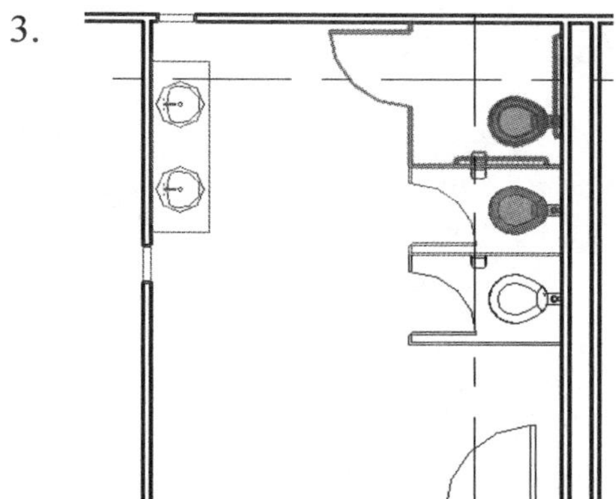

   Hold down the Control key and select the top two stalls or just window around them.

   They should highlight in red.
   Select the countertop with sinks, the trash receptacle, the mirror and the towel dispenser.

   Everything is selected EXCEPT one toilet stall.
4. 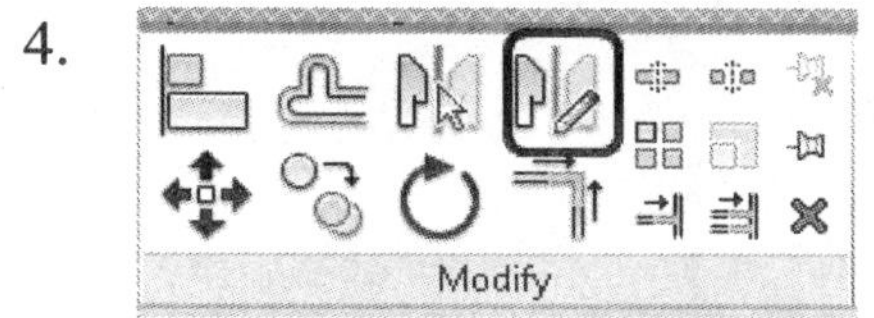

   Select the **Mirror→Draw Mirror Axis** tool under the Modify panel.
5. 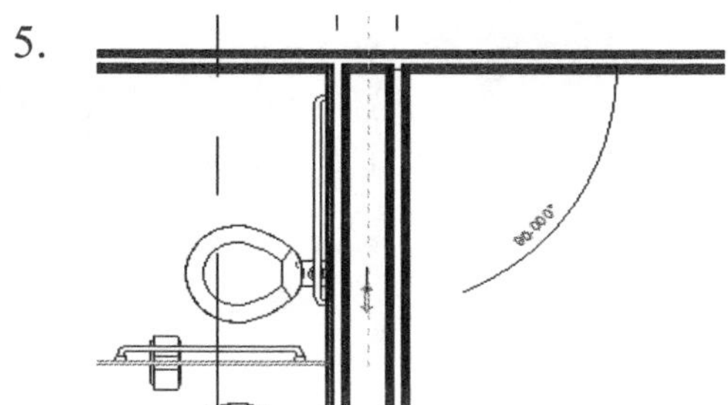

   Start a line at the midpoint into the wall space.

   Then pick a point directly below the first point selected.

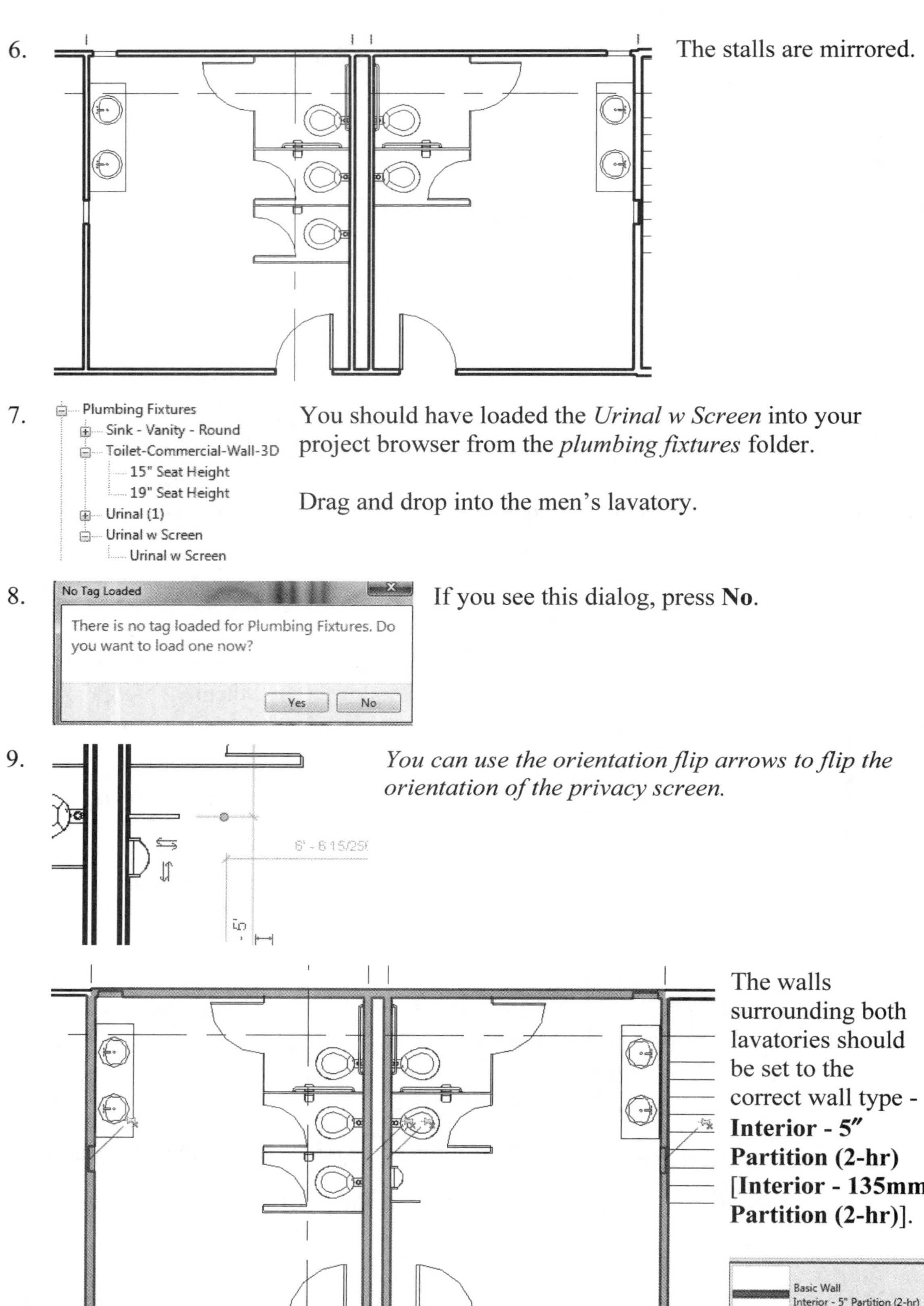

6. The stalls are mirrored.

7. You should have loaded the *Urinal w Screen* into your project browser from the *plumbing fixtures* folder.

   Drag and drop into the men's lavatory.

8. If you see this dialog, press **No**.

9. *You can use the orientation flip arrows to flip the orientation of the privacy screen.*

The walls surrounding both lavatories should be set to the correct wall type - **Interior - 5″ Partition (2-hr) [Interior - 135mm Partition (2-hr)]**.

10. Select the **Split** tool from the Modify panel on the Modify ribbon.

11. Split the walls at the points indicated.

Select the lavatory walls.

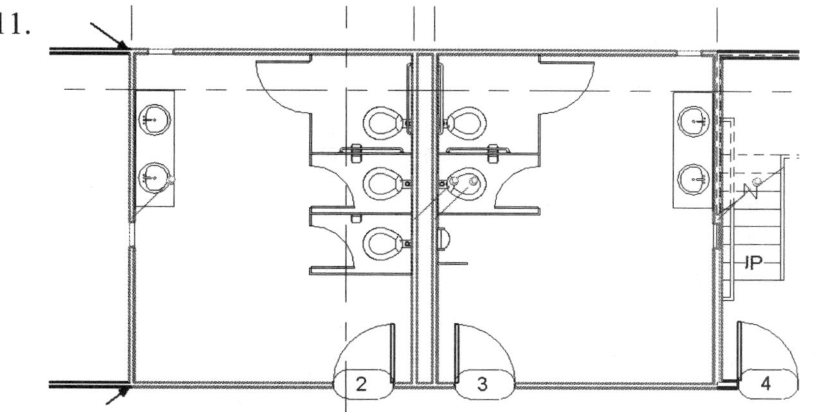

12. Use **FILTER** to only select walls.

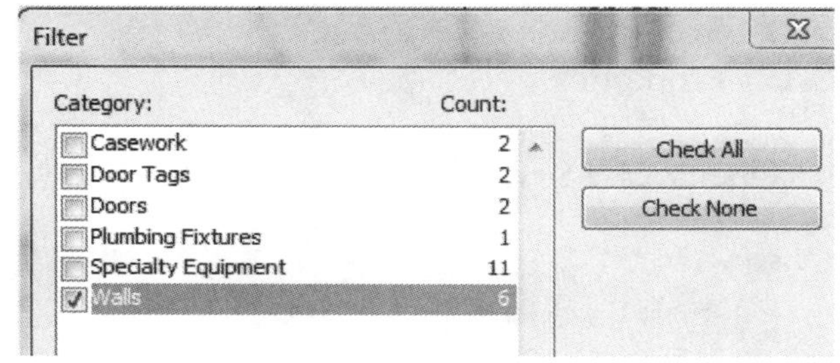

13. Set the walls to the correct type:

Interior - 5″ Partition (2-hr) [Interior - 135mm Partition (2-hr)] using the Properties pane type selector.

14. Use ALIGN from the Modify panel on the Modify ribbon to align the lavatory walls.

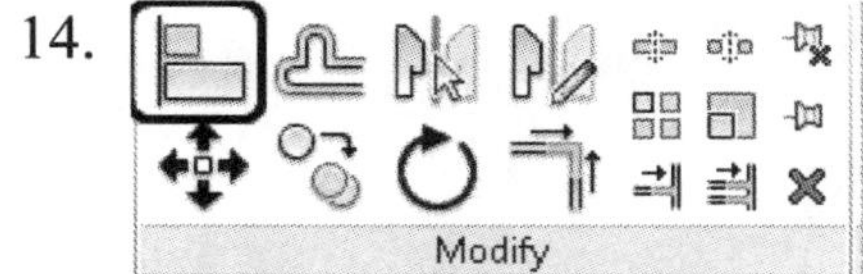

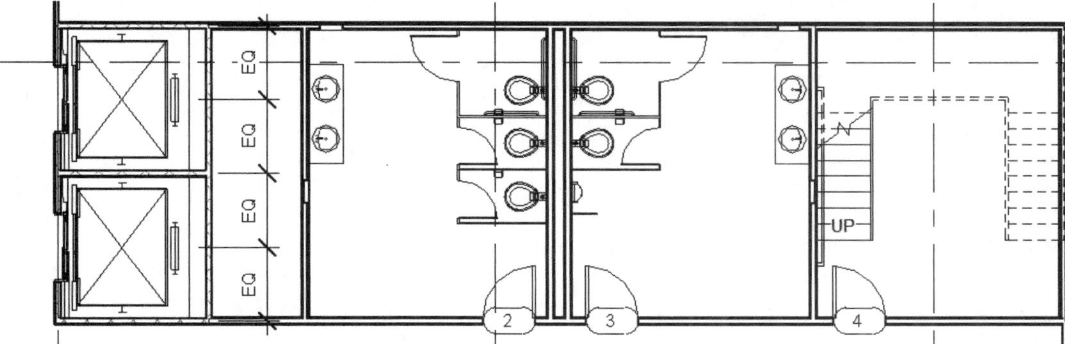

15. Save the file as *ex3-15.rvt.*

To re-select the previous selection set, hit the left arrow key.

Exercise 3-16
Create a 3D View

Drawing Name: ex3-15.rvt
Estimated Time: 10 minutes

This exercise reinforces the following skills:

- 3D view
- Section Box
- Properties

1. Open *ex3-15.rvt.*

2. 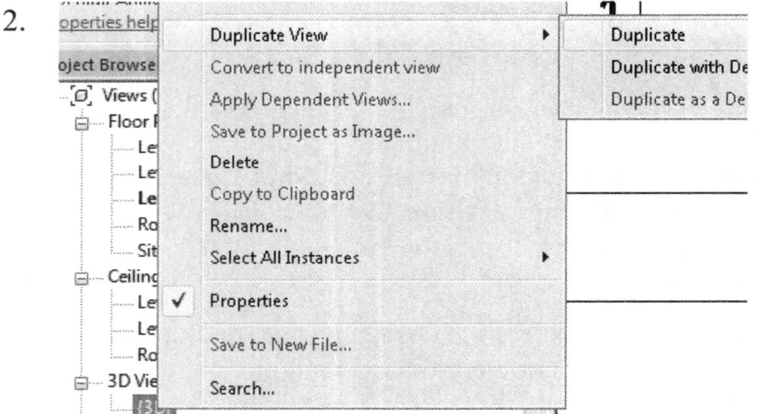

Highlight the 3D view in the Project Browser.

Right click and select **Duplicate View→ Duplicate**.

3. 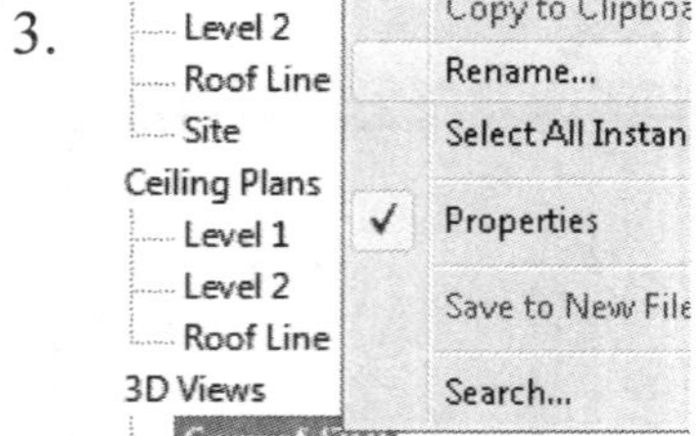

Right click on the new 3D view and select **Rename**.

4. Name: 3D- Lavatory

Type **3D - Lavatory**.

Press **OK**.

5.

Extents	
Crop View	☐
Crop Region Visible	☐
Annotation Crop	☐
Far Clip Active	☐
Section Box	☑

Scroll down the Properties pane.

Enable **Section Box**.

Press **OK**.

6.

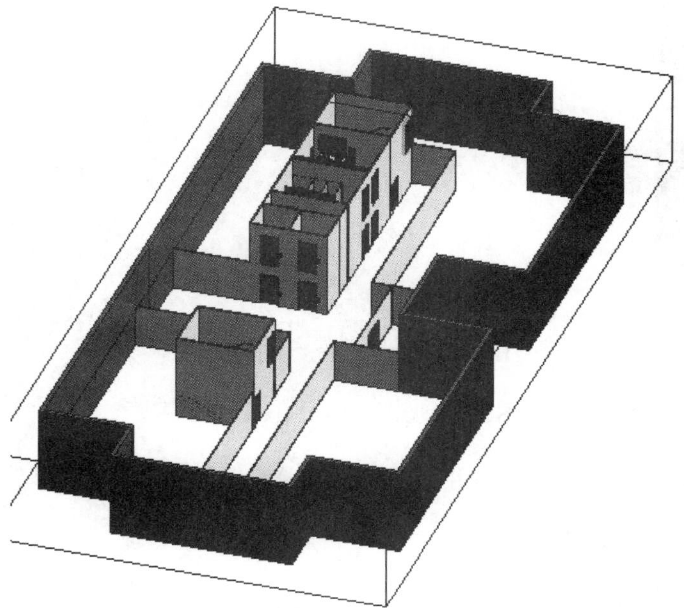

A clear box appears around the model. Left click to select the box.

There are grips indicated by arrows on the box.

7.

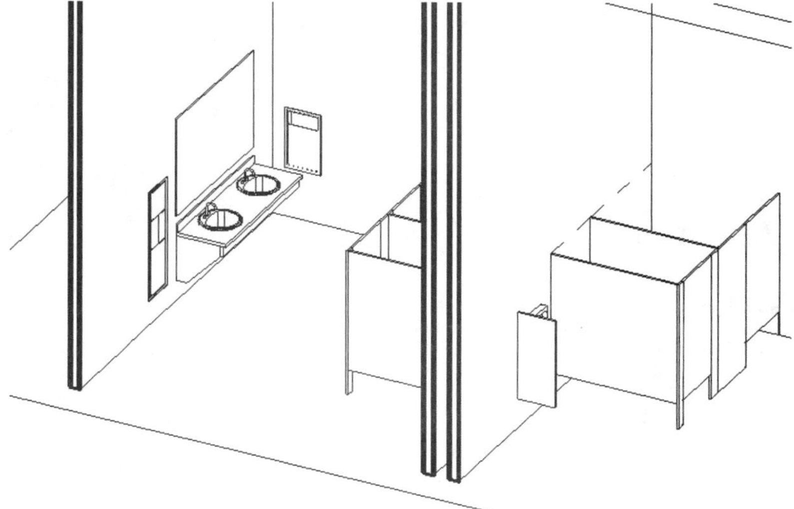

Select the grips and reduce the size of the box, so only the lavatories are shown.

Use the **SPIN** tool to rotate your view so you can inspect the lavatories.

If you hold down the SHIFT key and middle mouse button at the same time, you can orbit the model.

8. 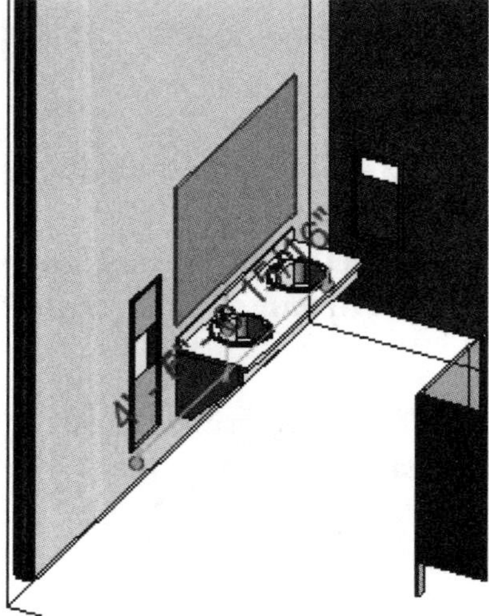

If you need to adjust the elevation/height of the mirror:

Select the mirror.

9. 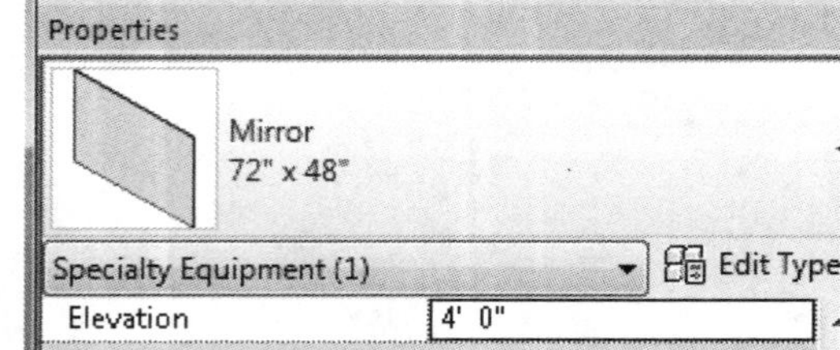

In the Properties pane:

Set the elevation to **4′ 0″**.

Press **Apply**.

10. Save as *ex3-16.rvt.*

Exercise 3-17
Copying Lavatory Layouts

Drawing Name: ex3-16.rvt
Estimated Time: 10 minutes

This exercise reinforces the following skills:

- Filter
- Group
- Copy Aligned

1. Open *ex3-16.rvt.*
2. Activate **Level 1**.
3. Select the components used in the lavatory layout.

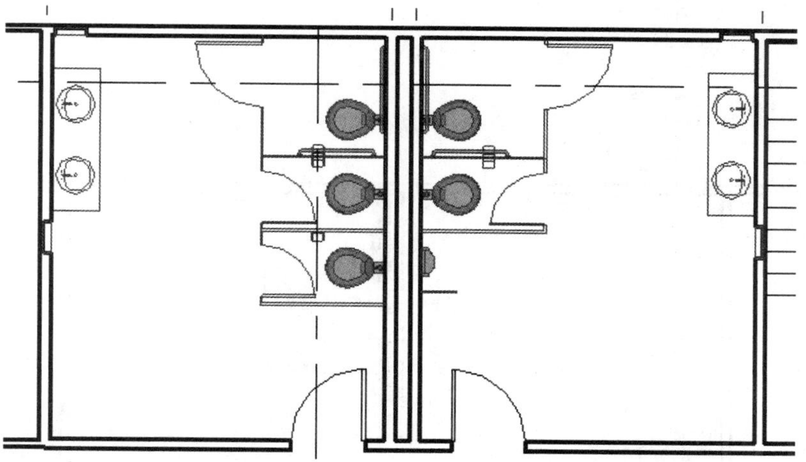

4. 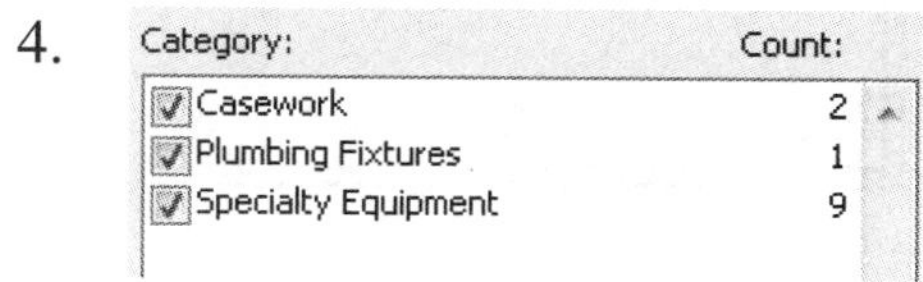

Filter **Hint: Use the Filter tool to select only the Casework, Plumbing Fixtures and Specialty Equipment.**

5. Select the **Create Group** tool from the Create panel.

6. 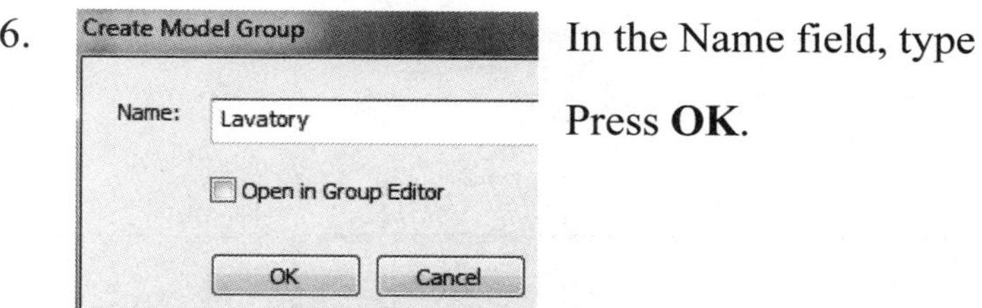

In the Name field, type **Lavatory**.

Press **OK**.

7. Select **Copy to Clipboard** from the Clipboard panel.

8. 

Select **Paste→Aligned to Selected Levels** from the Clipboard panel.

9. 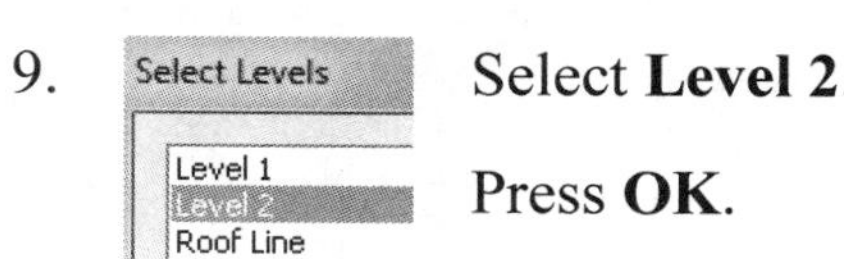

Select **Level 2**.

Press **OK**.

10. Switch to **Level 2**.

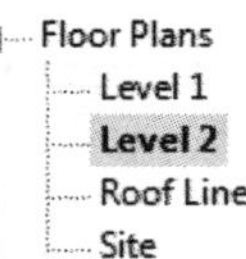

The lavatory should be placed.

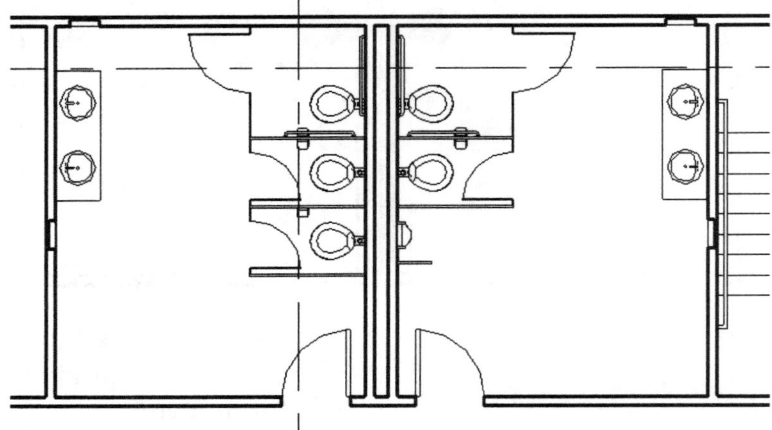

11. Save the file as *ex3-17.rvt.*

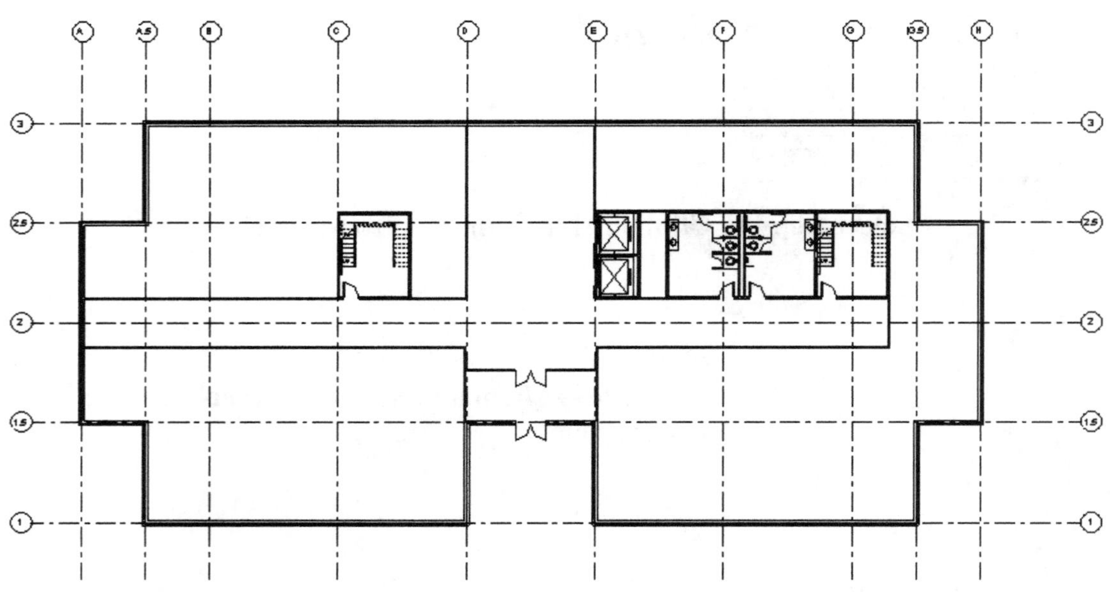

Level 1

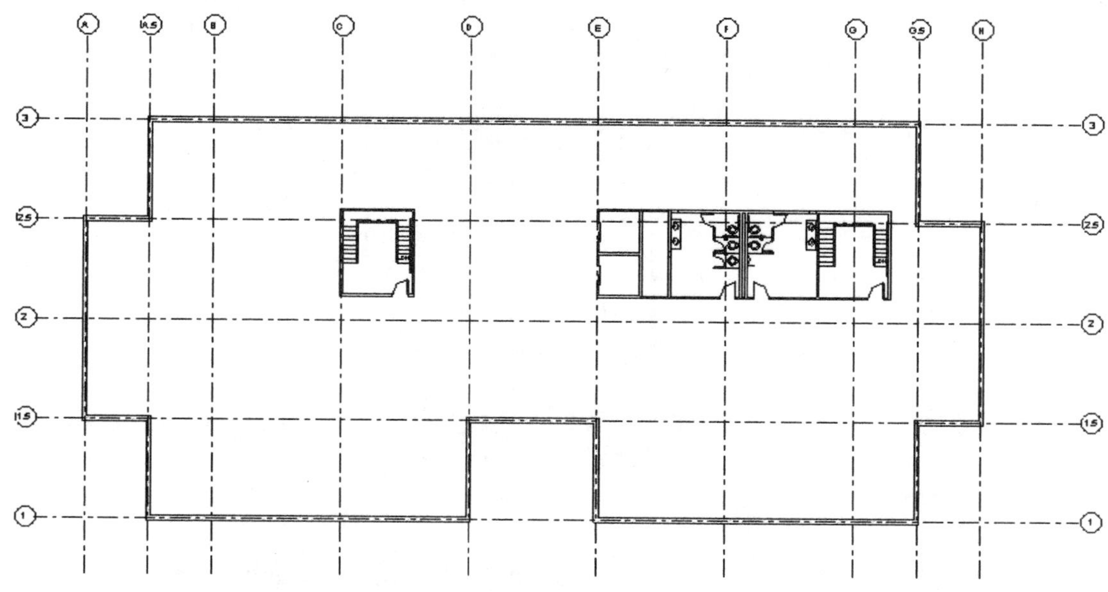

Level 2

Exercise 3-18

Add a Door to a Curtain Wall

Drawing Name: ex3-17.rvt
Estimated Time: 30 minutes

This exercise reinforces the following skills:

- Curtain Wall
- Modify Wall Curtain Wall
- Elevations
- Grid Lines
- Load Family
- Properties
- Type Selector

1. Open *ex3-17.rvt.*

2. Views (all)
Floor Plans
Level 1

   Activate **Level 1** Floor Plan.

3. Select the East Wall.

4. Select the **Storefront** Curtain Wall using the Type Selector on the Properties pane.

5. Type **VV** to launch the Visibility/Graphics dialog.
Enable **Elevations**.
Press **OK**.

6. 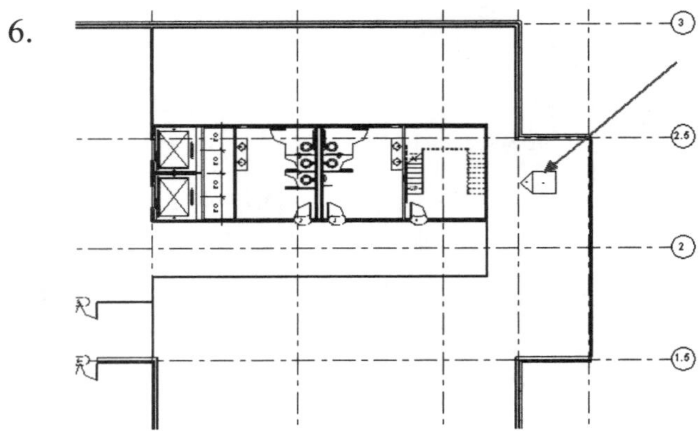

Locate your East Elevation marker. In this case the marker is inside the building.

7. 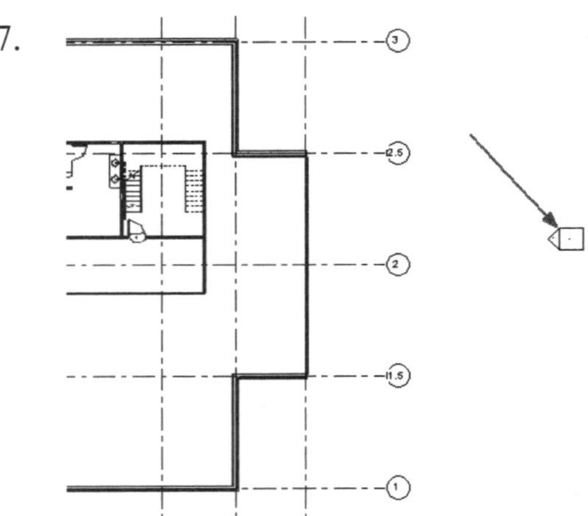

Place your cursor over the square part of the elevation marker. Hold down your left mouse button. Drag the marker so it is outside the building.

8. Left click on the triangle part of the elevation. A blue line will appear to indicate the depth of the elevation view.

Move the blue line so it is outside the building.

Double left click on the triangle to open the East Elevation view or select East elevation in the Project Browser.

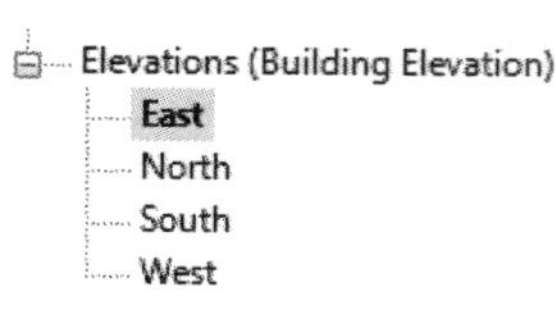

9. 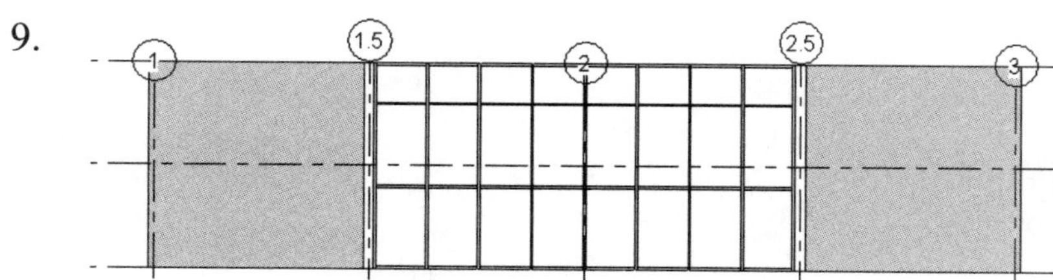

This is the east elevation view when the marker is outside the building and the depth is outside the building.

10. 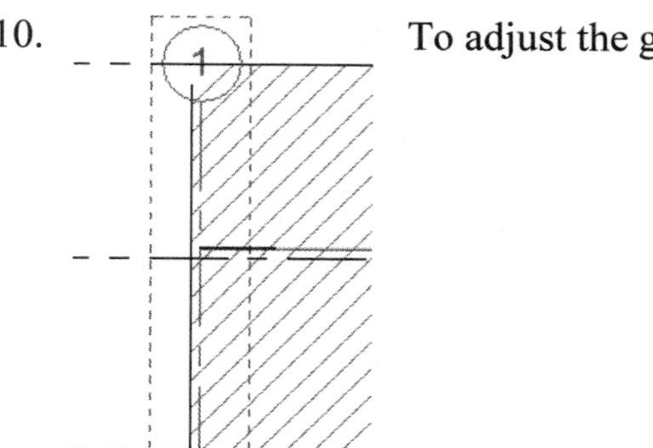

To adjust the grid lines, select the first grid line.

11. 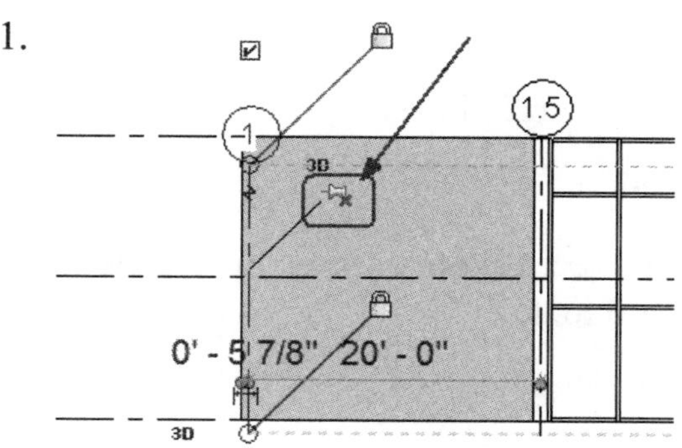

Unpin the grid line, if it has a pin on it.

12. Select the grid line again.

Drag the bubble using the small circle above the building model.

13. 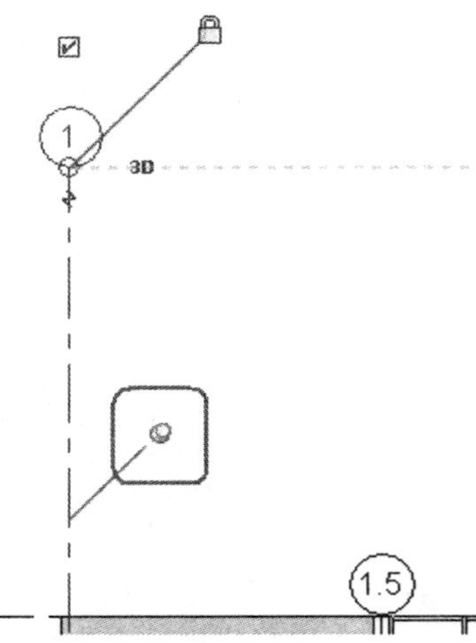

Left click to re-enable the pin.

14. 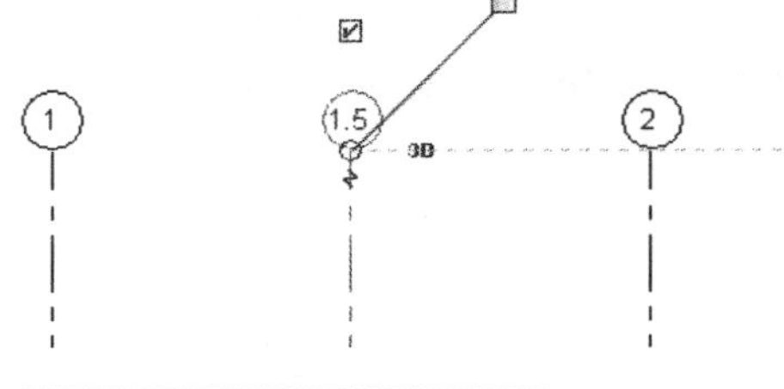

The group will adjust. Drag the remaining gridlines so the bubbles are aligned with the grid line group.

15. 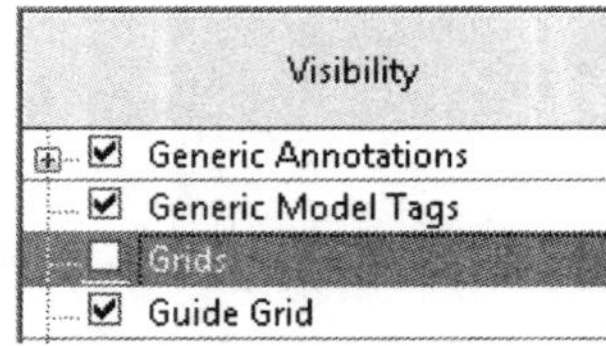

Type VV to launch the Visibility/Graphics dialog. Turn off visibility of grids.

Press **OK**.

16. 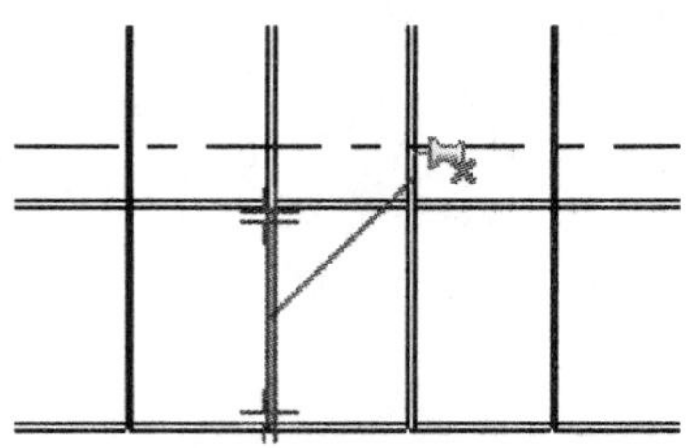

Select the center mullion.
Use the TAB key to cycle select.

Unpin the selection.

Right click and select **Delete** or press the **Delete** key on your keyboard to delete.

17. Select the grid line.

18. Select the **Add/Remove Segments** tool from the ribbon.

19. 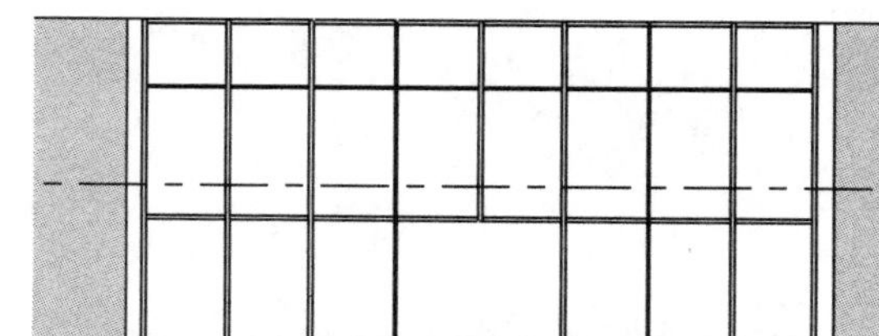

Select the grid line to be removed.

Left click below the building to accept.

There will now be a wide pane to be used to create a door.

20. Select the **Load Family** tool from the Load from Library panel on the Insert ribbon.

21. Locate the **Curtain Wall Dbl Glass [M_Curtain Wall Dbl Glass]** family from the *Doors* folder. Press **Open**.

22. Hover your cursor over the edge of the panel.

DO NOT CLICK.

23. Press the tab.

Repeat until only the glass pane is highlighted.

24. 

You should see **System Panel Glazed** in the Properties pane.

It is grayed out because it is pinned which prevents editing.

25. 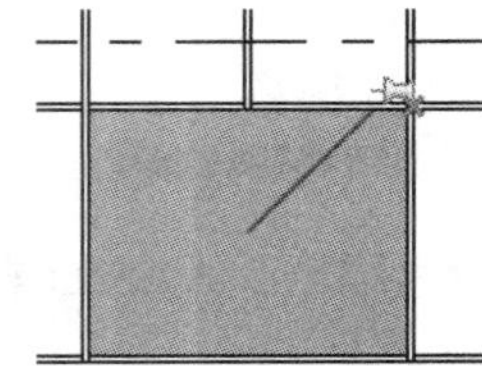

Unpin the glazing.

26. 

From the Properties pane:
Assign the Curtain Wall Dbl Glass door to the selected element.

Left click to complete the command.

27. You will now see a door in your curtain wall.

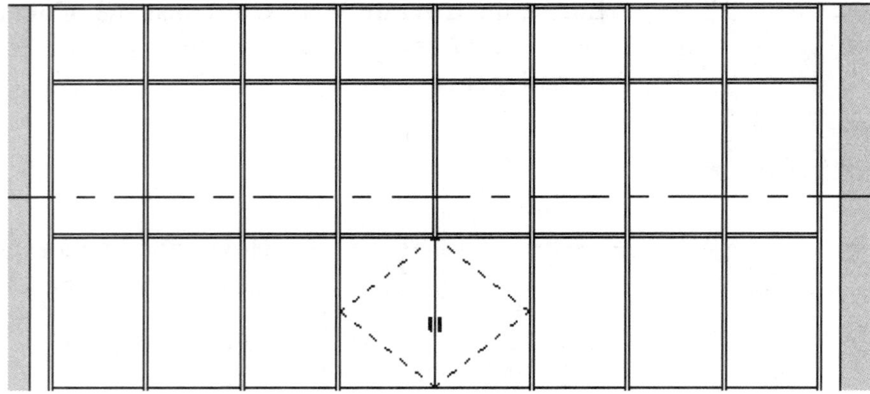

28. Save as *ex3-18.rvt.*

Exercise 3-19
Modifying a Curtain Wall

Drawing Name: ex3-18.rvt
Estimated Time: 30 minutes

This exercise reinforces the following skills:

- Curtain Wall
- Curtain Wall Grids
- Curtain Wall Doors

Several students complained that the door was too big and asked how to make it a smaller size.

1. Open *ex3-18.rvt.*

2. Elevations (Building Elevation)
   East
   North
   South
   West

   Switch to the **East** elevation view.

3. 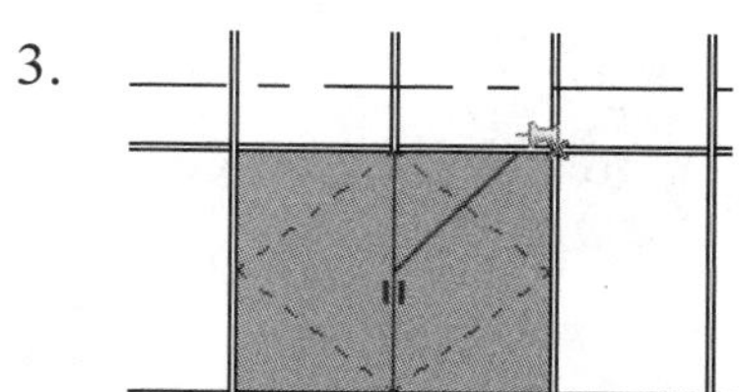

   Select the Curtain Wall door.

4. 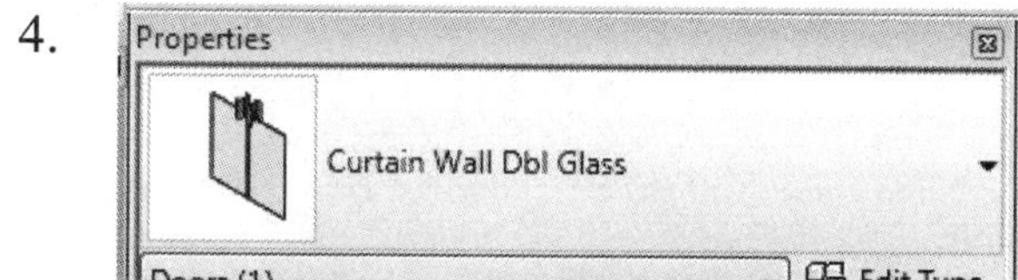

   You should see Curtain Wall Dbl Glass in the Properties pane.

5. 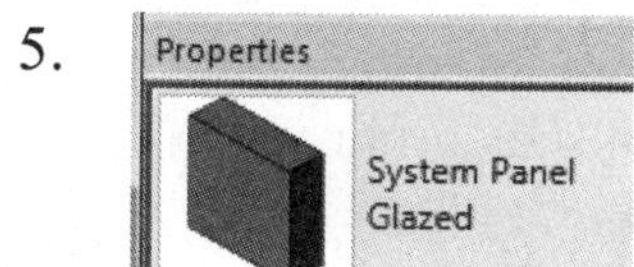

   Using the Type Selector, change the door to a **System Panel - Glazed.**

   Left click below the window to complete the command.

6. 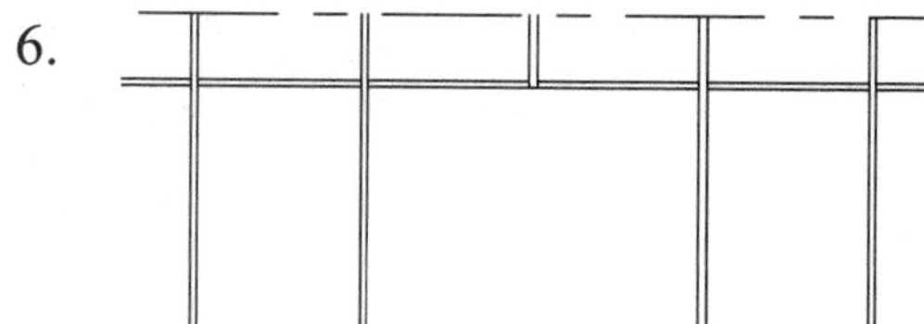

   The curtain wall now has a glass panel instead of a door.

7. Curtain Grid

   Activate the Architecture ribbon.

   Select the **Curtain Grid** tool.

8. 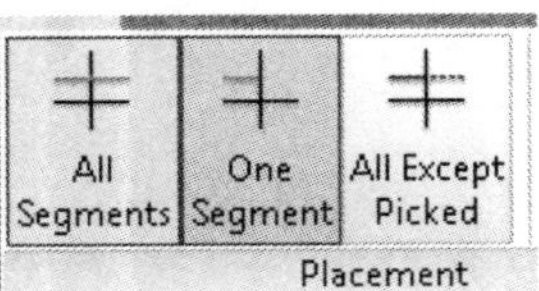

On the ribbon:

Look for the Placement panel.

Select **One Segment**.

9. 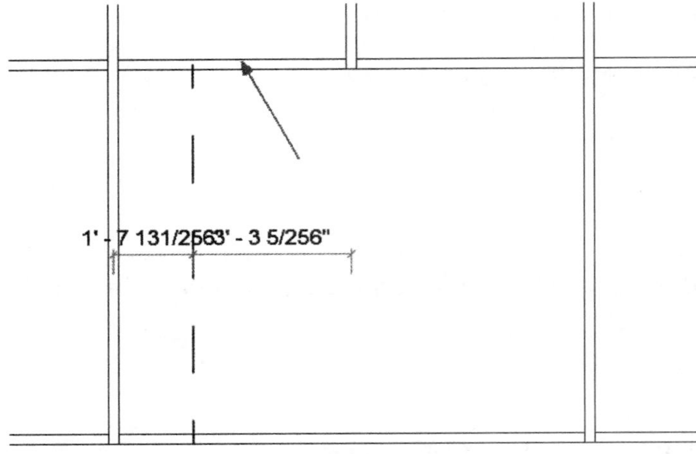

Hover your mouse over the horizontal mullion on the left side of the pane to preview the placement of the curtain grid.

Note that you use the horizontal mullion to place a vertical grid and a vertical mullion to place a horizontal grid.

10. 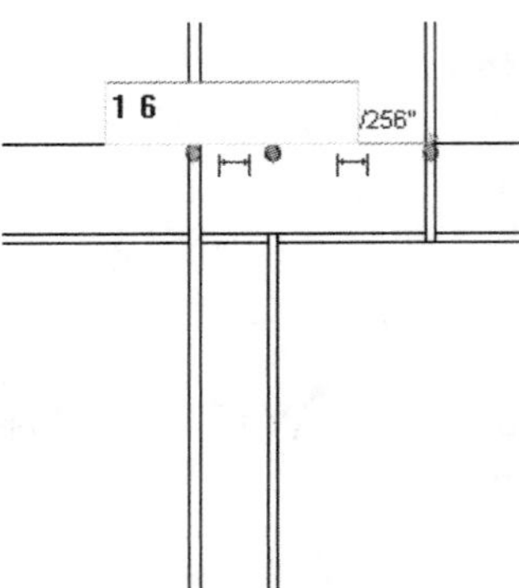

Left click to place.

Click on the temporary dimension to adjust the placement of the mullion. Set the distance to **1′ 6″**.

11. 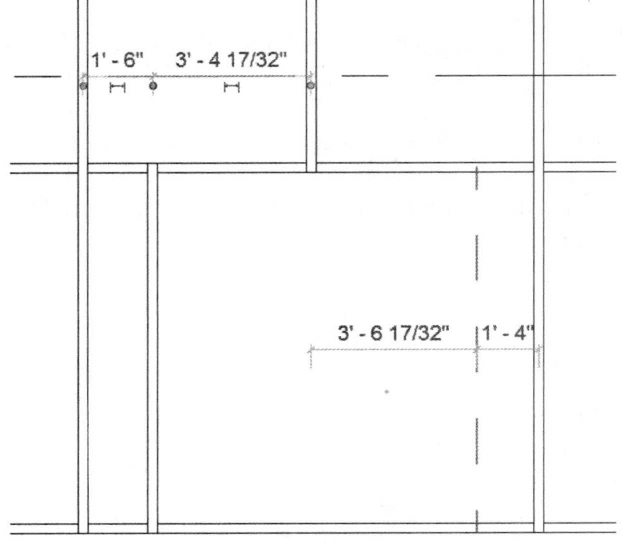

Hover your mouse over the horizontal mullion to preview the placement of the curtain grid on the right side.

12.

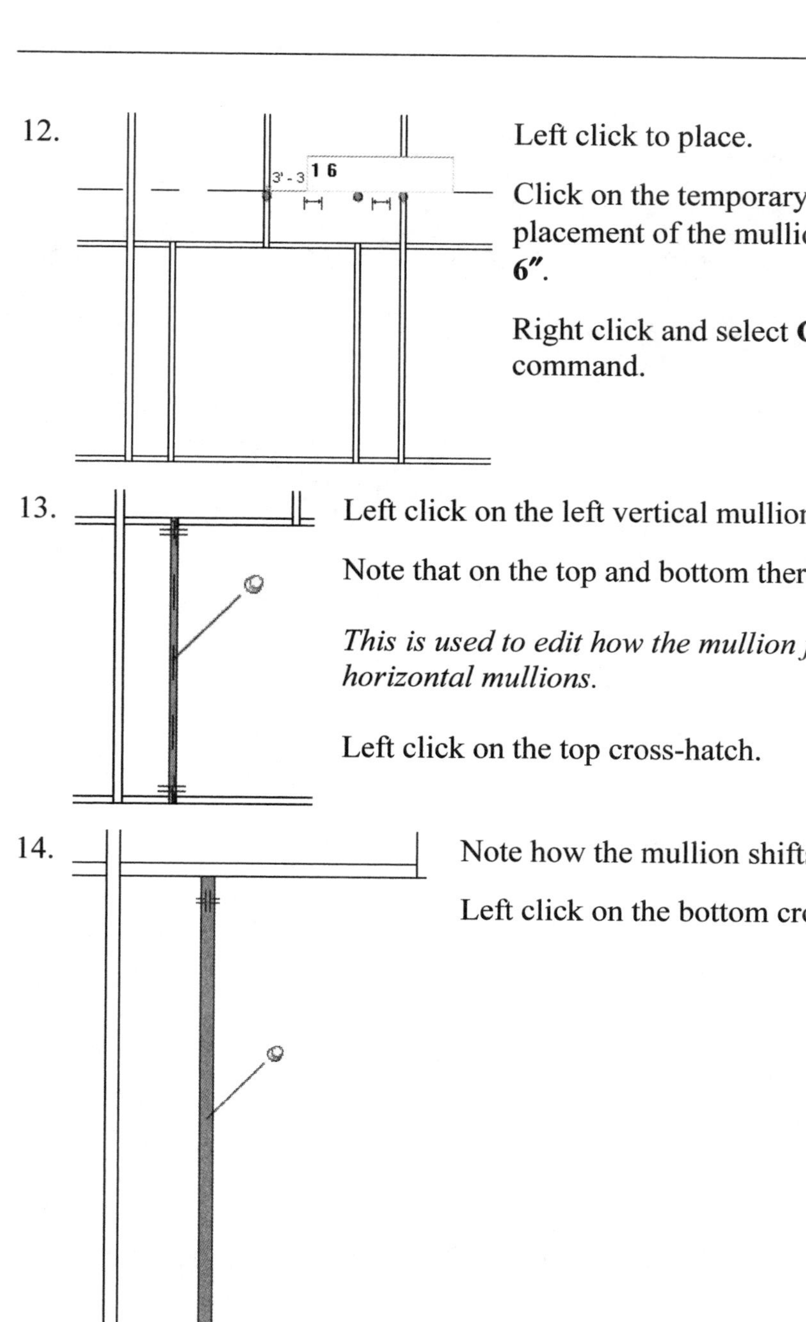

Left click to place.

Click on the temporary dimension to adjust the placement of the mullion. Set the distance to **1′ 6″**.

Right click and select **Cancel** to exit the command.

13. Left click on the left vertical mullion.

Note that on the top and bottom there is a cross-hatch icon.

This is used to edit how the mullion joins/intersects the horizontal mullions.

Left click on the top cross-hatch.

14. Note how the mullion shifts position.

Left click on the bottom cross-hatch.

15. Note how the mullion on the left has been adjusted.

Repeat on the right mullion using the cross-hatch icons.

16. 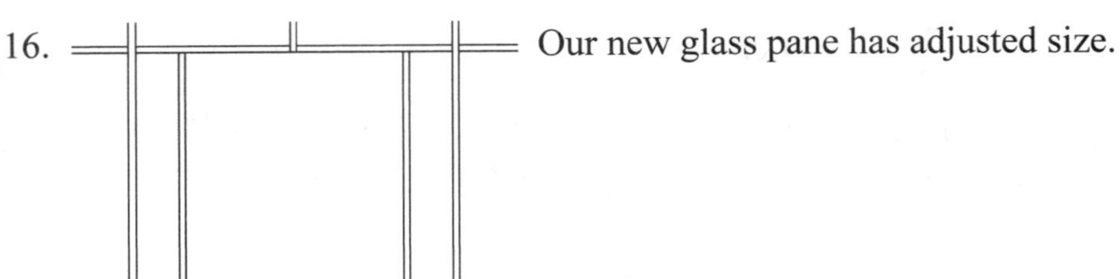
Our new glass pane has adjusted size.

17. 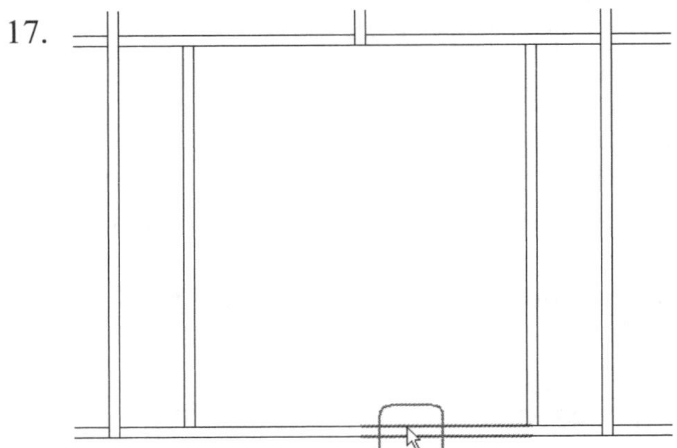
Hover your cursor over the edge of the panel.

DO NOT CLICK.

18. Press the tab.

Repeat until only the glass pane is highlighted.

Left click to select the glass pane.

19. You should see **System Panel Glazed** in the Properties pane.

20. From the Properties pane:
Assign the Curtain Wall Dbl Glass door to the selected element using the Type Selector.

Left click to complete the command.

21. You will now see a door in your curtain wall.

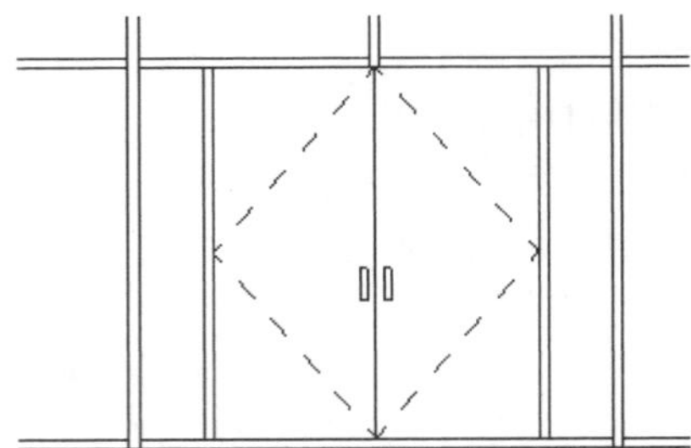

22. Save as *ex3-19.rvt.*

Exercise 3-20

Curtain Wall with Spiders

Drawing Name: ex3-19.rvt
Estimated Time: 15 minutes

This exercise reinforces the following skills:

- Curtain Walls
- System Families
- Properties

1. Open *ex3-19.rvt.*

2. 

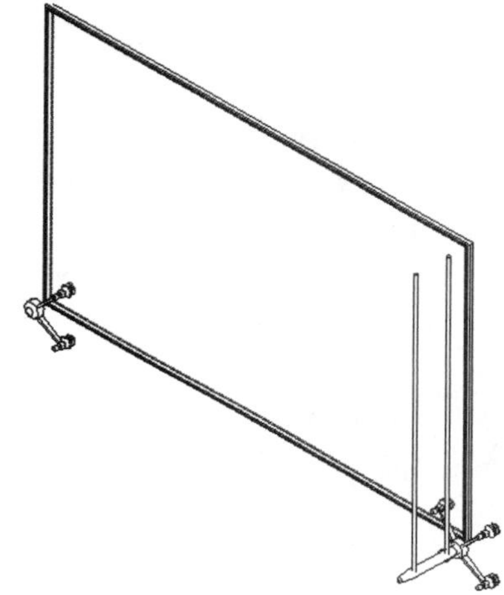

We are going to replace the existing panels in the curtain wall with a panel using spiders.

In order to use the panel with spiders, we need to load the family into the project.

3. Load Family | Load as Group | Load from Library

Go to the **Insert** ribbon. Select **Load Family**.

4. File name: spider clips
Files of type: All Supported Files (*.rfa, *.adsk)

Browse to where you are storing the exercise files.
Select the *spider clips.rfa.*
Press **Open**.

5. 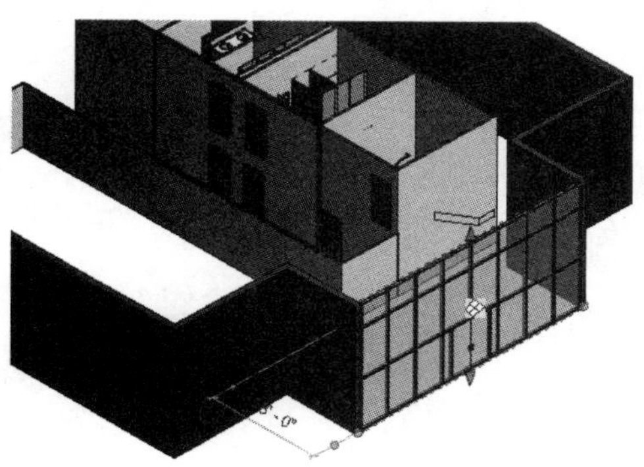

Select the curtain wall so that it highlights.

6. Edit Type — Select **Edit Type** from the Properties panel.

7. Duplicate... — Select **Duplicate**.

8. Name: Curtain Wall with Spiders — Rename ***Curtain Wall with Spiders.*** Press **OK**.

9. 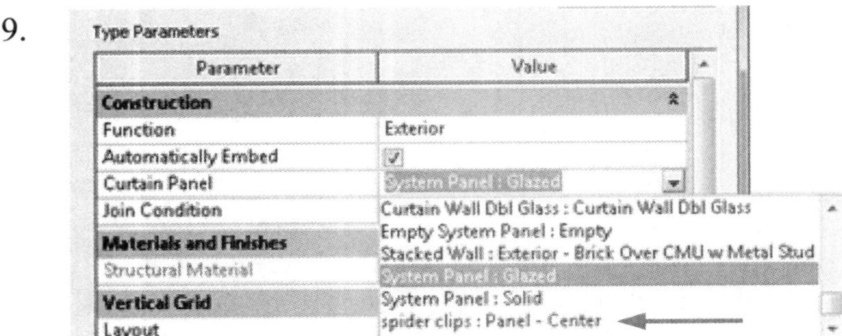

Locate the Curtain Panel parameter.

Select the drop-down arrow.

Select the spider clips: Panel - Center family.

10. You should see the spider clips panel family listed as assigned to the Curtain Panel.

Parameter	Value
Construction	
Function	Exterior
Automatically Embed	☑
Curtain Panel	spider clips : Panel - Center
Join Condition	Vertical Grid Continuous

11. Scroll down the dialog box and locate the Vertical and Horizontal Mullions.

Vertical Mullions	
Interior Type	Rectangular Mullion : 2.5" x 5" rec
Border 1 Type	Rectangular Mullion : 2.5" x 5" rec
Border 2 Type	Rectangular Mullion : 2.5" x 5" rec
Horizontal Mullions	
Interior Type	Rectangular Mullion : 2.5" x 5" rec
Border 1 Type	Rectangular Mullion : 2.5" x 5" rec
Border 2 Type	Rectangular Mullion : 2.5" x 5" rec

12. Use the drop-down selector to set all the Mullions to **None**.

Adjust for Mullion Size; Vertical Mullions: Interior Type, Border 1 Type, Border 2 Type; Horizontal Mullions: Interior Type, Border 1 Type, Border 2 Type; Identity Data: Keynote

Drop-down options:
- Rectangular Mullion : 2.5" x 5" rectangular
- None
- Circular Mullion : 2.5" Circular
- Rectangular Mullion : 1" Square
- Rectangular Mullion : 1.5" x 2.5" rectangular
- Rectangular Mullion : 2.5" x 5" rectangular
- Rectangular Mullion : 2.5" x 5" rectangular
- Rectangular Mullion : 2.5" x 5" rectangular

13. Verify that all the mullions are set to **None**.

Vertical Mullions	
Interior Type	None
Border 1 Type	None
Border 2 Type	None
Horizontal Mullions	
Interior Type	None
Border 1 Type	None
Border 2 Type	None

14. 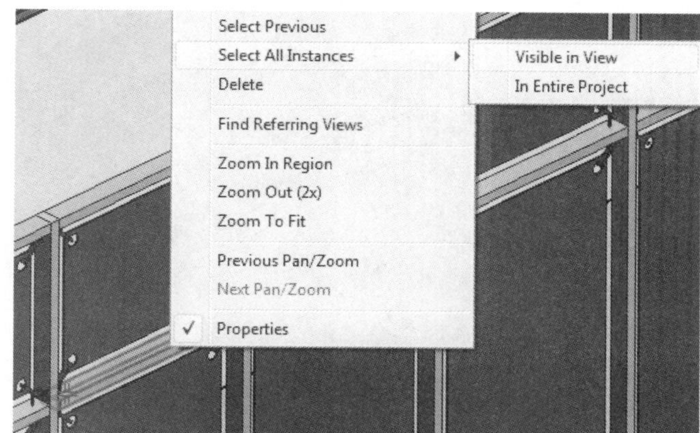

If you still see mullions…

Select one of the mullions. Right click and use **Select All Instances→Visible in View**.

Then press the Delete key on your keyboard.

15. 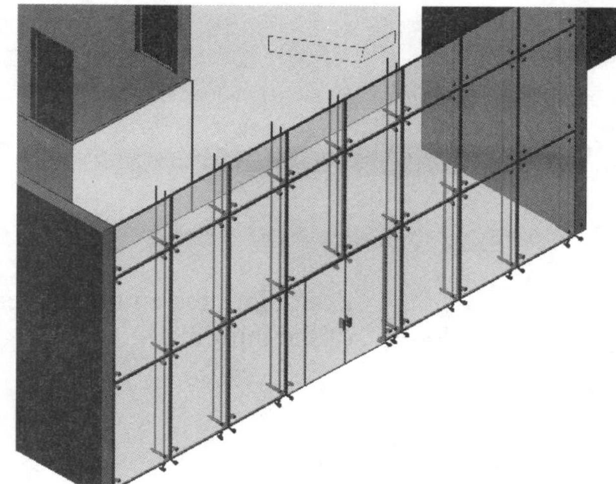

The curtain wall with spiders and no mullions is displayed.

16. Save as *ex3-20.rvt.*

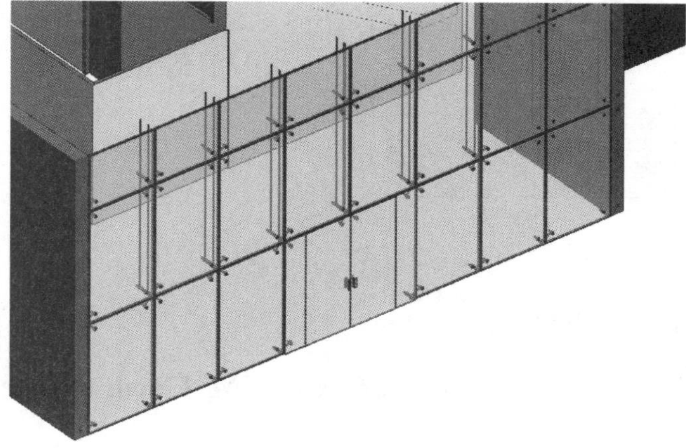

Extra: Replace the bottom panels with the Spider Panel – End Panel family to create a cleaner looking curtain wall.

Hint: *Load the Spider Panel – End Panel family and replace each bottom panel with the new family using the Type Selector (similar to placing the curtain wall door).*

Exercise 3-21

Adding Windows

Drawing Name: ex3-20.rvt
Estimated Time: 60 minutes

This exercise reinforces the following skills:

- Window
- Window Properties
- Array
- Mirror
- Copy-Move

1. Open *ex3-20.rvt.*

2. Elevations (Building Elevation)
   East
   North
   South
   West

   Switch to a **South** elevation view.

3. 

   Zoom into the entrance area of the building.

   Display is set to Coarse, Hidden Line.

4. Window

   Select the **Architecture** ribbon.

   Select the **Window** tool from the Build panel.

5. 

   Set the Window Type to **Fixed: 36″ x 48″** [**M_Fixed: 0915 x 1220mm**].

6. Place two windows **5′ 6″** [**170 cm**] from the door's midpoint.

7. In plan view, the windows will be located as shown.

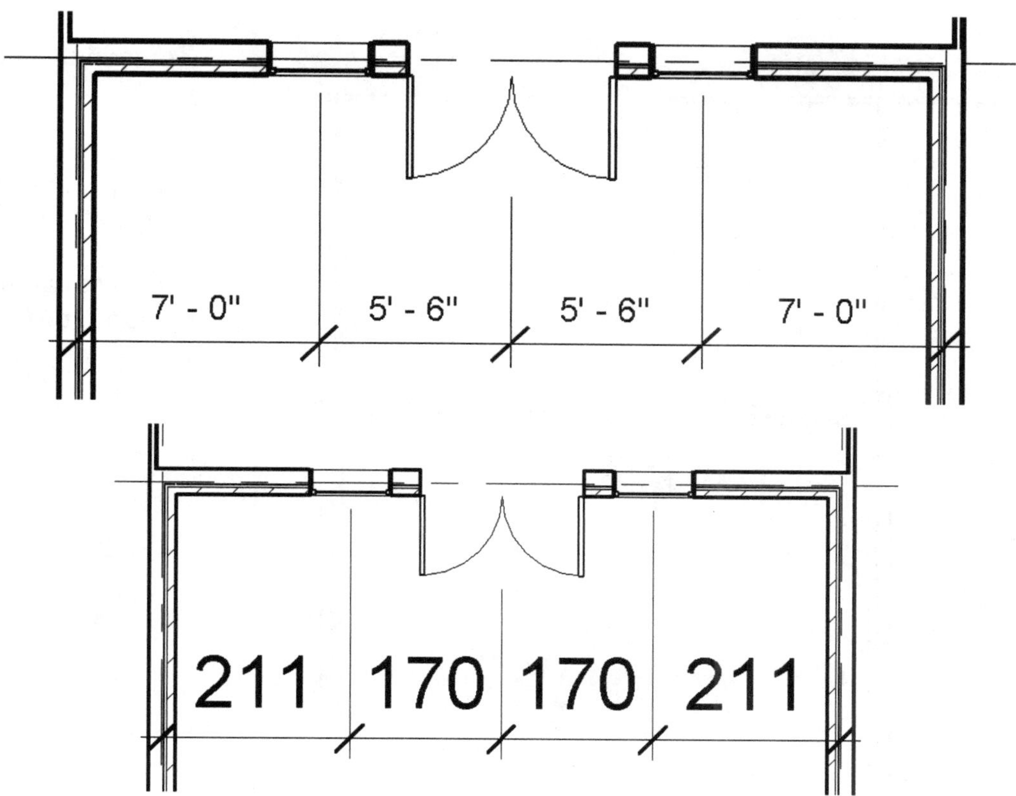

8. Activate the **South** Elevation.

9. Zoom into the entrance area.

10. Use the **ALIGN** tool to align the top of the windows with the top of the door.
Select the **Align** tool on the Modify panel on the Modify ribbon.

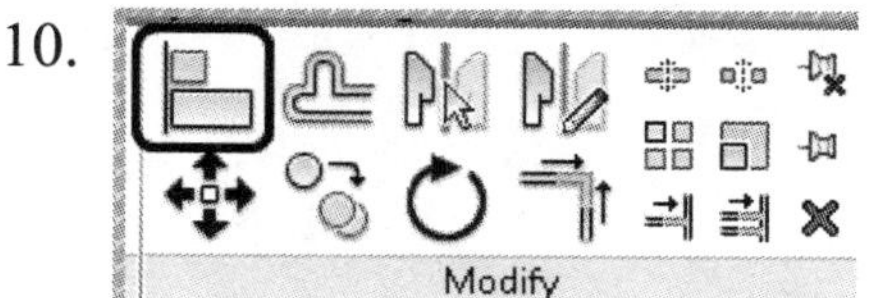

11. Enable **Multiple Alignment** on the Options bar.

12. Select the top of the door, then the top of the left window. Then, select the top of the second window.

    Right click and select **Cancel** twice to exit the command.

13. 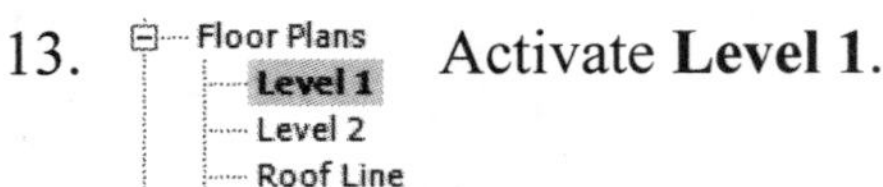

Activate **Level 1**.

14. 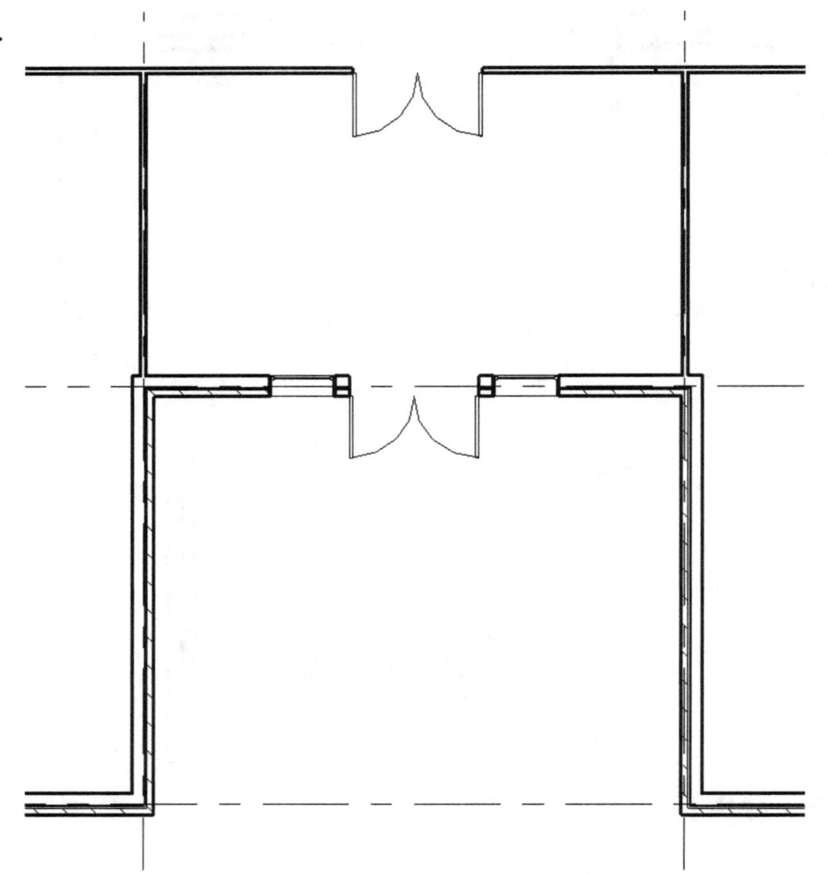

Zoom into the entry area.

We want the exterior walls to be centered on the grid lines.

We want the interior walls aligned to the interior face of the exterior walls.

15. 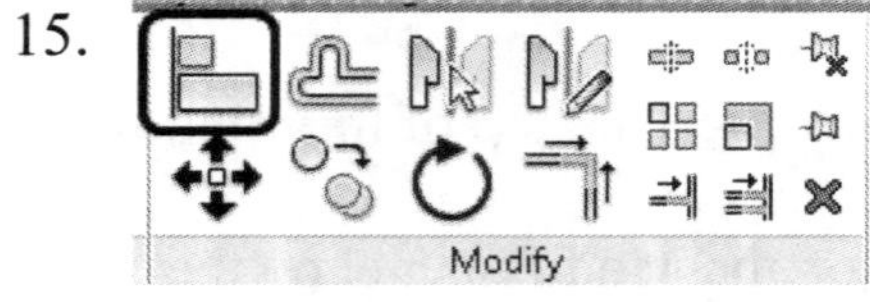

Activate the **Modify** ribbon.

Select the **ALIGN** tool.

16. Multiple Alignment Prefer: Wall faces

On the Options bar:
Set Prefer to Wall faces.

17. Select the interior face on the exterior wall.

Then select the corresponding face on the interior wall.

Repeat for the other side.

18. Activate the South elevation.

Elevations (Building Elevation)
East
North
South
West

19. Place a **Fixed: 36″ x 48″** [**M_Fixed: 0915 x 1220mm**] window on the Level 2 wall.

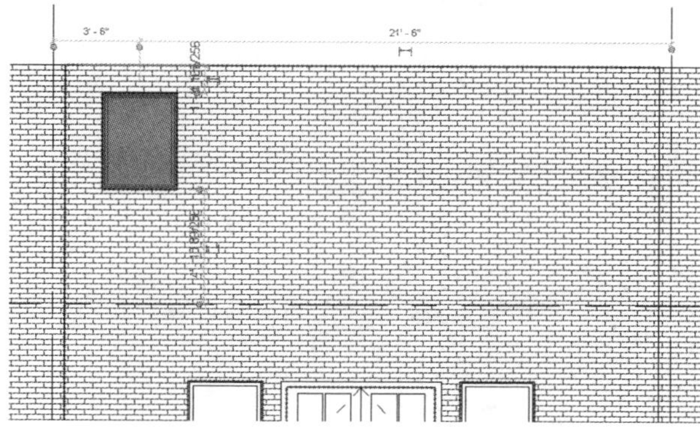

Locate the window 3′ 6″ [110 cm] to the right of grid D.

20. Select the window.
Select the **Array** tool from the Modify panel.

Modify

21. Enable **Group and Associate**.

Set the Number to **4**.
Enable Move to: **Last**.
Enable **Constrain**. *This forces your cursor to move orthogonally.*

22. Pick the midpoint of the top of the window as the base points.

Move the cursor 18′ [542 cm] towards the right.
Pick to place.

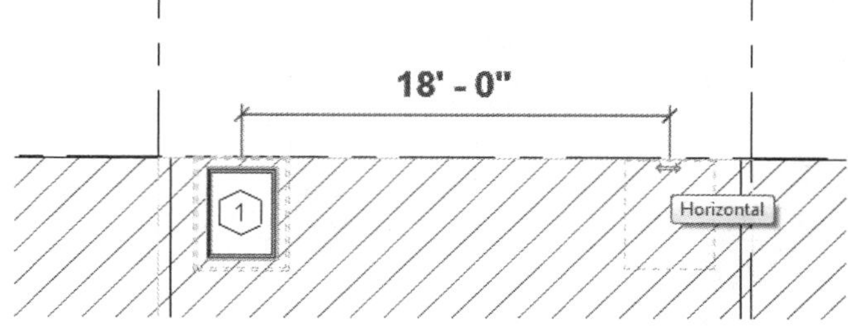

23. Press ENTER to accept the preview.

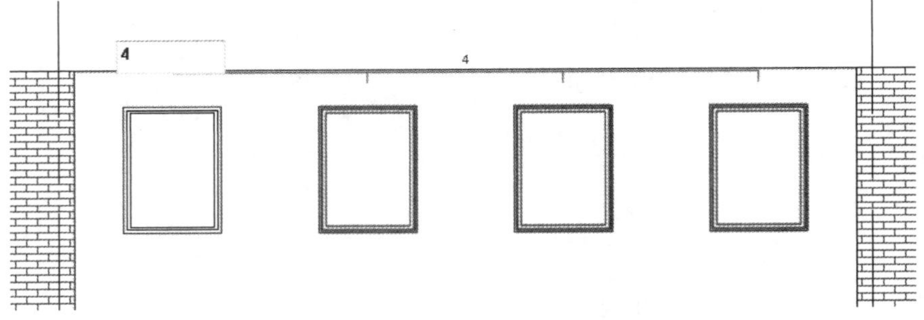

Left click anywhere in the display window to exit the command.

24. 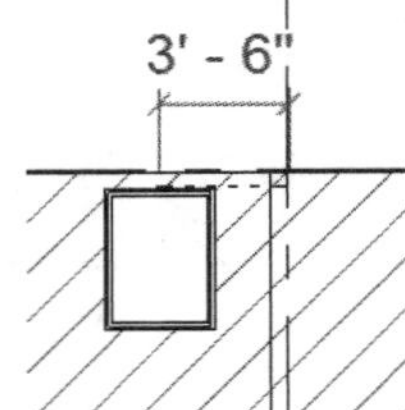

Use the **Measure** tool from the Quick Access tool bar to verify that the last window is 3′ 6″ [1110 cm] from grid E.

Verify that the four windows are equally spaced using the Measure tool.

25. 

Select the window group.

Select **Edit Group** from the Group panel.

26. 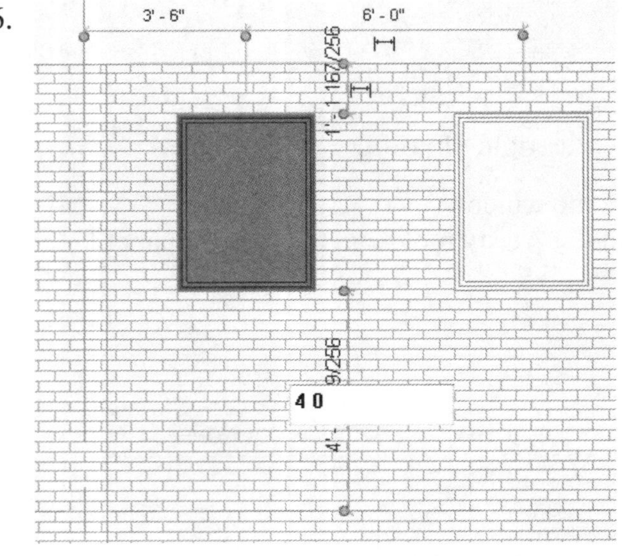

Select the first window.

27. 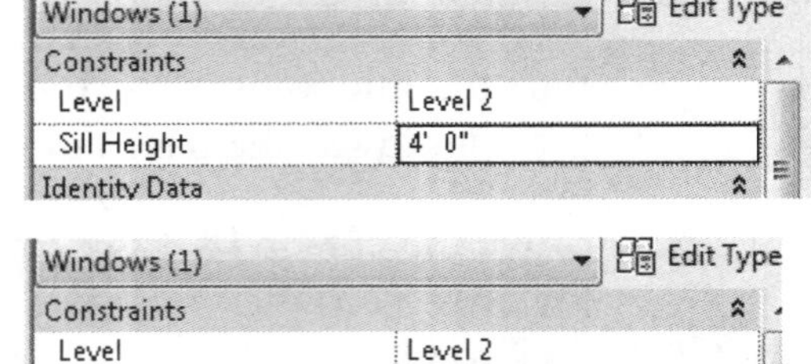

In the Properties pane:
Set the Sill Height to **4′ 0″** [**120 cm**].

28. 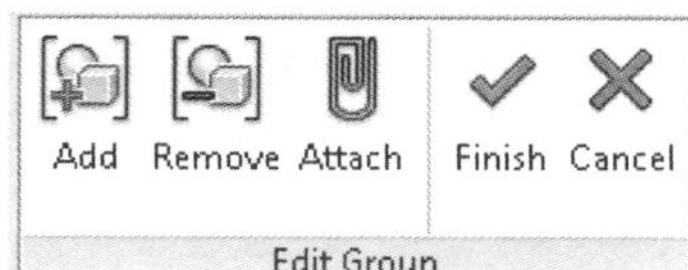

Select **Finish** from the Edit group toolbar.

29. The entire group of window adjusts.

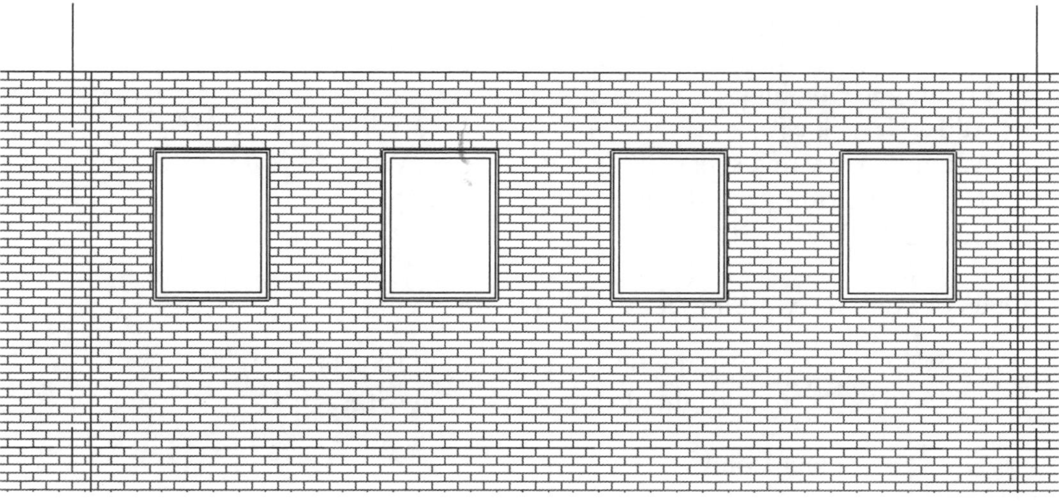

30. Save the file as *ex3-21.rvt.*

Challenge Exercise:

Add additional windows to complete the project.
Use the MIRROR and ARRAY tools to place windows.

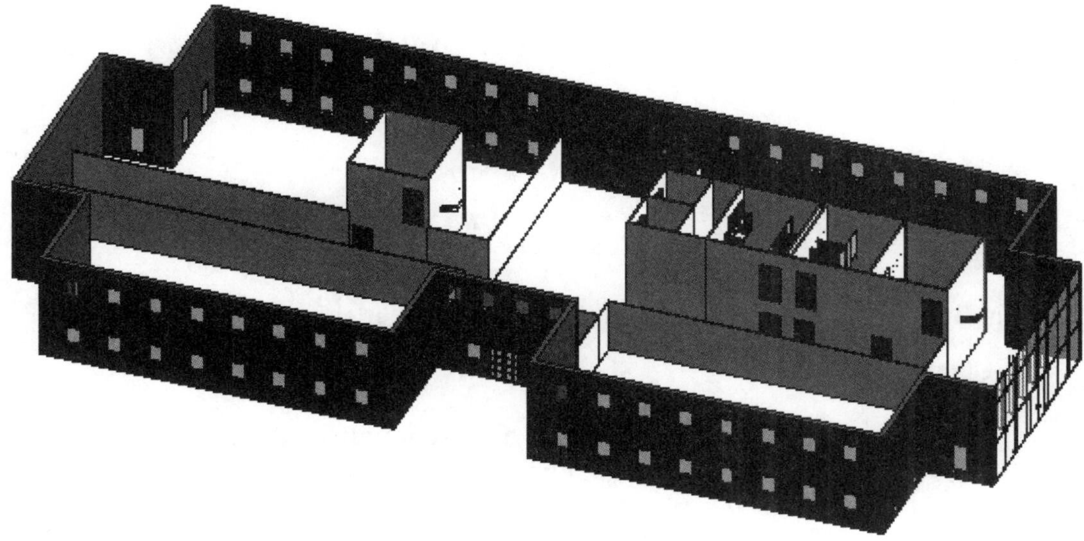

Elements can only be arrayed on the same work face.

Exercise 3-22:
Floor Plan Layout

Drawing Name: ex3-21.rvt
Estimated Time: 20 minutes

This exercise reinforces the following skills:

- Loading a Title block
- Add a New Sheet
- Adding a view to a sheet
- Adjusting Gridlines and Labels
- Hiding the Viewport

1. Open or continue working in *ex3-21.rvt.*

2. In the browser, highlight **Sheets**. Right click and select **New Sheet**.

3. Select **Load**.

4. 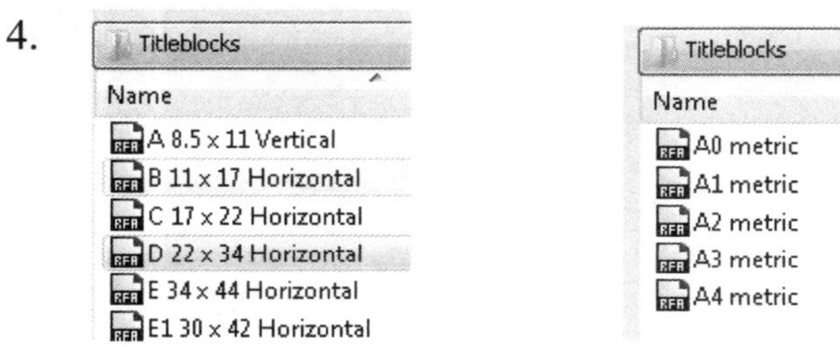

Browse to the *Titleblocks* folder.

Select the **D 22 x 34 Horizontal** [**A3 metric**] Titleblock.

Press **Open**.

5. 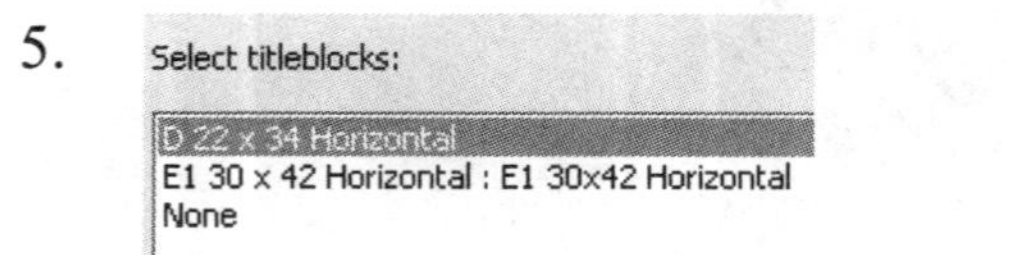

Highlight the **D 22 x 34 Horizontal** [**A3 metric**] Titleblock.

Press **OK**.

6. Highlight **A101-Unnamed** in the browser. Right click and select **Rename**.

7. 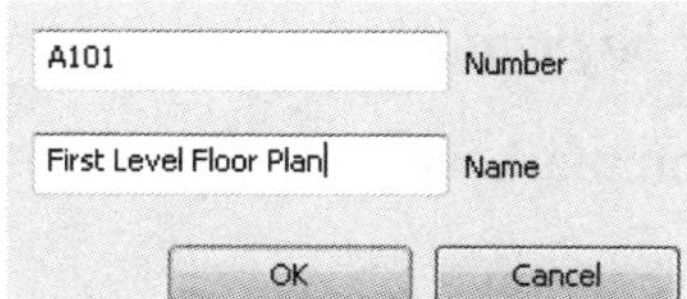

Change the Name of the Sheet to **First Level Floor Plan** and then press **OK**.

8. Drag and drop the Level 1 Floor Plan from the browser into the sheet.

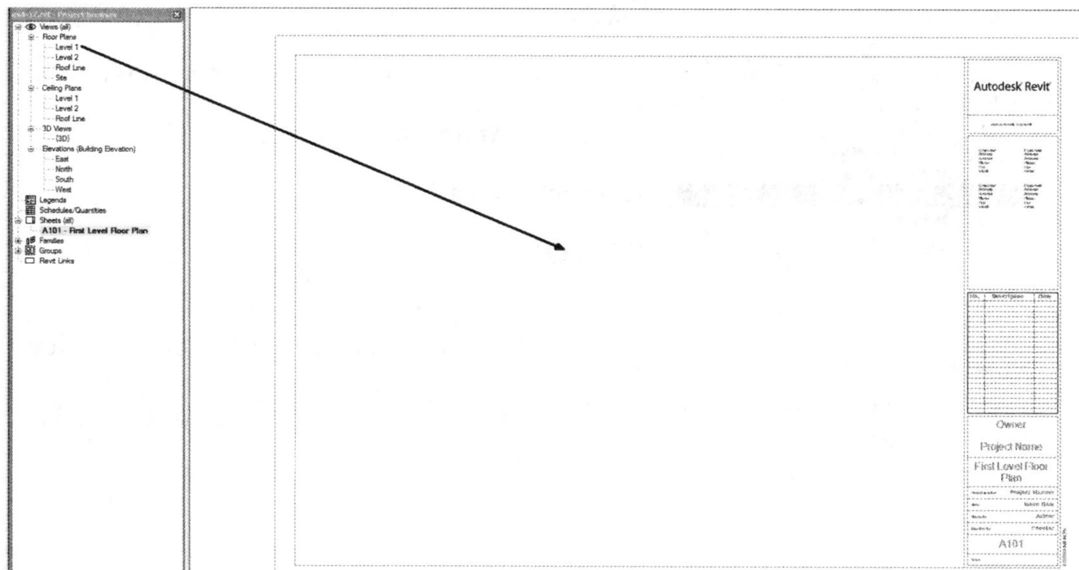

9. 1 Level 1
1/8" = 1'-0"

If you zoom into the View label, you see the scale is set to *1/8″= 1′-0″*.

You can adjust the position of the label, by picking on the label to activate the blue grip. Then hold the grip down with the left mouse button and drag to the desired location.

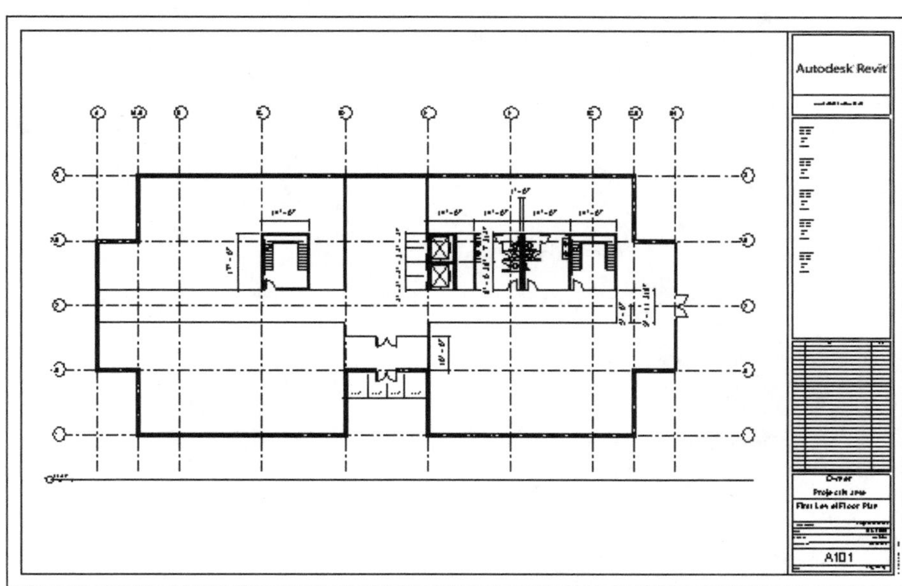

10. 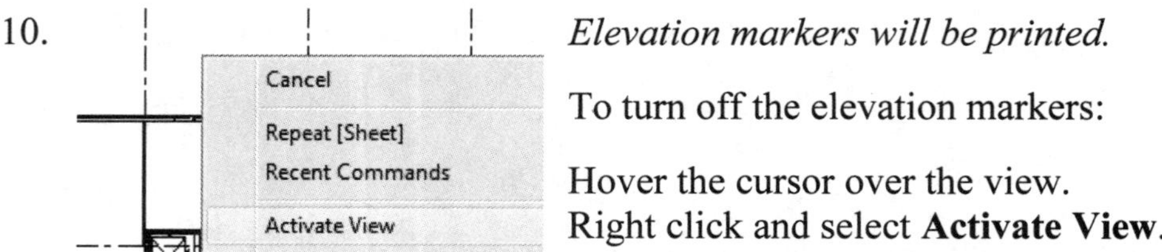

Elevation markers will be printed.

To turn off the elevation markers:

Hover the cursor over the view.
Right click and select **Activate View**.

This is similar to activating model space in AutoCAD.

11. 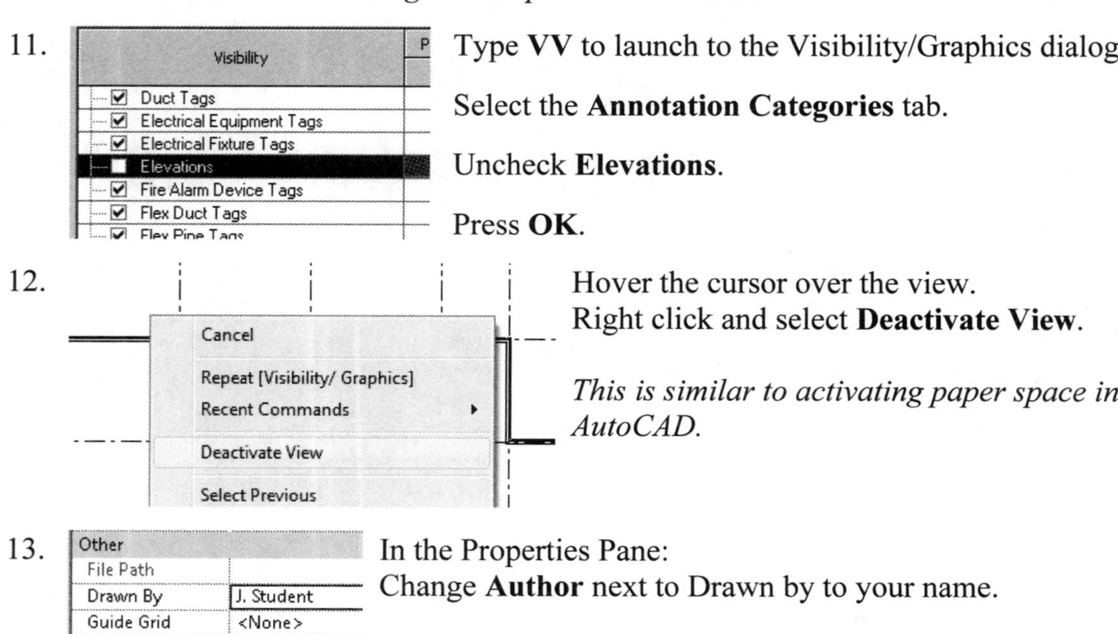

Type **VV** to launch to the Visibility/Graphics dialog.

Select the **Annotation Categories** tab.

Uncheck **Elevations**.

Press **OK**.

12. Hover the cursor over the view.
Right click and select **Deactivate View**.

This is similar to activating paper space in AutoCAD.

13. In the Properties Pane:
Change **Author** next to Drawn by to your name.

14. The title block updates with your name.

15. Save as *ex3-22.rvt*.

Additional Projects

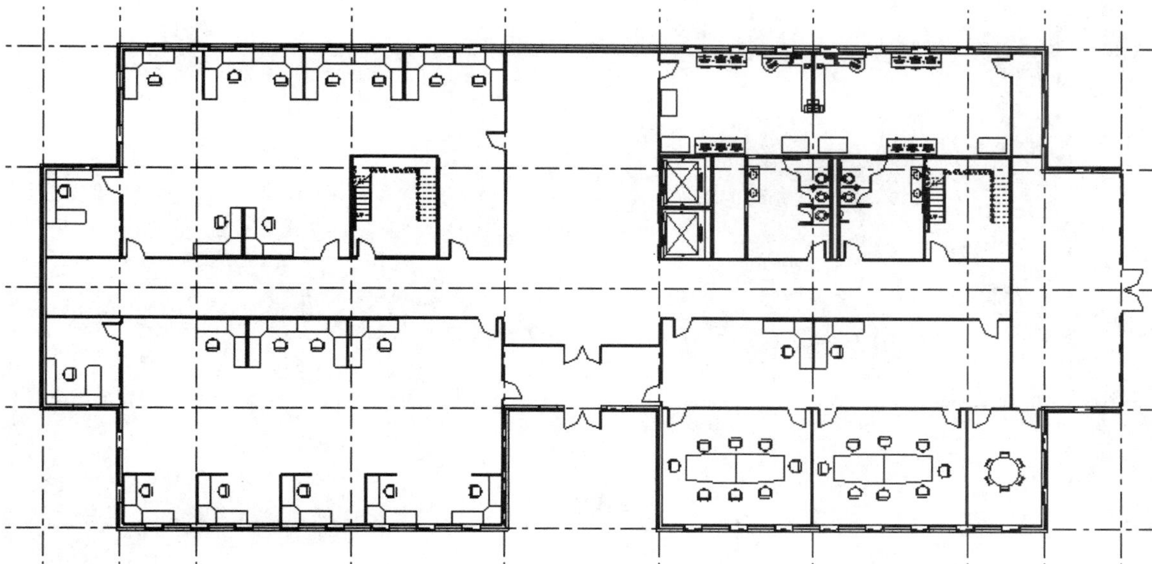

1) Duplicate the Level 1 Floor plan and create an office layout similar to the one shown.

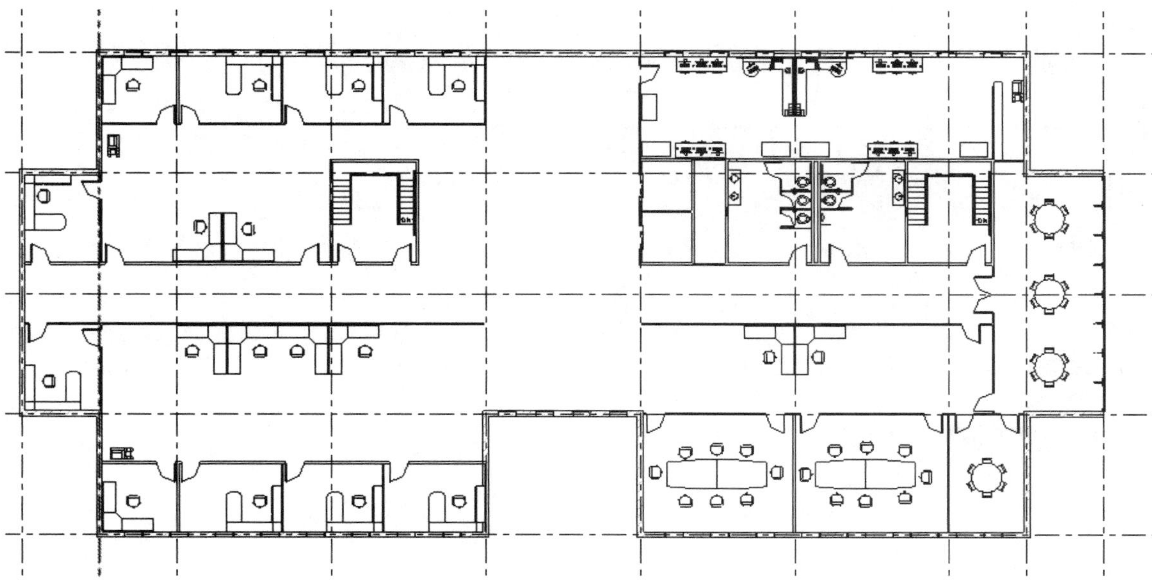

2) Duplicate the Level 2 Floor plan and create an office layout similar to the one shown.

3) On Level 2, in the cafeteria area add furniture groups using a table and chairs. Add vending machines. (Families can be located on the publisher's website.)

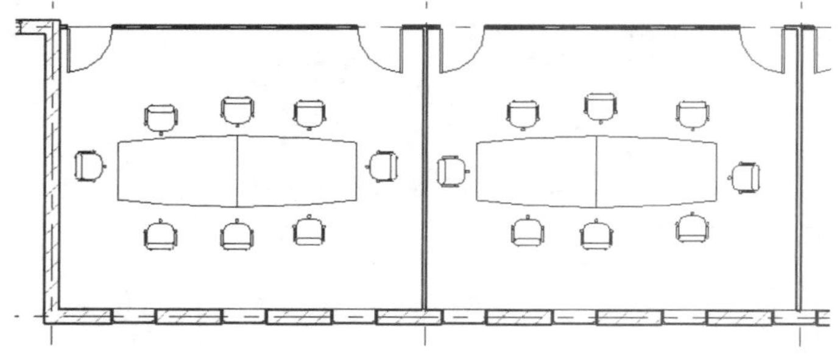

4) Furnish the two conference rooms on Level 2.

Add tables and chairs to the two conference room areas.

Use Group to create furniture combinations that you can easily copy and move.

There are conference table group families available on the publisher's website.

5) Furnish the office cubicles. Families can be found on the publisher's website.

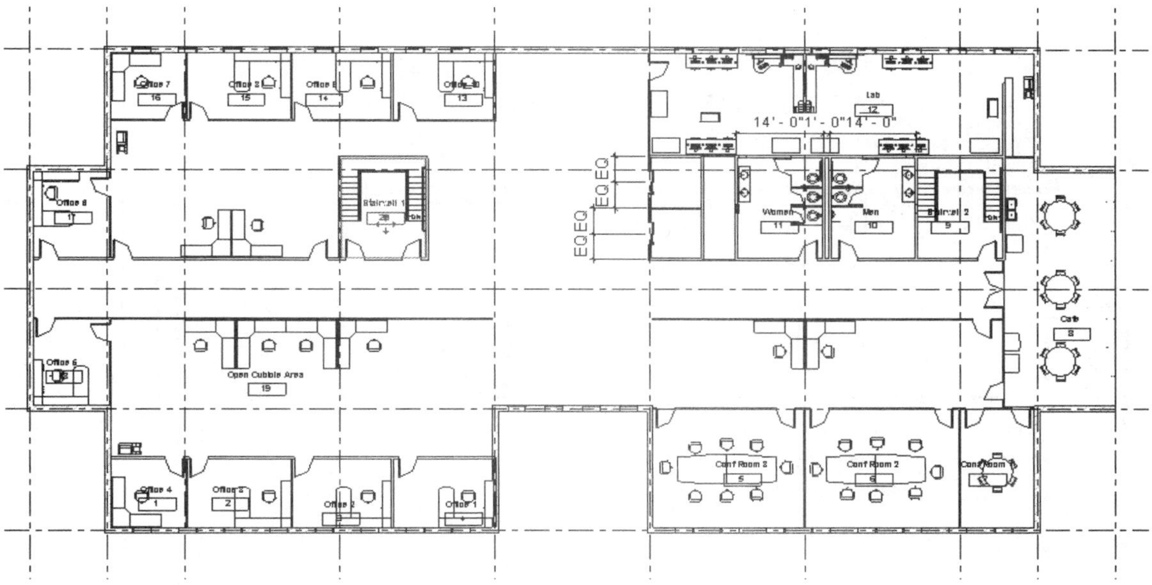

6) Add room tags to the rooms on Level 2.
Create a room schedule

<Room Schedule>		
A	B	C
Number	Name	Area
1	Office 4	136 SF
2	Office 3	187 SF
3	Office 2	181 SF
4	Office 1	183 SF
5	Conf Room 3	470 SF
6	Conf Room 2	479 SF
7	Conf Room 1	233 SF
8	Cafe	708 SF
9	Stairwell 2	229 SF
10	Men	228 SF
11	Women	228 SF
12	Lab	1058 SF
13	Office 10	183 SF
14	Office 9	181 SF
15	Office 8	187 SF
16	Office 7	136 SF
17	Office 6	176 SF
18	Office 5	176 SF
19	Open Cubicle A	6168 SF
20	Stairwell 1	225 SF

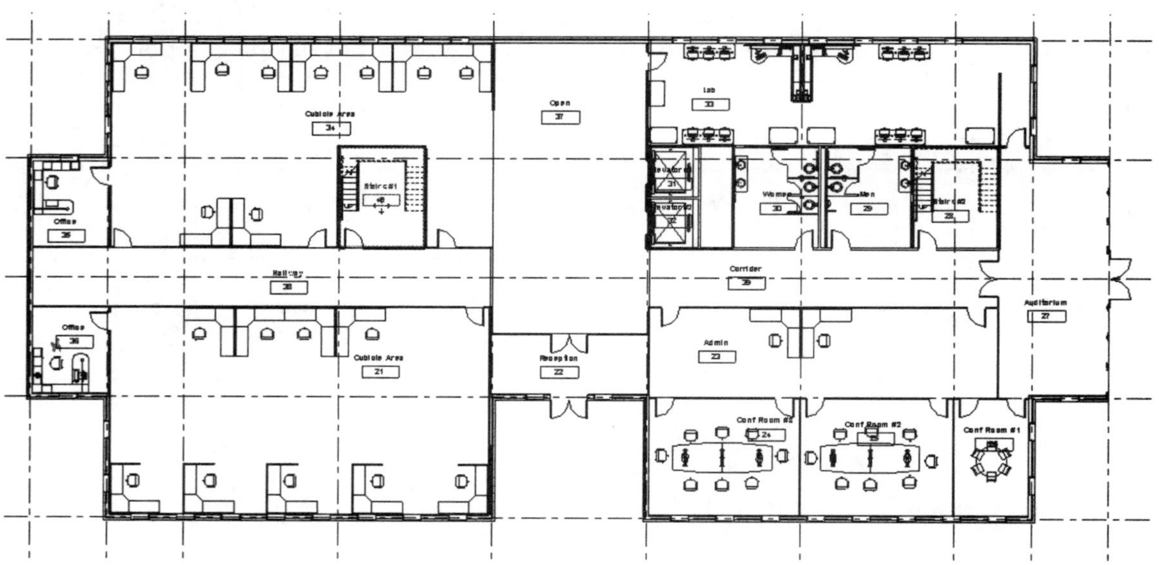

7) Use the Room Separator tool and the Room Tag tool to add rooms and room tags to Level 1.

Lesson 3 Quiz

True or False

1. Changes in the settings for one view do not affect other views.

Multiple Choice

2. When placing doors, which key is pressed to flip orientation?
   Choose one answer.

   A. Ctl+S
   B. H
   C. Spacebar
   D. F
   E. L or R

3. Which of the following is NOT an example of bidirectional associativity?
   Choose one answer.

   A. Draw a wall in plan and it appears in all other views
   B. Add an annotation in a view
   C. Change a door type in a schedule and all the views update
   D. Flip a section line and all views update

4. Curtain Grids can be defined using all of the following except:
   Choose one answer.

   A. Vertical line
   B. Angled line
   C. Horizontal line
   D. Partial line

5. Which of the following are part of the sketch when you create custom stairs?
   Choose two answers.

   A. Run
   B. Railing
   C. Riser
   D. Boundary
   E. Tread width

6. Which command is used to place a free-standing element, such as furniture?
   Choose one answer.

   A. Detail Component
   B. Load Family
   C. Repeating Detail
   D. Model In Place
   E. Place a Component

7. Select the TWO which are Type properties of a wall:
   Choose at least two answers.

   A. FUNCTION
   B. COARSE FILL PATTERN
   C. BASE CONSTRAINT
   D. TOP CONSTRAINT
   E. LOCATION LINE

8. Which is NOT true about placing windows?
   Choose one answer.

   A. Windows require a wall as a host
   B. Windows cut an opening in the wall when placed
   C. The location of the exterior side of the window can be selected
   D. Sill height is adjustable in plan view

ANSWERS:

1) T; 2) C; 3) B; 4) B; 5) C & D; 6) E; 7) A & B; 8) D

Lesson 4
Materials

Materials are used:

- For Rendering
- For Scheduling
- To control hatch patterns
- To control appearance of objects

Revit divides materials into TWO locations:

- Materials in the Project
- Autodesk Asset Library

You can also create one or more custom libraries for materials you want to use in more than one project. You can only edit materials in the project or in the custom library – Autodesk Materials are read-only.

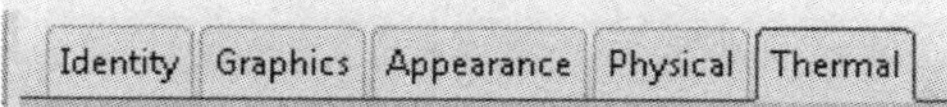

Materials have FIVE asset definitions – Identity, Graphics, Appearance, Physical and Thermal. Materials do not have to be fully defined to be used – YOU DON'T HAVE TO DEFINE ALL FIVE ASSETS. Each asset contributes to the definition of a single material.

You can define Appearance, Physical, and Thermal Assets independently without assigning/associating it to a material. You can assign the same assets to different materials. An asset can exist without being assigned to a material BUT a material must have at least THREE assets (Identity, Graphics, and Appearance). Assets can be deleted from a material in a project or in a user library, but you cannot remove or delete assets from materials in locked material libraries, such as the Autodesk Materials library, the AEC Materials library, or any locked user library. You can delete assets from a user library – BUT be careful because that asset might be used somewhere!

You can only duplicate, replace or delete an asset if it is in the project or in a user library. The Autodesk Asset Library is "read-only" and can only be used to check-out or create materials.

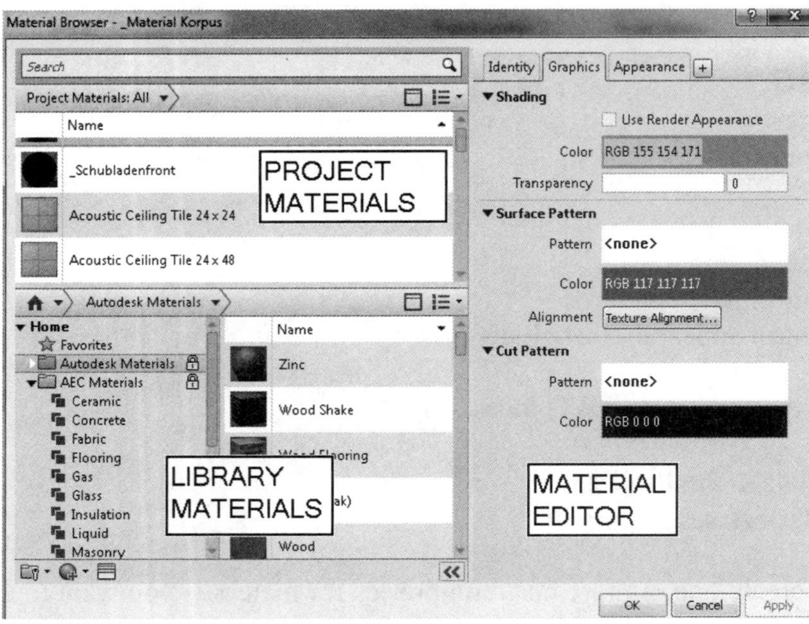

The Material Browser is divided into three distinct panels.
The Project Materials panel lists all the materials available in the project.
The Material Libraries list any libraries available.
The Material Editor allows you to modify the definition of materials in the project or in custom libraries.

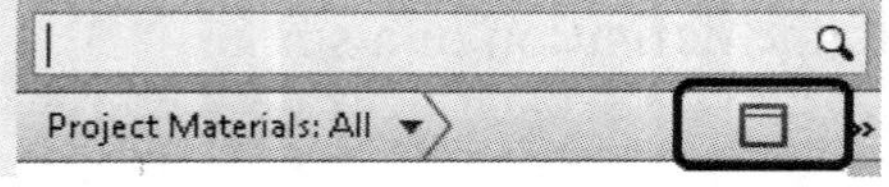

The search field allows you to search materials using keywords, description or comments.

The button indicated toggles the display of the Material Libraries panel.

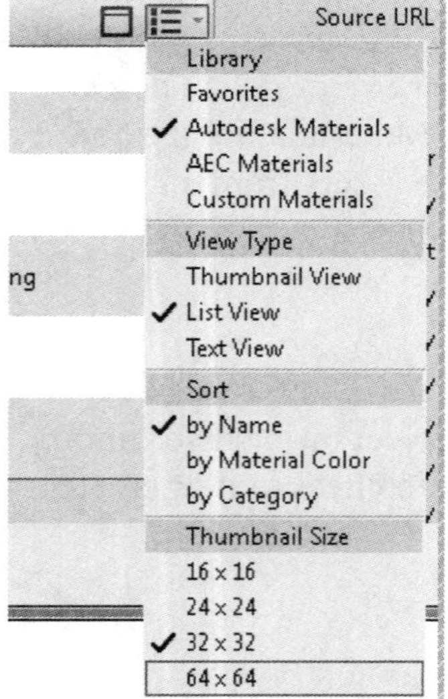

The View control button allows you to control how materials are sorted and displayed in the Material Libraries panel.

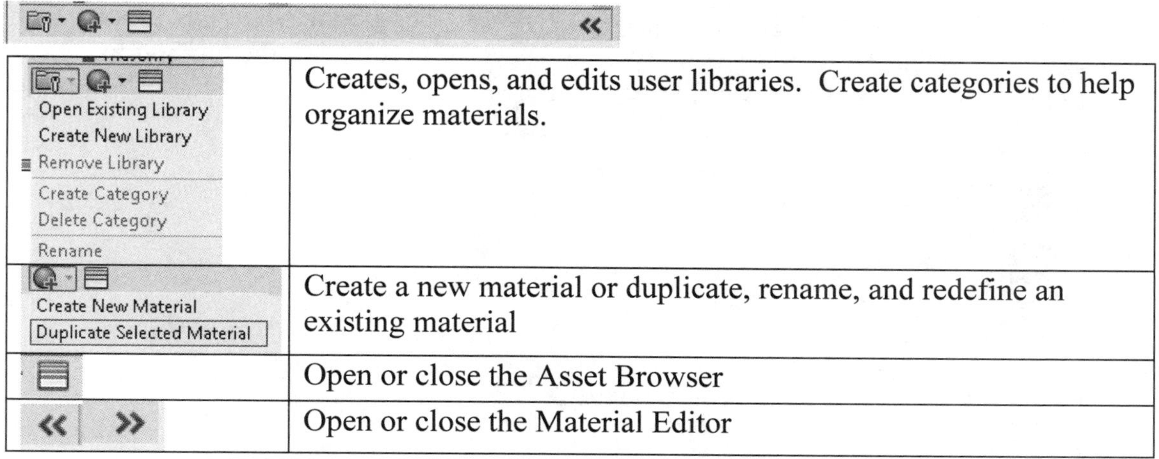

Open Existing Library Create New Library Remove Library Create Category Delete Category Rename	Creates, opens, and edits user libraries. Create categories to help organize materials.
Create New Material Duplicate Selected Material	Create a new material or duplicate, rename, and redefine an existing material
	Open or close the Asset Browser
« »	Open or close the Material Editor

Exercise 4-1

Modifying the Material Browser Interface

Drawing Name: ex3-22.rvt
Estimated Time: 10 minutes

This exercise reinforces the following skills:

- Navigating the Material Browser and Asset Browser

1. Activate the **Manage** ribbon.

   Select the **Materials** tool.

2. Make the Material Browser appear as shown.

   Toggle the Materials Library pane OFF by selecting the top button.

   Collapse the Material Editor by selecting the << Arrow on the bottom of the dialog.

3. 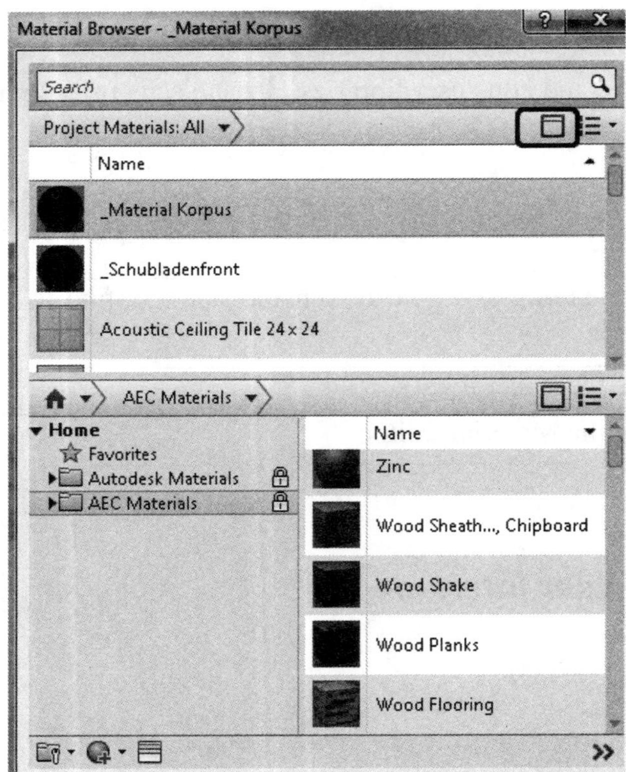

Toggle the Materials Library ON by selecting the top button.

4. Select the toggle button indicated to hide the library names.

5. 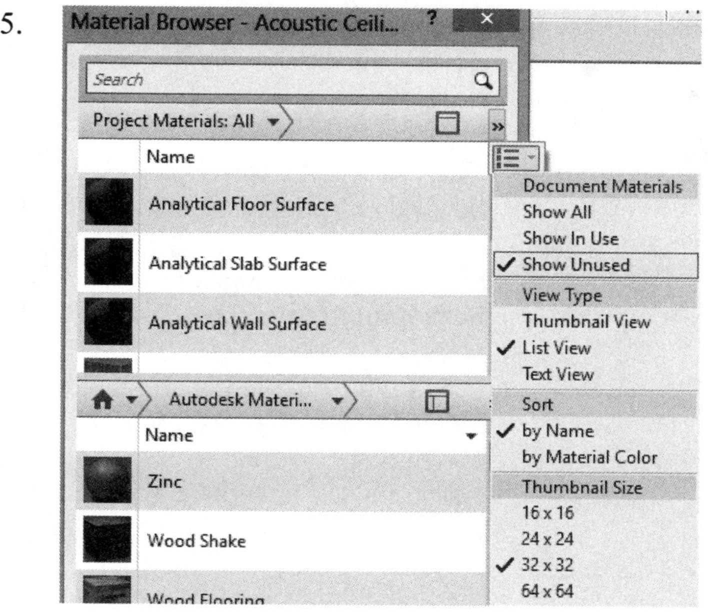

In the Project Materials panel, set the view to **Show Unused**.

Scroll through the list to see what materials are not being used in your project.

6. 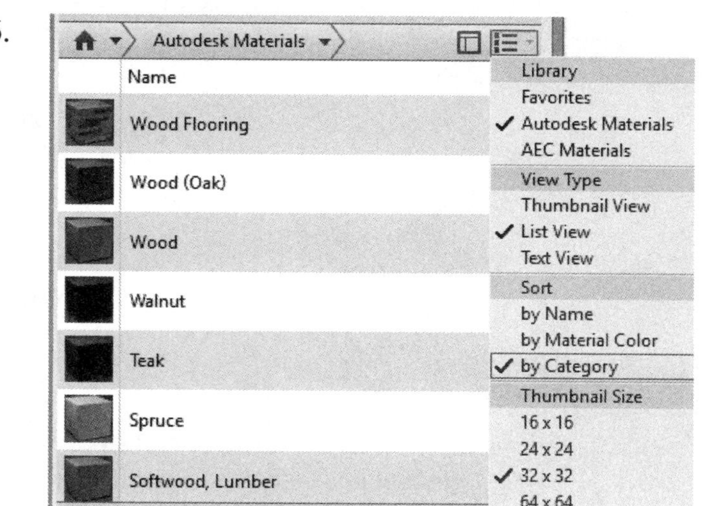

In the Material Library pane, change the view to **sort by Category**.

7. Close the Material dialog.

The Asset Browser has up to five tabs.

The Identity Tab

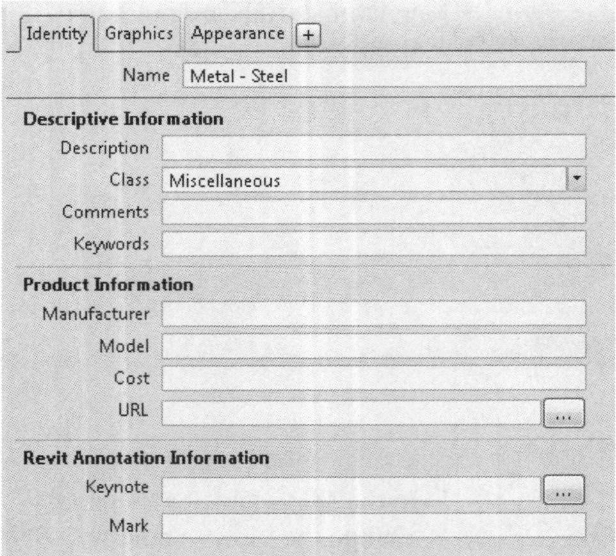

The value in the Description field can be used in Material tags.

Using comments and keywords can be helpful for searches.

Product Information is useful for material take-off scheduling

Assigning the keynote and a mark for the legend makes keynote creation easier.

The Graphics Tab

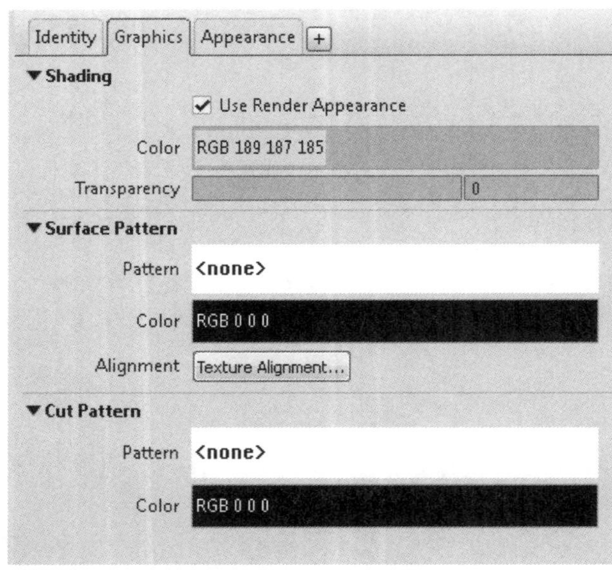

Shading –
Determines the color and appearance of a material when view mode is SHADED.

If you have Use Render Appearance unchecked – then the material will show a color of the material when the display is set to Shaded.

If Use Render Appearance is checked – then the material uses the Render Appearance Color when the display is set to Shaded.

Comparing the appearance of the model when Render Appearance is disabled or enabled:

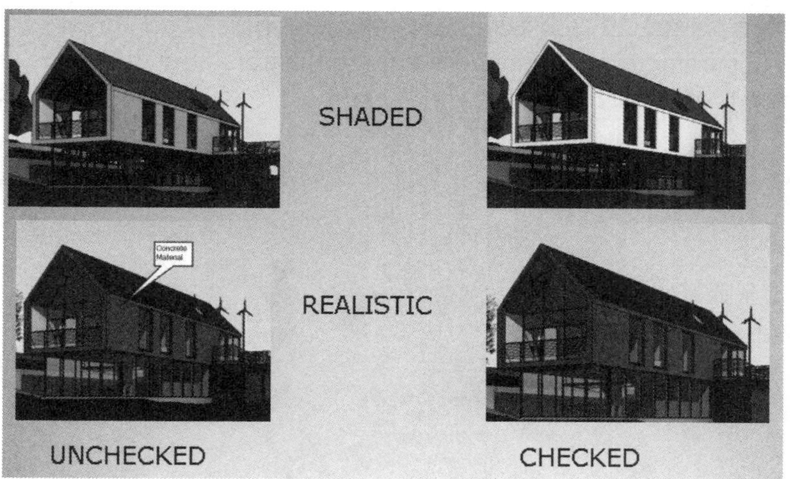

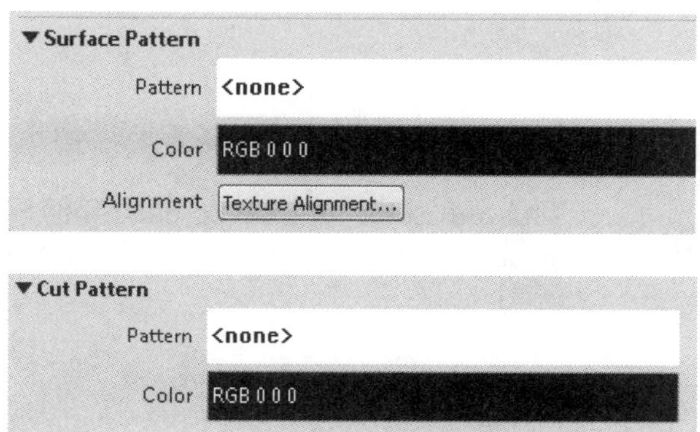

Surface Pattern will be displayed in all the following Display settings: Wireframe/Hidden/Shaded/Realistic/ Consistent Colors.

Cut Patterns appear in section views.

The Appearance Tab

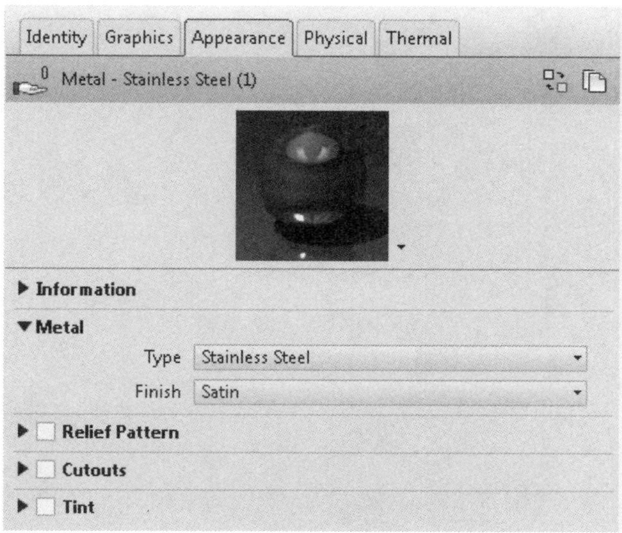

Appearance controls how material is displayed in a rendered view, Realistic view, or Ray Trace view.

A zero next to the hand means that only the active/selected material uses the appearance definition.

Different material types can have different appearance parameters.

The assigned class controls what parameters are assigned to the material. If you create a custom class, it will use generic parameters. The images below illustrate how different classes use different appearance parameters.

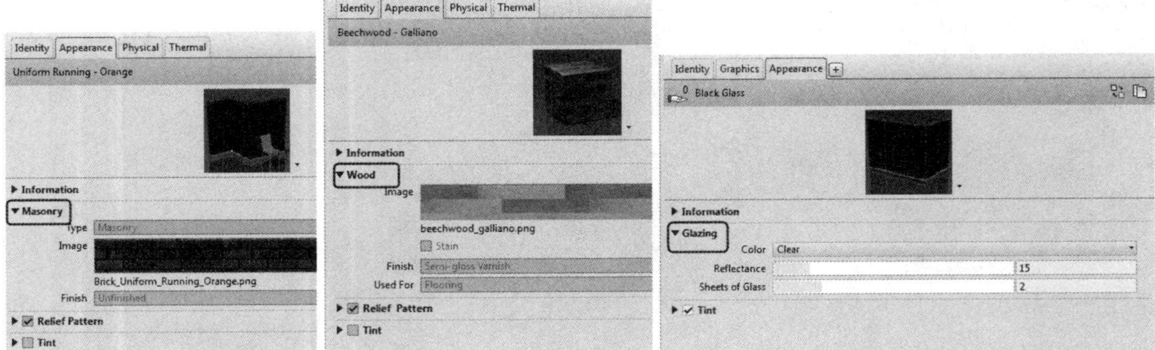

The Physical Tab

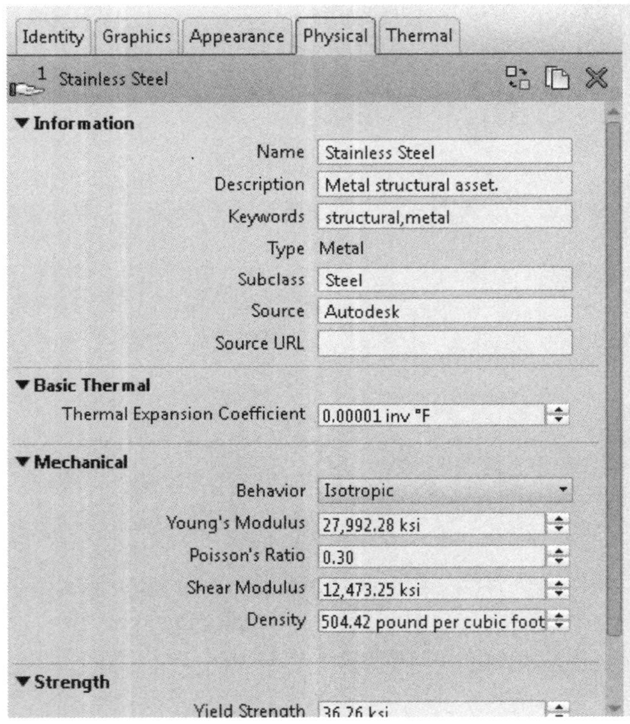

This information may be used for structural and thermal analysis of the model.

You can only modify physical properties of materials in the project or in a user library.

The Thermal Tab

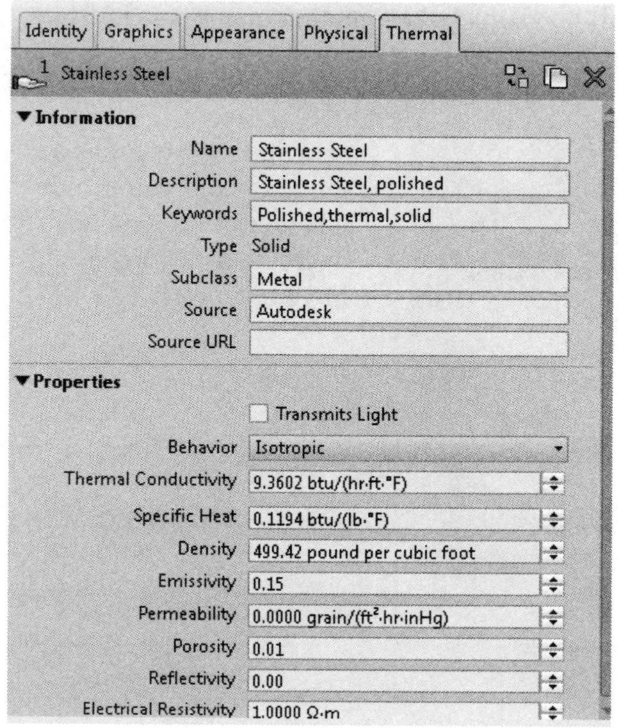

The Thermal tab is only available in Revit. (The Autodesk Material Library is shared by any installed Autodesk software, such as AutoCAD.)

This information is used for thermal analysis and energy consumption.

Material libraries organize materials by category or class.

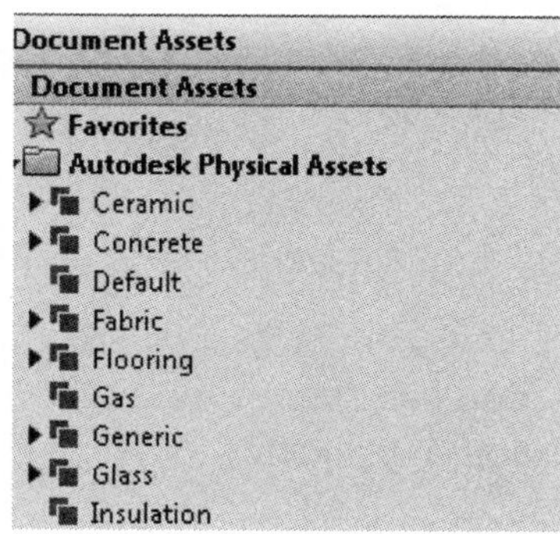

Material structural classes are organized into the following types:

- Basic
- Generic
- Metal
- Concrete
- Wood
- Liquid
- Gas
- Plastic

This family parameter controls the hidden view display of structural elements. If the Structural Material Class of an element is set to Concrete or Precast, then it will display as hidden. If it is set to Steel or Wood, it will be visible when another element is in front of it. If it is set to Unassigned, the element will not display if hidden by another element.

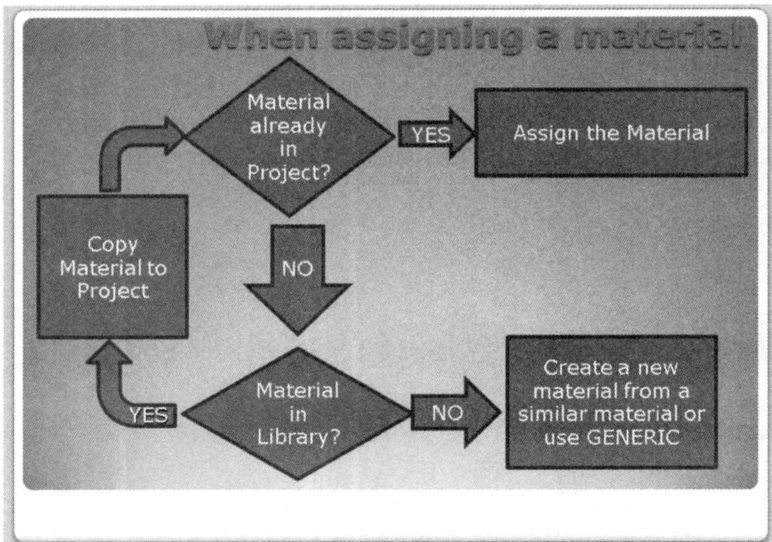

Use this flow chart as a guide to help you decide whether or not you need to create a new material in your project.

Exercise 4-2

Copy a Material from a Library to a Project

Drawing Name: ex3-22.rvt
Estimated Time: 10 minutes

In order to use or assign a material, it must exist in the project. You can search for a material and, if one exists in one of the libraries, copy it to your active project.

This exercise reinforces the following skills:

- Copying materials from the Materials Library
- Modifying materials in the project

1. Go to the Manage ribbon.
2. Materials — Select the **Materials** tool.
3. oak — Type **oak** in the search field.

4. The active project has one oak material called Oak Flooring.

5. 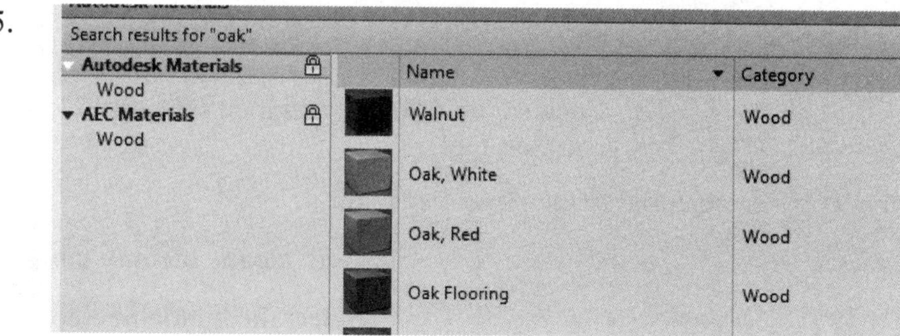

If you look in the Materials Library pane, you see that more oak materials are listed.

6. 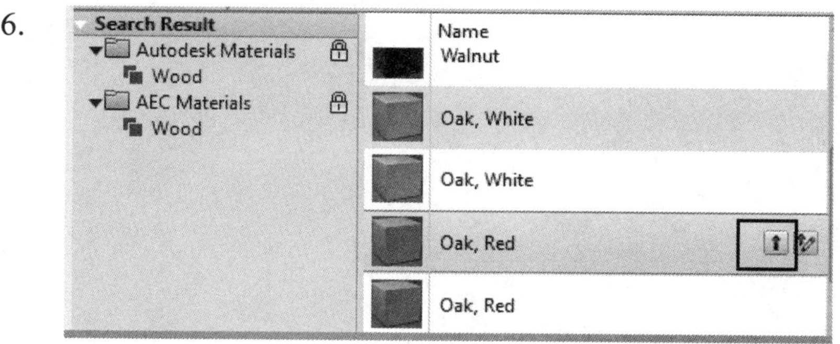

Select the Up arrow to copy the Oak, Red material from the library to the active project.

7. 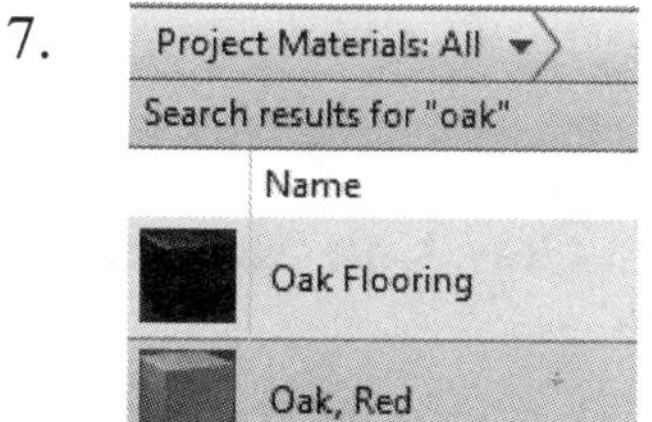

The material is now available for use in the project.

8. Type **brick** in the search field.

9. There are one or two brick materials in the project.

Users working in metric will only see one brick material because only one brick material is pre-loaded in the metric template.

10. 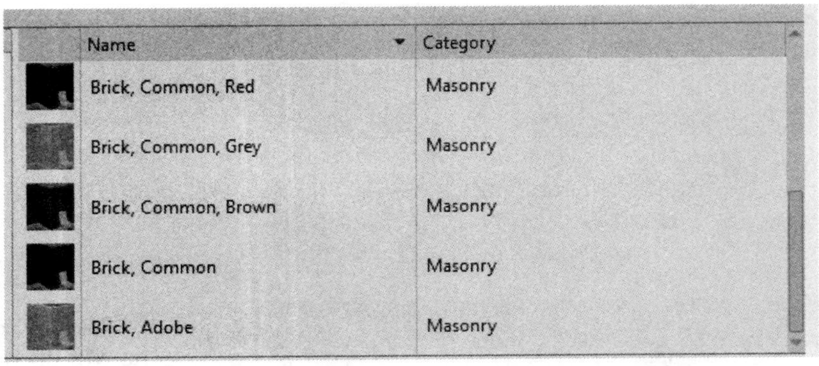 There are several more brick materials in the library.

11.  Locate Brick, Adobe and then select the Copy and Edit tool.

This allows you to copy the material to the project and edit it.

12. 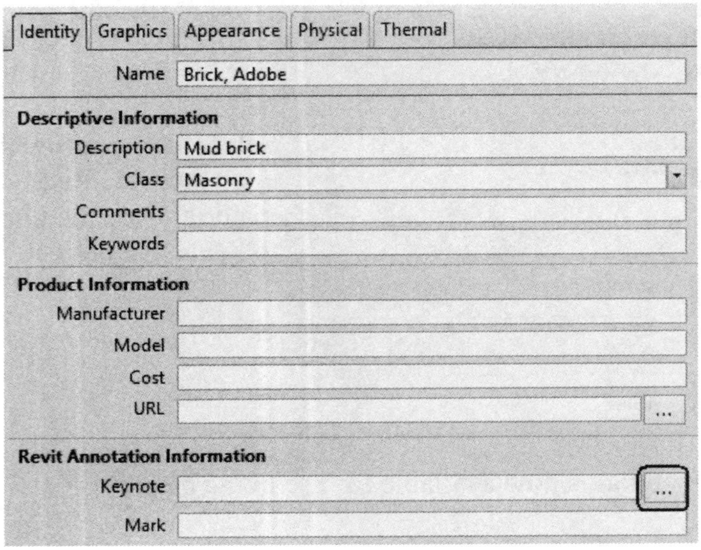 Activate the Identity tab.

Select the button next to **Keynote**.

13. 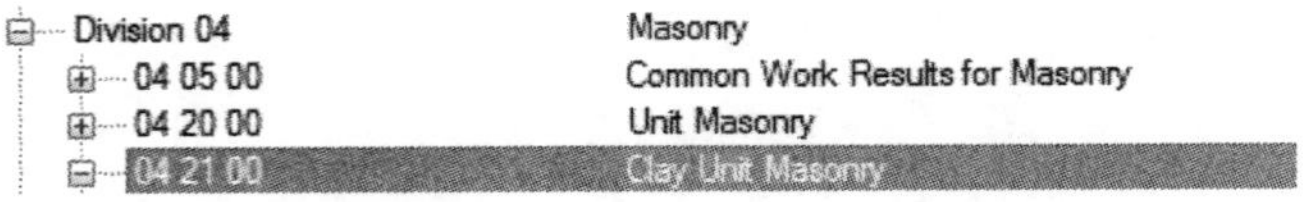 Highlight **Clay Unit Masonry**. Press **OK**.

14. 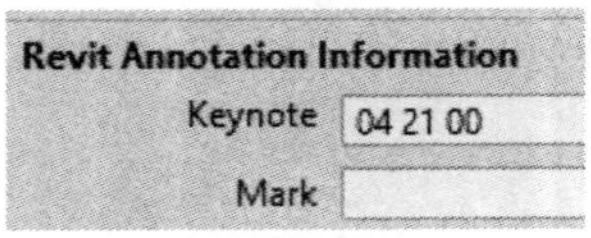 The keynote number auto-fills the text box.

15. 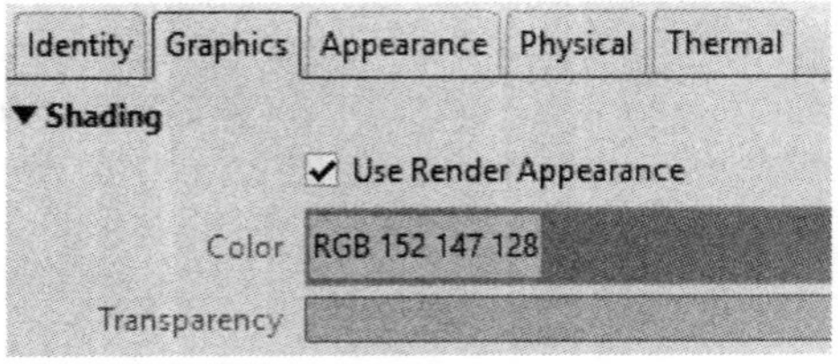 Activate the Graphics tab.
Enable **Use Render Appearance**.

16. Left click on **<none>** in the Pattern box under Surface Pattern and select **Masonry – Brick**.

    Press **OK**.

17. 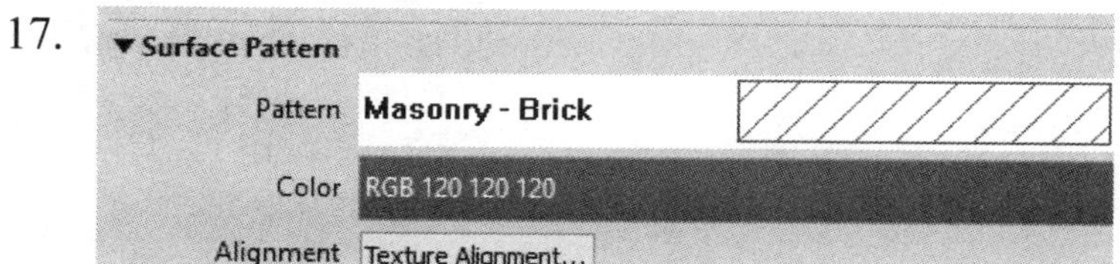

    The fill pattern now appears in the Pattern box.

18. 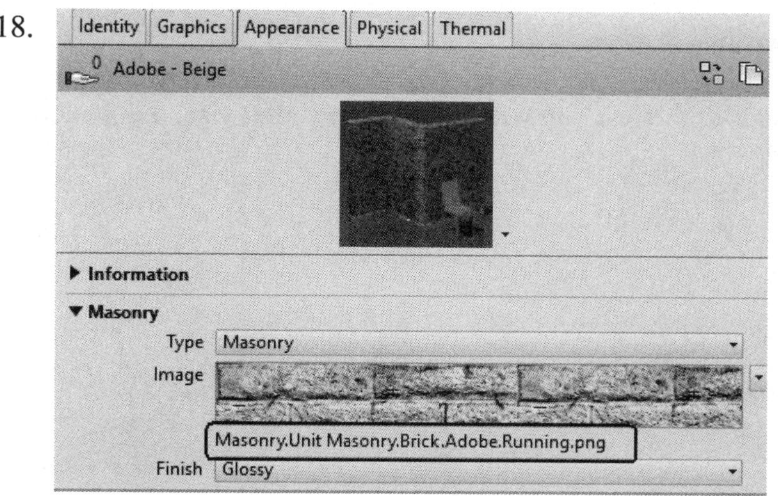

    Activate the **Appearance** tab.

    Left click on the image name.

19. Locate the *adobe brick* image file.
    Press **Open**.

20. Change the Finish to **Unfinished**.

    Press **OK**.

21. Close the Materials dialog.

22. Save as *ex4-2.rvt*.

You have modified the material definition in the project ONLY and not in the Materials library.

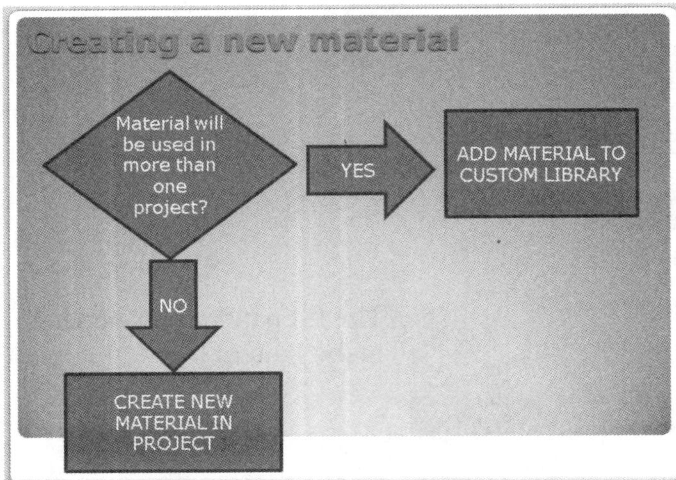

If you need to create a new material, you should first consider whether the material might be used in more than one project.

If the material may be used again, add the material to your custom library.

Steps for creating a new material:

1. Locate a material similar to the one you want, if you can (otherwise, use Generic)
2. Duplicate the material
3. Rename
4. Modify the Identity, Graphics, and Appearance tabs
5. Apply to the object
6. Preview using Realistic or Raytrace
7. Adjust the definition as needed

Exercise 4-3
Create a Custom Material Library

Drawing Name: ex3-22.rvt
Estimated Time: 5 minutes

This exercise reinforces the following skills:

- Materials Library

1. Go to the Manage ribbon.
2. Select the **Materials** tool.
3. At the bottom of the dialog:

   Select **Create New Library**.
4. Browse to where you are storing your work. Assign your materials file a name, like *Custom Materials*.

   Press **Save**.
5. 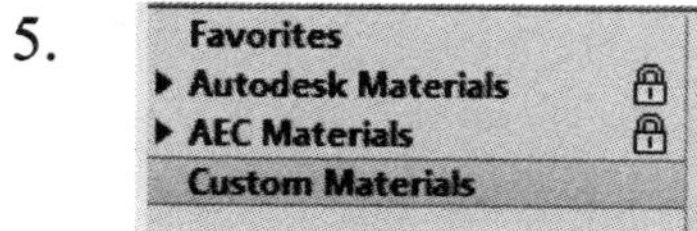

   The custom library is now listed in the Libraries pane.

   Note that there is no lock next to the Custom Materials library because this library can be edited.

Exercise 4-4
Create Paint Materials

Drawing Name: ex3-22.rvt
Estimated Time: 30 minutes

This exercise reinforces the following skills:

- Materials

1. Go to the Manage ribbon.
2.  Materials — Select the **Materials** tool.
3. 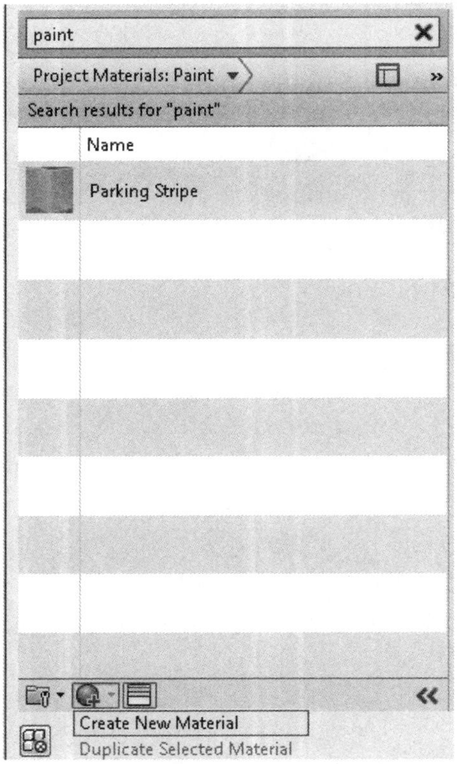 Type **Paint** in the search text box.

   There are no paints currently defined in the project.

   Select the Create **New Material** tool at the bottom of the dialog.

paint
Project Materials: Paint
Search results for "paint"
Name
Parking Stripe
Create New Material
Duplicate Selected Material

4. Activate the **Identity** tab.
In the Name field, type **Paint - SW6126NavajoWhite**.
In the Description field, type **Sherwin Williams Paint – Interior**.
Select **Paint** for the Class under the drop-down list.
In the Manufacturer field, type **Sherwin Williams**.
In the Model field, type **SW6126NavajoWhite**.

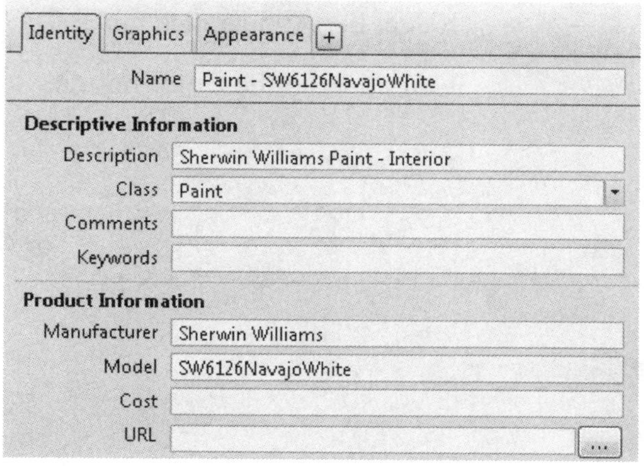

5. Select the **... browse** button next to Keynote.

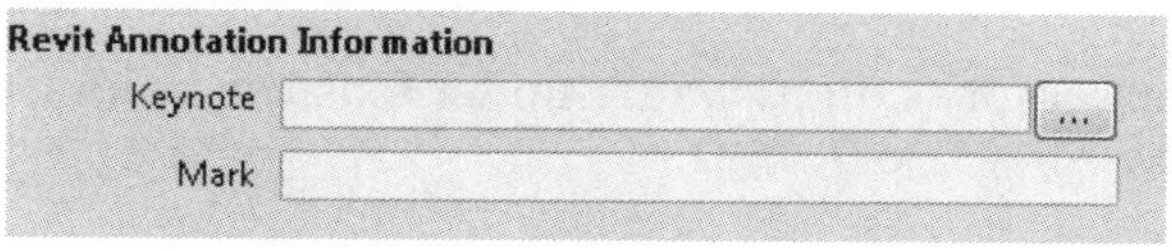

6. Select the **09 91 00.A2 Semi-Gloss Paint Finish** in the list.

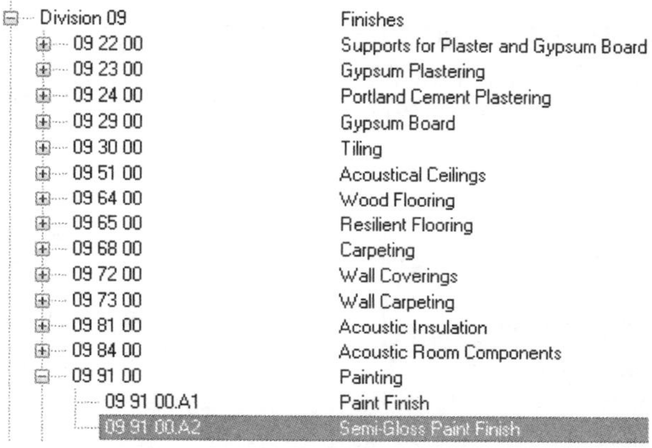

   Press **OK**.

7. Note the keynote information auto-fills based on the selection.

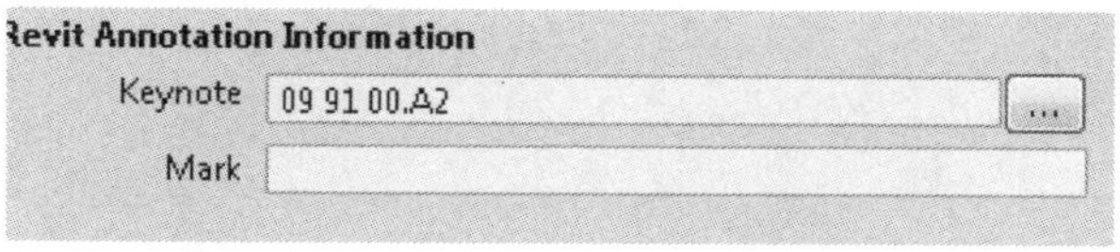

8. Activate the Graphics tab.

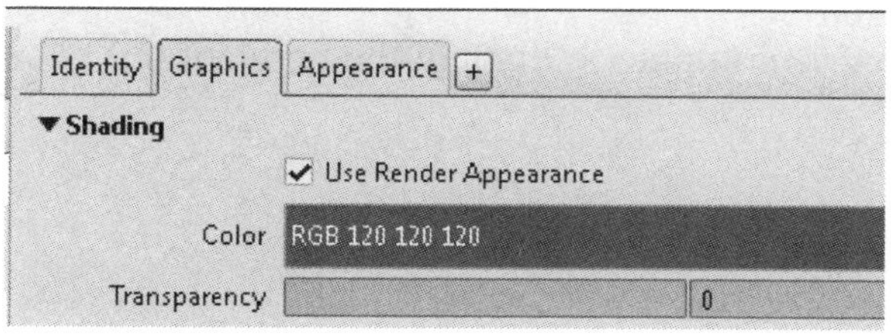

   Place a check on **Use Render Appearance for Shading**.

9. 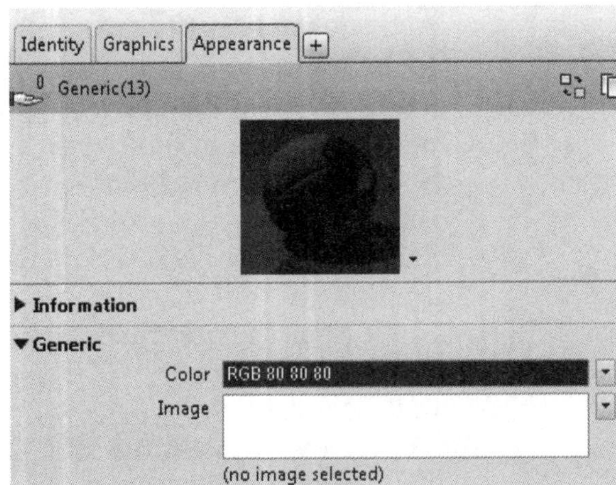

Select the Appearance tab.

Left click on the Color button.

10. Select an empty color swatch under Custom colors.

11. In the Red field, enter **234**.
In the Green field, enter **223**.
In the Blue field, enter **203**.

Press **Add**.

This matches Sherwin William's Navajo White, SW6126.

12. Select the color swatch.

Press **OK**.

13. The preview will update to display the new color.

Press **OK**.

14. Click on the bottom of the Material Browser to add a material.

15. On the Identity tab:

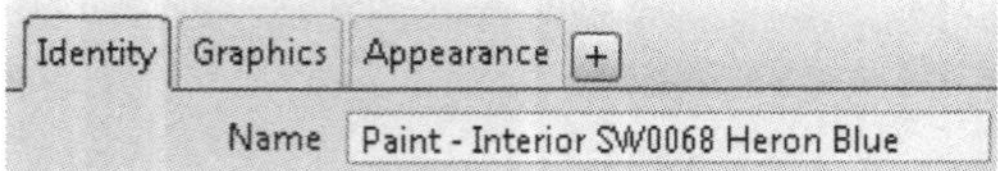

Type **Paint - Interior-SW0068 Heron Blue** for the name of the material.

16. Enter the Description in the field.

You can use Copy and Paste to copy the Name to the Description field.

Enter the Manufacturer and Model information.

17. Select the **...** browse button next to Keynote.

18. Locate the **Semi-Gloss Paint Finish**. Press **OK**.

19. The Identity tab should appear as shown.

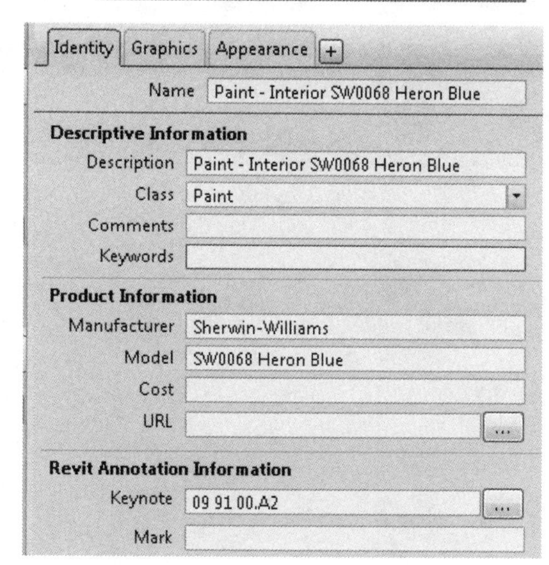

20. Activate the **Graphics** tab.

Enable **Use Render Appearance**.

21. On the drop-down list, select **Appearance**.

22. Select the down arrow next to Color to edit the color.

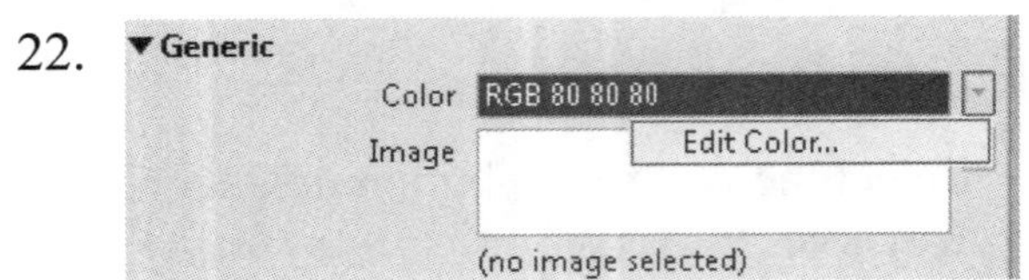

23. Select an empty slot under Custom Colors.

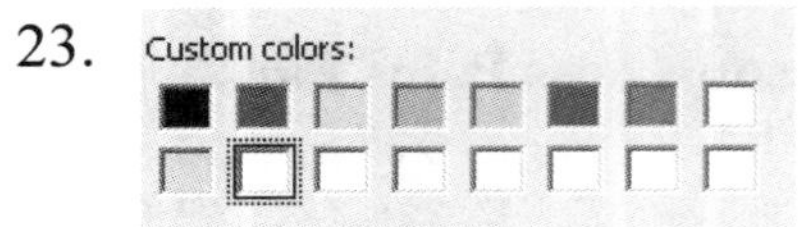

Set Red to 173.
Set Green to 216.
Set Blue to 228.

Press Add.

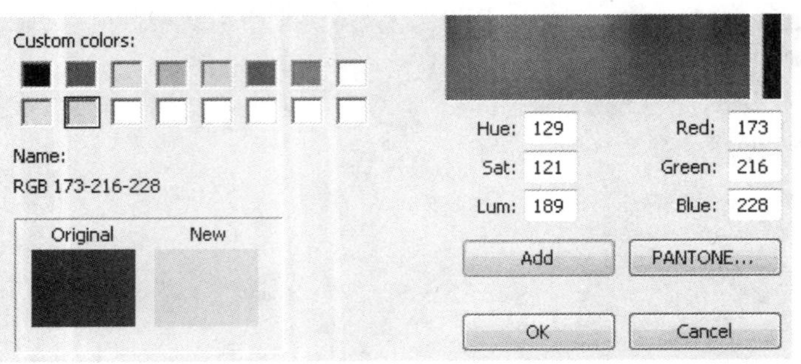

24. Select the custom color.

Press **OK**.

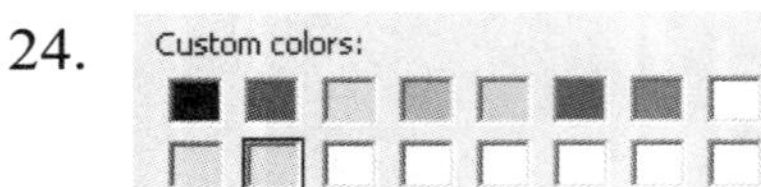

25. The color is previewed.

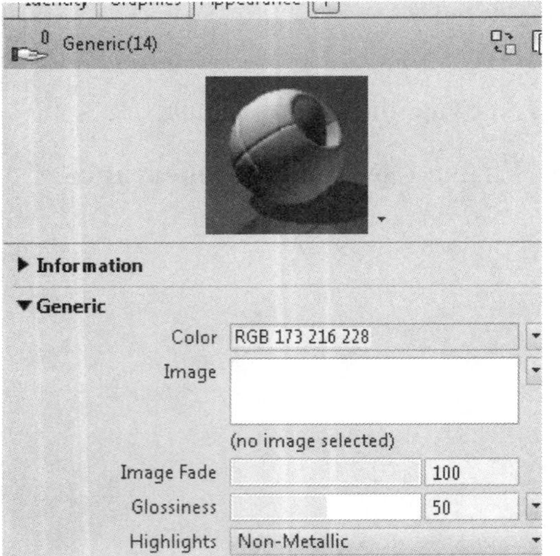

26. If you return to the Graphics tab, you see that the Color has been updated.

27. Press **OK** to close the Materials dialog.

28. Save as *ex4-4.rvt*.

Exercise 4-5

Add Categories and Materials to a Custom Library

Drawing Name: ex4-3.rvt
Estimated Time: 10 minutes

This exercise reinforces the following skills:

- ❑ Material Libraries
- ❑ Create Library Categories
- ❑ Add Materials to Custom Libraries

1. Go to the Manage ribbon.

2. Select the **Materials** tool.

3. 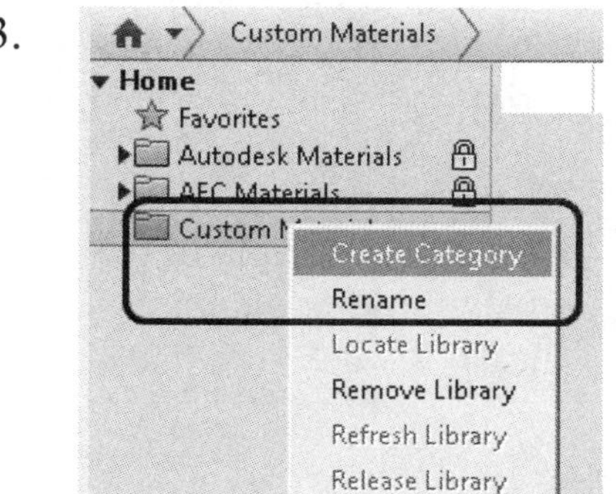

In the Library Pane:

Highlight the Custom Materials library. Right click and select **Create Category**.

4. 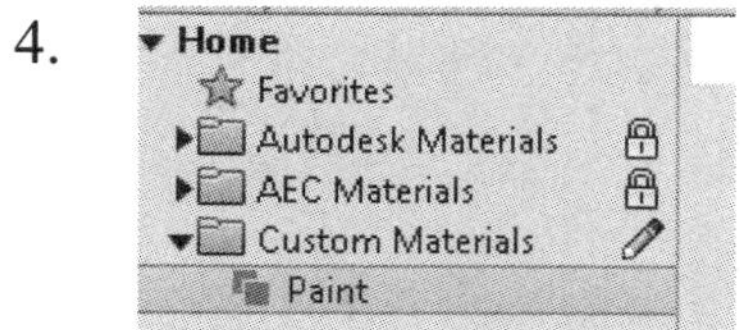

Type over the category name and rename it to **Paint**.

5. Locate the Navajo White paint in the Project Materials list.

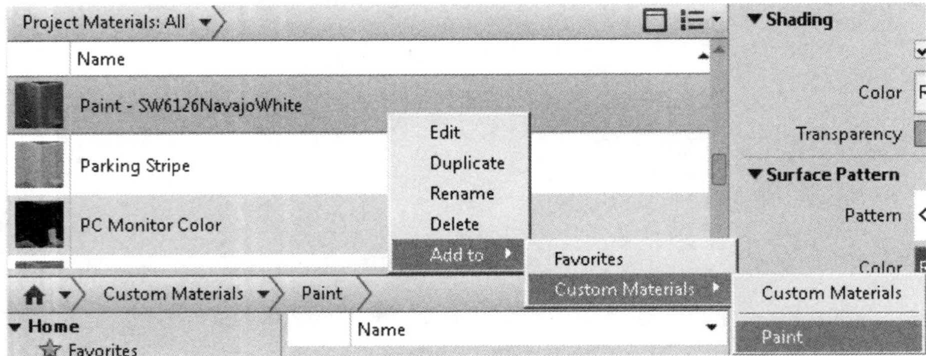

Right click and select **Add to → Custom Materials → Paint**.

6. 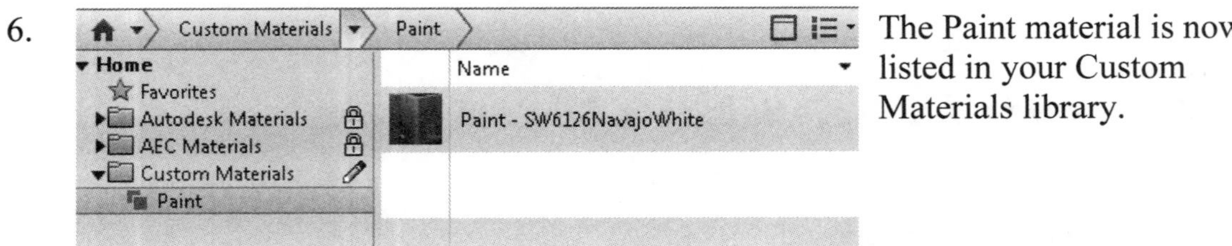

The Paint material is now listed in your Custom Materials library.

The material will now be available for use in other projects.

7. Locate Heron Blue paint in the Project Materials list.

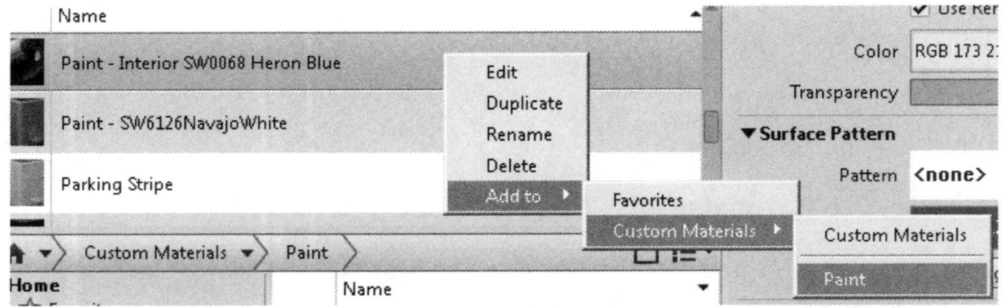

Right click and select **Add to → Custom Materials → Paint**.

8. 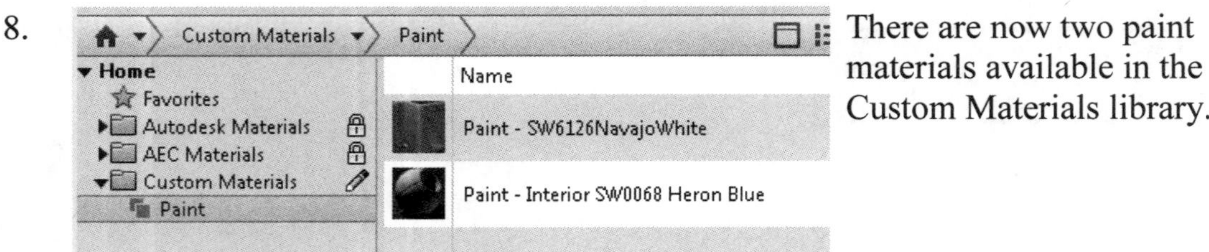

There are now two paint materials available in the Custom Materials library.

9. Close the Materials Manager.

Exercise 4-6

Defining Wallpaper Materials

Drawing Name: ex4-4.rvt
Estimated Time: 15 minutes

This exercise reinforces the following skills:

- Materials
- Defining a new class
- Using the Asset Manager

1. Materials — Go to **Manage→Materials**.

2. wallpaper — Type **Wallpaper** for the name of the material.

3. No search result for "wallpaper" — There are no wallpaper materials in the project or the library.

4. 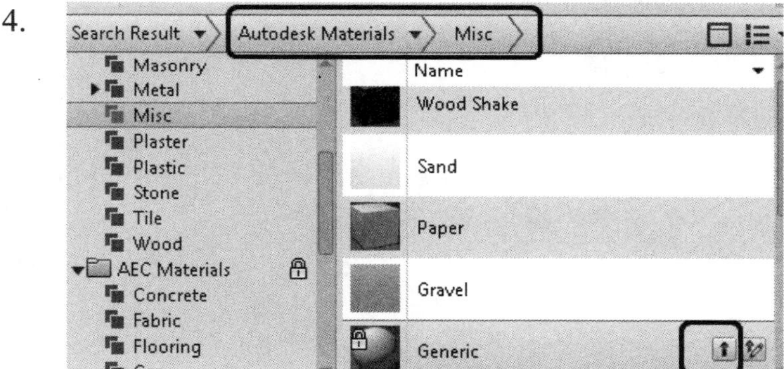

Locate the **Generic** material in the *Autodesk Materials* library under *Misc*.

Add it to the project.

5. 

Highlight the **Generic** material. Right click and select **Rename**.

6. Wallpaper - Striped — Rename to **Wallpaper- Striped**.

7. 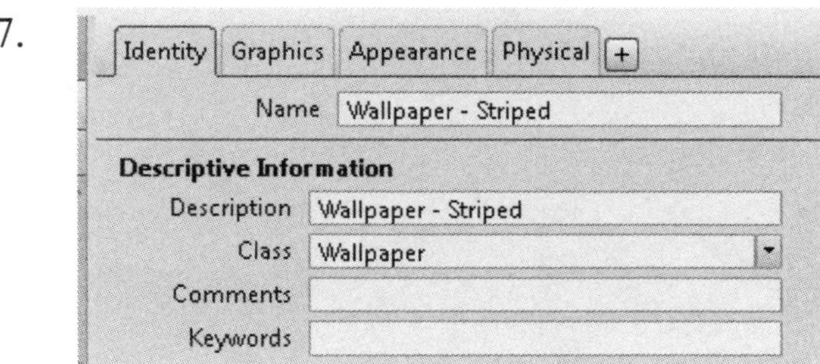

Activate the Identity tab.
In the Name field: type **Wallpaper – Striped**.
In the Description field: type **Wallpaper – Striped**.
In the Class field: type **Wallpaper**.

This adds Wallpaper to the Class drop-down list automatically.

8. Browse to assign a keynote.

9. 

Locate the **Vinyl Wallcovering** keynote. Press **OK**.

10. 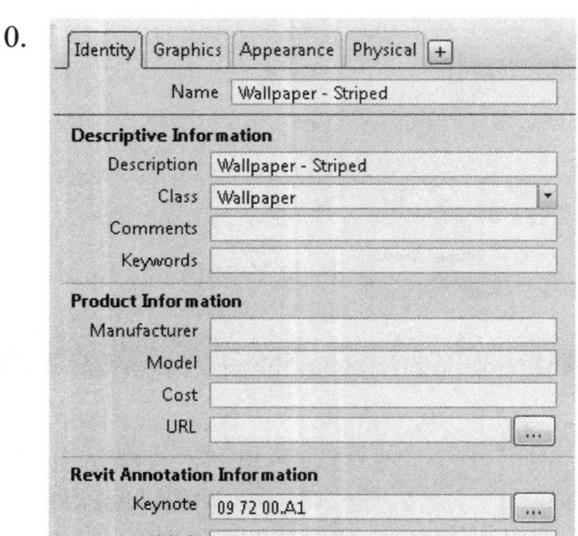

The Identity tab should appear as shown.

11. 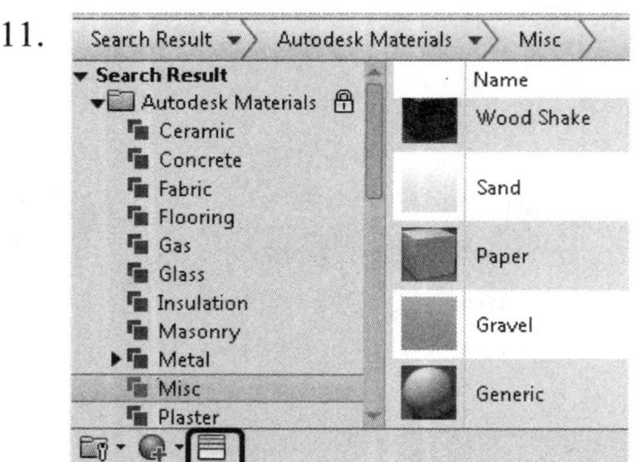

Launch the **Asset Browser** by pressing the button on the dialog.

12. Type **stripes** in the search field.

13. Highlight Wall Covering.
There are several materials available.

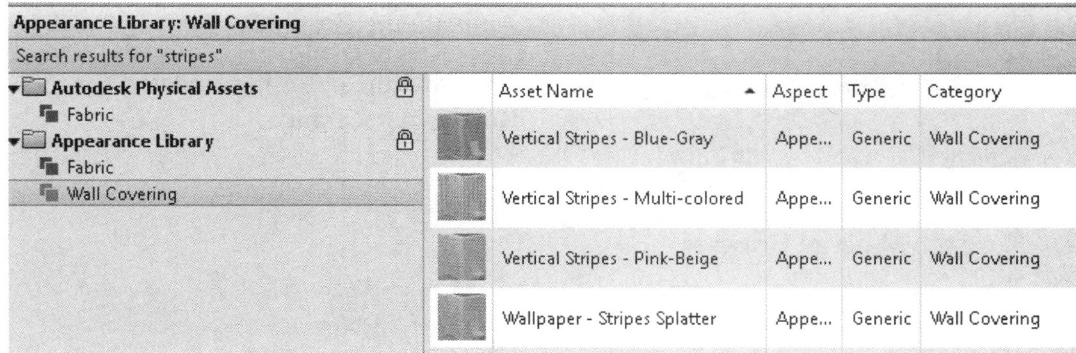

Highlight the **Vertical Stripes – Blue-Gray**.

14. Select the button on the far right.

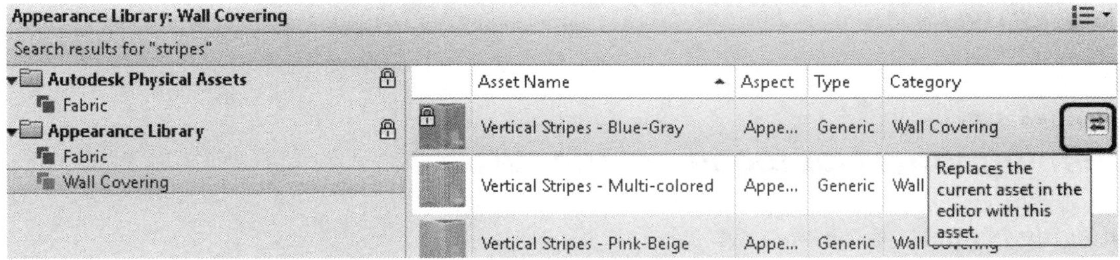

This copies the asset properties over to the material being edited – the Wallpaper-Striped.

15. Activate the Appearance tab.

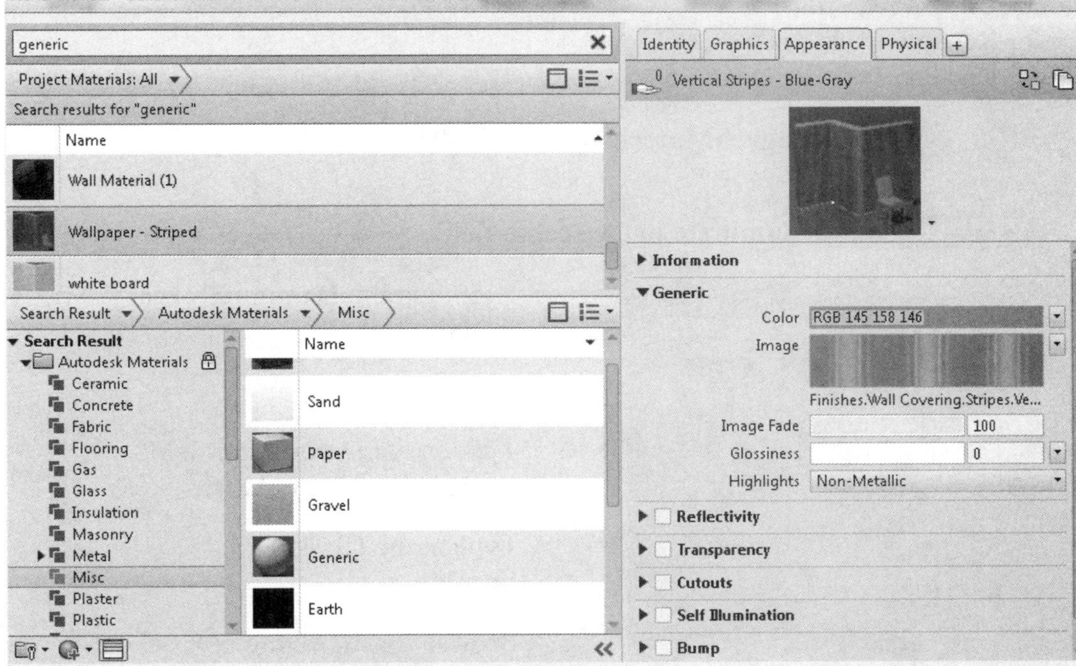

Note how the appearance has updated.

16. Activate the Graphics tab.

Note that the color has updated for the Render Appearance.

17. Close the Material Browser.

18. Save as *ex4-6.rvt*.

***Extra**: Create a Wallpaper – Floral material using the Asset Browser.*

Note: The materials you defined are local only to this project. To reuse these materials in a different project, they should be added to a custom library or use Transfer Project Standards on the Manage ribbon.

Exercise 4-7

Defining Vinyl Composition Tile (VCT)

Drawing Name: ex4-5.rvt
Estimated Time: 30 minutes

This exercise reinforces the following skills:

- Materials
- Copy a material
- Rename a material
- Use the Asset Browser

1. Go to **Manage→Materials**.

2. Type **laminate** in the search field.

3. 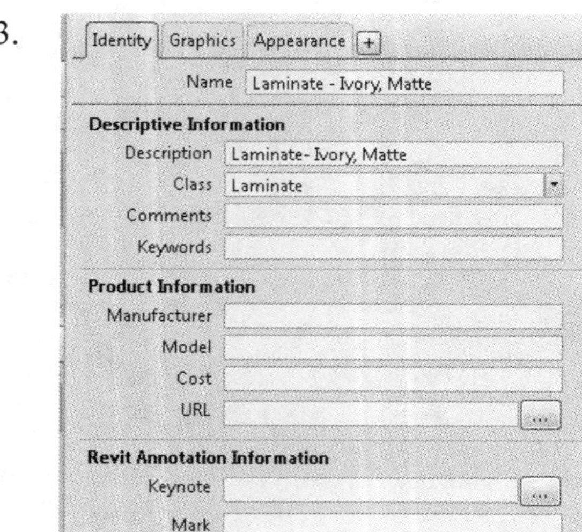

Highlight the **Laminate - Ivory, Matte** material.

On the Identity tab:

Type in the Description field: **Laminate - Ivory, Matte**

Type in the Class field: **Laminate**.

Browse for the keynote.

4. 

Select the keynote for **Resilient Flooring**.

Press **OK**.

5. 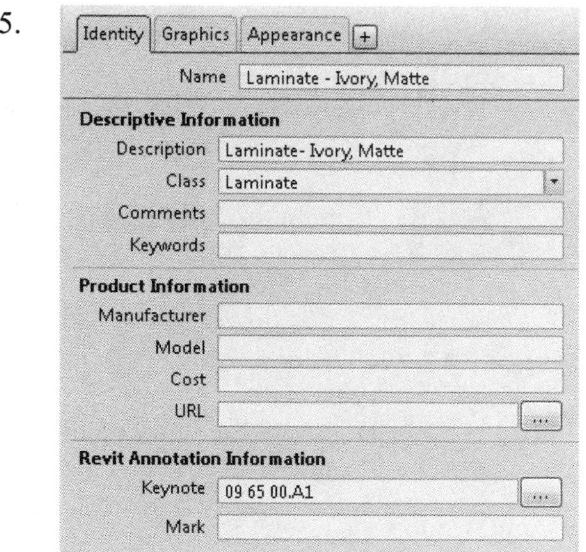

The Identity tab should appear as shown.

6. 

On the Graphics tab:
Enable **Use Render Appearance**.

7. 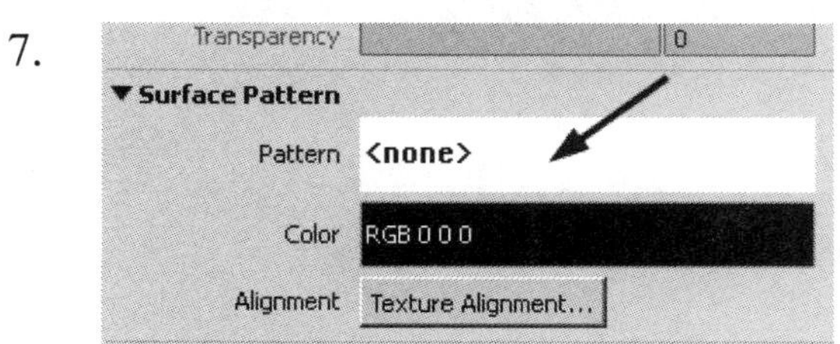

Select the Pattern button under Surface Pattern to assign a hatch pattern.

8. 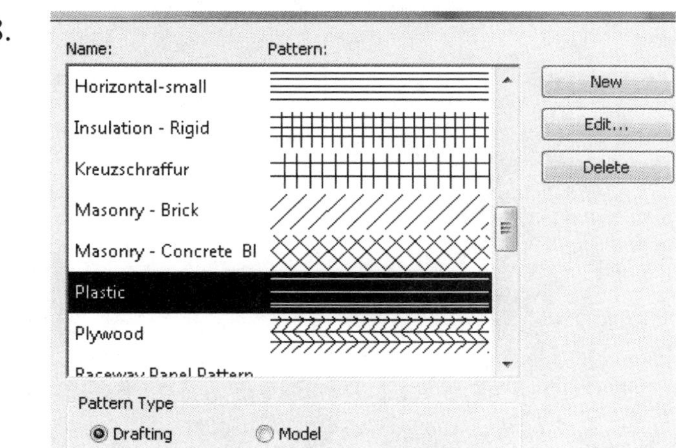

Scroll down and select the **Plastic** fill pattern.

Press **OK**.

9. Activate the **Appearance** tab.

Select **Edit Color** from the color drop-down.

10. Select an empty color swatch.

11. 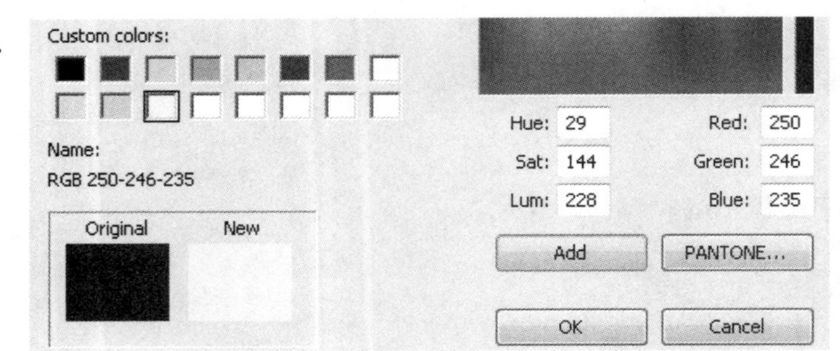

Type in the following values:

Red: 250
Green: 246
Blue: 235

Press **Add**.
Highlight the ivory color.
Press **OK**.

12. 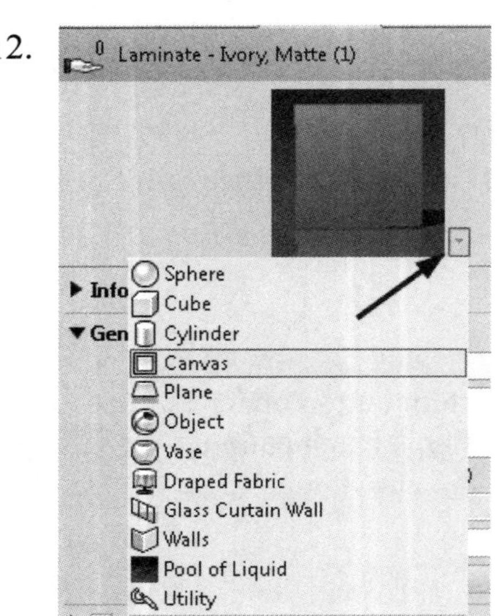

In the Preview window:

Select the down arrow.
Highlight Canvas to switch the preview to display a canvas.

13. 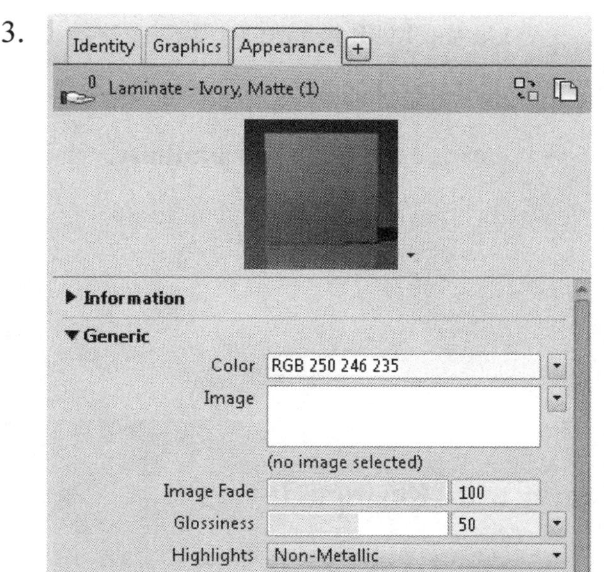

The Appearance tab should look as shown.

14. 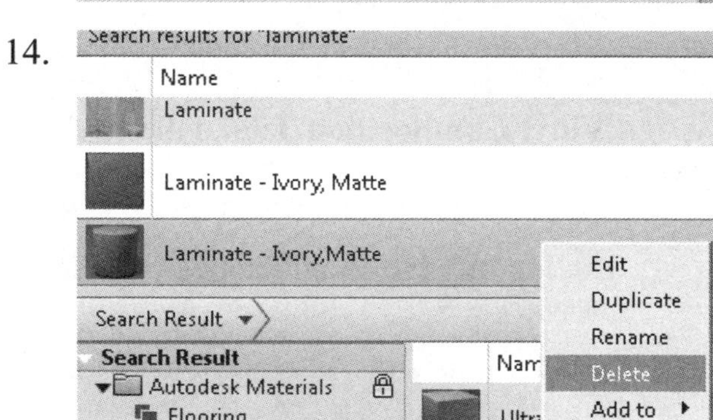

There are multiple Ivory, Matte laminate materials in the Project.

Highlight the ones which were not modified.

Right click and press **Delete**.

15. 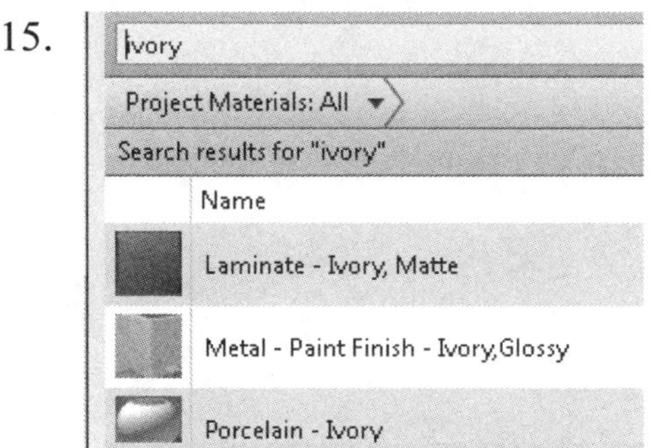

Verify that there is only one Ivory, Matte laminate material in the project by doing a search on ivory.

16. Type **tile** in the search box.

17. 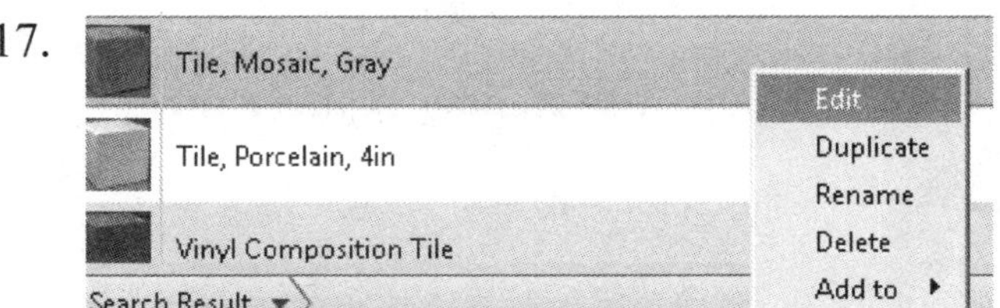

Highlight the **Tile, Mosaic, Gray**.

Right click and select **Edit**.

18. 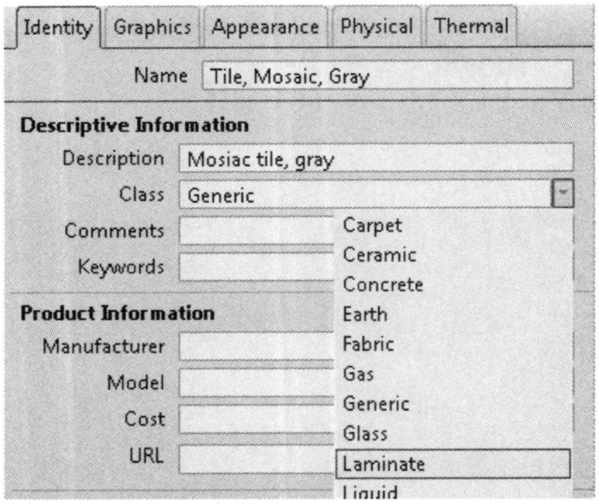 On the Identity tab:

Add a Description.

Change the Class to **Laminate**.

19. 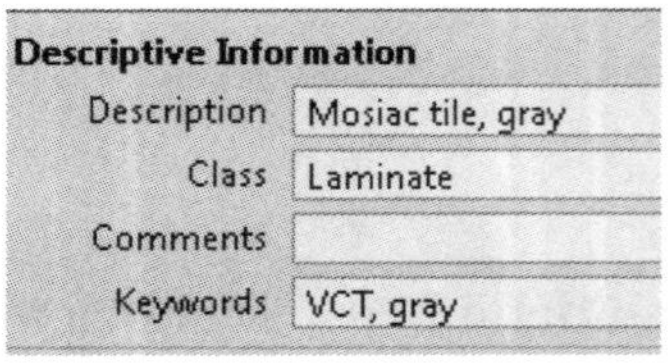 Add **VCT, gray** to the Keywords list.

20. 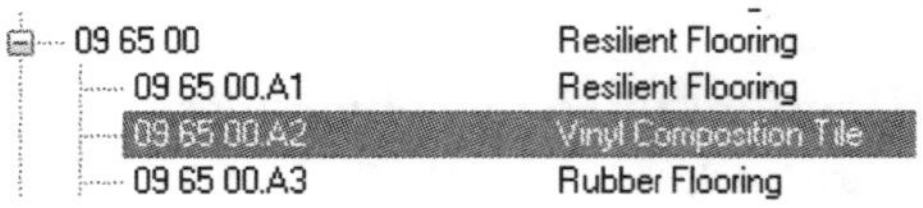 Assign **Vinyl Composition Tile** to the keynote.

21. 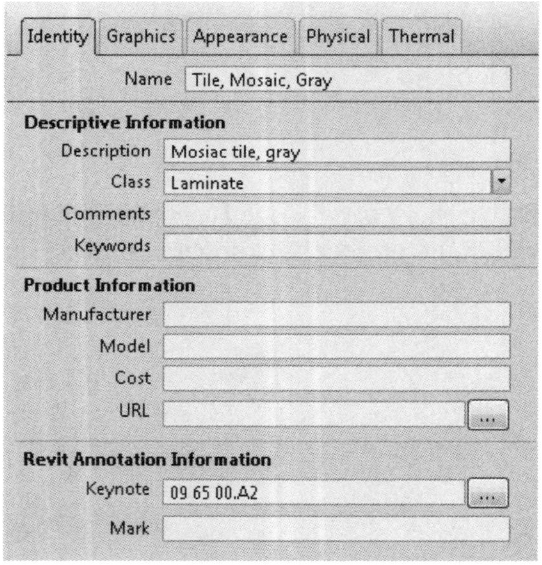 The Identity tab should appear as shown.

22. 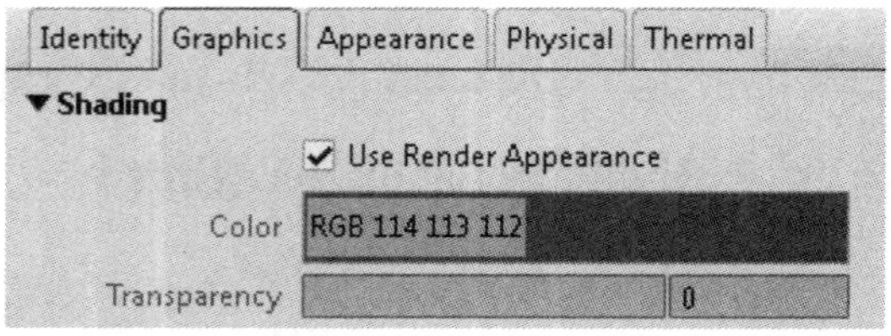 On the Graphics tab:

Enable **Use Render Appearance**.

23. Select the Pattern button under Surface Pattern to assign a hatch pattern.

24. Scroll down and select the **Crosshatch** fill pattern.

Press **OK**.

25. 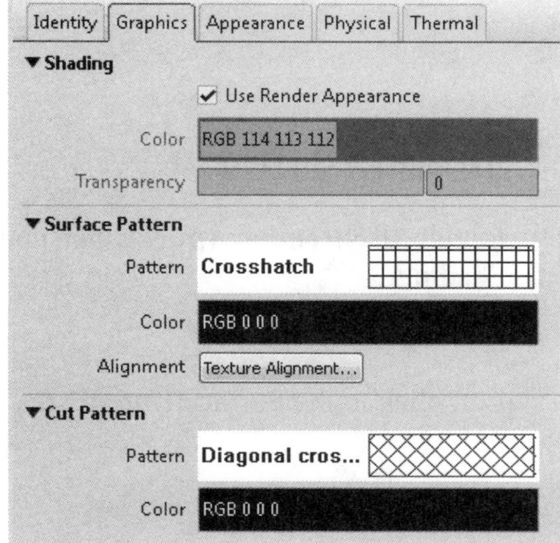

The Graphics tab should appear as shown.

26. Type **TILE** in the search field.

27. Scroll down the Document materials and locate the Vinyl Composition Tile.

Right click and select **Rename**.

28. 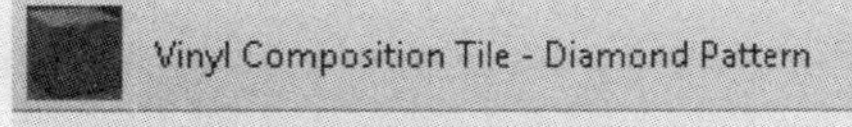

Name the new material **Vinyl Composition Tile - Diamond Pattern**.

29. Activate the Identity tab.

In the Description field: Type **VCT-Diamond Pattern**.
Set the Class to **Laminate**.
Enter **VCT, Diamond** for Keywords.

Assign **09 65 00.A2** as the Keynote.

30. 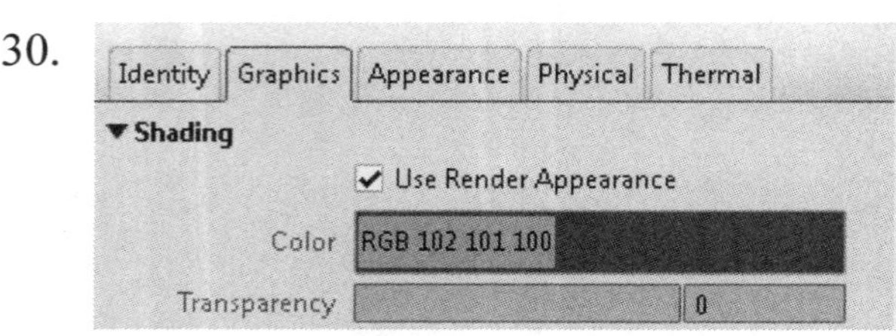

Activate the Graphics tab.

Enable **Use Render Appearance** under Shading.

31. 

Left click in the Surface Pattern area.

32. 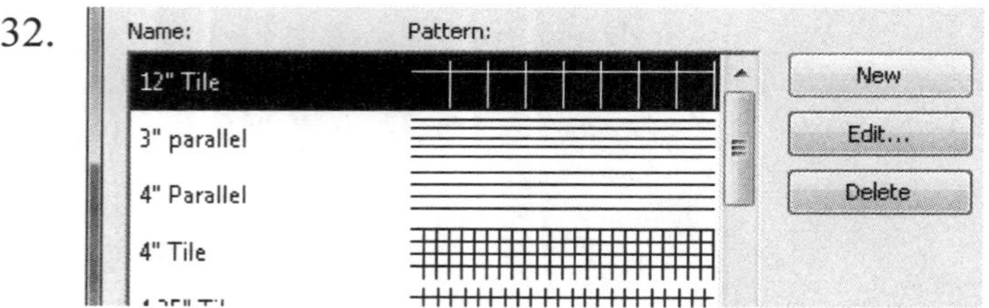

Select the **New** button.

33. 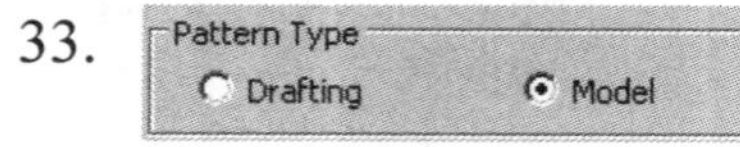

Enable **Model**.

34. Enable **Simple**.

In the Name field, enter **Diamond 12″** [**Diamond 300**].

Set the Line Space 1: to **12″** [**300**].
Set the Line Space 2: to **12″** [**300**].
Enable **Crosshatch**.

Press **OK**.

35. The new hatch pattern is listed.

Highlight to select and press **OK**.

36. The new hatch pattern is displayed.

37. Launch the Asset Browser.

38. In the Assets drop-down list, select **Browse**.

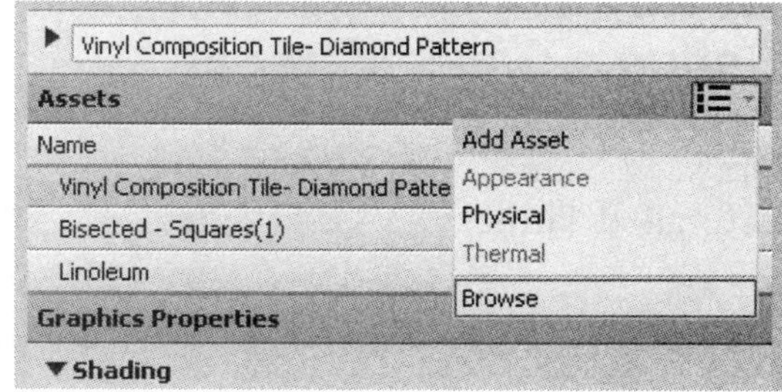

39. Type diamond in the search box at the top of the Asset Browser dialog.

40. Locate the **Diamonds1** property set.

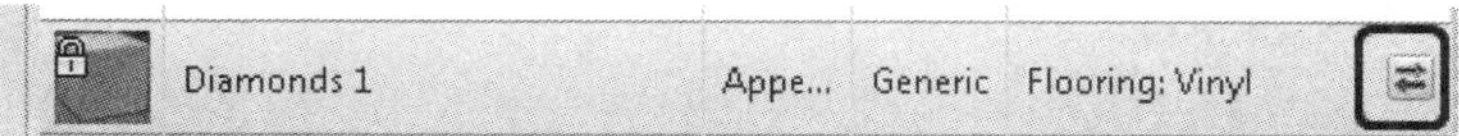

At the far left, you should see a button that says replace the current asset in the editor with this asset.

41. The Appearance tab will update with the new asset information.

42. 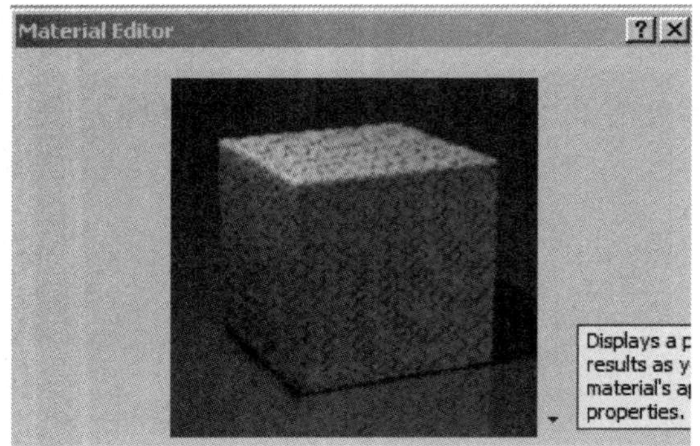

The Material Editor will update.

Close the Asset Browser.

43. Save as *ex4-7.rvt*.

Exercise 4-8

Define a Glass Material

Drawing Name: ex3-22.rvt
Estimated Time: 20 minutes

This exercise reinforces the following skills:

- Materials
- Use the Asset Browser
- Duplicate a Material

1. Materials Go to **Manage→Materials**.

2. glass Type glass in the search field.

3. 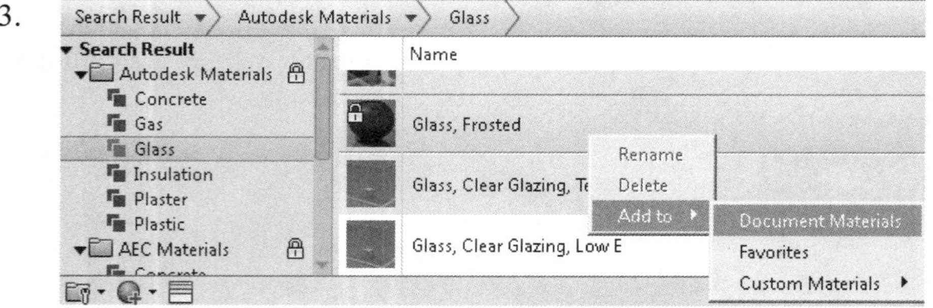

Locate the **Glass, Frosted** material in the Library pane.

Right click and select **Add to→ Document Materials**.

4. 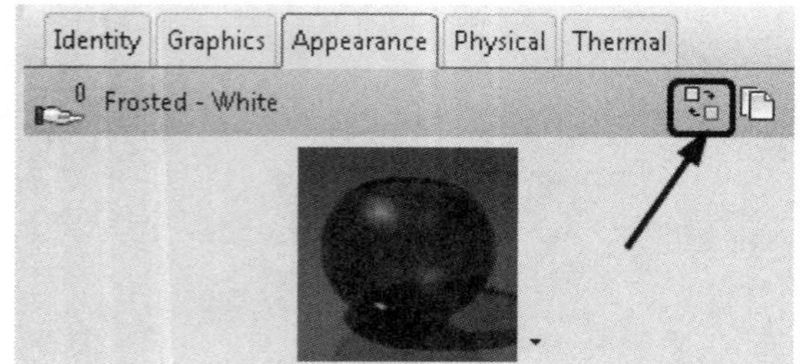

Activate the Appearance tab.

Select **Replace this asset**.

This will launch the Asset Browser.

5. The Asset Browser will launch.

   Type **glass** in the search field.

   Highlight Glass under Appearance Library and scroll through to see all the different glass colors.

   Select **Clear - Amber**.

   Select the Replace asset tool on the far right.

6. Identity | Graphics | Appearance | Physical | Thermal

   Name: Glass, Frosted Amber

   Descriptive Information

   Description: Frosted glass, Amber

   Class: Glass

   Comments:

   Keywords: amber, glass, frosted

   Product Information

   Manufacturer:

   Model:

   Cost:

   URL:

   Revit Annotation Information

   Keynote: 08 81 00.A1

   Mark:

   On the Identity tab:
   Set the fields:

   Name: Glass, Frosted Amber
   Description: Frosted glass, Amber
   Class: Glass
   Keywords: amber, glass, frosted
   Keynote: 08 81 00.A1

7. On the Graphics tab:

Enable **Use Render Appearance**.

8. 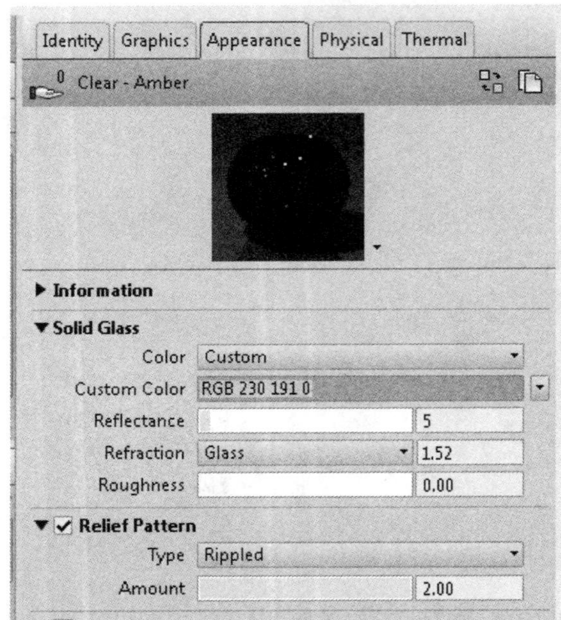

On the Appearance tab:

Under Relief Pattern:

Set the Type to **Rippled**.
Set the Amount to **2.0**.

Press **Apply**.

Apply saves the changes and keeps the dialog box open.
OK saves the changes and closes the dialog box.

9. Highlight the **Glass, Frosted Amber** material in the Project Materials pane. Right click and select **Duplicate**.

10. Highlight the duplicated material.
Right click and select **Rename**.

11. Change the name to **Glass, Frosted Green**.

12. 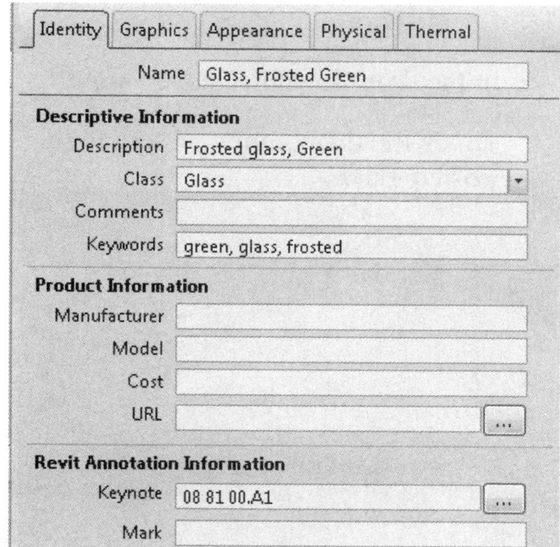

On the Identity tab:
Set the fields:

Name: Glass, Frosted Green
Description: Frosted glass, Green
Class: Glass
Keywords: green, glass, frosted
Keynote: 08 81 00.A1

13. In the Asset Browser:
In the Appearance Library

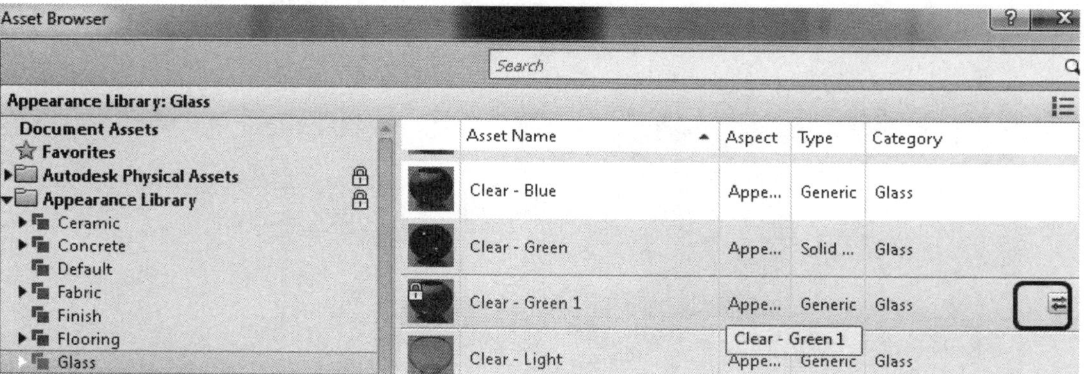

Locate the **Clear - Green 1** glass and select the double arrows to assign that material appearance to the Glass, Frosted Green material.

14. 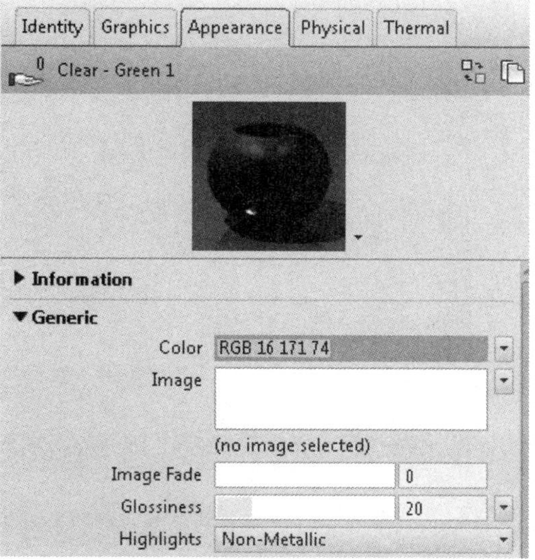

The Appearance properties will update.

15. Enable **Bump**.

In the drop-down list select **Noise**.

This will add a bumpy pattern to the frosted glass.

16. 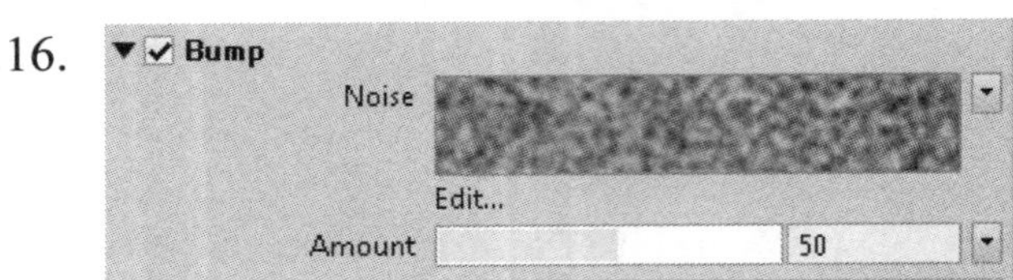

Set the Amount to **50**.

17. 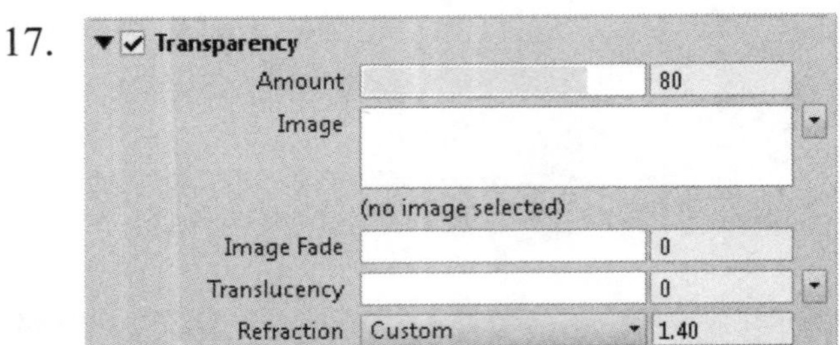

Set the Transparency to **80**.

18. 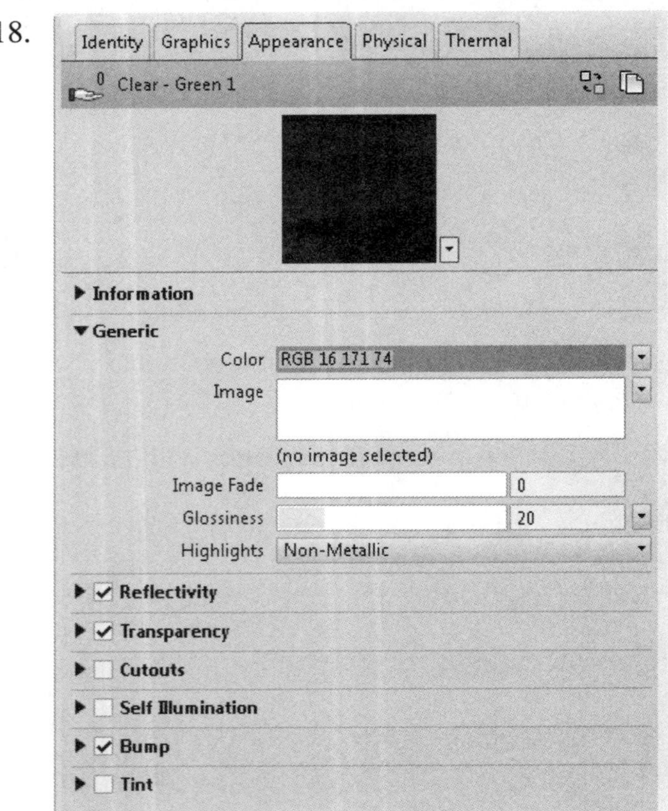

Check the preview image and verify that the material looks good.

Adjust the appearance settings to your preferences.

19. Activate the Graphics tab.

Enable **Use Render Appearance**.

Press **Apply** to save the settings.

Exercise 4-9

Defining Wood Materials

Drawing Name: ex3-22.rvt
Estimated Time: 5 minutes

This exercise reinforces the following skills:

- Materials
- Appearance Settings
- Identity Settings
- Copying from Library to Project Materials

1. Go to **Manage→Materials.**

2. Type **oak** in the search field.

3. There is one oak material available in the Project Materials.

4. Locate the **Oak, Red** in the Autodesk Materials Library.

Add it to the Project Materials.

5. 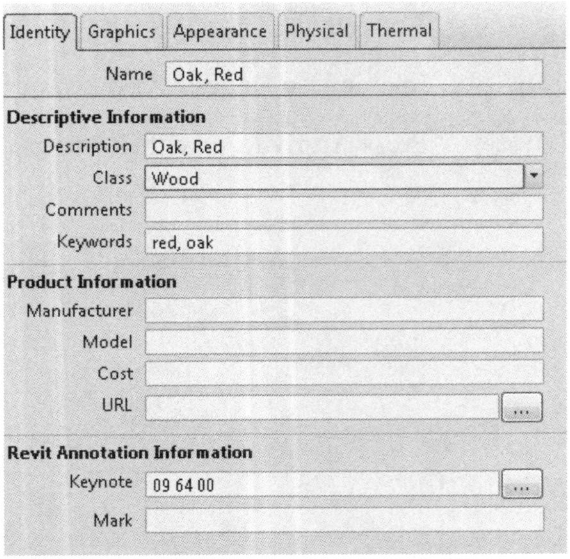 In the Identity tab:

Name: Oak, Red
Description: Oak, Red
Class: Wood
Keywords: red, oak
Keynote: 09 64.00

6. 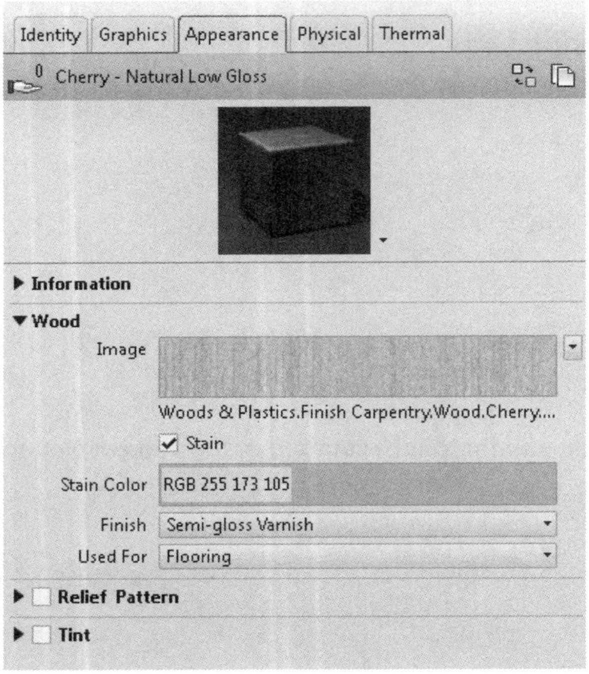 On the Appearance tab:

Enable **Stain**.
Set the Finish to **Semi-gloss Varnish**.
Set Used For to **Flooring**.

7. 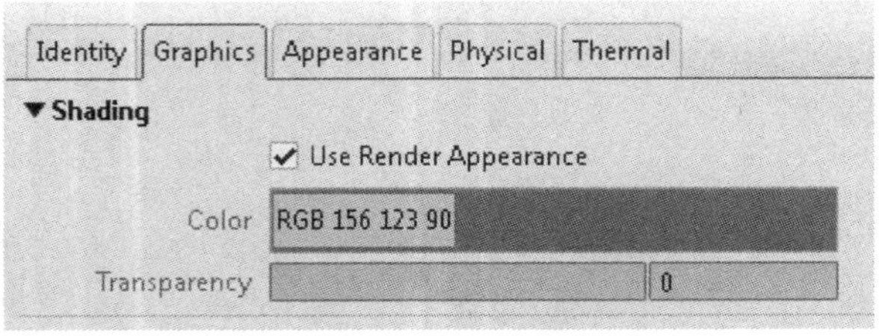 On the Graphics tab:

Enable **Use Render Appearance**.

8.

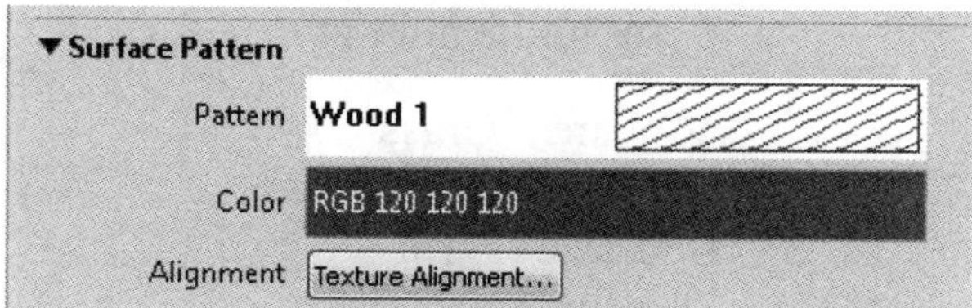

Set the Surface Pattern to **Wood 1**.

Press Apply to save the settings.

Exercise 4-10

Defining Site Materials

Drawing Name: ex3-22.rvt
Estimated Time: 15 minutes

This exercise reinforces the following skills:

- ❑ Copying Materials from the Library to Document
- ❑ Editing Materials
- ❑ Using the Asset Browser
- ❑ Assigning a custom image to a material

1. Materials Go to **Manage→Materials**.

2. grass Type **grass** in the search field at the top of the Material browser.

3.

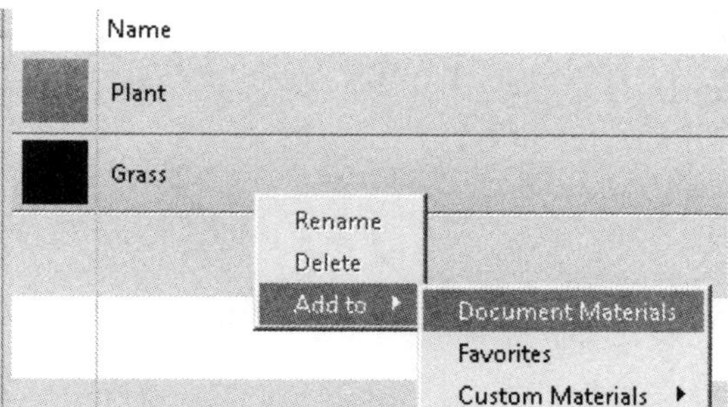

Grass is listed in the lower pane.

Highlight **grass**.
Right click and select **Add to→ Document Materials**.

4. 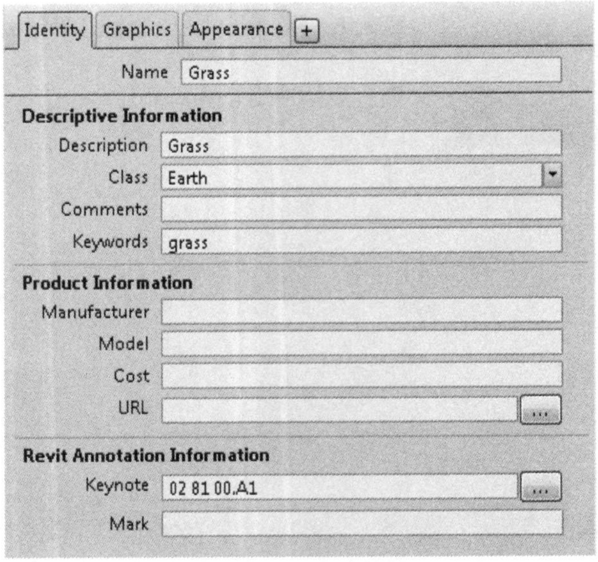 In the Identity tab:

Name: Grass
Description: Grass
Class: Earth
Keywords: grass
Keynote: 02 81 00.A1

5. 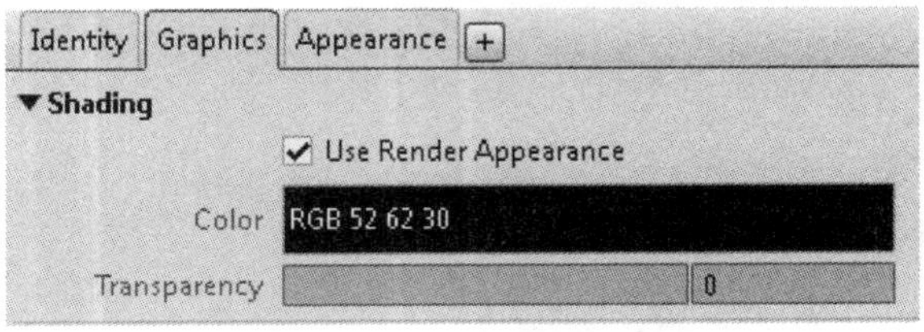 On the Graphics tab:

Enable **Use Render Appearance**.

6. 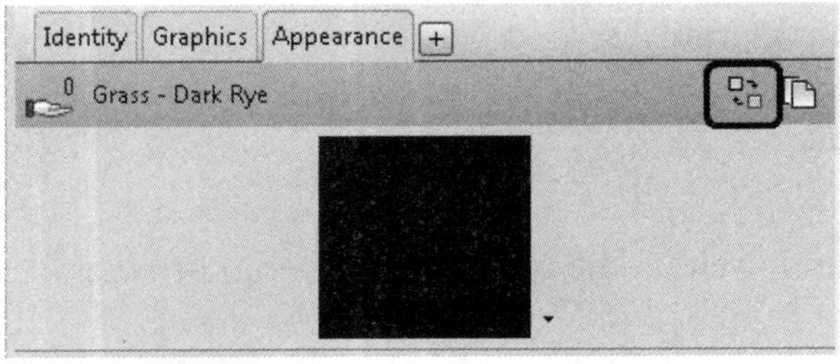 On the Appearance tab.

Select **Replaces this asset**.

7.  Type **grass** in the search field.

8. 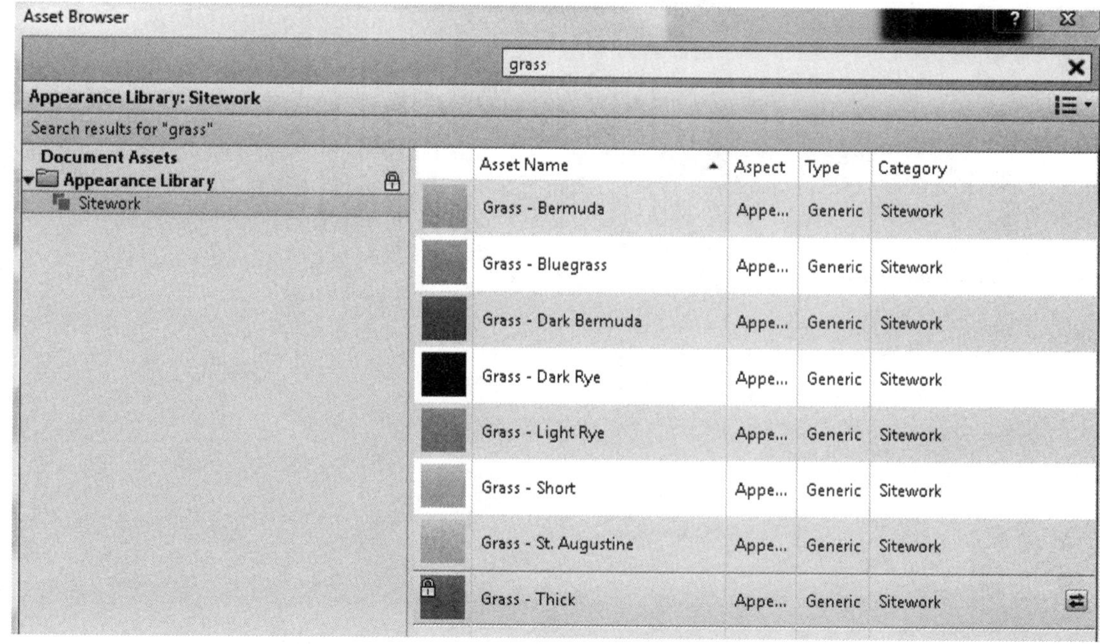

You have a selection of grasses to select from.

9. 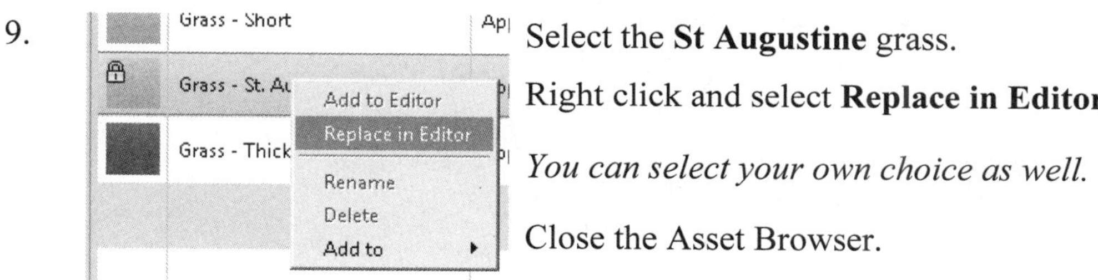

Select the **St Augustine** grass.

Right click and select **Replace in Editor**.

You can select your own choice as well.

Close the Asset Browser.

10. 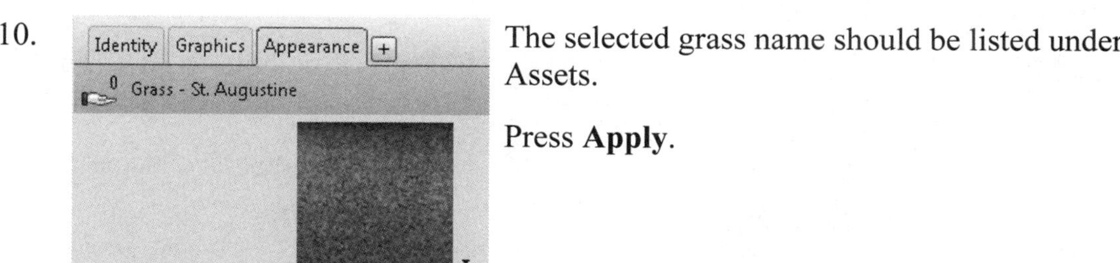

The selected grass name should be listed under Assets.

Press **Apply**.

11. gravel Do a search for **gravel** in the Material Browser.

12. 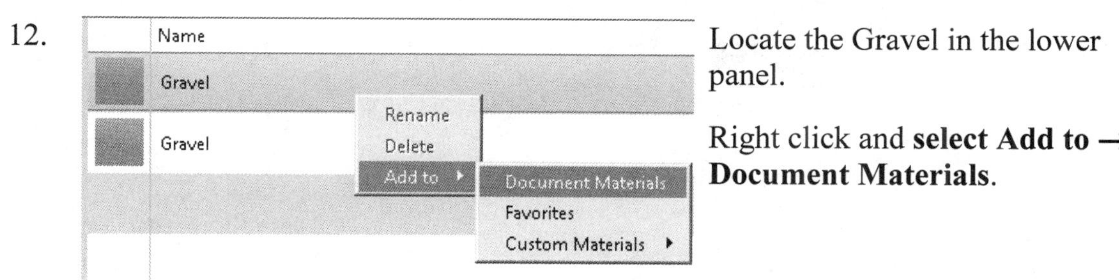

Locate the Gravel in the lower panel.

Right click and **select Add to → Document Materials**.

13. 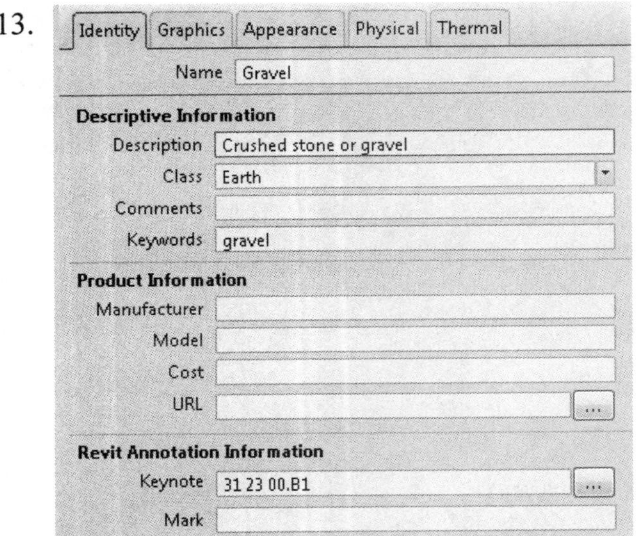

In the Identity tab:

Name: Gravel
Description: Crushed stone or gravel
Class: Earth
Keywords: gravel
Keynote: 31 23 00.B1

14. In the Graphics tab:

Enable **Use Render Appearance**.

Assign the **Sand Dense** hatch pattern to the Surface Pattern.

15. 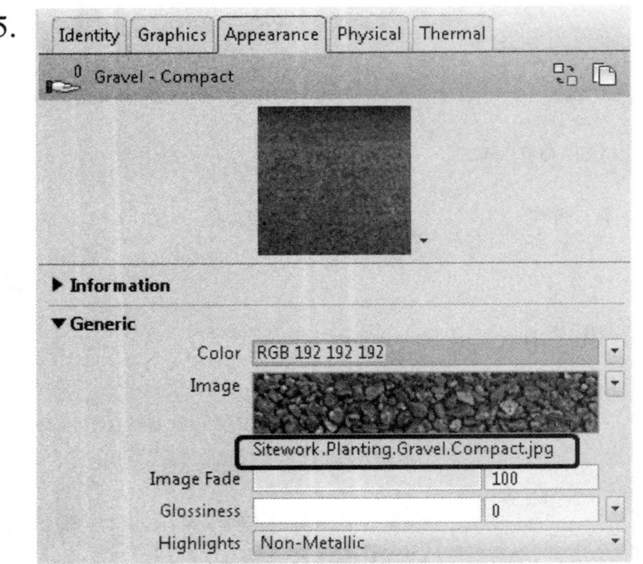

On the Appearance tab:

Change the color to **RGB 192 192 192**.

Left click on the image name.

16. 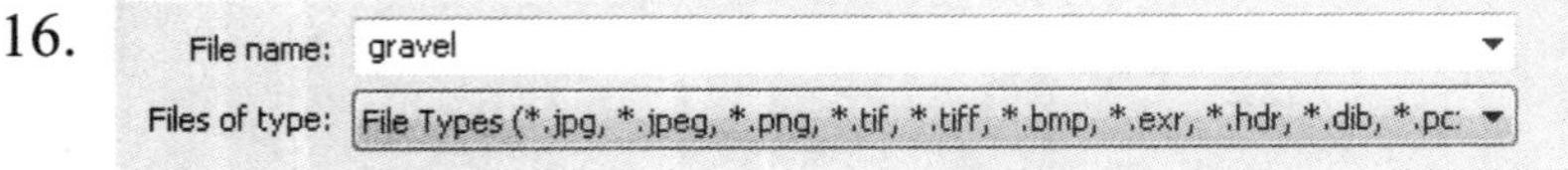

Locate the *gravel* image file in the exercise files.

Press **Open**.

17. 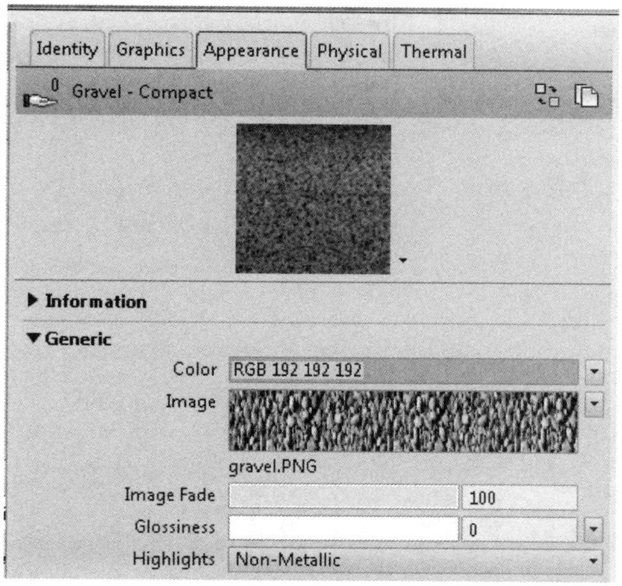 The Appearance will update.

Press **Apply** to save the changes.

Exercise 4-11

Defining Masonry Materials

Drawing Name: ex3-22.rvt
Estimated Time: 15 minutes

This exercise reinforces the following skills:

- Copying Materials from the Library to the Document Materials
- Using the Asset Browser

1.  Go to **Manage→Materials.**

2.  Type **masonry** in the search field.

3. 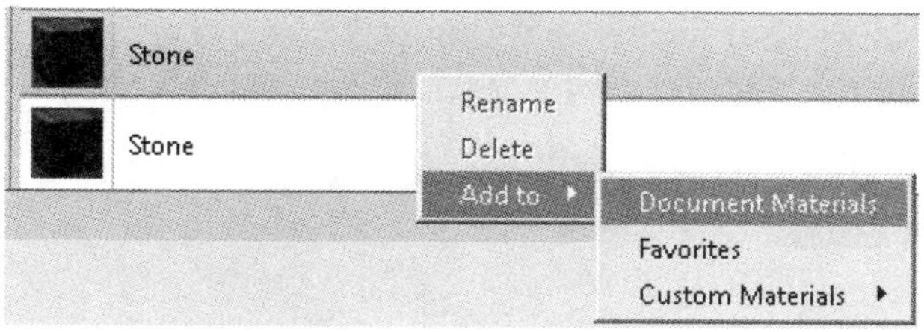 Highlight **Stone** in the Libraries pane.
Right click and select **Add to → Document Materials**.

4. In the Identity tab:

Name: Stone, River Rock
Description: Stone, River Rock
Class: Stone
Keywords: stone, river rock
Keynote: 32 14 00.D4

5. 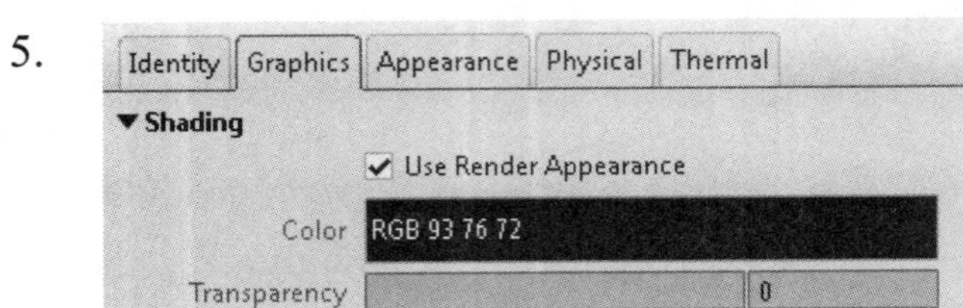

In the Graphics tab:

Enable **Use Render Appearance for Shading**.

6. 

Select the Pattern button to assign a fill pattern.

7. Select New to create a new fill pattern.

8. 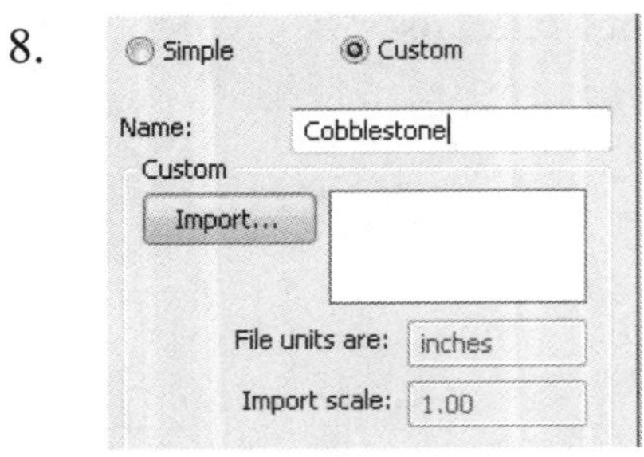

Type **Cobblestone** in the Name field.

Enable **Custom**.

Press the **Import** button under Custom.

9. Locate the *cobblestone.pat* file in the exercise files on the publisher's website.

Press **Open**.

10. 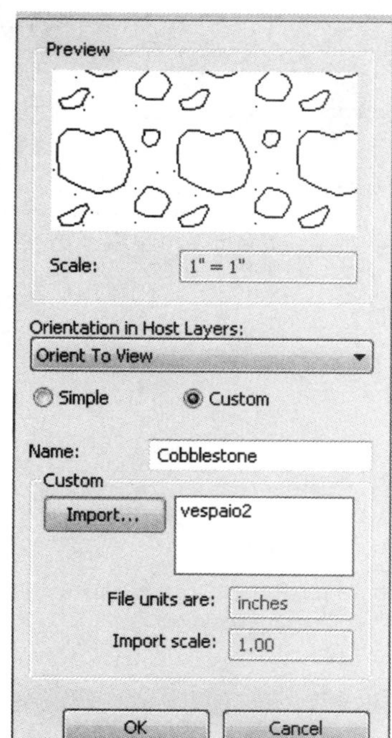

You will see a preview of the pattern.

Verify that the name is set to **Cobblestone**.

Press **OK**.

11. 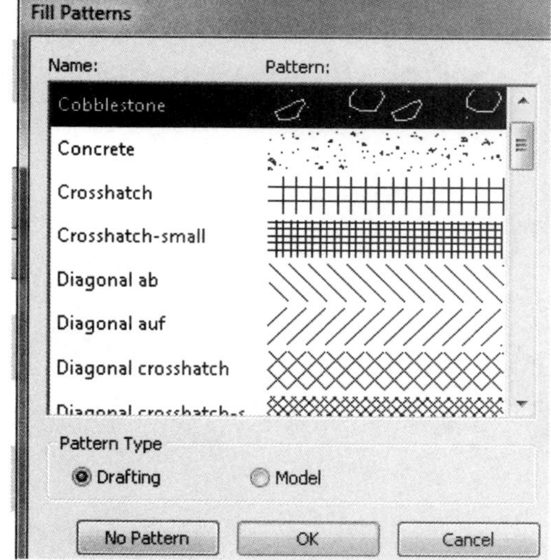

Highlight **Cobblestone**.

Press **OK**.

Revit allows you to use any AutoCAD pat file as a fill pattern.

12. 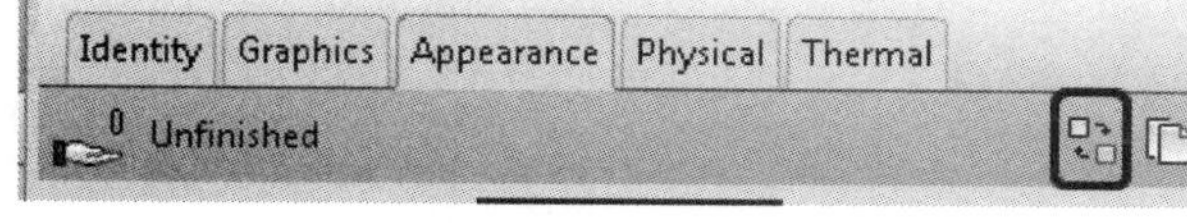

On the Appearance tab:

Select **Replaces this asset**.

13. Type **rock** in the search field.

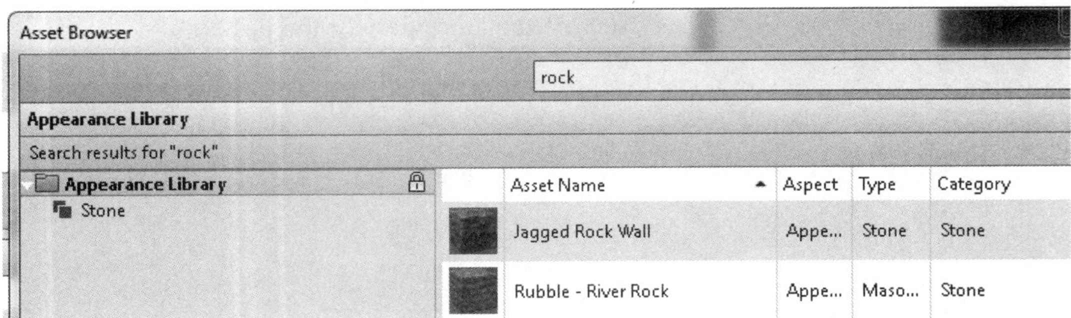

Locate the **Rubble - River Rock**.

14. 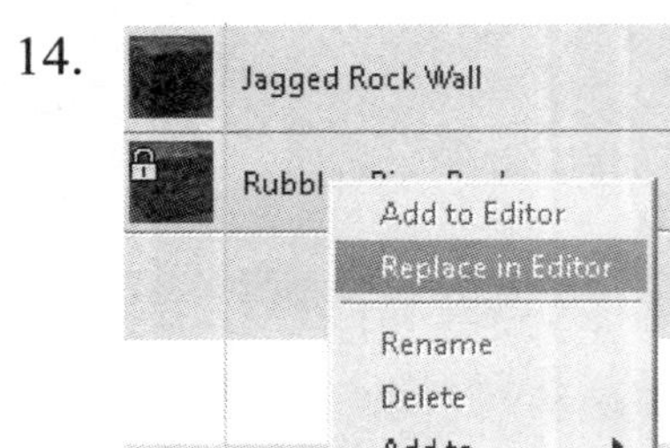

Highlight the **Rubble - River Rock**.

Right click and select **Replace in Editor**.

15. 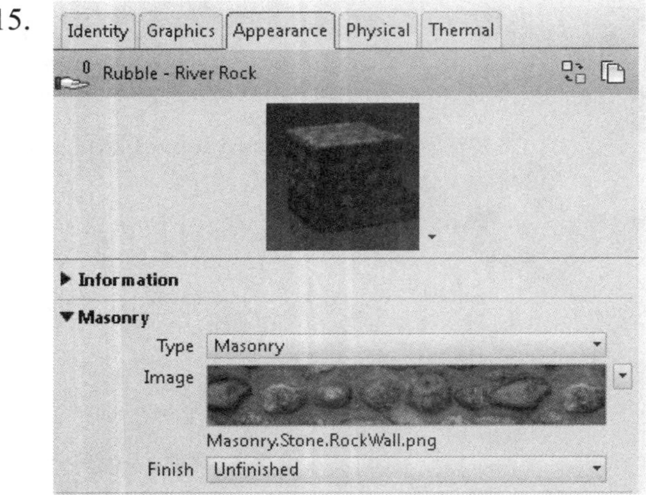

The Material Editor updates.

Press **OK** to save the changes and close the dialog.

Exercise 4-12
Assigning Materials to Stairs

Drawing Name: ex3-22.rvt
Estimated Time: 20 minutes

This exercise reinforces the following skills:

- ❑ Floor
- ❑ Floor Properties

1. Open *ex3-22.rvt.*
2. Activate **Level 1**.
3. Select the stairs.

   Select **Edit Type** on the Properties pane.
4. Select **Duplicate**.
5. 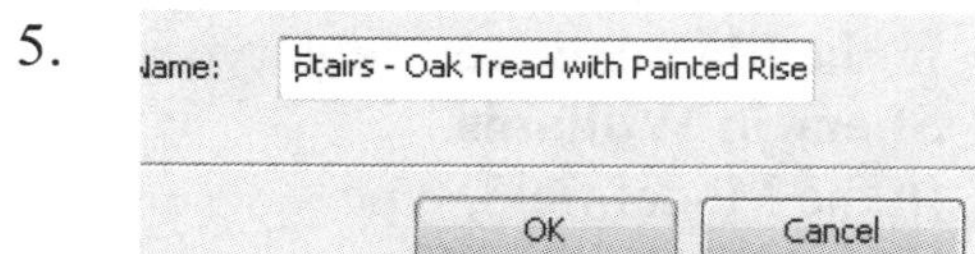

   Type **Stairs - Oak Tread with Painted Riser**.

   Press **OK**.
6.

Materials and Finishes	
Tread Material	<By Category>
Riser Material	<By Category>
Stringer Material	<By Category>
Monolithic Material	<By Category>

   Scroll down to the Materials and Finishes category.

   Select the **Tread Material** column.
7. Type **oak** in the search field.
   Select the **Oak, Red** material.

   Press **OK**.

8.

Materials and Finishes	
Tread Material	Oak Flooring
Riser Material	<By Category>
Stringer Material	<By Category>
Monolithic Material	<By Category>

   Select the **Riser Material** column.

9. Type **white** in the search field.

   Locate the **SW6126NavajoWhite** material.

   Press **OK**.

10. 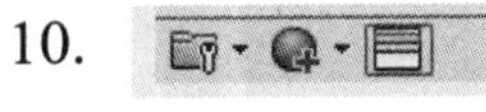
    Enable the **Asset Browser** on the bottom of the Material Browser dialog.

11. Activate the **Identity** tab.
    In the Name field, type **Paint - SW6126NavajoWhite**.
    In the Description field, type **Sherwin Williams Paint - Interior**.
    Select **Paint** for the Class under the drop-down list.
    In the Manufacturer field, type **Sherwin Williams**.
    In the Model field, type **SW6126NavajoWhite**.

12. Select the **... browse** button next to Keynote.

13. Note the keynote information auto-fills based on the selection.

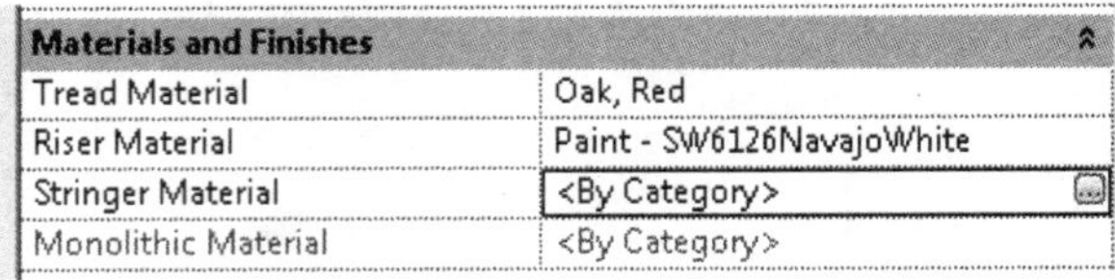

Materials and Finishes	
Tread Material	Oak, Red
Riser Material	Paint - SW6126NavajoWhite
Stringer Material	<By Category>
Monolithic Material	<By Category>

Select the **Stringer Material** column.

14. 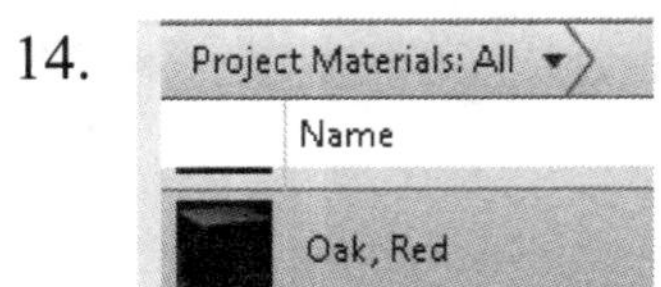

    Select the **Oak, Red** material.

    Press **OK**.

15. Press **OK** to close the dialog.

16. Switch to a **3D** view.

17. Graphic Display Options...
Wireframe
Hidden Line
Shaded
Consistent Colors
Realistic
Ray Trace

Change the display to **Realistic**.

Orbit around the model to inspect the stairs.

18. 

Observe how the assigned materials affect the stairs' appearance.

Some users may not see the wood pattern on their stairs. This is a graphics card issue. I use a high-end graphics card.

19. If you want the boards to be oriented horizontally instead of vertically on the treads:

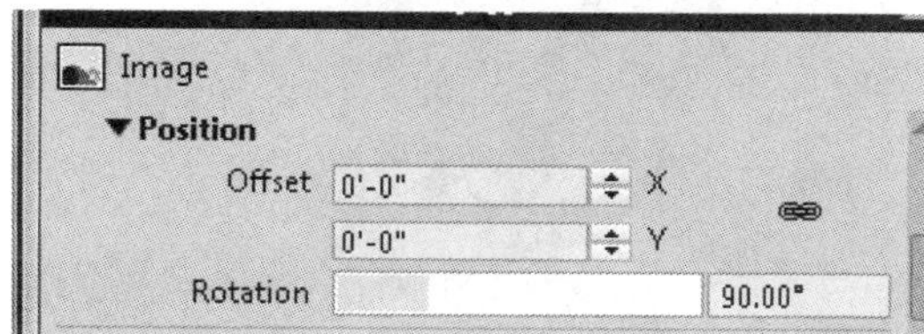

Select the stairs.
Edit Type.
Select the Tread Material.
Select the Appearance tab.

Next to the image picture, select Edit Image from the drop down list.
Expand the Transform area.
Set the Rotation to 90 degree.
Press Done.

20. Save as *ex4-12.rvt*.

Some students have expressed concern about the railing joins at the corners. This is due to the change in elevation at those joins. If you adjust the riser position, you can clean up those areas.

With the riser position adjusted.

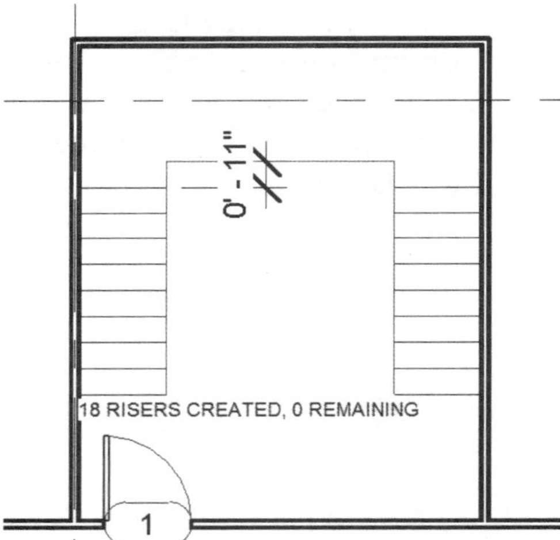

Verify that you have offset the riser a minimum of a tread-width to allow for the railing adjustment.

Extra: Add all the custom materials to the Custom Materials library.

Define a custom wallpaper, a custom brick, and a custom wood material using assets from the Asset Browser.

Additional Projects

1) Create a material for the following Sherwin-Williams paints:

SW 6049 Gorgeous White
Interior/Exterior

Color Collection	Soft and Sheer
Color Family	Whites
Color Strip	8
RGB Value	R-232 | G-220 | B-212
Hexadecimal Value	# E8DCD4
LRV	73

SW 6050 Abalone Shell
Interior/Exterior

Color Family	Reds
Color Strip	8
RGB Value	R-219 | G-201 | B-190
Hexadecimal Value	# DBC9BE
LRV	60

SW 6052 Sandbank
Interior/Exterior

Color Family	Reds
Color Strip	8
RGB Value	R-196 | G-166 | B-152
Hexadecimal Value	# C4A698
LRV	41

2) Create a wallpaper material using appearances from the Asset Browser.

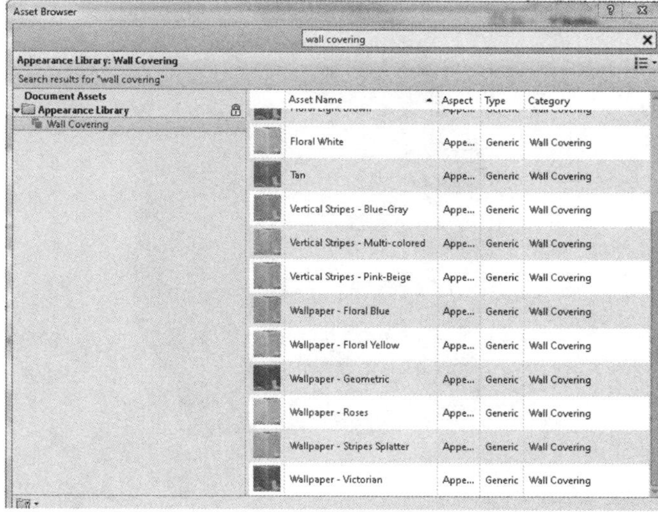

3) Create three different type s of carpeting materials using appearances from the Asset Browser.

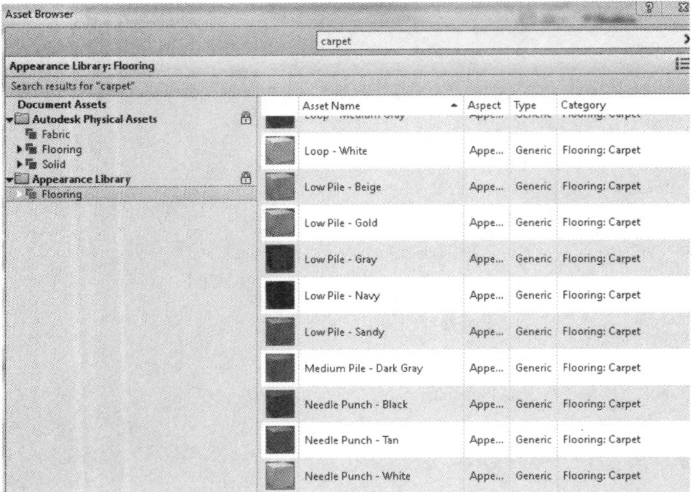

4) On Level 2, in the cafeteria area: apply paint to the walls and modify the floor to use a VCT material.

5) Apply paints to the walls in the conference rooms. Modify the floors to use a carpet material by creating parts.

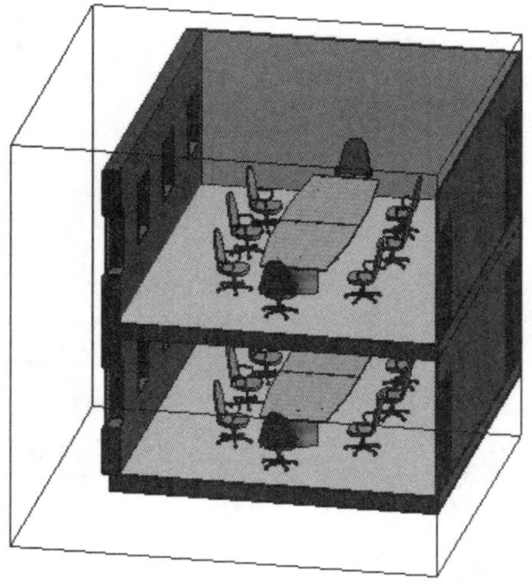

Lesson 4 Quiz

True or False

1. Materials in Material Libraries can be modified.
2. Only materials in the current project can be edited.
3. A material can have up to five assets, but only one of each type of asset.

Multiple Choice

4. Which of the following is NOT a Material asset?

   A. Identity
   B. Graphics
   C. Appearance
   D. Structural
   E. Thermal

5. Identify the numbers.

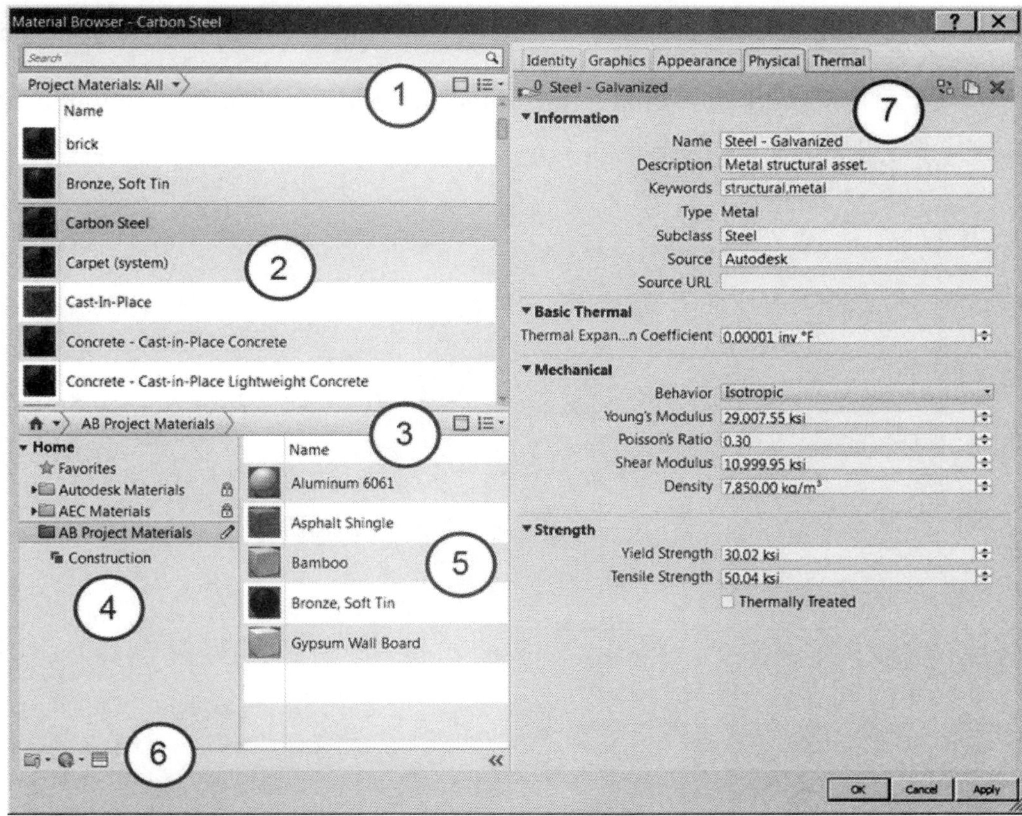

Material Browser

6. The lock icon next to the Material Library indicates the library is:

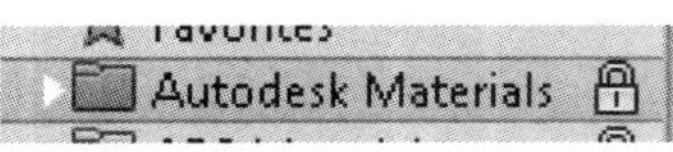

   A. Secure
   B. Closed
   C. "read-only"
   D. Unable to be moved

7. To access Materials, use this ribbon:

   A. Manage
   B. View
   C. Architecture
   D. Annotate
   E. Materials

8. To add a material to the current project:

   A. Double left click the material in the library list
   B. Drag and drop the material from the library list into the project materials list
   C. Right click the material and use the Add to Document materials short-cut menu
   D. Select the material in the library list and click the Add button located on the far right
   E. All of the above

ANSWERS:
1) F; 2) T; 3) T; 4) D; 5) 1- Show/Hide library panel button, 2- Property materials list, 3-Show/Hide library button, 4- Library list, 5- Library materials list, 6- Material Browser toolbar, 7- Asset panel; 6) C; 7) A; 8) E

Lesson 5
Floors and Ceilings

Ceiling Plans are used to let the contractor how the ceiling is supposed to look.

When drafting a reflected ceiling plan, imagine that you are looking down on the floor, which is acting as a mirror showing a reflection of the ceiling. You want to locate lighting, vents, sprinkler heads, and soffits.

We start by placing the floors that are going to reflect the ceilings. (Reflected ceiling plans look down, not up. They are the mirror image of what you would see looking up, as if the ceiling were reflected in the floor.)

Exercise 5-1
Creating Floors

Drawing Name: ex4-12.rvt
Estimated Time: 35 minutes

This exercise reinforces the following skills:

- Floors
- Floor Properties
- Materials

1. Open *ex4-12.rvt.*

2. 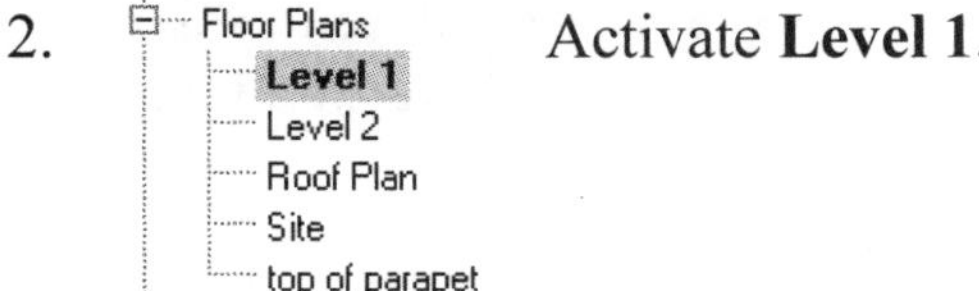

Activate **Level 1**.

3. In the browser, locate the exterior wall that is used in the project.

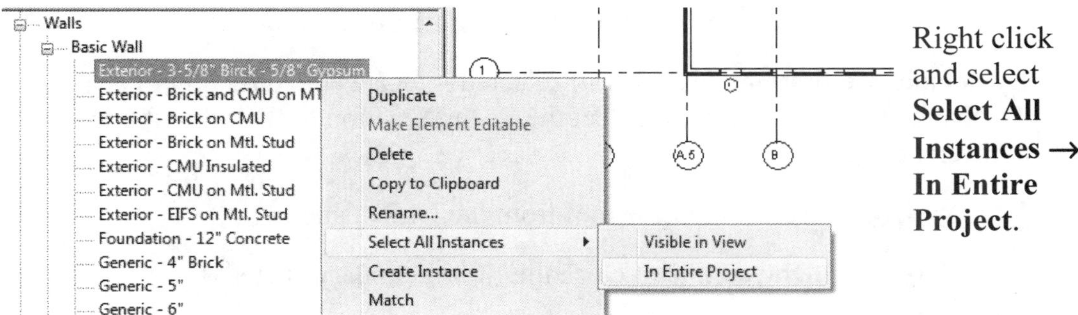

Right click and select **Select All Instances → In Entire Project**.

4. On the status bar:
Select **Isolate element**.

This will turn off the visibility of all elements except for the exterior walls, which will make selecting the walls easier.

5. You should see the top view of your model with only the exterior walls visible.

There are gaps where there are doors, windows, and the curtain wall.

6. Activate the **Architecture** ribbon.

Select the **Floor: Architectural** tool under the Build panel.

7. Select all the exterior walls.

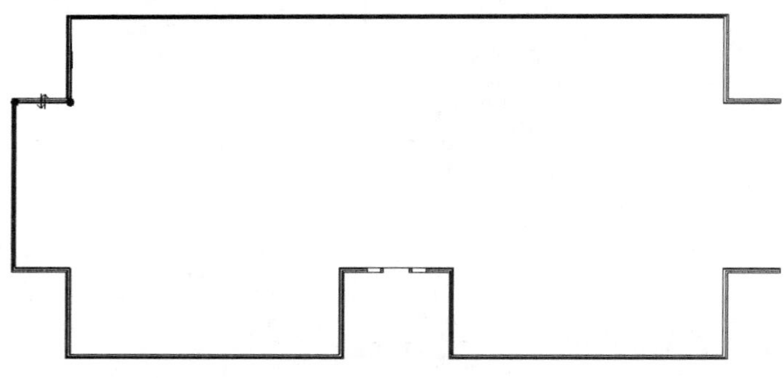

The curtain wall can not be selected.

In order to close the sketch, you need to draw a line.

The parallel lines indicate the direction of span.

By default, the first line placed/wall selected indicates the direction of span.
To change the span direction, select the Span Direction tool on the ribbon and select a different line.

8. Select the Line tool from the Draw panel.

Draw a line to close the floor boundary sketch.

9. Verify that your floor boundary has no gaps or intersecting lines.

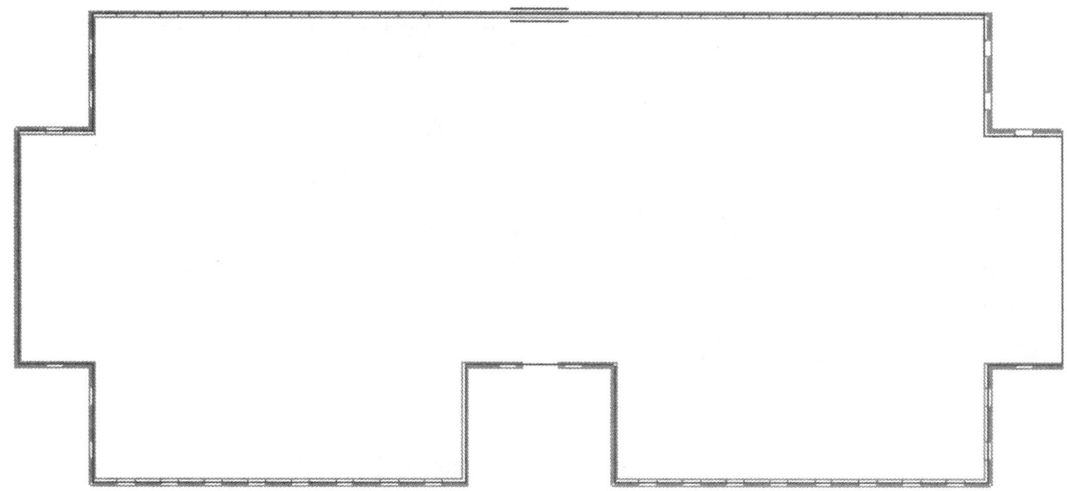

10. Select **Edit Type** from the Properties pane.

11. Select **Wood Truss Joist 12″ - Carpet Finish** from the Type drop-down list.

12. Select **Duplicate**.

13. Change the Name to **Wood Truss Joist 12″ - VCT**.

Press **OK**.

14. Select **Edit** under Structure.

15. For Layer 1: Finish 1 [4]:
Select the *browse* button in the Material column.

16. 

Type **vct** in the search field.

The Tile, Mosaic Gray is listed because you added vct to the keywords.

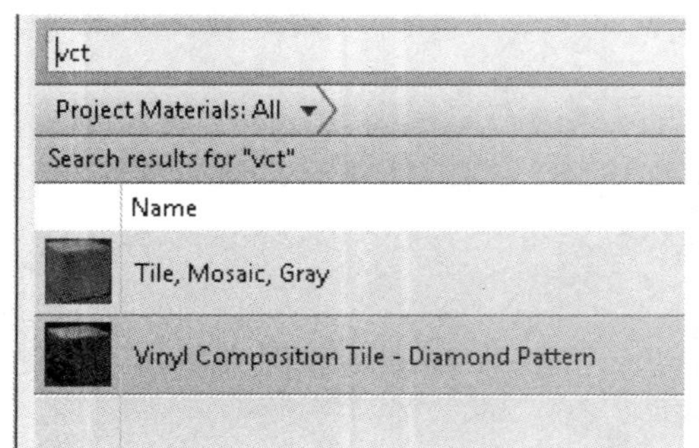

Highlight **the Vinyl Composition Tile – Diamond Pattern** to select.

Press **OK**.

17. Done — Select the Done button at the bottom of the Material Editor.

18. Layers

	Function	Material	Thickness
1	Finish 1 [4]	Vinyl Composition Tile - Diamond Pattern	0' 0 1/8"
2	**Core Boundary**	**Layers Above Wrap**	**0' 0"**
3	Structure [1]	Plywood, Sheathing	0' 0 3/4"

You should see the new material listed.

Press **OK**.

19.

Graphics	
Coarse Scale Fill Pattern	Diagonal crosshatch
Coarse Scale Fill Color	Black

Set the Coarse Scale Fill Pattern to **Diagonal crosshatch**.

Press **OK** to close the dialog.

20. 

Select the **Green Check** under Mode to finish the floor.

If you get a dialog box indicating an error with the Floor Sketch, press the 'Show' button. Revit will zoom into the area where the lines are not meeting properly. Press 'Continue' and use Trim/Extend to correct the problem.

21.  Switch to a 3D View.

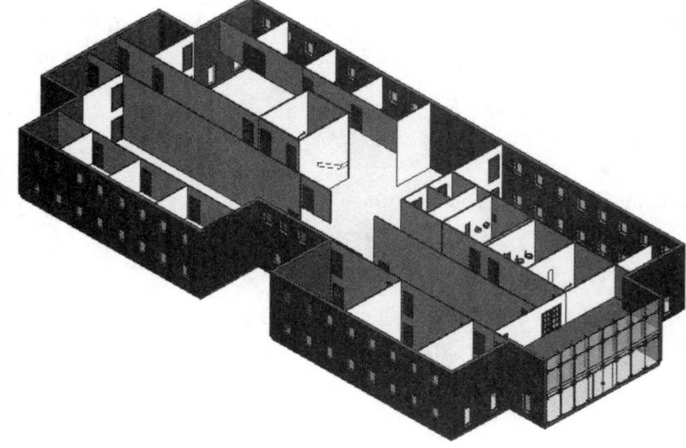

22. Activate **Level 1**.

23. Select **Reset Temporary Hide/Isolate** to restore the elements in the Level 1 floor plan.

24. Save as *ex5-1.rvt*.

Exercise 5-2

Copying Floors

Drawing Name: ex5-1.rvt
Estimated Time: 5 minutes

This exercise reinforces the following skills:

- Copy
- Paste Aligned
- Opening
- Shaft Opening
- Opening Properties

1. Open *ex5-1.rvt*

2. Switch to a 3D View.

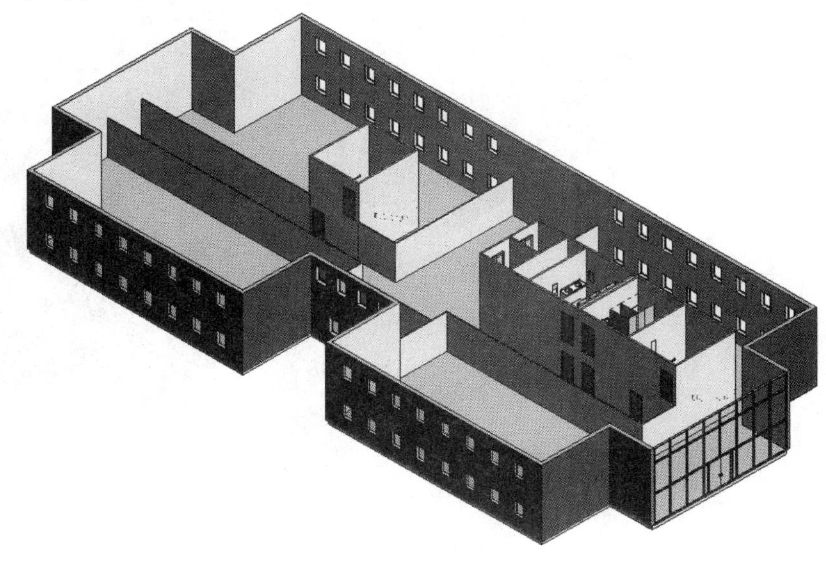

3. 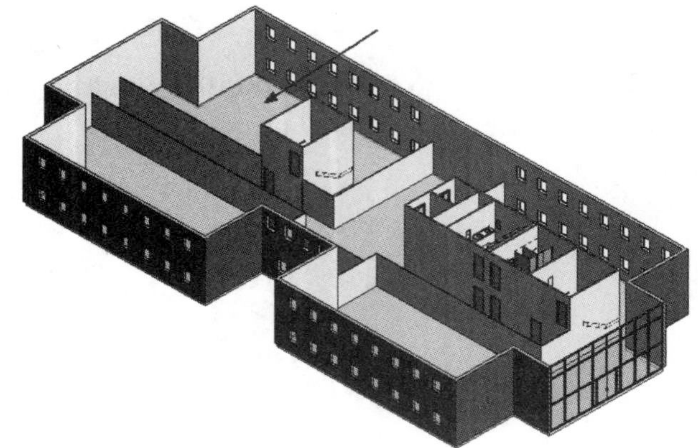

Left click to select the floor.

4. Select **Copy** from the Clipboard panel.

5. 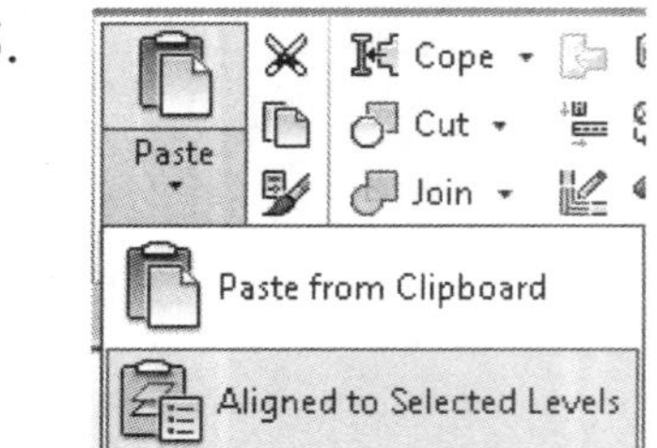

Select **Paste→Aligned to Selected Levels**.

6. Select **Level 2**.

Press **OK**.

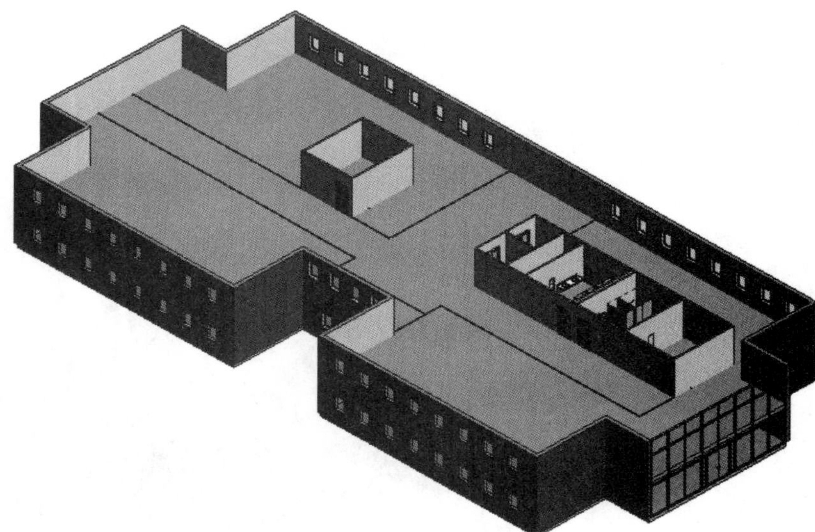

7. Left click in the window to release the selection.

8. Save as *ex5-2.rvt*.

Exercise 5-3

Creating a Shaft Opening

Drawing Name: ex5-2.rvt
Estimated Time: 15 minutes

This exercise reinforces the following skills:

- Shaft Opening
- Opening Properties
- Symbolic Lines

1. Open *ex5-2.rvt*

2. We need to create openings in the Level 2 floor for the elevators.
   Activate **Level 2**.

3. 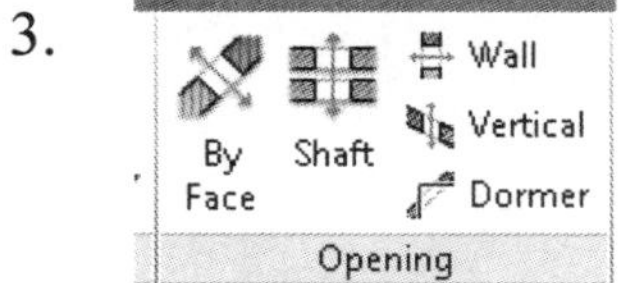

   Select the **Shaft Opening** tool under the Opening panel on the Architecture ribbon.

4. 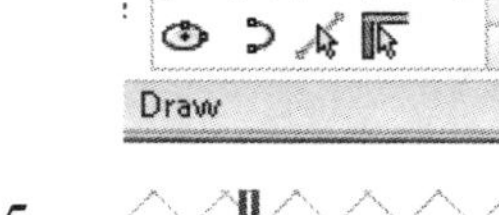

   Select the **Rectangle** tool from the Draw panel.

5. 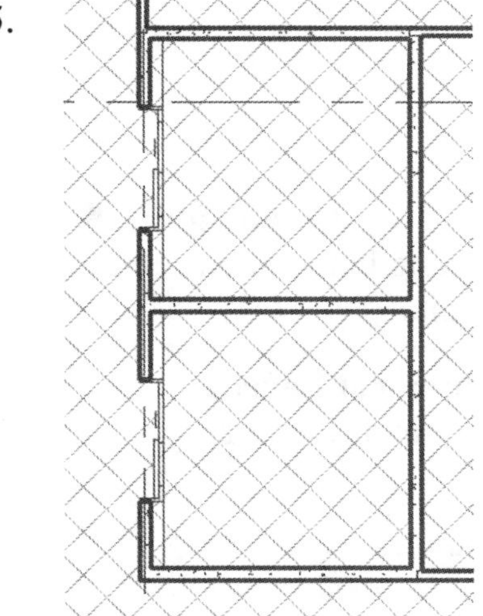

   Zoom into the elevator area.

   Draw two rectangles for the elevator shafts.

   Align the rectangles to the finish face of the inside walls and behind the elevator doors.

   The shaft will cut through any geometry, so be careful not to overlap any elements you want to keep.

6. Select the **Symbolic Line** tool.

7. Disable **Chain** on the Options bar.

8. Select the **Line** tool.

9. 

Place an X in each elevator shafts using the corners of the rectangle sketch.

The symbolic lines will appear in the floor plan to designate an opening.

10. 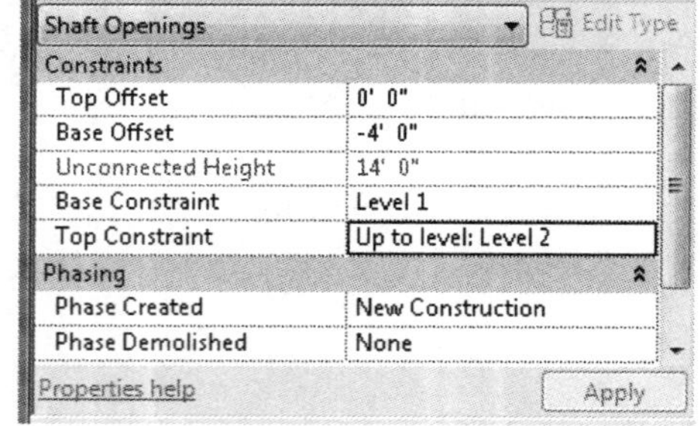

On the Properties pane:

Set the Base Offset at **-4′ 0″ [600 mm]**. This starts the opening below the floor to create an elevator pit.

Set the Base Constraint at **Level 1**.
Set the Top Constraint at **Level 2**.

11. 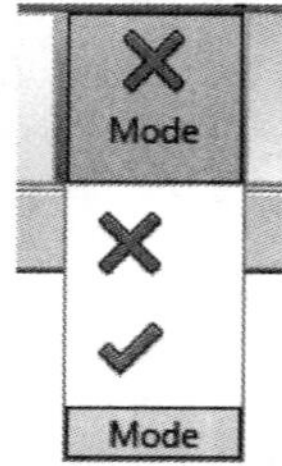

Select the **Green Check** under the Mode panel.

12. Switch to a 3D view.
Orbit around to inspect the model.

13. 

Inspect the elevator shafts.

Note that the shafts go through the bottom floor.

14. Floor Plans
- Level 1
- Level 2
- Roof Line
- Site

Activate **Level 1**.

The symbolic lines are visible.

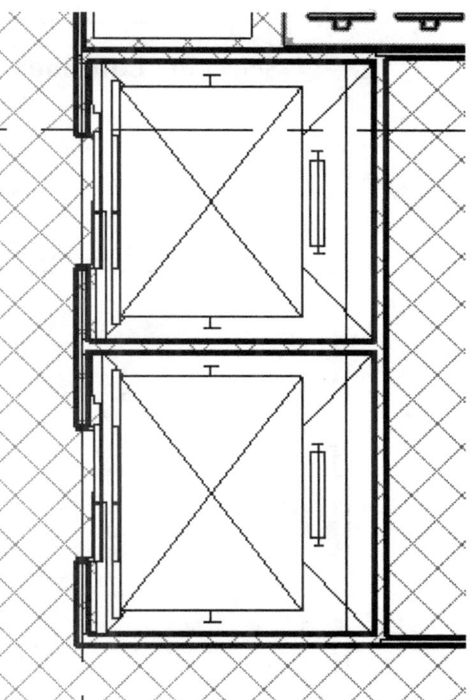

15. Save as *ex5-3.rvt*.

Exercise 5-4

Adding an Opening to a Floor

Drawing Name: ex5-3.rvt
Estimated Time: 20 minutes

This exercise reinforces the following skills:

- Opening
- Modify Floor

1. Open *ex5-3.rvt*
2. We need to create openings in the Level 2 floor for the stairs.
   Activate **Level 2**.
3. Properties
   Floor
   Wood Truss Joist 12" -VCT

   Select the floor.

   If it is selected, you should see it listed in the Properties pane.
4. 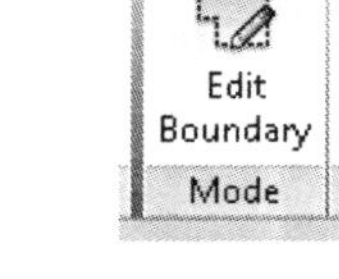

   Select the **Edit Boundary** tool on the ribbon.
5. 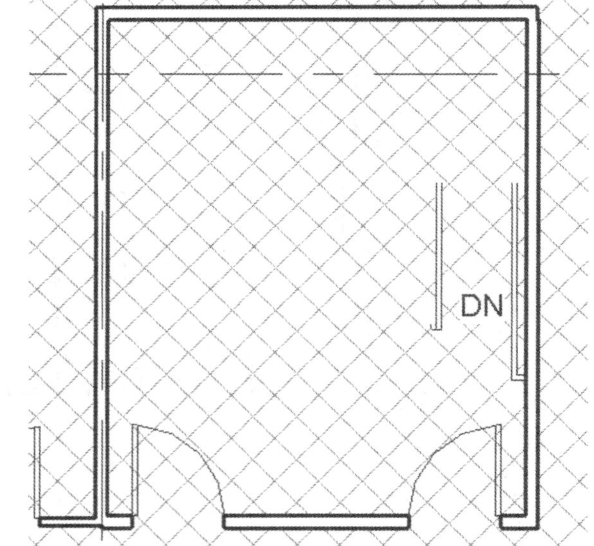

   Zoom into the first set of stairs.
6. Boundary Line
   Slope Arrow
   Span Direction
   Draw

   Select the **Rectangle** tool on the Draw panel.

7. 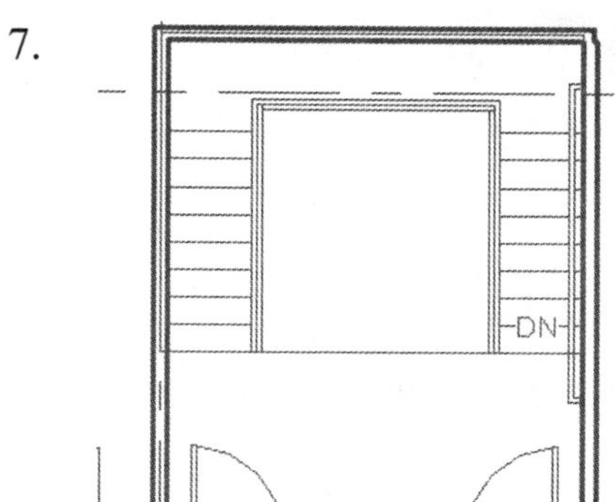

Place the rectangle so it is aligned to the inner walls and the stair risers.

8. 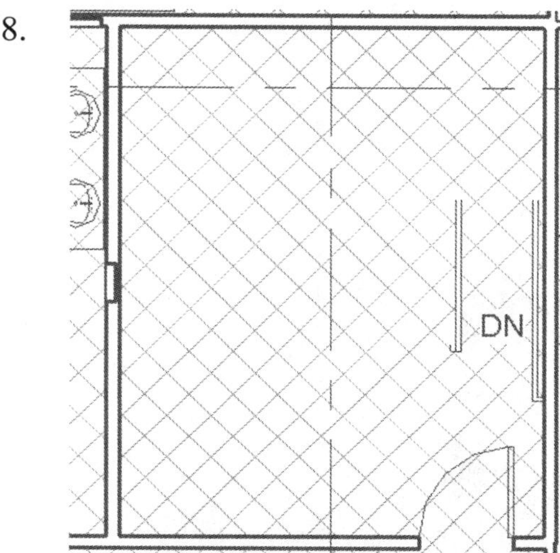

Zoom and pan over to the second set of stairs.

9. 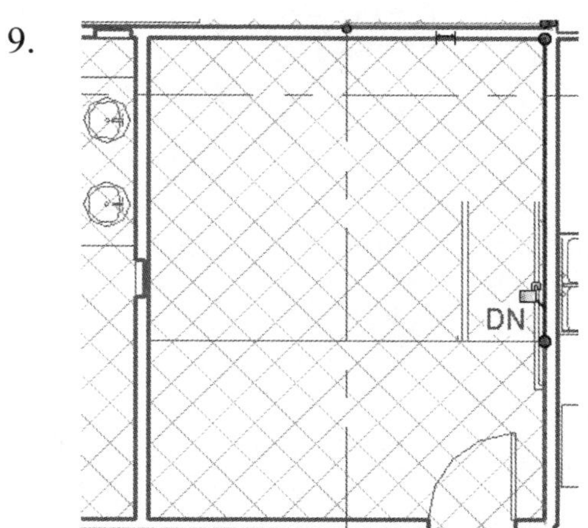

Place the rectangle so it is aligned to the inner walls and the stair risers.

10. 

Select the **Green Check** to finish modifying the floor.

11. 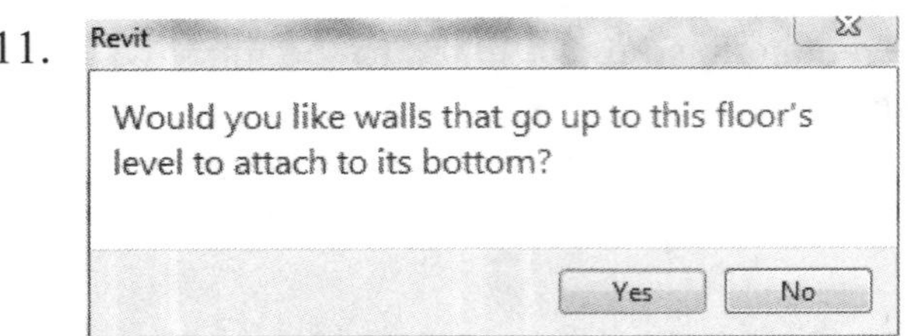

Press **No**.

12. Revit

The floor/roof overlaps the highlighted wall(s). Would you like to join geometry and cut the overlapping volume out of the wall(s)?

Yes No

If you see this dialog, press **No**.

13. 

Left click to release the selection.

Switch to a 3D view and inspect the openings in the floor.

14. Save as *ex5-4.rvt*.

Challenge Question:

When is it a good idea to use a Shaft Opening to cut a floor and when should you modify the floor boundary?

Shaft Openings can be used to cut through more than one floor at a time. Modifying the floor boundary creates an opening only in the floor selected.

Exercise 5-5
Creating Parts

Drawing Name: ex5-4.rvt
Estimated Time: 30 minutes

This exercise reinforces the following skills:

- Parts
- Dividing an Element
- Assigning materials to parts
- Modifying materials.

1. Open *ex5-4.rvt*.

   Switch to a 3D view.

2. 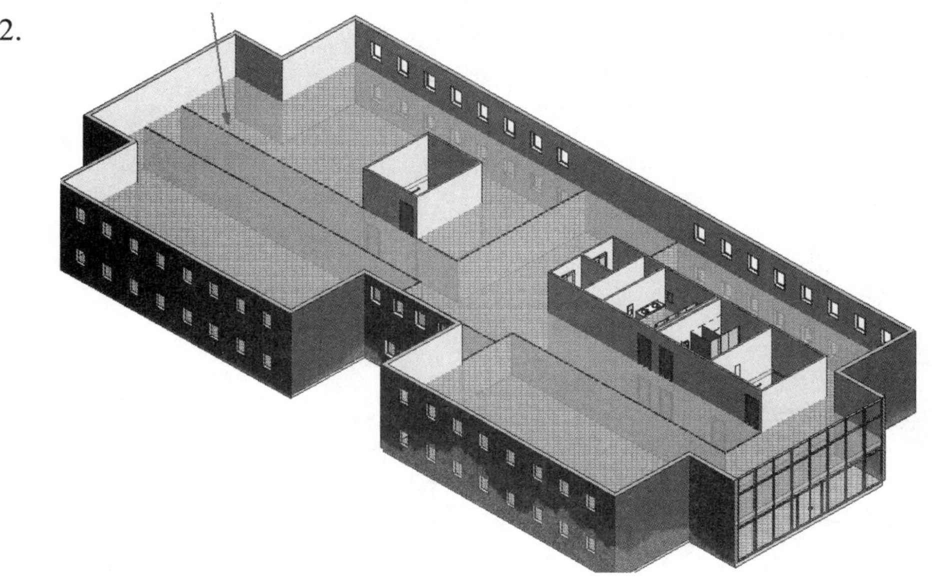

   Select the floor on the second level.

3. 

   Select the **Create Parts** tool under the Create panel.

4. Select **Divide Parts** from the Part panel.

   Divide Parts

5. 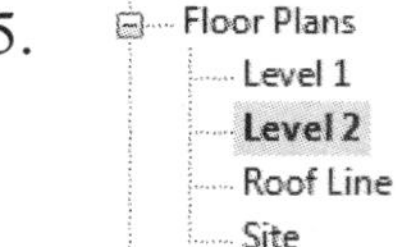

   Activate **Level 2**.

6. 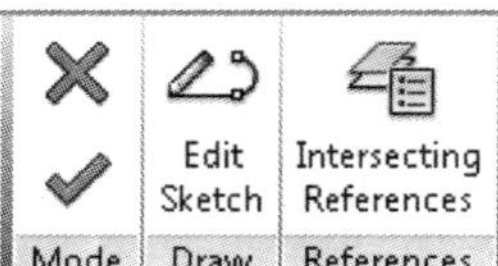

Select **Edit Sketch**.

7. 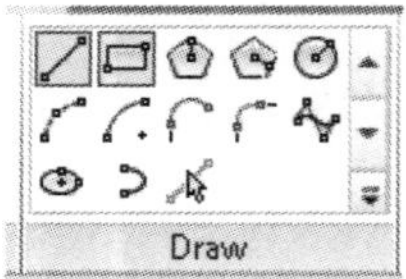

Select the rectangle tool from the Draw panel.

8. 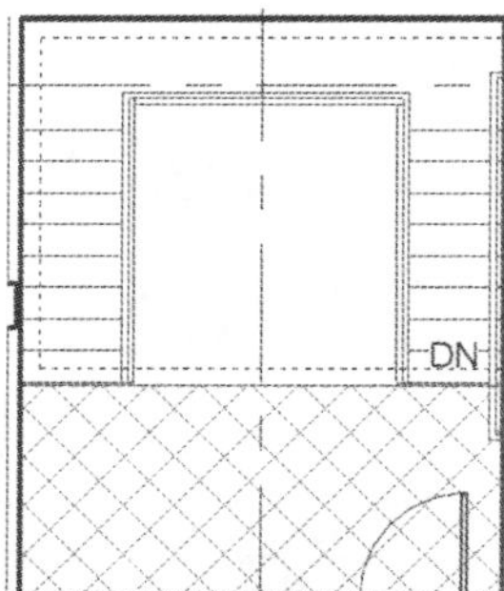

Draw a rectangle to define the landing for the stairwell.

9. 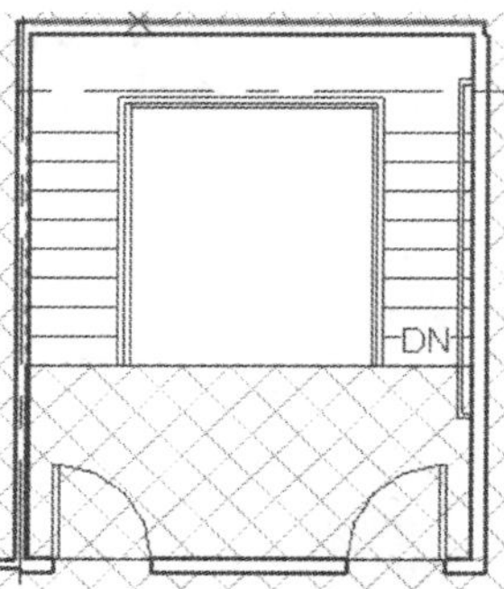

Repeat for the other stairwell.

10. 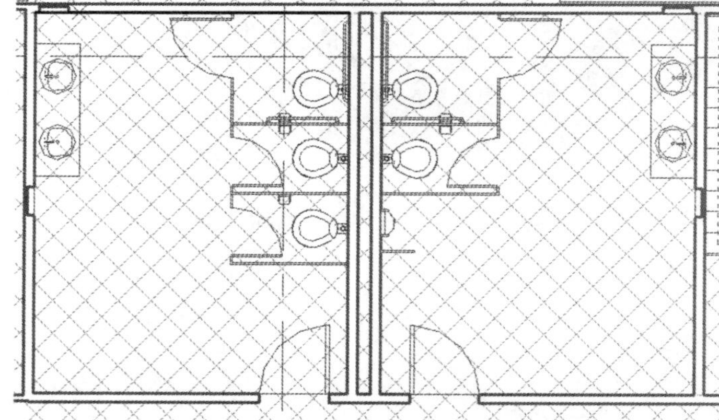
Draw a rectangle using the finish faces of the walls in the lavatories.

11. 

Select the **Green Check** under Mode twice.

12.  Switch to a 3D View.

13.

Graphics	
View Scale	1/8" = 1'-0"
Scale Value 1:	96
Detail Level	Medium
Parts Visibility	Show Parts
Visibility/Graphics Overri...	Edit...
Graphic Display Options	Edit...
Discipline	Architectural
Default Analysis Display S...	None

In the Properties pane for the view:

Under Parts Visibility: Enable **Show Parts**.

In order to see the parts in a view, you need to enable the visibility of the parts.

14.

Select the landing of the first stairwell.

You will see that it is identified as a part.

15.

Original Type	Wood Truss Joist 12" - Vinyl
Material By Original	☐
Material	VCT - Vinyl Composition Tile Diamond Patte...
Construction	Finish

In the Properties pane:

Uncheck **Material by Original**.
Left click in the Material field.

16.

Project Materials: All

Name
Gypsum Wall Board
Iron, Ductile
Laminate
Laminate - Ivory, Matte
Laminate - Linen,Matte

Scroll up and select the **Laminate - Ivory, Matte** material.

Press **OK**.

17.

Original Type	Wood Truss Joist 12" -VCT
Material By Original	☐
Material	Laminate - Ivory, Matte
Construction	Finish

The new material is now listed in the Properties pane.
Left click in the window to release the selection.

18. Pan over to the lavatory area.

Hold down the Control key.

Select the lavatory floor in both lavatories.

Note that it is now identified as a part.

19. 

Uncheck **Material by Original**.
Left click inside the Material field.

20. 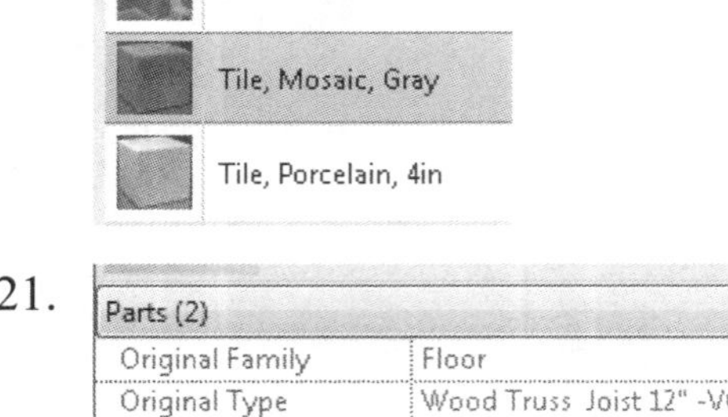

Locate the **Tile, Mosaic, Gray** material.

Press **OK**.

21. 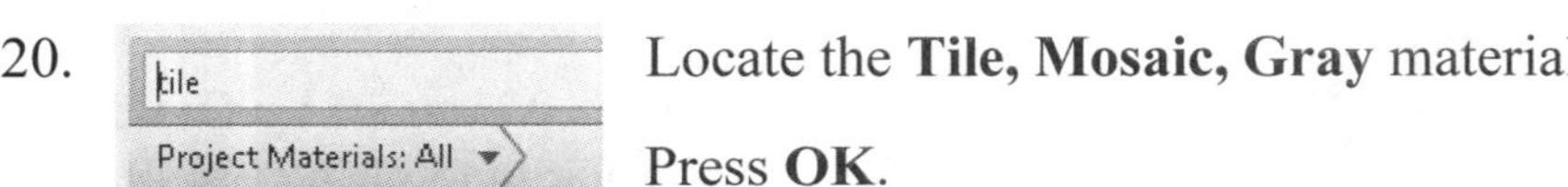

The lavatory parts are now set to the Tile material.
Left click in the window to release the selection.

22. 

Pan over to the second stairwell.

Select the landing.

Note that it is now identified as a part.

23. 

Uncheck **Material by Original**. Left click inside the Material field.

24.

conc
Project Materials: All
Search results for "conc"
Name
Concrete Masonry Units
Concrete, Cast-in-Place gray
Concrete, Lightweight
Concrete, Precast

Scroll up in the Material library.
Locate the **Concrete - Cast in-Place gray** material.

Press **OK**.

25. 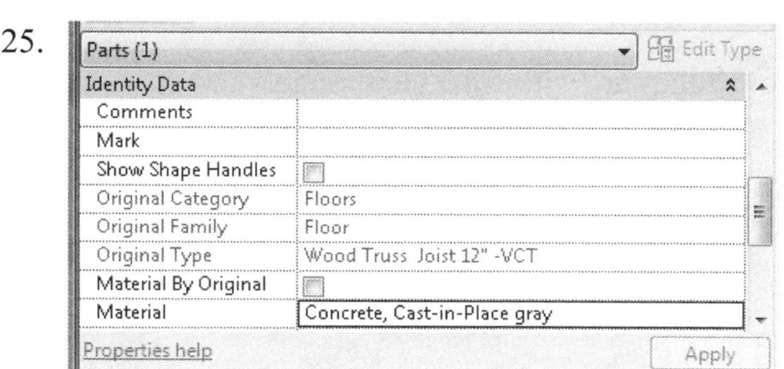

Verify that the landing has been assigned the correct material in the Properties pane.

26. Left click in the window to release the selection.

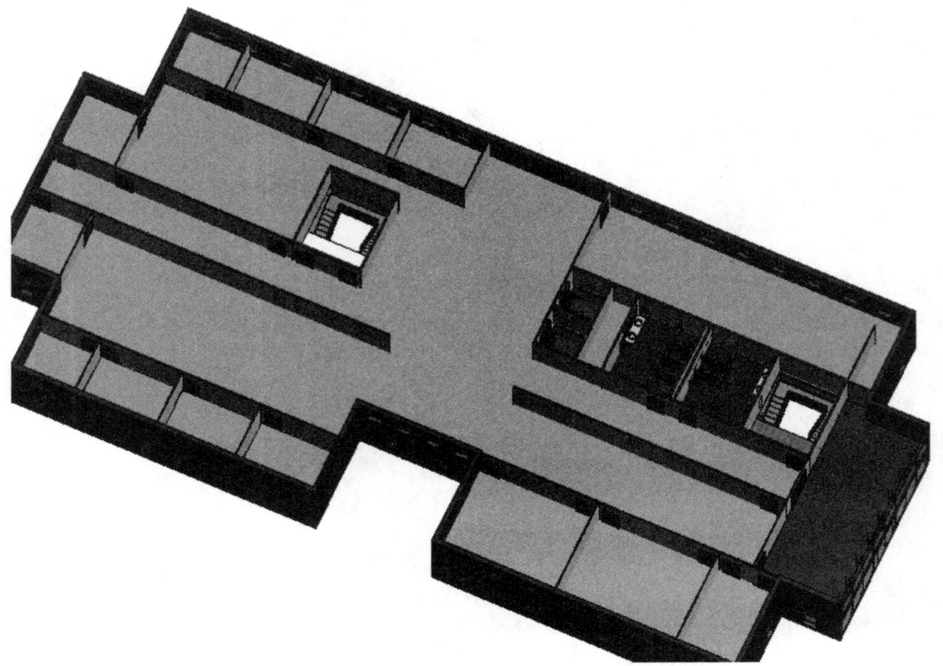

The different materials are displayed in the view.

27. Save as *ex5-5.rvt.*

Exercise 5-6
Viewing Parts in a Floor Plan View

Drawing Name: ex5-5.rvt
Estimated Time: 10 minutes

This exercise reinforces the following skills:

- View Range
- Parts

Parts can only be displayed in a view if they are within the view range.

1. Open *ex5-5.rvt.*

2. 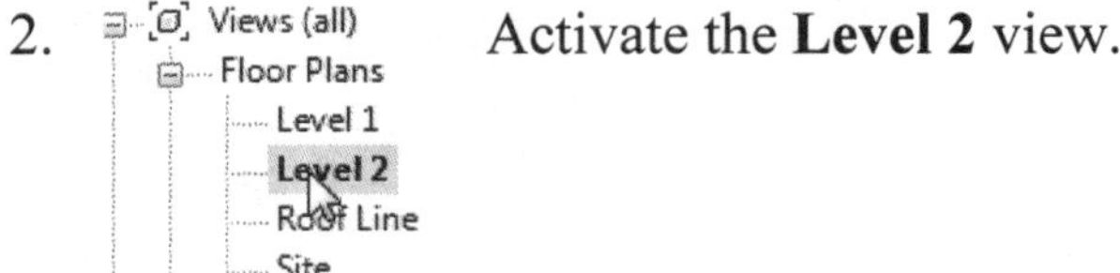

Activate the **Level 2** view.

3. 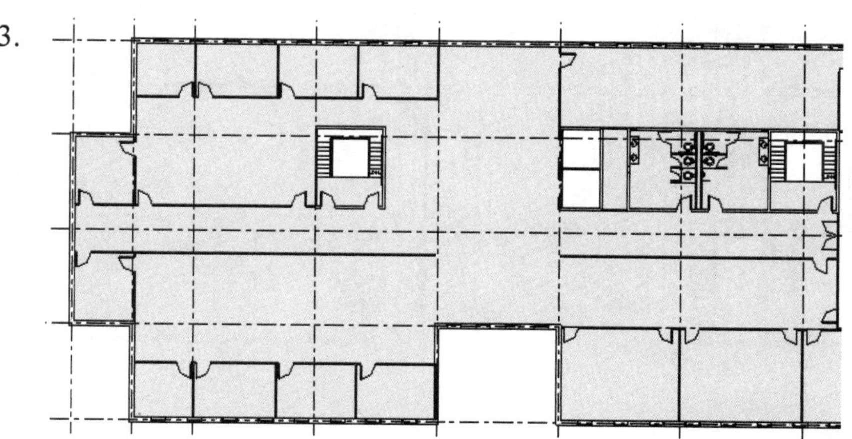

The hatch patterns for the parts are not visible.

4. In the Properties pane:

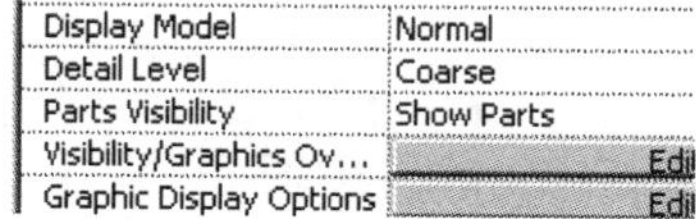

Set the Parts Visibility to **Show Parts**.

The floor disappears.

5. 1/8" = 1'-0"

Set the View Display to **Coarse** with **Hidden Lines**.

The view display does not change.

6.

Extents	
Crop View	☐
Crop Region Visible	☐
Annotation Crop	☐
View Range	Edit...
Associated Level	Level 2
Scope Box	None

Scroll down the Properties pane.

Press **Edit** next to the View Range field.

7. View Range

Primary Range

Top:	Associated Level (Level 2)	Offset:	7' 6"
Cut plane:	Associated Level (Level 2)	Offset:	4' 0"
Bottom:	Associated Level (Level 2)	Offset:	0' 0"

View Depth

Level:	Associated Level (Level 2)	Offset:	-1' 0"

OK Cancel Apply Help

Set the Top Offset to **7′ 6″ [228.6]**.
Set the Cut plane Offset to **4′ 0″ [121.92]**.
Set the Bottom Offset to **4′ 0″ [121.92]**.
Set the View Depth Level to Level 1.
Set the View Depth Offset to **-1′ 0″ [-60.0]**.
Press **Apply**.

8. The parts now display properly.

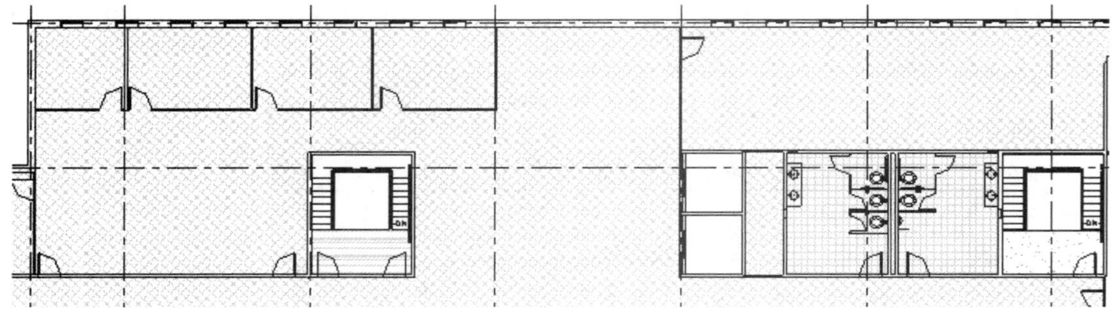

Save as *ex5-6.rvt*.

Understanding View Range

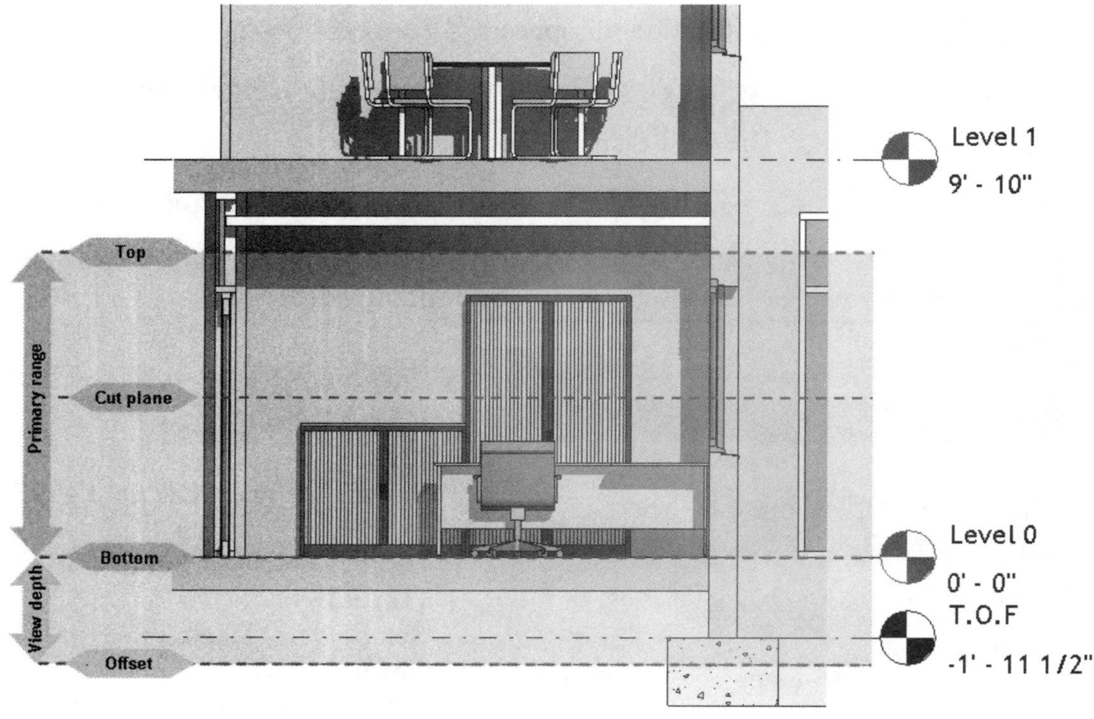

This figure shows an elevation view of a view range setting.

- Elements within the boundaries of the primary range that are not cut are drawn in the element's projection line style.
- Elements that are cut are drawn in the element's cut line style.

  Note: Not all elements can display as cut.
- Elements that are within the view depth are drawn in the beyond line style – that is a solid line.

Exercise 5-7
Adding a Railing

Drawing Name: ex5-6.rvt
Estimated Time: 15 minutes

This exercise reinforces the following skills:

- Railing
- Railing Properties
- Re-Host

1. Open *ex5-6.rvt.*

2. 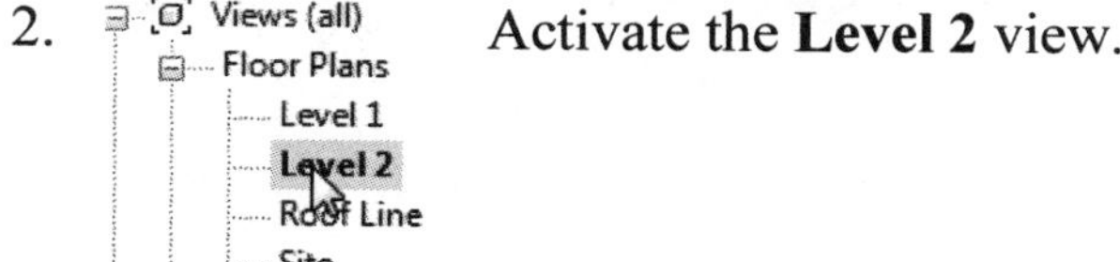

Activate the **Level 2** view.

3. 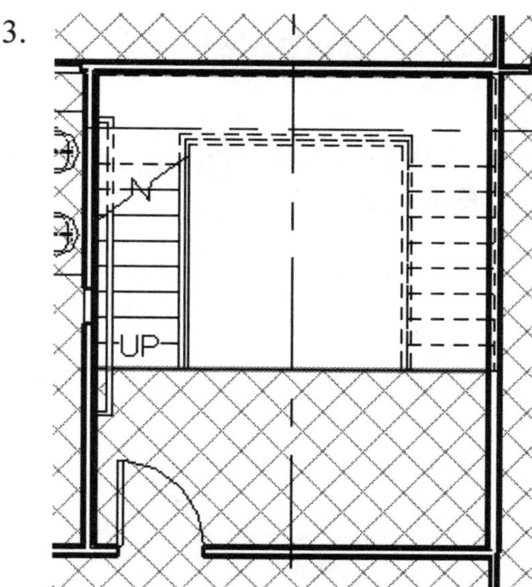

Zoom into the concrete landing next to the lavatories.

4. 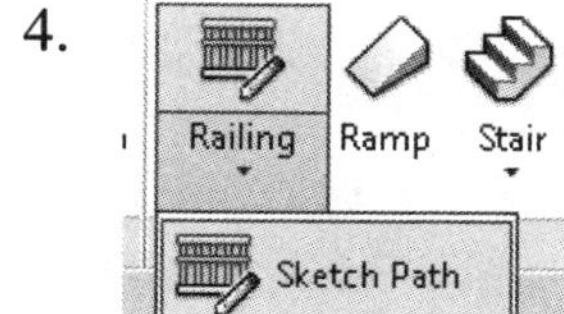

Select the **Railing→Sketch Path** tool under the Circulation panel on the Architecture ribbon.

5. 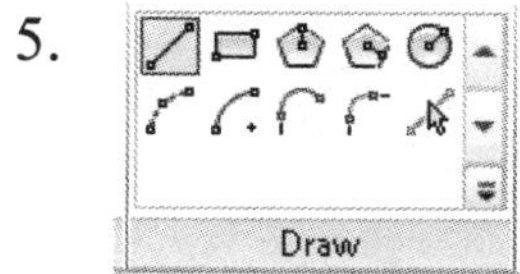

Draw the railing using the **Line** tool from the Draw panel.

   Use the end points of the existing rails to locate it.

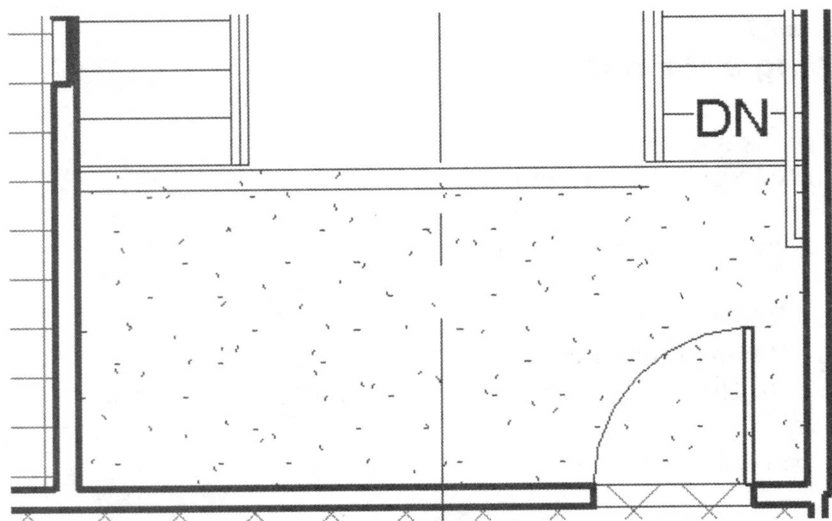

6. Edit Type Select **Edit Type** from the Properties pane.

7. Duplicate... Select **Duplicate**.

8. Name: Guardrail - Landing Name the new railing style – **Guardrail-Landing**.

Press **OK**.

9. Select the **Edit** button next to Rail Structure.

Type Parameters

Parameter	Value
Construction	
Railing Height	3' 0"
Rail Structure (Non-Continuous)	Edit...
Baluster Placement	Edit...

10. Insert Press the **Insert** button two times to add two rails.

11. Name the rails.
Set Rail 1 to **Middle Rail**.
Set Rail 2 to **Bottom Rail**.

Rails

	Name
1	Middle Rail
2	Bottom Rail

12.

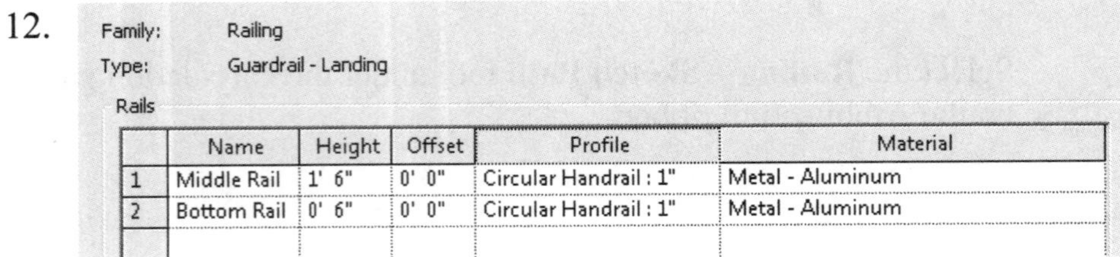

Family: Railing
Type: Guardrail - Landing
Rails

	Name	Height	Offset	Profile	Material
1	Middle Rail	1' 6"	0' 0"	Circular Handrail : 1"	Metal - Aluminum
2	Bottom Rail	0' 6"	0' 0"	Circular Handrail : 1"	Metal - Aluminum

Set the rail heights to **1′-6″** [**600**], and **6″** [**150 mm**].
Set the profiles to **Circular Handrail: 1″** [**M_Circular Handrail: 30 m**].
Set the material to **Metal - Aluminum**.
Press **OK**.

13. 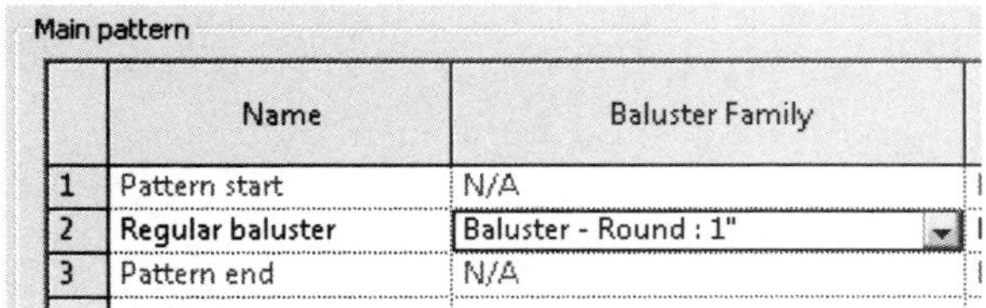

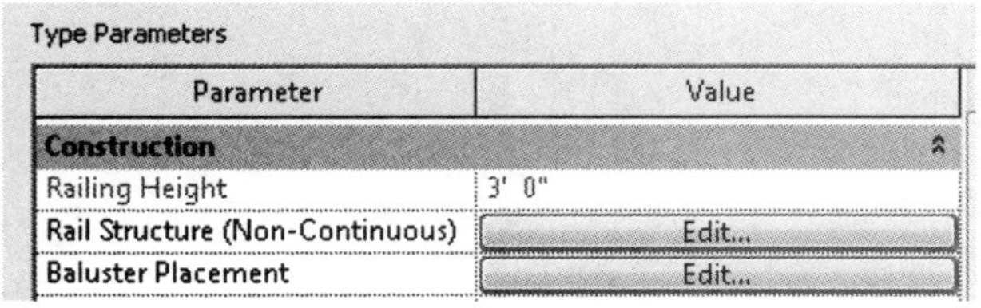

Select **Edit** next to Baluster Placement.

14. 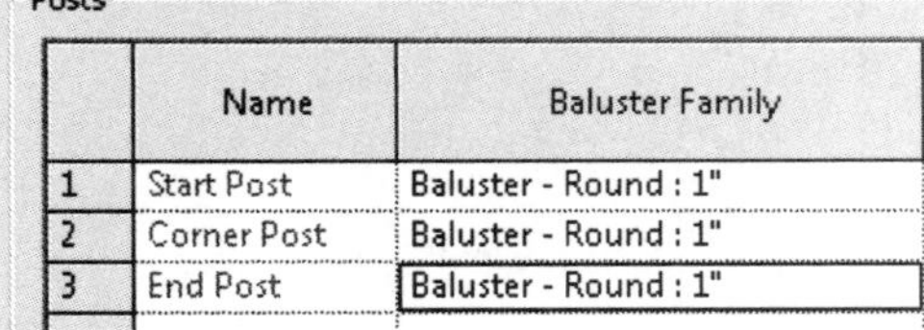

Under Main Pattern:

Set the Baluster Family to **Baluster - Round 1″**.

15. Under Posts:

Set the Baluster Family to **Baluster - Round 1″**.

16. 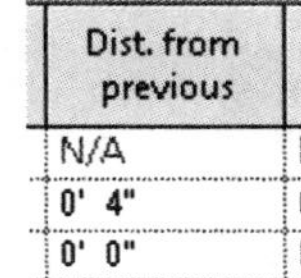

In the Dist. from previous column, set the distance to **4″ [150]**. Press **OK**.

Close the dialog.

17. 

Select the **Green Check** under Mode to finish the railing.

18. Switch to a 3D view to inspect the railing.

Repeat the exercise to place a railing at the other stair landing.

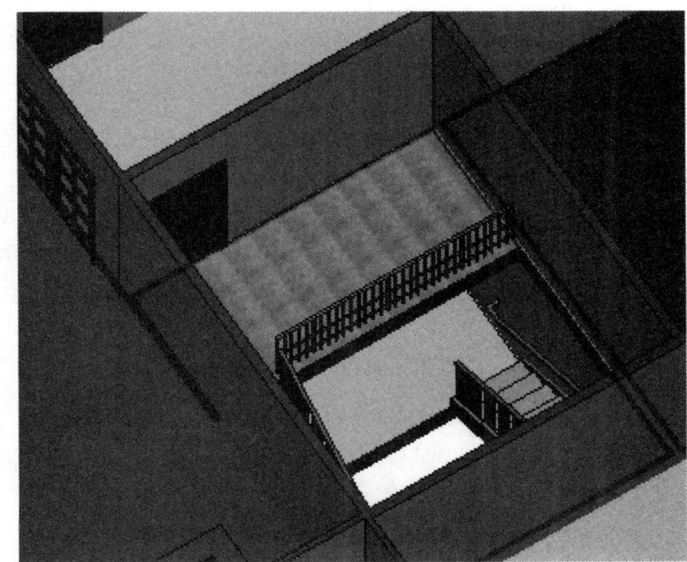

19. Save the file as *ex5-7.rvt.*

Exercise 5-8
Creating Ceilings

Drawing Name: ex5-7.rvt
Estimated Time: 10 minutes

This exercise reinforces the following skills:

- ❑ Ceilings
- ❑ Visibility of Annotation Elements

1. Open *ex5-7.rvt.*

2. Ceiling Plans / Level 1 / Level 2 / Roof Line — Activate **Level 1** under Ceiling Plans.

3. Type **VV**.

4. 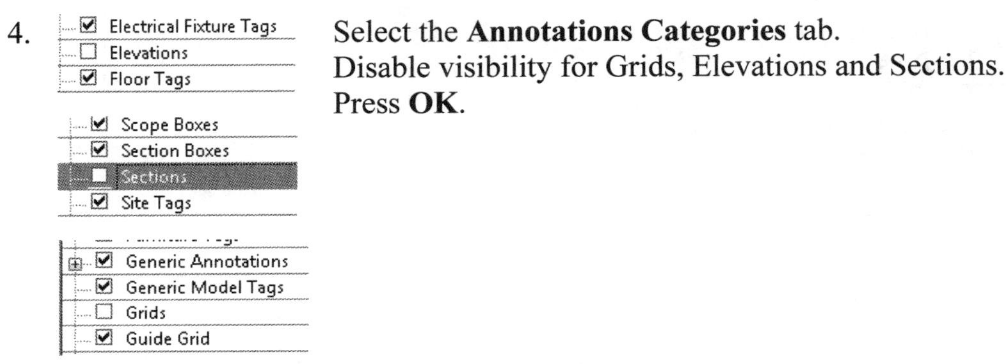

Select the **Annotations Categories** tab.
Disable visibility for Grids, Elevations and Sections.
Press **OK**.

5. The view display should update.

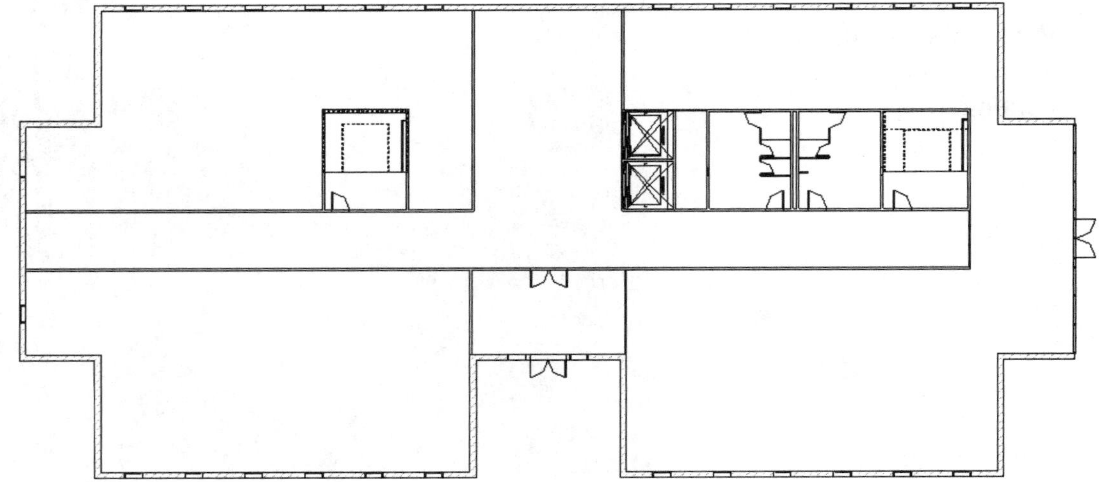

6. Ceiling — Select the **Ceiling** tool from Build panel on the Architecture ribbon.

7. Select the **Ceiling: 2′ × 4′ ACT System [Compound Ceiling: 600 x 1200 mm Grid]** from the Properties pane.

8. Left click in the building entry to place a ceiling.

The ceiling is placed.

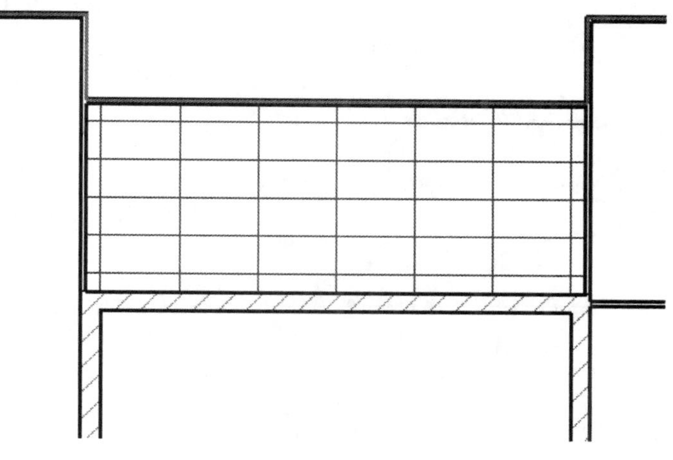

9. Save as *ex5-8.rvt*.

Exercise 5-9

Adding Lighting Fixtures

Drawing Name: ex5-8.rvt
Estimated Time: 10 minutes

This exercise reinforces the following skills:

- Add Component
- Load From Library

1. Open or continue working in *ex5-8.rvt*.

2. Activate **Level 1 Ceiling Plan**.

3. Activate the **Architecture** ribbon.

Select the **Component→Place a Component** tool from the Build panel.

4. Select **Load Family** from the Mode panel.

5. 

Browse to the *Lighting/Architectural/Internal* folder.

6. 

Locate the *Ceiling-Linear Box.rfa [M_ Ceiling-Linear Box.rfa]*. Press **Open**.

7. 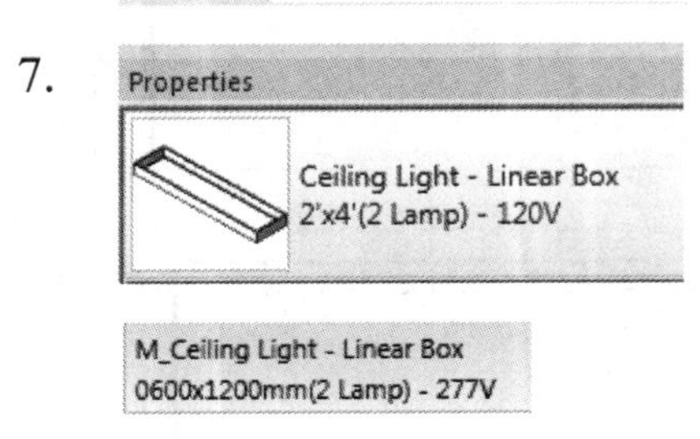

Select the **2′x 4′ (Lamp) [0600x 1200mm (2 Lamp) – 277V]** for the element type.

8. Place fixtures on the grid.

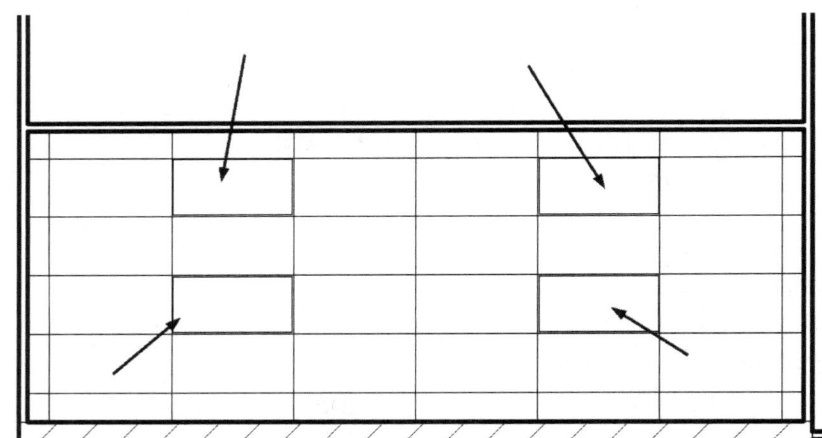

Use the ALIGN tool to position the fixtures in the ceiling grid.

9. Save the file as *ex5-9.rvt.*

Challenge Exercise:

Add ceilings to Level 1 and Level 2.

Define new ceiling types using stucco material.

Exercise 5-10

Applying Paints and Wallpaper to Walls

Drawing Name: ex5-9.rvt
Estimated Time: 30 minutes

This exercise reinforces the following skills:

- Views
- Section Box
- View Properties
- Materials
- Load From Library
- Render Appearance Library

1. Open or continue working in *ex5-9.rvt.*

2. 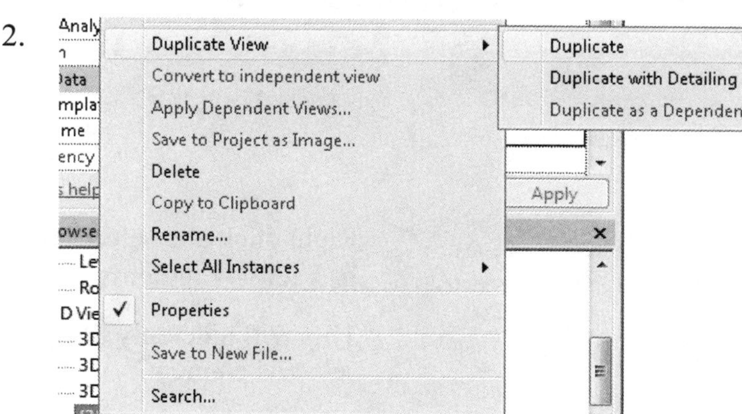

Highlight the {3D} view in the Project Browser.

Right click and select **Duplicate View → Duplicate**.

3. 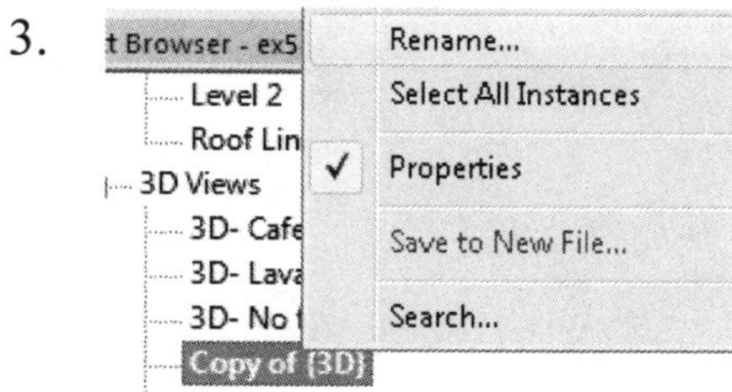

Right click on the new view.

Select **Rename**.

4. 

Type **3D-Lobby**.

Press **OK**.

5. Set Parts Visibility to **Show Original**.

3D View: 3D- Lobby	
Graphics	
View Scale	1/8" = 1'-0"
Scale Value 1:	96
Detail Level	Medium
Parts Visibility	Show Original

6. Enable Section Box in the Properties panel.

Extents	
Crop View	☐
Crop Region Visible	☐
Annotation Crop	☐
Far Clip Active	☐
Section Box	☑

7. Using the grips on the section box, reduce the view to just the lobby area.

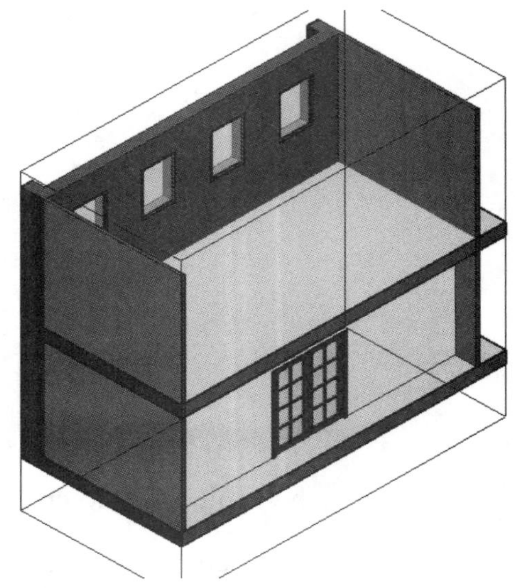

8. Select the floor on Level 2.

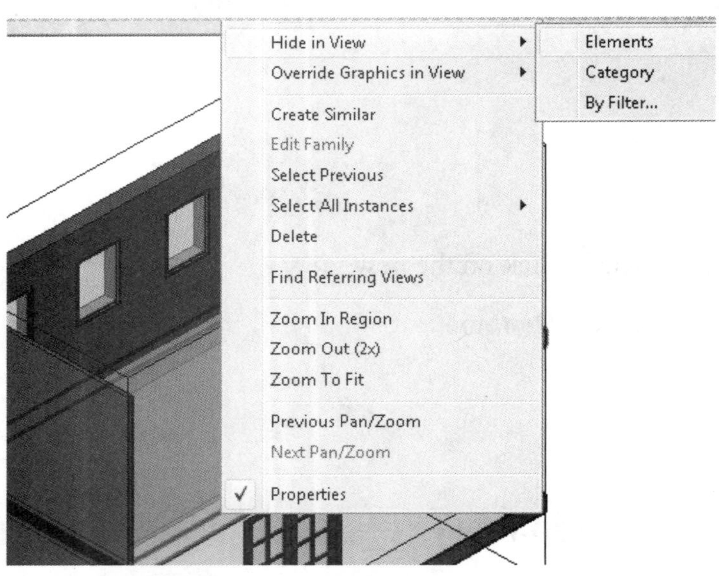

Right click and select **Hide in View→Elements**.

This will hide only the selected element.

9. Select the ceiling. Right click and select **Hide in View → Elements**.

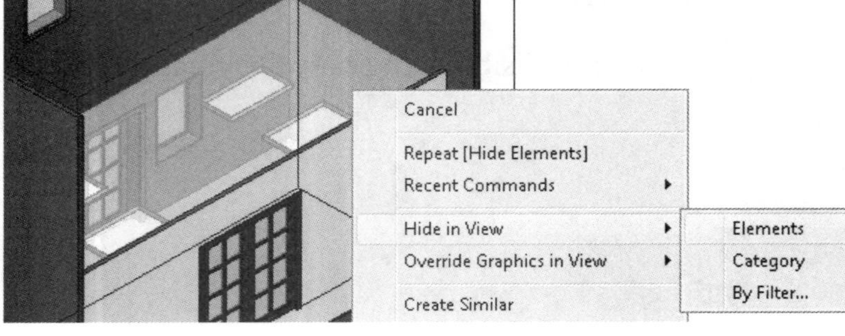

This will hide only the selected element.

10. The lighting fixtures in the ceiling are still visible but can be ignored.

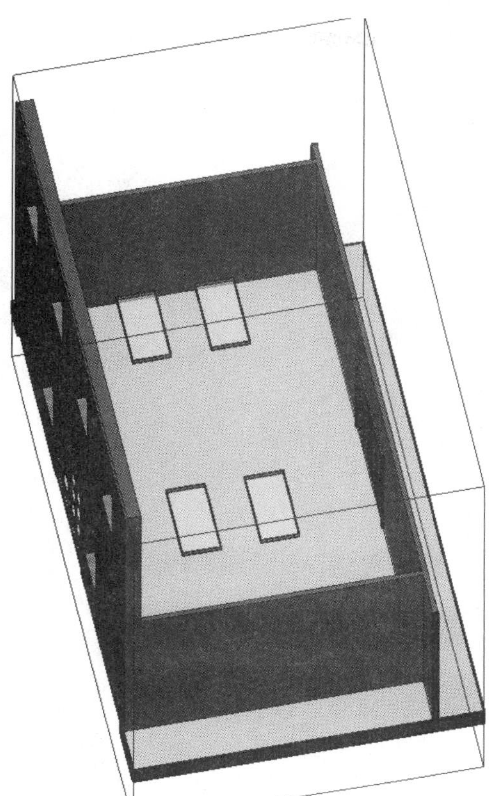

11. Activate the Modify ribbon.

Select the **Split Face** tool on the Geometry panel.

12.

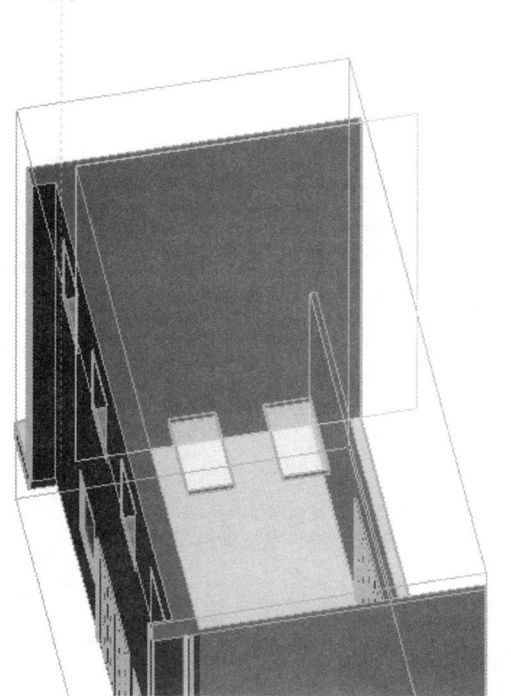

13. 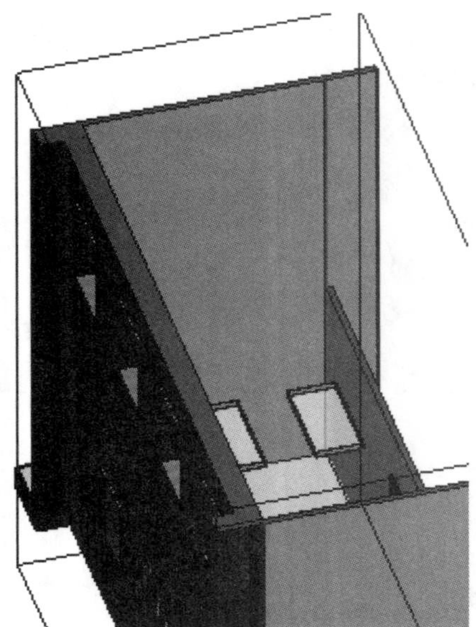

Draw a line on the corner of the room to indicate where the wall should be split.

14. 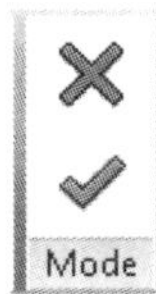

Select the **Green check**.

15. 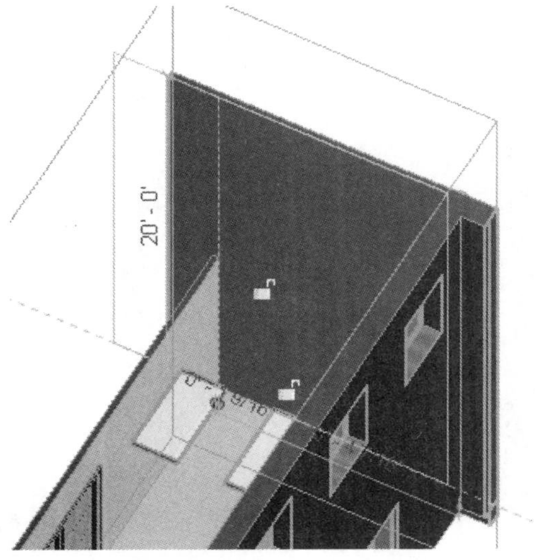

Repeat for the wall on the other side of the lobby.

16. 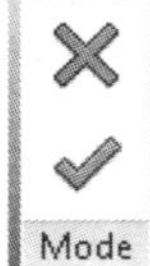

Select the **Green check**.

17. 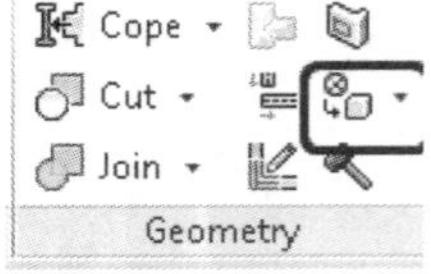

Select the **Paint** tool on the Geometry panel.

18. Locate the **Finish – Paint - SW0068 Heron Blue** from the Material Browser list.

Material Browser - Metal - Aluminum
paint
Project Materials: All
Search results for "paint"
Metal - Paint...sh -
Paint - Inter...0068
Paint - SW61...hite
Steel, Paint Finis...ory,

19. Select the walls indicated.

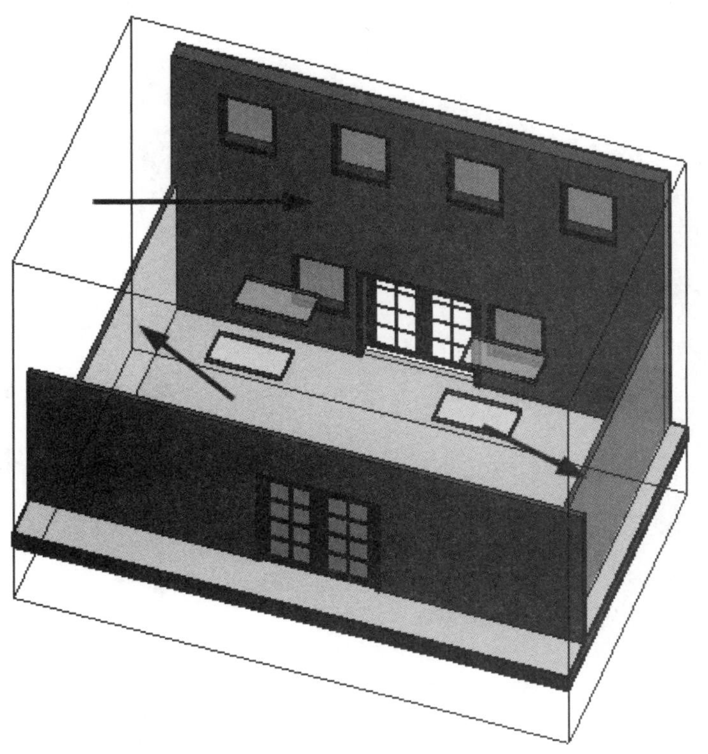

20. Locate the Wallpaper you defined earlier.

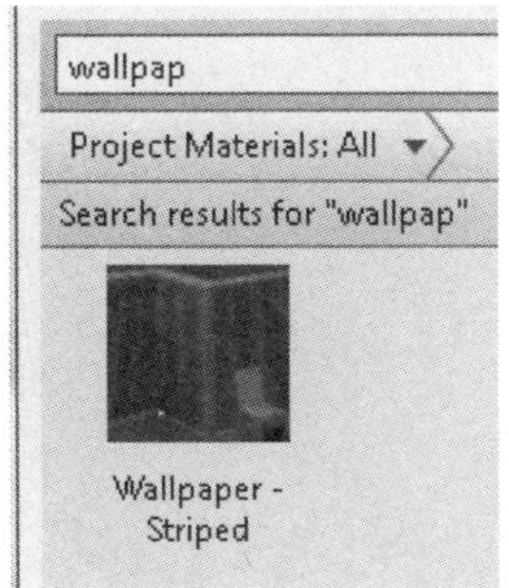

21. 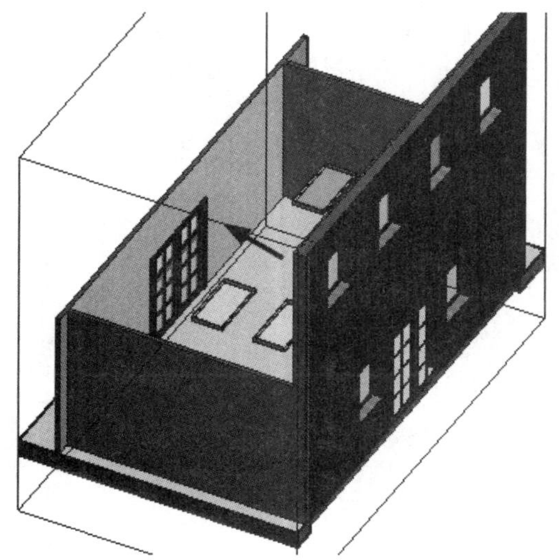

Apply the wallpaper to the inner lobby back wall.

22. 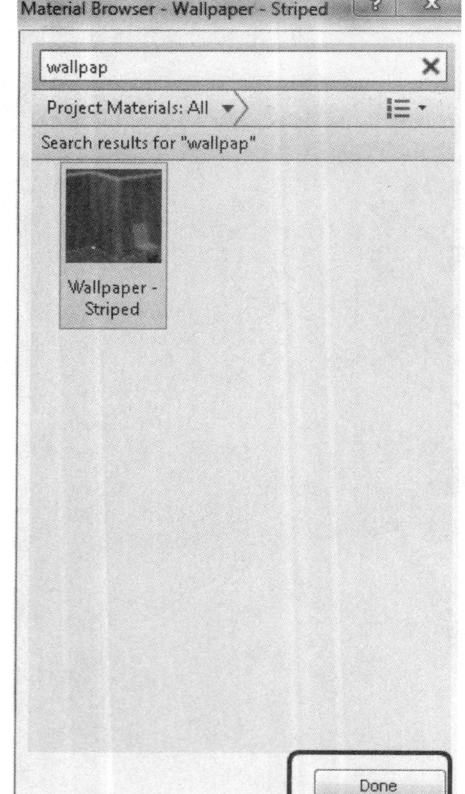

Select the **Done** button at the bottom of the Material Browser.

23. 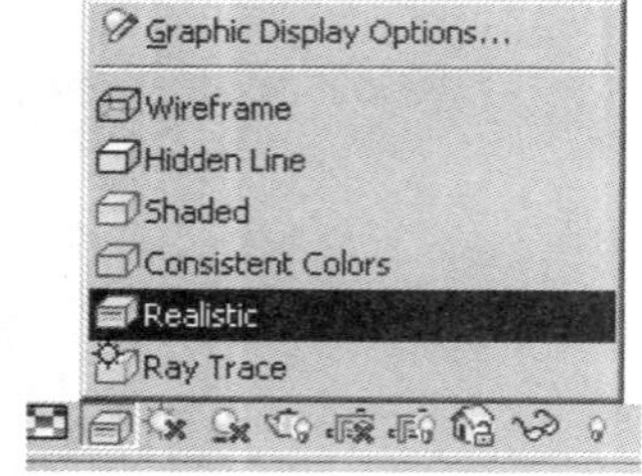

Change the display to **Realistic** so you can see the paint color applied.

24. Save as *ex5-10.rvt*.

Additional Projects

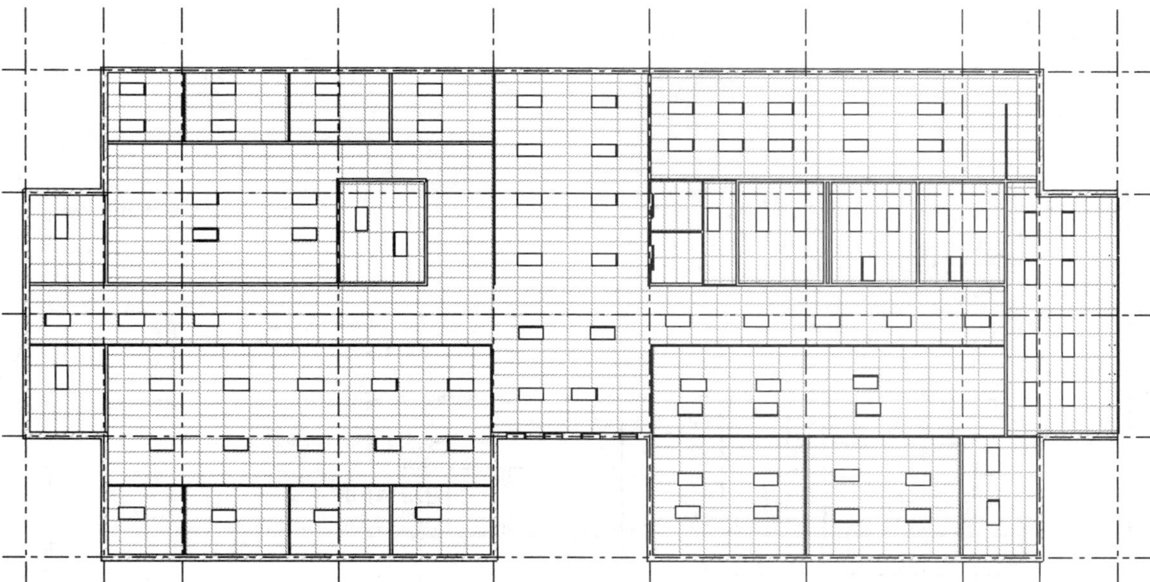

1) Add light fixtures and ceilings to the Second Level Ceiling Plan.
   Create a Ceiling Plan layout/sheet.

2) Load the Lighting Fixture Tag-Mark – Boxed (This family is in the exercise files) using File→Load Family.
   Use Tag All Not Tagged to tag all the lighting fixtures.
   Create a schedule of lighting fixtures.
   Add to your reflected ceiling plan sheet.

<Lighting Fixture Schedule>			
A	B	C	D
Type	Wattage	Level	Count
2'x4'(2 Lamp) - 120V	80 W	Level 2	93

Sort by Level and then by Type to get a schedule like this. Filter to only display Level 2 fixtures.

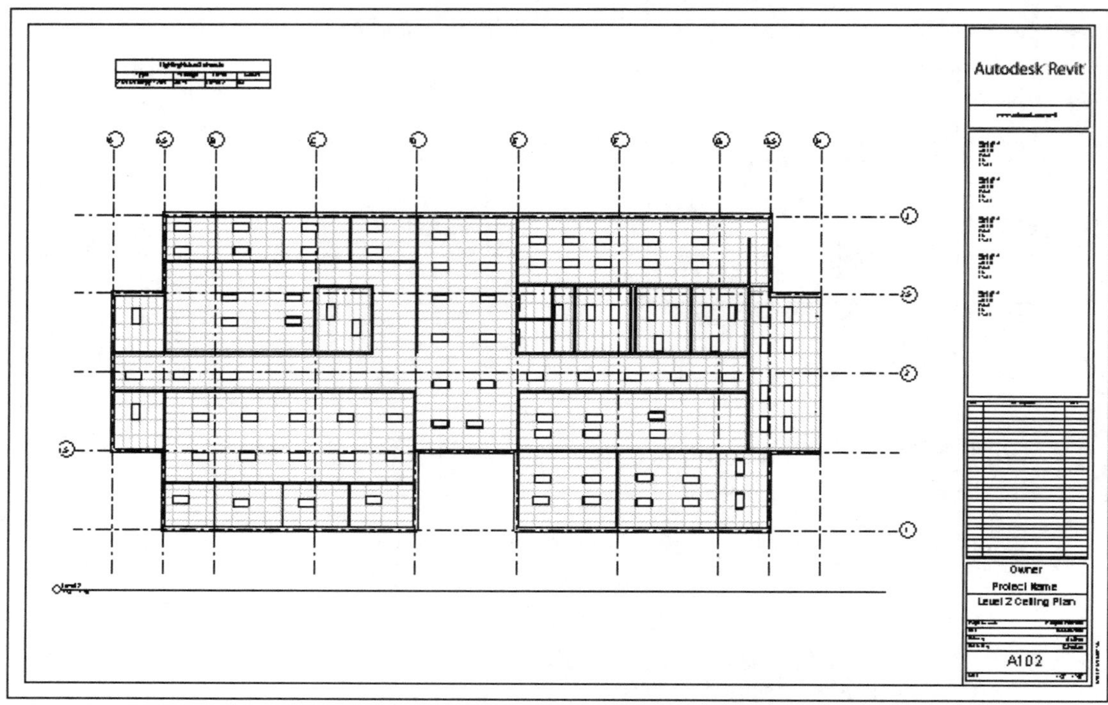

Lesson 5 Quiz

True or False

1. Ceilings are not visible on the Floor Plan view.
2. Ceilings are visible on the Ceiling Plan view.
3. In order to place a ceiling-based light fixture, the model must have a ceiling.
4. To create an opening in a floor, use EDIT BOUNDARY.
5. Floors and ceilings are level-based.
6. Floors and ceilings can be offset from a level.
7. The boundaries for a floor or ceiling must be closed, non-intersecting loops.

Multiple Choice

8. When a floor is placed:

   A. The top of the floor is aligned to the level on which it is placed with the thickness projecting downward.
   B. The bottom of the floor is aligned to the level on which it is placed with the thickness projecting upwards.
   C. The direction of the thickness can be flipped going up or down.
   D. The floor offset can be above or below the level.

9. The structure of a floor is determined by its:

   A. Family type
   B. Placement
   C. Instance
   D. Geometry

10. Floors can be created by these two methods:
    Pick two answers.

    A. Sketching a closed polygon
    B. Picking Walls
    C. Place Component
    D. Drawing boundary lines

11. Ceilings are:
    Pick one answer.

    A. Level-based
    B. Floor-based
    C. Floating
    D. Non-hosted

12. Paint can be applied using the Paint tool which is located on this ribbon:

    A. Architecture
    B. Modify
    C. Rendering
    D. View

13. New materials are created using:

    A. Manage→ Materials.
    B. View→Materials
    C. Architecture→Create→Materials
    D. Architecture→Render→Materials

14. This icon:

    A. Adjusts the brightness of a view.
    B. Temporarily isolates selected elements or categories
    C. Turns off visibility of elements
    D. Zooms into an element

15. To place a Shaft Opening, activate the ____________________ ribbon.

    A. Modify
    B. View
    C. Manage
    D. Architecture

16. In order for parts to be visible in a view:

    A. Parts should be enabled on the Materials ribbon
    B. Parts should be enabled in the Visibility/Graphics dialog
    C. Show Parts should be enabled in the Properties pane for the view
    D. The view display should be set to Shaded

ANSWERS:

1) T; 2) T; 3) T; 4) T; 5) T; 6) T; 7) T; 8) A; 9) A; 10) A & B; 11) A; 12) B; 13) A; 14) B 15) D; 16) C

Lesson 6
Schedules

Revit proves its power in the way it manages schedules. Schedules are automatically updated whenever the model changes. In this lesson, users learn how to add custom parameters to elements to be used in schedules, how to create and apply keynotes, and how to place schedules on sheets.

Tags are annotations and they are **view-specific**. This means if you add a tag in one view, they are not automatically visible in another view.

Tags are Revit families. Tags use parameter data. For example, a Room tag might display the room name and the room area. The room name and room area are both parameters.

A schedule is a tabular view of information, using the parameters of elements in a project. You can organize a schedule using levels, types of elements, etc. You can filter a schedule so it only displays the elements of a specific type or located on a specific level.

Because schedules are views, they are listed in the Project Browser in the view area. Schedules are placed on sheets, just like any other view; simply drag and drop from the Project Browser.

You cannot import schedules from Excel, but you can export schedules to Excel.

Exercise 6-1
Adding Door Tags

Drawing Name: ex5-11.rvt
Estimated Time: 10 minutes

This exercise reinforces the following skills:

- Door Tags

1. Floor Plans / Level 1 / Level 2 / Roof Line / Site — Activate Level 1.

2. The floor plan has several doors.

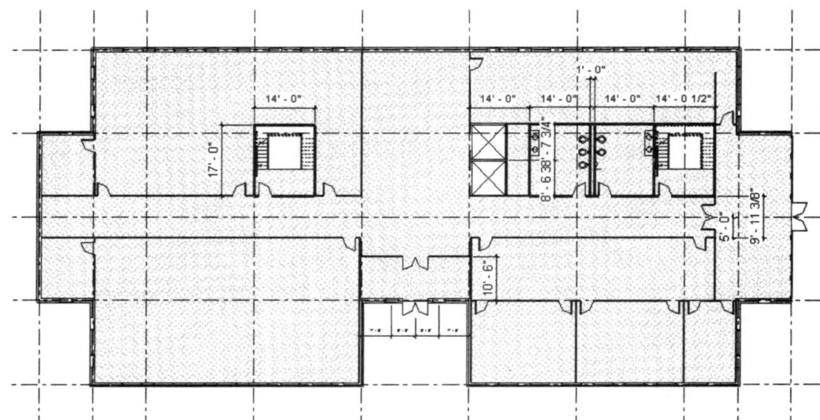

The additional rooms and doors were added in the additional practice exercises.

3. Activate the **Annotate** ribbon.

   Tag All — Select **Tag All**.

4. 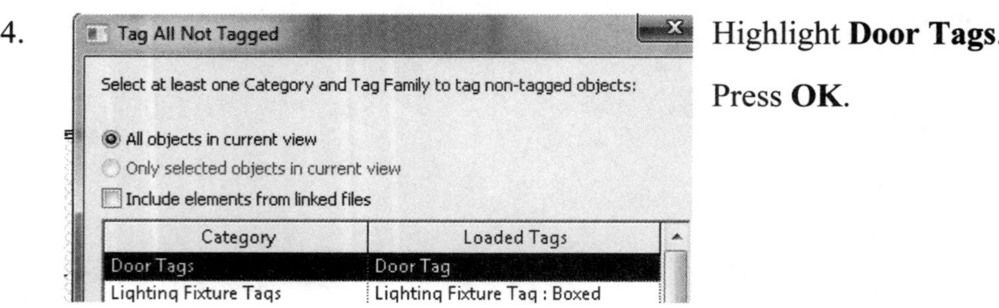

   Highlight **Door Tags**.

   Press **OK**.

5. Door Tags are added to the doors.

   Select the exterior double door.

6. Identity Data

Identity Data	
Comments	
Mark	5

Go to the **Properties** panel.

Locate the **Mark** parameter under Identity Data.

The Mark or Door Number can be modified in the Properties panel.

You cannot use the same door number twice. You will see an error message if you attempt to assign a door number already in use.

If you delete a door and add a new door, the door will be assigned the next mark number. It will not use the deleted door's mark number. Many users wait until the design is complete and then re-number all the doors on each level.

7. Floor Plans
   - Level 1
   - Level 2
   - Roof Line
   - Site

   Activate **Level 2**.

8. Activate the **Annotate** ribbon.

   Tag All

   Select **Tag All**.

9. | Category | Loaded Tags |
   |---|---|
   | Door Tags | Door Tag |
   | Lighting Fixture Tags | Lighting Fixture Tag : Boxed |

   Highlight **Door Tags**.

   Press **OK**.

10. Door tags are added to all the doors.

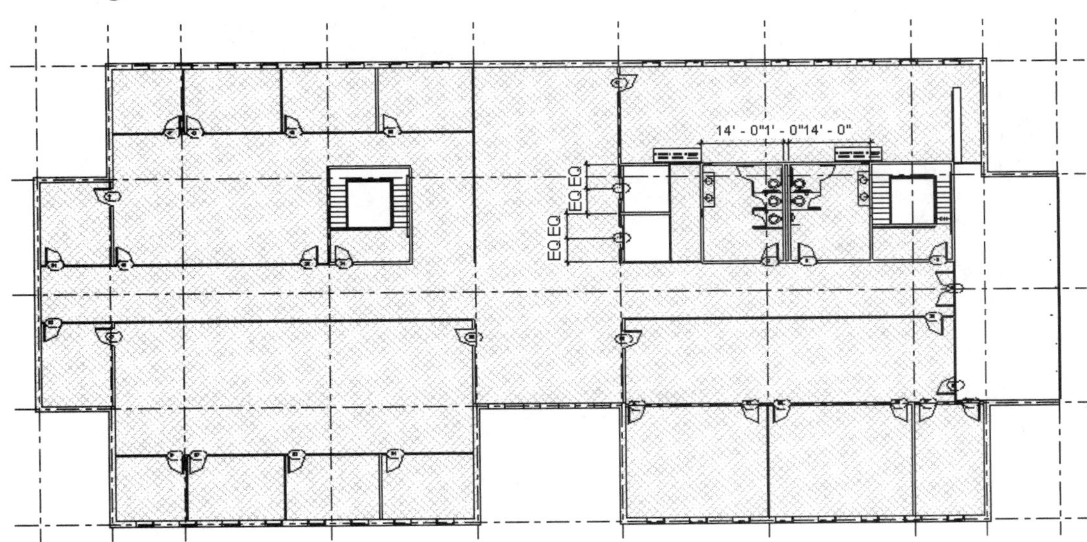

11. Save as *ex6-1.rvt*.

Exercise 6-2
Creating a Door Schedule

Drawing Name: ex6-1.rvt
Estimated Time: 30 minutes

This exercise reinforces the following skills:

- Door Tags
- Schedules

1. Activate the View ribbon.

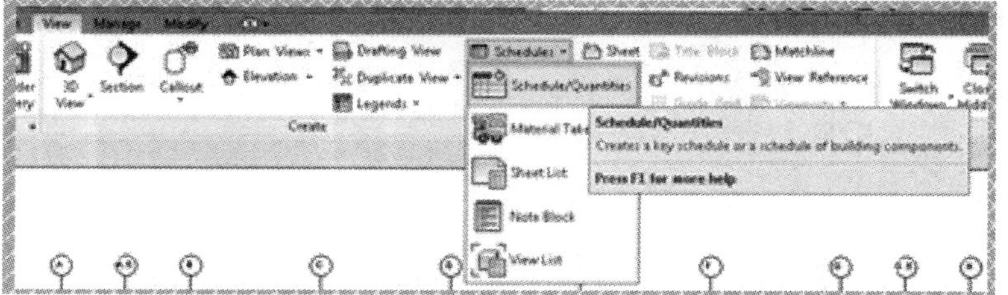

Select **Schedules → Schedules/Quantities**.

2. 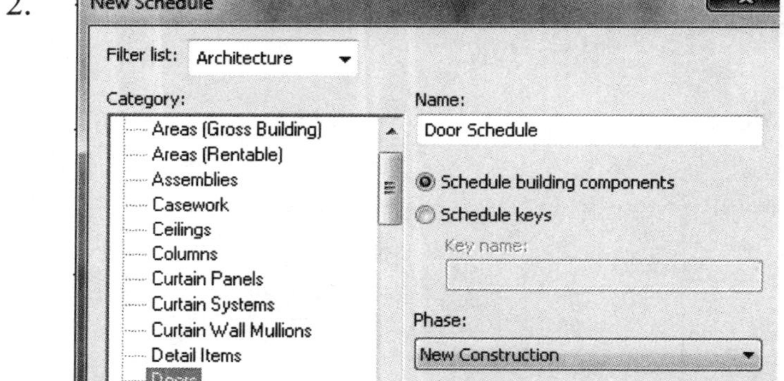

Under Filter list:
Select Architecture.

Select **Doors**.

Press **OK**.

3. The available fields are Parameters assigned to the door families.

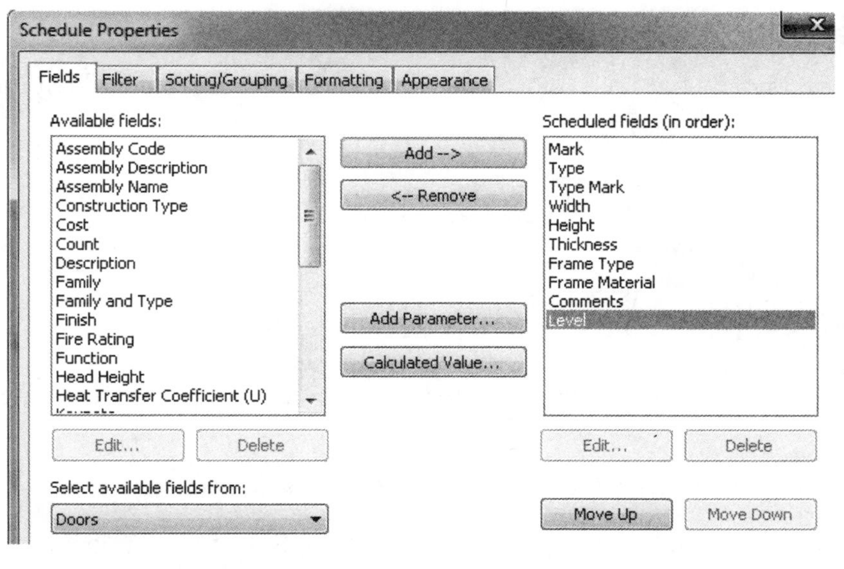

You can add which parameters to use in the schedule by highlighting and selecting the Add button.

The order the fields appear in the right pane is the order the columns will appear in the schedule.

4. 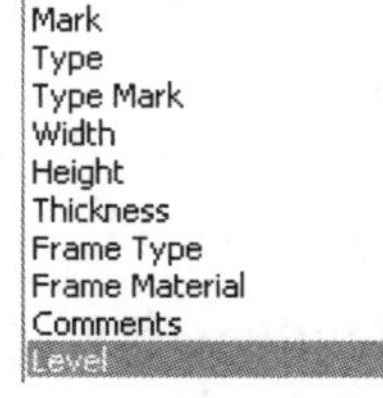

Select the following fields in this order:

Mark	Height	Frame Material
Type	Thickness	Comments
Type Mark	Frame Type	Level
Width		

5. 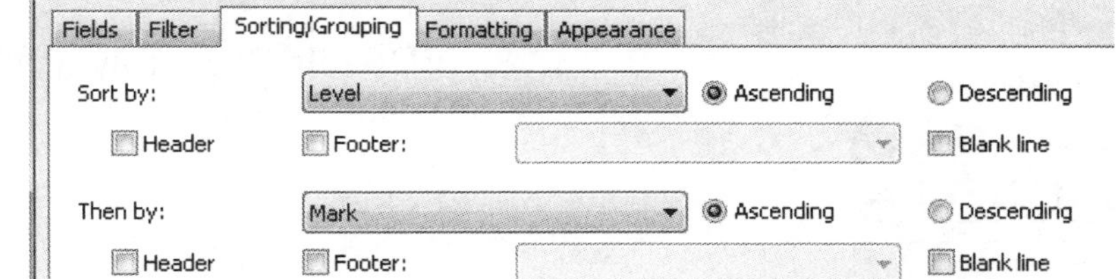

Select the Sorting/ Grouping tab. Sort by Level. Then by Mark.

6. 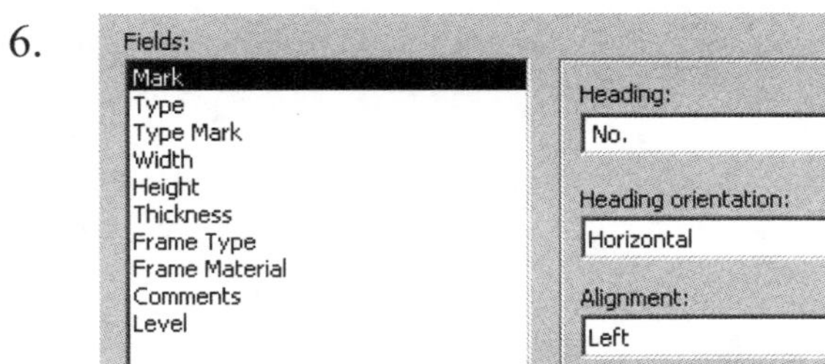

The Formatting Column allows you to rename the Column Header.

Rename Mark to **No**.

7. 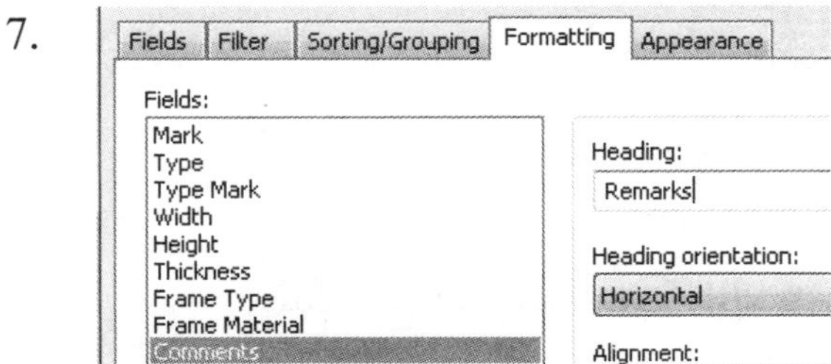

Highlight **Comments**.

Rename the Heading to **Remarks**.

8. 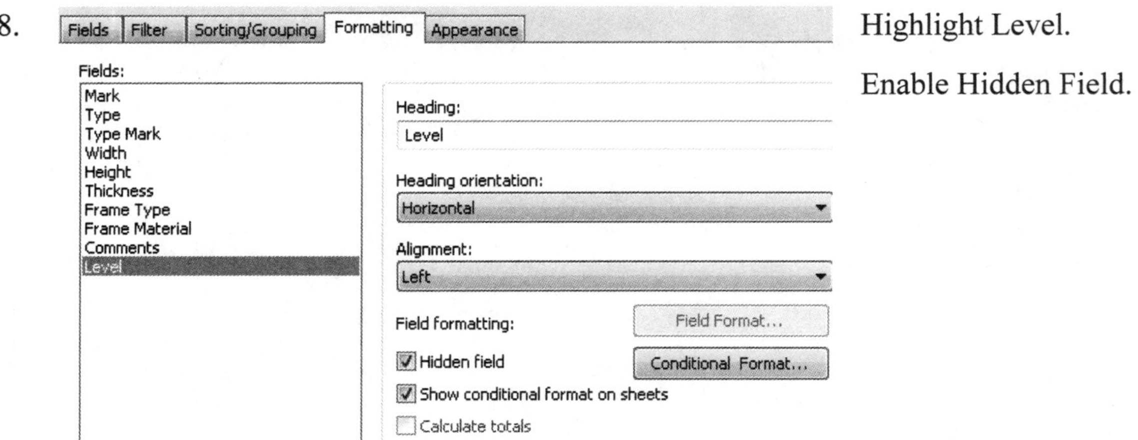

Highlight Level.

Enable Hidden Field.

This allows us to sort by the Level without showing it in the schedule.

9. 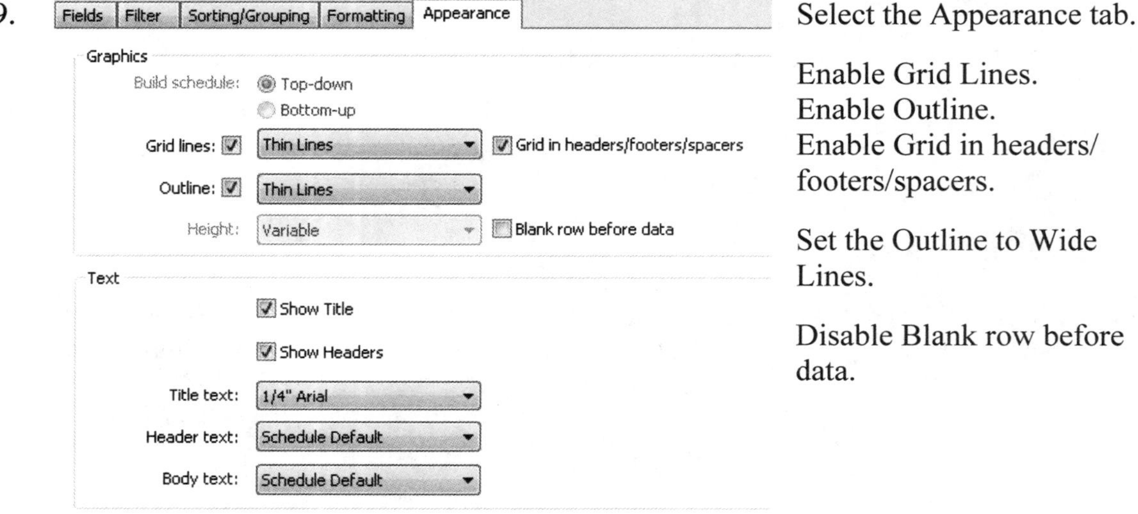

Select the Appearance tab.

Enable Grid Lines.
Enable Outline.
Enable Grid in headers/footers/spacers.

Set the Outline to Wide Lines.

Disable Blank row before data.

Enable Show Title.
Enable Show Headers.
Set the Title Text to 1/4″ Arial.
Press **OK**.

10. A view opens with the schedule.

<Door Schedule>								
A	B	C	D	E	F	G	H	I
Mark	Type	Type Mark	Width	Height	Thickness	Frame Type	Frame Material	Remarks
	Curtain Wall Dbl Glass	14	6' - 9 1/8"	8' - 0"				
1	36" x 84"	1	3' - 0"	7' - 0"	0' - 2"			
2	36" x 84"	1	3' - 0"	7' - 0"	0' - 2"			
3	36" x 84"	1	3' - 0"	7' - 0"	0' - 2"			
4	36" x 84"	1	3' - 0"	7' - 0"	0' - 2"			
5	72" x 78"	8	6' - 0"	6' - 6"	0' - 2"			

Now, you can see where you may need to modify or tweak the schedule.

11. 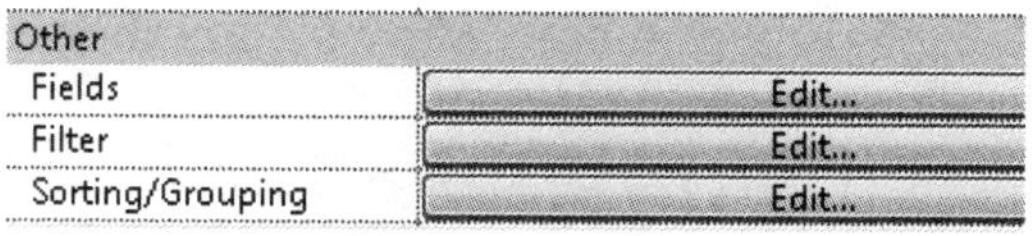 In the Properties pane:

Select **Edit** next to Sorting/Grouping.

12. 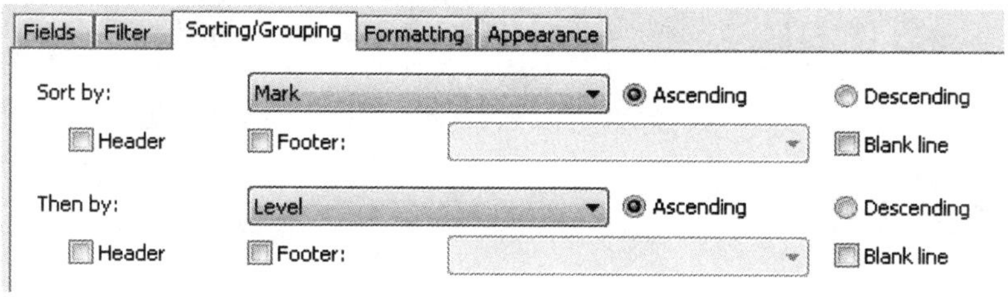 Sort by **Mark** and then by **Level**.

Press **OK**.

13. 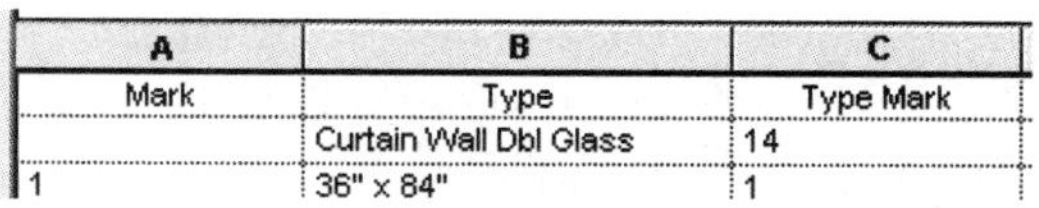 The schedule updates.

Note that the Curtain Wall Dbl Glass Door is missing a mark or door tag.

14. 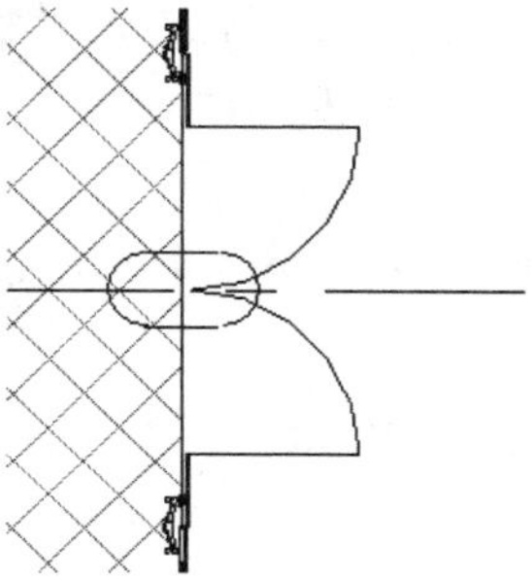 Activate Level 1.

Zoom into the curtain wall double door.

We see the door tag, but no number.

Select the door.

15. 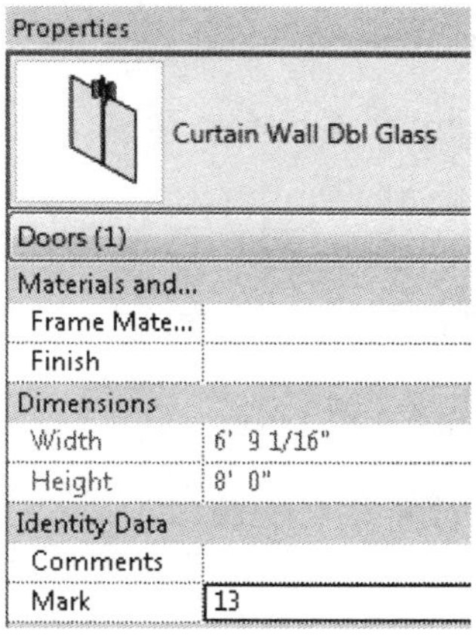 In the Properties pane:

Locate the Mark field.

Enter the number **13**.

Press **Apply**.

The tag should update with the number.

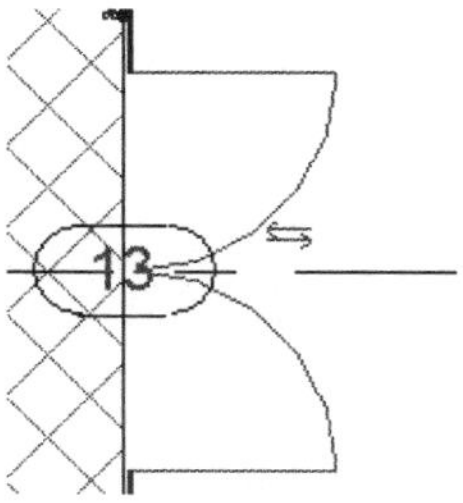

16. 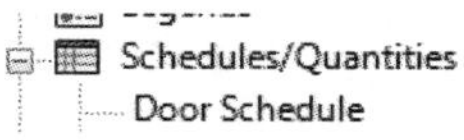 Locate the Door Schedule in the Project Browser.

Double left click on the Door Schedule to activate/open the view.

17.

A	B	C	
Mark	Type	Type Mark	
1	36" x 84"	1	3' -
2	36" x 84"	1	3' -
3	36" x 84"	1	3' -
4	36" x 84"	1	3' -
5	72" x 78"	8	6' -
6	72" x 78"	8	6' -
8	36" x 84"	1	3' -
9	36" x 84"	1	3' -
10	36" x 84"	1	3' -
11	12000 x 2290 Opening	13	2' -
12	12000 x 2290 Opening	13	2' -
13	Curtain Wall Dbl Glass	14	6' -
14	36" x 84"	1	3' -
15	36" x 84"	1	3' -

The schedule now shows a number for the curtain wall door.

Notice that the schedule re-sorted to place the curtain wall in the correct order.

18.

Other	
Fields	Edit...
Filter	Edit...
Sorting/Gro...	Edit...

In the Properties Pane:

Select **Edit** next to Fields.

19.

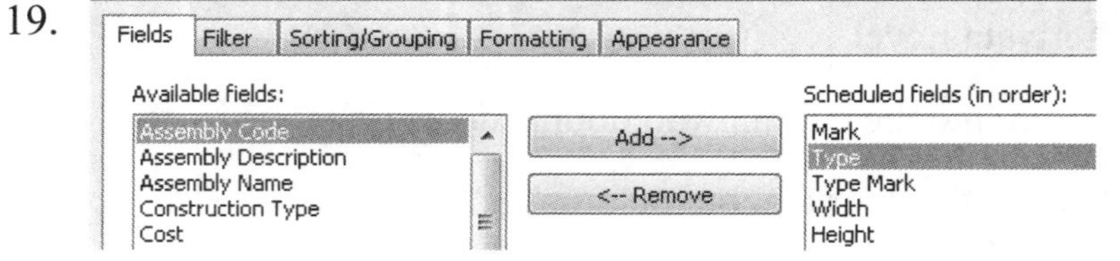

Highlight **Type** in the Scheduled fields list.

Select **Remove** to remove from the list.

20.

Fields | Filter | Sorting/Grouping | Formatting | Appearance

Fields: Mark, Type Mark, Width, Height, Thickness, Frame Type, Frame Material, Comments, Level

Heading: Type

Heading orientation: Horizontal

Alignment: Center

Select the Formatting tab.

Highlight **Type Mark**.

Change the Heading to **Type**.

Set Alignment to **Center**.

21.

Fields | Filter | Sorting/Grouping | Formatting | Appearance

Fields: Mark, Type Mark, Width, Height, Thickness, Frame Type, Frame Material, Comments, Level

Heading: No.

Heading orientation: Horizontal

Alignment: Center

Highlight **Mark**.

Change the Heading to **No.**

Set the Alignment to **Center**.

Press **OK**.

22. The schedule updates.

<Door Schedule>

A	B	C	D	E	F	G	H
No.	Type	Width	Height	Thickness	Frame Type	Frame Material	Remarks
1	1	3' - 0"	7' - 0"	0' - 2"			
2	1	3' - 0"	7' - 0"	0' - 2"			
3	1	3' - 0"	7' - 0"	0' - 2"			
4	1	3' - 0"	7' - 0"	0' - 2"			

23. 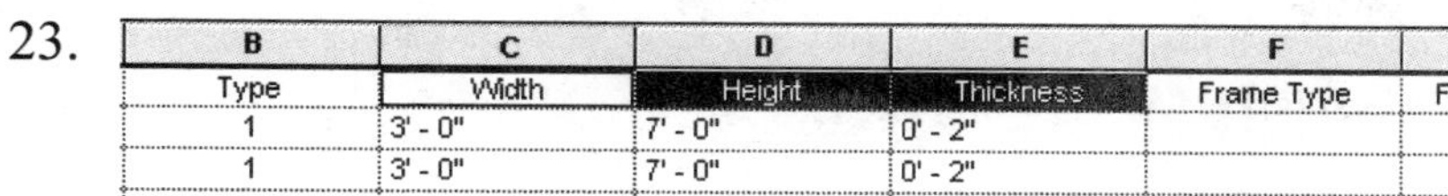

Drag the mouse across the Width, Height, and Thickness columns.

24. Select **Group** on the Titles & Headers panel on the ribbon.

25. 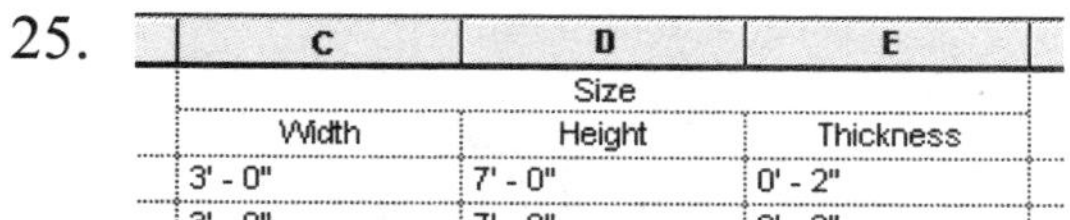

Type **Size** as the header in the sub-header.

26. 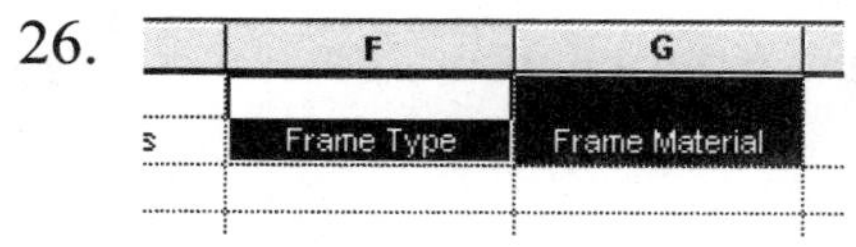

Drag the mouse across the Frame Type and Frame Material columns.

27. 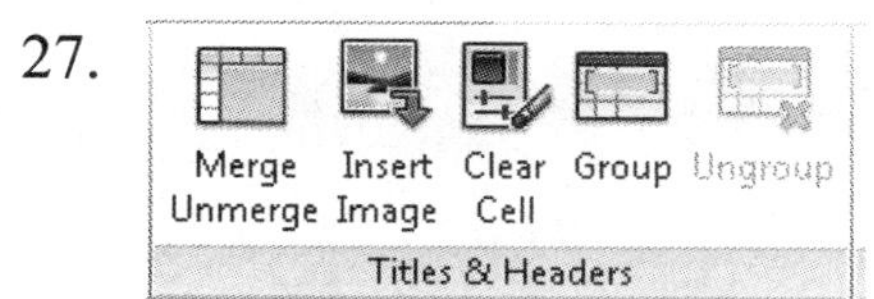

Select **Group** on the Titles & Headers panel on the ribbon.

28. 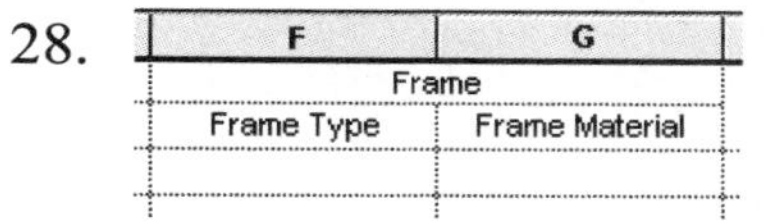

Type **Frame** as the header in the sub-header.

29. Save as ***ex6-2.rvt***.

The door schedule is missing information. Many architects prefer to use letter designations for door types and not numbers. To modify the information and update the schedule, we need to update the parameters. The values displayed in schedules are the values stored in family parameters.

Revit uses two types of parameters: *instance* and *type*. Instance parameters can be modified in the Properties pane. They are unique to each **instance** of an element. Examples of instance parameters might be level, hardware, or sill height. Type parameters do not change regardless of where the element is placed. Examples of type parameters are size, material, and assembly code. To modify a type parameter, you must **edit type**.

Exercise 6-3
Modifying Family Parameters

Drawing Name: ex6-2.rvt
Estimated Time: 10 minutes

This exercise reinforces the following skills:

- Family Parameters
- Schedules

1. 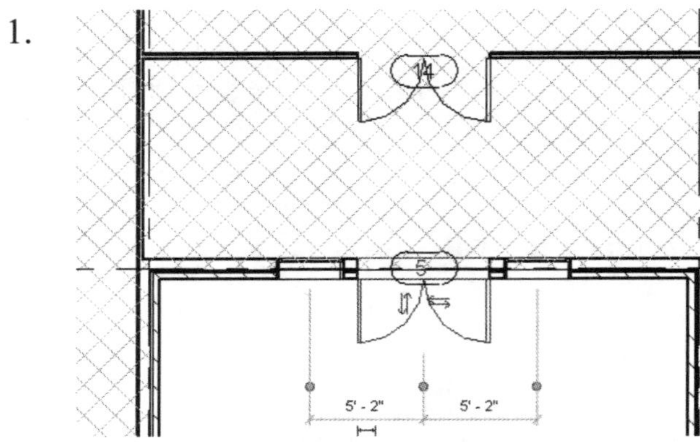

Activate the Level 1 floor plan.

Select the exterior front door.

2.

Doors (1)	
Level	Level 1
Sill Height	0' 0"
Construction	
Frame Type	1
Materials and Finishes	
Frame Material	WD
Finish	
Identity Data	
Comments	BY MFR
Mark	5

Fill in the Frame Type as 1.

Fill in Frame Material as **WD**.
WD is the designator for wood.
Fill in Comments as **BY MFR**.

Press **Apply** to save the changes.

These are instance parameters, so they only affect each element selected.

3. Open the Door Schedule.

5	8	6' - 0"	6' - 6"	0' - 2"	1	WD	BY MFR
6	8	6' - 0"	6' - 6"	0' - 2"			

The schedule has updated with the information, but it only affected the one door. That is because the parameters that were changed in the Properties were *instance* parameters.

4. 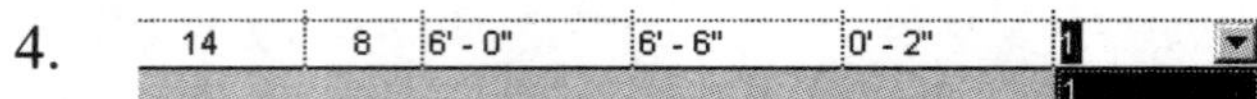

14	8	6' - 0"	6' - 6"	0' - 2"	1
					1

Locate the Door Type 8 which is the same type as the first exterior double door.

5. If you click in the Frame Type column, you can select the same values.

6.

4	1	3' - 0"	7' - 0"	0' - 2"			
5	8	6' - 0"	6' - 6"	0' - 2"	1	WD	BY MFR
6	8	6' - 0"	6' - 6"	0' - 2"	1	WD	BY MFR
8	1	3' - 0"	7' - 0"	0' - 2"			

Modify the schedule so that the two exterior doors show the same information.

7. Activate **Level 2**.

8. 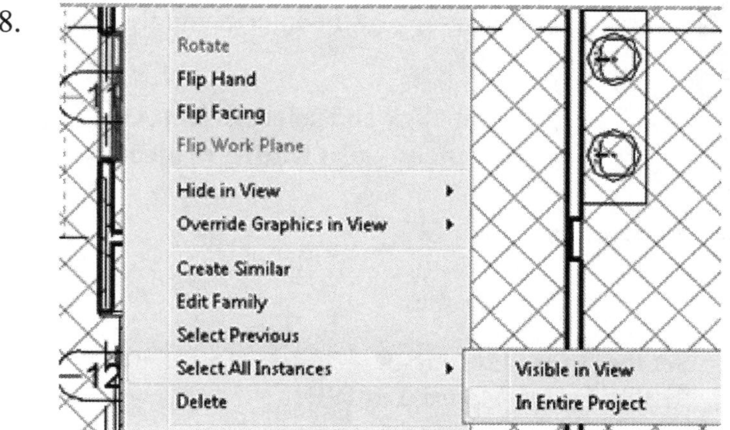

Zoom into the area where the two elevators are located.

Select one of the elevator doors.

Right click and select **Select All Instances → In Entire Project**.

9. 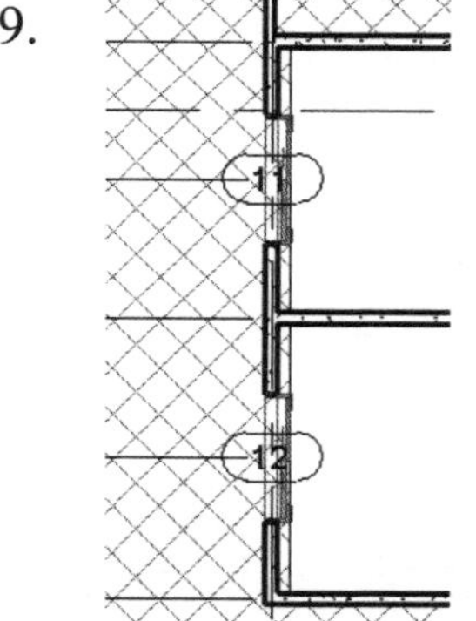

Both elevator doors on both levels are selected.

10.

Properties	
Door-Elevator 12000 x 2290 Opening	
Doors (2)	Edit Type
Constraints	
Level	Level 2
Sill Height	0' 0"
Construction	
Frame Type	2
Graphics	
Elevator Call B...	☐
Elevator Call B...	☑
Materials and Fi...	
Frame Material	AL
Finish	

In the Properties pane:

Set the Frame Type to **2**.
Set the Frame Material to **AL**.

AL is the designator for aluminum.

Press **Apply**.

11.

	0' - 2"		
	0' - 1 1/8"	2	AL
	0' - 1 1/8"	2	AL

Check the Door Schedule.

It has updated with the new information.

12. Activate **Level 1**.

Zoom into the area where the lavatories are located.

Select one of the interior single flush doors.

Right click and select **Select All Instances → In Entire Project**.

13. 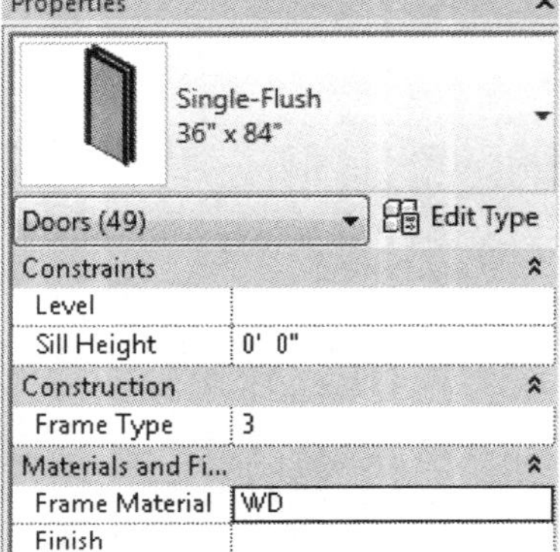

In the Properties pane:

Set the Frame Type to **3**.
Set the Frame Material to **WD**.
WD is the designator for wood.
Press **Apply**.

14. Check the Door Schedule.

No.	Type	Size			Frame		Remarks
		Width	Height	Thickness	Frame Type	Frame Material	
1	1	3' - 0"	7' - 0"	0' - 2"	3	WD	
2	1	3' - 0"	7' - 0"	0' - 2"	3	WD	
3	1	3' - 0"	7' - 0"	0' - 2"	3	WD	
4	1	3' - 0"	7' - 0"	0' - 2"	3	WD	
5	8	6' - 0"	6' - 6"	0' - 2"	1	WD	BY MFR
6	8	6' - 0"	6' - 6"	0' - 2"	1	WD	BY MFR
8	1	3' - 0"	7' - 0"	0' - 2"	3	WD	
9	1	3' - 0"	7' - 0"	0' - 2"	3	WD	
10	1	3' - 0"	7' - 0"	0' - 2"	3	WD	
11	13	2' - 11 3/8"	7' - 6 1/8"	0' - 1 1/8"	2	AL	
12	13	2' - 11 3/8"	7' - 6 1/8"	0' - 1 1/8"	2	AL	

It has updated with the new information.

15. 

Activate **Level 1**.

Select one of the lavatory doors.

In the Properties Pane, select **Edit Type**.

16.

Identity Data	
Assembly Code	C1020
Keynote	
Model	
Manufacturer	
Type Comments	
URL	
Description	
Assembly Description	Interior Doors
Type Mark	A
Fire Rating	
Cost	
OmniClass Number	23.30.10.00
OmniClass Title	Doors

Scroll down to locate the Type Mark.

Change the Type Mark to **A**.

This only changes the parameter value for the doors loaded in the project.

If you would like to change the parameter for the door family so that it will always show a specific value whenever it is loaded into a family, you have to edit the door family.

Press OK.

Release the door selection.

17. Check the Door Schedule.

A	B	C	D
		Size	
No.	Type	Width	Height
1	A	3' - 0"	7' - 0"
2	A	3' - 0"	7' - 0"
3	A	3' - 0"	7' - 0"
4	A	3' - 0"	7' - 0"
5	8	6' - 0"	6' - 6"
6	8	6' - 0"	6' - 6"
8	A	3' - 0"	7' - 0"
9	A	3' - 0"	7' - 0"
10	A	3' - 0"	7' - 0"
11	13	2' - 11 3/8"	7' - 6 1/8"
12	13	2' - 11 3/8"	7' - 6 1/8"

It has updated with the new information.

Notice that all the single flush doors updated with the new Type Mark value.

*Because this was a **type** parameter, not an **instance** parameter, all doors that are the same type are affected.*

18.

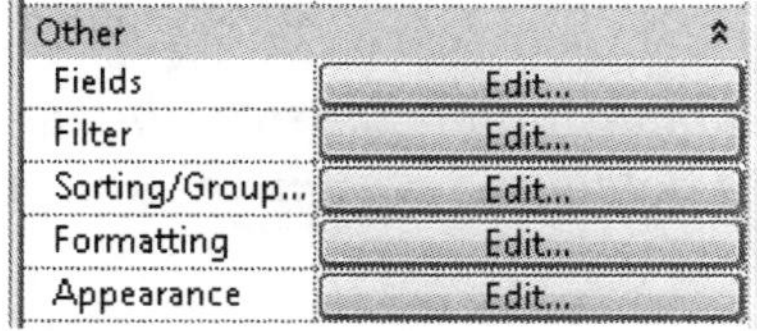

Other	
Fields	Edit...
Filter	Edit...
Sorting/Group...	Edit...
Formatting	Edit...
Appearance	Edit...

Select the **Edit** tab next to Fields.

We want to add a parameter for hardware.

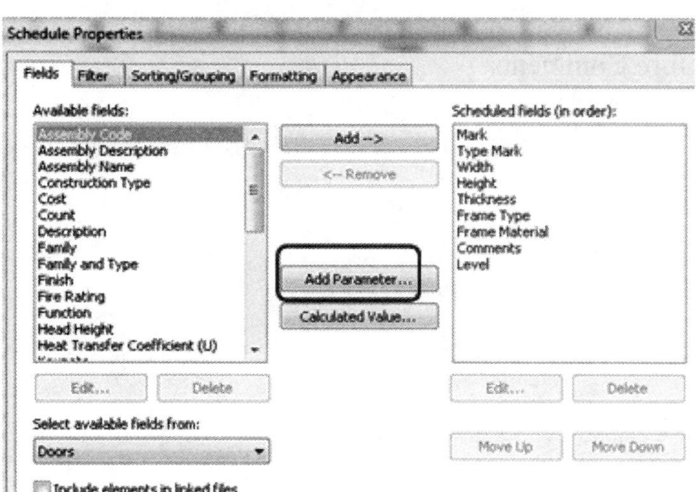

If you look in the available fields, you will see that Hardware is not listed.

So, we have to create that parameter.

19. Select the **Add Parameter** button.

20. 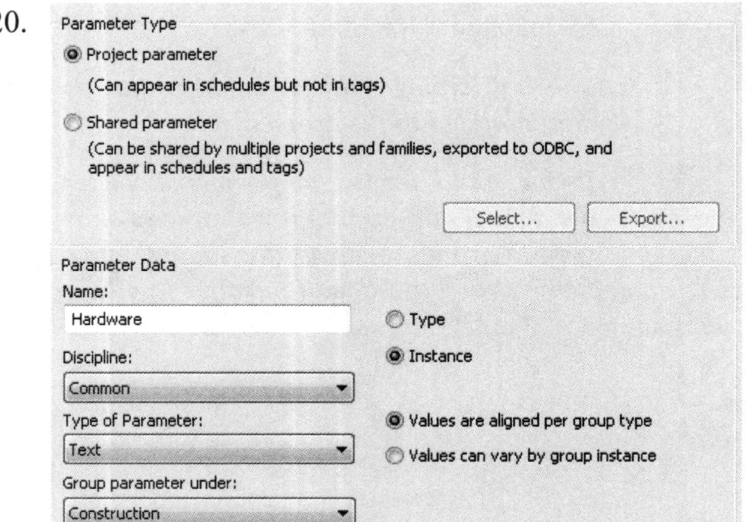

Enable **Project parameter**.

This means the parameter is only available in this project. If you wanted to create a parameter which could be used in any project or family, you would use a shared parameter.

21. Under Parameter Data:
Type **Hardware** for the Name.
Select **Text** for the Type of Parameter.
Group the parameter under **Construction**.
Enable **Instance**.
Press **OK**.

By default parameters are set to length, which is a dimension parameter. If you do not set the type of parameter to text, you will have to delete the parameter and re-create it.

22. Scheduled fields (in order):
Mark
Type Mark
Width
Height
Thickness
Frame Type
Frame Material
Comments
Level
Hardware
Edit...
Delete
Move Up
Move Down

Hardware is now listed in the Scheduled fields list.

Use the **Move Up** button to position the Hardware column before Comments.

23. 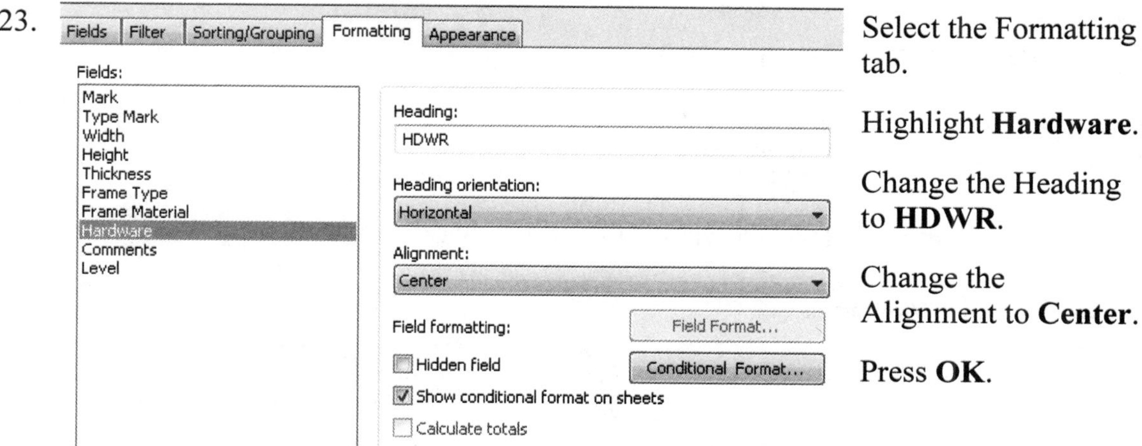

Select the Formatting tab.

Highlight **Hardware**.

Change the Heading to **HDWR**.

Change the Alignment to **Center**.

Press **OK**.

24. The Hardware column is added to the schedule.

Door Schedule

	Door				Frame			
No.	Type	Width	Height	Thickness	Frame Type	Frame Material	HDWR	Comments
1	A	3' - 0"	7' - 0"	0' - 2"	3	OAK		
2	A	3' - 0"	7' - 0"	0' - 2"	3	OAK		
3	A	3' - 0"	7' - 0"	0' - 2"	3	OAK		
4	A	3' - 0"	7' - 0"	0' - 2"	3	OAK		
5	8	6' - 0"	6' - 6"	0' - 2"	1	OAK		BY MFR
7	A	3' - 0"	7' - 0"	0' - 2"	3	OAK		
8	A	3' - 0"	7' - 0"	0' - 2"	3	OAK		
9	A	3' - 0"	7' - 0"	0' - 2"	3	OAK		
10	A	3' - 0"	7' - 0"	0' - 2"	3	OAK		
11	13	2' - 11 7/16"	7' - 6 5/32"	0' - 1 3/16"	2	ALUMINUM		
12	13	2' - 11 7/16"	7' - 6 5/32"	0' - 1 3/16"	2	ALUMINUM		
13	14	6' - 6 9/16"	7' - 8 1/4"					
14	8	6' - 0"	6' - 6"	0' - 2"	1	OAK		BY MFR

25. Select a door on Level 1.

26. 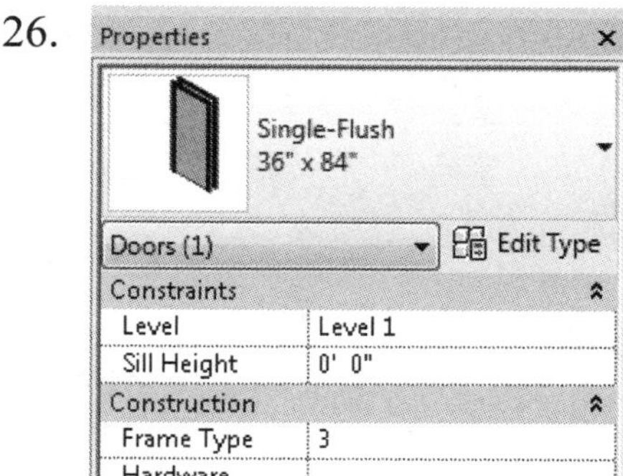

Note that Hardware is now available as a parameter in the Properties pane.

*It is available in the Properties palette because it was designated as an **instance** parameter.*

27. Save as *ex6-3.rvt.*

Exercise 6-4
Creating Shared Parameters

Drawing Name: ex6-3.rvt
Estimated Time: 30 minutes

This exercise reinforces the following skills:

- Shared Parameters
- Schedules
- Family Properties

Many architectural firms have a specific format for schedules. The parameters for these schedules may not be included in the pre-defined parameters in Revit. If you are going to be working in multiple projects, you can define a single file to store parameters to be used in any schedule in any project.

1. Activate the **Manage** ribbon.

2. Select the **Shared Parameters** tool from the Settings panel.

3. 

Press **Create** to create a file where you will store your parameters.

4. Locate the folder where you want to store your file.
Set the file name to *custom parameters.txt.*
Press '**Save**'.

Note that this is a txt file.

5. 

Under Groups, select **New**.

6. 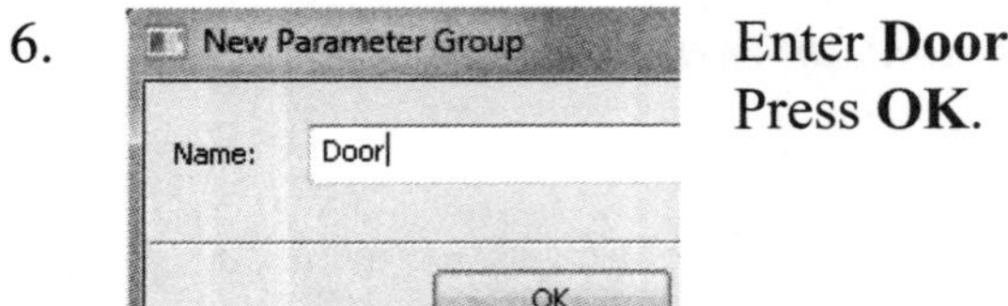

Enter **Door**.
Press **OK**.

7. Under Parameters, select **New**.

8. Enter **Head Detail** for Name.

In the Type field, we have a drop-down list.
Select '**Text**'.

Press '**OK**'.

9. 

Notice that we have a Parameter Group called **Door** now.

There is one parameter listed.

Select **New** under Parameters.

10. 

Enter **Jamb Detail** for Name.
In the Type of Parameter field, select **Text**.
Press **OK**.

Select **New** under Parameters.

Hint: *By default, parameters are set to Length. If you rush and don't set the Type of Parameter, you will have to delete it and re-do that parameter.*

11. 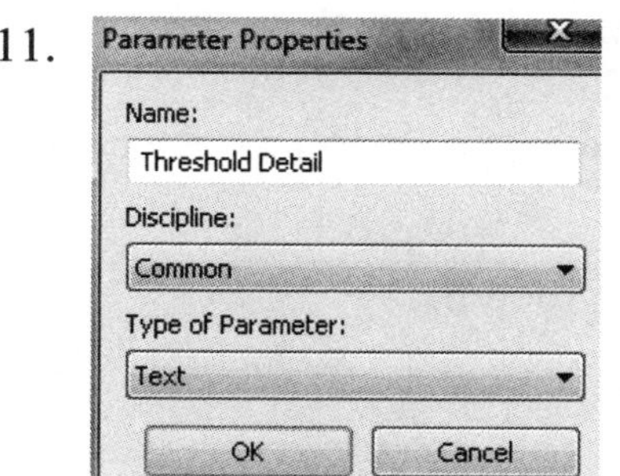

Enter **Threshold Detail** for Name.
In the Type field, select **Text**.
Press **OK**.

Select **New** under Parameters.

12. 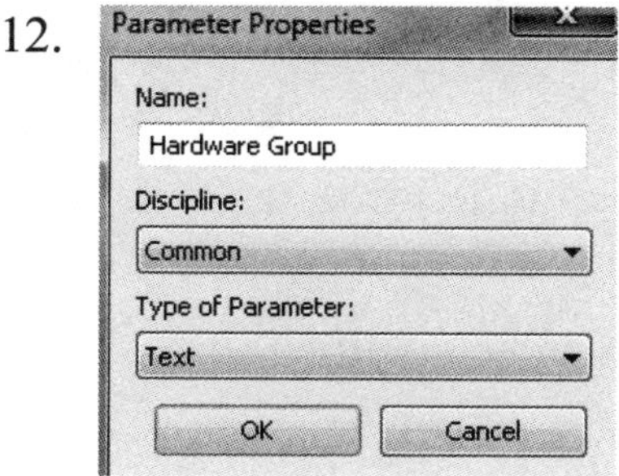

Enter **Hardware Group** for Name.
In the Type field, select **Text**.
Press **OK**.

Select **New** under Parameters.

13. Select **New** under Groups.

14. 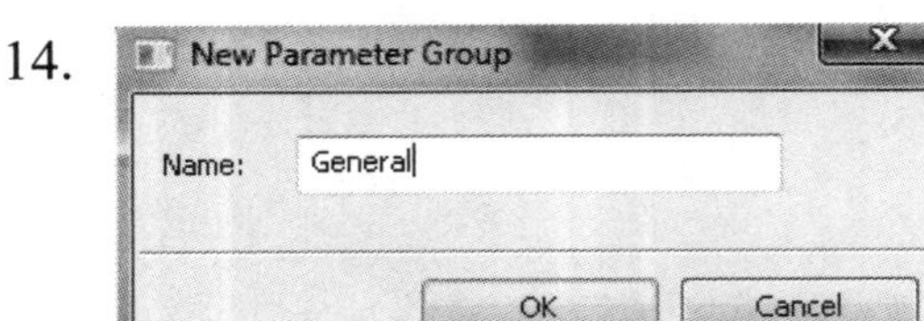

Name the new group '**General**'.
Press '**OK**'.

15. We now have two groups listed under Parameter group.

Select **Door**.

16. 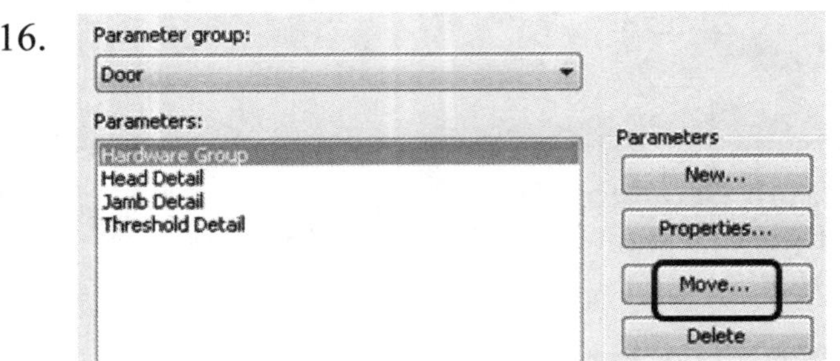

Highlight the **Hardware Group** field.

Select **Move**.

17. Select **General** from the drop-down list.
Press **OK**.

18. **Hardware Group** is no longer listed in the Door parameter group.

Select **General** from the Parameter group list.

19. We see **Hardware Group** listed.

Highlight **Hardware Group**.

Select **Properties**.

20. We see how **Hardware Group** is defined.
Press **OK**.

Notice that the properties cannot be modified.

21. Locate the *custom parameters.txt* file using Windows Explorer.

22. Right click and select **Open**.

This should open the file using Notepad and assumes that you have associated txt files with Notepad.

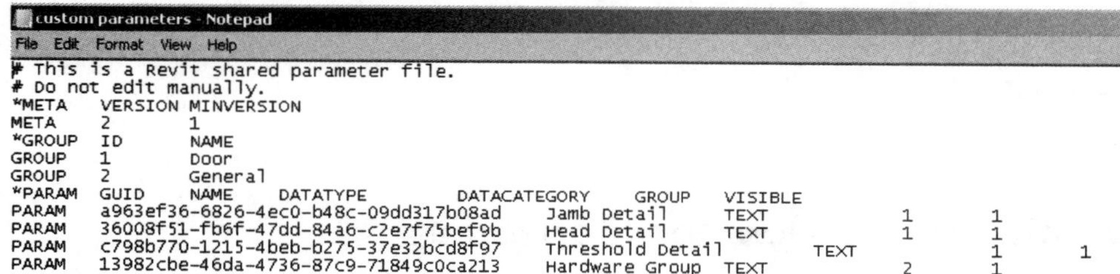

```
custom parameters - Notepad
File  Edit  Format  View  Help
# This is a Revit shared parameter file.
# Do not edit manually.
*META   VERSION MINVERSION
META    2       1
*GROUP  ID      NAME
GROUP   1       Door
GROUP   2       General
*PARAM  GUID    NAME    DATATYPE        DATACATEGORY    GROUP   VISIBLE
PARAM   a963ef36-6826-4ec0-b48c-09dd317b08ad    Jamb Detail     TEXT            1       1
PARAM   36008f51-fb6f-47dd-84a6-c2e7f75bef9b    Head Detail     TEXT            1       1
PARAM   c798b770-1215-4beb-b275-37e32bcd8f97    Threshold Detail        TEXT            1       1
PARAM   13982cbe-46da-4736-87c9-71849c0ca213    Hardware Group  TEXT            2       1
```

We see the format of the parameter file.
Note that we are advised not to edit manually.
However, currently this is the only place you can modify the parameter type from Text to Integer, etc.

23. Change the data type to **INTEGER** for Hardware Group.

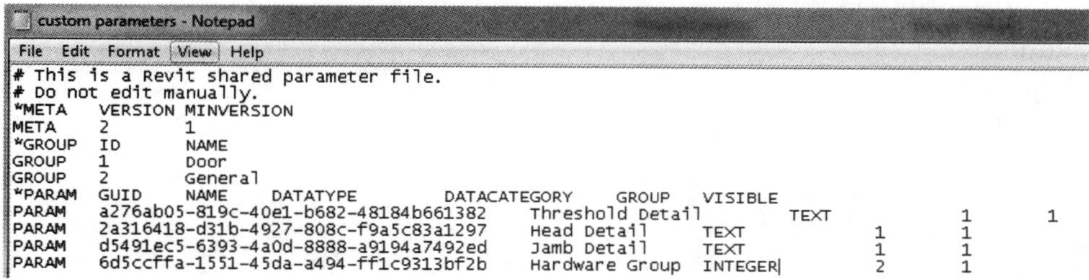

```
custom parameters - Notepad
File  Edit  Format  View  Help
# This is a Revit shared parameter file.
# Do not edit manually.
*META   VERSION MINVERSION
META    2       1
*GROUP  ID      NAME
GROUP   1       Door
GROUP   2       General
*PARAM  GUID    NAME    DATATYPE        DATACATEGORY    GROUP   VISIBLE
PARAM   a276ab05-819c-40e1-b682-48184b661382    Threshold Detail        TEXT            1       1
PARAM   2a316418-d31b-4927-808c-f9a5c83a1297    Head Detail     TEXT            1       1
PARAM   d5491ec5-6393-4a0d-8888-a9194a7492ed    Jamb Detail     TEXT            1       1
PARAM   6d5ccffa-1551-45da-a494-ff1c9313bf2b    Hardware Group  INTEGER         2       1
```

Do not delete any of the spaces!

24. Save the text file and close.

25. Select the **Shared Parameters** tool.

If you get an error message when you attempt to open the file, it means that you made an error when you edited the file. Re-open the file and check it.

26. 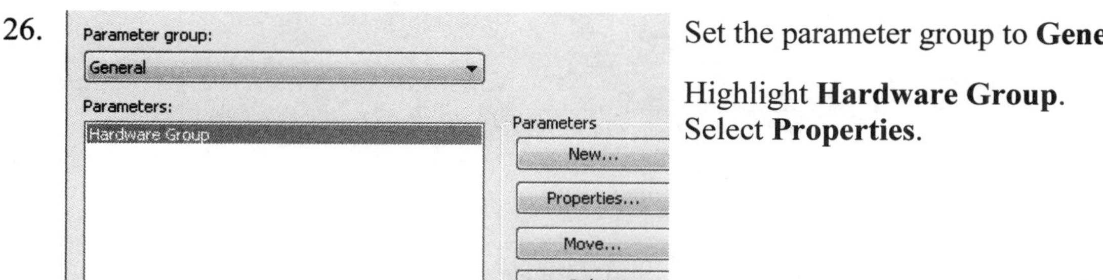

Set the parameter group to **General**.

Highlight **Hardware Group**.
Select **Properties**.

27. 

Note that Hardware Group is now defined as an Integer.

Press **OK** twice to exit the Shared Parameters dialog.

28. Save as *ex6-4.rvt.*

Exercise 6-5

Adding Shared Parameters to a Schedule

Drawing Name: ex6-4.rvt
Estimated Time: 30 minutes

This exercise reinforces the following skills:

- ❑ Shared Parameters
- ❑ Family Properties
- ❑ Schedules

1. Open *ex6-4.rvt.*

   View Activate the **View** ribbon.

2. Select **Create→Schedule/ Quantities.**

3. 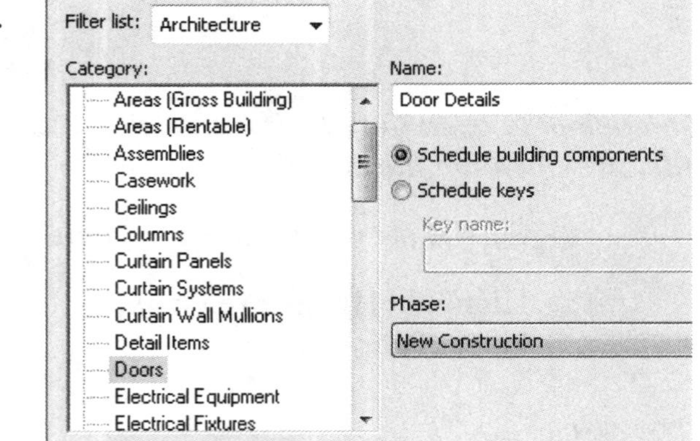

Highlight **Doors.**

Enter **Door Details** for the schedule name.

Press **OK.**

Note that you can create a schedule for each phase of construction.

4. Add **Mark, Type, Width, Height,** and **Thickness.**

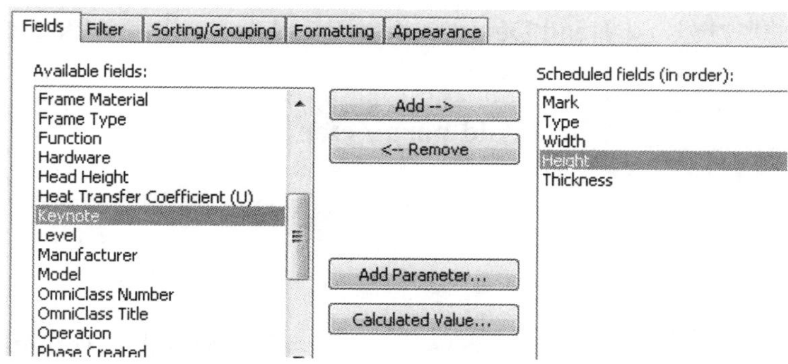

The order of the fields is important. The first field is the first column, etc. You can use the Move Up and Move Down buttons to sort the columns.

5. Add Parameter... Select the **Add Parameter** button.

6. 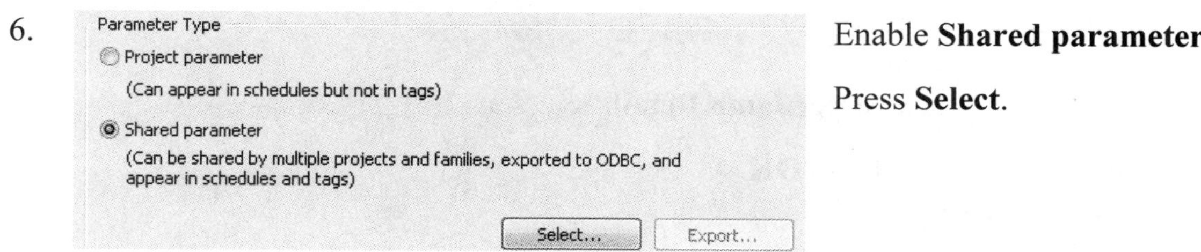

Enable **Shared parameter**.

Press **Select**.

*If you don't see any shared parameters, you need to browse for the shared parameters.txt file to load it. Go to **Shared Parameters** on the Manage ribbon and browse for the file.*

7. 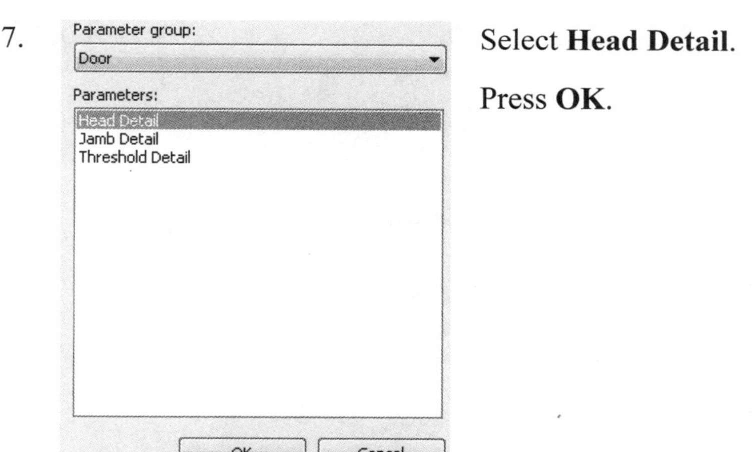

Select **Head Detail**.

Press **OK**.

8. Parameter Data
Name: Head Detail
Discipline: Common
Type of Parameter: Text
Group parameter under: Construction

Group it under **Construction**.

Press **OK**.

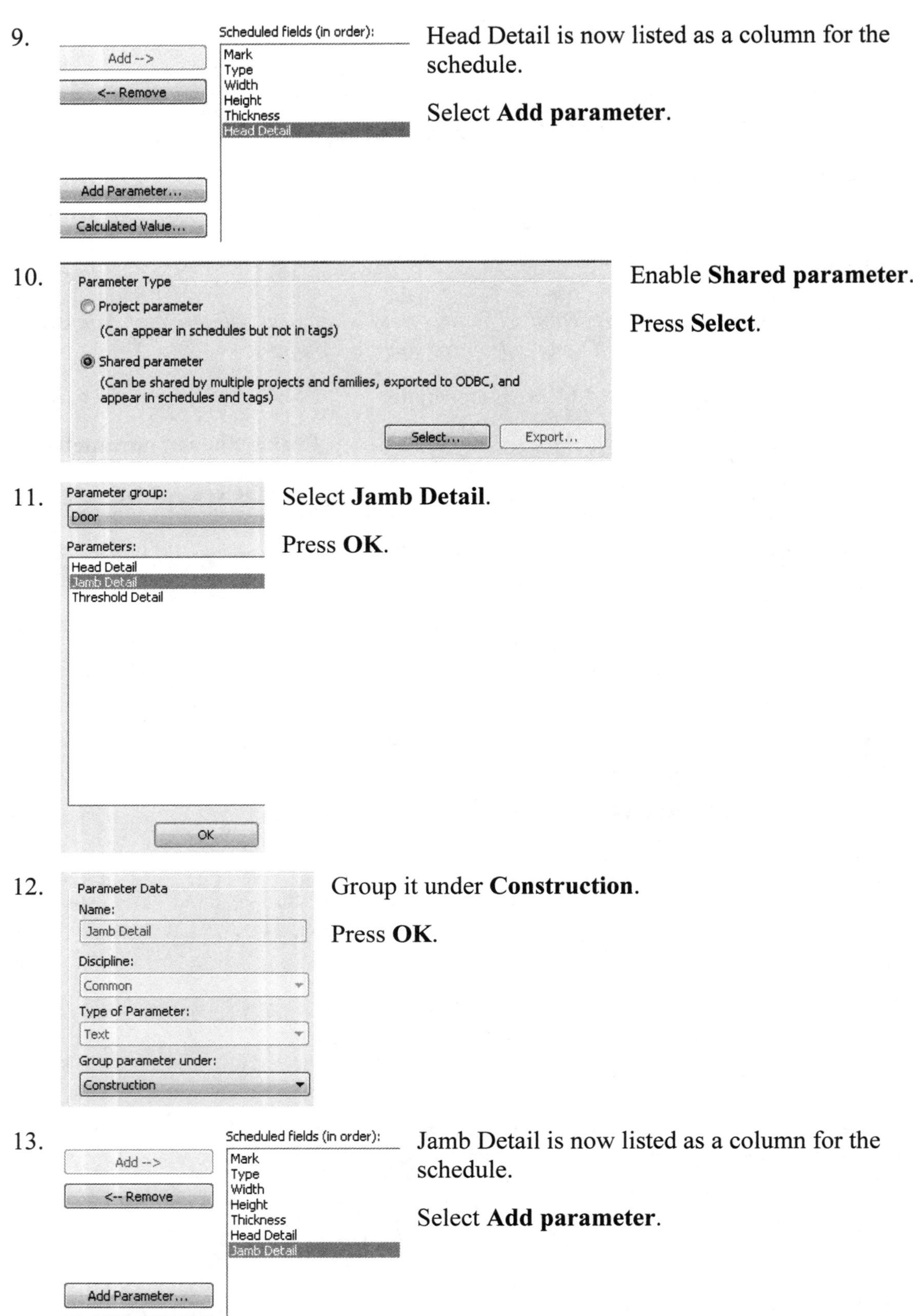

9. Head Detail is now listed as a column for the schedule.

   Select **Add parameter**.

10. Enable **Shared parameter**.

    Press **Select**.

11. Select **Jamb Detail**.

    Press **OK**.

12. Group it under **Construction**.

    Press **OK**.

13. Jamb Detail is now listed as a column for the schedule.

    Select **Add parameter**.

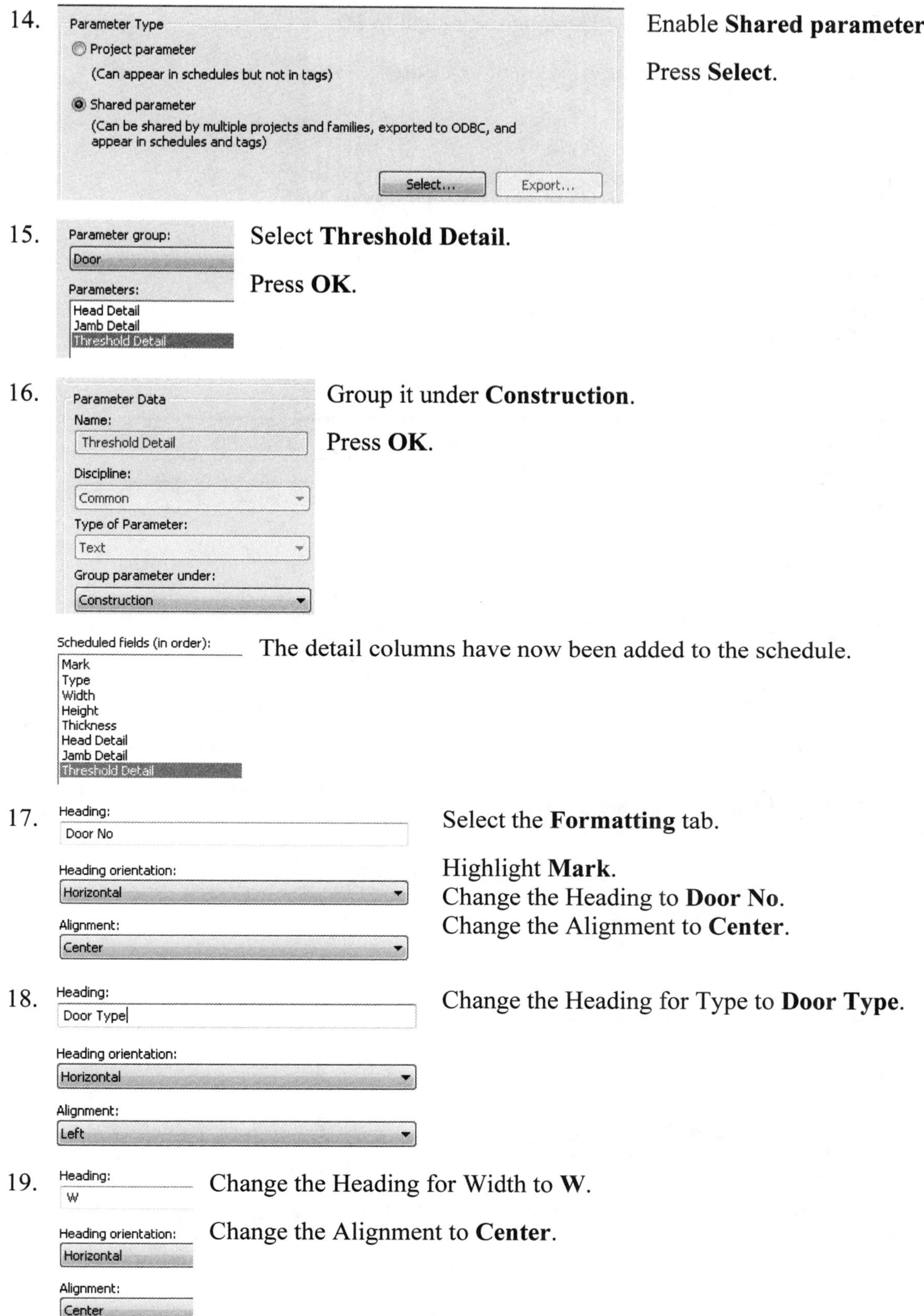

14. Enable **Shared parameter**.

    Press **Select**.

15. Select **Threshold Detail**.

    Press **OK**.

16. Group it under **Construction**.

    Press **OK**.

The detail columns have now been added to the schedule.

17. Select the **Formatting** tab.

    Highlight **Mark**.
    Change the Heading to **Door No**.
    Change the Alignment to **Center**.

18. Change the Heading for Type to **Door Type**.

19. Change the Heading for Width to **W**.

    Change the Alignment to **Center**.

20. Change the Heading for Height to **H**.

Change the Alignment to **Center**.

21. Change the Heading for Thickness to **THK**.

Change the Alignment to **Center**.

Press **OK**.

22. A window will appear with your new schedule.

Door Details							
Door No.	Door Type	W	H	THK	Head Detail	Jamb Detail	Threshold Det
1	36" x 84"	3' - 0"	7' - 0"	0' - 2"			
2	36" x 84"	3' - 0"	7' - 0"	0' - 2"			
3	36" x 84"	3' - 0"	7' - 0"	0' - 2"			
4	36" x 84"	3' - 0"	7' - 0"	0' - 2"			
5	72" x 78"	6' - 0"	6' - 6"	0' - 2"			
7	36" x 84"	3' - 0"	7' - 0"	0' - 2"			
8	36" x 84"	3' - 0"	7' - 0"	0' - 2"			
9	36" x 84"	3' - 0"	7' - 0"	0' - 2"			
10	36" x 84"	3' - 0"	7' - 0"	0' - 2"			
11	12000 x 2	2' - 11 7/16"	7' - 6 5/32"	0' - 1 3/16"			
12	12000 x 2	2' - 11 7/16"	7' - 6 5/32"	0' - 1 3/16"			
13	Curtain W	6' - 6 9/16"	7' - 8 1/4"				
14	72" x 78"	6' - 0"	6' - 6"	0' - 2"			

23. Select the W column, then drag your mouse to the right to highlight the H and THK columns.

24. 

Select **Titles & Headers→Group**.

25. 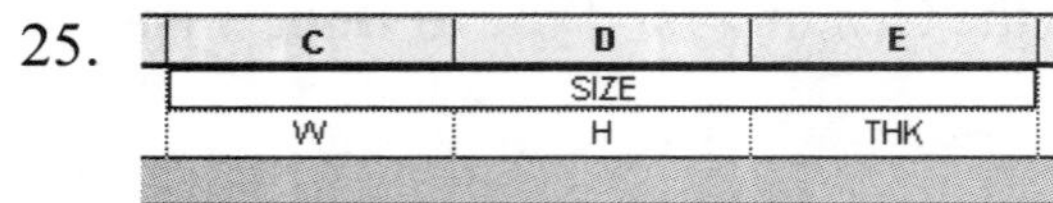

Type '**SIZE**' as the header for the three columns.

26. 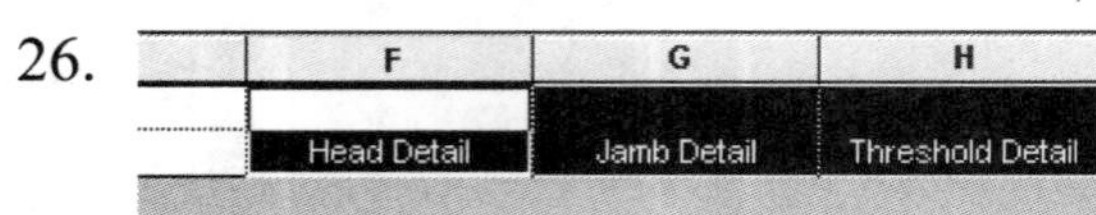

Select the Head Detail column, then drag your mouse to the right to highlight the Jamb Detail and Threshold Detail columns.

27. 

Select **Titles & Headers→Group**.

28.

F	G	H
	DETAILS	
Head Detail	Jamb Detail	Threshold Detail

Type '**DETAILS**' as the header for the three columns.

29. Our schedule now appears in the desired format.

<Door Details>

A	B	C	D	E	F	G	H
		SIZE			DETAILS		
Door No	Door Type	W	H	THK	Head Detail	Jamb Detail	Threshold Detail
1	36" x 84"	3' - 0"	7' - 0"	0' - 2"			
2	36" x 84"	3' - 0"	7' - 0"	0' - 2"			
3	36" x 84"	3' - 0"	7' - 0"	0' - 2"			
4	36" x 84"	3' - 0"	7' - 0"	0' - 2"			
5	72" x 78"	6' - 0"	6' - 6"	0' - 2"			
6	72" x 78"	6' - 0"	6' - 6"	0' - 2"			
8	36" x 84"	3' - 0"	7' - 0"	0' - 2"			
9	36" x 84"	3' - 0"	7' - 0"	0' - 2"			
10	36" x 84"	3' - 0"	7' - 0"	0' - 2"			
11	12000 x 2290	2' - 11 3/8"	7' - 6 1/8"	0' - 1 1/8"			
12	12000 x 2290	2' - 11 3/8"	7' - 6 1/8"	0' - 1 1/8"			
13	Curtain Wall Dbl	6' - 9 1/8"	8' - 0"				
14	36" x 84"	3' - 0"	7' - 0"	0' - 2"			

30. Save as *ex6-5.rvt.*

Exercise 6-6

Adding Shared Parameters to Families

Drawing Name: ex6-5.rvt
Estimated Time: 25 minutes

In order to add data to the shared parameters, we have to add those shared parameters to the families used in the projects. We have four door families in use.

This exercise reinforces the following skills:

- ❑ Shared Parameters
- ❑ Families

1. Open *ex6-5.rvt.*

2.

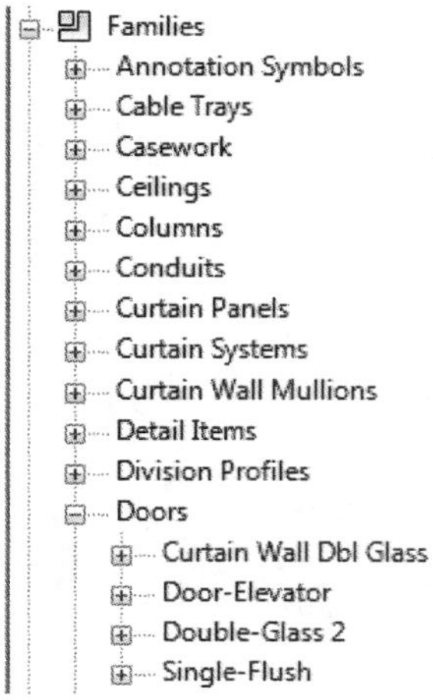

Families
- Annotation Symbols
- Cable Trays
- Casework
- Ceilings
- Columns
- Conduits
- Curtain Panels
- Curtain Systems
- Curtain Wall Mullions
- Detail Items
- Division Profiles
- Doors
  - Curtain Wall Dbl Glass
  - Door-Elevator
  - Double-Glass 2
  - Single-Flush

In the Project Browser:

Locate the **Families** category.

Expand the **Doors** folder.

The four door families used in the project are listed.

3. Highlight the **Curtain Wall Dbl Glass** door.

Right click and select **Edit**.

4. The door family will open for editing.

Select the **Family Types** tool on the ribbon.

5. We see the parameters available.

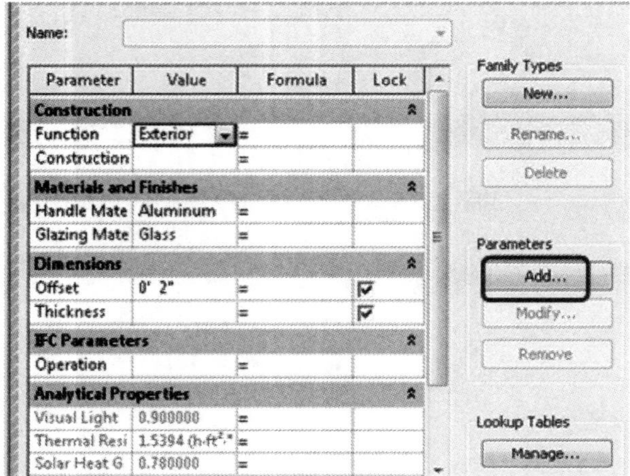

Select **Add** under the Parameters heading.

6. Enable **Shared Parameter**. Press **Select**.

7. Highlight **Head Detail**.

Press **OK**.

8. Select **Other** from the Group parameter drop-down list. Enable **Type**.

Press **OK**.

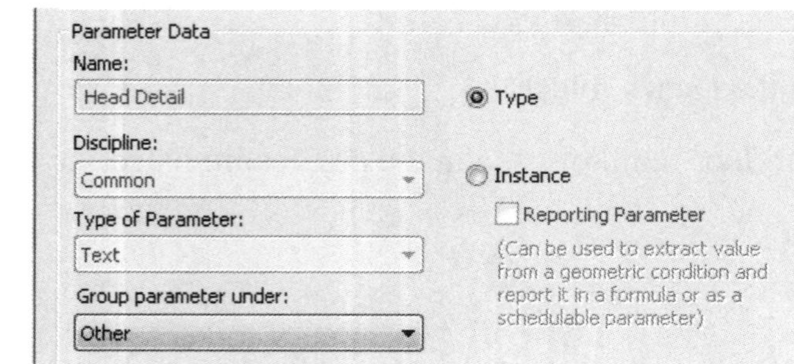

9. 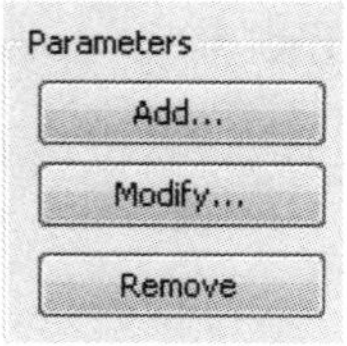 Select **Add** under Parameters.

10.  Enable **Shared Parameter**.
Press **Select**.

11. 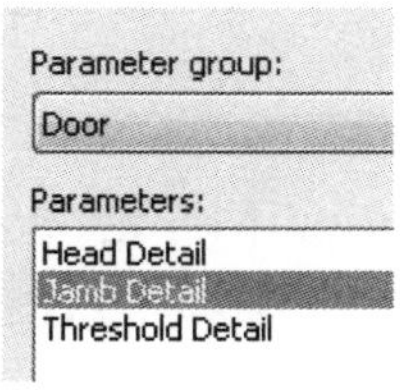 Highlight **Jamb Detail**.

Press **OK**.

12. 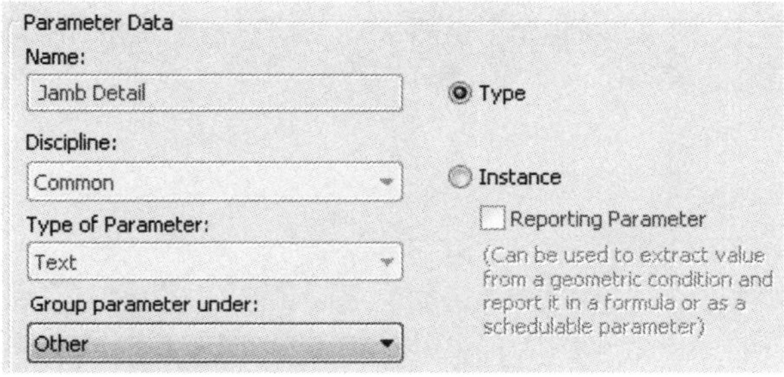 Select **Other** from the Group parameter drop-down list.
Enable **Type**.

Press **OK**.

13. 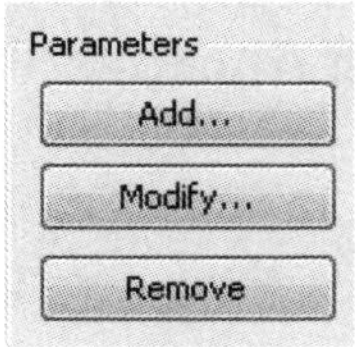 Select **Add** under Parameters.

14.  Enable **Shared Parameter**.
Press **Select**.

15. 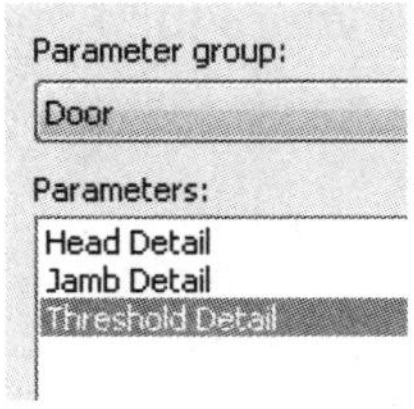 Highlight **Threshold Detail**.

Press **OK.**

16. Parameter Data
Name: Threshold Detail
Discipline: Common
Type of Parameter: Text
Group parameter under: Other
Type
Instance
Reporting Parameter
(Can be used to extract value from a geometric condition and report it in a formula or as a schedulable parameter)

Select **Other** from the drop-down list.
Enable **Type**.

Press **OK**.

17.

Other		
Threshold Detail	TD1	=
Jamb Detail	JD1	=
Head Detail	HD1	=

In the shared parameter fields, enter **TD1** for Threshold Detail, **JD1** for Jamb Detail, and **HD1** for Head Detail. Press **OK**.

18. 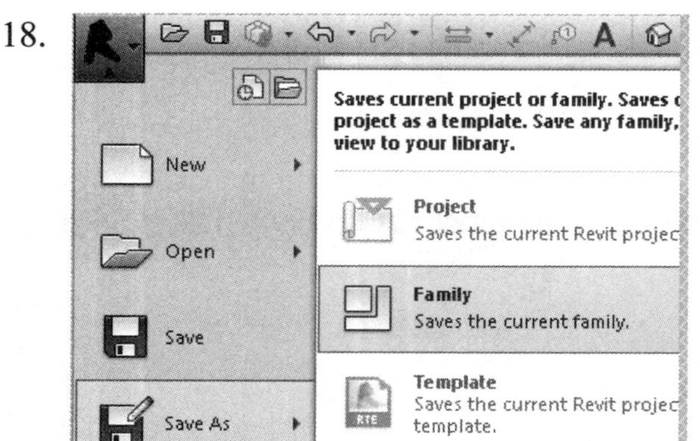

Go to the File Application Menu.

Select **Save As→Family**.

19. File name: Curtain Wall Dbl Glass-Custom
Files of type: Family Files (*.rfa)

Browse to your work folder.
Rename the family **Curtain Wall Dbl Glass Custom**.rfa

Press **Save**.

20. Load into Project
Family Editor

Select **Load into Projects** from the Family Editor panel.

21. Load into Projects
Check the open Projects/Families you want to load the edited Family into
ex6-5.rvt

A dialog will appear if you have more than one project open.

Select the project to load the family file.
Press **OK**.

22. Doors
Curtain Wall Dbl Glass
Curtain Wall Dbl Glass-Custom
Door-Elevator
Double-Glass 2
Single-Flush

Go to the Doors category in the Families folder of the browser.

You should see the Custom family you just edited listed.

23. Double-G
Double-G
Single-Flu
Floors
Floor
3" LW
Gener
New Type
Make Workset Editabl
Delete
Rename...
Edit

Repeat the steps to add the shared parameters to the Door-Elevator, the Double-Glass 2 door and the Single-Flush Doors.

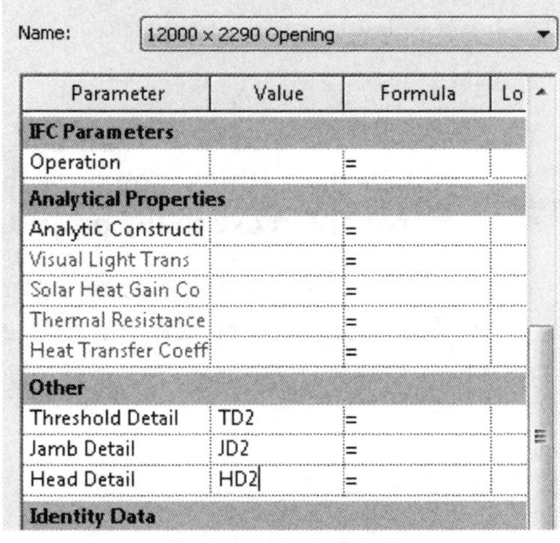

You have to add parameters to each size of door (door type) in each family.

For the elevator door, enter in the data for each detail under Other.

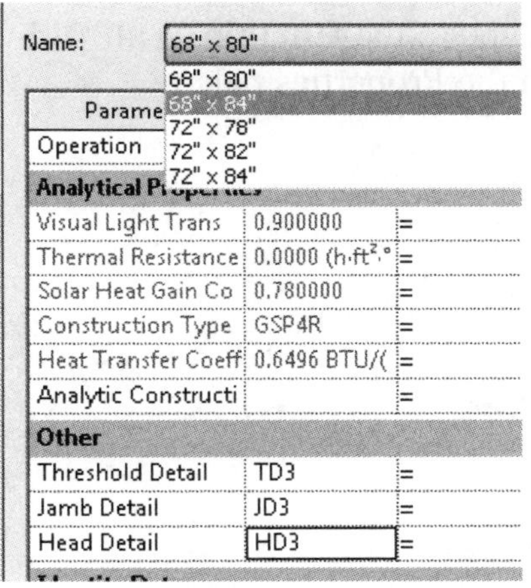

For the Double Glass 2 Door, you have to select each size door and fill in the data for the details under Other.

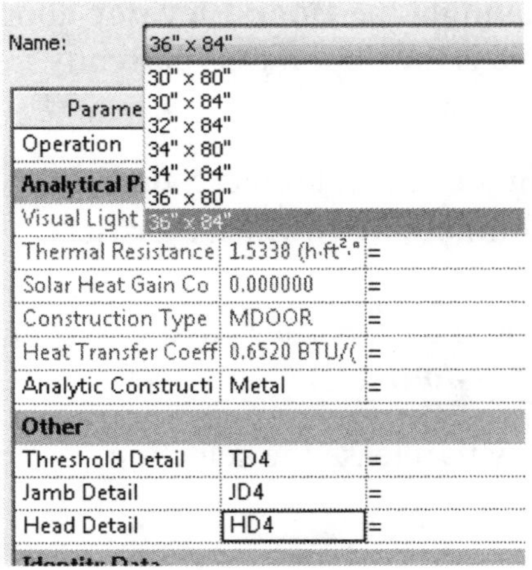

For the Single-Flush Door, you have to select each size door and fill in the data for the details under Other.

- Doors
  - Curtain Wall Dbl Glass
  - Curtain Wall Dbl Glass-Custom
  - Door-Elevator
  - Door-Elevator Custom
  - Double-Glass 2
  - Double-Glass 2- Custom
  - Single-Flush
  - Single-Flush Custom

Verify that you have loaded the custom version of each door in the Project Browser.

The custom versions should have the shared parameters added.

24. Activate **Level 1 Floor Plan**.

25. 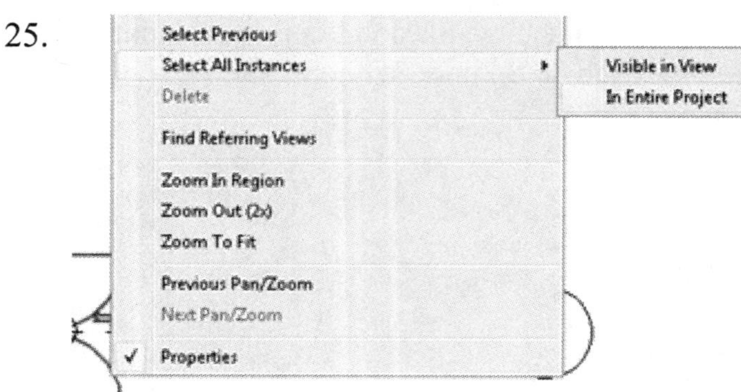

Select the **Curtain Wall Dbl Glass** door (this is the door that is currently in use in the project.

Right click and select **Select All Instances → In Entire Project**.

26. 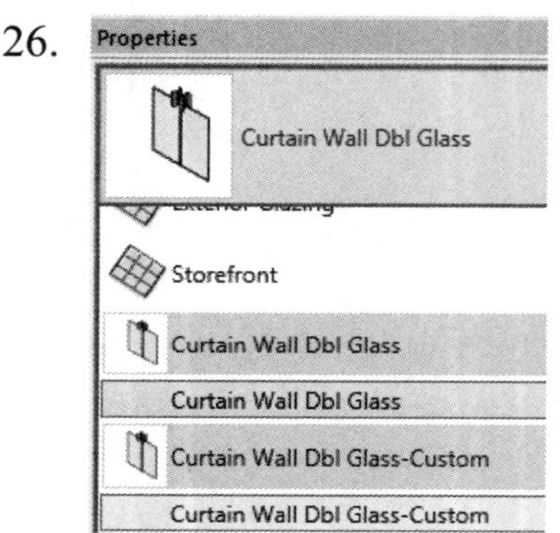

Change the Element Type to the **Curtain Wall Dbl Glass Custom** door in the Properties palette.

27. In the Project Browser:

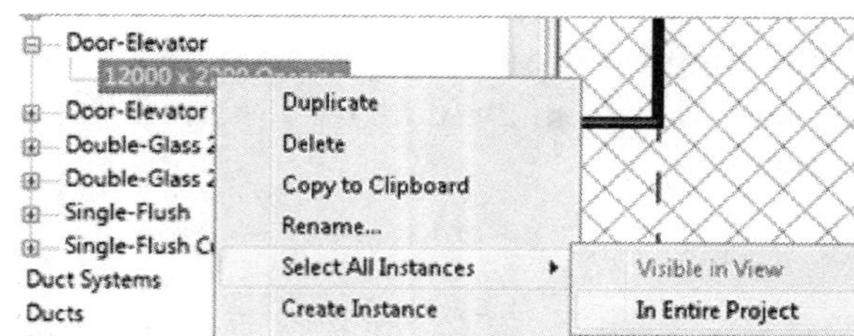

Highlight the **Door-Elevator** door (this is the door that is currently in use in the project.

Right click and select **Select All Instances → In Entire Project**.

28. 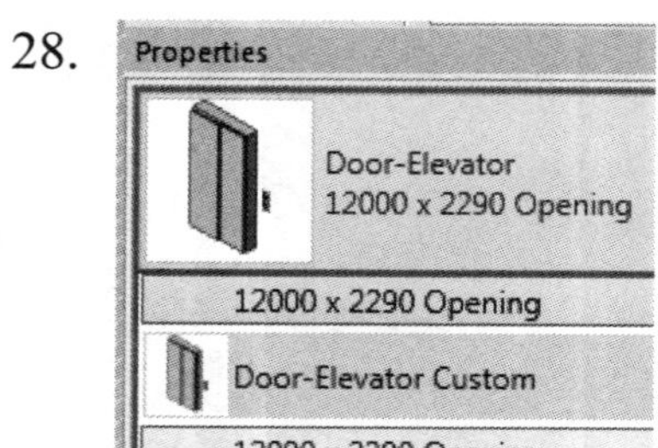

Use the Type Selector in the Properties palette to change to the **Door-Elevator Custom** door.

Left click in the window to release the selection.

29. Select the **Double-Glass 2 72″ x 78″** door (this is the door that is currently in use in the project).

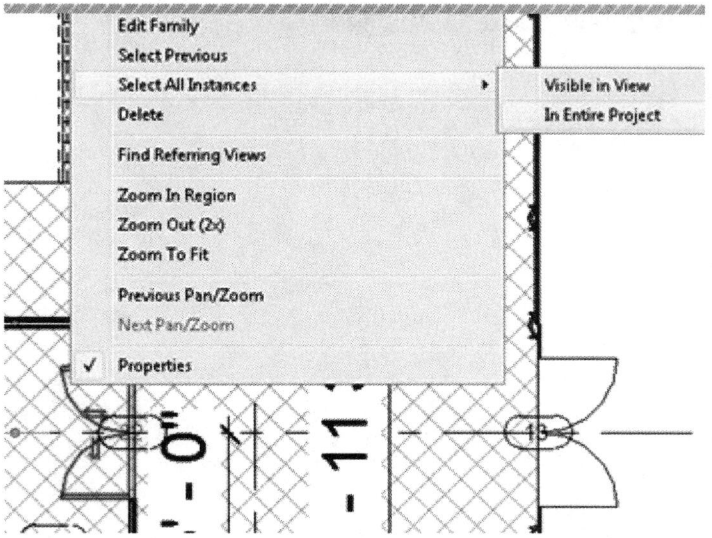

Right click and select **Select All Instances → In Entire Project**.

30. 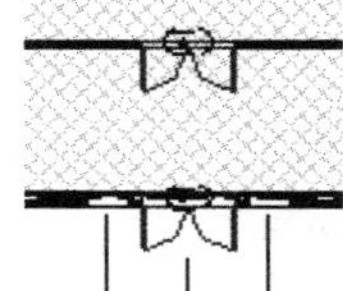

The doors will highlight in the display window.

31.
Double-Glass 2
72" x 82"
72" x 82"
72" x 84"
Double-Glass 2- Custom
68" x 80"
68" x 84"
72" x 78"

Change the Element Type to the **Double- Glass 2 Custom** door that is the same size.

Left click in the window to release the selection.

32. 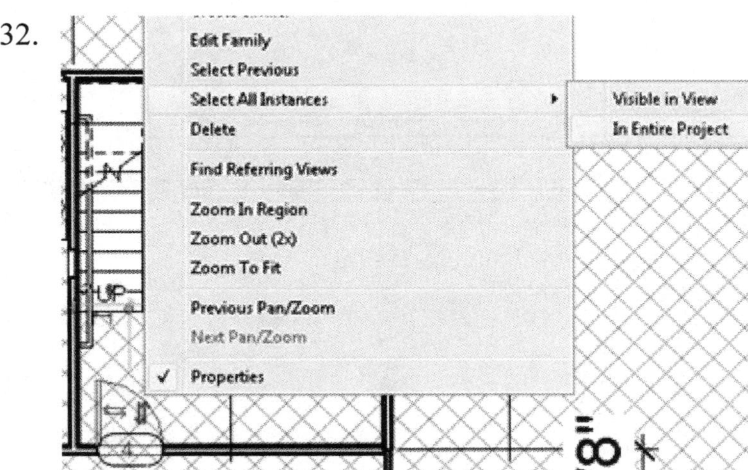

Select the **Single Flush** door located in the first stairwell.

Right click and select **Select All Instances→In Entire Project**.

33. The doors will highlight in the display window.

34. 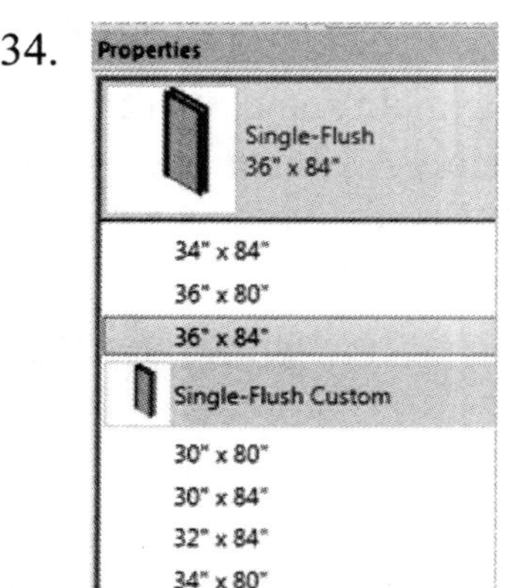

Change the Element Type to the **Single-Flush custom** door that is the same size: **36″ x 84″**.

35. Activate the **Manage** ribbon.

Purge Unused Select **Settings → Purge Unused** from the Manage ribbon.

36. Check None Press **Check None**.

37. 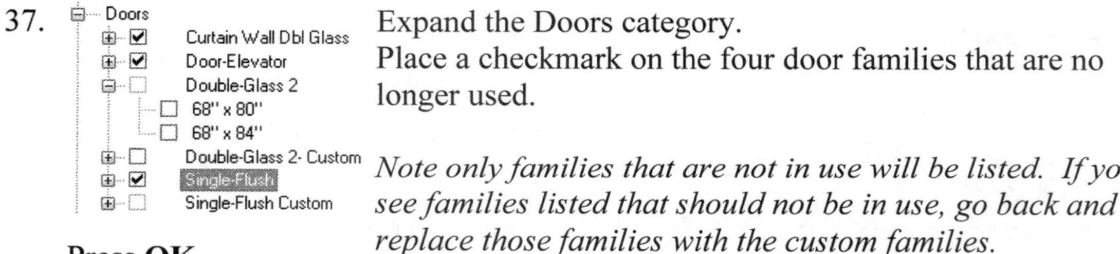

Expand the Doors category.
Place a checkmark on the four door families that are no longer used.

Note only families that are not in use will be listed. If you see families listed that should not be in use, go back and replace those families with the custom families.

Press **OK**.

38. Doors
Curtain Wall Dbl Glass-Custom
Door-Elevator Custom
Double-Glass 2- Custom
Single-Flush Custom

The browser now only lists the doors which are used.

39. Activate the Door Details schedule.

<Door Details>

A	B	C	D	E	F	G	H
		SIZE			DETAILS		
Door No	Door Type	W	H	THK	Head Detail	Jamb Detail	Threshold Detail
1	36" x 84"	3' - 0"	7' - 0"	0' - 2"	HD4	JD4	TD4
2	36" x 84"	3' - 0"	7' - 0"	0' - 2"	HD4	JD4	TD4
3	36" x 84"	3' - 0"	7' - 0"	0' - 2"	HD4	JD4	TD4
4	36" x 84"	3' - 0"	7' - 0"	0' - 2"	HD4	JD4	TD4
5	72" x 78"	6' - 0"	6' - 6"	0' - 2"	HD3	JD3	TD3
6	72" x 78"	6' - 0"	6' - 6"	0' - 2"	HD3	JD3	TD3
8	36" x 84"	3' - 0"	7' - 0"	0' - 2"	HD4	JD4	TD4
9	36" x 84"	3' - 0"	7' - 0"	0' - 2"	HD4	JD4	TD4
10	36" x 84"	3' - 0"	7' - 0"	0' - 2"	HD4	JD4	TD4

40. Save as *ex6-6.rvt*.

Exercise 6-7
Creating a Custom Window Schedule

Drawing Name: ex6-6.rvt
Estimated Time: 25 minutes

This exercise reinforces the following skills:

- Shared Parameters
- Schedule/Quantities

Glazing Schedule							
WINDOW NO	FRAME TYPE	SIZE		SILL	DETAILS		REMARKS
		W	H		HEAD	JAMB	
1	36"	3' - 0"	4' - 0"	2' - 9"			
1	36"	3' - 0"	4' - 0"	2' - 9"			
1	36"	3' - 0"	4' - 0"	4' - 0"			
1	36"	3' - 0"	4' - 0"	4' - 0"			

We want our window schedule to appear as shown.

1. Open *ex6-6.rvt*.

2. 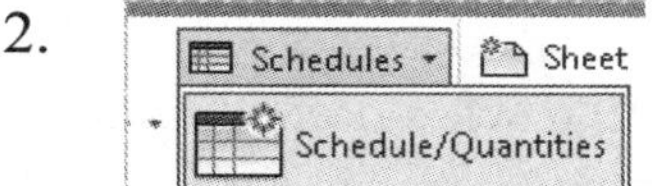

Activate the **View** ribbon.

Select **Create → Schedule/Quantities**.

3. 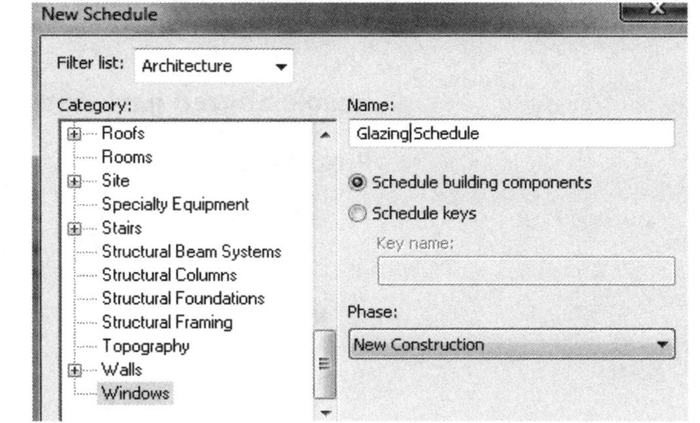

Highlight **Windows**.

Change the Schedule name to **Glazing Schedule**.

Press **OK**.

4. Add the following fields from the Available Fields.

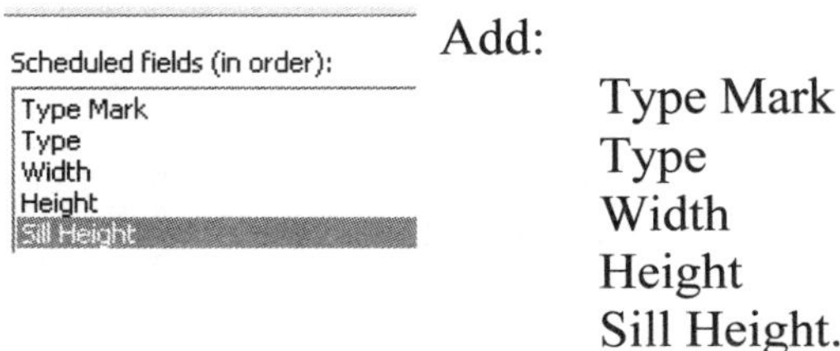

Add:

Type Mark
Type
Width
Height
Sill Height.

Select **Add Parameter**.

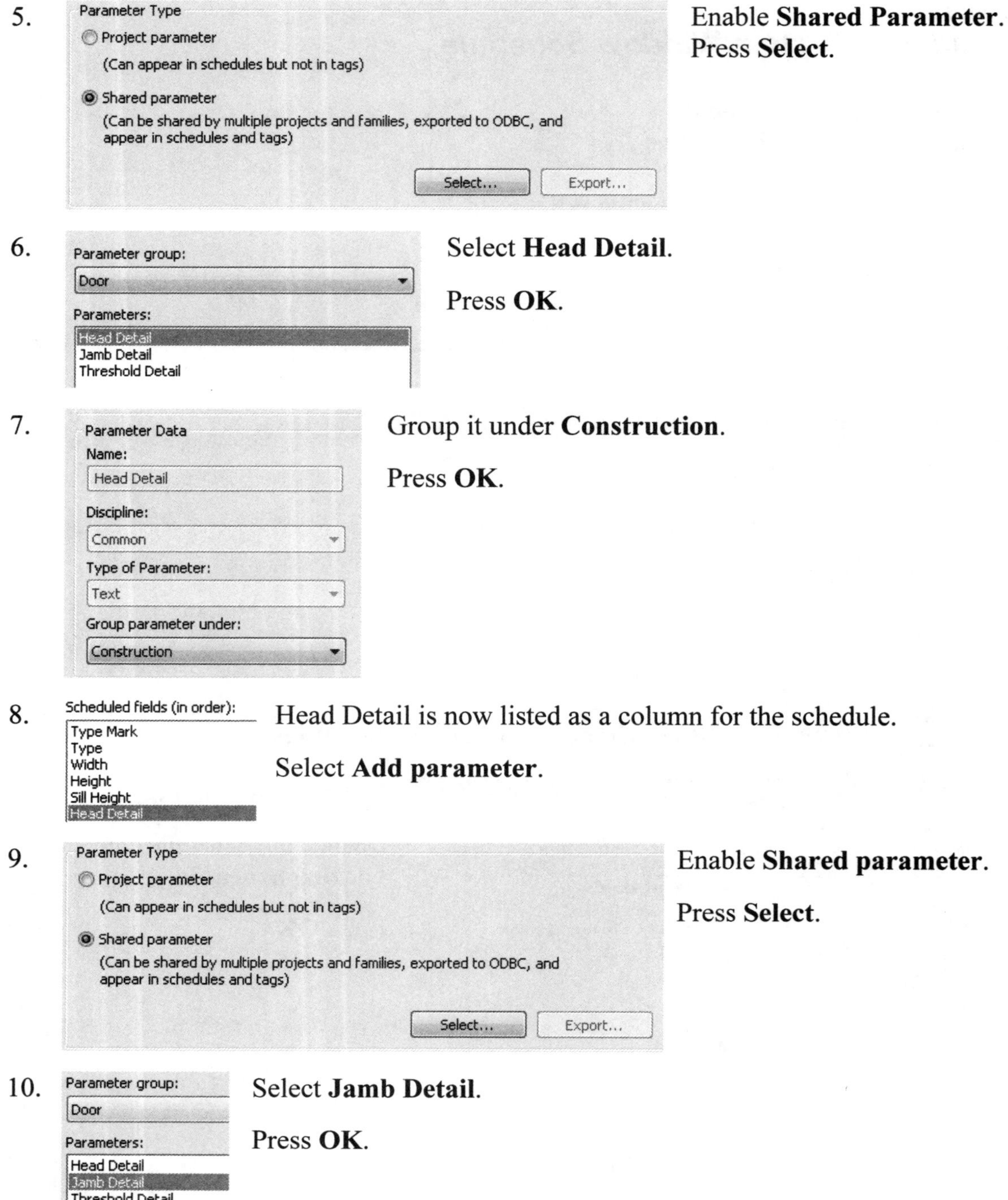

5. Enable **Shared Parameter**.
Press **Select**.

6. Select **Head Detail**.

Press **OK**.

7. Group it under **Construction**.

Press **OK**.

8. Head Detail is now listed as a column for the schedule.

Select **Add parameter**.

9. Enable **Shared parameter**.

Press **Select**.

10. Select **Jamb Detail**.

Press **OK**.

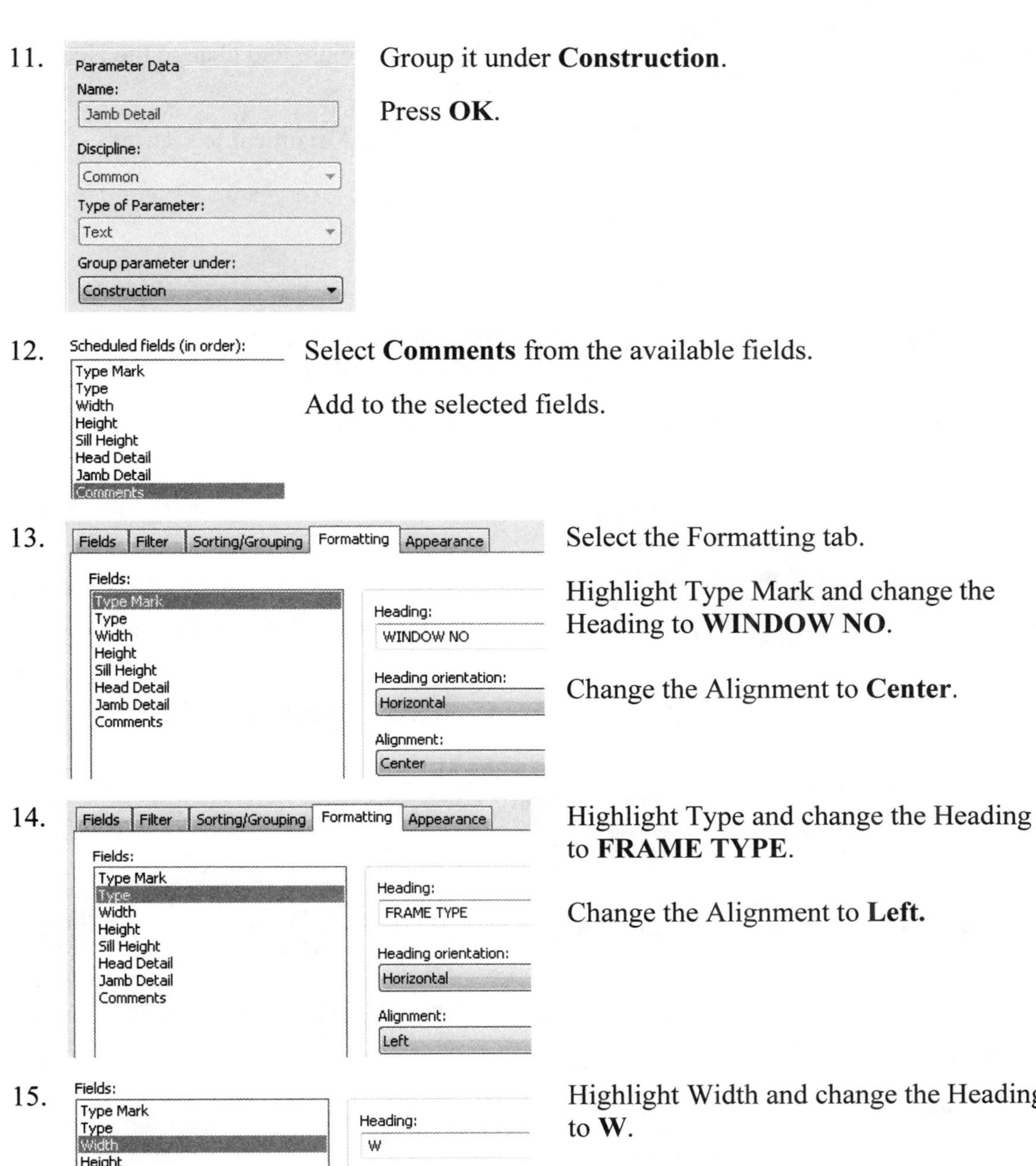

11. Group it under **Construction**.

    Press **OK**.

12. Select **Comments** from the available fields.

    Add to the selected fields.

13. Select the Formatting tab.

    Highlight Type Mark and change the Heading to **WINDOW NO**.

    Change the Alignment to **Center**.

14. Highlight Type and change the Heading to **FRAME TYPE**.

    Change the Alignment to **Left.**

15. Highlight Width and change the Heading to **W**.

    Change the Alignment to **Center**.

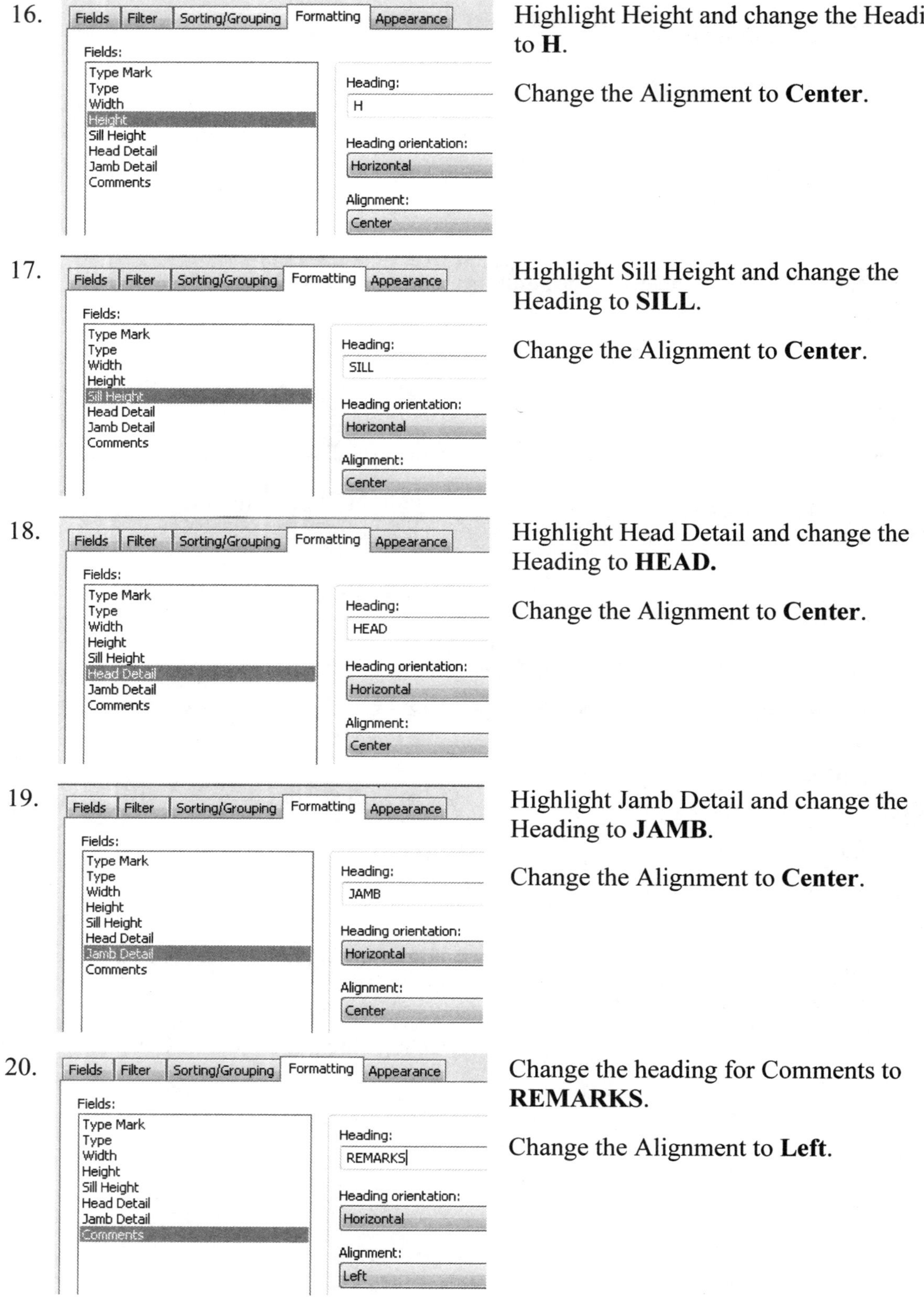

16. Highlight Height and change the Heading to **H**.

    Change the Alignment to **Center**.

17. Highlight Sill Height and change the Heading to **SILL**.

    Change the Alignment to **Center**.

18. Highlight Head Detail and change the Heading to **HEAD.**

    Change the Alignment to **Center**.

19. Highlight Jamb Detail and change the Heading to **JAMB**.

    Change the Alignment to **Center**.

20. Change the heading for Comments to **REMARKS**.

    Change the Alignment to **Left**.

21. Press **OK** to create the schedule.

22. Select the W and H columns to group.

23. Select **Titles & Headers→Group**.

24. Add a header called **SIZE** above the W and H columns.

25. Group the Head and Jamb columns.

26. Add the header DETAILS over the Head/Jamb group.

<Glazing Schedule>							
A	B	C	D	E	F	G	H
		SIZE			DETAILS		
WINDOW NO	FRAME TYPE	W	H	SILL	HEAD	JAMB	REMARKS
1	36" x 48"	3' - 0"	4' - 0"	2' - 9"			
1	36" x 48"	3' - 0"	4' - 0"	2' - 9"			
1	36" x 48"	3' - 0"	4' - 0"	4' - 0"			
1	36" x 48"	3' - 0"	4' - 0"	4' - 0"			

27. Save as *ex6-7.rvt.*

Exercise 6-8

Create a Finish Schedule

Drawing Name: ex6-7.rvt
Estimated Time: 15 minutes

This exercise reinforces the following skills:

- Schedule/Quantities
- Rooms
- Materials

1. Open *ex6-7.rvt.*

2. 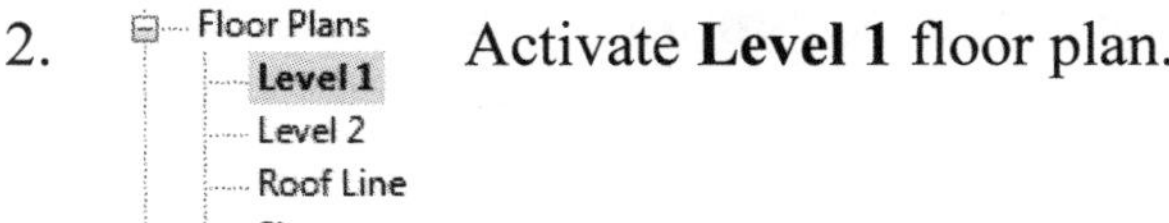

Activate **Level 1** floor plan.

3. Activate the Architecture ribbon.

Select **Room** from the Room & Area panel.

4. 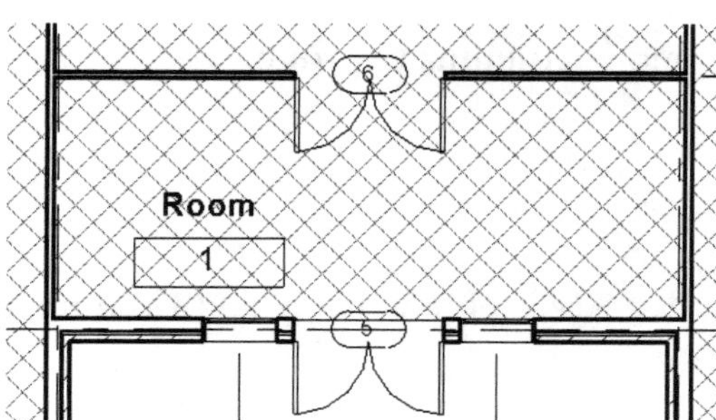

Place a room in the Lobby Area.

Left click outside the building to release the ROOM command.

Materials were applied in Lesson 4. If you skipped those exercises, you should do Lesson 4 before you do this exercise or use the exercise file available on the publisher's website.

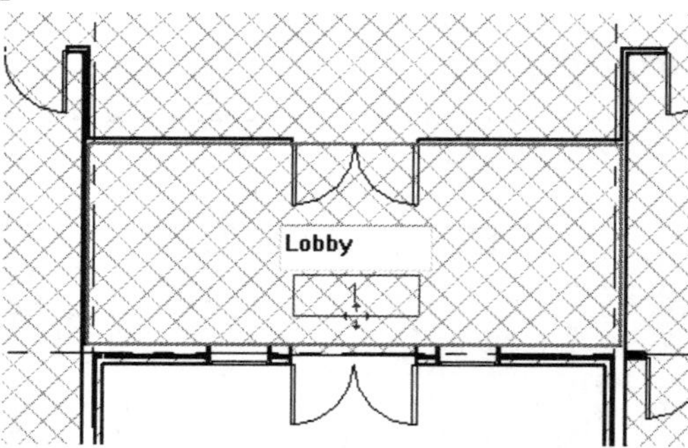

To rename the room, simply left click on the label and type.

5. 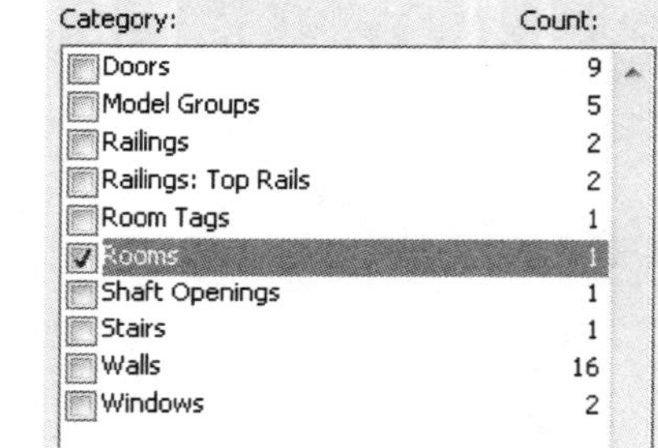

Category:	Count:
Doors	9
Model Groups	5
Railings	2
Railings: Top Rails	2
Room Tags	1
Rooms	1
Shaft Openings	1
Stairs	1
Walls	16
Windows	2

Select the Room using the FILTER tool or TAB SELECT.

6. 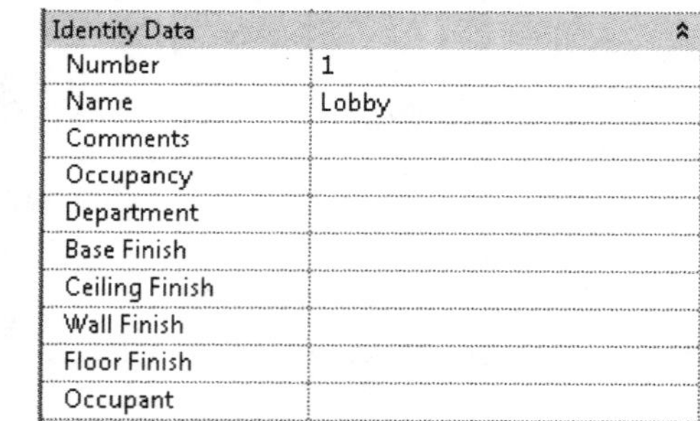

Identity Data	
Number	1
Name	Lobby
Comments	
Occupancy	
Department	
Base Finish	
Ceiling Finish	
Wall Finish	
Floor Finish	
Occupant	

Note there are parameters for finish in the Properties list.

7. 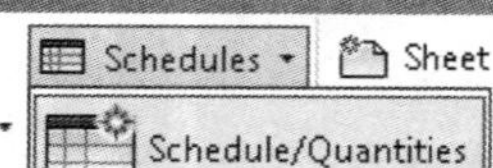

Activate the View ribbon.

Select **Create → Schedules/Quantities**.

8. 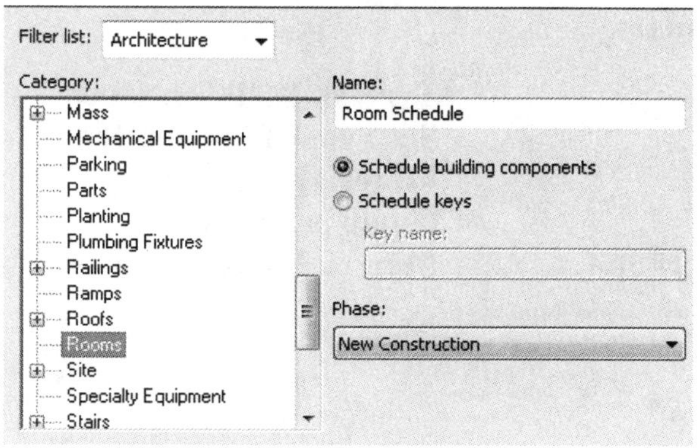 Highlight **Rooms** in the left pane.

Enable **Schedule Building components**.

Press **OK**.

9. 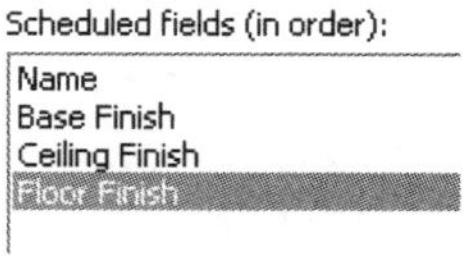 Add the following Room parameters:
   - Name
   - Base Finish
   - Ceiling Finish
   - Floor Finish

10. 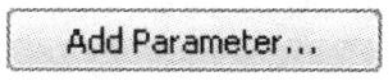 Select **Add Parameter**.

11. 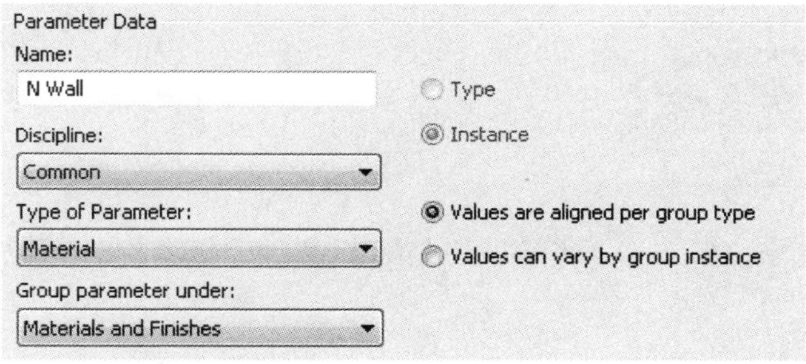 Type **N Wall** for Name.
Set Type of Parameter to **Material**.
Group parameter under **Materials and Finishes**.

Press **OK**.

12.  Select **Add Parameter**.

13. 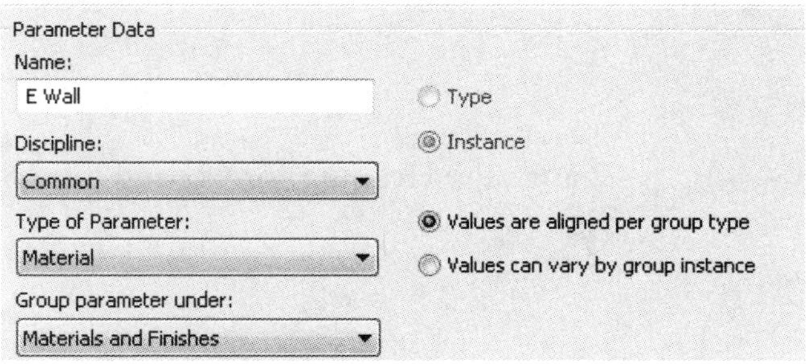 Type **E Wall** for Name.
Set Type of Parameter to **Material**.
Group parameter under **Materials and Finishes**.

Press **OK**.

14. 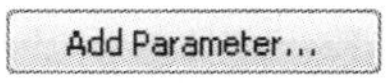 Select **Add Parameter**.

15. 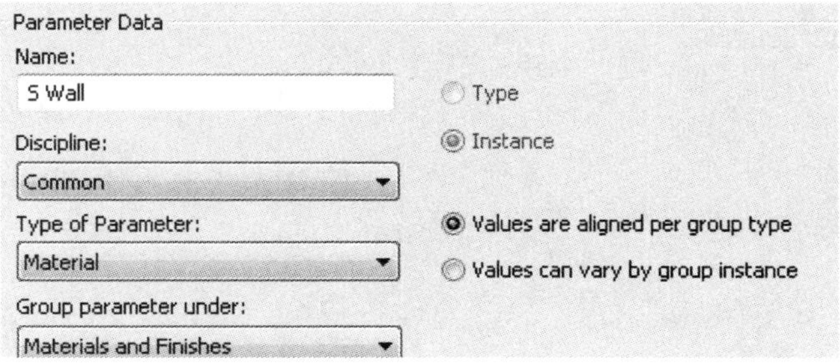 Type **S Wall** for Name.
Set Type of Parameter to **Material**.
Group parameter under **Materials and Finishes**.

Press **OK**.

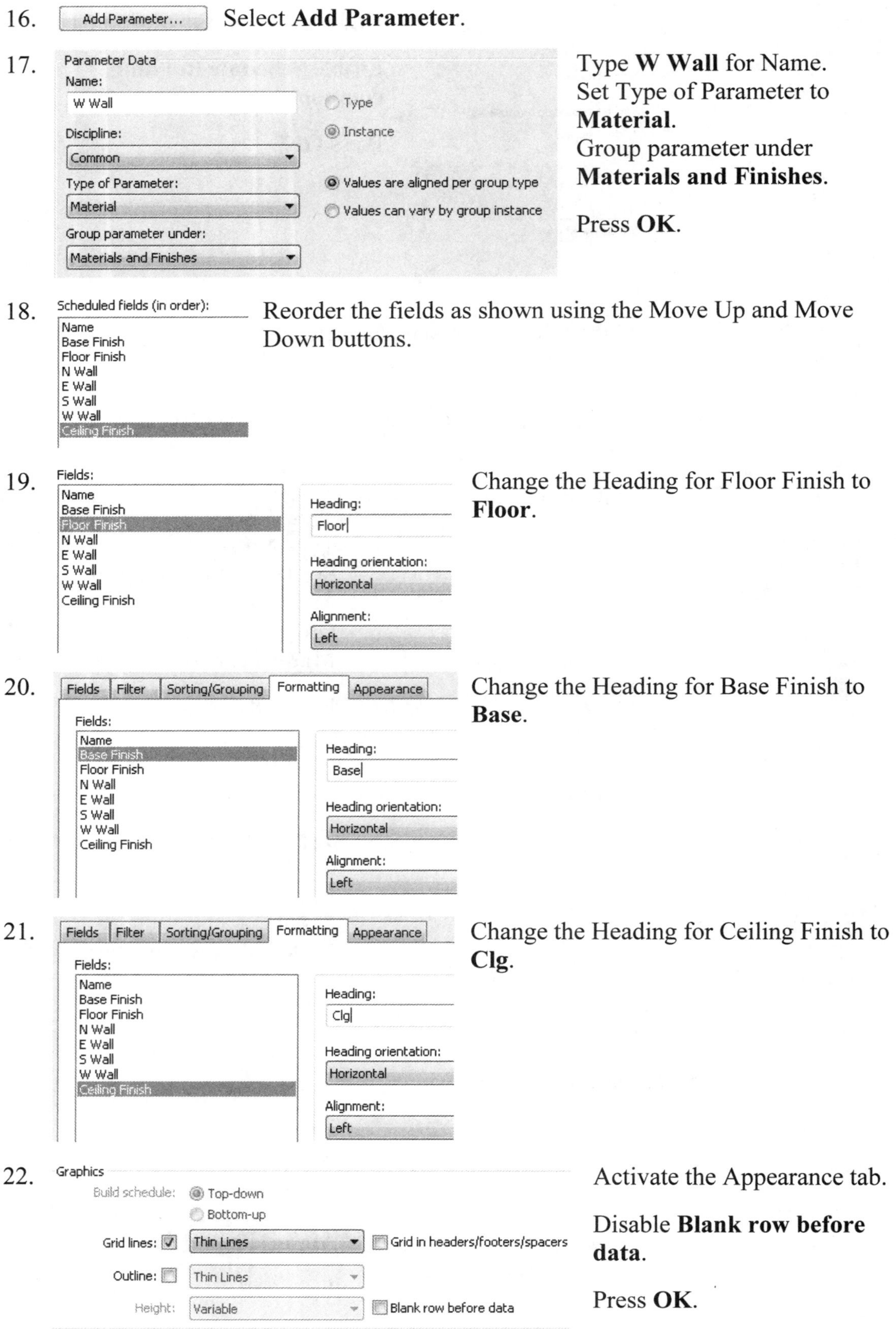

16. Select **Add Parameter**.

17. Type **W Wall** for Name.
Set Type of Parameter to **Material**.
Group parameter under **Materials and Finishes**.

    Press **OK**.

18. Reorder the fields as shown using the Move Up and Move Down buttons.

19. Change the Heading for Floor Finish to **Floor**.

20. Change the Heading for Base Finish to **Base**.

21. Change the Heading for Ceiling Finish to **Clg**.

22. Activate the Appearance tab.

    Disable **Blank row before data**.

    Press **OK**.

23. The schedule is displayed.

<Room Schedule>

A	B	C	D	E	F	G	H
Name	Base	Floor	N Wall	E Wall	S Wall	W Wall	Clg
Lobby							

24. 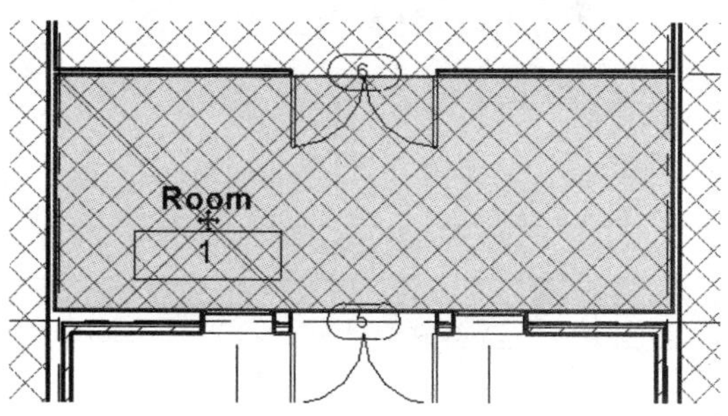

Activate **Level 1**.

25. Repeat [Schedule/Quantities]
Recent Commands
Select Previous
Find Referring Views

Right click in the window and **Select Previous** from the shortcut menu.

26. Rooms (1)

Area	244.43 SF

The room should re-appear in the Properties pane as selected.

27. Rooms (1) Edit Type

Constraints	
Level	Level 1
Upper Limit	Level 1
Limit Offset	10' 0"
Base Offset	0' 0"
Materials and Finishes	
N Wall	
E Wall	
S Wall	
W Wall	
Dimensions	

Note the parameters added now appear in the Properties panel.

28.

Materials and Finishes	
N Wall	Paint - Interior SW0068 Heron Blue
E Wall	Wallpaper - Striped
S Wall	Paint - Interior SW0068 Heron Blue
W Wall	Paint - Interior SW0068 Heron Blue
Dimensions	

Select in the material column and assign the appropriate material for each wall.

29.

Identity Data	
Number	1
Name	Lobby
Comments	
Occupancy	
Department	
Base Finish	A
Ceiling Finish	B
Wall Finish	C
Floor Finish	D
Occupant	

Under Identity Data:

Assign letters to each of the remaining finish elements.

30.  In the Project Browser, select the **Room Schedule**.

31.  Change the View Name to **FINISH SCHEDULE**.

The title of the schedule will update.

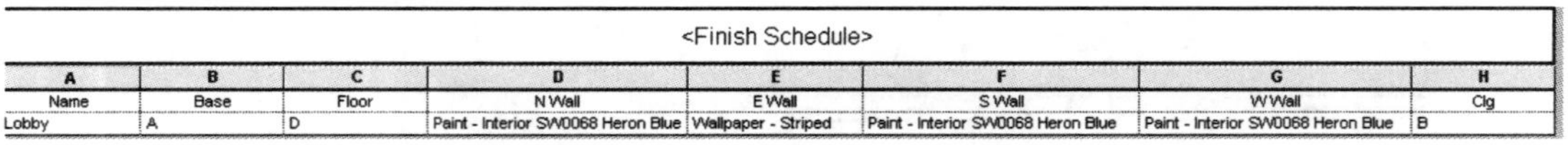

<Finish Schedule>							
A	B	C	D	E	F	G	H
Name	Base	Floor	N Wall	E Wall	S Wall	W Wall	Clg
Lobby	A	D	Paint - Interior SW0068 Heron Blue	Wallpaper - Striped	Paint - Interior SW0068 Heron Blue	Paint - Interior SW0068 Heron Blue	B

32. Save as *ex6-8.rvt*.

Exercise 6-9

Adding Schedules and Tables to Sheets

Drawing Name: ex6-8.rvt
Estimated Time: 15 minutes

This exercise reinforces the following skills:

- Shared Parameters
- Schedule/Quantities
- Sheets

1. Open *ex6-8.rvt.*

2.  Right click on Sheets and select **New Sheet**.

3. 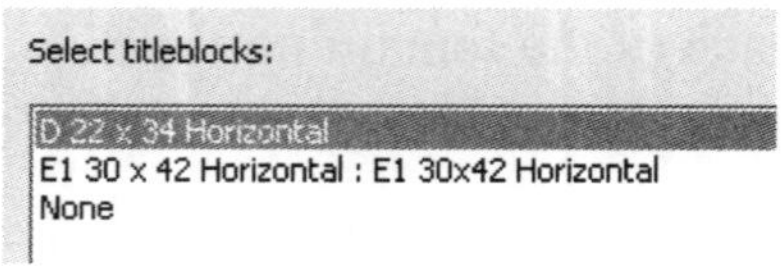 Highlight the D 22 x 34 Horizontal title block.

   Press **OK**.

4. Drag and drop the door schedule from the browser onto the sheet.

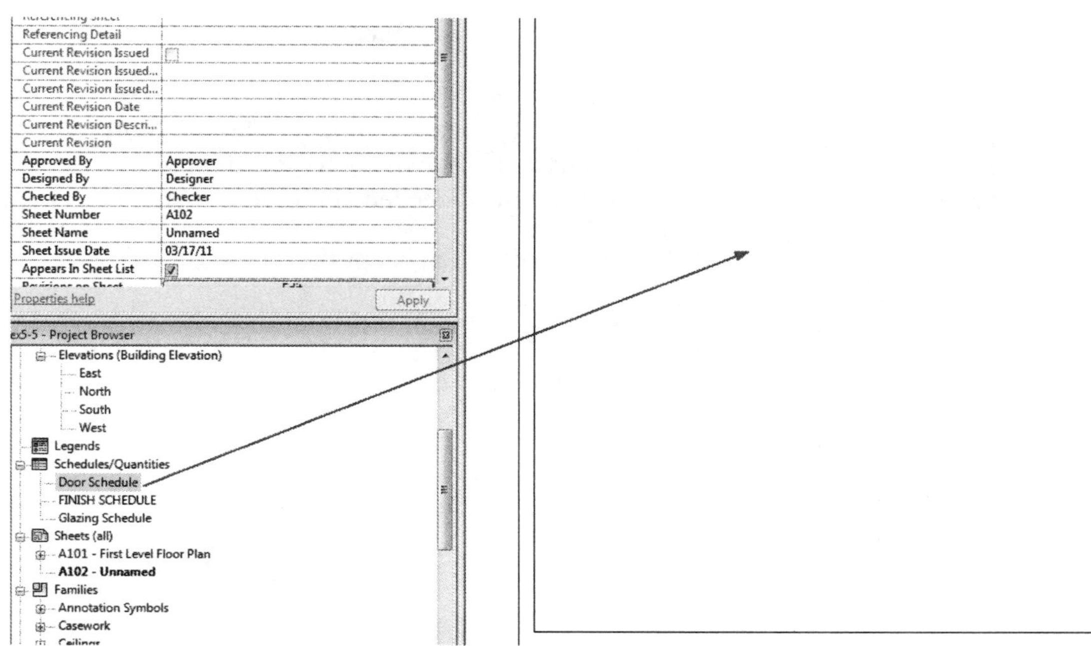

5. Use the blue grips to widen or shorten the columns.

Door Schedule								
	Door				Frame			
No.	Type	Width	Height	Thickness	Frame Type	Frame Material	HDWR	Remarks
1	A	3' - 0"	7' - 0"	0' - 2"	3	WD		
2	A	3' - 0"	7' - 0"	0' - 2"	3	WD		
3	A	3' - 0"	7' - 0"	0' - 2"	3	WD		
4	A	3' - 0"	7' - 0"	0' - 2"	3	WD		
5	8	6' - 0"	6' - 6"	0' - 2"	1	WD		BY MFR
7	A	3' - 0"	7' - 0"	0' - 2"	3	WD		
8	A	3' - 0"	7' - 0"	0' - 2"	3	WD		
9	A	3' - 0"	7' - 0"	0' - 2"	3	WD		
10	A	3' - 0"	7' - 0"	0' - 2"	3	WD		
11	13	2' - 11 7/16"	7' - 6 5/32"	0' - 1 3/16"	2	AL		
12	13	2' - 11 7/16"	7' - 6 5/32"	0' - 1 3/16"	2	AL		
13	14	6' - 5 9/16"	7' - 8 1/4"					
14	8	6' - 0"	6' - 6"	0' - 2"	1	WD		BY MFR

6.

Current Revision	
Approved By	M. Instructor
Designed By	J. Student
Checked By	M. Teacher
Sheet Number	A601
Sheet Name	Door Schedule
Sheet Issue Date	06/22/13
Appears In Sheet List	☑
Revisions on Sheet	Edit...
Other	
File Path	
Drawn By	J. Student
Guide Grid	<None>

On the Properties pane:

Change the Sheet Number to **A601**.
Change the Sheet Name to **Door Schedule**.
Add your name to the Designed by and Drawn by fields.
Add your instructor's name to the Approved by and Checked by fields.

7. View Activate the **View** ribbon.

8. Sheet Select the **New Sheet** tool from the Sheet Composition panel.

Highlight the D 22 x 34 Horizontal title block.

Press **OK**.

9.

Current Revision	
Approved By	M. Instructor
Designed By	J. Student
Checked By	M. Teacher
Sheet Number	A602
Sheet Name	Glazing Schedule
Sheet Issue Date	06/22/13
Appears In Sheet List	☑
Revisions on Sheet	Edit...
Other	
File Path	
Drawn By	J. Student
Guide Grid	<None>

In the Properties pane:

Change the Sheet Number to **A602**.
Change the Sheet Name to **Glazing Schedule**.
Change the Drawn By to your name.
Change the Checked By to your instructor's name.

Press **Apply** to accept the changes.

10. 

Zoom into the title block and you see that some of the fields have updated.

11. Manage Activate the **Manage** ribbon.

12. Project Information Select **Project Information** from the Settings panel.

13. Instance Parameters - Control selected or to-be-created instance

Parameter	Value
Identity Data	
Organization Name	
Organization Description	
Building Name	Brown Offices
Author	J. Student
Energy Analysis	
Energy Settings	Edit...
Other	
Project Issue Date	06-01-2014
Project Status	In Design
Client Name	B. Brown
Project Address	Edit...
Project Name	Brown Office Building
Project Number	P0101

Fill in the Project Data.
Press **OK**.

14. Note that the title block updates.

B. Brown
Brown Office Building
Glazing Schedule

Project number	P0101
Date	06-01-2014
Drawn by	J. Student
Checked by	M. Teacher

A602

Scale

Sheets (all)
- A101 - First Level Floor Plan
- A102 - Door Schedule
- **A103 - Glazing Schedule**

Activate the other sheets and note that the project information has updated on all sheets in the project.

15. Drag and drop the **Glazing Schedule** onto the A602 sheet.

Break the schedule into two parts by using the break control.

16. The schedule should be divided into two sections.

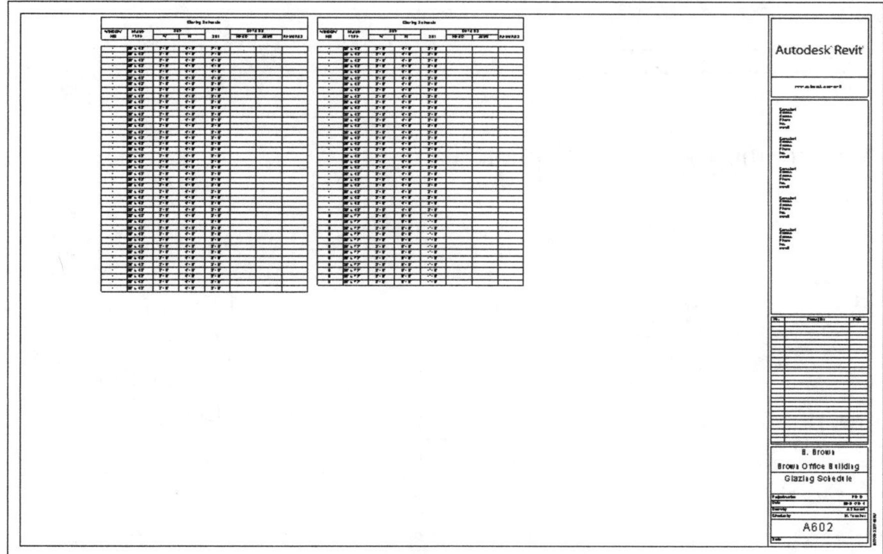

To put the two sections back together, just drag and drop one section on top of the other.

17. Save the file as *ex6-9.rvt*.

Exercise 6-10
Using Keynotes

Drawing Name: ex6-9.rvt
Estimated Time: 30 minutes

This exercise reinforces the following skills:

- Keynotes
- Duplicate Views
- Cropping a View

1. Open *ex6-9.rvt.*

2. View Activate the **View** ribbon.

3. Sheet Select the **New Sheet** tool from the Sheet Composition panel.

4. Select titleblocks:
   D 22 x 34 Horizontal
   E1 30 x 42 Horizontal : E1 30x42 Horizontal
   None

   Highlight the D 22 x 34 Horizontal titleblock.

   Press **OK**.

5.

Current Revision	
Approved By	M. Instructor
Designed By	J. Student
Checked By	M. Instructor
Sheet Number	A603
Sheet Name	Lobby Keynotes
Sheet Issue Date	06/22/13
Appears In Sheet List	☑
Revisions on Sheet	Edit...
Other	
File Path	
Drawn By	J. Student
Guide Grid	<None>

   In the Properties pane:

   Change the Sheet Name to **LOBBY KEYNOTES**.
   Change the Drawn By to your name.
   Change the Checked By to your instructor's name.

6. Floor Plans / Level 1 / Level 2 / Roof Line / Site

   Activate the **Level 1** floor plan.

7. 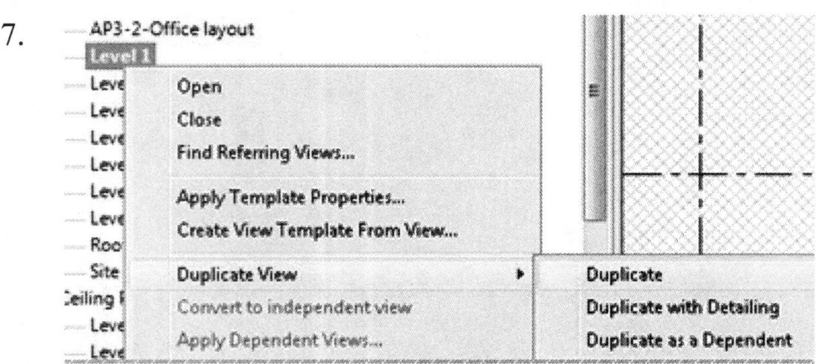

   Highlight **Level 1**.
   Right click and select **Duplicate View → Duplicate**.

8. Name: Level 1- Lobby Detail

   Rename the duplicate view **Level 1 - Lobby Detail**.

9. In the Properties palette:

Extents	
Crop View	☑
Crop Region Visible	☑
Annotation Crop	☐

Enable **Crop View**.
Enable **Crop Region Visible**.

10. Zoom out to see the crop region.

Select the rectangle surrounding the view. This is the crop region.

11. Use the blue circle grips to crop the view so that only the lobby area is displayed.

12. 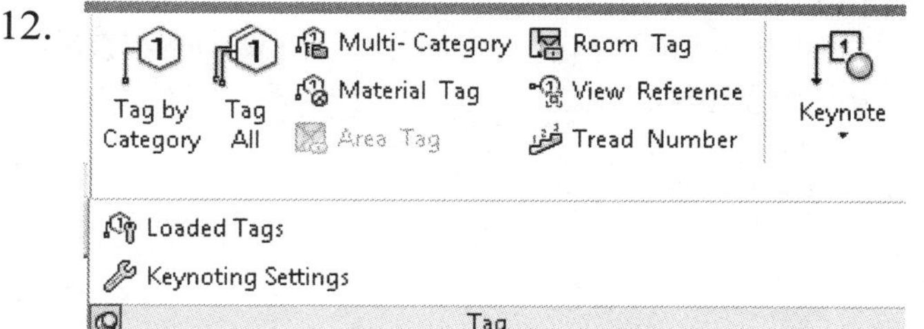

Activate the **Annotate** ribbon.

Select **Tag dropdown → Keynoting Settings**.

13. Keynote Table:
Full Path: ies\US Imperial\RevitKeynotes_Imperial_2004.txt
Browse...
Saved Path: RevitKeynotes_Imperial_2004.txt
View...
Reload
Path Type: Absolute / Relative / At Library Locations
Numbering Method: By keynote / By sheet

This shows the path for the keynote database.

This is a txt file that can be edited using Notepad. You can modify the txt file or select a different txt file for keynote use.

The file can be placed on a server in team environments.

Press **OK**.

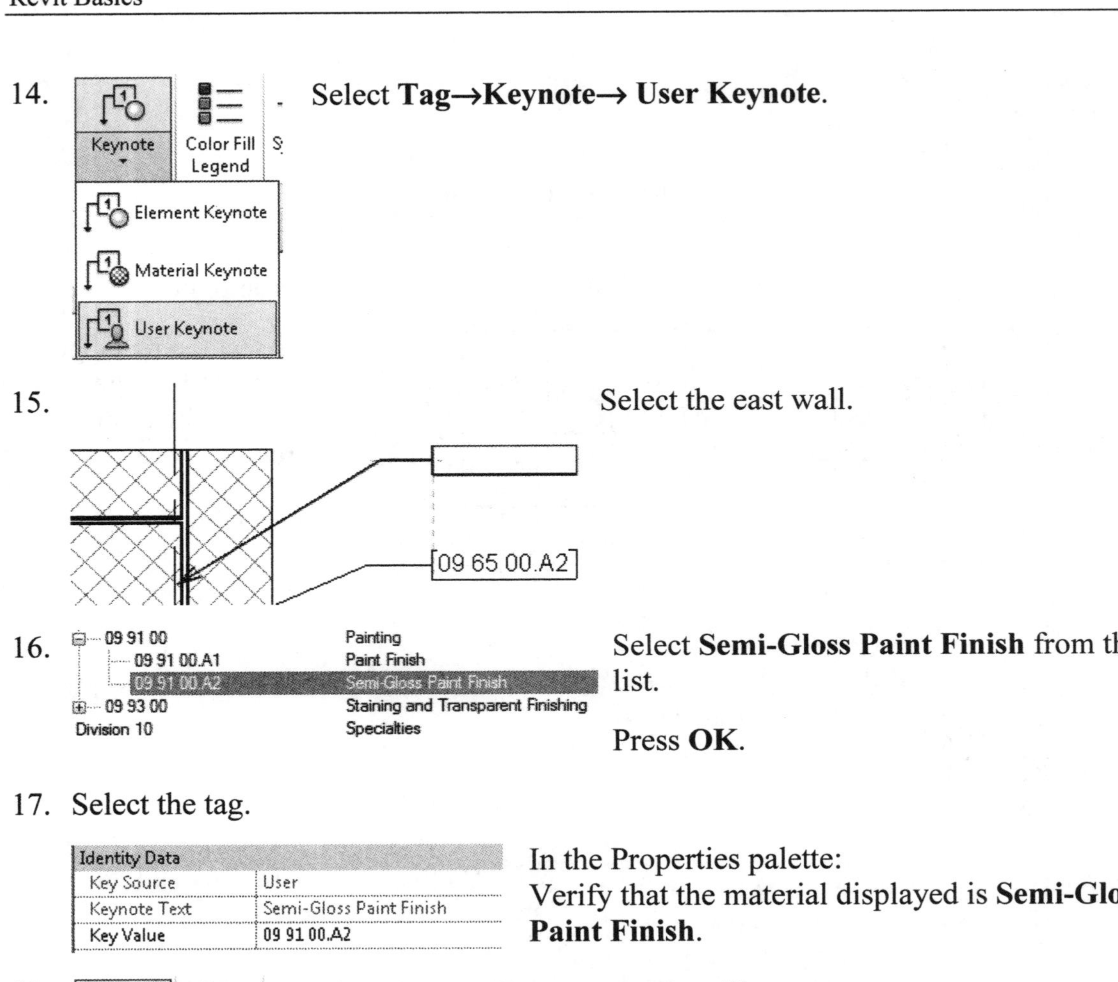

14. Select **Tag→Keynote→ User Keynote.**

15. Select the east wall.

16. Select **Semi-Gloss Paint Finish** from the list.

    Press **OK.**

17. Select the tag.

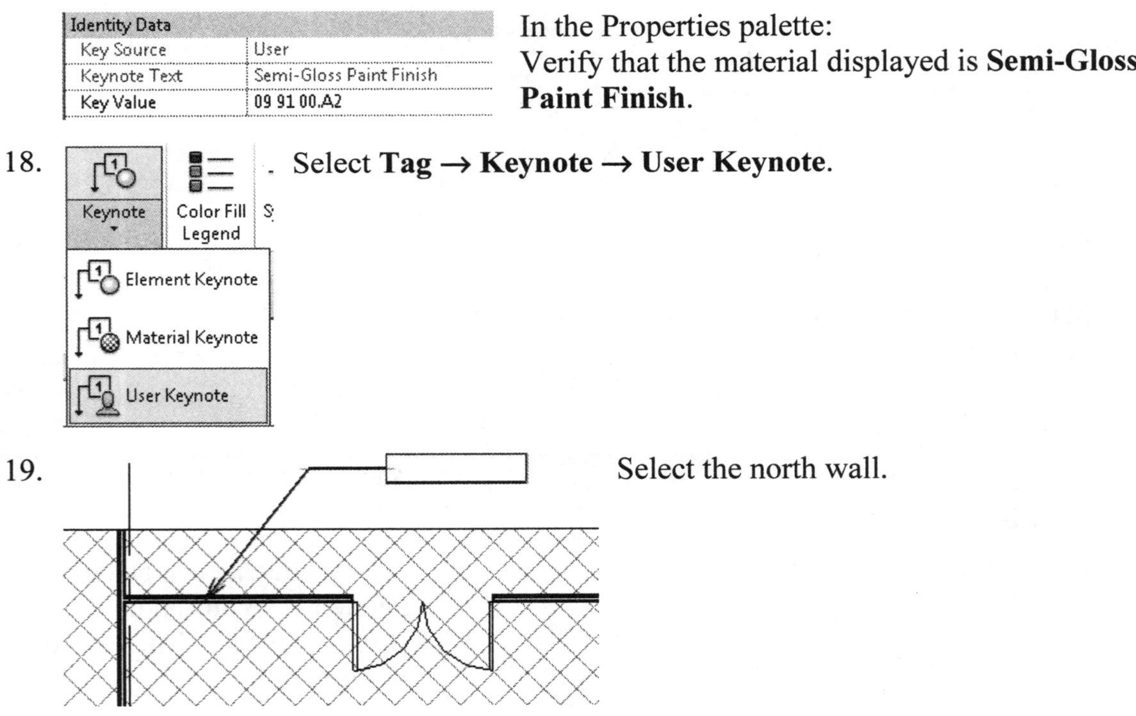

In the Properties palette:
Verify that the material displayed is **Semi-Gloss Paint Finish.**

18. Select **Tag → Keynote → User Keynote.**

19. Select the north wall.

20. Select **Vinyl Wallcovering** from the list.
    Press **OK.**

21. Select the west wall.

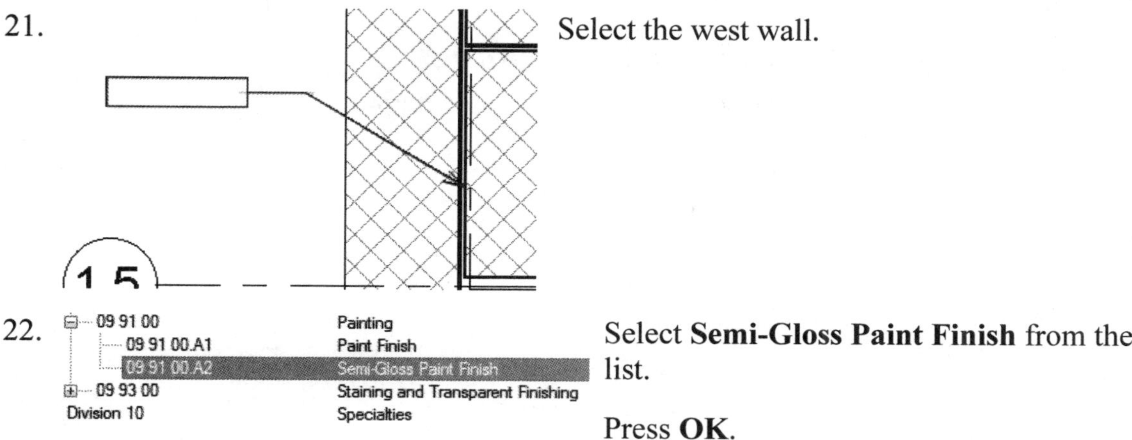

22. Select **Semi-Gloss Paint Finish** from the list.

Press **OK**.

23. Select the South wall to add a tag.

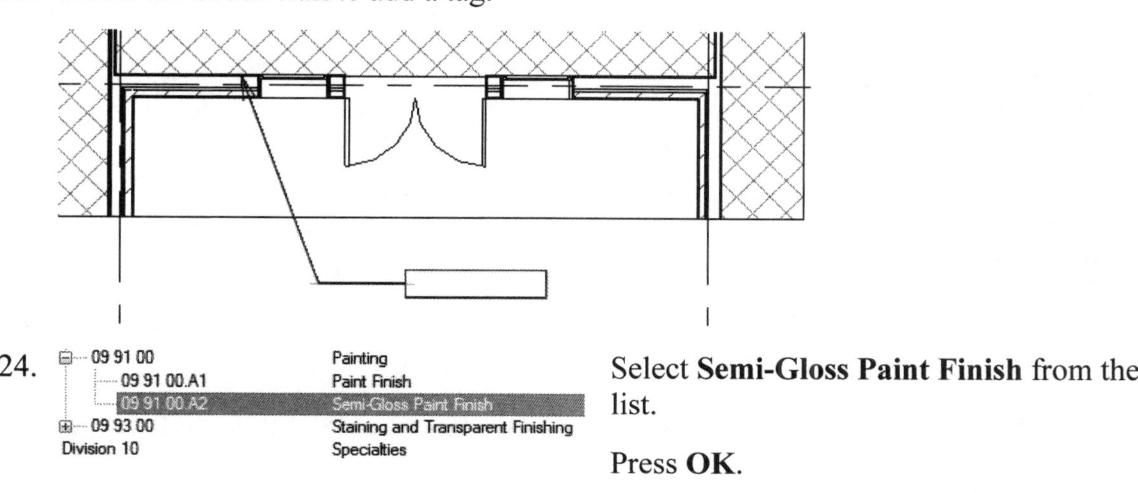

24. Select **Semi-Gloss Paint Finish** from the list.

Press **OK**.

25. The view should appear as shown.

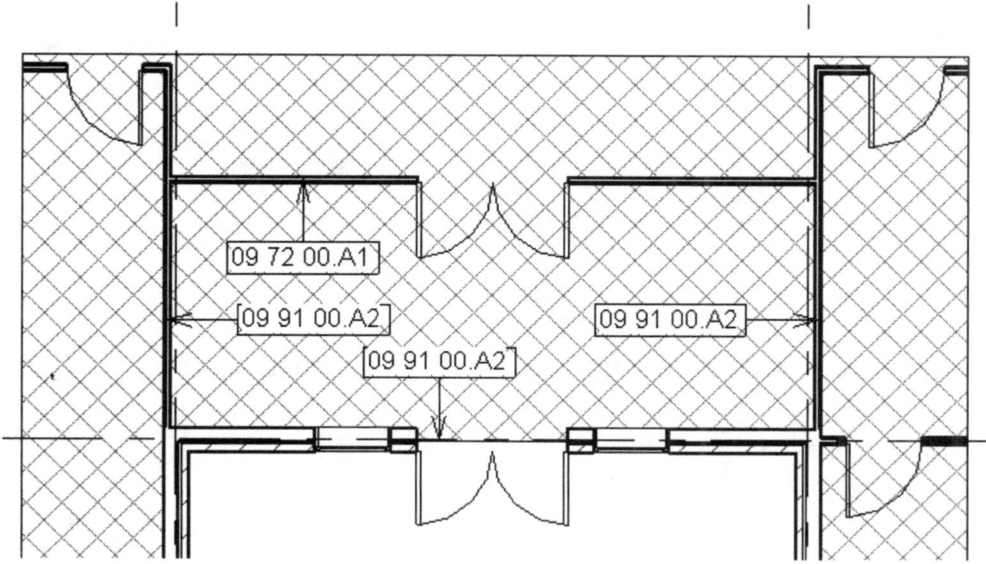

Save as *ex6-10.rvt*.

Exercise 6-11

Create a Building Elevation with Keynotes

Drawing Name: ex6-10.rvt
Estimated Time: 30 minutes

This exercise reinforces the following skills:

- Elevation View
- Cropping a View
- Keynote Tags

1. Open *ex6-10.rvt*.

2. Activate the **Level 1 - Lobby Detail** view.

3. Type **VV** to bring up the Visibility/Graphics dialog.

   Activate the **Annotation Categories** tab.

   Enable the visibility of Elevations.

4. Activate the View ribbon.

   Select **Elevation→ Elevation**.

5. Check in the Properties palette.

   You should see that you are placing a Building Elevation.

6. Place an elevation marker as shown.

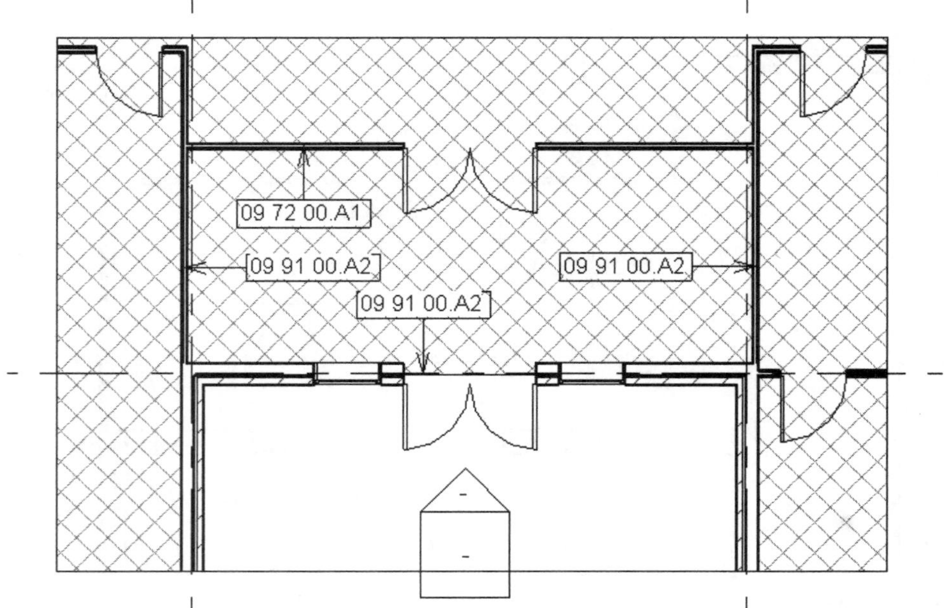

7.

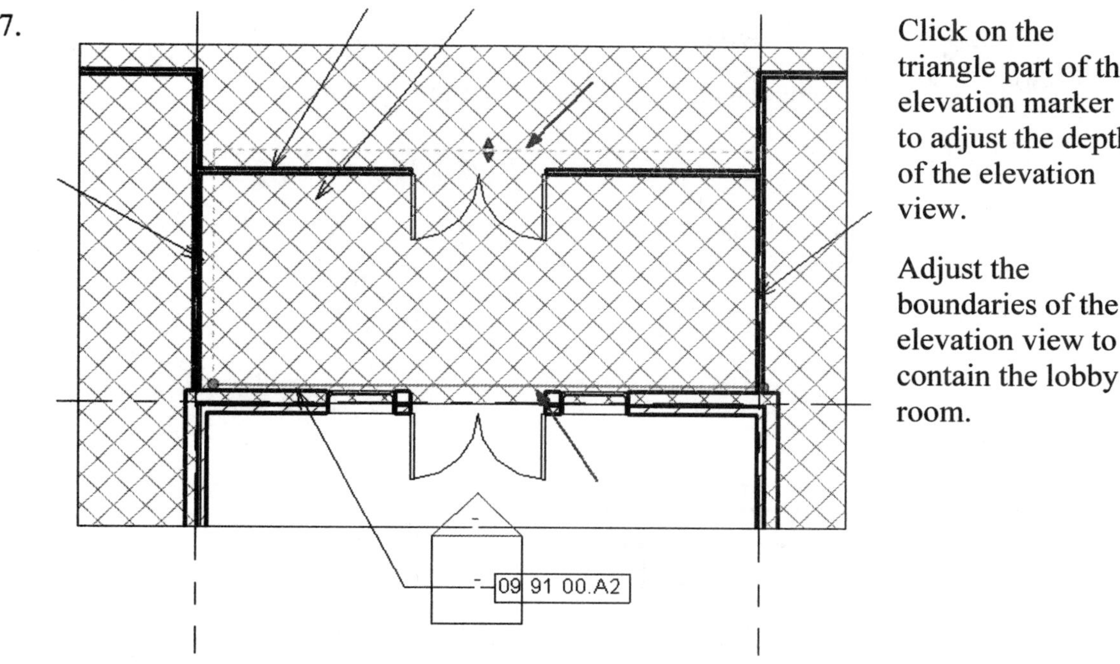

Click on the triangle part of the elevation marker to adjust the depth of the elevation view.

Adjust the boundaries of the elevation view to contain the lobby room.

8. Name: South Lobby

Locate the elevation in the Project Browser.

Rename to **South - Lobby**.

9. Elevations (Building Elevation)
- East
- North
- South
- South Lobby
- West

Activate the **South - Lobby** view.

10. Adjust the crop region to show the entire lobby including floor and ceiling.

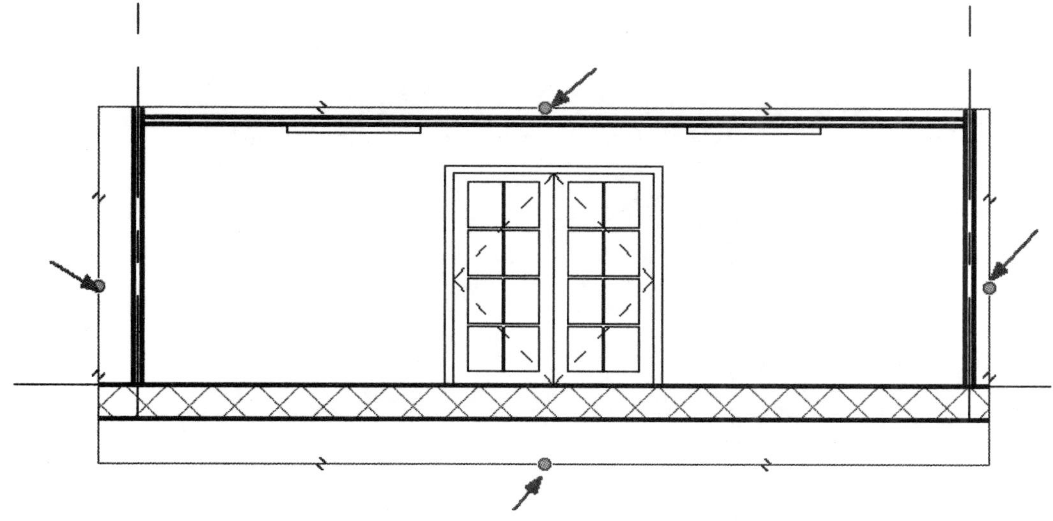

You may need to return to the Lobby Detail floor plan to adjust the location of the elevation view until it appears like the view shown.

11. Keynote | Color Fill Legend | Element Keynote

Activate the Annotation ribbon.

Select **Tag→Keynote→Element Keynote.**

12. Keynote Tag: Keynote Number

From the Properties palette:
Set the Keynote Tag to **Keynote Number**.

13. Select the ceiling.

14.

09 51 00	Acoustical Ceilings
09 51 00.A1	Square Edge (3/4 x 12 x 12)
09 51 00.A2	Square Edge (3/4 x 12 x 18)
09 51 00.A3	Square Edge (3/4 x 18 x 18)
09 51 00.A4	Square Edge (3/4 x 24 x 12)
09 51 00.A5	Square Edge (3/4 x 24 x 24)
09 51 00.A6	Square Edge (3/4 x 24 x 48)
09 51 00.A7	Tegular Edge (3/4 x 12 x 12)
09 51 00.A8	Tegular Edge (3/4 x 12 x 18)

Select the keynote under **Acoustical Ceilings: Square Edge (3/4 x 24 x 48).**

Press **OK**.

15. ?

Select the Lighting Fixture.

A ? indicates that Revit needs you to assign the keynote value.

16. 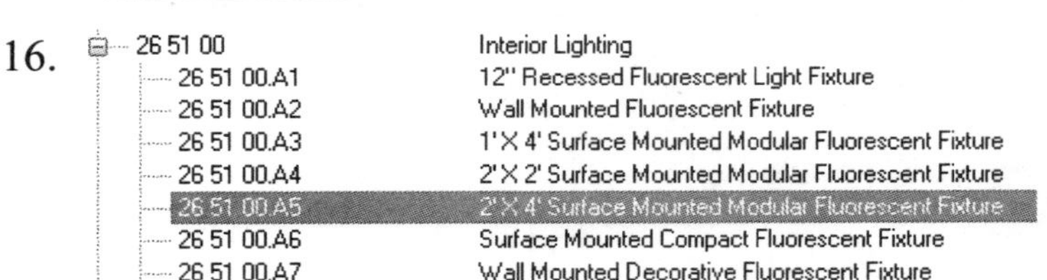

Locate the **2′ x 4′ Surface Mounted Modular Fluorescent Fixture**.

Press **OK**.

17. 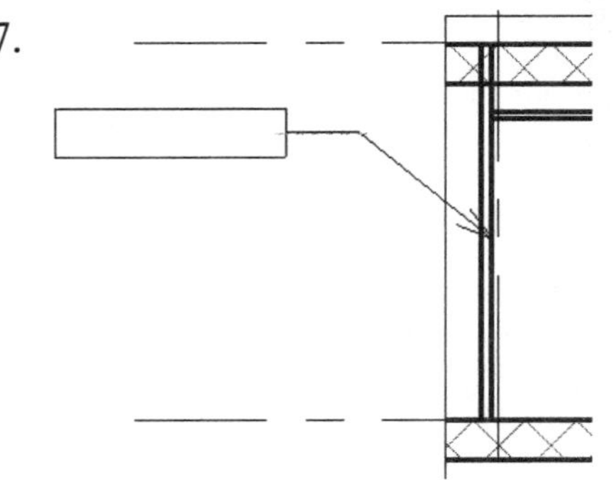

Select the west wall.

18.

09 84 00	Acoustic Room Components
09 91 00	Painting
09 91 00.A1	Paint Finish
09 91 00.A2	Semi-Gloss Paint Finish
09 93 00	Staining and Transparent Finishing

Locate the **Semi-Gloss Paint Finish**.

Press **OK**.

19. 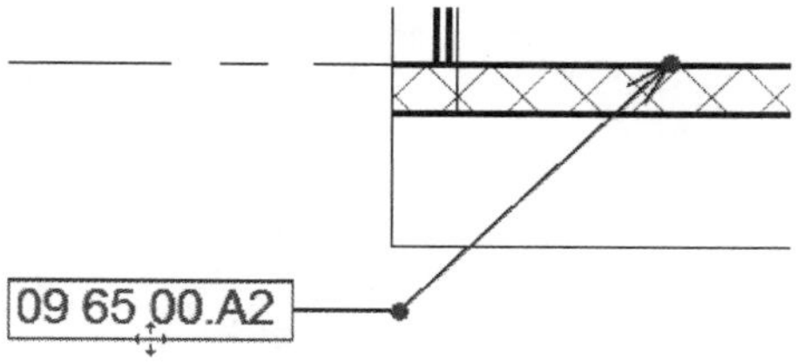 Select the Floor.

20. 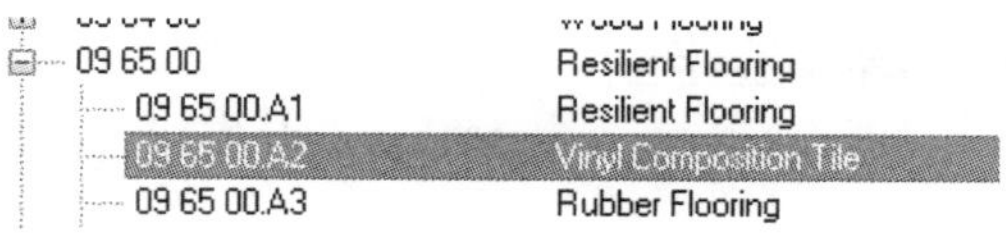 Locate the **Vinyl Composition Tile.**

Press **OK**.

21. 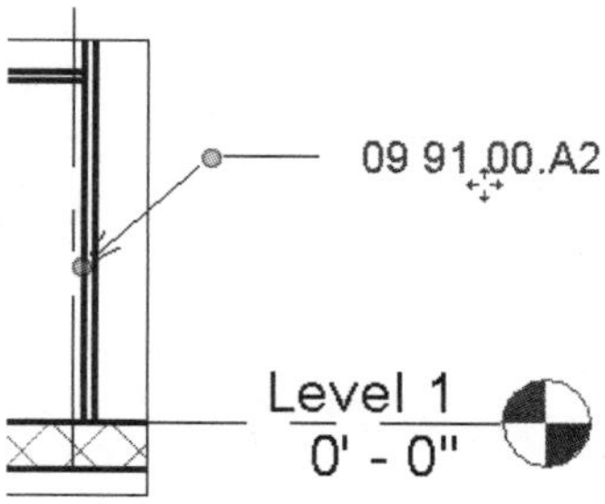 Select the East Wall.

Because you have already assigned a keynote to a similar wall, Revit remembers what was assigned.

22. 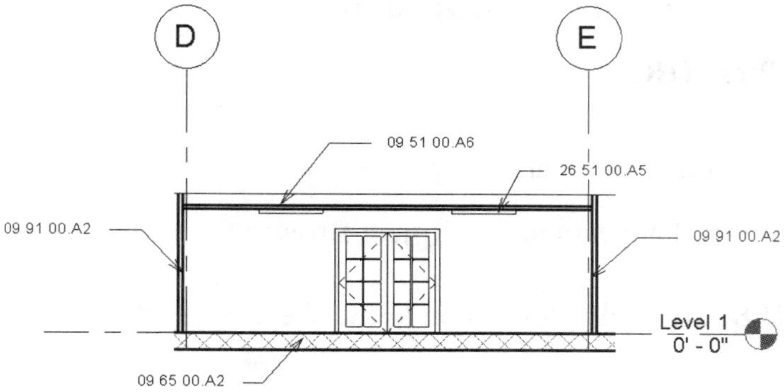 Disable **Crop Region Visible** in the Properties pane.

Your view should look similar to the one shown.

23.  Activate the **A603 - LOBBY KEYNOTES** sheet.

24. 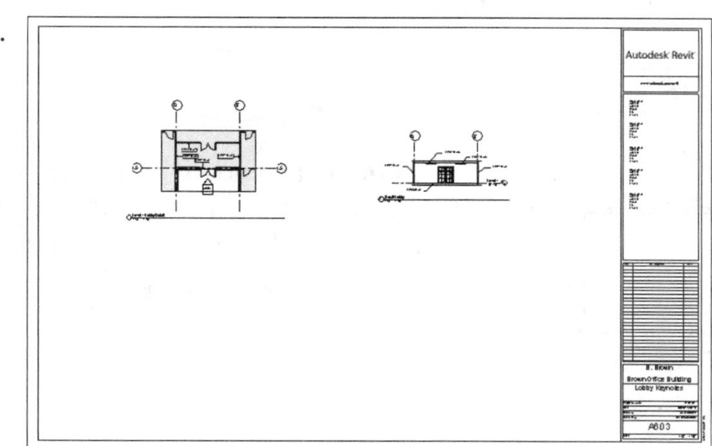

Add the **Level 1 - Lobby Detail** view to the sheet.

Add the **South Lobby Elevation** view to the sheet.

25. Add the Finish Schedule to the sheet.

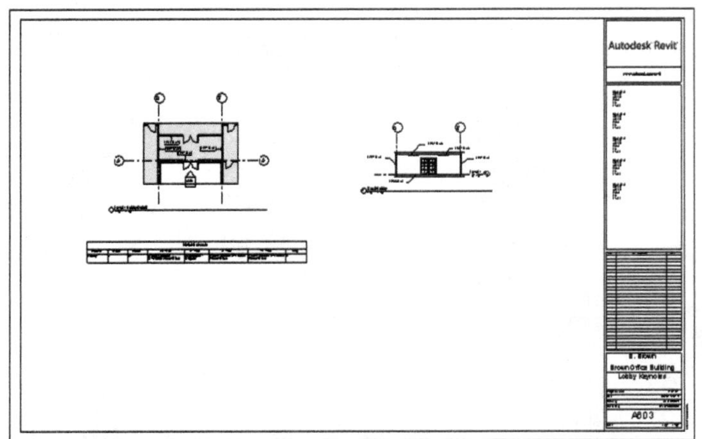

26. Activate the View ribbon.

Select **Create→Keynote Legend**.

27. Type **FINISH SCHEDULE KEYS**.

Press **OK**.

28. Press **OK** to accept the default legend created.

29. The legend appears in the Project Browser.

30. Drag and drop the FINISH SCHEDULE KEYS on to the sheet.

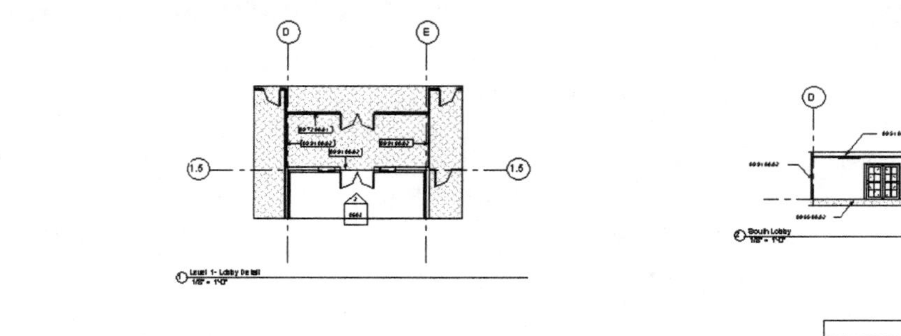

31. Zoom in and you will see the elevation marker now indicates the Sheet Number and View Number.

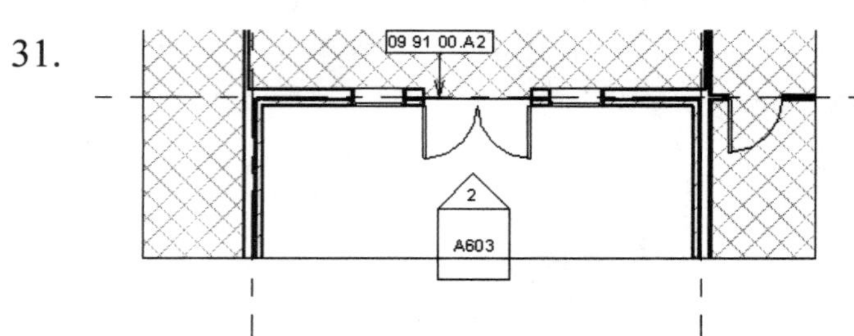

2 South - Lobby
1/8" = 1'-0"

32. Save as *ex6-11.rvt*.

Exercise 6-12

Find and Replace Families

Drawing Name: ex6-11.rvt
Estimated Time: 5 minutes

This exercise reinforces the following skills:

- Families
- Project Browser

1. Open *ex6-11.rvt.*

2. 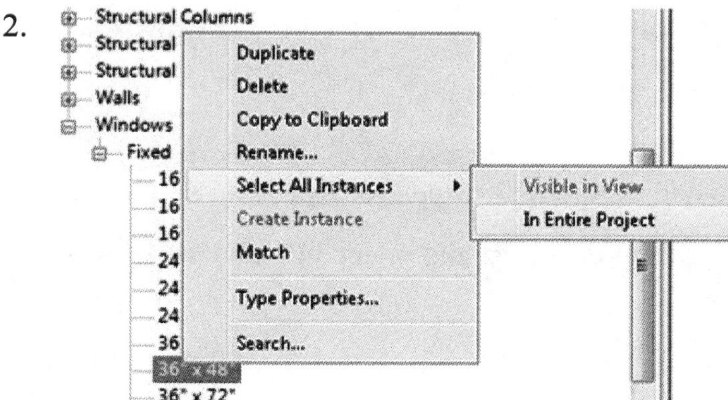

In the Project Browser, locate the *Windows* category under Families.

Highlight **36″ x 48″** [**0915 x 1220mm**].

Right click and select **Select All Instances→In Entire Project**.

3. Properties
Fixed
36" x 24"
Windows (69)

Select **Fixed: 36″ x 24″** [**M_Fixed: 0915 x 0610mm**] from the Properties pane Type selector.

4. All the selected windows have been replaced with the new type.

5. FINISH SCHEDULE KEYS
Schedules/Quantities
Door Details
Door Schedule
Finish Schedule
Glazing Schedule
Lighting Fixture Schedule

Activate the Glazing Schedule.

6.

8	36" x 24"	3' - 0"
8	36" x 24"	3' - 0"
8	36" x 24"	3' - 0"
8	36" x 24"	3' - 0"
8	36" x 24"	3' - 0"

Zoom into the window schedule and you will see that it has automatically updated.

7. Save as *ex6-12.rvt.*

Exercise 6-13
Modifying Family Types in a Schedule

Drawing Name: ex6-12.rvt
Estimated Time: 10 minutes

This exercise reinforces the following skills:

- Families
- Schedules

1. Open *ex6-12.rvt.*
2. 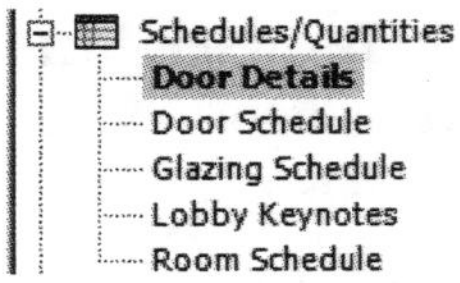 Activate the **Door Details** schedule in the Project Browser.
3. 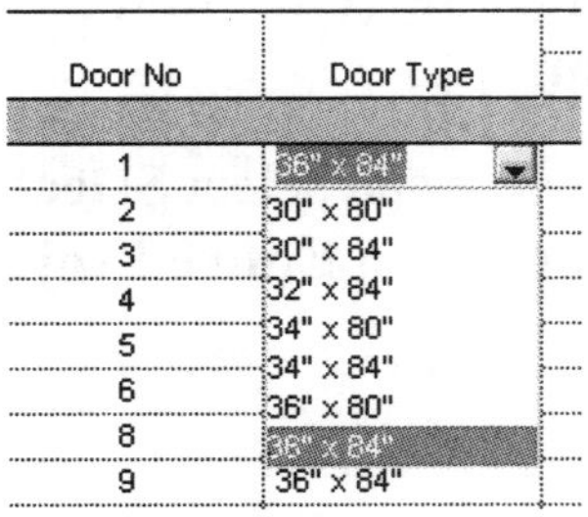 Click inside the Door Type cell for Row 1.

   Select the drop-down list and select **34″ x 84″** door type.
4. 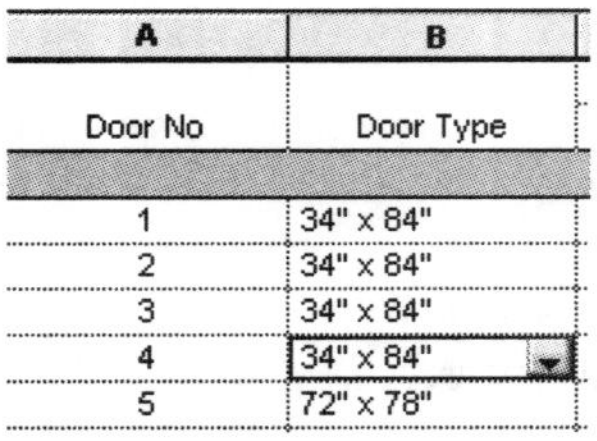 Set the first four doors to the **34″ x 84″** door type.
5. 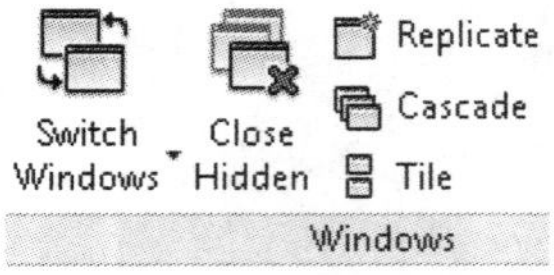 Activate the **View** ribbon.

   Select **Close Hidden** on the Windows panel.
6. Activate **Level 1**.
7. 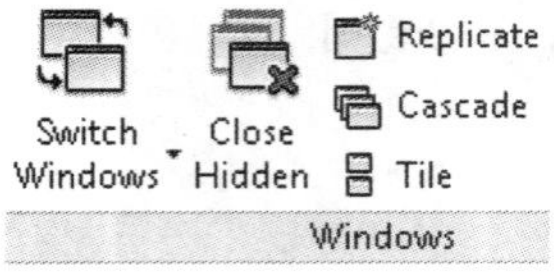 Activate the **View** ribbon.

   Select **Tile** on the Windows panel.
8. There should be two windows: The Level 1 floor plan and the Door Details schedule.

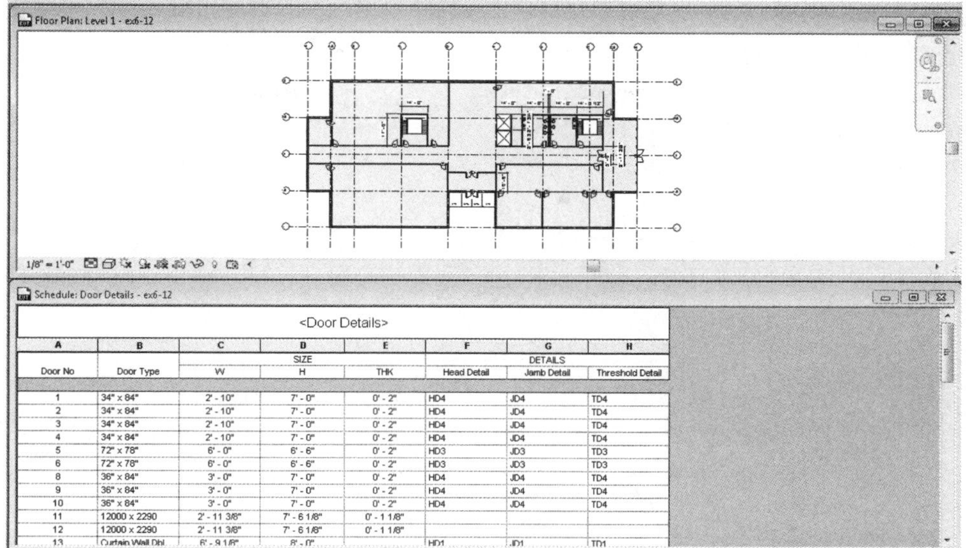

<Door Details>

A	B	C	D	E	F	G	H
		SIZE			DETAILS		
Door No	Door Type	W	H	THK	Head Detail	Jamb Detail	Threshold Detail
1	34" x 84"	2' - 10"	7' - 0"	0' - 2"	HD4	JD4	TD4
2	34" x 84"	2' - 10"	7' - 0"	0' - 2"	HD4	JD4	TD4
3	34" x 84"	2' - 10"	7' - 0"	0' - 2"	HD4	JD4	TD4
4	34" x 84"	2' - 10"	7' - 0"	0' - 2"	HD4	JD4	TD4
5	72" x 78"	6' - 0"	6' - 6"	0' - 2"	HD3	JD3	TD3
6	72" x 78"	6' - 0"	6' - 6"	0' - 2"	HD3	JD3	TD3
8	36" x 84"	3' - 0"	7' - 0"	0' - 2"	HD4	JD4	TD4
9	36" x 84"	3' - 0"	7' - 0"	0' - 2"	HD4	JD4	TD4
10	36" x 84"	3' - 0"	7' - 0"	0' - 2"	HD4	JD4	TD4
11	12000 x 2290	2' - 11 3/8"	7' - 6 1/8"	0' - 1 1/8"			
12	12000 x 2290	2' - 11 3/8"	7' - 6 1/8"	0' - 1 1/8"			
13	Curtain Wall Dbl	6' - 9 1/8"	8' - 0"		HD1	JD1	TD1

9.

Door No	Door Type
1	34" x 84"

Place your cursor in the cell with the number 1 under Door No.

10. Highlight in Model — Element

Select **Highlight in Model** from the ribbon.

11. 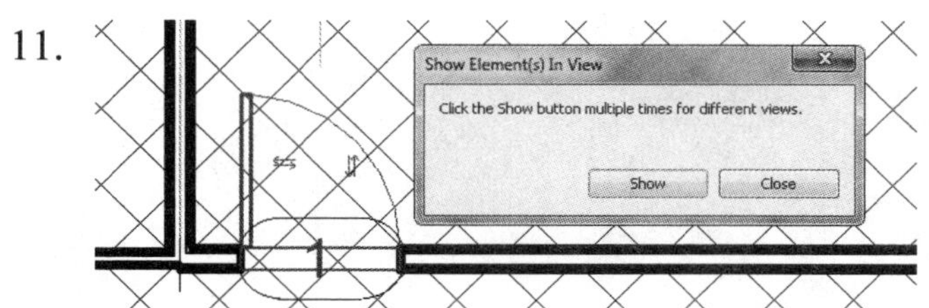

The floor plan view will zoom into the door. The door is automatically selected.

Press **Close**.

12. Properties — Single-Flush Custom 34" x 84"

In the Properties palette:

Note that the door is now 34″ x 84″.

13. Properties — Single-Flush Custom 36" x 84"

Use the Type Selector to change the door back to **36″ x 84″**.

Left click in the window to release the selection.

14.

A	B	C
Door No	Door Type	W
1	36" x 84"	3' - 0"
2	34" x 84"	2' - 10"
3	34" x 84"	2' - 10"
4	34" x 84"	2' - 10"

Note that the door details schedule has updated.

15. Save as *ex6-13.rvt*.

Exercise 6-14
Export a Schedule

Drawing Name: ex6-13.rvt
Estimated Time: 5 minutes

This exercise reinforces the following skills:

- Schedules

1. Open *ex6-13.rvt.*

2. 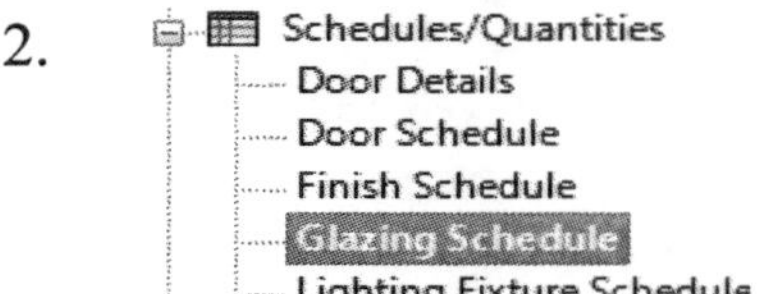

Activate the **Glazing Schedule**.

3. 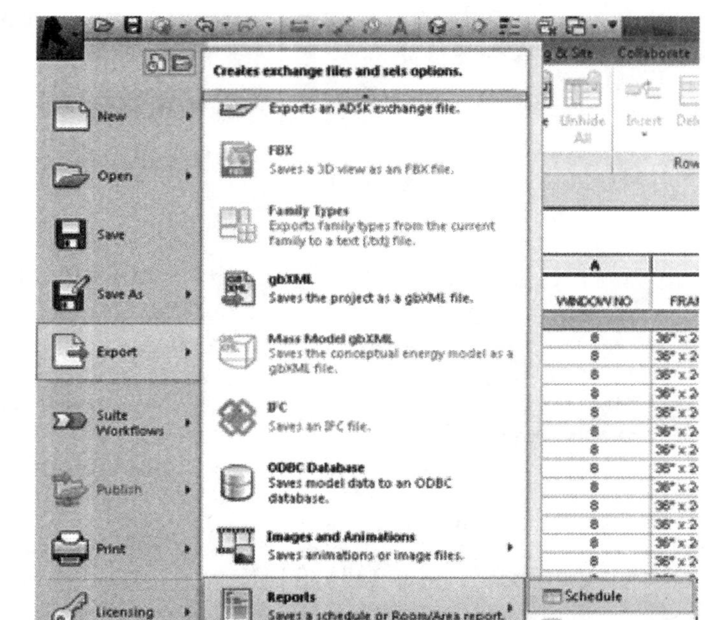

Go to the Applications Menu.

Select **File → Export → Reports → Schedule**.

4. File name: Glazing Schedule.txt
Files of type: Delimited text (*.txt)

The schedule will be saved as a comma delimited text file.

Browse to your exercise folder.
Press **Save**.

5. Press **OK**.

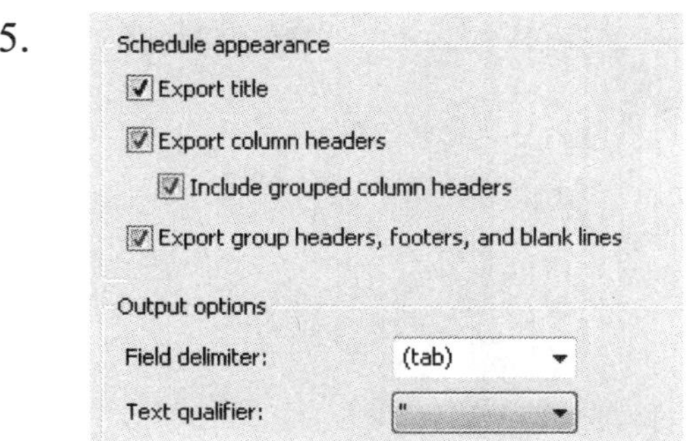

6. Launch **Excel**.

7. Open Select **Open**.

8. Text Files Set the file types to Text **Files**.

9. File name: Glazing Schedule Text Files Tools Open Cancel

Browse to where you saved the file and select it. Press **Open**.

10. Press **Next**.

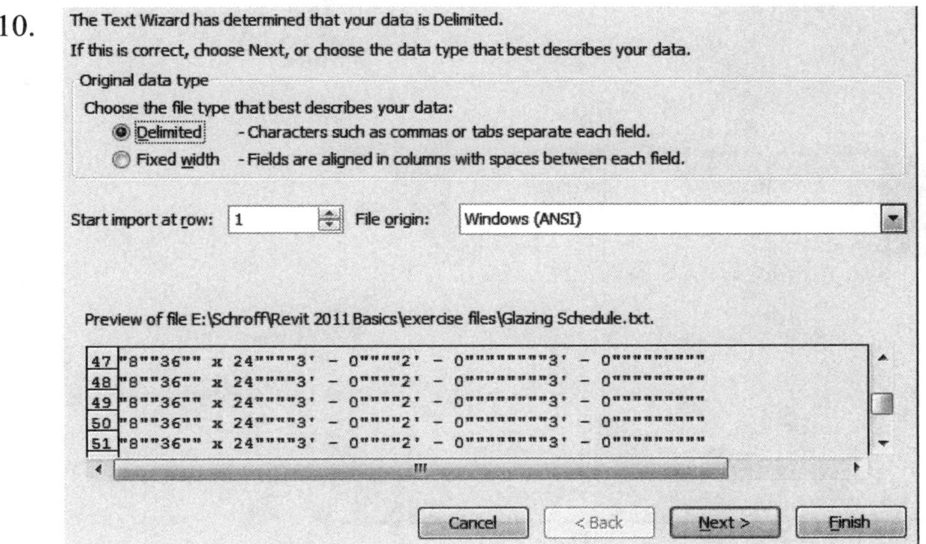

11. 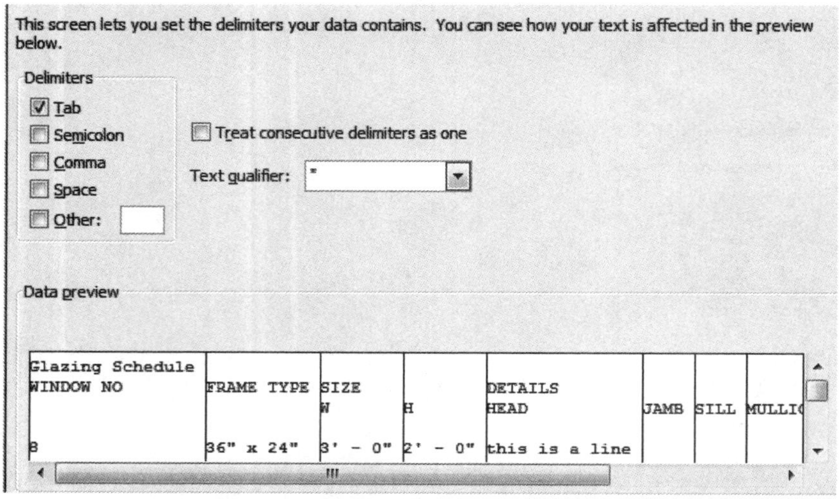 This screen lets you set the delimiters your data contains. You can see how your text is affected in the preview below.

Delimiters

- [x] Tab
- [ ] Semicolon
- [ ] Comma
- [ ] Space
- [ ] Other:

[ ] Treat consecutive delimiters as one

Text qualifier: "

Data preview

Glazing Schedule WINDOW NO	FRAME TYPE	SIZE W	H	DETAILS HEAD	JAMB	SILL	MULLI
8	36" x 24"	3' - 0"	2' - 0"	this is a line			

Press **Next**.

12. 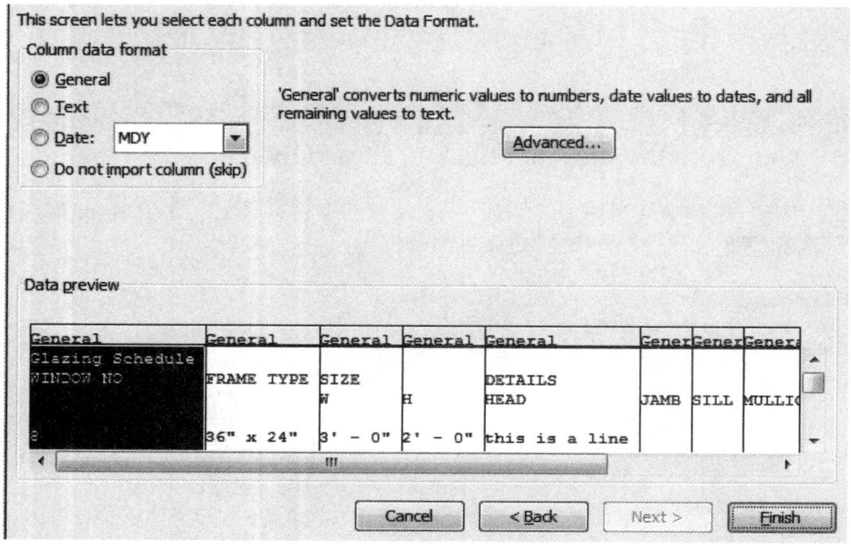 This screen lets you select each column and set the Data Format.

Column data format

- (•) General
- ( ) Text
- ( ) Date: MDY
- ( ) Do not import column (skip)

'General' converts numeric values to numbers, date values to dates, and all remaining values to text.

Advanced...

Data preview

General	General	General	General	General	Gener	Gener	Gener
Glazing Schedule WINDOW NO	FRAME TYPE	SIZE W	H	DETAILS HEAD	JAMB	SILL	MULLI
8	36" x 24"	3' - 0"	2' - 0"	this is a line			

Cancel | < Back | Next > | Finish

Press **Finish**.

13. The spreadsheet opens.

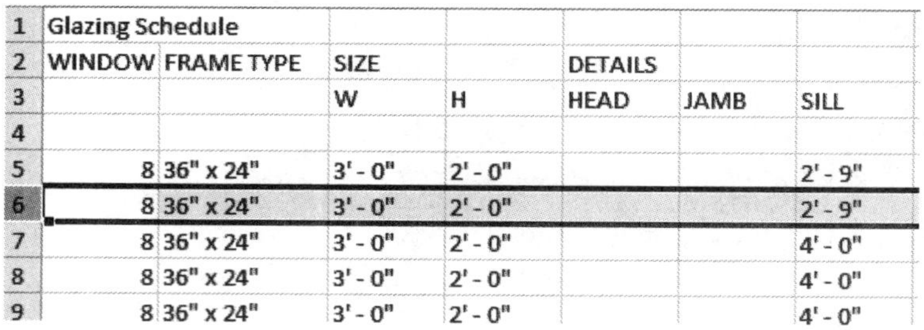

1	Glazing Schedule						
2	WINDOW	FRAME TYPE	SIZE		DETAILS		
3			W	H	HEAD	JAMB	SILL
4							
5	8	36" x 24"	3' - 0"	2' - 0"			2' - 9"
6	8	36" x 24"	3' - 0"	2' - 0"			2' - 9"
7	8	36" x 24"	3' - 0"	2' - 0"			4' - 0"
8	8	36" x 24"	3' - 0"	2' - 0"			4' - 0"
9	8	36" x 24"	3' - 0"	2' - 0"			4' - 0"

14. Close the Revit and Excel files without saving.

Exercise 6-15

Assigning Fonts to a Schedule

Drawing Name: ex6-13.rvt
Estimated Time: 5 minutes

This exercise reinforces the following skills:

- Schedules
- Text Styles

1. Open *ex6-13.rvt*.

2. Activate the Annotate ribbon.

3. Select the small arrow located in the bottom corner of the Text panel.

4. Select **Duplicate**.

5. 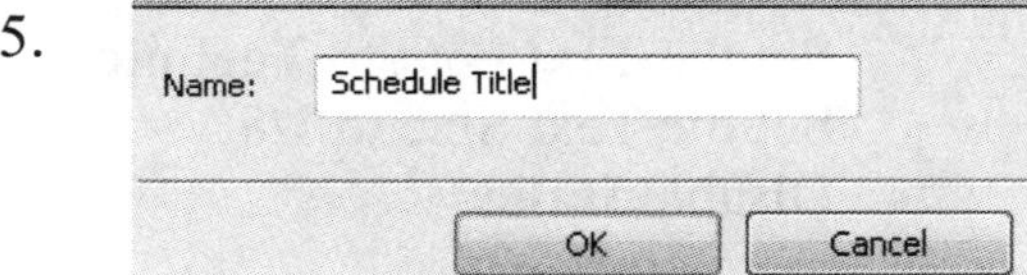

Enter **Schedule Title**.
Press **OK**.

6. 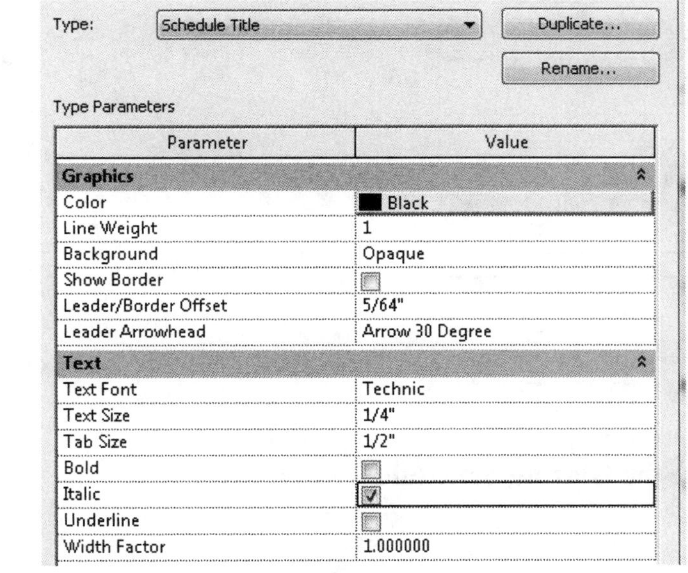

Set the Text Font to **Technic**.
Set the Text Size to ¼″.
Enable **Italic**.

Any Windows font can be used to create a Revit text style.

7. Select **Duplicate**.

8. Enter **Schedule Header**.
Press **OK**.

9. 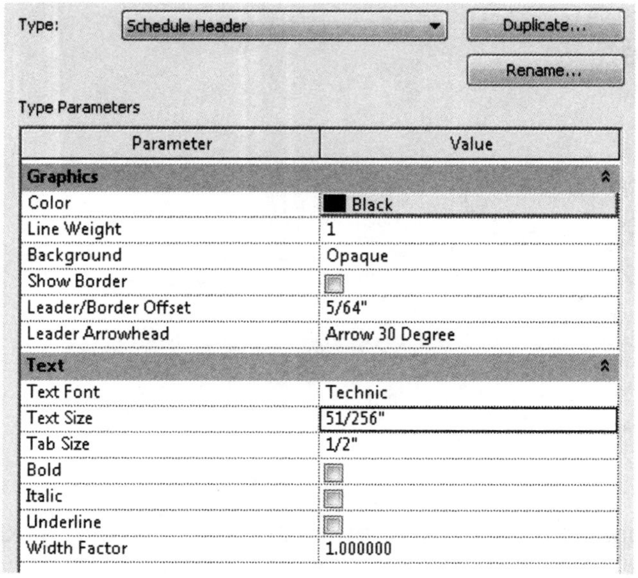 Type: Schedule Header | Duplicate... | Rename...

Type Parameters

Parameter	Value
Graphics	
Color	Black
Line Weight	1
Background	Opaque
Show Border	☐
Leader/Border Offset	5/64"
Leader Arrowhead	Arrow 30 Degree
Text	
Text Font	Technic
Text Size	51/256"
Tab Size	1/2"
Bold	☐
Italic	☐
Underline	☐
Width Factor	1.000000

Set the Text Font to **Technic**.
Set the Text Size to **0.2″**.
Disable **Italic**.

10. 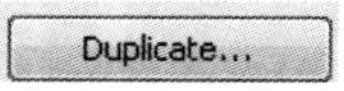 Duplicate...

Select **Duplicate**.

11. 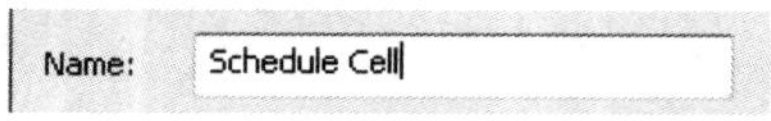 Name: Schedule Cell

Enter **Schedule Cell**.
Press **OK**.

12. 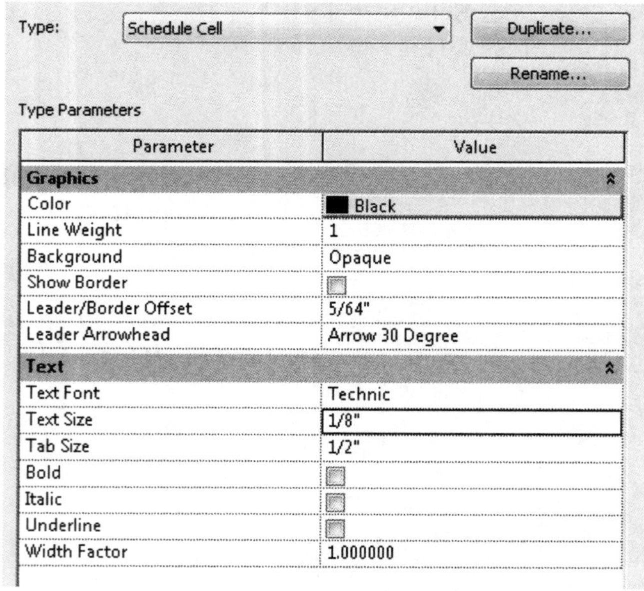 Type: Schedule Cell | Duplicate... | Rename...

Type Parameters

Parameter	Value
Graphics	
Color	Black
Line Weight	1
Background	Opaque
Show Border	☐
Leader/Border Offset	5/64"
Leader Arrowhead	Arrow 30 Degree
Text	
Text Font	Technic
Text Size	1/8"
Tab Size	1/2"
Bold	☐
Italic	☐
Underline	☐
Width Factor	1.000000

Set the Text Font to **Technic**.
Set the Text Size to **1/8″**.
Disable **Italic**.

13. 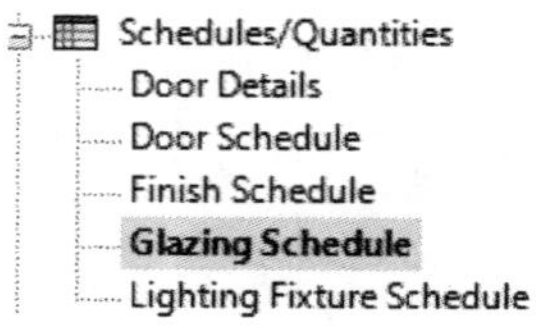 Schedules/Quantities
- Door Details
- Door Schedule
- Finish Schedule
- **Glazing Schedule**
- Lighting Fixture Schedule

Activate the **Glazing Schedule**.

14. 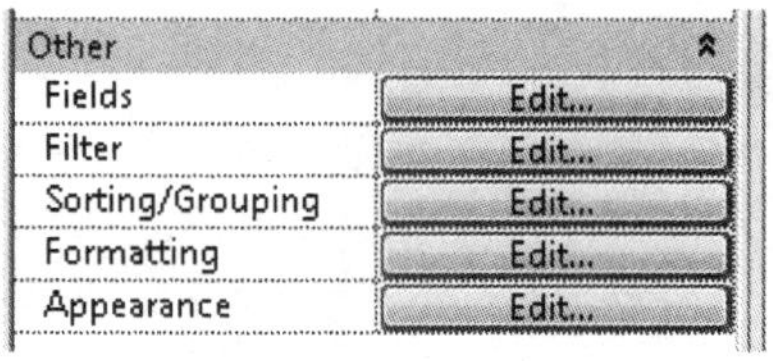 Select **Edit** next to Appearance.

15. 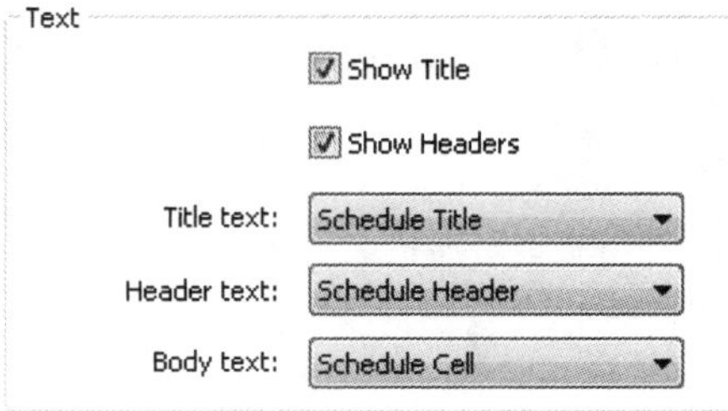 Set the Title text to **Schedule Title**.
Set the Header text to **Schedule Header**.
Set the Body text to **Schedule Cell.**

Press **OK.**

16. 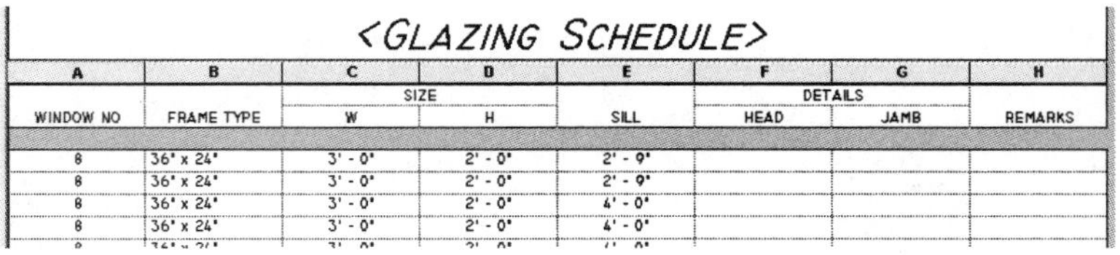 The schedule updates with the new fonts assigned.

17. Save as *ex6-15.rvt.*

Exercise 6-16

Using a View Template for a Schedule

Drawing Name: ex6-15.rvt
Estimated Time: 5 minutes

This exercise reinforces the following skills:

- Schedules
- Text Styles

1. Open *ex6-15.rvt.*

2. 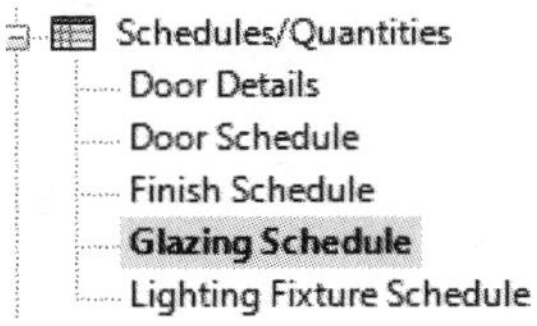 Activate the **Glazing Schedule**.

3. 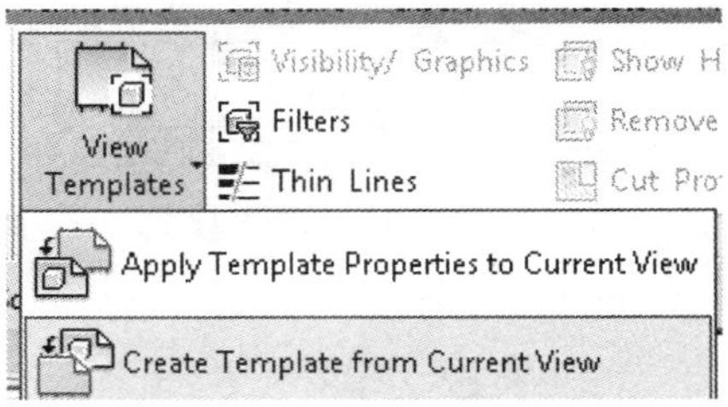 Activate the **View** ribbon.

Select **Create Template from Current View**.

4. Type **Schedule using Technic Fonts.**

   Press **OK**.

5. Note that you can use a View Template to control the appearance of a schedule, but not for selecting fields, etc.

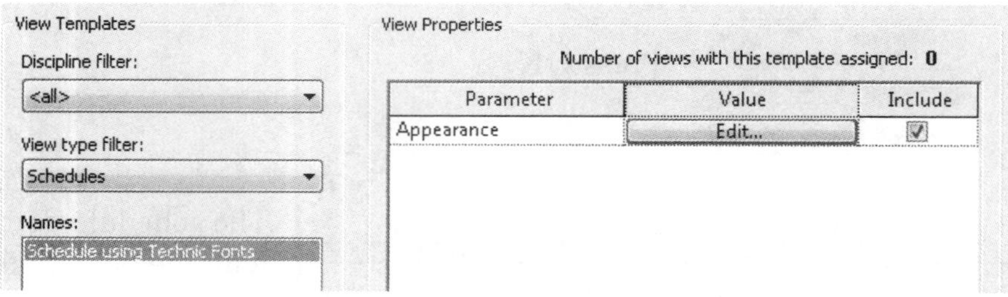

   Press **OK**.

6. Activate the **Door Details** schedule.

7. On the Properties palette:

   Select the **<None>** button next to View Template.

8. 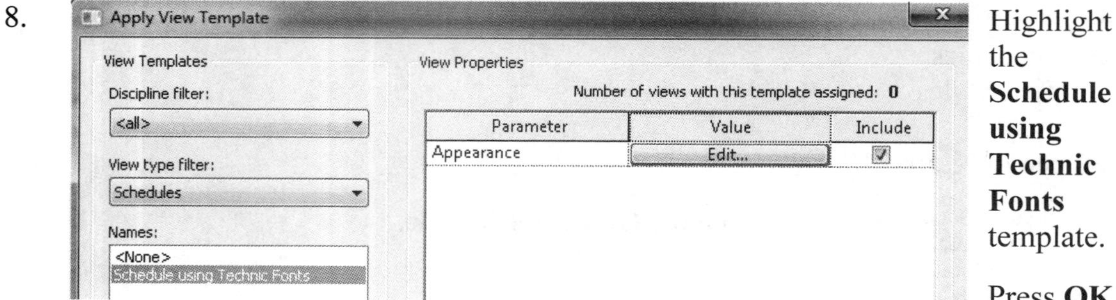

   Highlight the **Schedule using Technic Fonts** template.

   Press **OK**.

9. The schedule updates with the new appearance.

<DOOR DETAILS>

A	B	C	D	E	F	G	H
		SIZE			DETAILS		
DOOR NO	DOOR TYPE	W	H	THK	HEAD DETAIL	JAMB DETAIL	THRESHOLD DETAIL
1	36" x 84"	3' - 0"	7' - 0"	0' - 2"	HD4	JD4	TD4
2	34" x 84"	2' - 10"	7' - 0"	0' - 2"	HD4	JD4	TD4

10. Save as *ex6-16.rvt*

Additional Projects

FINISH SCHEDULE																
	ROOM	FLOOR		BASE		NORTH WALL		EAST WALL		SOUTH WALL		WEST WALL		CLG		
NO	NAME	MAT	FIN	MAT	FIN	MAT	FIN	MAT	FIN	MAT	FIN	MAT	FIN	MAT	FIN	REMARKS

1) Using Shared Parameters, create a Finish Schedule for the lavatories.

Door Schedule - Ver 2			
Mark	Type	Count	Remarks
1	36" x 84"	1	Single-Flush
2	36" x 84"	1	Single-Flush
3	36" x 84"	1	Single-Flush
4	36" x 84"	1	Single-Flush
5	72" x 78"	1	Double-Exterior
6	72" x 78"	1	Double-Exterior
7	36" x 84"	1	Single-Flush
8	36" x 84"	1	Single-Flush
9	36" x 84"	1	Single-Flush
10	36" x 84"	1	Single-Flush
	Curtain Wall Dbl Glass	1	Double Glazed

2) Create a door schedule

Door Schedule 2							
			Rough Opening				
Mark	Type	Level	Rough Height	Rough Width	Material	Lock Jamb	Swing
1	36" x 84"	Level 1			ULTEX/WOOD	CENTER	RIGHT
2	36" x 84"	Level 1			ULTEX/WOOD	THROW	RIGHT
3	36" x 84"	Level 1			ULTEX/WOOD	THROW	LEFT
4	36" x 84"	Level 1			ULTEX/WOOD	THROW	LEFT
5	72" x 78"	Level 1			ULTEX/WOOD	THROW	CENTER
6	72" x 78"	Level 1			ULTEX/WOOD	THROW	CENTER
	Curtain Wall Dbl	Level 1			ULTEX/WOOD	THROW	CENTER
7	36" x 84"	Level 2			ULTEX/WOOD	THROW	LEFT
8	36" x 84"	Level 2			ULTEX/WOOD	THROW	RIGHT
9	36" x 84"	Level 2			ULTEX/WOOD	THROW	RIGHT
10	36" x 84"	Level 2			ULTEX/WOOD	THROW	RIGHT

3) Create this door schedule.

4) Create three new fonts for Schedule Title, Schedule Header, and Cell text. Apply them to a schedule.

5) Create a view template using the schedule with your custom fonts.

Lesson 6 Quiz

True or False

1. A schedule displays information about elements in a building project in a tabular form.
2. Each property of an element is represented as a field in a schedule.
3. If you replace a model element, the schedule for that element will automatically update.
4. Shared parameters are saved in an Excel spreadsheet.
5. A component schedule is a live view of a model.

Multiple Choice

6. Select the three types of schedules you can create in Revit:

   A. Component
   B. Multi-Category
   C. Key
   D. Symbol

7. Keynotes can be attached to the following:
   Select THREE answers.

   A. Model elements
   B. Detail Components
   C. Materials
   D. Datum

8. Select the tab which is not available on the Schedule Properties dialog:

   A. Fields
   B. Filter
   C. Sorting/Grouping
   D. Formatting
   E. Parameters

9. Schedules are exported in this file format:

   A. Excel
   B. Comma-delimited text
   C. ASCII
   D. DXF

10. To export a schedule:

    A. Right click on a schedule and select **Export**.
    B. Place a schedule on a sheet, select the sheet in the Project Browser, right click and select Export.
    C. Go to the Manage ribbon and select the Export Schedule tool.
    D. On the Application Menu, go to File→Export→Reports→Schedule.

ANSWERS:

1) T; 2) T; 3) T; 4) F; 5) T; 6) A, B, and C; 7) A, B, and C; 8) E; 9) B; 10) D

Lesson 7
Roofs

Revit provides three methods for creating Roofs: By extrusion or footprint or by face. The extrusion method requires you to sketch an open outline. The footprint method uses exterior walls or a sketch. The face method requires a mass.

A roof cannot cut through windows or doors.

Exercise 7-1
Creating a Roof Using Footprint

Drawing Name: ex6-16.rvt
Estimated Time: 15 minutes

This exercise reinforces the following skills:

- Level
- Roof
- Roof Properties
- Roof Options
- Isolate Element
- Select All Instances
- 3D View

1. Open *ex6-16.rvt.*

2. 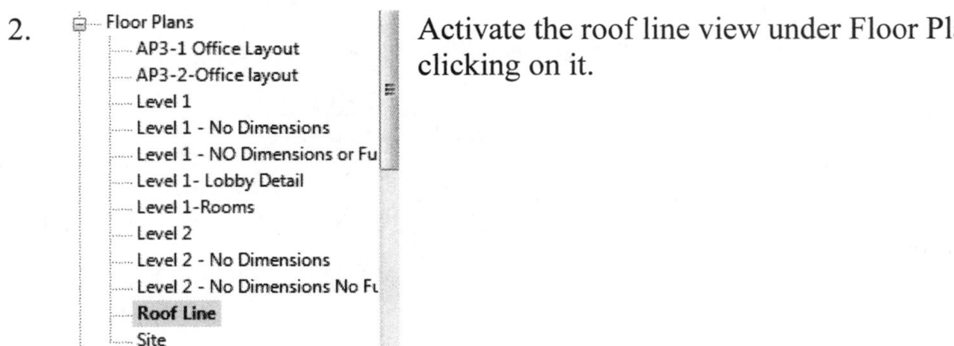

Activate the roof line view under Floor Plans by double clicking on it.

3. 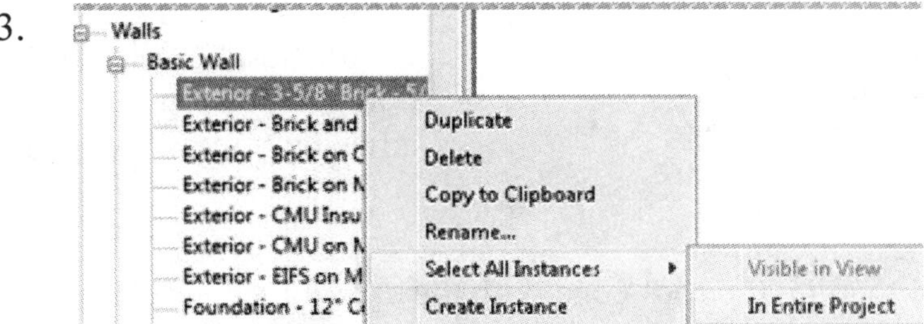

In the browser, locate the exterior wall that is used in the project.

Right click and select **Select All Instances → In Entire Project**.

4. 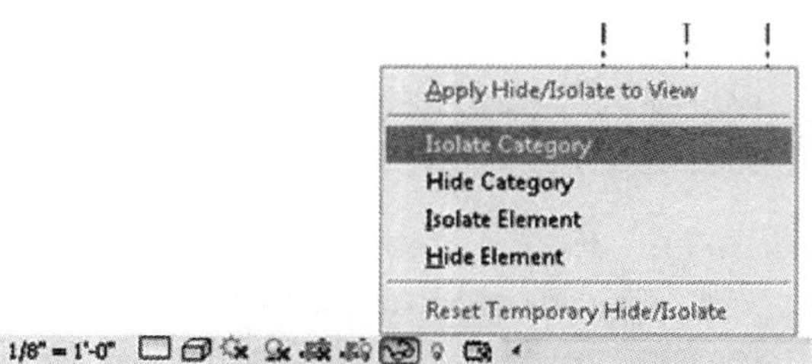

On the Display bar:

Left click on the icon that looks like sunglasses.

Select **Isolate element**.

This will turn off the visibility of all elements except for the exterior walls. This will make selecting the walls easier.

You should see the top view of your model with only the exterior walls visible.

You won't see the curtain wall because it is a different wall style.

5. Left click in the display window to release the selection set.

6. Select **Build→Roof→Roof by Footprint** from the Architecture ribbon.

Notice that **Pick Walls** is the active mode.

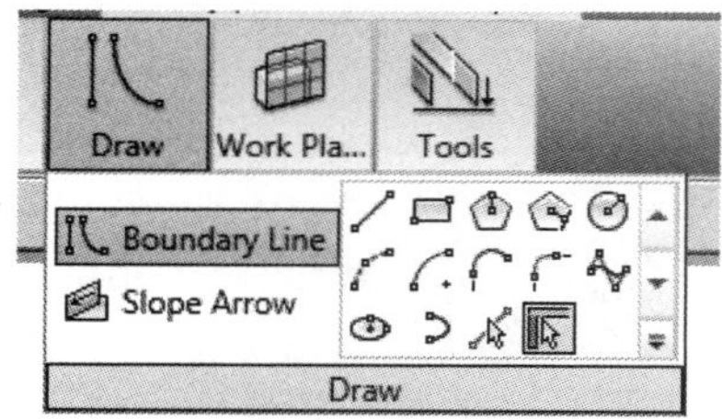

7. 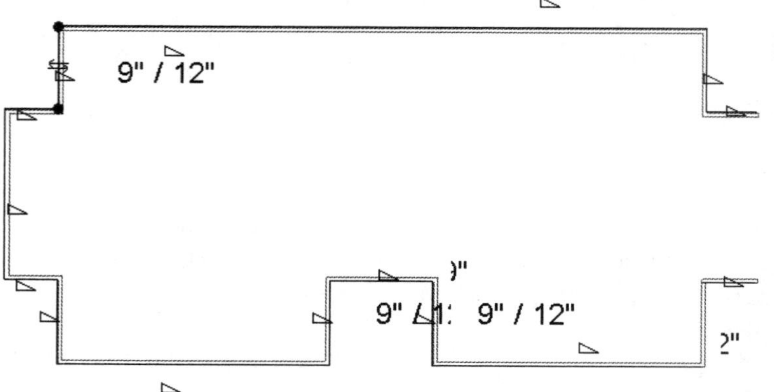

You can zoom in and select the exterior walls.

You can pan or scroll to move around the screen to select the walls.

If you miss a wall, you will get a dialog box advising you of the error.

You can use the ALIGN tool to align the roof edge with the exterior side of the wall.

8. Defines slope | Overhang: 0' 6" | Extend to wall core

Defines slope | Overhang: 60.00 | Extend to wall core

On the options bar, enable **Defines slope.**
Set the Overhang to **6″ [60**].
Enable **Extend to wall core.**
It is very important to enable the **Extend into wall (to core)** if you want your roof overhang to reference the structure of your wall.

For example, if you want a 2′-0″ overhang from the face of the stud, not face of the finish, you want this box checked. The overhang is located based on your pick point. If your pick point is the inside face, the overhang will be calculated from the interior finish face.

The angle symbols indicate the roof slope.

9. Draw

Select the **Line** tool from the Draw panel.

10. 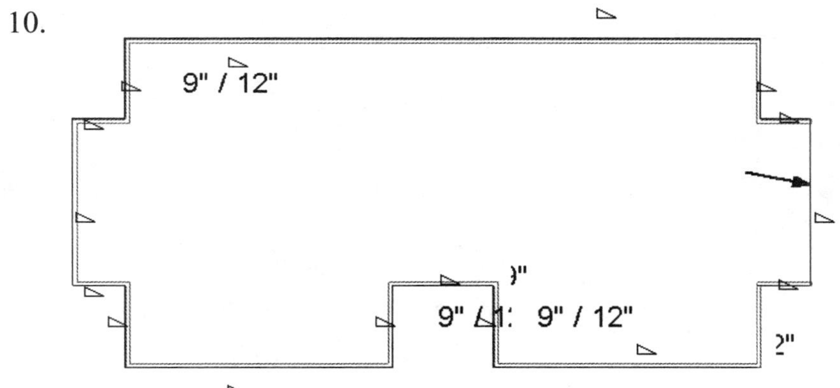

Draw a line to close the sketch.

Check the sketch to make sure there are no gaps or intersecting lines.

11. 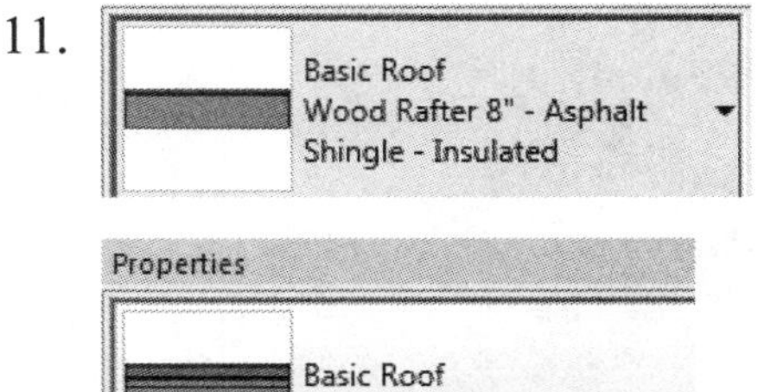

Properties
Basic Roof
Warm Roof - Timber

On the Properties palette:

Select the **Wood Rafter 8″ – Asphalt Shingle – Insulated** [**Warm Roof - Timber**] from the Type Selector.

12. Mode

Select **Green Check** under Mode.

13. This dialog will appear if you missed a wall.

You can press the **Show** button and Revit will highlight the wall you missed.

14. If this dialog appears. Press **Yes**.

15. If you get an error message like this, press **Delete Elements** to delete any conflicting elements.

16. On the Display bar:

Left click on the sunglasses.

Select **Reset Temporary Hide/Isolate**.

17. Go to **3D View**.

18. Enable **View → Realistic**.

We can now inspect our roof.

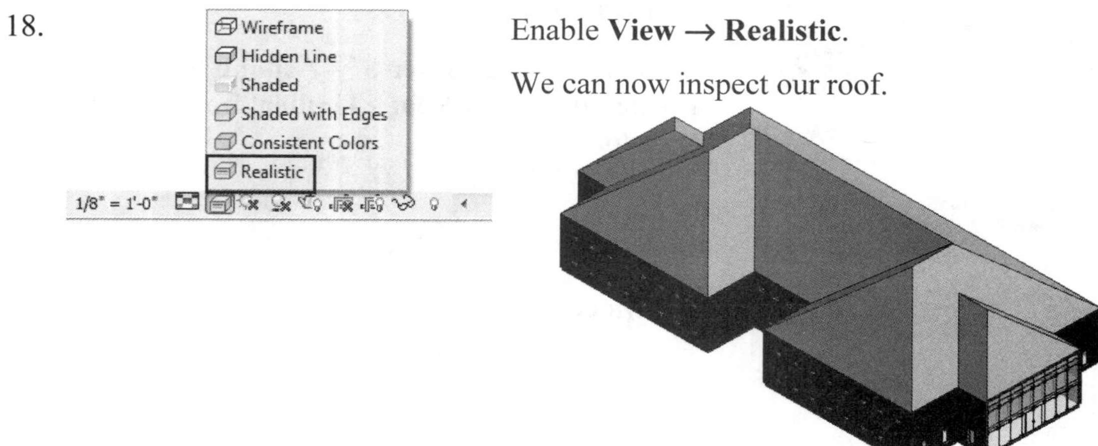

19. Save as *ex7-1.rvt.*

The Cutoff Level Property defines the distance above or below the level at which the roof is cut off.

Roofs (1)	
Constraints	
Base Level	Roof Line
Room Bounding	☑
Related to Mass	☐
Base Offset From Level	0' 0"
Cutoff Level	None
Cutoff Offset	0' 0"

Exercise 7-2

Modifying a Roof

Drawing Name: ex7-1.rvt
Estimated Time: 10 minutes

This exercise reinforces the following skills:

- ❑ Modifying Roofs
- ❑ Edit Sketch
- ❑ Align Eaves
- ❑ Roof
- ❑ Work Plane

1. Open or continue working in *ex7-1.rvt*.

2. Elevations (Building Elevation)
   - East
   - North
   - South
   - South Lobby
   - West

   Activate the East elevation.

3. Level
   Grid
   Datum

   Select the **Level** tool from the Datum panel on the Architecture ribbon.

4. Add a level 10′ 6″ [270mm] above the Roof Line level.

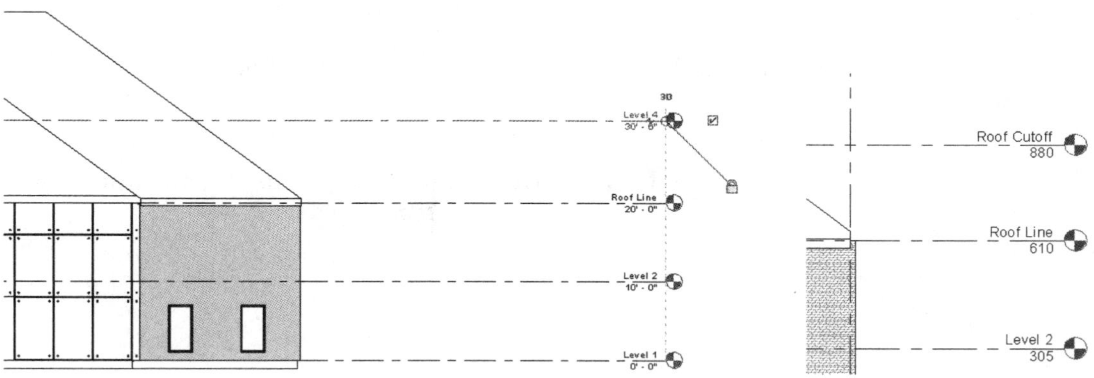

5. Rename the Level **Roof Cutoff**.

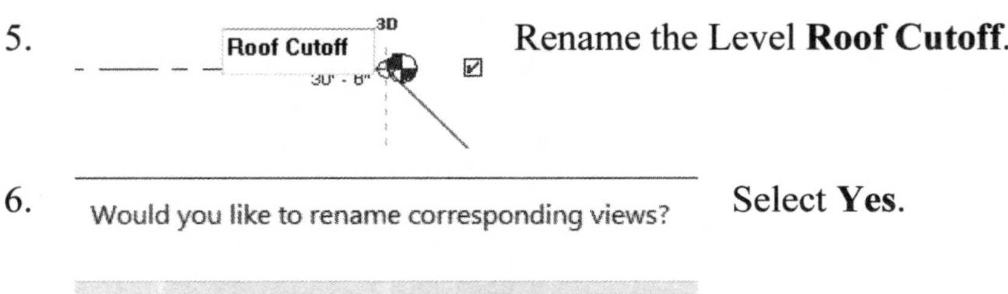

6. Select **Yes**.

7. Select the roof so it is highlighted.

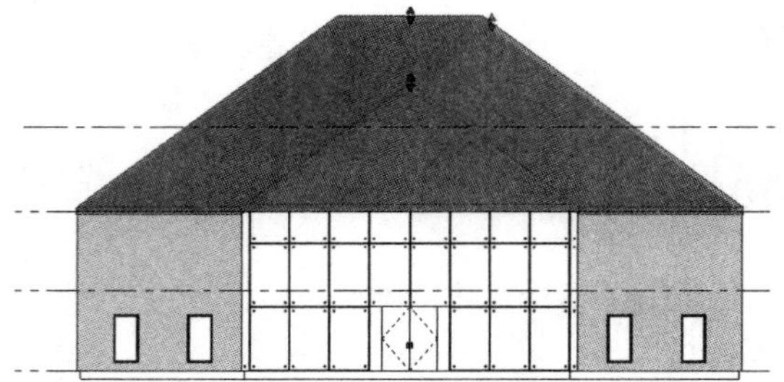

8. On the Properties pane:

Properties

Basic Roof
Wood Rafter 8" - Asphalt Shingle - Insulated

Roofs (1) Edit Type

Constraints	
Base Level	Roof Line
Room Bounding	☑
Related to Mass	☐
Base Offset From L...	0' 0"
Cutoff Level	Roof Cutoff
Cutoff Offset	0' 0"

Set the Cutoff Level to **Roof Cutoff**.

9. Note how the roof adjusts.

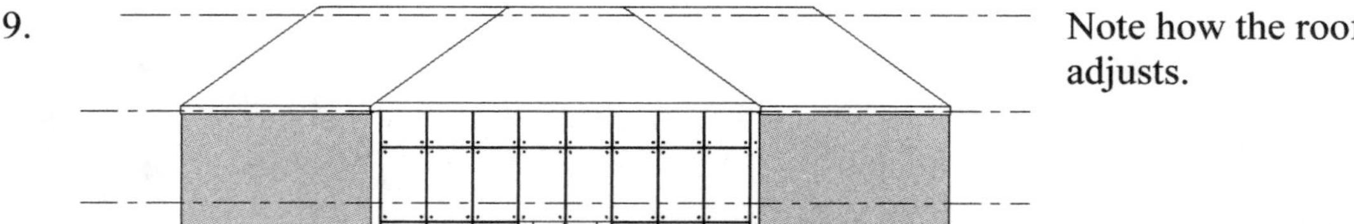

10. Activate the **Roof Cutoff** view under Floor Plans.

Level 2 - No Dime
Roof Cutoff
Roof Line
Site

11. Select **Roof→Roof by Footprint** from the Architecture ribbon.

Roof Ceiling Floor
Roof by Footprint

12. Select **Pick Lines** from the Draw panel.

13. Disable **Defines slope** on the Options bar.

14. 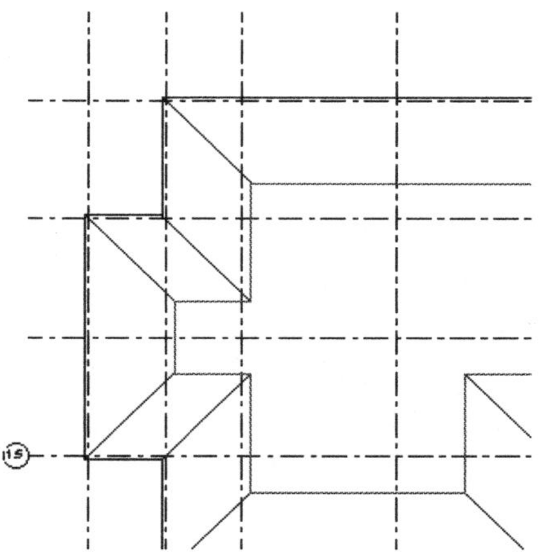

Pick an edge.

You won't see a slope symbol because slope has been disabled.

15. To remove a slope from a line, simply select the line and uncheck Defines slope on the Options bar.

16. 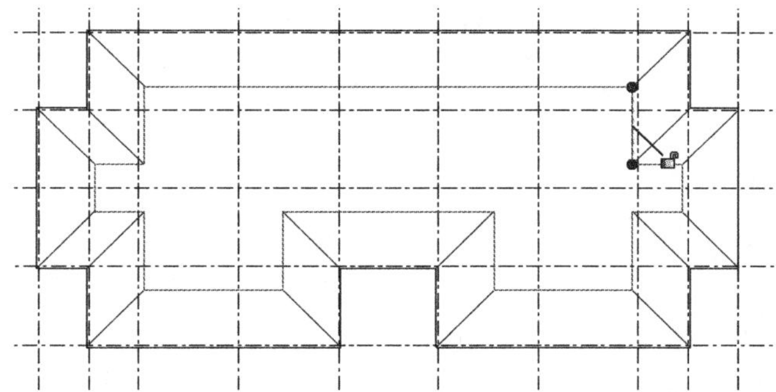

Select the edges to form a closed sketch.

Note that none of the lines have a slope defined.

17. 

Select **Edit Type** from the Properties pane.

18. 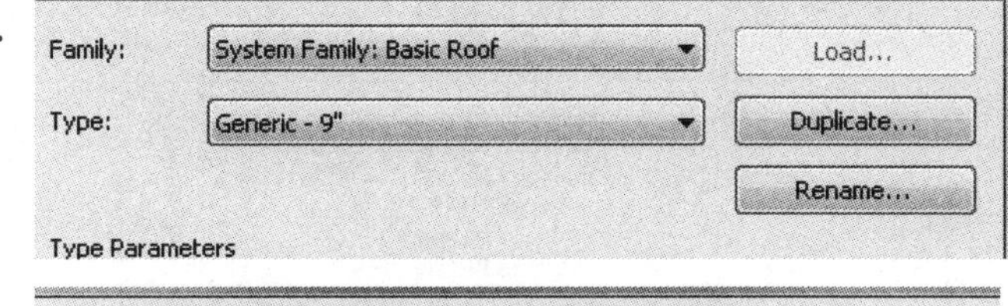

Select the **Generic - 9″ [Generic 400mm]** roof from the drop-down list.

Select **Duplicate**.

19. Enter **Tar and Gravel**.

    Press **OK**.

20. Select **Edit** next to Structure.

21. Insert three layers.

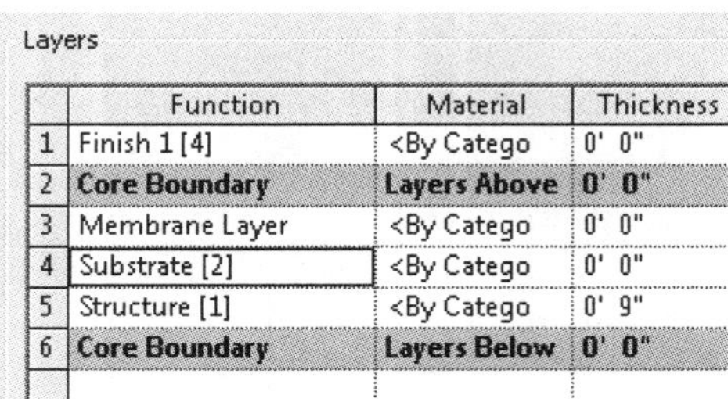

	Function	Material	Thickness
1	Finish 1 [4]	<By Catego	0' 0"
2	Core Boundary	Layers Above	0' 0"
3	Membrane Layer	<By Catego	0' 0"
4	Substrate [2]	<By Catego	0' 0"
5	Structure [1]	<By Catego	0' 9"
6	Core Boundary	Layers Below	0' 0"

Arrange the layers so:
Layer 1 is set to Finish 1 [4].
Layer 2 is Core Boundary.
Layer 3 is Membrane Layer.
Layer 4 is Substrate [2]
Layer 5 is Structure [1]
Layer 6 is Core Boundary.

22. Select the Material column for **Finish 1 [4]**.

23. Locate the **gravel** material in the Document materials.

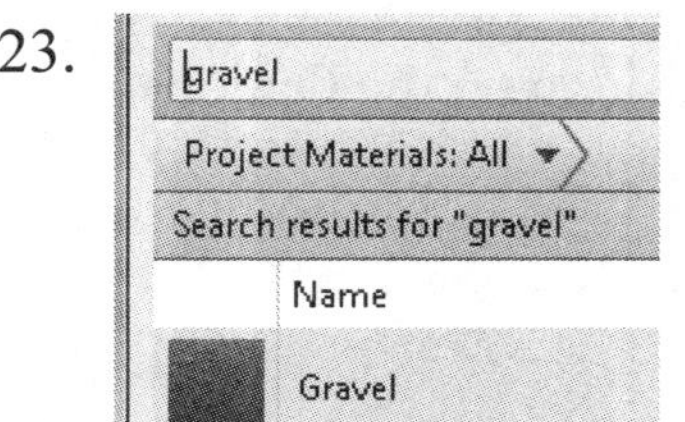

24. Set the thickness to **1/4″** [6].

25. Select the Material column for **Membrane Layer**.

    Do a search for **membrane**.

26. Set the Material to **Roofing - EPDM Membrane**.

    Set the Membrane thickness to **0″**.

	Function	Material	Thickness
1	Finish 1 [4]	Gravel	0' 0 1/4"
2	Core Boundary	Layers Above Wrap	0' 0"
3	Membrane Layer	Roofing - EPDM Membrane	0' 0"
4	Substrate [2]	<By Category>	0' 0"
5	Structure [1]	<By Category>	0' 9"
6	Core Boundary	Layers Below Wrap	0' 0"

27. 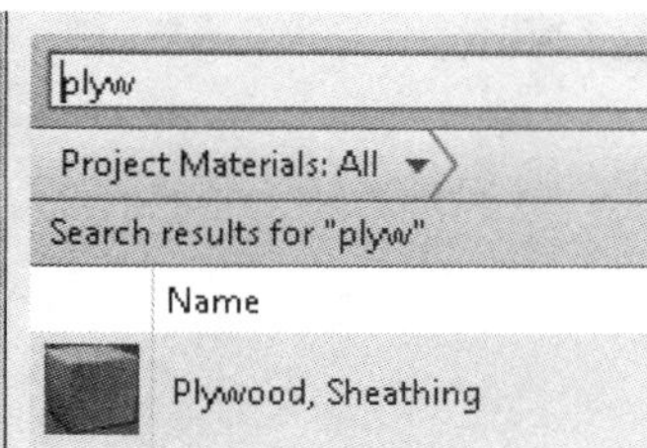

Set Layer 4 Substrate [2] to **Plywood, Sheathing** with a thickness of **5/8″ [16]**.

28. 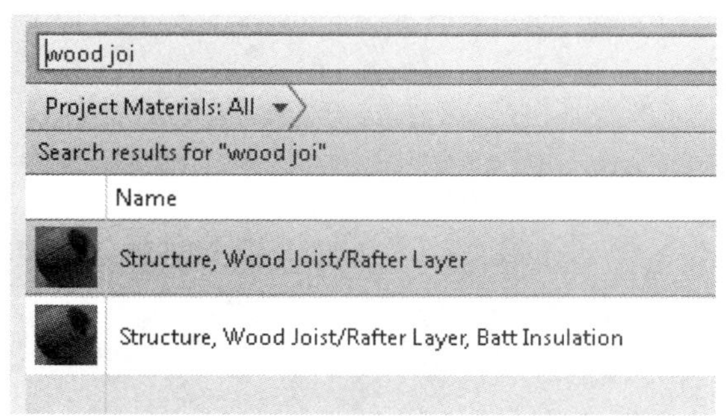

Set Layer 5 Structure [1] to **Structure-Wood Joist/ Rafter Layer [Structure, Timber Joist/Rafter Layer]** with a thickness of **7 ½″ [200]**.

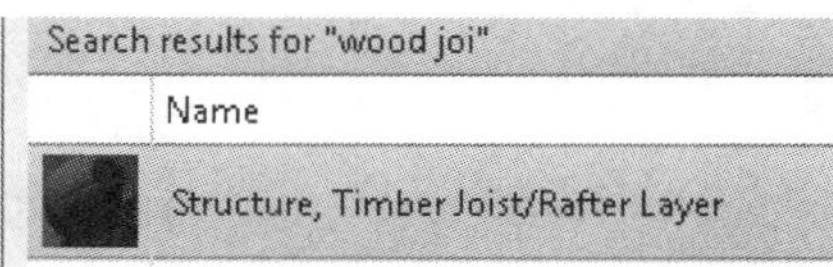

29. Press **OK**.

Family: Basic Roof
Type: Tar and Gravel
Total thickness: 0' 8 3/8" (Default)
Resistance (R): 44.0217 (h·ft²·°F)/BTU
Thermal Mass: 2.0023 BTU/°F

Layers

	Function	Material	Thickness	Wi
1	Finish 1 [4]	Gravel	0' 0 1/4"	
2	**Core Boundary**	**Layers Above Wrap**	**0' 0"**	
3	Membrane Layer	Roofing, EPDM Membrane	0' 0"	
4	Substrate [2]	Roofing, EPDM Membrane	0' 0 5/8"	
5	Structure [1]	Structure, Wood Joist/Rafter Layer	0' 7 1/2"	
6	**Core Boundary**	**Layers Below Wrap**	**0' 0"**	

Layers

	Function	Material	Thickness
1	Finish 1 [4]	Gravel	6.0
2	**Core Boundary**	**Layers Above Wrap**	**0.0**
3	Membrane Layer	Roofing, EPDM Me	0.0
4	Substrate [2]	Plywood, Sheathin	16.0
5	Structure [1]	Structure, Timber J	200
6	**Core Boundary**	**Layers Below Wrap**	**0.0**

30. 

Press the Browse button in the Coarse Scale Fill Pattern to assign a fill pattern.

31. 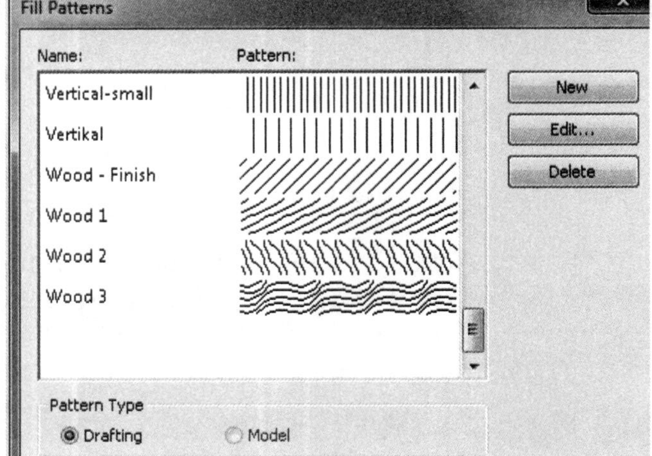

Press **New**.

32. Orientation in Host Layers:
Orient To View
Simple
Custom
Name: New pattern name
Custom
Import...
File units are: inches
Import scale: 1.00

Enable **Custom**.

Press **Import**.

33. File name: gravel
Files of type: Hatch Patterns (*.pat)

Select the *gravel* hatch pattern in the exercise files.

34. 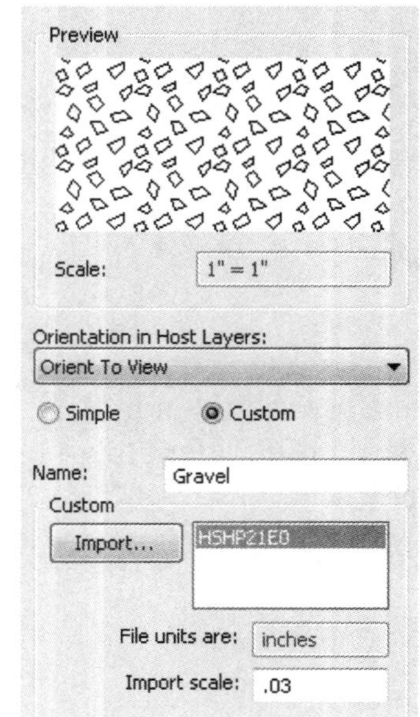

Change the Name to **Gravel**.

Set the Import scale to **0.03**.

Note how the preview changes.

Press **OK**.

35. Highlight Gravel.

Press **OK**.

36. Assign the **Gravel** pattern to the Coarse Scale Fill Pattern.

Press **OK**.

37. Select the **Green Check** under the Model panel to **Finish Roof**.

38. 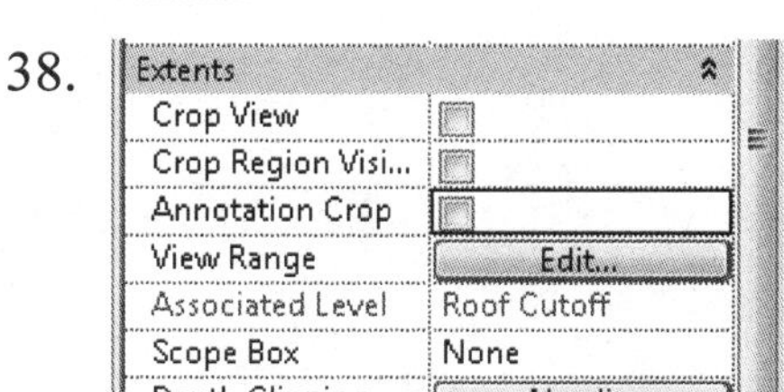

To see the fill pattern in the Roof Cutout floor plan, we need to adjust the view range.

Select **Edit** next to View Range in the Properties palette.

39. 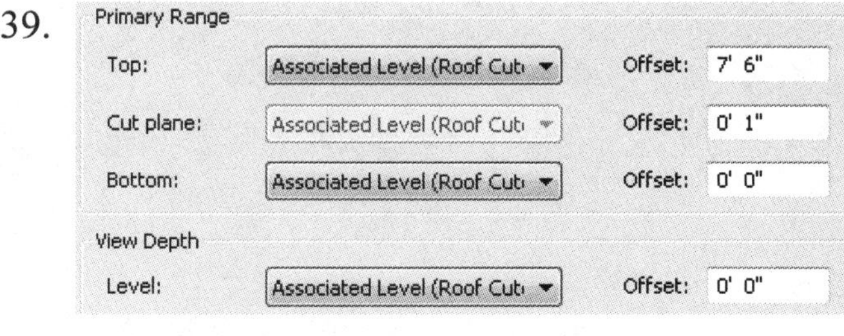

Change the View Range.
Set the Top Offset to 7′ 6″ [230].
Set the Cut Plane to 1″ [3].
Set the Bottom to 0′.
Set the View Depth to 0″.

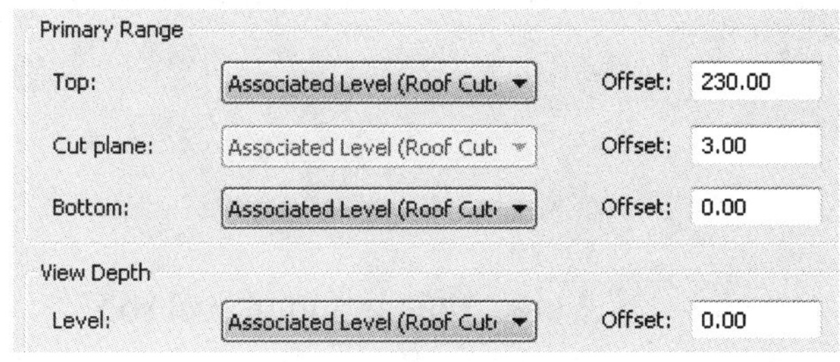

40. The fill pattern is now visible.

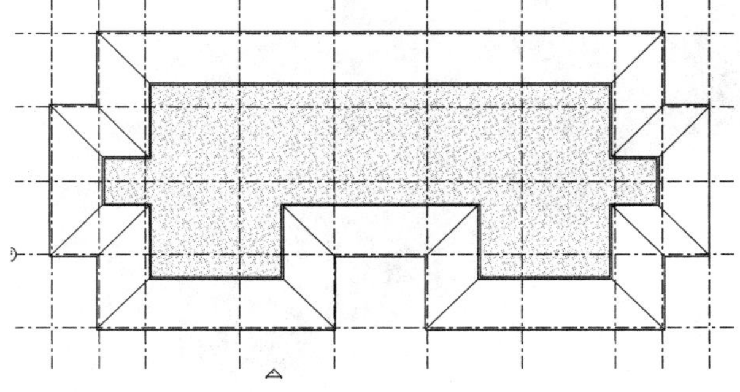

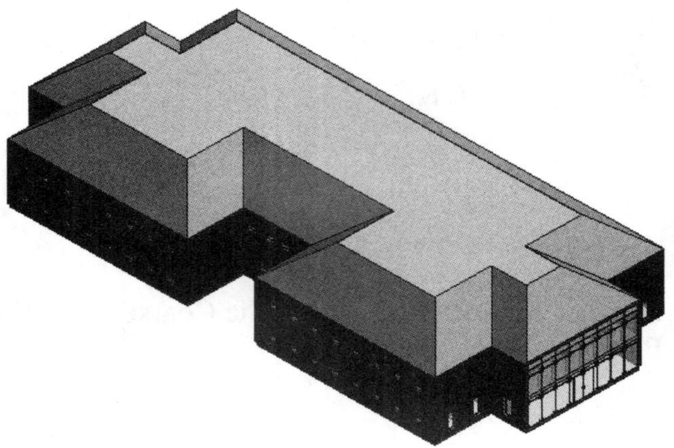

41. Save as *ex7-2.rvt.*

Exercise 7-3

Modifying a Roof Form

Drawing Name: ex7-2.rvt
Estimated Time: 10 minutes

This exercise reinforces the following skills:

- Shape Editing
- Window
- Load from Library
- Array

1. Open or continue working in *ex7-2.rvt.*

2. 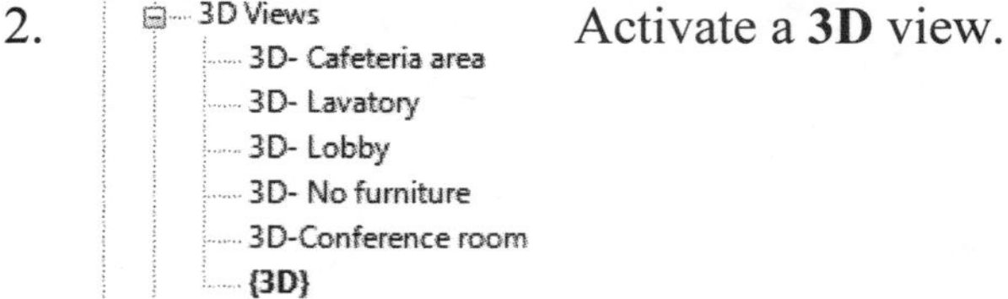

Activate a **3D** view.

3. 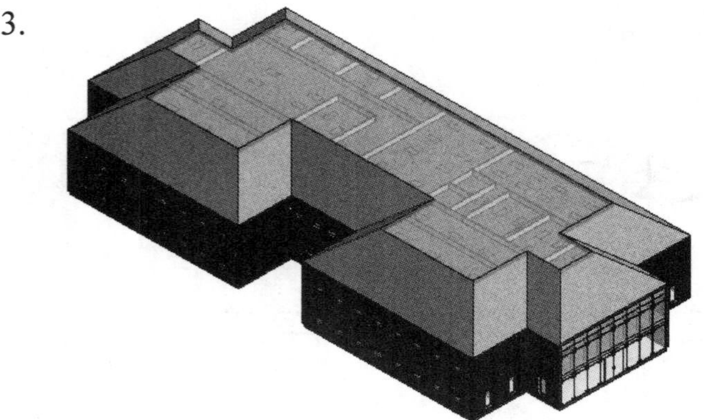

Select the tar and gravel roof.

It will highlight in blue and appear to be transparent.

4. 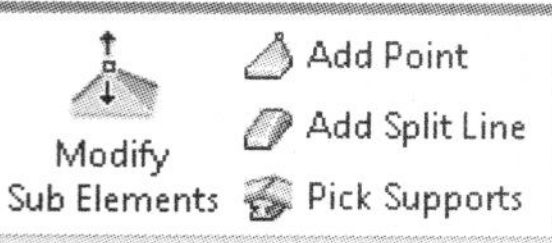

Select the **Add Point** tool on the **Shape Editing** panel on the ribbon.

5. 

Place points as shown.

6. Modify Sub Elements

Select **Modify Sub Elements**.

7. 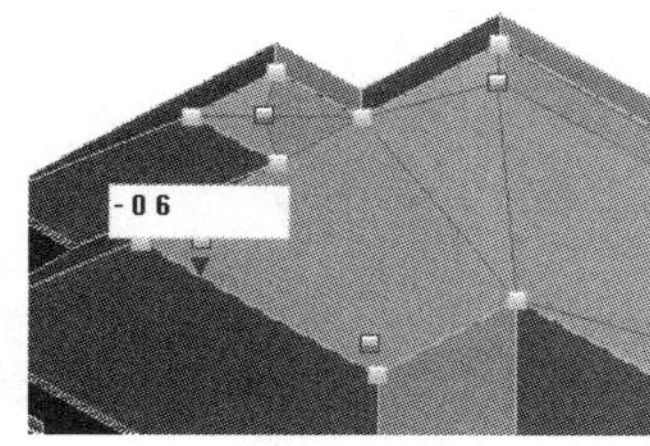

Select each point and set them to **-0′ 6″ [-15]**.

These will be drain holes.

Right click and select Cancel when you are done.

8. The roof surface will show the drainage areas.

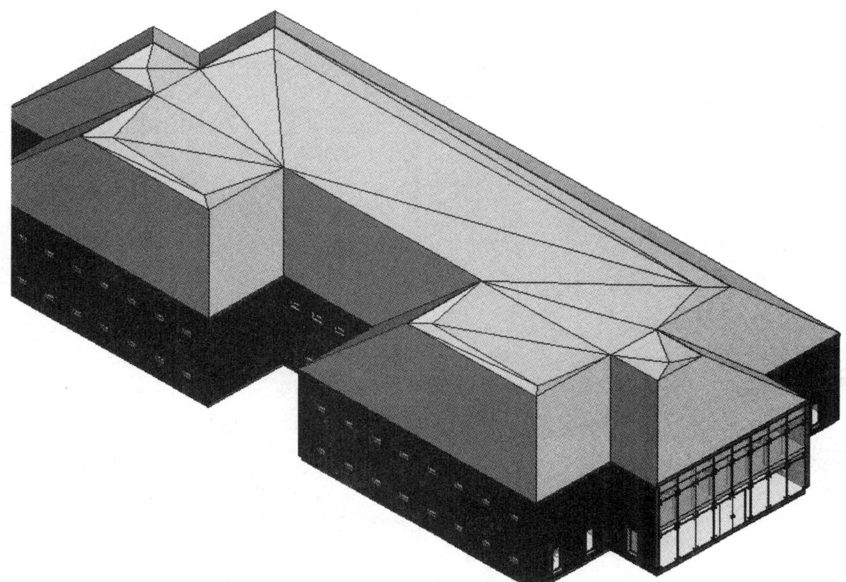

9. Save as *ex7-3.rvt.*

Exercise 7-4
Adding Roof Drains

Drawing Name: ex7-3.rvt
Estimated Time: 10 minutes

This exercise reinforces the following skills:

- Component
- Load Family

1. Open or continue working in *ex7-3.rvt.*

2. 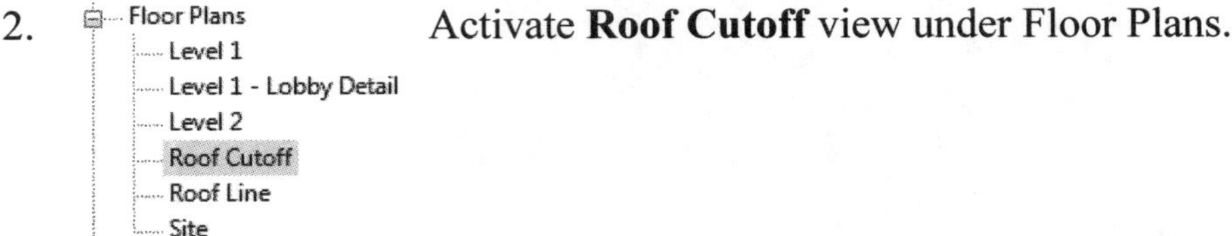

Activate **Roof Cutoff** view under Floor Plans.

3. Change the display settings to **Medium, Wireframe.**

4. Select **Place a Component** from the Build panel on the Architecture ribbon.

5. Select **Load Family** under the Mode panel.

6. 

Locate the *Drain- Roof* from the exercise files on the publisher's website.

   Press **Open**.

7. If a dialog appears asking if you want to load a tag for Plumbing Fixtures, press **No**.

8. Place roof drains coincident to the points placed earlier.

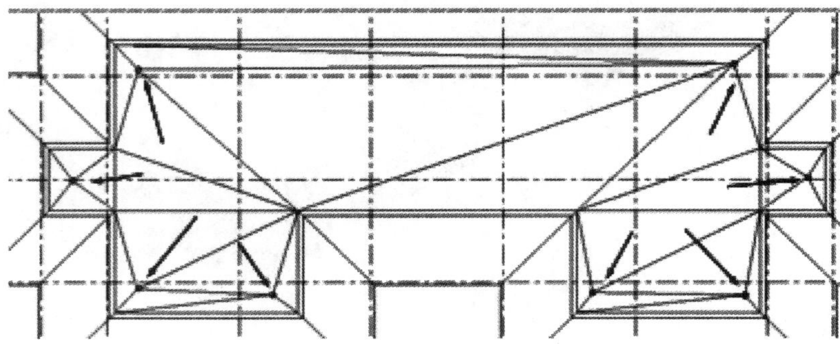

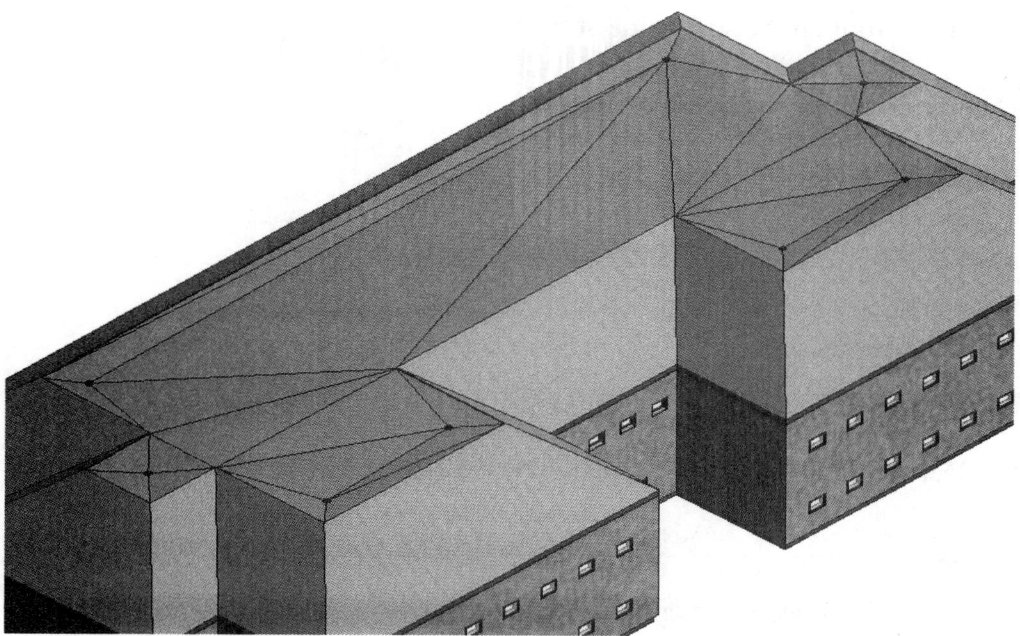

9. Save the file as *ex7-4.rvt.*

Exercise 7-5

Adding a Dormer by Modifying a Roof Sketch

Drawing Name: ex7-4.rvt
Estimated Time: 10 minutes

This exercise reinforces the following skills:

- Modify a Roof Sketch

A video for this exercise is available on my MossDesigns station on Youtube.com or a link is provided on my website at http://www.mossdesigns.com/Pages/Tutorials.aspx.

1. Open or continue working in *ex7-4.rvt.*
2. Roof Cutoff / Roof Line / Site — Activate the **Roof Line** view under Floor Plans.
3. Edit Footprint / Mode — Select the Wood/Timber roof.

   Select **Edit Footprint** from the ribbon.

   This returns you to sketch mode.
4. Select the **Split** tool on the Modify panel.

5. Split the roof on the south side at the Grids B & C.

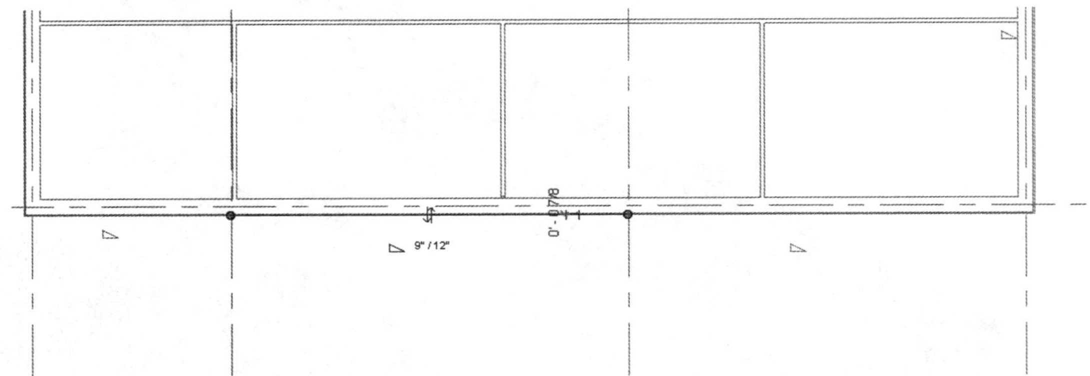

6. Select the new line segment created by the split.

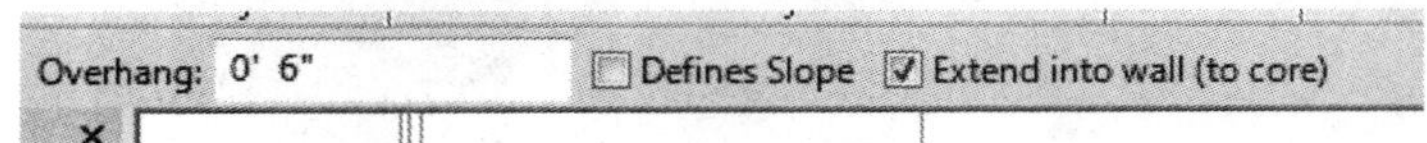

   Uncheck **Defines Slope** on the option bar.

7. Slope Arrow Select the **Slope Arrow** tool on the ribbon.

8. Select the left end point of the line and the midpoint of the line to place the slope.

9. Slope Arrow Select the **Slope Arrow** tool on the ribbon.

10. Select the right end point of the line and the midpoint of the line to place the slope.

11. The sketch should appear as shown.

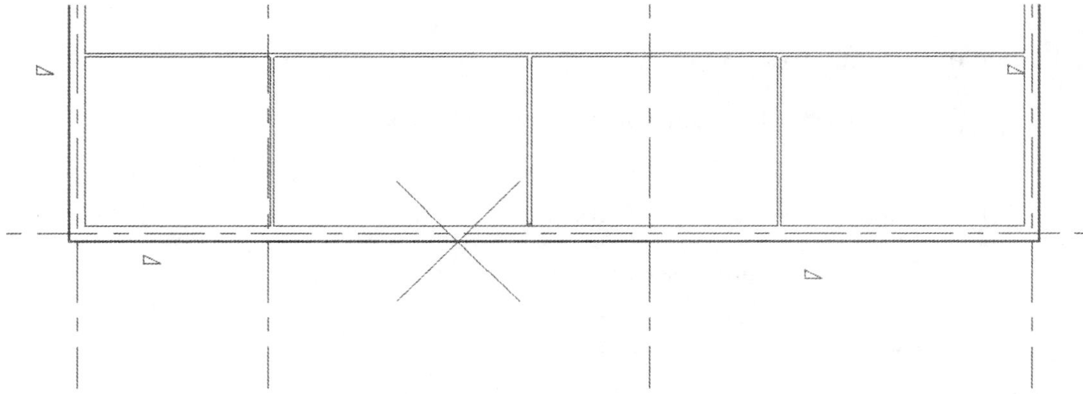

12. 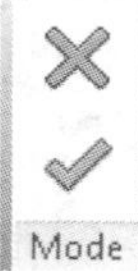

Select the green check to exit sketch mode.

13. Switch to a 3D view and orbit to inspect the new dormer.

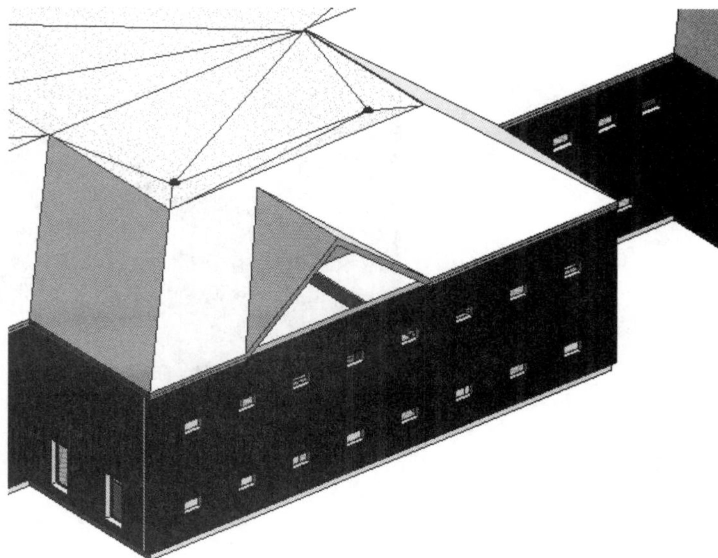

14. 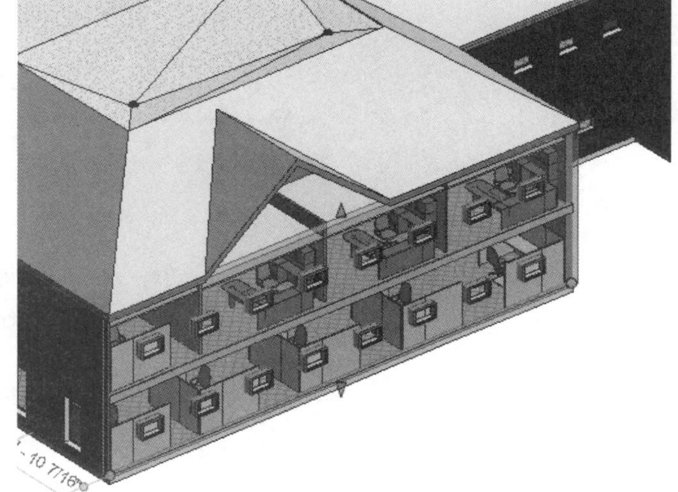

Select the southwest wall.

15. 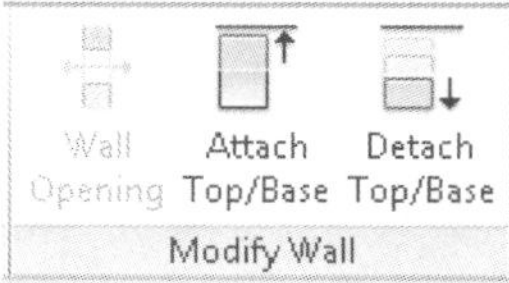

Select **Attach Top/Base** on the ribbon.

Select the roof with the dormer.

Left click anywhere in the window to release the selection.

16. The wall updates.

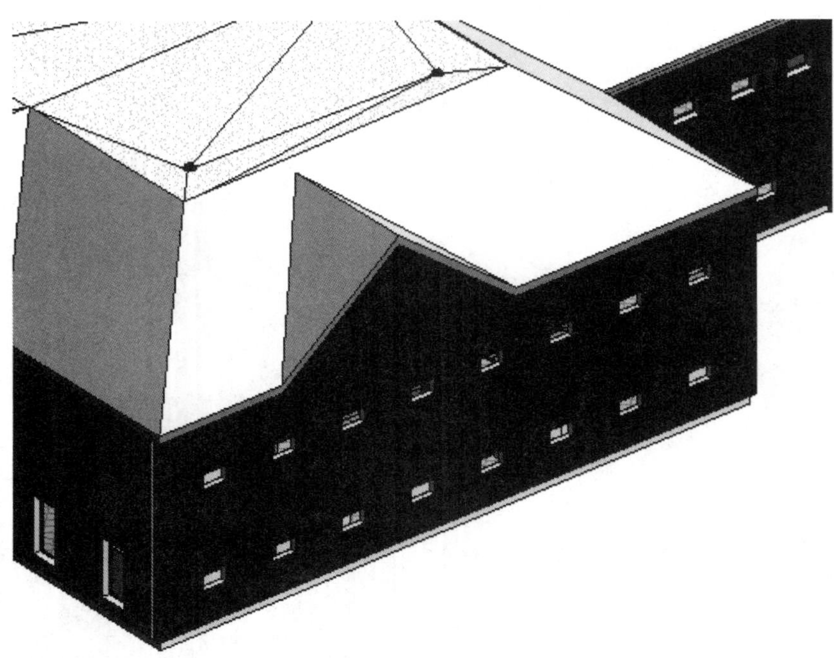

17. Save as *ex7-5.rvt*.

Additional Projects

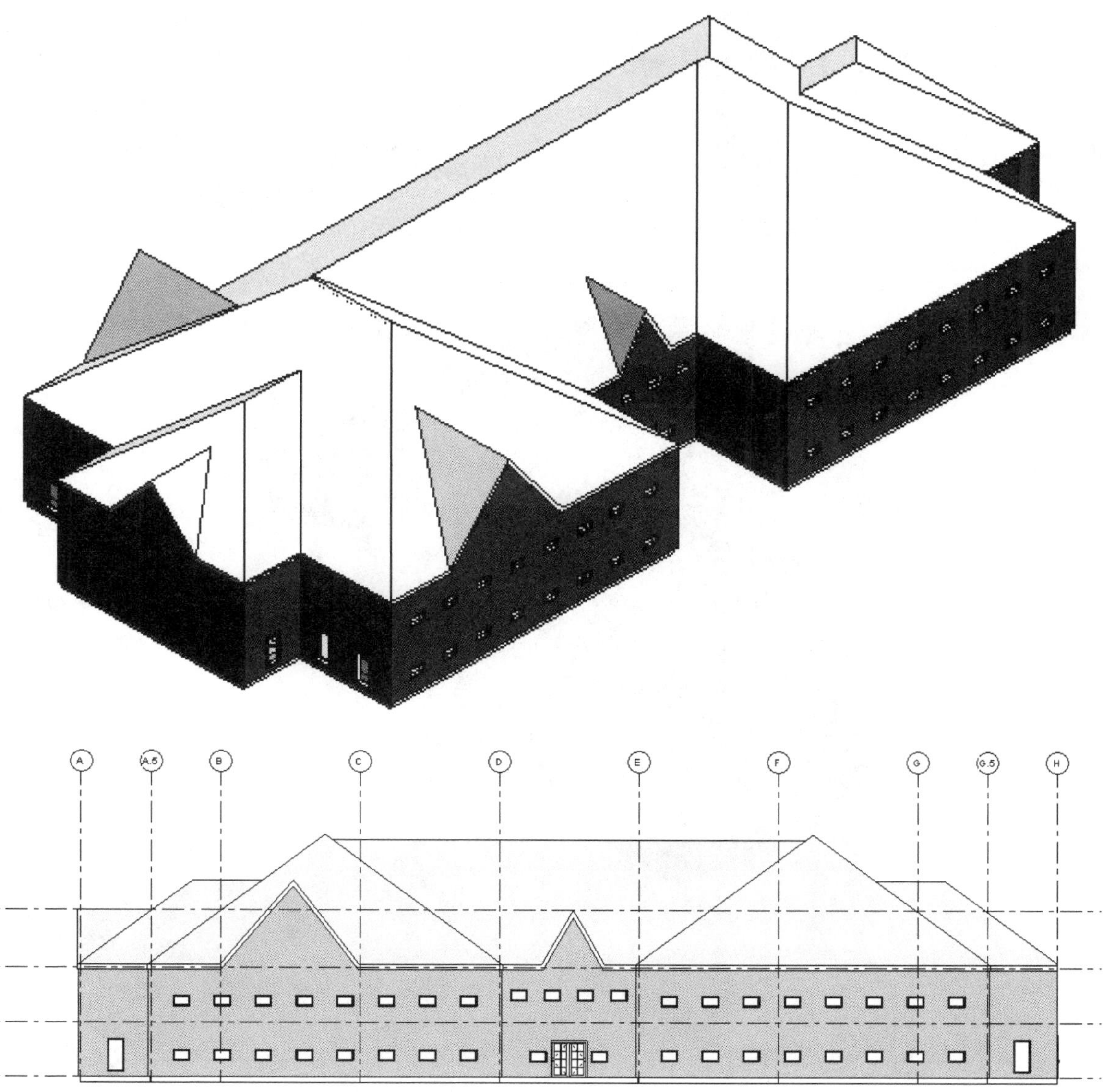

1) Create a roof with several dormers

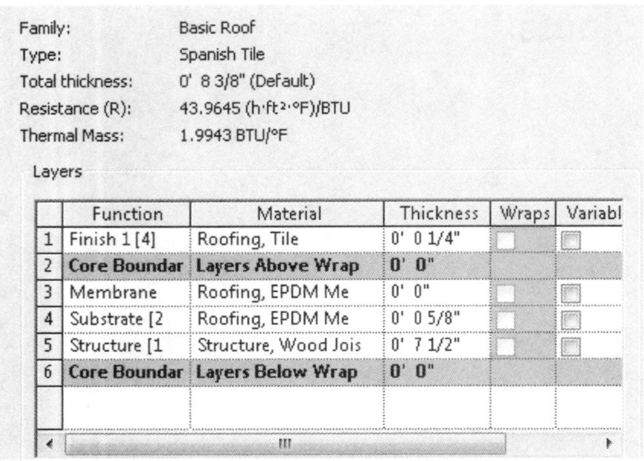
Family: Basic Roof
Type: Spanish Tile
Total thickness: 0' 8 3/8" (Default)
Resistance (R): 43.9645 (h·ft²·°F)/BTU
Thermal Mass: 1.9943 BTU/°F

Layers

	Function	Material	Thickness	Wraps	Variabl
1	Finish 1 [4]	Roofing, Tile	0' 0 1/4"	☐	☐
2	**Core Boundar**	**Layers Above Wrap**	**0' 0"**		
3	Membrane	Roofing, EPDM Me	0' 0"	☐	☐
4	Substrate [2	Roofing, EPDM Me	0' 0 5/8"	☐	☐
5	Structure [1	Structure, Wood Jois	0' 7 1/2"	☐	☐
6	**Core Boundar**	**Layers Below Wrap**	**0' 0"**		

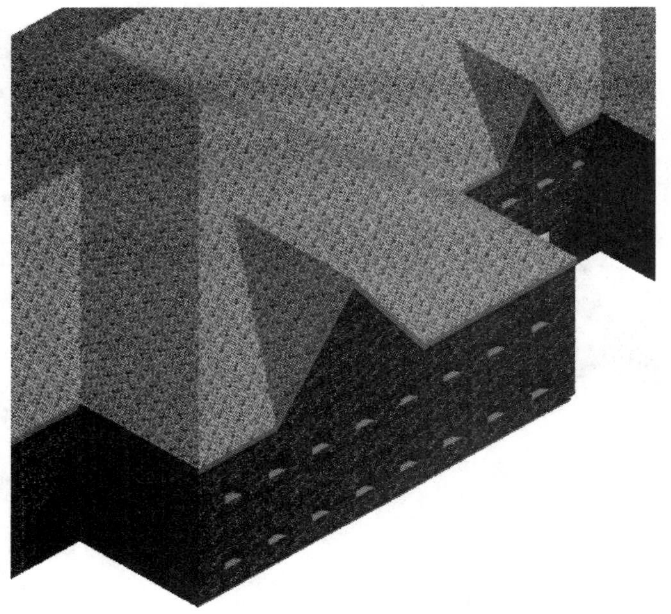

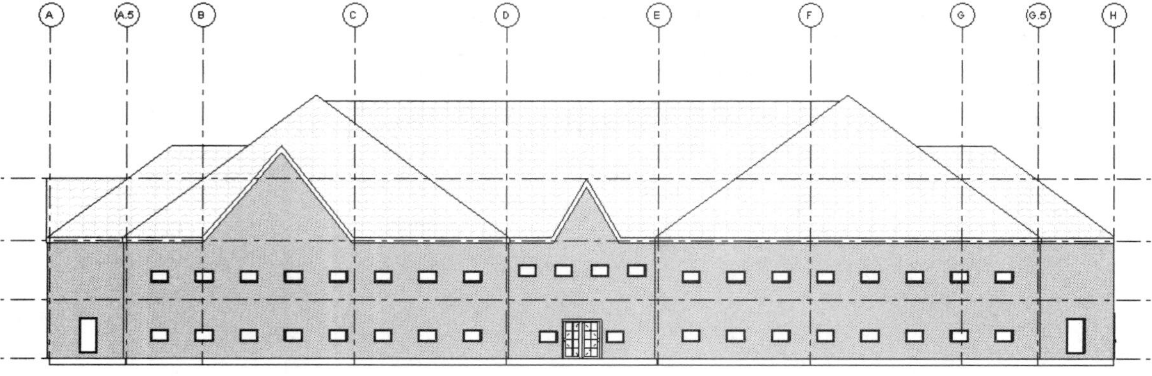

2) Create a roof family using Spanish tile material.

Lesson 7 Quiz

True or False

1. A roof footprint is a 2-D sketch.
2. When creating a roof by extrusion, the sketch must be closed.
3. When placing a roof by footprint, you must specify the work plane to place the sketch.
4. When you create a roof by extrusion, you can extend the extrusion toward or away from the view.
5. The Join/Unjoin Roof tool can be used to join two roofs together.

Multiple Choice

6. Roofs can be created using the following options:
   Select three:

   A. Roof by footprint
   B. Roof by extrusion
   C. Roof by face
   D. Roof by sketch

7. The Join/Unjoin roof tool is located:

   A. On the Modify panel of the Modify ribbon.
   B. On the Build panel of the Home ribbon.
   C. On the Geometry panel of the Modify ribbon.
   D. On the right shortcut menu when the roof is selected.

8. When creating a roof sketch you can use any of the following EXCEPT:

   A. Pick wall.
   B. Lines
   C. Arcs
   D. Circles

9. In order to attach a wall to a roof which is above the wall, you should use this option:

   A. Base Attach
   B. Top Attach
   C. Edit Profile
   D. Join/Unjoin

10. The Properties pane for a roof displays the roof:

    A. Area
    B. Weight
    C. Elevation
    D. Function

ANSWERS:

1) T; 2) F; 3) F; 4) T; 5) T; 6) A, B, & C; 7) C; 8) D; 9) B; 10) A

Lesson 8
Elevations, Details & Plans

Exercise 8-1
Creating Elevation Documents

Drawing Name: 7-5.rvt
Estimated Time: 10 minutes

This exercise reinforces the following skills:

- Sheet
- Add View
- Changing View Properties

1. Open *ex7-5.rvt.*

2. View — Activate the **View** ribbon.

3. Sheet — Select **Sheet** from Sheet Composition panel to add a new sheet.

4. File name: D 22 x 34 Horizontal.rfa — Select the **D 22 x 34 Horizontal [A3 metric]** title block.

   File name: A3 metric.rfa

5. Select a titleblock: D 22 x 34 Horizontal; E1 30 x 42 Horizontal : E1 30x42 Horizontal — Select **D 22 x 34 Horizontal [A3 metric]** title block. Press **OK**.

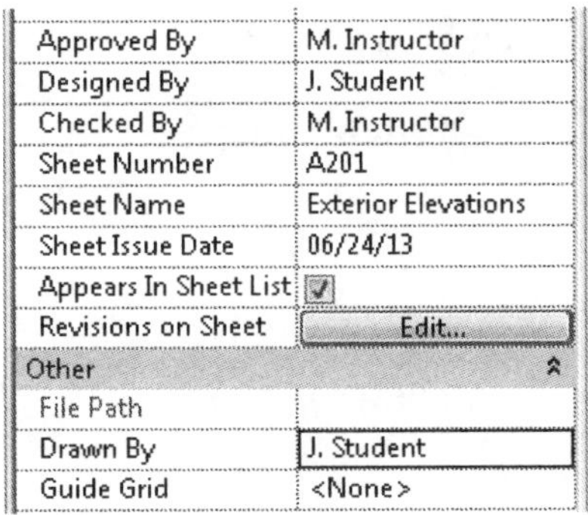

Approved By	M. Instructor
Designed By	J. Student
Checked By	M. Instructor
Sheet Number	A201
Sheet Name	Exterior Elevations
Sheet Issue Date	06/24/13
Appears In Sheet List	☑
Revisions on Sheet	Edit...
Other	
File Path	
Drawn By	J. Student
Guide Grid	<None>

In the Properties pane:

Change Approved by to your instructor's name.
Change Designed by to your name.
Change Checked by to your instructor's name.
Change the Sheet Number to **A201**.
Change the Sheet Name to **Exterior Elevations**.
Change Drawn by to your name.

6. Elevations (Building Elevation): East, North, South, South Lobby, West — Locate the North and South Elevations in the Project Browser.

7. 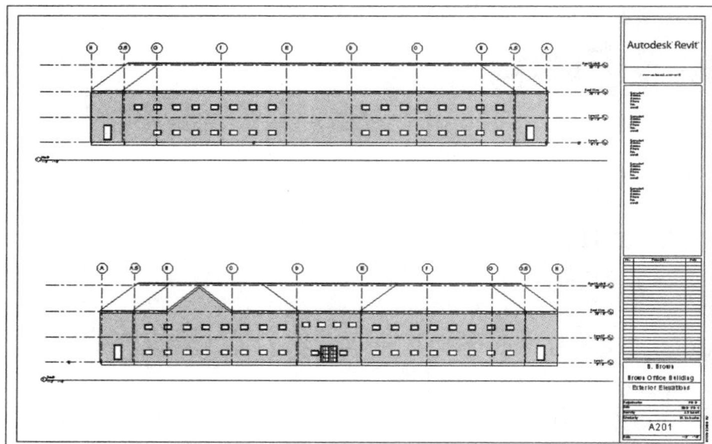

Drag and drop the North and South Elevations from the browser onto the sheet. The top elevation will be the North elevation. The bottom elevation will be the South Elevation.

You may notice that some entities are visible in the view, which you do not want to see, like the stairs inside.

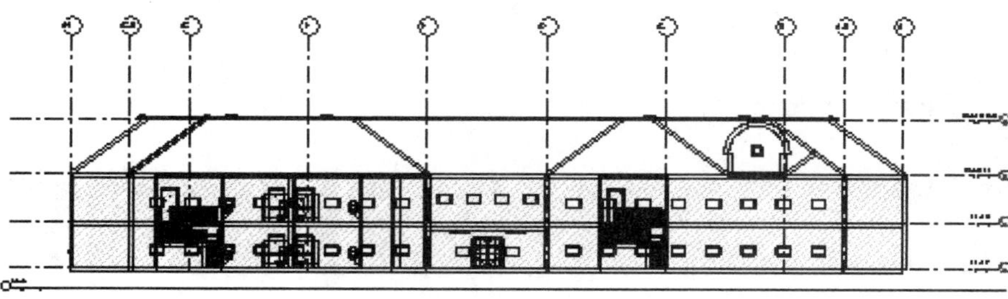

Let's look at the **North** Elevation first.

8.

Rotation on Sheet	None
Visibility/Graphics Overri...	Edit...
Graphic Display Options	Edit...
Hide at scales coarser than	1" = 400'-0"
Discipline	Architectural

Select the **North** Elevation View on the sheet.

In the Properties pane:
Select the **Edit** button next to Graphic Display Options.

9.

Model Display
Style: Hidden Line
Show Edges
Transparency: 0
Silhouettes: <none>

Under Model Display:

Set Surfaces to **Hidden Line**.

Press **OK**.

10.

Rotation on Sheet	None
Visibility/Graphics Overri...	Edit...
Graphic Display Options	Edit...
Hide at scales coarser than	1" = 400'-0"

Select **Edit** next to Visibility/Graphics Overrides.

11.

Model Categories | Annotation Categories | Anal
Show annotation categories in this view
Filter list: Architecture

Visibility
☑ Generic Model Tags
☐ Grids
☑ Guide Grid

Under Annotation Categories, disable Grids and Sections.

Press **OK**.

12. 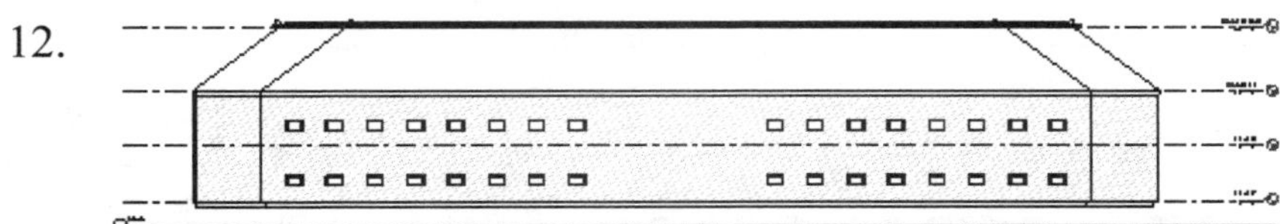

The North Elevation now looks more appropriate.

13. Select the **South** Elevation View on the sheet.

In the Properties pane:

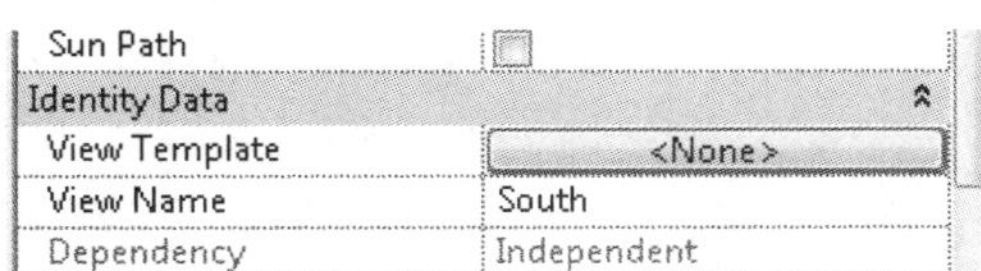

Select the View Template column.

14. View Templates
Discipline filter:
<all>
View type filter:
Elevations, Sections, Detail Views
Names:
<None>
Architectural Elevation
Architectural Presentation Elevation
Architectural Section
Site Section
Structural Framing Elevation
Structural Section

Set the View Template to **Architectural Presentation Elevation**.
Press **Apply**.

15. V/G Overrides Model — Edit...
V/G Overrides Annotation — Edit...
V/G Overrides Analytical Model — Edit...
V/G Overrides Import — Edit...

Select **Edit** next to V/G Overrides Annotation.

16. 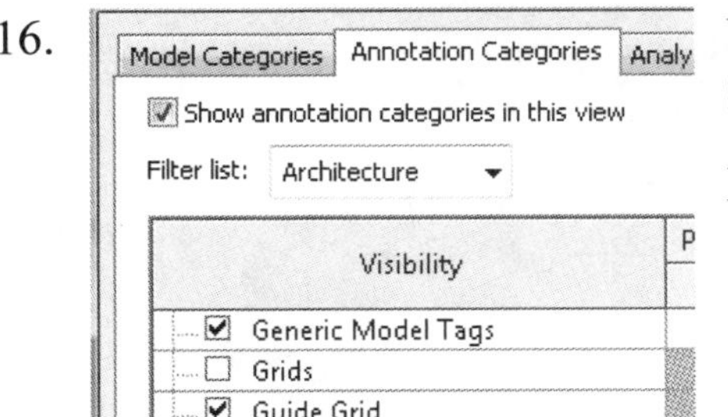

Under Annotation Categories, disable Grids and Sections.

Press **OK**.

17. V/G Overrides Filters — Edit...
Model Display — Edit...
Shadows — Edit...
Lighting — Edit...

Select **Edit** next to Shadows.

18. Shadows
Cast Shadows
Show Ambient Shadows

Enable **Cast Shadows**.
Enable **Show Ambient Shadows**.
Press OK.

Close the dialog.

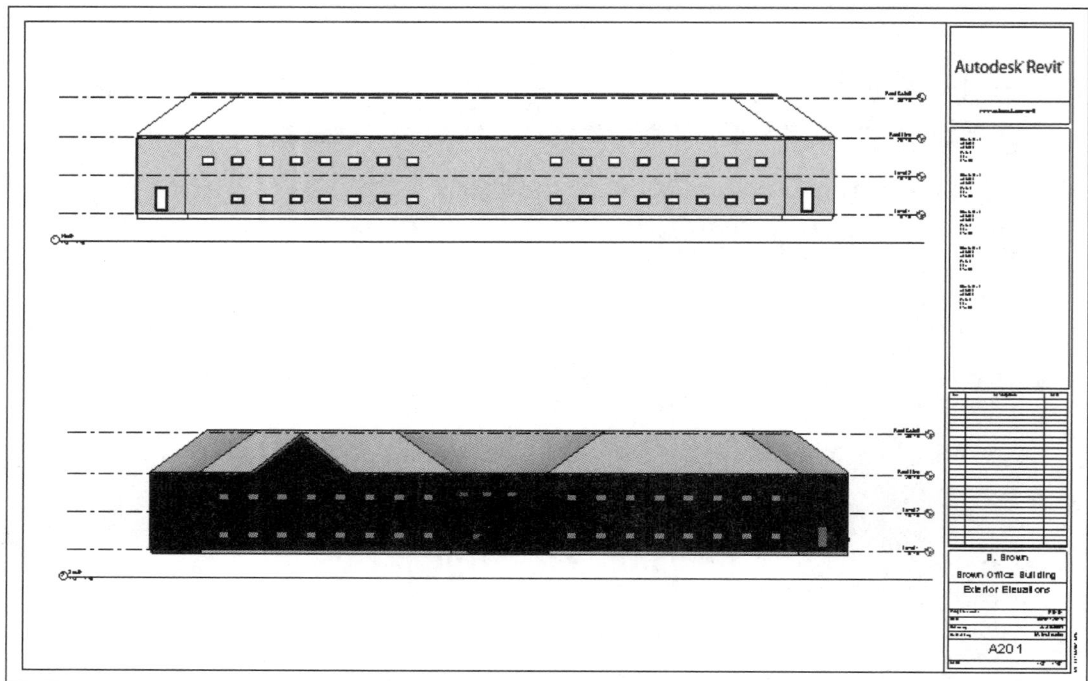

19. Save as *ex8-1.rvt.*

Exercise 8-2
Using Line Work

Drawing Name: 8-1.rvt
Estimated Time: 15 minutes

This exercise reinforces the following skills:

- ❑ Activate View
- ❑ Linework tool
- ❑ Line Styles
- ❑ Line Weight

1. Open *ex8-1.rvt.*

2. Activate the **Exterior Elevations** sheet.

Sheets (all)
- A101 - First Level Floor Plan
- A102 - Level 2 Ceiling Plan
- **A201 - Exterior Elevations**
- A601 - Door Schedule
- A602 - Glazing Schedule
- A603 - Lobby Keynotes

3. 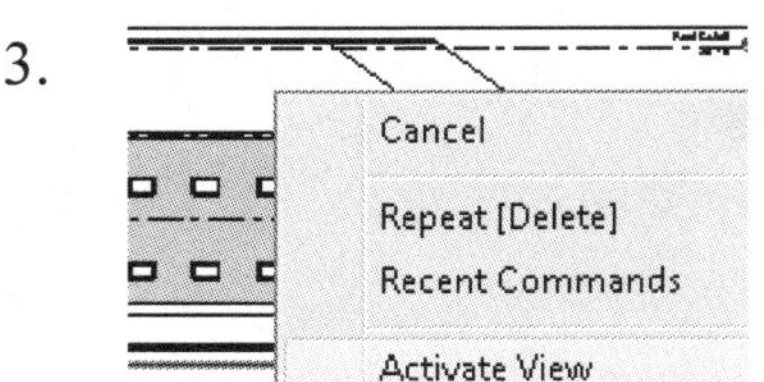

Select the top elevation view (**North**). Right click and select **Activate View**.

Activate View works similarly to Model Space/Paper Space mode in AutoCAD.

4. Select the **Modify** ribbon.

5. Select the **Linework** tool from the View panel.

6. 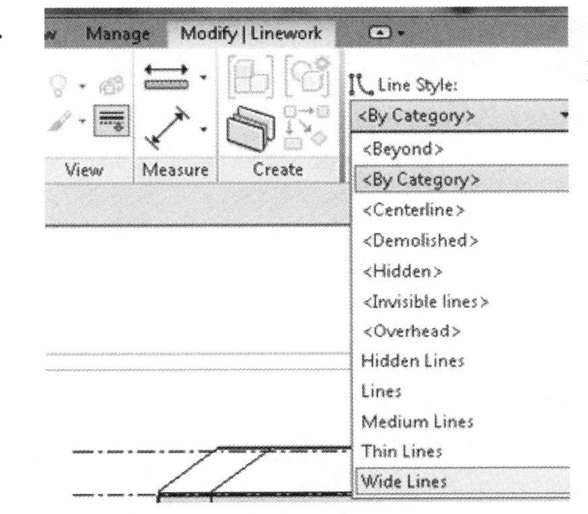

Select **Wide Lines** from the Line Style panel on the ribbon.

7. 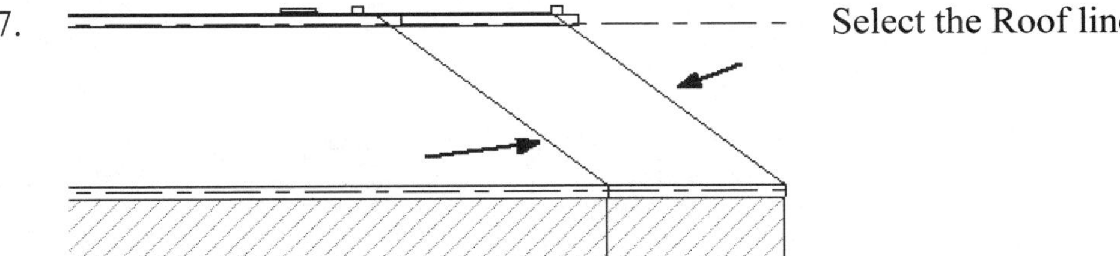
Select the Roof lines.

8. 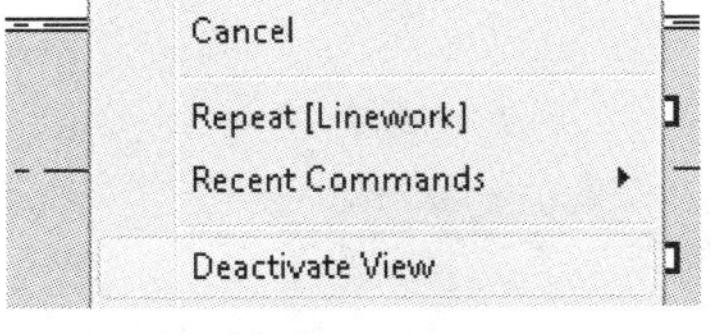

Right click in the graphics area. Select **Deactivate View**.

9. Activate the **Manage** ribbon.

10. Go to **Settings→Additional Settings→Line Styles**.

    Move the dialog out of the way so you can see what happens when you apply the new line weight.

11. Set the Line Weight for Wide Lines to **16**.
    Press **Apply**.

12. Our rooflines have dramatically changed.

13. Set the Wide Lines Line Weight to **12**.
    Press **Apply**.
    Press **OK**.

14. Note that both views updated with the new line style applied.

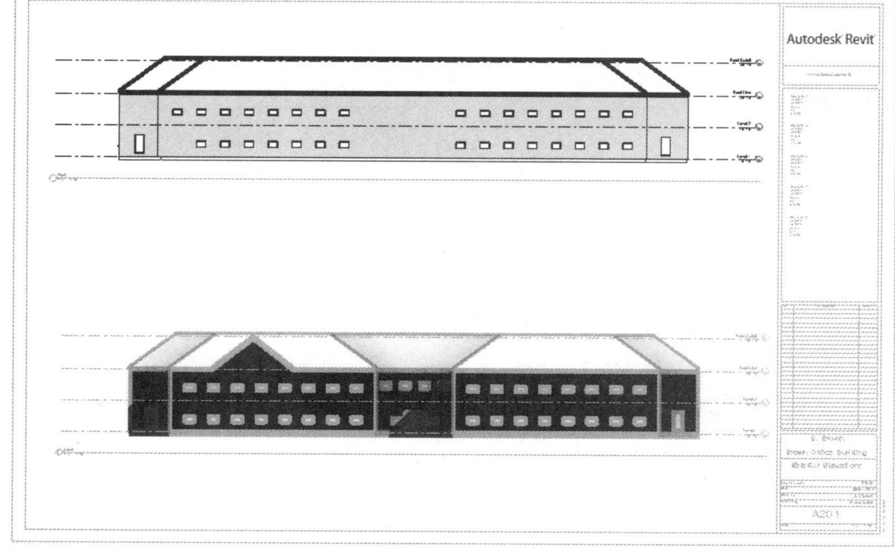

15. Save the file as *ex8-2.rvt.*

You can use invisible lines to hide any lines you don't want visible in your view.Linework is specific to each view. If you duplicate the view, any linework edits you applied will be lost.

Exercise 8-3
Creating a Section View

Drawing Name: 8-2.rvt
Estimated Time: 15 minutes

This exercise reinforces the following skills:

- Activate View
- Add Section Symbol

1. Open *ex8-2.rvt.*

2. Floor Plans
   - AP3-1 Office Layout
   - AP3-2-Office layout
   - **Level 1**
   - Level 1 - No Dimensions
   - Level 1 - NO Dimensions or Furniture
   - Level 1- Lobby Detail

   Activate **Level 1**.

3. View Activate the **View** ribbon.

4. 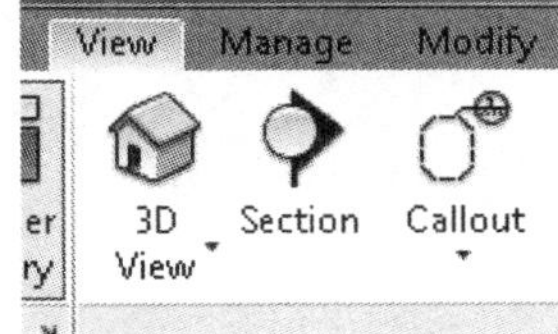

   Select the **Section** tool from the Create panel.

5. 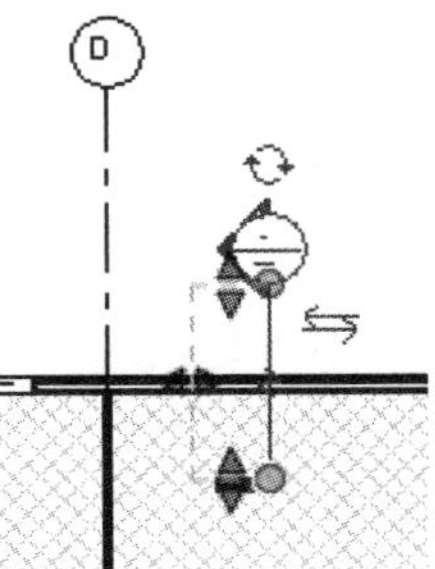

   Place a section on the north exterior wall.

   Adjust the clip range to show just the wall.

6. 

   On the Properties panel:

   Select **Wall Section** from the Type Selector drop-down list.

7. The new section appears in your Project Browser.

8. Rename the section view **North Exterior Wall**.

Activate the section view.

9. Set the Detail Level to **Fine**.
Set the Visual Style to **Consistent Colors**.

10. Adjust the crop region to display the wall as shown.

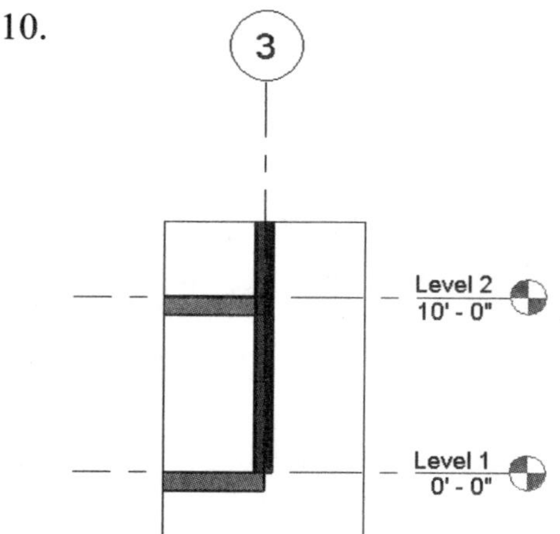

11. Select the **Annotate** ribbon.

Select **Detail Component**.

12. Select **Load Family**.

13.

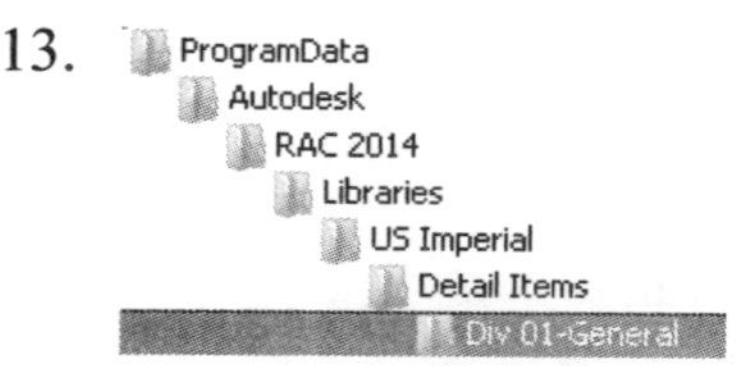

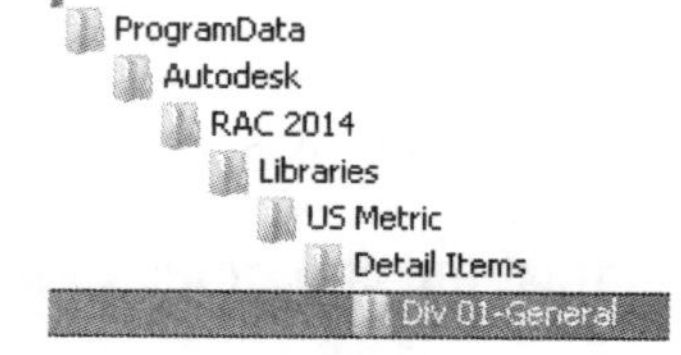

Browse to the *Detail Items\Div 01-General* folder.

Select the *Break Line [M_Break Line]*.

14. 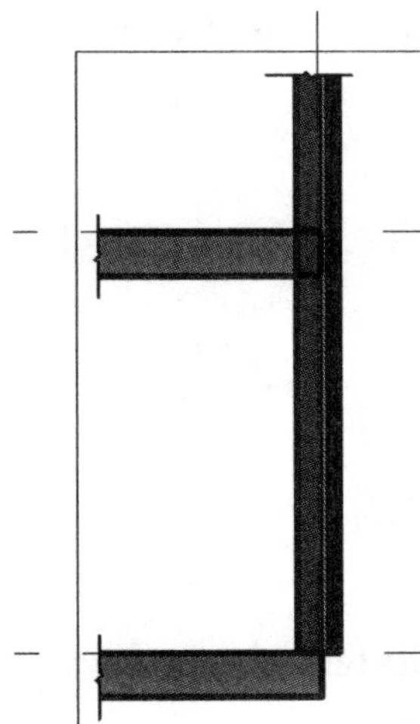

Add break lines to indicate that the top of the wall continues up, the floors and ceiling continue toward the right.

Press the SPACE BAR to rotate the break line symbol.

15. Select the **Filled Region** tool from the Annotation ribbon.

16. Enable **Chain** on the Options bar.

17. 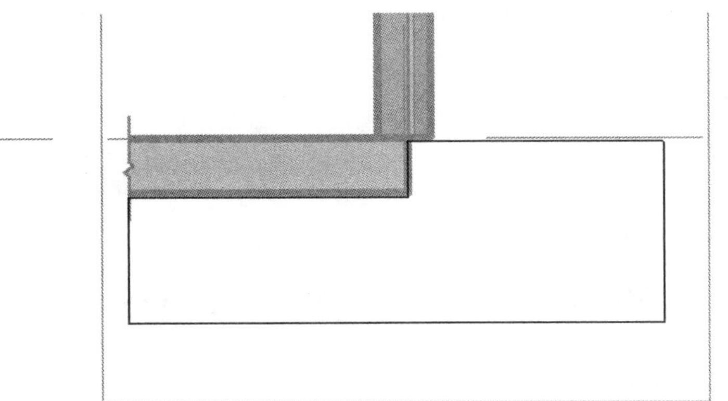

Draw the outline shown.

18. Press the Green Check to finish the filled region.

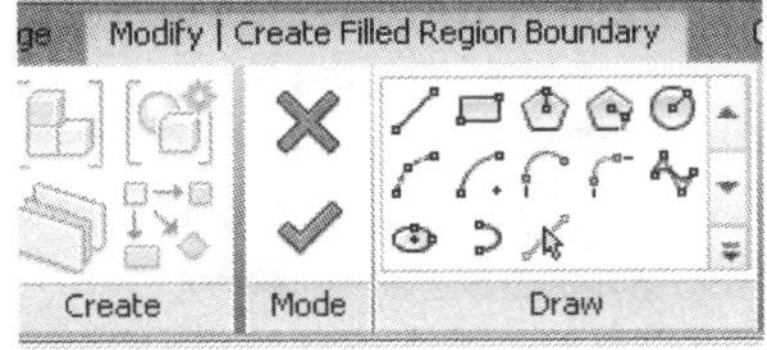

19. 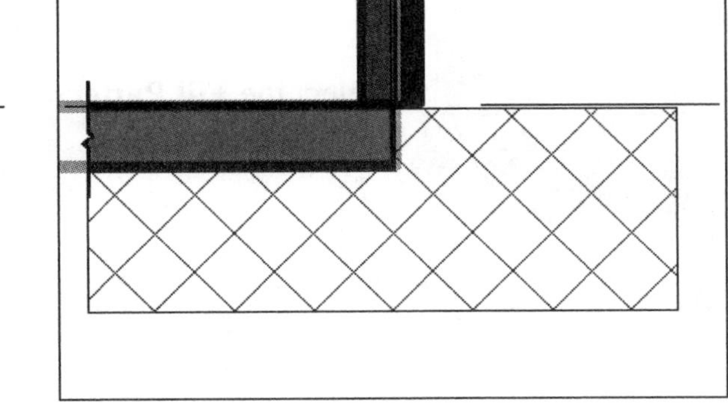

A filled region with a diagonal crosshatch pattern is placed.

20. Locate the **Filled region** under *Families/Detail Items* in the Project Browser.

Detail Items
Break Line
Brick Standard
Filled region
Diagonal Crosshatch
Diagonal Crosshatch - Transparent
Diagonal Down
Diagonal Down - Transparent
Diagonal Up
Horizontal Lines
Ortho Crosshatch
Solid Black
Vertical Lines
Wood 1
Wood 2

21. Highlight the **Diagonal Crosshatch**.
Right click and select **Duplicate**.

Filled region
Diagonal Crosshatch
Duplicate
Delete

22. Right click and select **Rename** to rename the copied fill region.

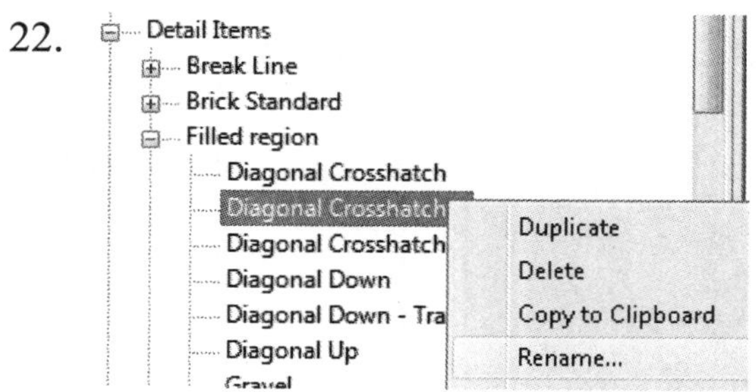

23. Gravel Rename **Gravel**.

24. Highlight **Gravel**.

Right click and select **Type Properties**.

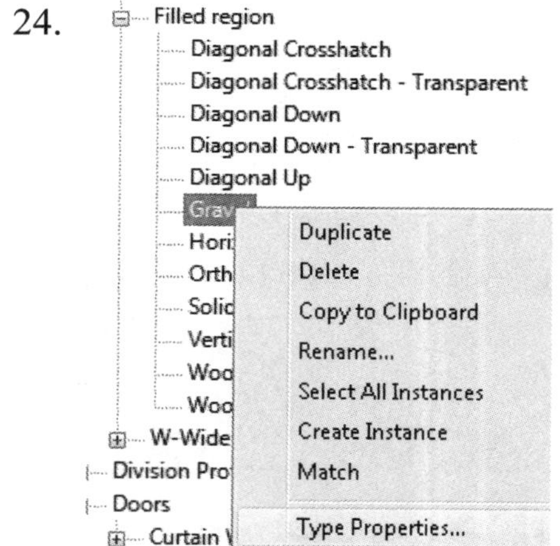

25. Select the **Fill Pattern**.

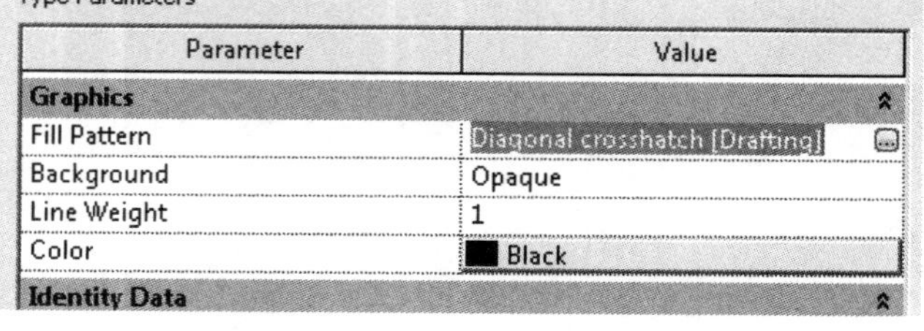

Type Parameters

Parameter	Value
Graphics	
Fill Pattern	Diagonal crosshatch [Drafting]
Background	Opaque
Line Weight	1
Color	Black
Identity Data	

26.

Fill Patterns
Name: Pattern:
Diagonal up
Diagonal up-small
Diagonale Kreuzschraff
Earth
Gravel
Gypsum-Plaster
Horizontal
New
Edit...
Delete
Pattern Type
Drafting
Model
OK
Cancel
Help

Locate the **Gravel** hatch pattern.

Press **OK**.

This fill pattern was defined in Exercise 7-2.

27.

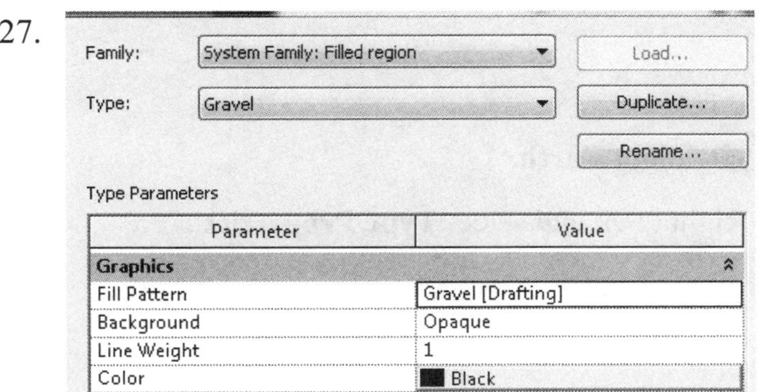

Verify that the Gravel fill pattern has been assigned.

Press **OK**.

28.

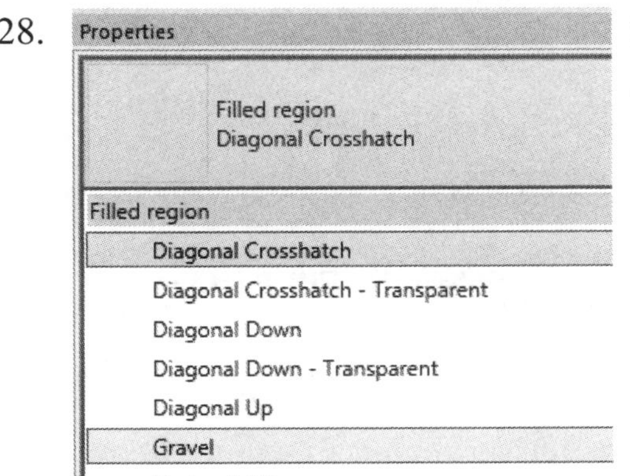

Select the Filled Region in the view.

Then select **Gravel** from the Type Selector.

29.

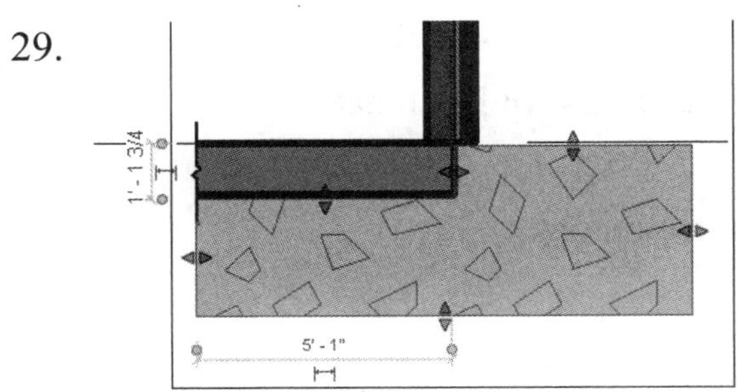

If you select the filled region you can use the grips to adjust the size.

30. Highlight the **Diagonal Crosshatch** filled region in the Project Browser.

Right click and select **Duplicate**.

31. 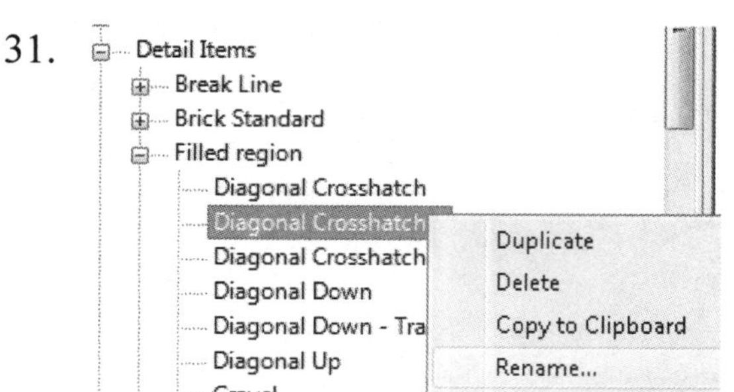

Right click and select **Rename** to rename the copied fill region.

32. 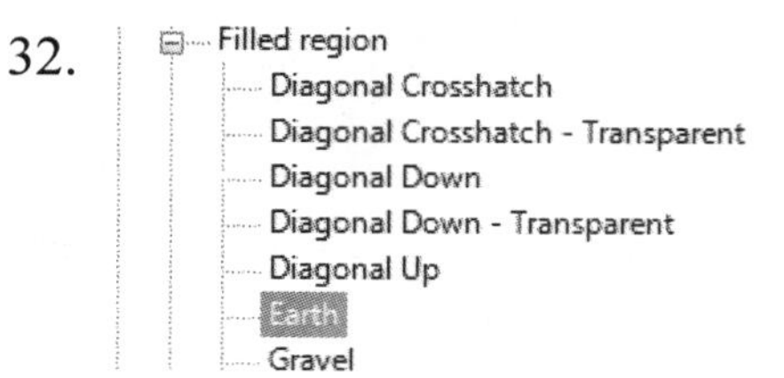

Rename **Earth**.

33. 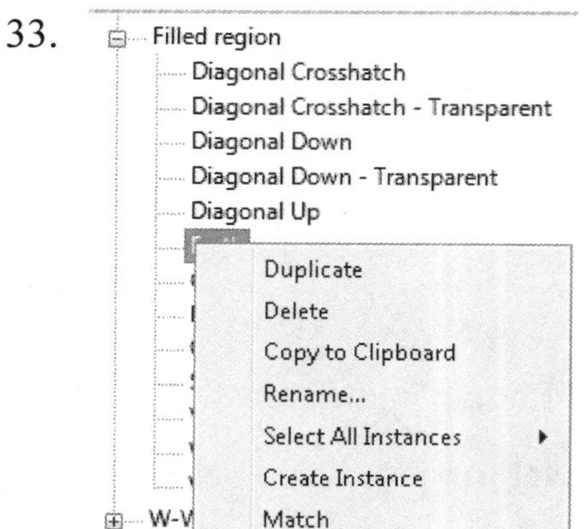

Highlight **Earth**.

Right click and select **Type Properties**.

34. Type Parameters

Parameter	Value
Graphics	
Fill Pattern	Diagonal crosshatch [Drafting]
Background	Opaque
Line Weight	1
Color	Black
Identity Data	

Select the **Fill Pattern**.

35. 

Select **the Earth** hatch pattern.
Press **OK**.

Exit the dialog.

36. 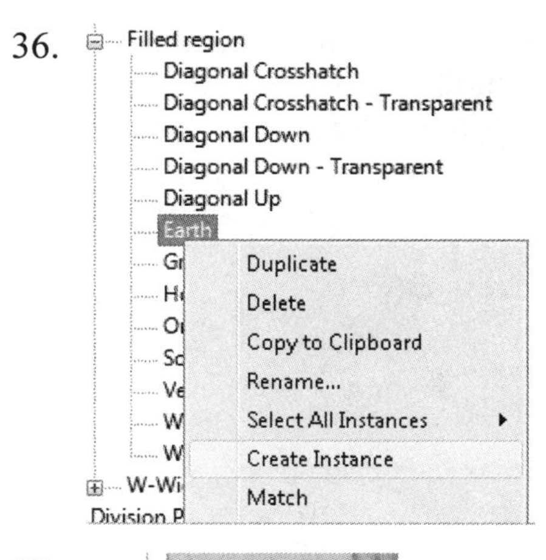

Highlight the Earth filled region in the Project Browser.

Right click and select **Create Instance**.

37. 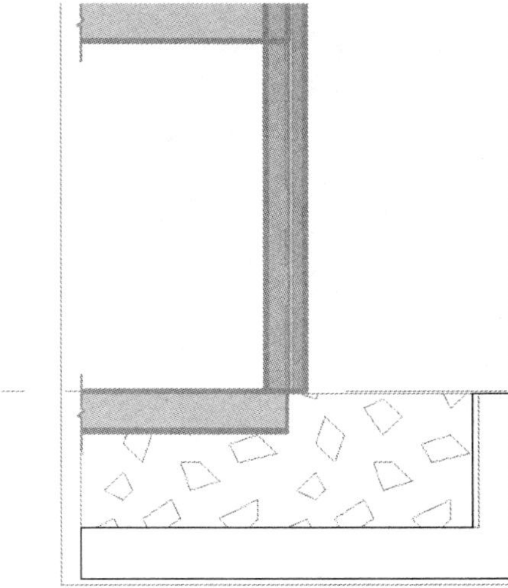

Draw an outline for the earth filled region.

Select the Green Check to complete.

38. 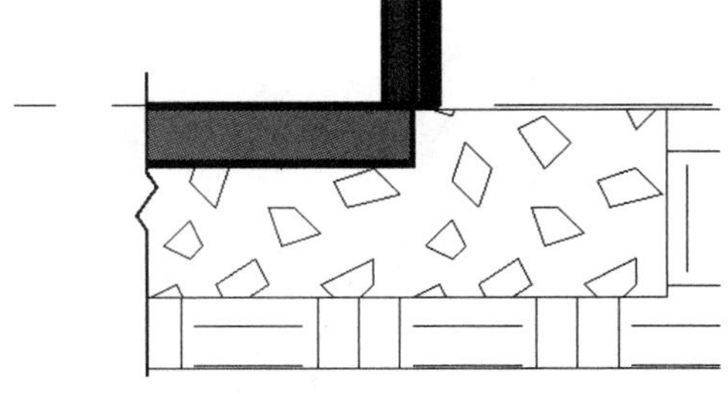

Adjust the break line to extend past the earth filled region.

39. 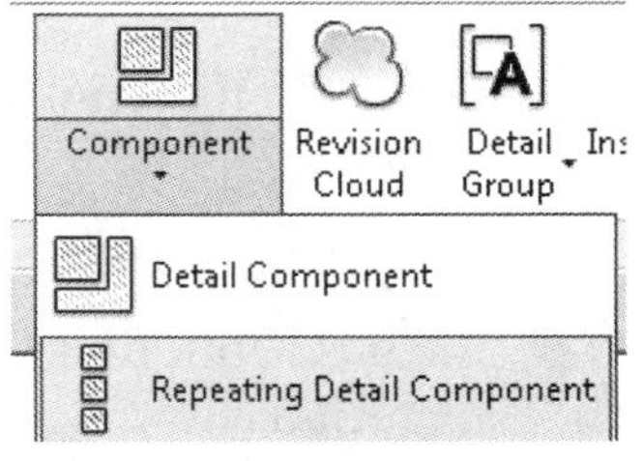

Select **Repeating Detail Component**.

40. 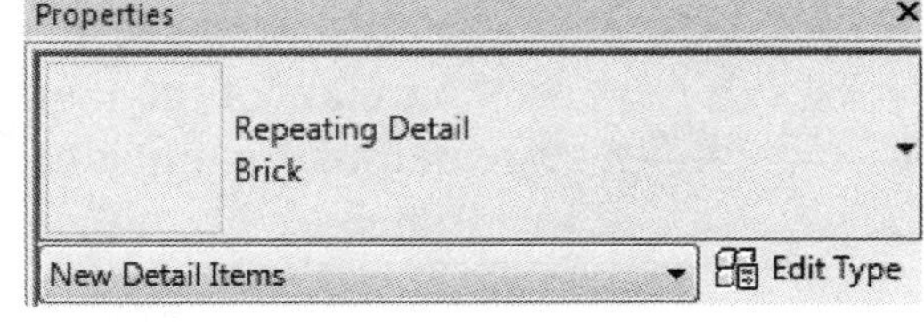

In the Properties Pane:
Verify that the Repeating Detail is **Brick**.
Select **Edit Type**.

41. 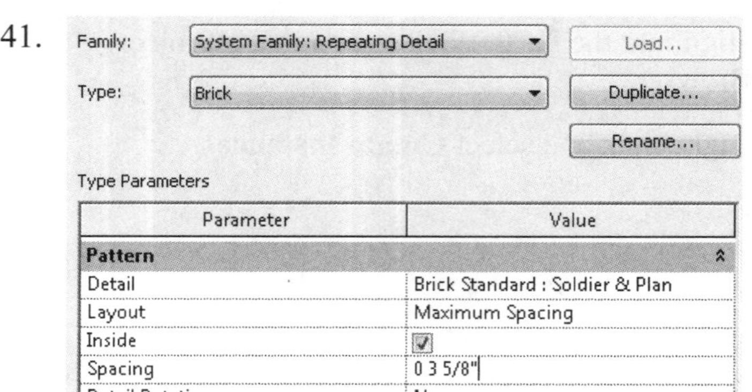

Set the Detail to **Brick Standard: Soldier & Plan.**
Set the Layout to **Maximum Spacing.**
Set the Spacing to **3 5/8″.**

Press **OK.**

42. 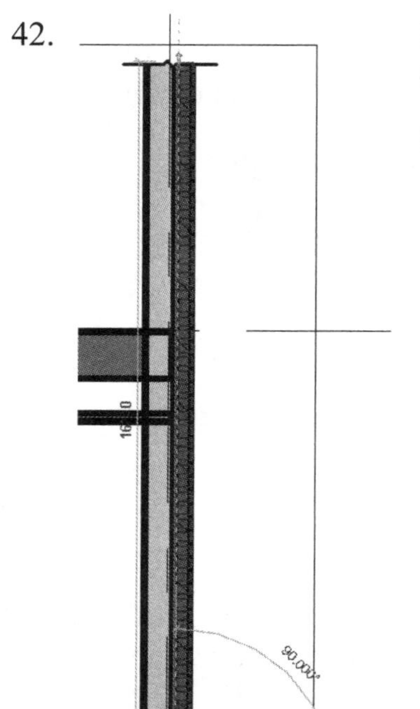

Select the interior bottom side for the start point of the brick detail.

Select the interior top side for the end point.

43. Hide the Crop Region.

44. Select the **Material Tag** tool from the Annotate ribbon.

45. 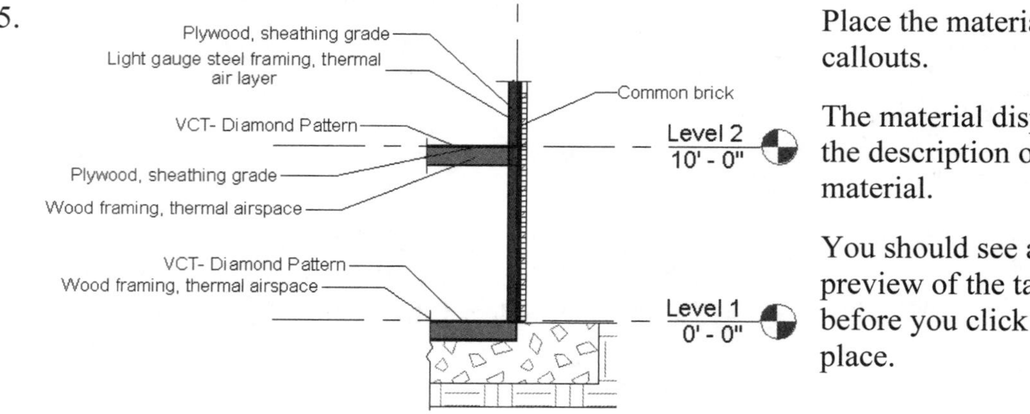

Place the material callouts.

The material displays the description of the material.

You should see a preview of the tag before you click to place.

46. View Activate the **View** ribbon.

47. Sheet Select **New Sheet** from the Sheet Composition panel.

48. Select titleblocks:
D 22 x 34 Horizontal
E1 30 x 42 Horizontal : E1 30x42 Horizontal
None

Select **D 22 x 34 Horizontal** [**A1 Metric**] titleblock. Press **OK**.

49.

Current Revision	
Approved By	M. Instructor
Designed By	J. Student
Checked By	M. Instructor
Sheet Number	AD501
Sheet Name	Details
Sheet Issue Date	06/24/13
Appears In Sheet List	☑
Revisions on Sheet	Edit...
Other	
File Path	
Drawn By	J. Student
Guide Grid	<None>

In the Properties pane:

Change the Sheet Number to **AD501**.

Change the Sheet Name to **Details**.

Modify the Drawn By field with your name.

Modify the Approved By field with your instructor's name.

50. Drag and drop the section view onto the sheet.

51.

Viewports (1)	Edit Type
Graphics	
View Scale	1/4" = 1'-0"
Scale Value 1:	48

Select the view.
In the Properties pane:
Set the View Scale to **1/4″ = 1′-0″**.

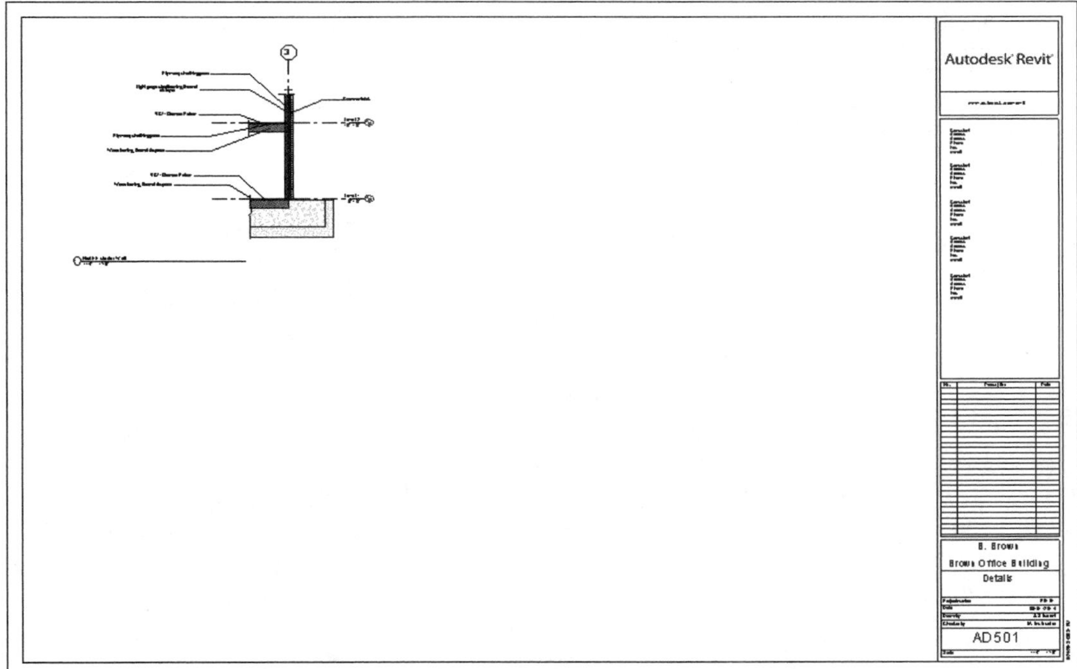

52. Save the file as *ex8-3.rvt*.

Any blue symbol will behave like a hyperlink on a web page and can be double clicked to switch to the referenced view. (Note: The blue will print black on your plots if you want it to.)

Exercise 8-4

Modifying Keynote Styles

Drawing Name: 8-3.rvt
Estimated Time: 15 minutes

This exercise reinforces the following skills:

- Keynotes
- Materials
- Edit Family

1. Open or continue working in *ex8-3.rvt*.

2. Activate the **Exterior Elevations** sheet.

   Sheets (all)
   - A101 - First Level Floor Plan
   - A102 - Door Schedule
   - A103 - Glazing Schedule
   - A104 - LOBBY KEYNOTES
   - A105 - Exterior Elevations
   - A106 - East Section

3. Activate the Southern Elevation view.

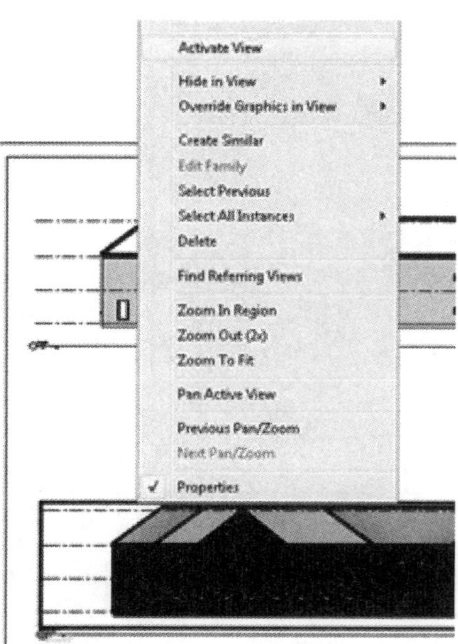

If you do not add the notes in Model Space, then the notes will not automatically scale and move with the view.

4. Annotate Activate the **Annotate** ribbon.

5. 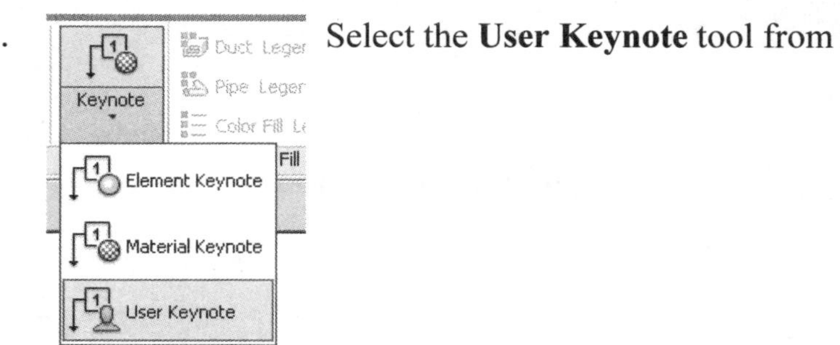

Select the **User Keynote** tool from the Tag panel.

Note: Revit only uses fonts available in the Windows fonts folder. If you are an AutoCAD user with legacy shx fonts, you need to locate ttf fonts that are equivalent to the fonts you want to use and load them into the Windows font folder. To convert shx fonts over to ttf, check with www.tcfonts.com.

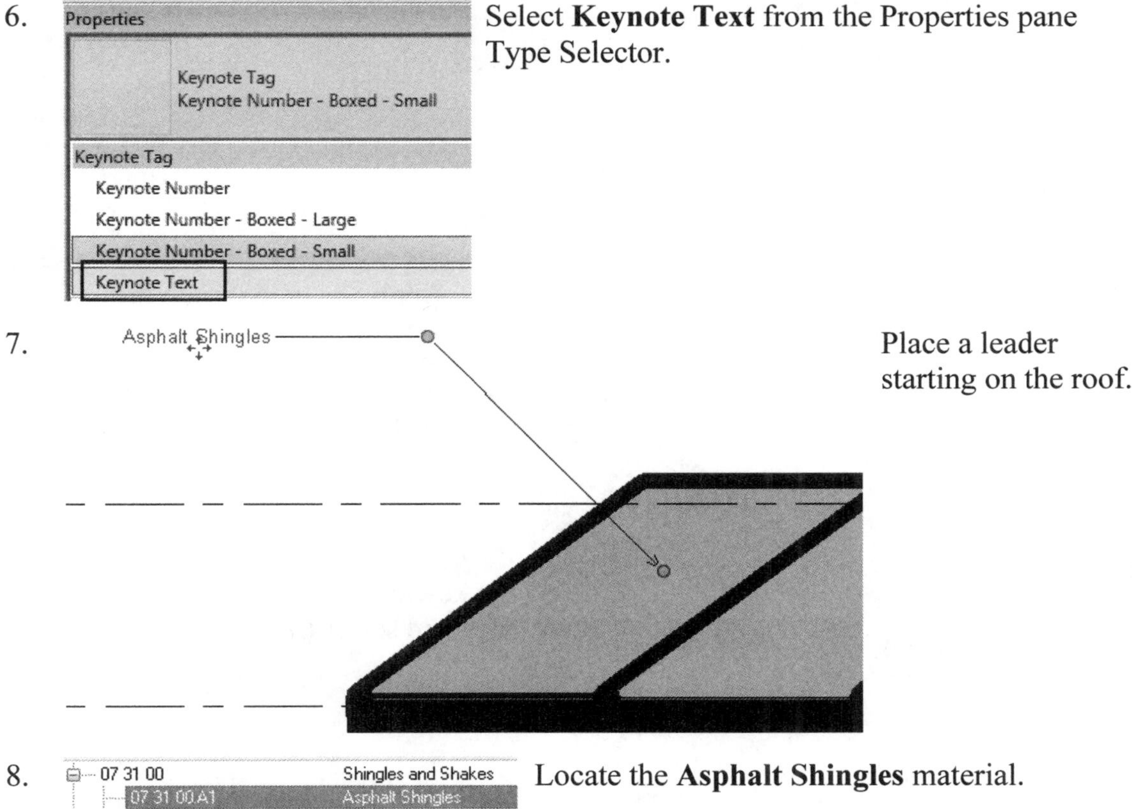

6. Select **Keynote Text** from the Properties pane Type Selector.

7. Place a leader starting on the roof.

8. Locate the **Asphalt Shingles** material.

Press **OK**.

Architects are particular about the size of text, and often about the alignment. Notes should not interfere with elevations, dimensions, etc. You can customize the appearance of keynotes.

9. 

Select the keynote that was placed.

Select **Edit Type** from the Properties panel.

10. Duplicate... Select **Duplicate**.

11. 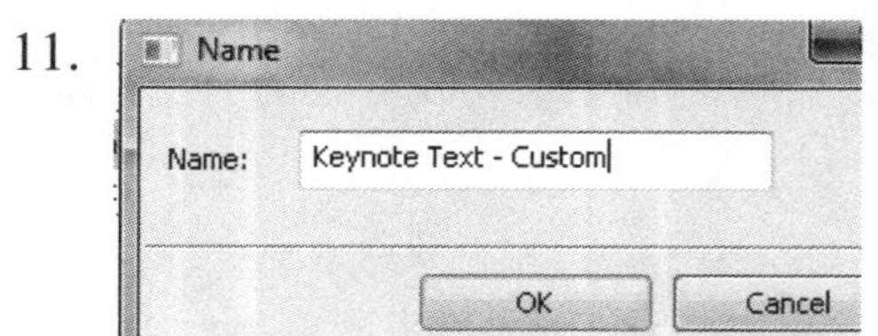

Enter **Keynote Text - Custom**.

Press **OK**.

12. 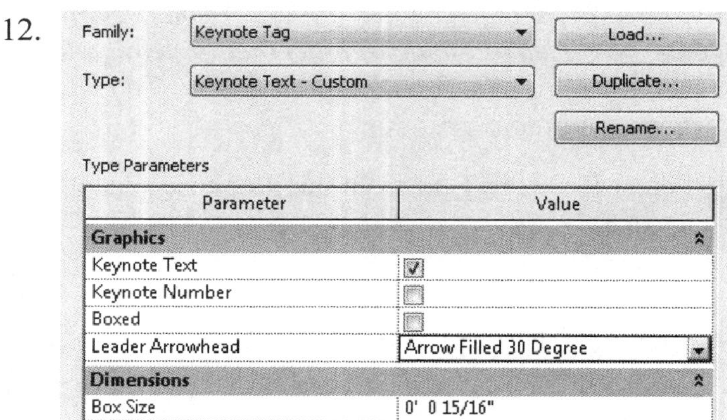

Change the Leader Arrowhead to **Arrow Filled 30 Degree**.

Press **OK**.

13. 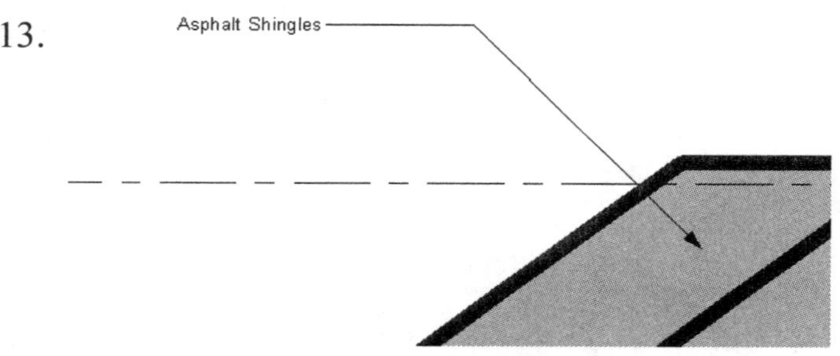

Apply the new type to the keynote.

Notice that the arrowhead changes

14. 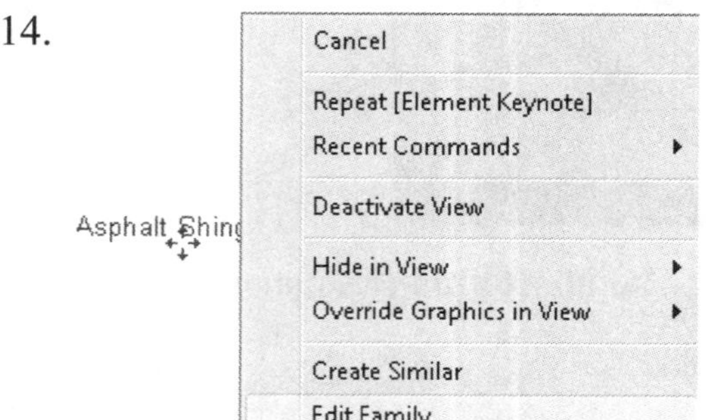

Select the keynote.
Right click and select **Edit Family**.

15. 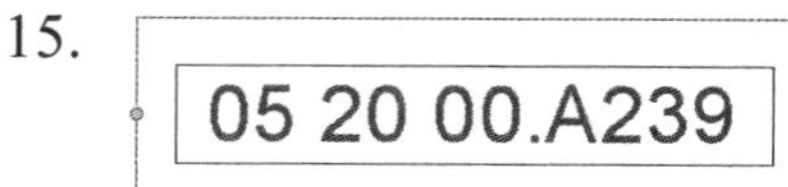

Select the text.

16.

Select **Edit Type**.

17. 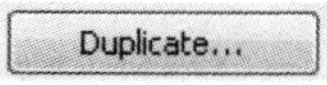

Select **Duplicate**.

18. 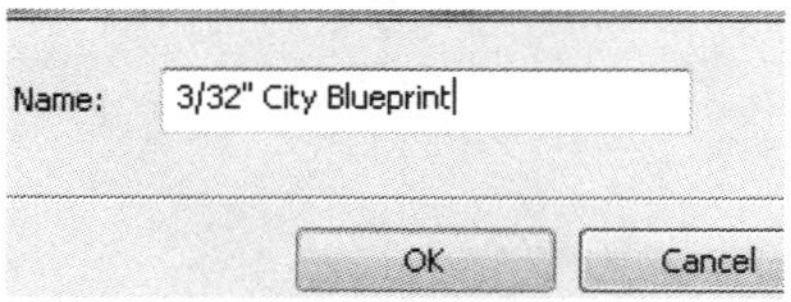

Change the name to **3/32" City Blueprint**.

Press **OK**.

19. 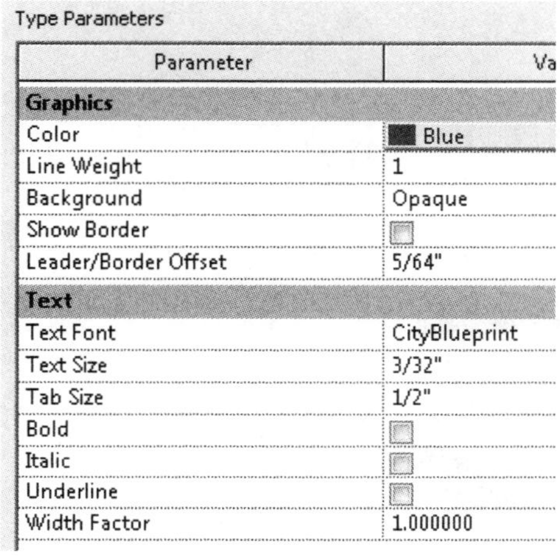

Type Parameters

Parameter	Va
Graphics	
Color	Blue
Line Weight	1
Background	Opaque
Show Border	☐
Leader/Border Offset	5/64"
Text	
Text Font	CityBlueprint
Text Size	3/32"
Tab Size	1/2"
Bold	☐
Italic	☐
Underline	☐
Width Factor	1.000000

Change the Color to **Blue**.

Change the Text Font to **City Blueprint**.

Press **OK**.

20. 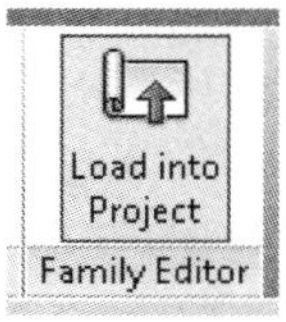

Save the file as *Keynote Tag CityBlueprint*.

Select Load into Project under the Family Editor panel.

21. 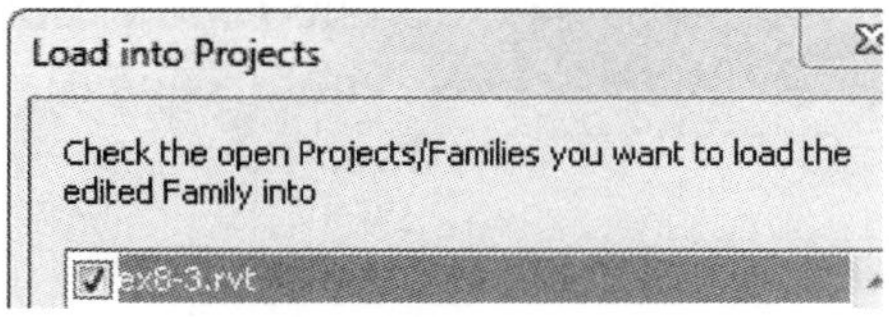

Place a check next to the project and press **OK**.

22. 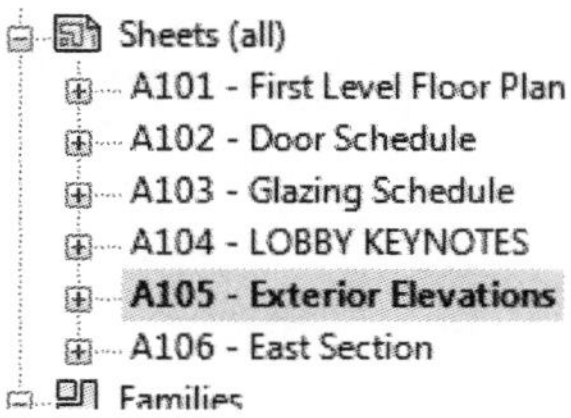

Return to the **Exterior Elevations** sheet.

Activate the South Elevation view.

23. 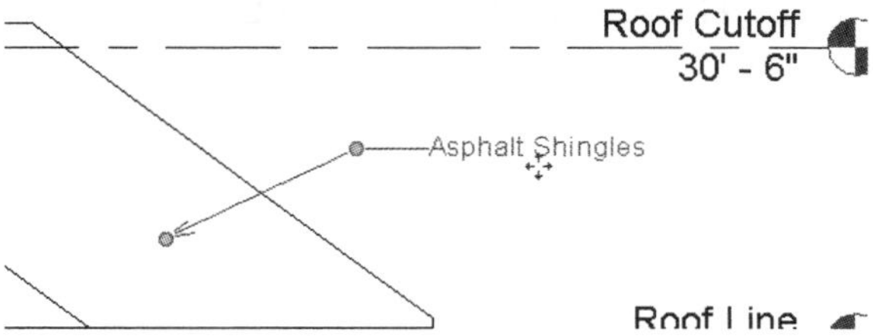

Select the keynote placed for the roof.

24. 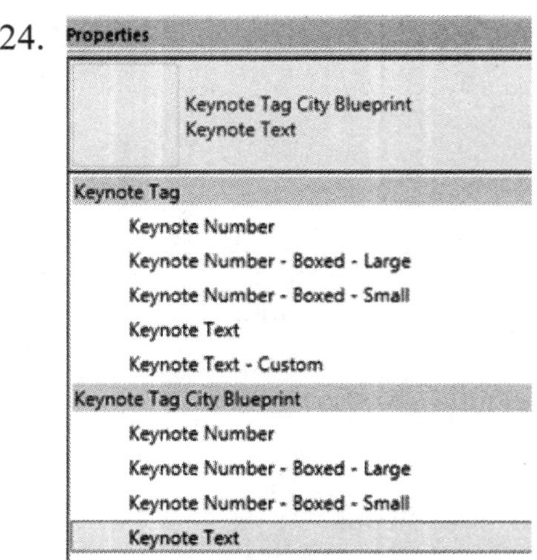

Using the Type Selector:

Locate the **Keynote Tag City Blueprint**.

Select the **Keynote Text** type for the Keynote Tag City Blueprint family.

25. 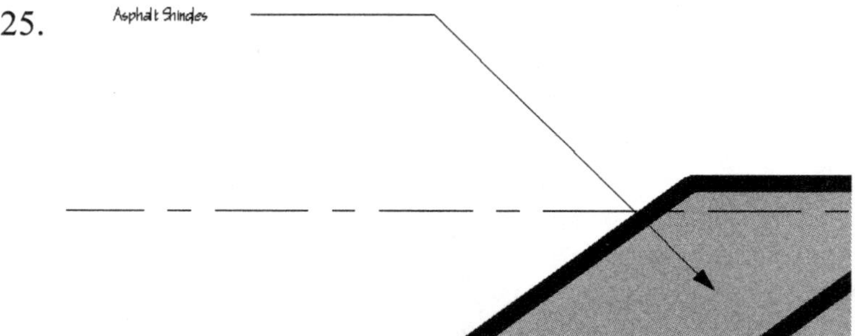

The keynote font updates.

26. Activate the Manage ribbon.

Object Styles

Select **Object Styles** under Settings.

27. 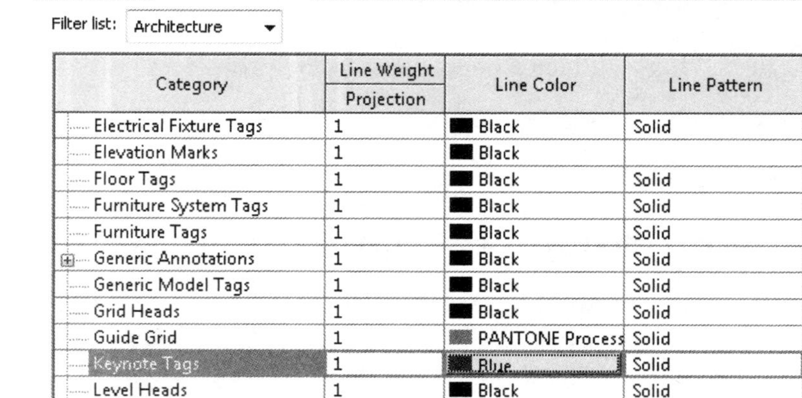

Model Objects | Annotation Objects | Analytical Model Objects | Imported Objects

Filter list: Architecture

Category	Line Weight Projection	Line Color	Line Pattern
Electrical Fixture Tags	1	Black	Solid
Elevation Marks	1	Black	
Floor Tags	1	Black	Solid
Furniture System Tags	1	Black	Solid
Furniture Tags	1	Black	Solid
Generic Annotations	1	Black	Solid
Generic Model Tags	1	Black	Solid
Grid Heads	1	Black	Solid
Guide Grid	1	PANTONE Process	Solid
Keynote Tags	1	Blue	Solid
Level Heads	1	Black	Solid

Select the Annotation Objects tab.
Set the Line Color for Keynote Tags to **Blue**.

Press **OK**.

28. 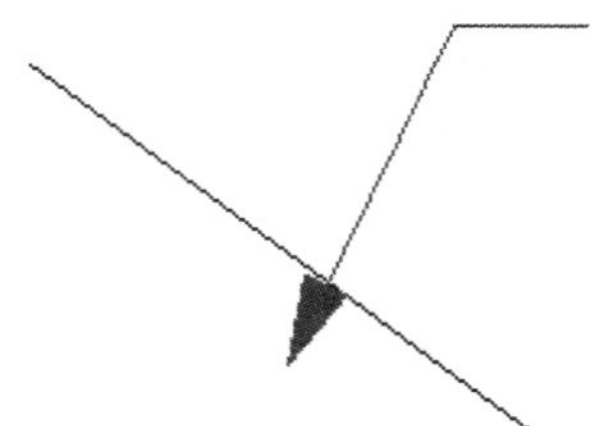

Asphalt Shingles The leader changes to blue.

29. Add additional keynotes.

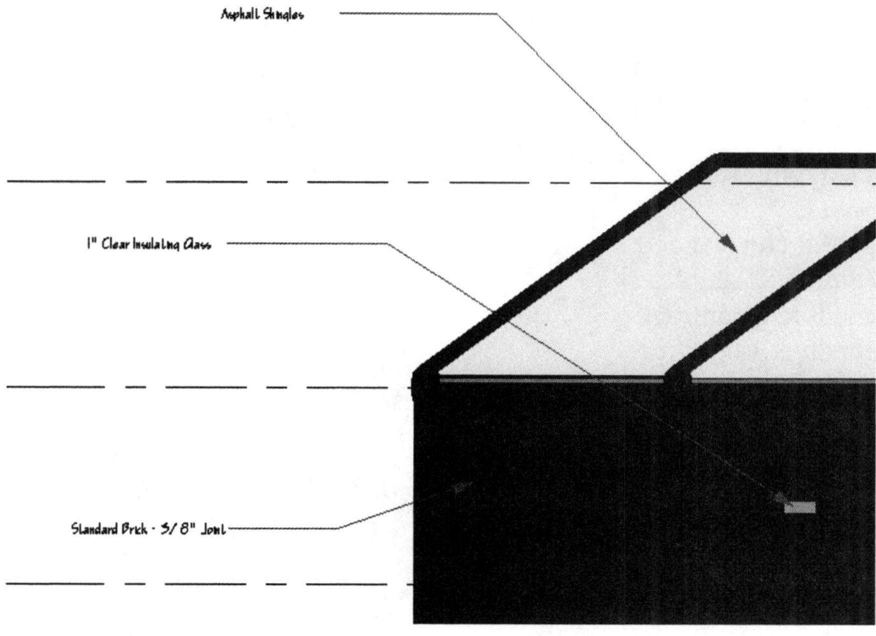

30. Deactivate the view.

31. Save the file *ex8-4.rvt*.

Once you assign an elevation view to a sheet, the elevation marker will update with the sheet number.

Exercise 8-5

Adding Window Tags

Drawing Name: 8-4.rvt
Estimated Time: 5 minutes

This exercise reinforces the following skills:

- Tag All Not Tagged
- Window Schedules
- Schedule/Quantities
- Schedule Properties

1. Open *ex8-4.rvt.*

2. Activate the **North Building Elevation**.

3. Activate the Annotate ribbon.

   Select the **Tag All** tool from the Tag panel.

4. 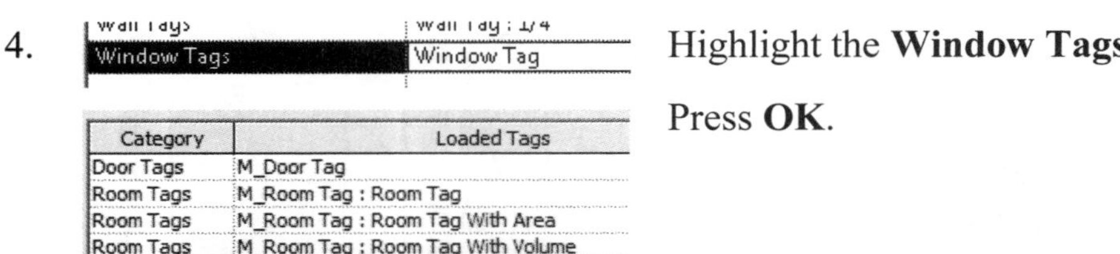

   Highlight the **Window Tags**.

   Press **OK**.

5. 

   Tags will appear on all the windows.

   The window tag uses the window type as an identifier, not the window mark. So all windows of the same type will display the same tag number.

6. Save the file as *ex8-5.rvt.*

Exercise 8-6
Changing Window Tags from Type to Instance

Drawing Name: 8-5.rvt
Estimated Time: 20 minutes

This exercise reinforces the following skills:

- Family Types
- Parameters
- Tags

In Exercise 8-5, we added a window tag that was linked to window type. So, all the tags displayed the same number for all windows of the same type. Some users want their tags to display by instance (individual placement). That way they can specify in their schedule the location of each window as well as the type. In this exercise, you learn how to modify Revit's window tag to link to an instance instead of a type.

1. Open *ex8-5.rvt.*

2. Activate the **North Building Elevation**.

3. Select one of the window tags.

   Make sure you don't select a window.

   The Window Tag will display in the Properties pane if it is selected.

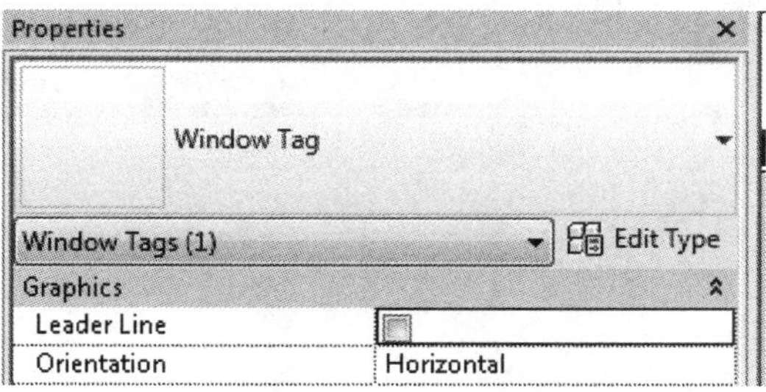

4. Right click and select **Edit Family**.

5. Select the label/text located in the center of the tag. Select **Edit Label** on the ribbon bar.

6. Highlight the Type Mark listed as the Label Parameters.

   This is linked to the type of window placed.

   Select the **Remove** button.

7. Locate **Mark** in the Category Parameters list. This parameter is linked to the instance or individual window.

   Select the **Add** button.

8. You should see the Mark parameter listed.

   Press **OK**.

9. On the Applications Menu:

   Go to **File → Save As → Family**.

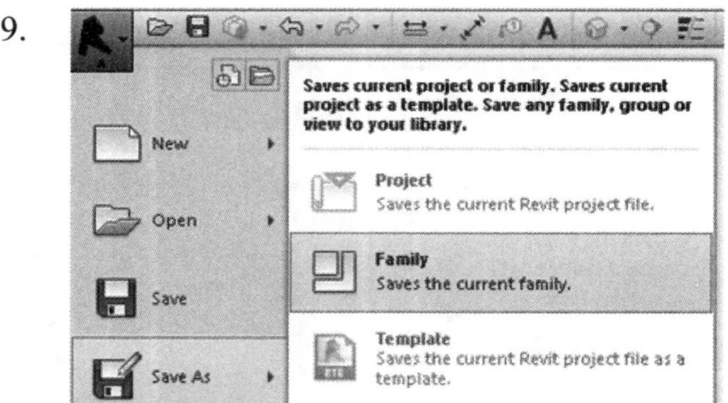

10. Save the file with a new file name – **Window Tag_Instance** – in your class work folder.

11. Select **Load into Project** to make the new tag available in the building model.

12. Place a check next to the project file.

    Press **OK**.

13. Close the window tag file.

14. Switch back to the *ex8-5.rvt* file.

15. 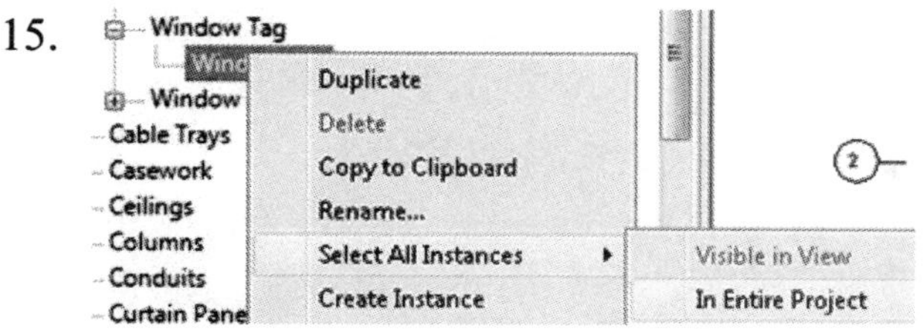

    In the Project Browser:
    Locate the **Window Tag** under the Annotation Symbols category.

    Right click and select **Select All Instances → In Entire Project**.

16. The window tags will be selected in all views.

    In the Properties Pane:

    Use the Type Selector to select the **Window Tag - Instance**.

17. Activate the North Exterior elevations.

    Zoom in to see that the windows are now renumbered using the Mark parameter.

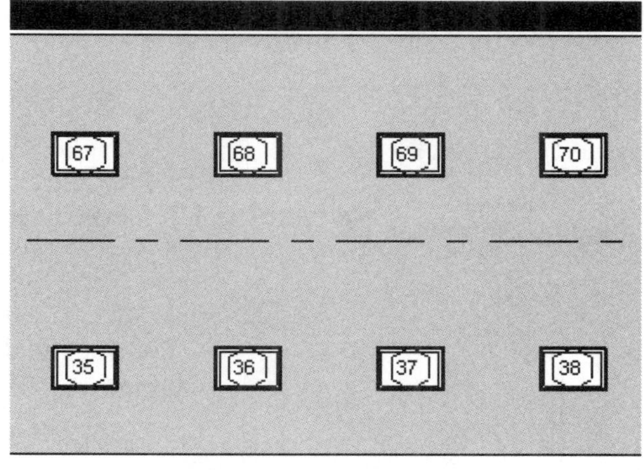

18. Save as 8-*6.rvt*.

Exercise 8-7
Creating a Plan Region View

Drawing Name: plan region view.rvt (This can be located on the publisher's website.)
Estimated Time: 20 minutes

Thanks to John Chan, one of my Revit students at SFSU for this project!

This exercise reinforces the following skills:

- Plan Region View
- Split Level Views
- Linework

Some floor plans are split levels. In those cases, users need to create a Plan Region View in order to create a good floor plan.

1. Open *plan region view.rvt.*

   If you switch to a 3D view, you see that this is a split-level floor plan.

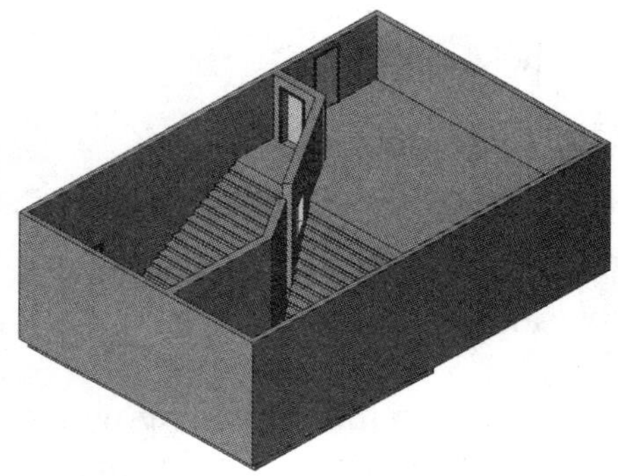

2. Floor Plans: **1/F Level 1**, 1/F Level 2, 2/F, Site

   Activate the **1/F Level 1** view under floor plans.

3. You see the door and window tags, but no doors or windows.

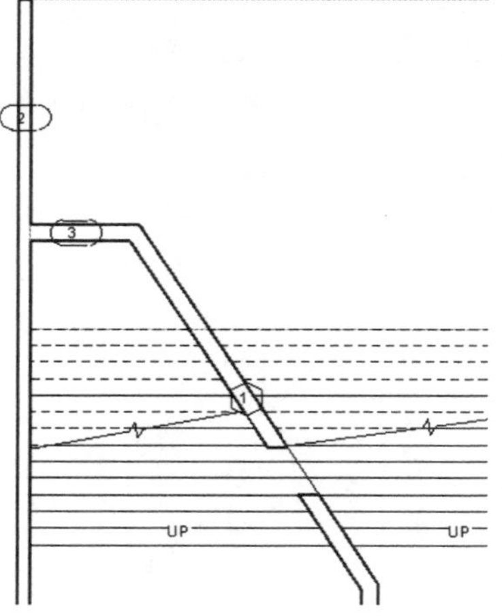

4. Activate the **View** ribbon.

5. 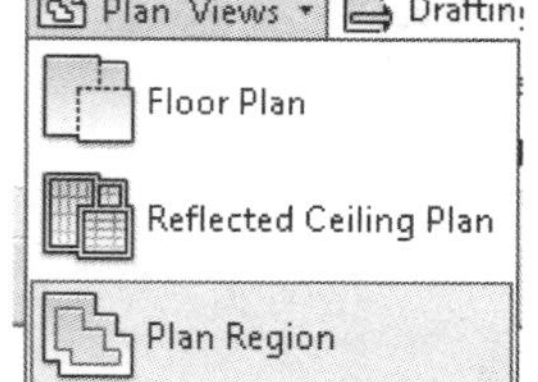

Select **Plan Views→Plan Region** tool on the Create panel.

6. 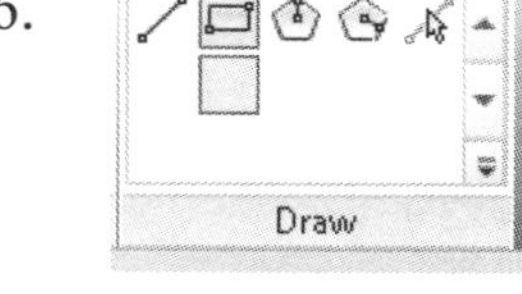

Select the **Rectangle** tool from the ribbon.

7. 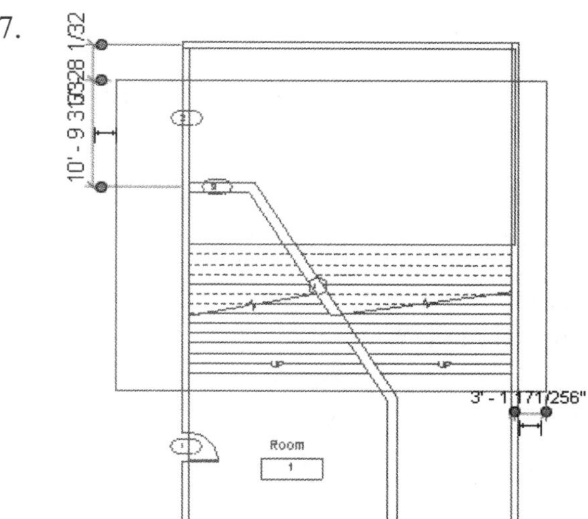

Draw a rectangle around the region where you want the doors and windows to be visible.

Be sure to extend the rectangle across the entire plan or the stairs may not appear properly.

8. 

Select the **Edit** button next to View Range on the Properties pane.

9. 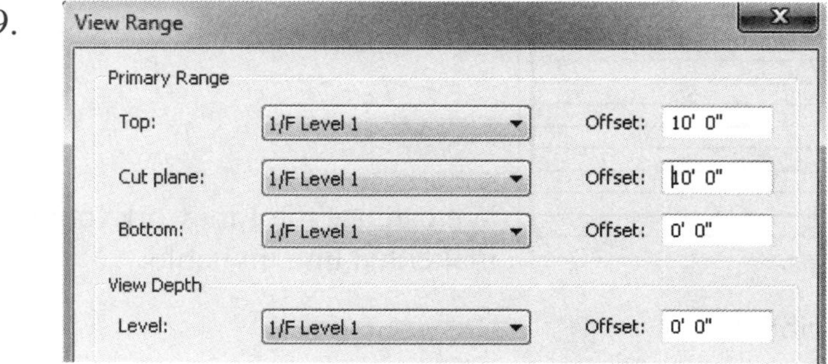

Set the Offset for the Top plane to **10′ 0″**.
Set the Cut Plane Offset to **10′ 0″**.

Press **OK**.

Note: Your dimension values may be different if you are using your own model.

10. Select the **Green Check** under the Mode panel to **Finish Plan Region**.

Mode

11. 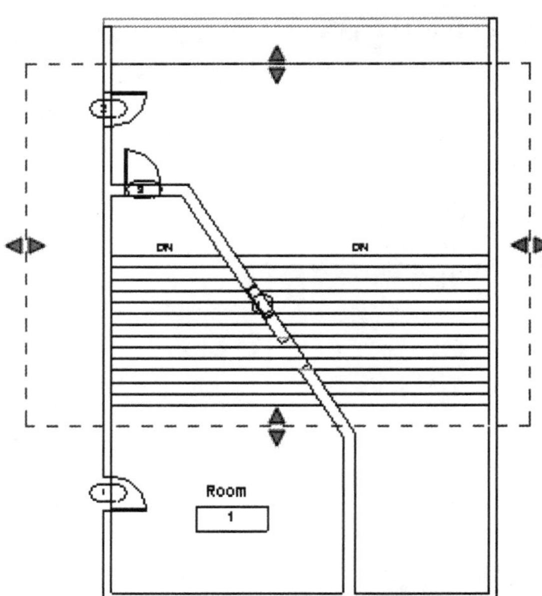

The doors and window are now visible.

12. To turn off the visibility of the Plan Region rectangle in the view, type **VG**.

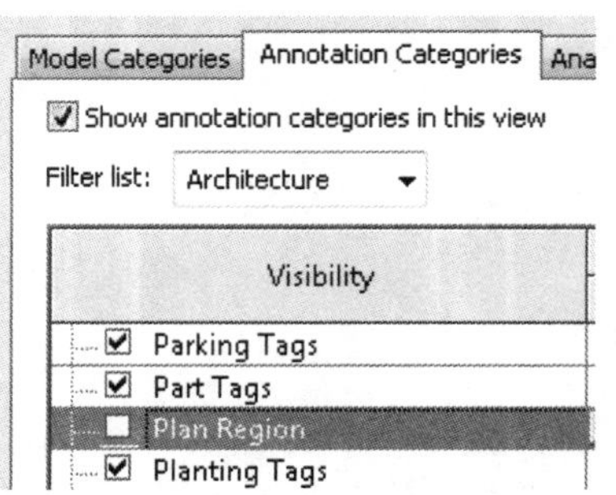

Select the Annotations tab.
Disable **Plan Region**.
Press **OK**.

13. 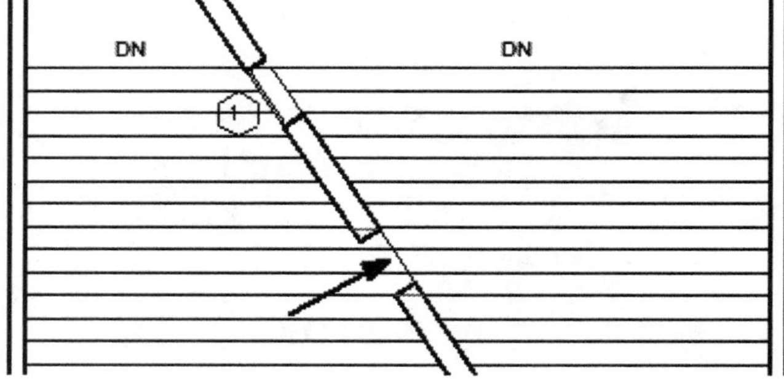

There is a line where the two stairs connect.

We can use the Linework tool to make this line invisible.

14. Activate the Modify ribbon.

15. Select the **Linework** tool under the View panel.

16. Select **Invisible Lines** from the Line Style drop-down list.

17. Select the lines you wish to make invisible.

18. The lines are now invisible.

19. Close without saving.

Exercise 8-8

Creating a Detail View

Drawing Name: ex8-6.rvt
Estimated Time: 40 minutes

This exercise reinforces the following skills:

- Detail Components
- Filled Regions
- Notes

1. Open *ex8-6.rvt.*

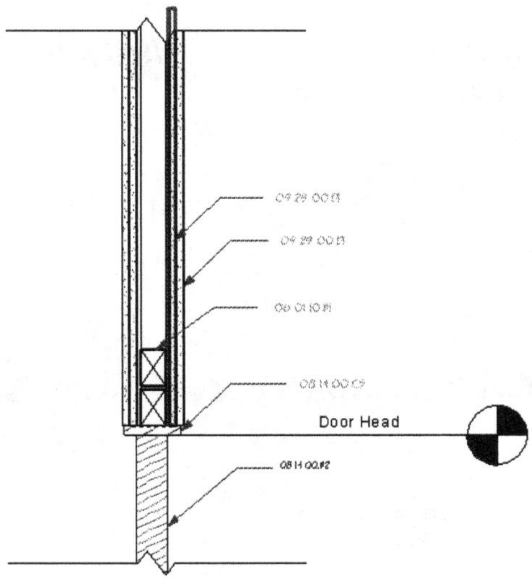

You will create this view of a Head Detail for an interior door using detail components, filled regions, and key notes.

2. Drafting View Activate the **View** ribbon.

   Select **Drafting View**.

3. 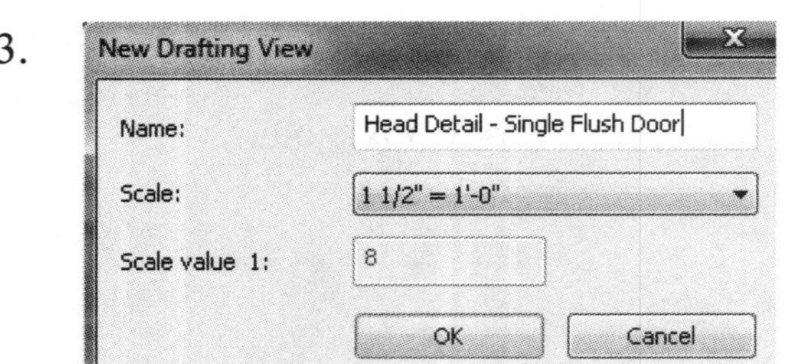

Type **Head Detail – Single Flush Door** for the name.

Press **OK**.

4. Activate the **Insert** Ribbon.

Select **Load Family**.

5. Browse to the *Detail Items* folder under the Imperial library.

6. You will want to load the following detail items:

Gypsum Wallboard - Section

C Studs - Side

Wood Door Frame - Section

To locate the detail components, use the keynotes in the image to guide you. The first four digits indicate the folders where they are located.

7. Load the ***Spot Elevation – Right Aligned*** family from the publisher's website.

When you place the detail components, be sure to use the Type Selector to select the correct size of component to be used.

The structure of the interior wall used in our project:

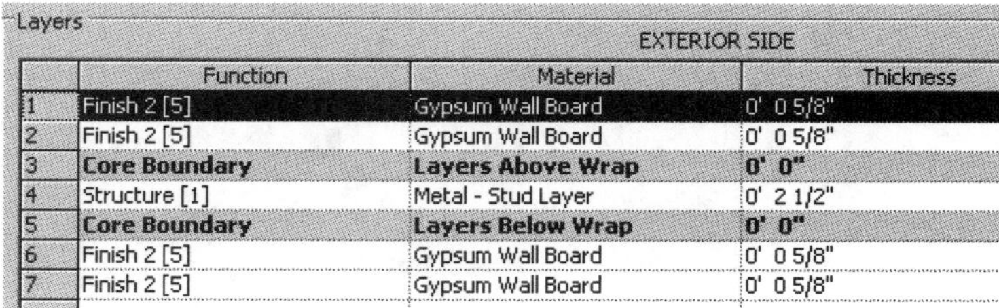

Layers

EXTERIOR SIDE

	Function	Material	Thickness
1	Finish 2 [5]	Gypsum Wall Board	0' 0 5/8"
2	Finish 2 [5]	Gypsum Wall Board	0' 0 5/8"
3	**Core Boundary**	**Layers Above Wrap**	**0' 0"**
4	Structure [1]	Metal - Stud Layer	0' 2 1/2"
5	**Core Boundary**	**Layers Below Wrap**	**0' 0"**
6	Finish 2 [5]	Gypsum Wall Board	0' 0 5/8"
7	Finish 2 [5]	Gypsum Wall Board	0' 0 5/8"

8. Select the **Detail Component** tool from the Annotate ribbon.

9. 

Select **Gypsum Wallboard – Section 5/8″** on the Properties palette.

10. Place two instances of gypsum wall board by drawing two vertical lines.

For the metric view, place one 13 mm section and one 6 mm section.

11. Select the **Detail Component** tool from the Annotate ribbon.

12. 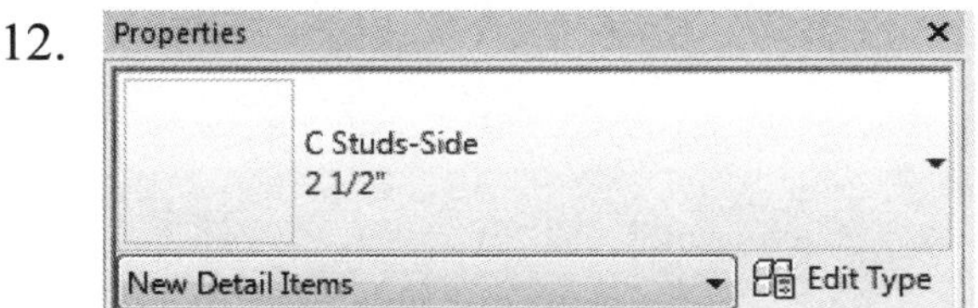

Select **C Studs – Side 2 1/2″** on the Properties palette.

13. 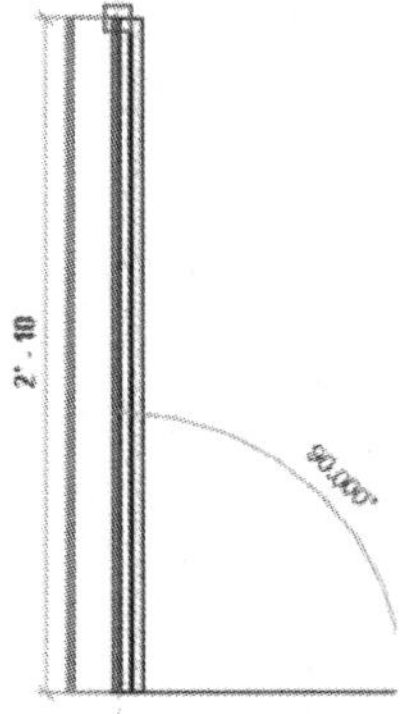

Draw the stud layer on the left side of the gypsum sections.

14. Add two more layers of 5/8″ gypsum wall board on the left side of the stud.

The detail view should show two layers of 5/8″ gypsum board on either side of the metal stud.

15. Select the **Detail Component** tool from the Annotate ribbon.

16. Select the **Load Family** tool from the ribbon.

17. 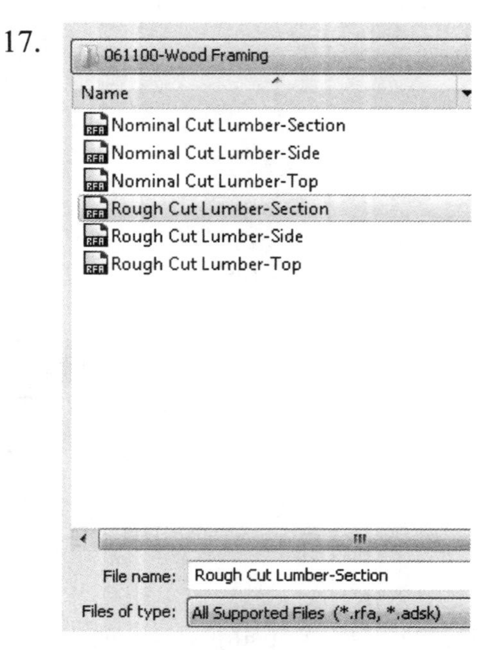

Browse to the *061100 – Wood Framing folder* under Detail Items.

Select **Rough Cut Lumber – Section**.

18. 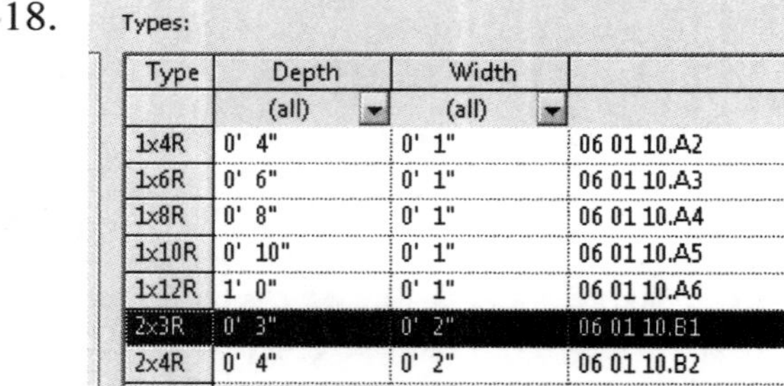

Types:

Type	Depth	Width	
	(all)	(all)	
1x4R	0' 4"	0' 1"	06 01 10.A2
1x6R	0' 6"	0' 1"	06 01 10.A3
1x8R	0' 8"	0' 1"	06 01 10.A4
1x10R	0' 10"	0' 1"	06 01 10.A5
1x12R	1' 0"	0' 1"	06 01 10.A6
2x3R	0' 3"	0' 2"	06 01 10.B1
2x4R	0' 4"	0' 2"	06 01 10.B2

right for each family listed on the left OK

Locate the **2x3R** size.

Press **OK**.

19. 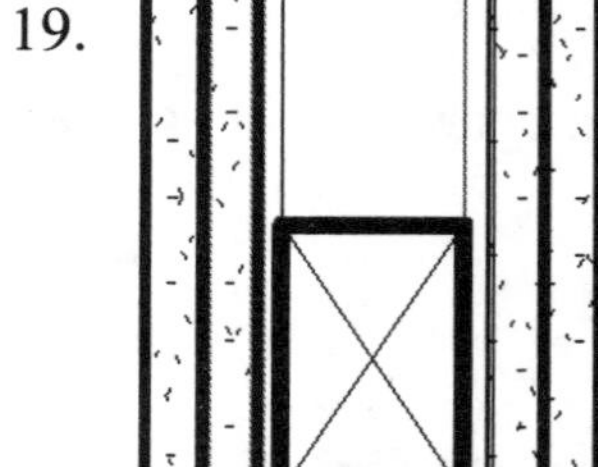

Place the headers between the gypsum board assemblies.

20. Select the **Detail Component** tool from the Annotate ribbon.

21. Select **Wood Door Frame Section 4 3/4″** from the Properties palette.

22. Place the door frame below the other detail components.

23. Select the **Filled Region** tool.

24. Select **Filled region: Wood 1** from the Properties palette.

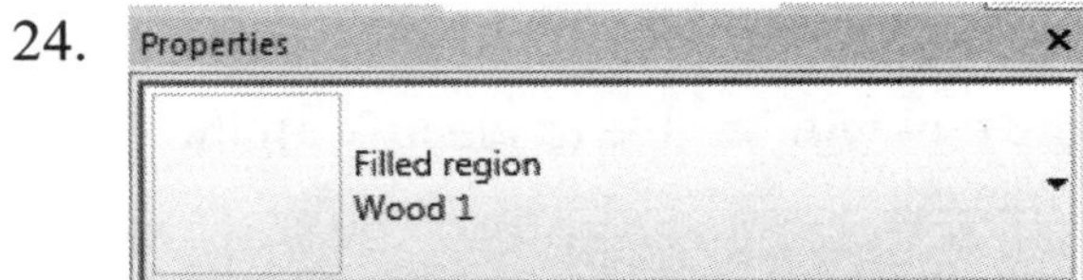

25. Select **rectangle** from the Draw panel on the ribbon.

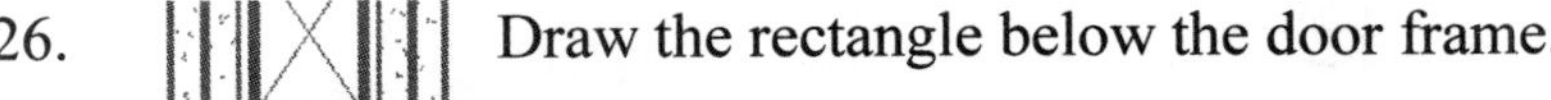

26. Draw the rectangle below the door frame.

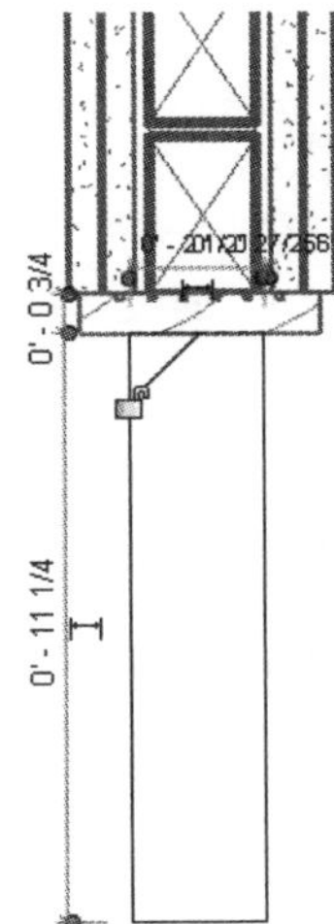

27. Select **Green Check** on the ribbon to exit filled region mode.

28. 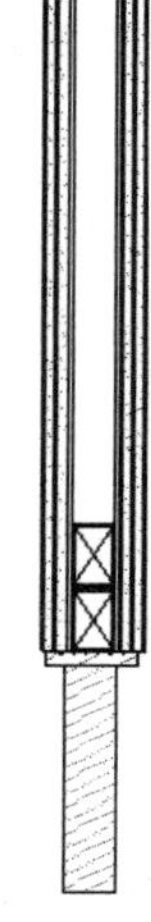 Place the door using a filled region with a wood fill pattern.

29. 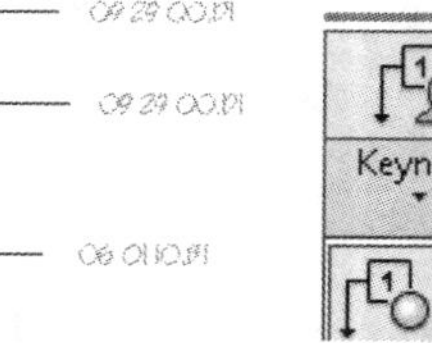

Add the keynotes.

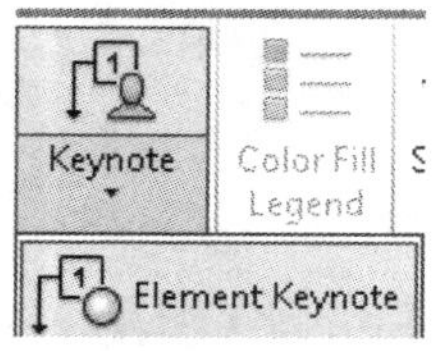

The element keynote tool will be able to identify all the detail components placed.

The filled region has to be identified using a text note.

30. 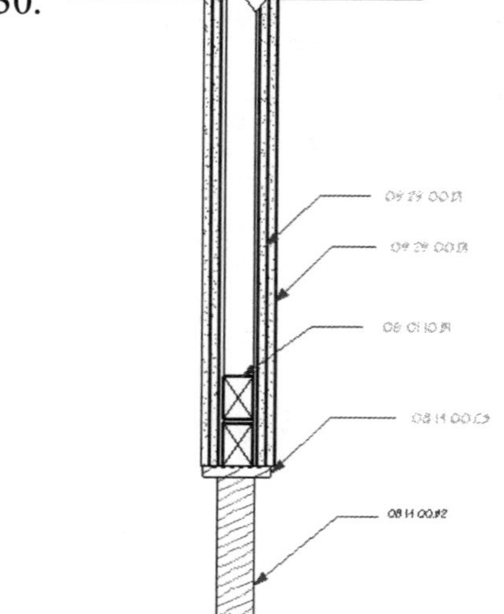

Add the break lines.

Select the Detail Component tool.

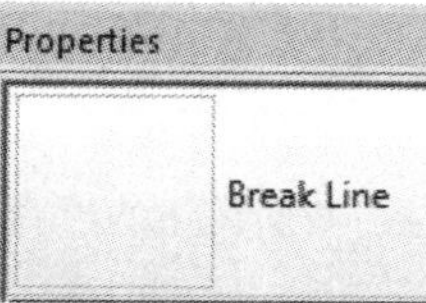

Select **Break Line** from the Properties palette.

31.  Symbol Select the Symbol tool from the Annotate ribbon.

32.  On the Properties palette:

Select *Spot Elevation – Right Aligned Label.*

33. 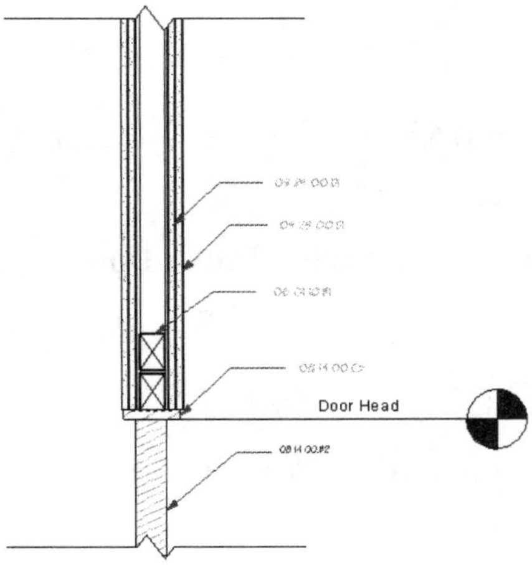 Place the symbol as shown.

34. Save as *ex8-8.rvt.*

Exercise 8-9
Adding a Callout

Drawing Name: ex8-8.rvt
Estimated Time: 10 minutes

This exercise reinforces the following skills:

- Detail Components
- Notes
- Callouts

This exercise assumes that the user has created the drafting view in Ex8-8.

1.  Open *ex8-8.rvt.'*

2. Activate **Level 1**.

3.  Section Activate the **View** ribbon.

Select the **Section** tool.

4. Place a section so it is creating a view of one of the single flush interior doors.

5. Activate **(Building Section) Section 1** in the browser.

6. Rename the section view **Single Flush Door Elevation**.

   Press **OK**.

7. Adjust the crop region for the view.

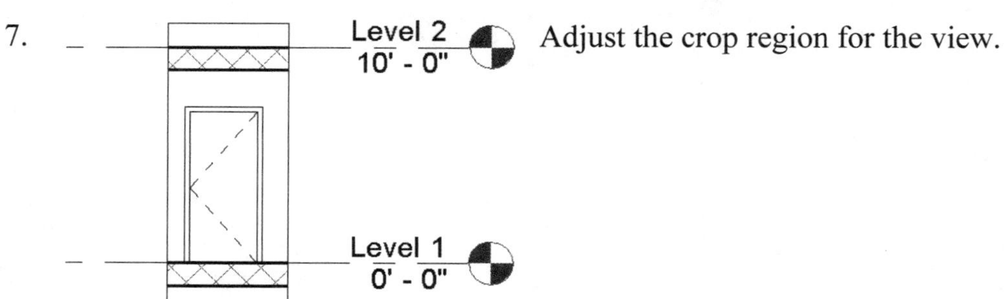

8. On the View ribbon, select the **Callout** tool on the Create panel.

9. On the Options bar:

Enable **Reference other view**:
Select the **Drafting View: Head Detail - Single Flush Door**.

10. Locate the callout to enclose the top of the interior door.

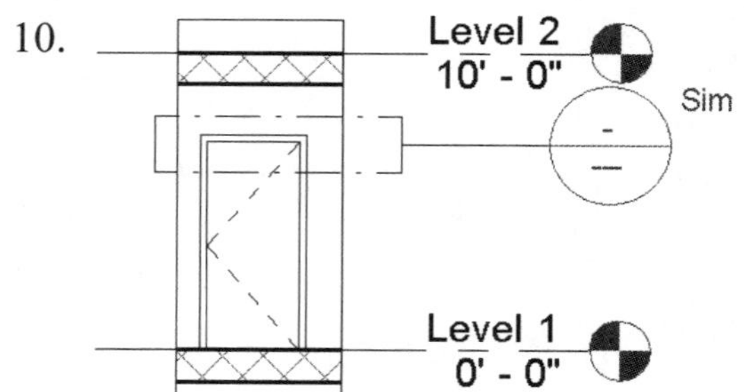

Use the grips to position the Detail Callout.

The detail number and sheet number will be filled out when you place the view on a sheet automatically.

11. Double click on the callout bubble to open the detail view.

12. Save as *ex8-9.rvt*.

Exercise 8-10

Adding a Detail to a Sheet

Drawing Name: ex8-9.rvt
Estimated Time: 15 minutes

This exercise reinforces the following skills:

- Views
- Sheets
- Schedules
- Keynote Legends

This exercise assumes that the user has created the drafting view in Ex8-8.

1. Open *ex8-9.rvt.*

2. Sheets (all)
   A101 - First Level Floor Plan
   A102 - Level 2 Ceiling Plan
   A201 - Exterior Elevations
   A601 - Door Schedule
   A602 - Glazing Schedule
   A603 - Lobby Keynotes
   AD501 - Details

   Activate **AD501 - Details** sheet.

3. Add the Head Detail onto the sheet.

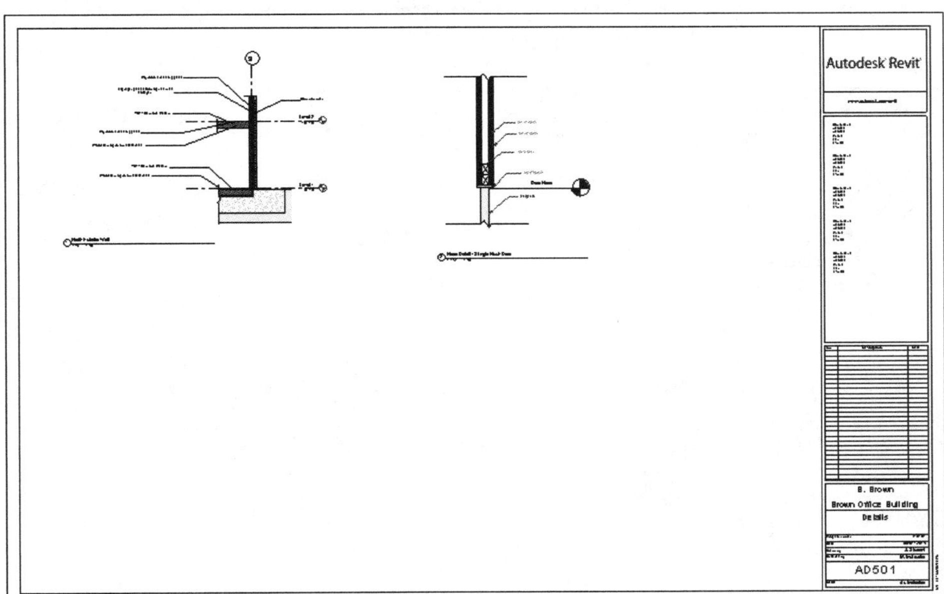

4. Legends
   Legend
   Keynote Legend
   Keynote Legend

   Activate the View ribbon.

   Select **Legend→Keynote Legend**.

5. Type **Single Flush Door Keynotes**.

Press **OK**.

6. 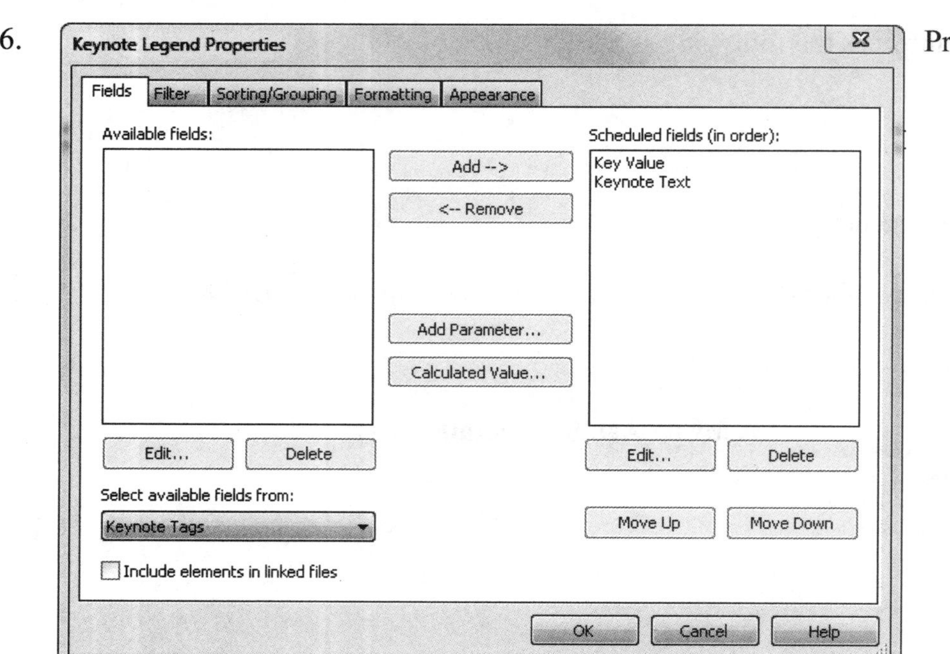

Press **OK**.

7. <Single Flush Door Keynotes>

A	B
Key Value	Keynote Text
04 21 00.A1	Standard Brick - 3/8" Joint
06 01 10.B1	2x3R
07 31 00.A1	Asphalt Shingles
08 14 00.C3	Wood Door Frame
08 81 00.F1	1" Clear Insulating Glass
09 29 00.D1	5/8" Gypsum Wallboard
09 51 00.A6	Square Edge (3/4 x 24 x 48)
09 65 00.A2	Vinyl Composition Tile
09 72 00.A1	Vinyl Wallcovering
09 91 00.A2	Semi-Gloss Paint Finish
26 51 00.A5	2' X 4' Surface Mounted Modular Fluorescent Fixture

The Keynote Legend appears in the view.

Note there are some materials listed we don't need to call out for the door.

8. 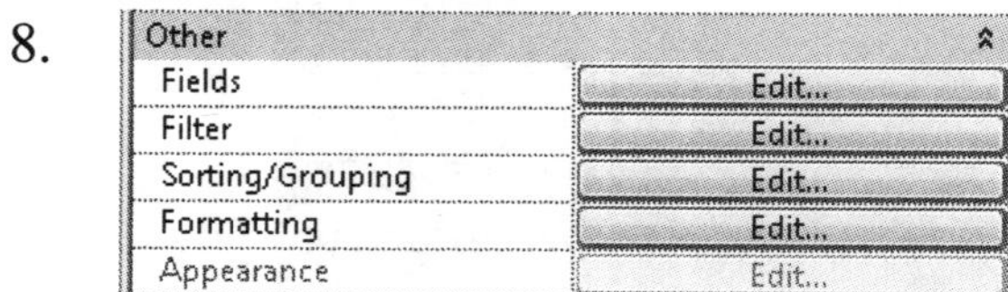

Select the **Edit** button next to Filter.

9.

Keynote Legend Properties

Fields | Filter | Sorting/Grouping | Formatting | Appearance

Filter by: (none)

And: (none)

And: (none)

And: (none)

Filter by sheet

Enable **Filter by sheet** at the bottom of the dialog.

Press **OK**.

10.

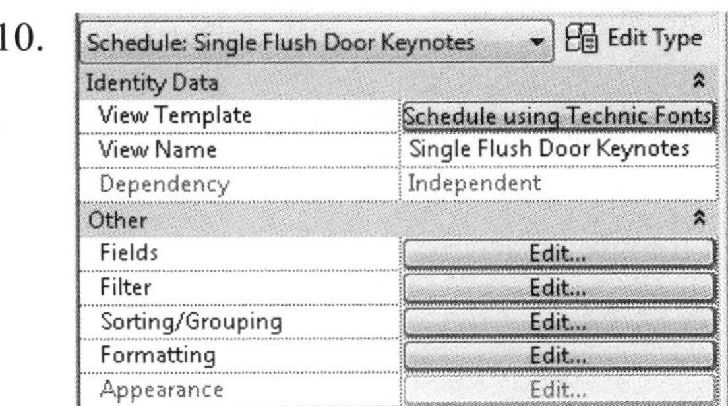

Apply the **Schedule using Technic Fonts** View Template.

11.

Sheets (all)
A101 - First Level Floor Plan
A201 - Exterior Elevations
A601 - Door Schedule
A602 - Glazing Schedule
A603 - LOBBY KEYNOTES
AD501 - Details
Families

Activate **AD501 - Details** sheet.

12.

Legends
FINISH SCHEDULE KEYS
Single Flush Door Keynotes

Locate the Keynote Legend.

13.

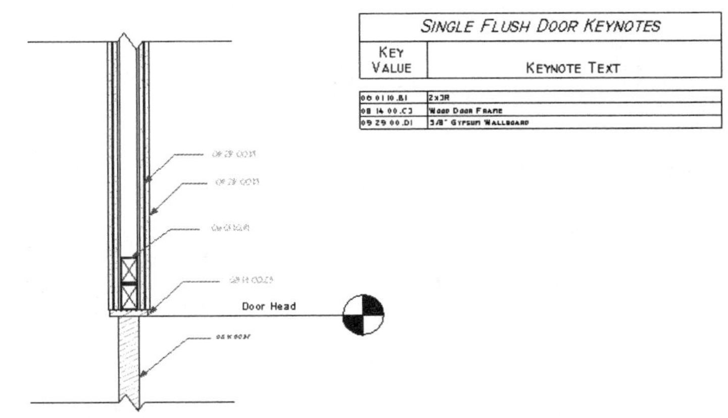

Drag and drop it onto the Details sheet.

Notice that the legend automatically changes to reflect the keynotes on the view on the sheet.

Legend views can be placed on multiple sheets.

14. Head Detail - Single Flush Door 1 1/2" = 1'-0" — Zoom into the Head Detail.

The bubble is filled in with the number 2. This is the detail number.

15. Schedules/Quantities: Door Details, Door Schedule, Glazing Schedule, Lobby Keynotes, Room Schedule — Activate the **Door Details** schedule.

16. Modify the detail number for the Head Detail for the interior single flush doors.

<DOOR DETAILS>

A	B	C	D	E	F	G	H
		SIZE			DETAILS		
Door No	Door Type	W	H	THK	Head Detail	Jamb Detail	Threshold D
1	36" x 84"	3' - 0"	7' - 0"	0' - 2"	HD2	JD4	TD4
2	34" x 84"	2' - 10"	7' - 0"	0' - 2"	HD2	JD4	TD4
3	34" x 84"	2' - 10"	7' - 0"	0' - 2"	HD2	JD4	TD4
4	34" x 84"	2' - 10"	7' - 0"	0' - 2"	HD2	JD4	TD4
5	72" x 78"	6' - 0"	6' - 6"	0' - 2"	HD3	JD3	TD3

17. Save as *ex8-10.rvt.*

Exercise 8-11

Importing a Detail View

Drawing Name: ex8-10.rvt
Estimated Time: 20 minutes

This exercise reinforces the following skills:

- Import CAD
- Sheets
- Detail Views

1. Open *ex8-10.rvt.*

2. 

Activate the Insert ribbon.

Select **Insert from File→Insert Views from File.**

3. File name: Curtain Wall Head Detail — Files of type: All Supported Files (*.rvt, *.adsk)

Locate the **Curtain Wall Head Detail** file available on the publisher's website. Press **Open**.

4. A preview of the detail will appear.

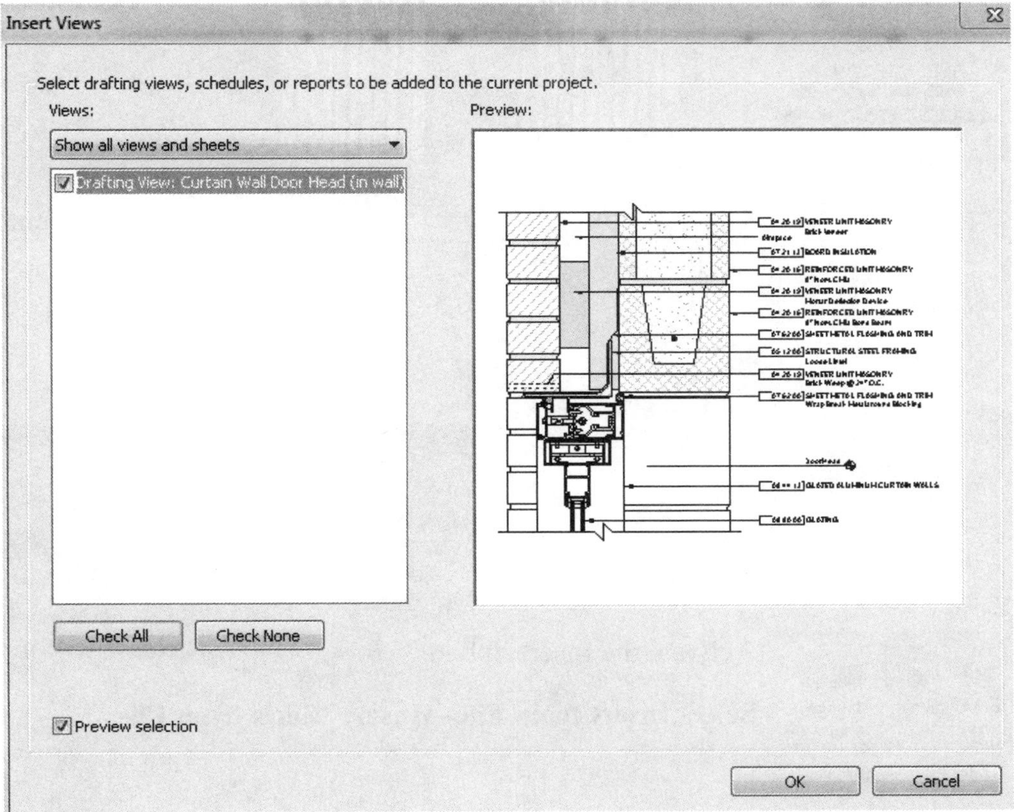

Press **OK**.

5. 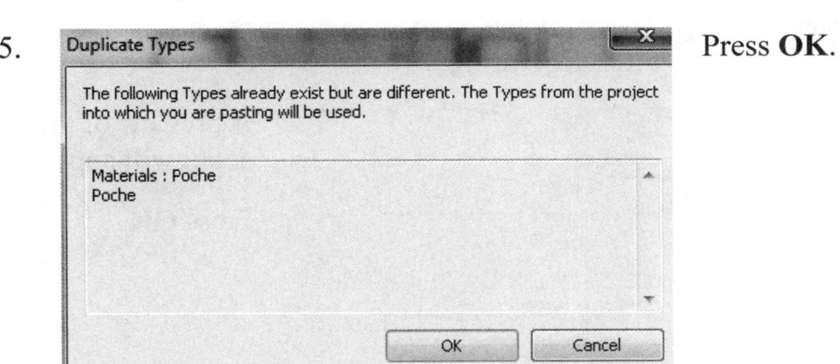

Press **OK**.

6. Properties
Drafting View
Detail
Drafting View: Curtain Wall Door Head (in
Edit Type

In the Type Selector, change the Drafting View to **Detail**.

7. Drafting Views (Detail)
Curtain Wall Door Head (in wall) Detail
Head Detail - Single Flush Door

The Drafting View is listed in the Project Browser.

8. Sheets (all)
A101 - First Level Floor Plan
A102 - Level 1 - East Wing
A103 - Level 1 - West Wing
A201 - Exterior Elevations
A601 - Door Schedule
A602 - Glazing Schedule
A603 - LOBBY KEYNOTES
AD501 - Details

Activate the **AD501 - Details** sheet.

9. 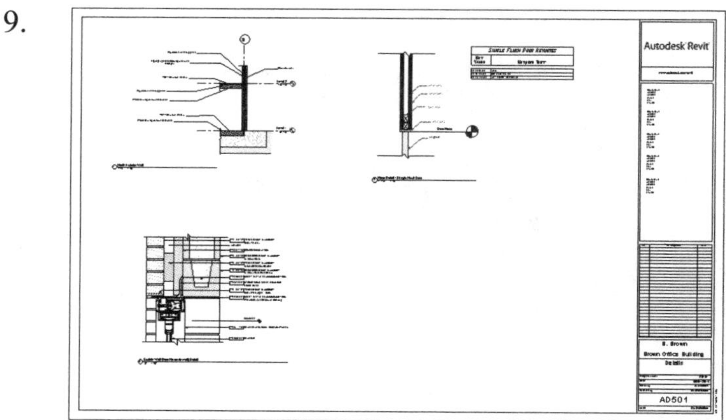

Drag and drop the view onto the sheet.

10. Insert from File
Image
Manage Images
Insert Views from File

Activate the Insert ribbon.

Select **Insert from File→Insert Views from File**.

11. File name: Curtain Wall Jamb Detail
Files of type: All Supported Files (*.rvt, *.adsk)

Locate the **Curtain Wall Jamb Detail** file available on the publisher's website.
Press **Open**.

12. 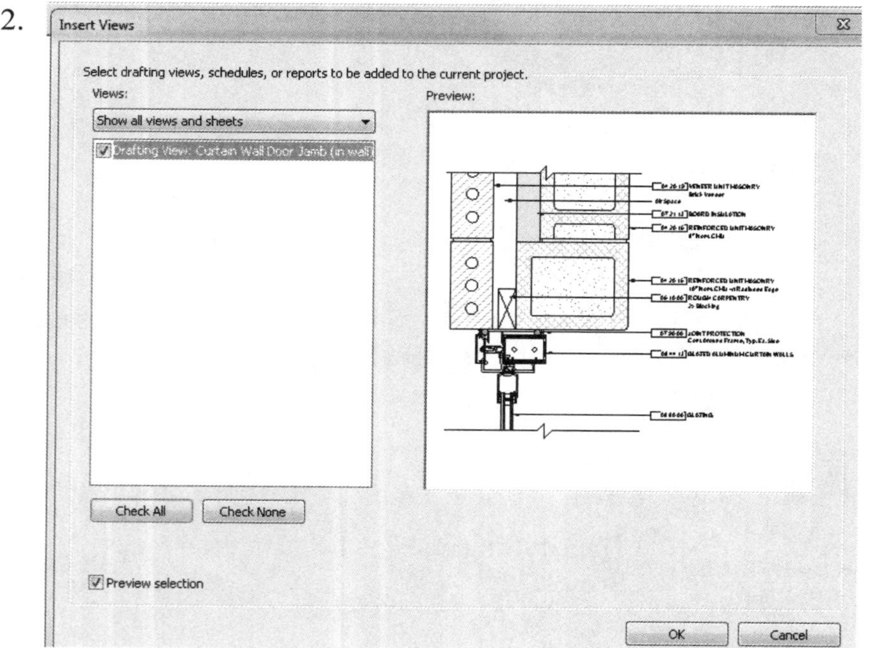

A preview of the detail will appear.

Press **OK**.

13. 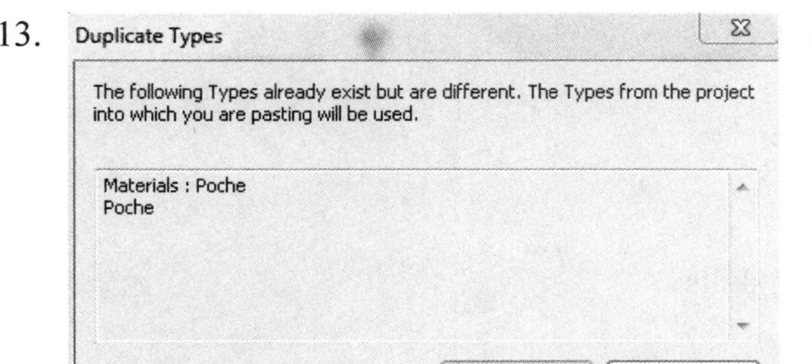

Press **OK**.

14. Properties
Drafting View
Detail
Drafting View: Curtain Wall Door Jamb (in
Edit Type

In the Type Selector, change the Drafting View to **Detail**.

15. Drafting Views (Detail)
Curtain Wall Door Head (in wall) Detail
Curtain Wall Door Jamb (in wall) Detail
Head Detail - Single Flush Door

The Drafting View is listed in the Project Browser.

16. Sheets (all)
A101 - First Level Floor Plan
A102 - Level 2 Ceiling Plan
A201 - Exterior Elevations
A601 - Door Schedule
A602 - Glazing Schedule
A603 - Lobby Keynotes
AD501 - Details

Activate the **AD501 - Details** sheet.

17. Drag and drop the **Curtain Wall Jamb Detail** view onto the sheet.

Note that the Curtain Wall Head Detail Number is 3. Note that the Curtain Wall Jamb Detail is 4.

18. Save as *ex8-11.rvt*.

Exercise 8-12
Using a Matchline

Drawing Name: ex8-11.rvt
Estimated Time: 30 minutes

This exercise reinforces the following skills:

- Matchline
- Sheets
- Views

1. Open *ex8-11.rvt.*

2. 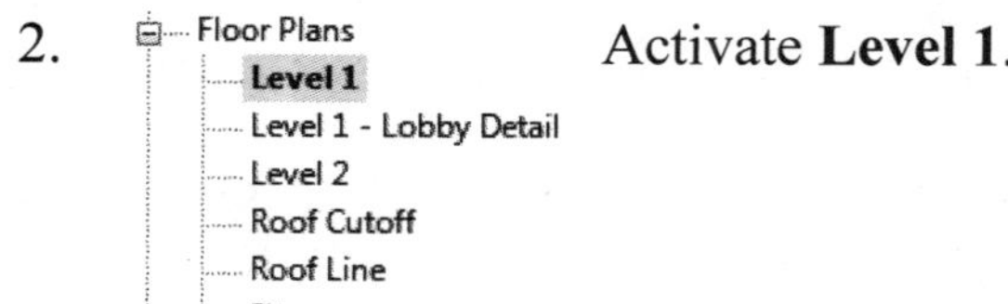

Activate **Level 1**.

3. Duplicate View | Convert to independent view | Apply Dependent Views... | Duplicate | Duplicate with Detailing | Duplicate as a Dependent

   Right click on **Level 1** in the browser.
   Select **Duplicate View→ Duplicate with Detailing**.

4. 

Rename the view **Level 1-East Wing**.

   Press **OK**.

5. 

Right click on **Level 1** in the browser.
Select **Duplicate View → Duplicate with Detailing**.

6. Name: Level 1 - West Wing | OK

   Rename the view **Level 1-West Wing**.

   Press **OK**.

7. 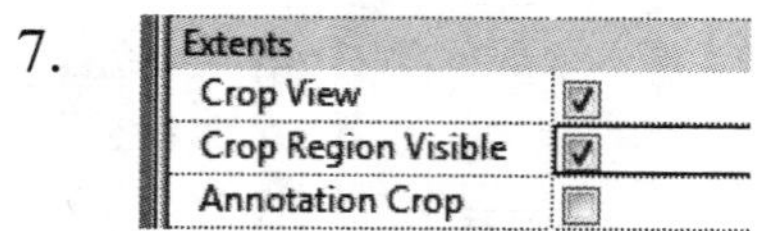

Activate the view **Level 1-West Wing** floor plan.

   In the Properties pane:
   Enable **Crop View**.
   Enable **Crop Region Visible**.

8. 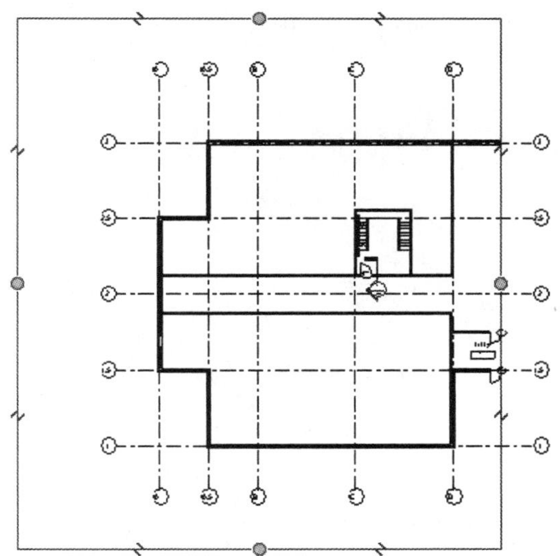

Use the grips on the crop region to only show the west side of the floor plan.

9. Level 1 - West Wing / Level 1- East Wing / Level 2

Activate **Level 1 - East Wing**.

10. 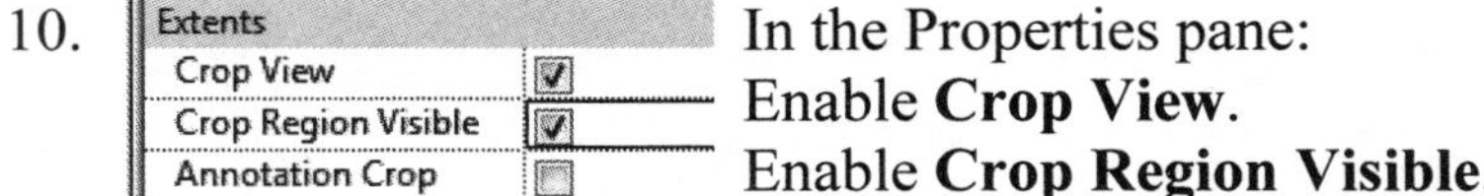

In the Properties pane:
Enable **Crop View**.
Enable **Crop Region Visible**.

11. Use the grips on the crop region to only show the east side of the floor plan.

12. View

Activate the **View** ribbon.

13. 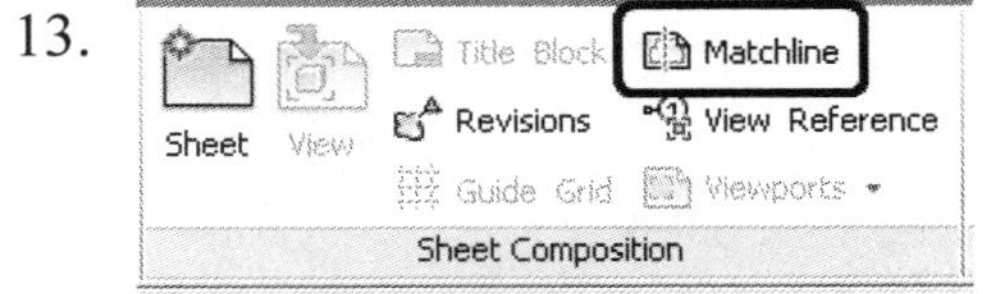

Under the Sheet Composition panel:

Select the **Matchline** tool.

14. 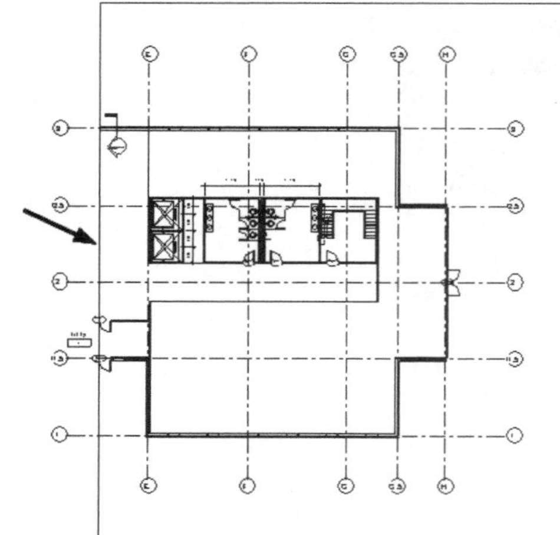

Draw a line where the view is cropped.

15. 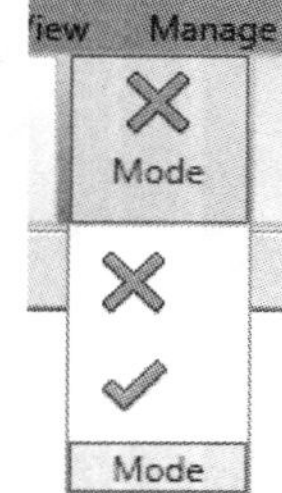

Select the **Green Check** under Mode to finish the matchline.

16. 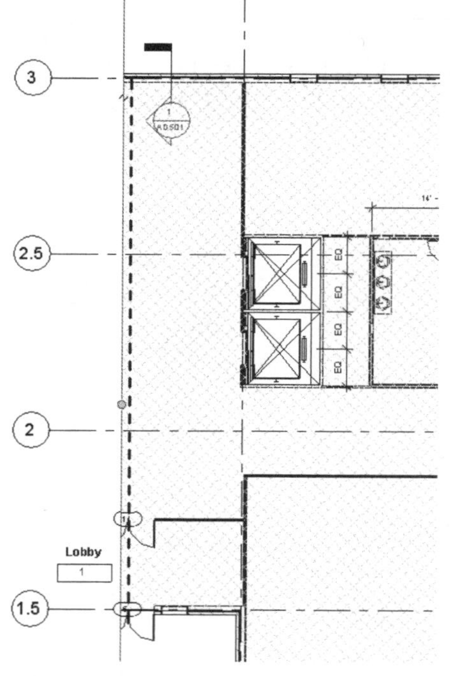

Adjust the crop region so that you see the match line.

17.

Extents	
Crop View	☑
Crop Region Visible	☐
Annotation Crop	☐

Disable **Crop Region Visible** in the Properties pane.

18.

Level 1 - Lobby Detail
Level 1 - West Wing
Level 1- East Wing

Activate the **Level 1 - West Wing** floor plan.

19. 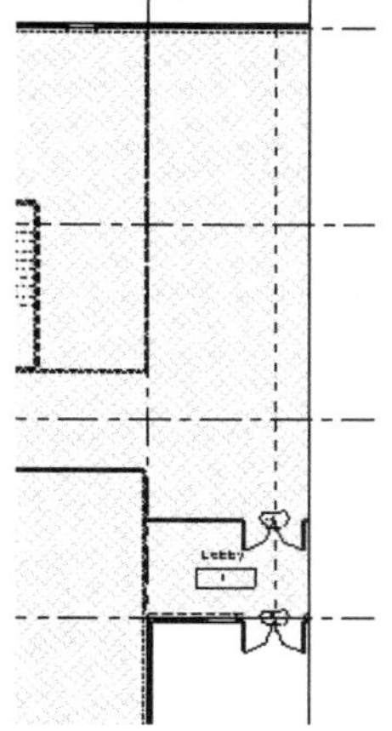

You should see a match line in this view as well.

20.

Extents	
Crop View	☑
Crop Region Visible	☐
Annotation Crop	☐

Disable **Crop Region Visible** in the Properties pane.

21.

Sheet Co... Windows
Sheet Title Block Matchline
View Revisions View Reference
Guide Grid Viewports
Sheet Composition

Add a new **Sheet** using the Sheet Composition panel on the View ribbon.

Press **OK** to accept the default title block.

22. 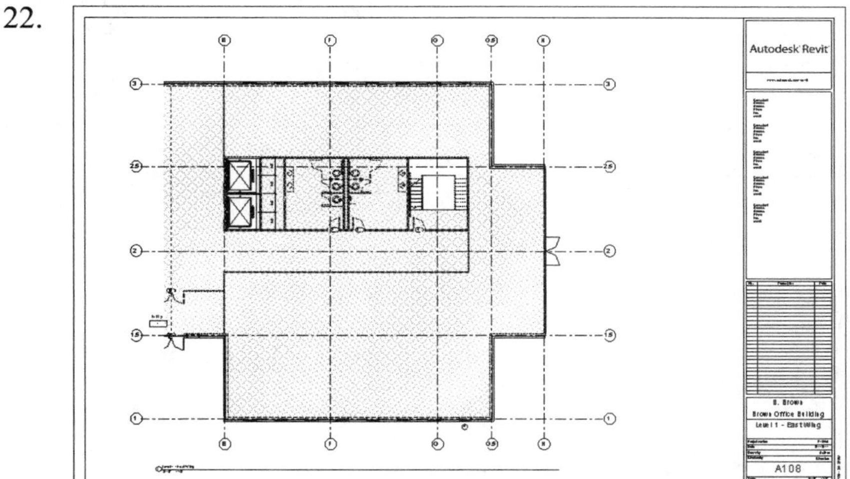

Place the **Level 1- East Wing** floor plan on the sheet.

Adjust the scale so it fills the sheet.

Adjust the grid lines, if needed.

Turn off the visibility of the elevation markers.

23.

Current Revision	
Approved By	M. Instructor
Designed By	J. Student
Checked By	M. Instructor
Sheet Number	A102
Sheet Name	Level 1 - East Wing
Sheet Issue Date	03/17/12
Appears In Sheet List	☑
Revisions on Sheet	Edit...
Other	
File Path	
Drawn By	J. Student
Guide Grid	<None>

Change the Sheet Number to **A102**.
Name the sheet **Level 1 - East Wing**.

Enter in your name and your instructor's name.

24. 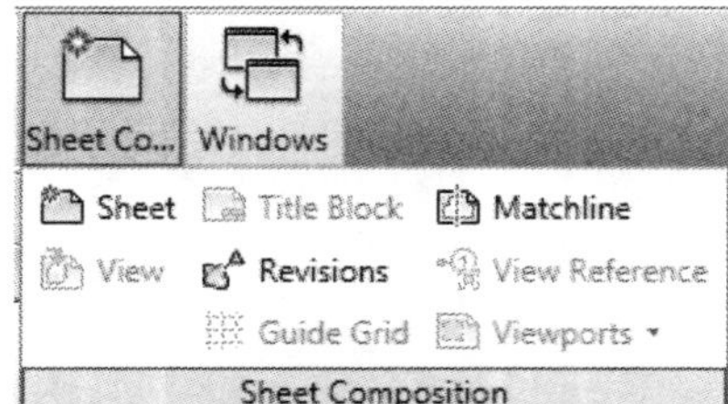

Add a new **Sheet** using the Sheet Composition panel on the View ribbon.

Press **OK** to accept the default title block.

25. Place the **Level 1- West Wing** floor plan on the sheet.

Adjust the scale so it fills the sheet.

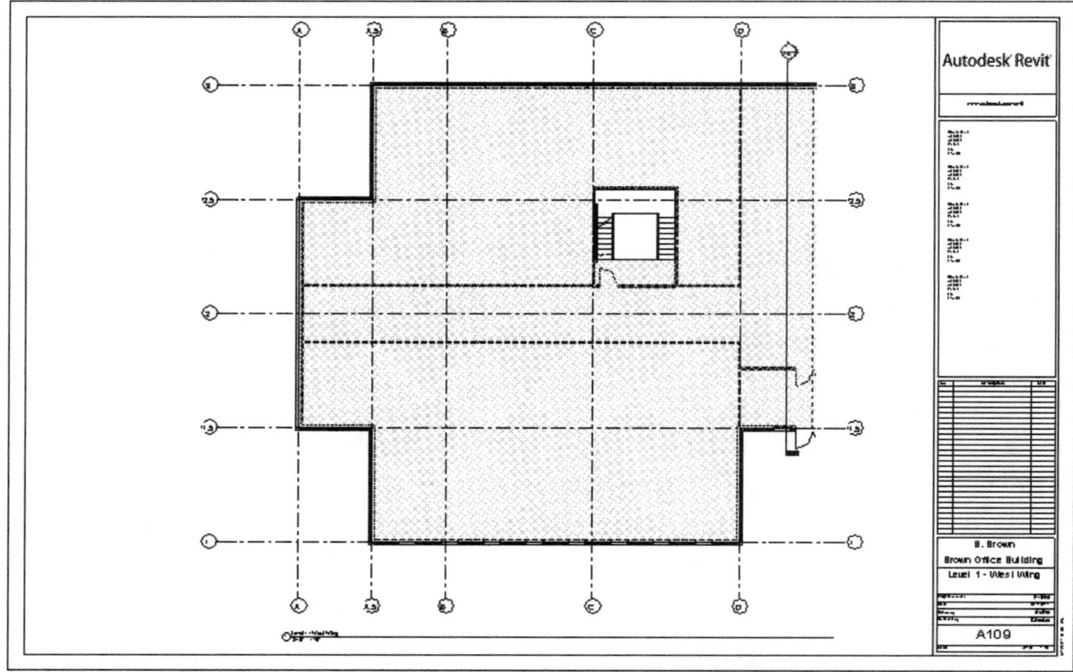

Turn off the visibility of the elevation markers.

26.

Current Revision	
Approved By	M. Instructor
Designed By	J. Student
Checked By	M. Instructor
Sheet Number	A103
Sheet Name	Level 1 - West Wing
Sheet Issue Date	03/17/12
Appears In Sheet List	☑
Revisions on Sheet	Edit...
Other	
File Path	
Drawn By	J. Student
Guide Grid	<None>

Change the Sheet Number to **A103**.

Name the sheet **Level 1 -West Wing**.

Enter in your name and your instructor's name.

27. Save the file as *ex8-12.rvt*.

Exercise 8-13
Updating a Schedule using Shared Parameters

Drawing Name: ex8-12.rvt
Estimated Time: 20 minutes

This exercise reinforces the following skills:

- ❑ Sheet List Schedule
- ❑ Sheets

1. Open *ex8-12.rvt.*

2. 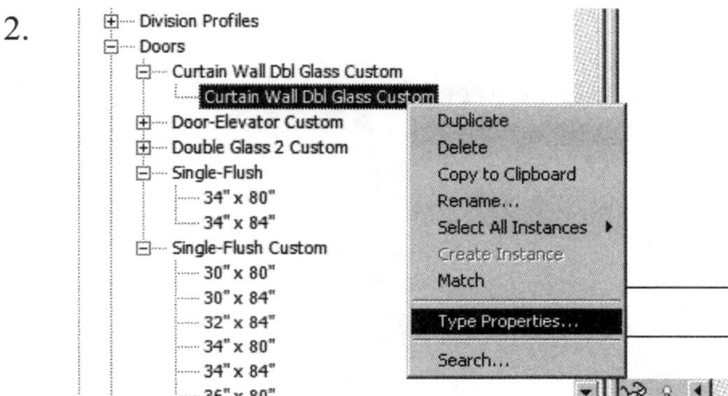

Locate the Curtain Wall Dbl Glass Custom in the Project Browser. Right click and select **Type Properties**.

3. 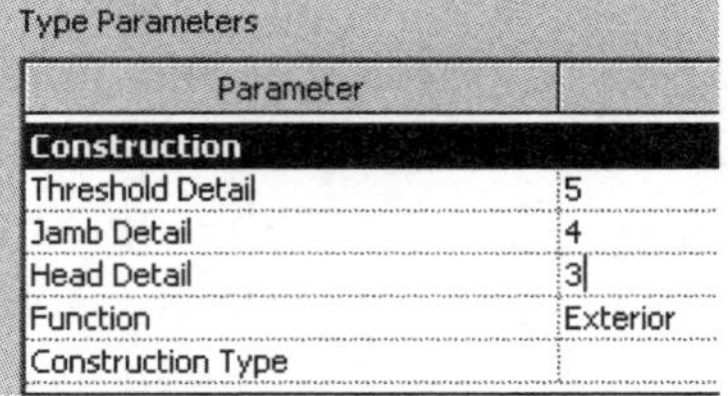

Enter in the correct numbers for the Threshold, Jamb and Head Details.

Press **OK**.

4. Schedules/Quantities
   - Door Details
   - Door Schedule
   - Glazing Schedule
   - Lobby Keynotes
   - Room Schedule

   Activate the **Door Details** schedule.

5. Door Details

		SIZE			DETAILS		
Door No.	Door Type	W	H	THK	Head	Jamb	Threshold
1	36" x 84"	3' - 0"	7' - 0"	0' - 2"	2		
2	34" x 84"	2' - 10"	7' - 0"	0' - 2"	2		
3	34" x 80"	2' - 10"	6' - 8"	0' - 2"	2		
4	34" x 84"	2' - 10"	7' - 0"	0' - 2"	2		
5	72" x 78"	6' - 0"	6' - 6"	0' - 2"			
7	36" x 84"	3' - 0"	7' - 0"	0' - 2"	2		
8	36" x 84"	3' - 0"	7' - 0"	0' - 2"	2		
9	36" x 84"	3' - 0"	7' - 0"	0' - 2"	2		
10	36" x 84"	3' - 0"	7' - 0"	0' - 2"	2		
11	12000 x 2290 Opening	2' - 11 7/16"	7' - 6 5/32"	0' - 1 3/16"			
12	12000 x 2290 Opening	2' - 11 7/16"	7' - 6 5/32"	0' - 1 3/16"			
13	Curtain Wall Dbl Glass C	6' - 6 9/16"	7' - 8 1/4"		3	4	5
14	72" x 78"	6' - 0"	6' - 6"	0' - 2"			

Notice that the schedule has updated.

6. Save as *ex8-13.rvt.*

Exercise 8-14
Create a Sheet List

Drawing Name: ex8-13.rvt
Estimated Time: 20 minutes

This exercise reinforces the following skills:

- Sheet List Schedule
- Sheets

1. Open *ex8-13.rvt.*

2. Activate the **View** ribbon.

   Select **Schedule→Sheet List**.

3. 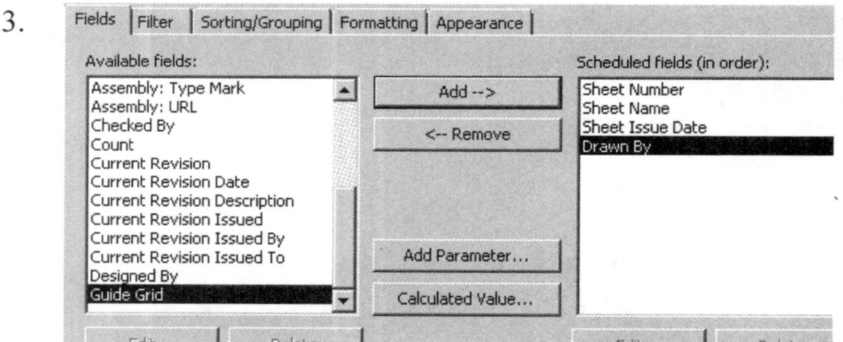

   Add the following fields in this order:
   - Sheet Number
   - Sheet Name
   - Sheet Issue Date
   - Drawn By

4. 

   Select the Sorting/Grouping tab.
   Sort by **Sheet Number**.

5. 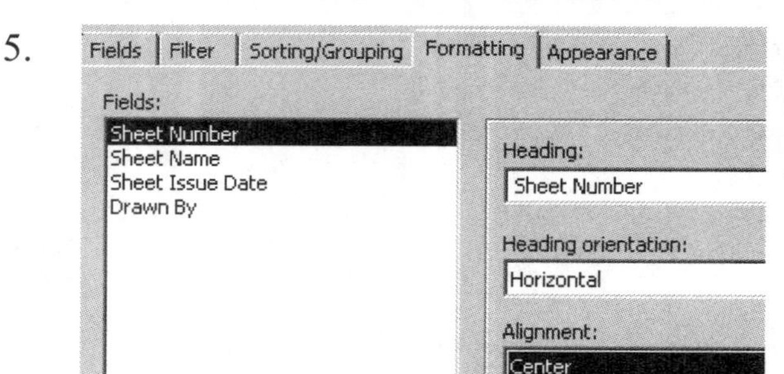

   Select the Formatting tab.

   Highlight the Sheet Number field.
   Change the Alignment to **Center**.

6. Highlight the Sheet Issue Date.
Change the Heading to **Issue Date**.
Change the Alignment to **Center**.

7. 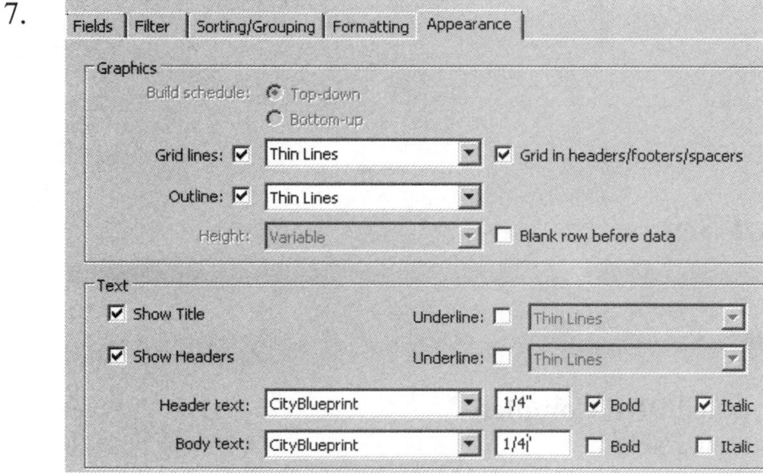

Select the Appearance tab.
Enable Grid lines.
Enable Outline
Enable Grid in headers/ footer/spacers.
Disable blank row before data.
Enable Show Title.
Enable Show Headers.
Change the font to CityBlueprint.
Change the font size to 1/4″.
Enable bold and italic for the header text.
Press **OK**.

8.

Sheet List			
Sheet Numbe	Sheet Name	Issue Date	Drawn By
A101	First Level Floor Plan	03/14/12	J. Student
A102	Level 1 - East Wing	03/17/12	Author
A103	Level 1 - West Wing	03/17/12	J. Student
A201	Exterior Elevations	03/16/12	J. Student
A601	Door Schedule	03/16/12	Author
A602	Glazing Schedule	03/16/12	J. Student
A603	LOBBY KEYNOTES	03/16/12	J STUDENT
AD501	Details	03/16/12	J. Student

The Sheet List appears.

This is a good way to check if you added your name as the Author to all sheets.

Can you find a sheet without your name?

9. Activate the **View** ribbon.
Select **New Sheet**.
Select the D-size title block.

10. Drag and drop the sheet list schedule on to the sheet.

Sheet List			
Sheet Number	***Sheet Name***	***Issue Date***	***Drawn By***
A101	First Level Floor Plan	03/14/12	J. Student
A102	Level 1 - East Wing	03/17/12	J. Student
A103	Level 1 - West Wing	03/17/12	J. Student
A104	Unnamed	03/17/12	Author
A201	Exterior Elevations	03/16/12	J. Student
A601	Door Schedule	03/16/12	J. Student
A602	Glazing Schedule	03/16/12	J. Student
A603	LOBBY KEYNOTES	03/16/12	J. Student
AD501	Details	03/16/12	J. Student

11.

Approved By	M. Instructor
Designed By	J. Student
Checked By	M. Instructor
Sheet Number	0.0
Sheet Name	Cover Sheet
Sheet Issue Date	03/17/12
Appears In Sheet List	☐
Revisions on Sheet	Edit...
Other	
File Path	
Drawn By	J. Student
Guide Grid	<None>

Fill in the properties for the sheet.
Sheet Number should be **0.0**.
Sheet Name should be **Cover Sheet**.
Uncheck **Appears in Sheet List**.

12. Save as *ex8-14.rvt*.

Exercise 8-15

Create a PDF Document Set

Drawing Name: ex8-14.rvt
Estimated Time: 10 minutes

Revit comes with a PDF writer called **PDF Complete**.
This exercise reinforces the following skills:

- Printing

1. Open *ex8-14.rvt*.

2. 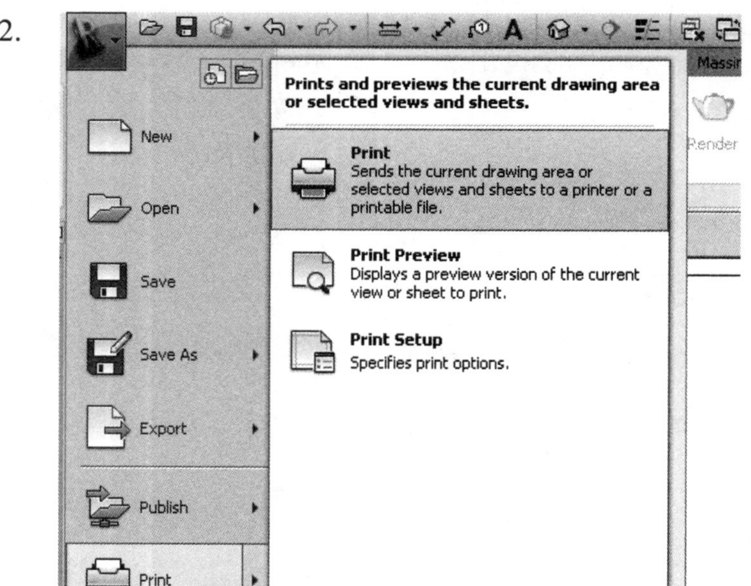

In the Application Menu:

Select **Print→Print**.

3. 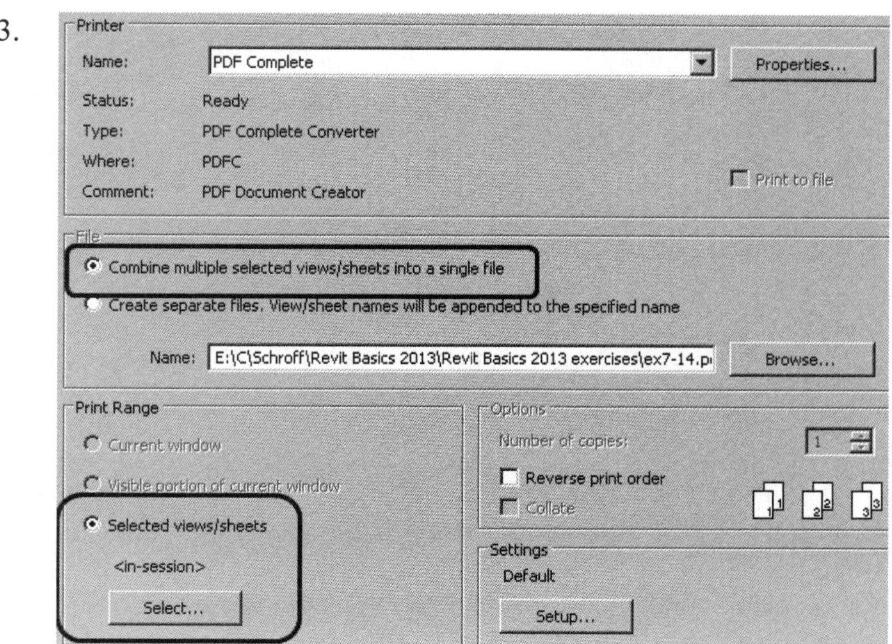

Select **PDF Complete** as the printer.

Enable **combine multiple selected views/ sheets into a single file**.

Enable **Selected views/sheets**.

Press the **Select** button to select which sheets to print.

4. On the bottom of the dialog, enable **Sheets** only.

5. 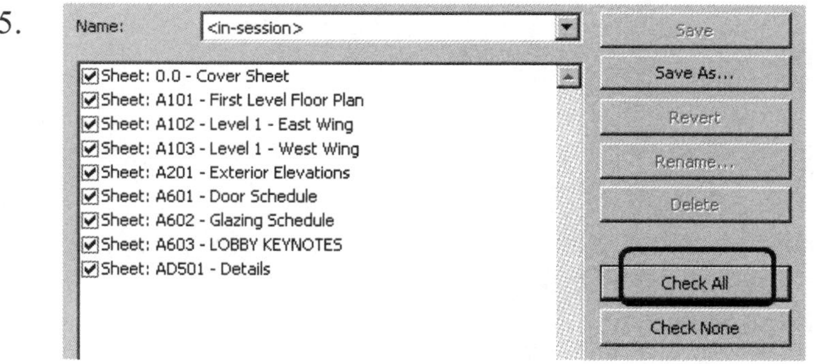

Select **Check All** to select all the sheets in your project.

Press **OK**.

6. 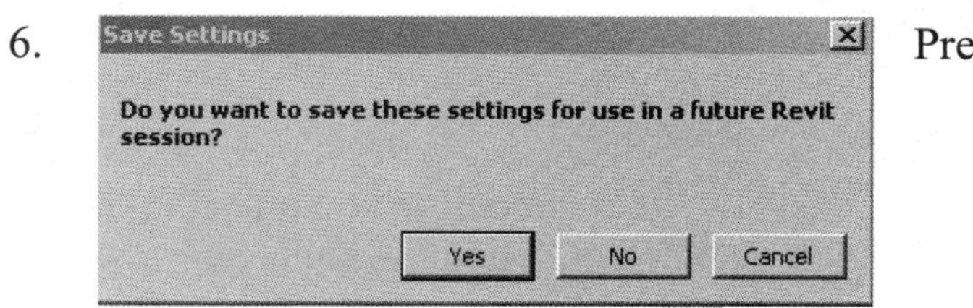

Press **No**.

7. Select the **Setup** next to Settings.

8. 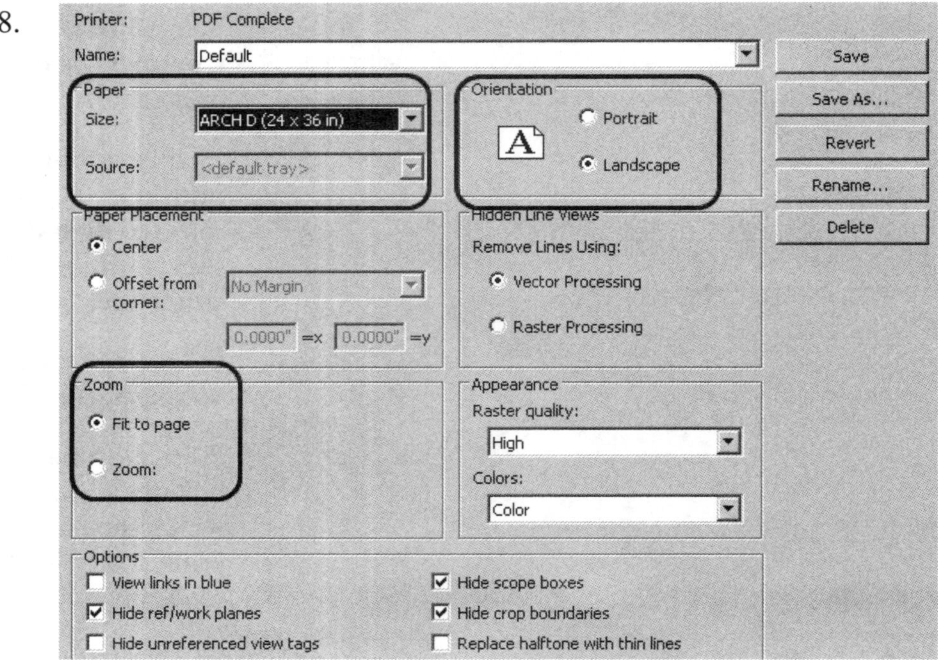

Set the Size to **Arch D**.
Set the Orientation to **Landscape**.
Set Zoom to **Fit to Page**.
Enable **Center** for Paper Placement.

Press **OK**.

9. Press **OK** to print.

10. File name: Bill Brown project
Save as type: PDF files (*.PDF)

Browse to the folder where you want to store the pdf file.
Name the file **Bill Brown project**.
Press **Save**.

You may want to save the file with your last name so your instructor can identify your work.

11. 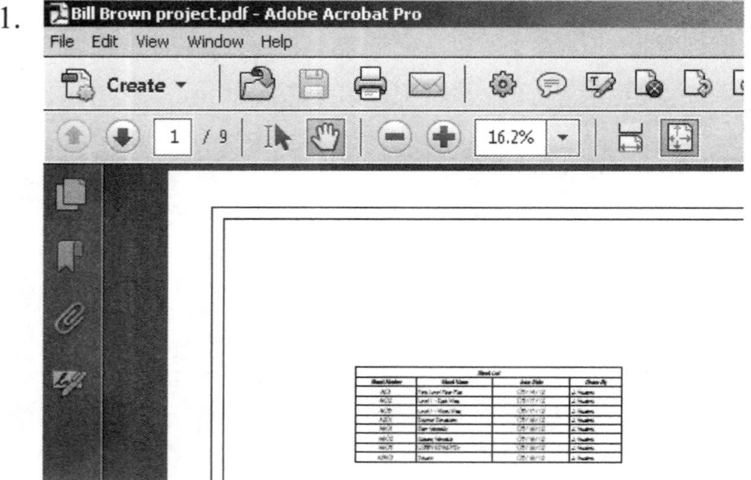

Locate the file and preview it before you turn it in or send it to someone.

Additional Projects

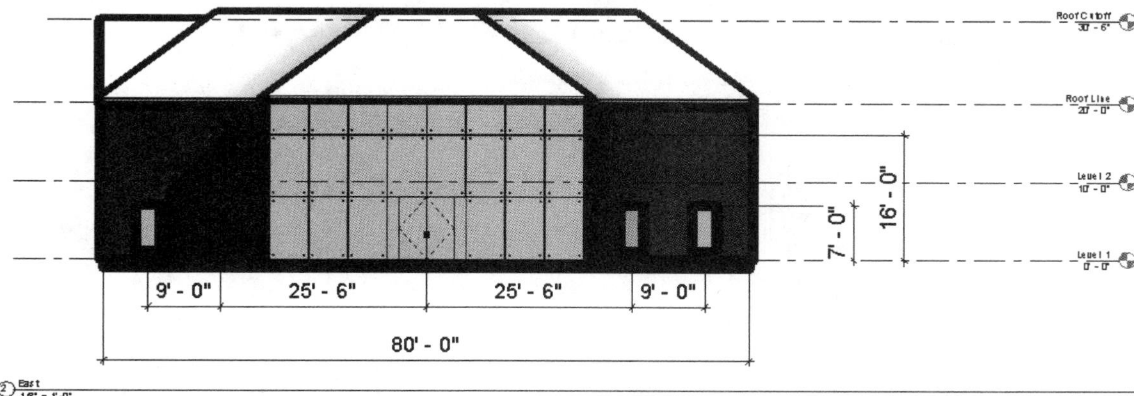

1) Create East & West Elevations view on a sheet.
   Add dimensions to the North Elevation view.

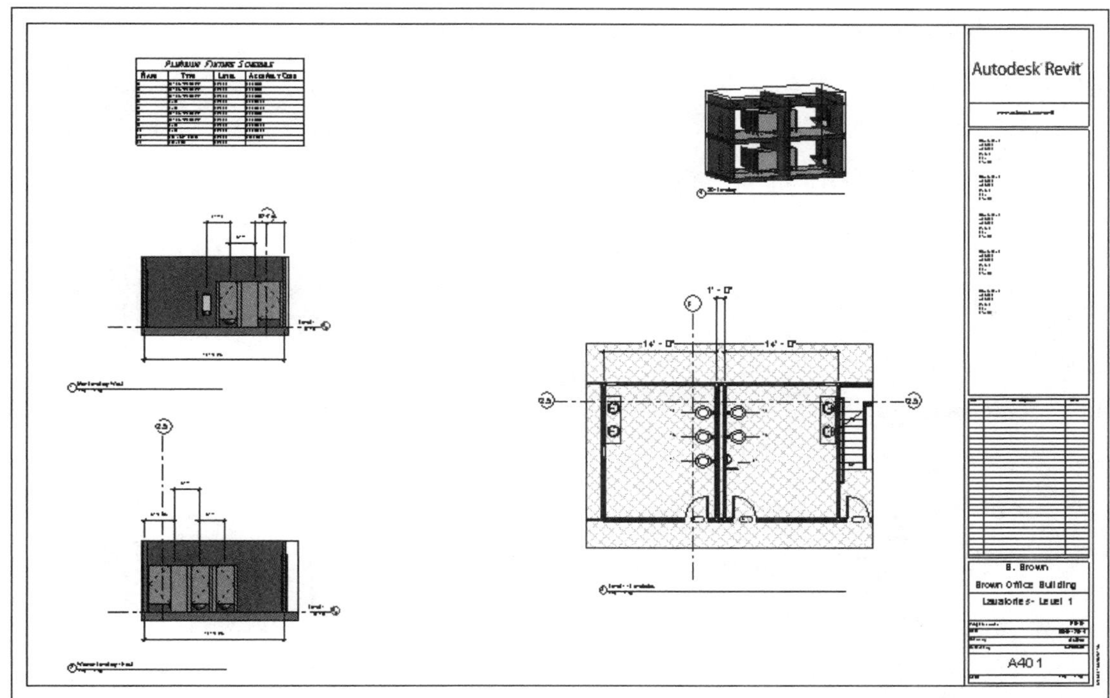

2) Create a sheet for the level 1 Lavatories. The sheet should have a plumbing fixture schedule, interior views for the men's and women's lavatories, a cropped view of the floor plan and the 3D view as shown.

3) Create Head, Threshold, and Jamb Details for the remaining doors and windows.

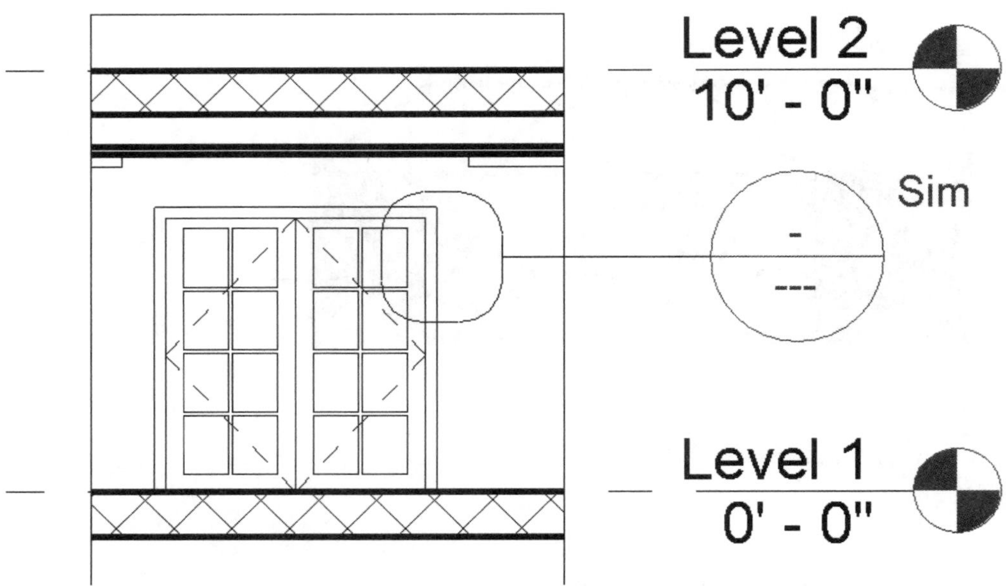

4) Create a sheet with elevations for each door and window.

5) Create a sheet with detail views for the doors and windows.

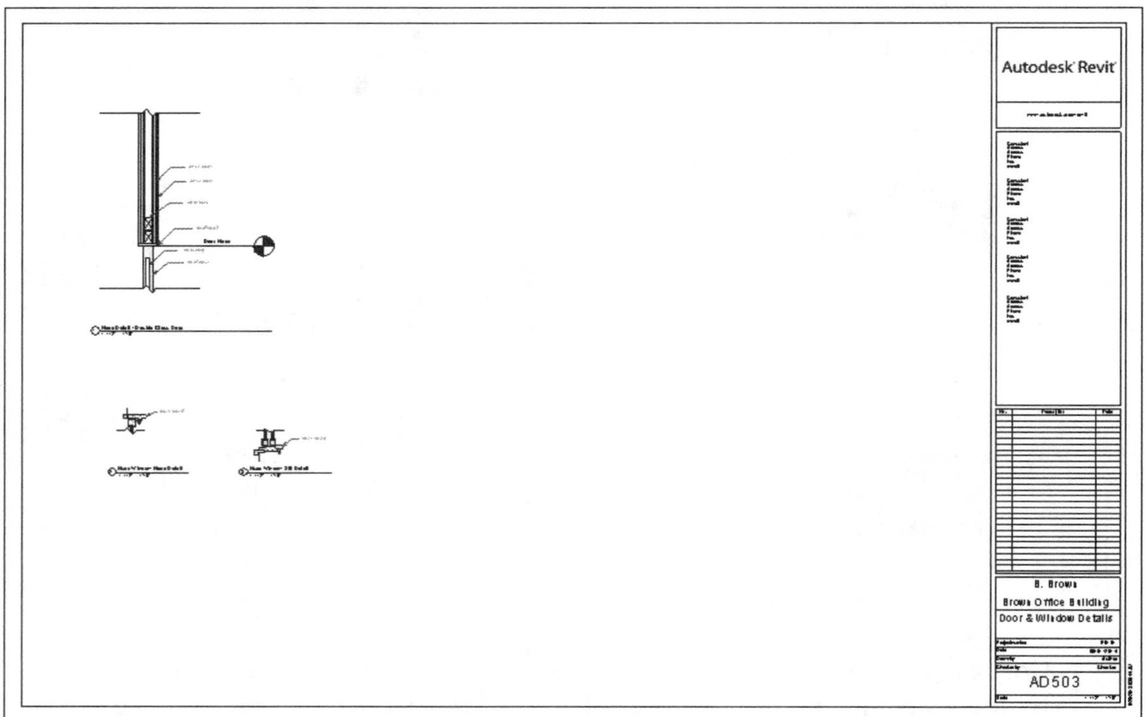

Lesson 8 Quiz

True or False

1. You have to deactivate a view before you can activate a different view.
2. When adding dimensions to an elevation, you add horizontal dimensions, not vertical dimensions
3. The Linework tool is used to change the line style of a line in a view
4. If you change the line style of a line in one view, it will automatically update in all views.
5. Double clicking on a blue symbol will automatically activate the view linked to that symbol.

Multiple Choice

6. To add a view to a sheet, you can:

   A. Drag and drop the view name from the browser onto the sheet
   B. Go to View→New→Add View
   C. Select 'Add View' from the View Design Bar
   D. All of the above

7. To add a sheet, you can:

   A. Select the New Sheet tool from the View ribbon.
   B. Right click on a sheet and select New Sheet.
   C. Highlight Sheets in the Browser, right click and select 'New Sheet'.
   D. Go to File→New Sheet.

8. To control the depth of an elevation view (visible objects behind objects):

   A. Change to Hidden Line mode
   B. Adjust the location of the elevation clip plane
   C. Adjust the Section Box
   D. Change the View Underlay

9. The keyboard shortcut key for Linework is:

   A. L
   B. LW
   C. LI
   D. LK

10. The text leader option NOT available is:

    A. Leader with no shoulder
    B. Leader with shoulder
    C. Curved Leader
    D. Spline Leader

11. The number 1 in the section symbol shown indicates:

    A. The sheet number
    B. The sheet scale
    C. The elevation number
    D. The detail number on the sheet

12. The values in the section symbol are automatically linked to:

    A. The browser
    B. The sheet where the section view is placed
    C. The text entered by the user
    D. The floor plan

13. To control the line weight of line styles:

    A. Go to Settings→Line Styles
    B. Go to Line Styles→Properties
    C. Pick the Line, right click and select 'Properties'.
    D. Go to Tools→Line Weights

ANSWERS:

1) T; 2) F; 3) T; 4) F; 5) T; 6) A & B; 7) A & C; 8) B; 9) B; 10) D; 11) D; 12) B; 13) A

Lesson 9
Rendering

Rendering is an acquired skill. It takes practice to set up scenes to get the results you want. It is helpful to become familiar with photography as many of the same lighting and shading theory is applicable. Getting the right scene is a matter of trial and error. It is a good idea to make small adjustments when setting up a scene as you often learn more about the effects of different settings.

Exercise 9-1
Create a Toposurface

Drawing Name: 8-11.rvt
Estimated Time: 15 minutes

This exercise reinforces the following skills:

- Site
- Toposurface

Before we can create some nice rendered views, we need to add some background scenery to our model.

1. Open *ex8-11.rvt.*

2. Roof Cutoff
   Roof Line
   Site

   Activate the **Site** floor plan view.

   Type **VV** to launch the Visibility/Graphics dialog.

   On the Annotations tab:
   Turn off the visibility of grids, elevations, and sections.

3. 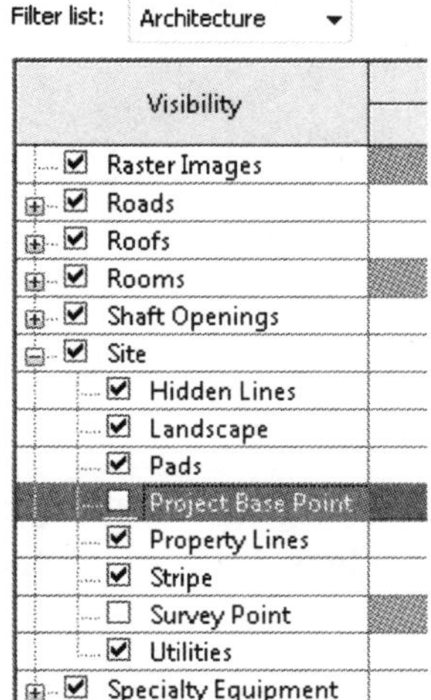

   Turn off the visibility of the Project Base Point and the Survey Point (located under Site) on the Model Categories tab.

4. 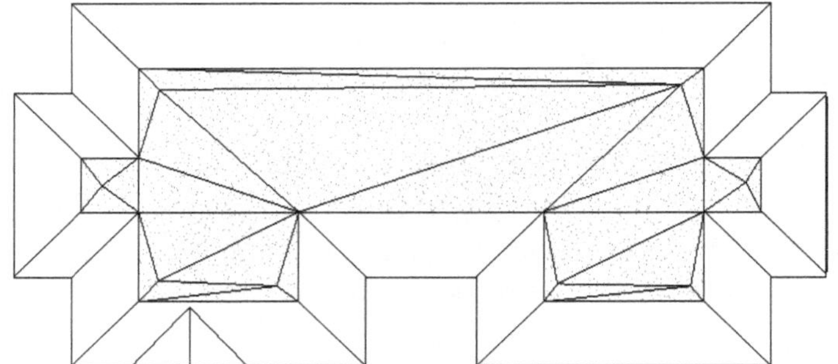

The site plan should just display the roof and building.

5. Massing & Site Activate the **Massing & Site** ribbon.

6. Toposurface Select the **Toposurface** tool from the Model Site panel.

7. Place Point Use the **Place Point** tool from the Tools panel to create an outline of a lawn surface.

7. Pick the points indicated to create a lawn expanse.
You can grab the points and drag to move into the correct position.

You are creating a toposurface around the existing building.

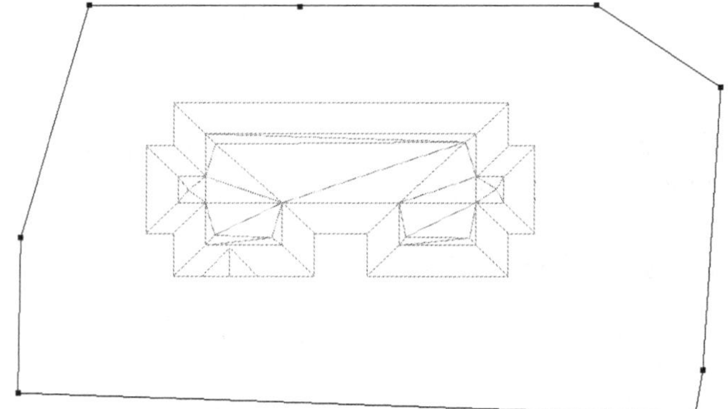

8. 

Select the **green check** on the Surface panel to **Finish Surface**.

9. 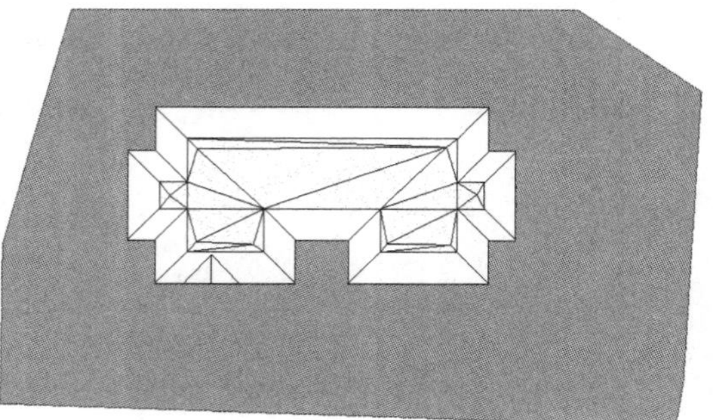

Select the toposurface.

10. 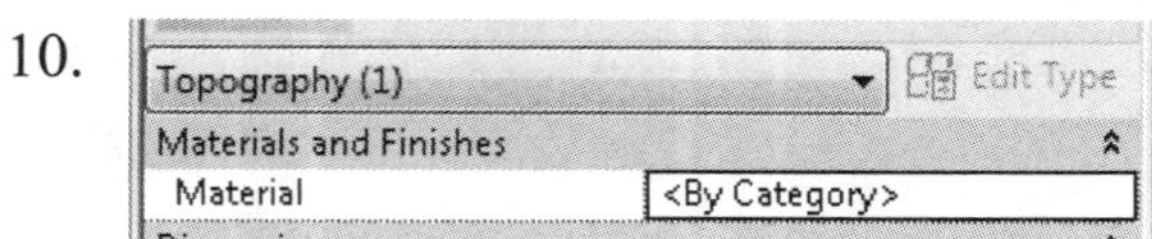

Left click in the **Materials** column on the Properties pane.

11. Locate the **grass** material that was defined in Lesson 5.

    Select and press **OK.**

12. Verify that Grass is now listed as the material for the toposurface.

13. 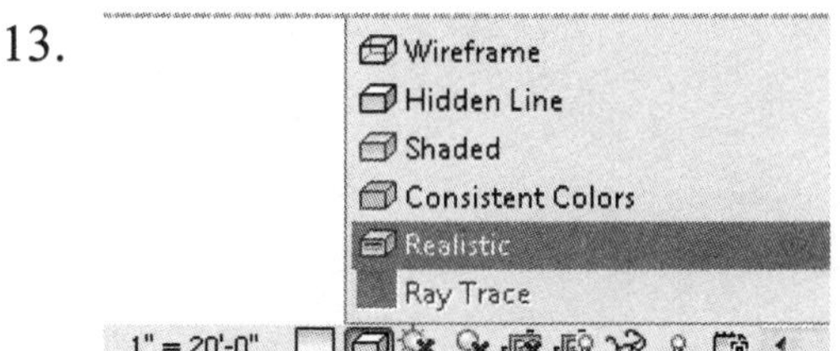

    Switch to **Realistic** to see the grass material.

    Ray trace is used to test render your view. Do not use this option unless you want to wait a significant amount of time while your system renders.

14. Save as *ex9-1.rvt.*

Exercise 9-2

Create a Split Region

Drawing Name: 9-1.rvt
Estimated Time: 20 minutes

This exercise reinforces the following skills:

- Site
- Toposurface
- Split a Toposurface

1. Open *ex9-1.rvt.*

2. Activate the **Site** floor plan.

3. 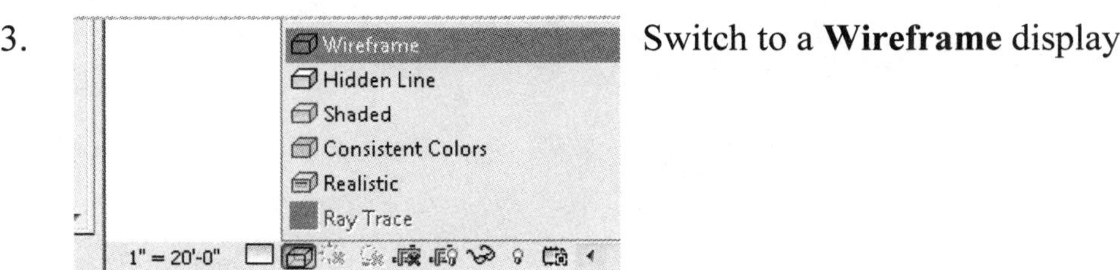

   Switch to a **Wireframe** display.

4. Activate the **Massing & Site** ribbon.

Select the **Split Surface** tool on the Modify Site panel.

Select the toposurface.

5. Select the Pick Line tool from the Draw panel.

6. Select the outline of the building.

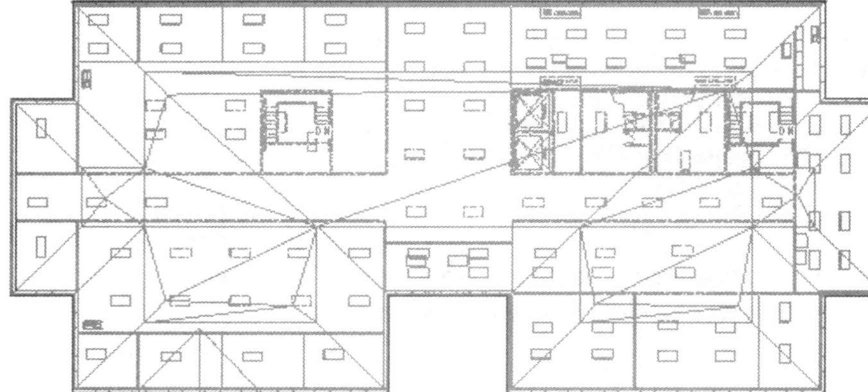

7. Left click in the Material field on the Properties pane.

8. Set the Material to **Concrete - Cast in-Place gray**.

Press **OK**.

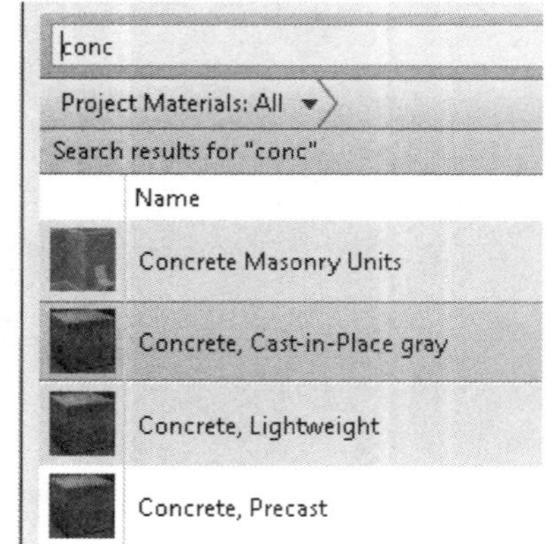

9. You will see a dialog stating that toposurfaces do not display hatch/fill patterns.

Press **OK**.

10. Select the **green check** on the Mode panel.

Mode

11. Error - cannot be ignored

The splitting boundary must divide the Surface into separate pieces. There may be a gap in the splitting Lines or the Sketch may be incomplete.

Show | More Info | Expand >>

If you get this error message, it means that the sketch is not closed or there are overlapping lines.

Close the dialog and inspect the sketch to correct any errors.

12. 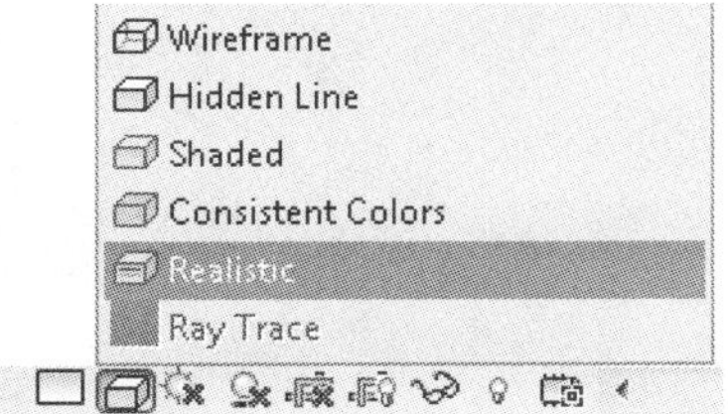

Switch to **Realistic** to see the new material.

13. If you orbit the 3D model, you will see the building foundation below the lawn.

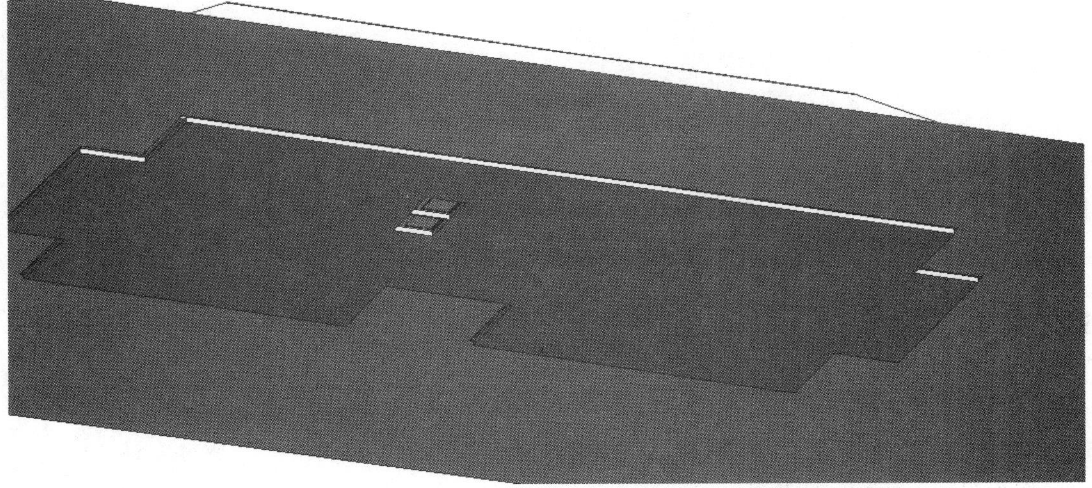

The openings are the shaft openings for the elevators.

14. Save as *ex9-2.rvt*.

Exercise 9-3
Create a Building Pad

Drawing Name: 9-2.rvt
Estimated Time: 30 minutes

This exercise reinforces the following skills:

- Site
- Toposurface
- Building Pad
- Materials
- Importing a Fill Pattern

1. Open *ex9-2.rvt.*

2. Activate the **Site** floor plan.

3. Switch to a **Wireframe** display.

4. Select the **Building Pad** tool on the Model Site panel.

Building Pad

5. Select the **Rectangle** tool from Draw panel on the ribbon.

6. Use the **Rectangle** tool on the Draw panel to create a sidewalk up to the building.

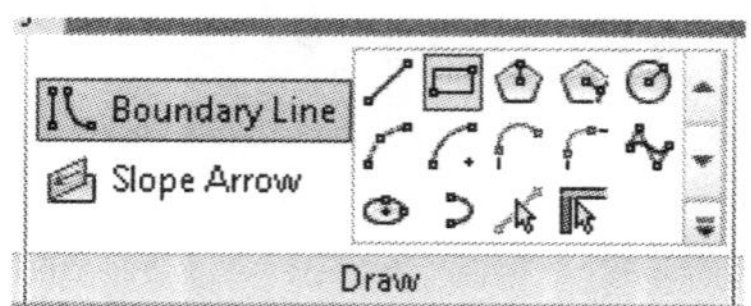

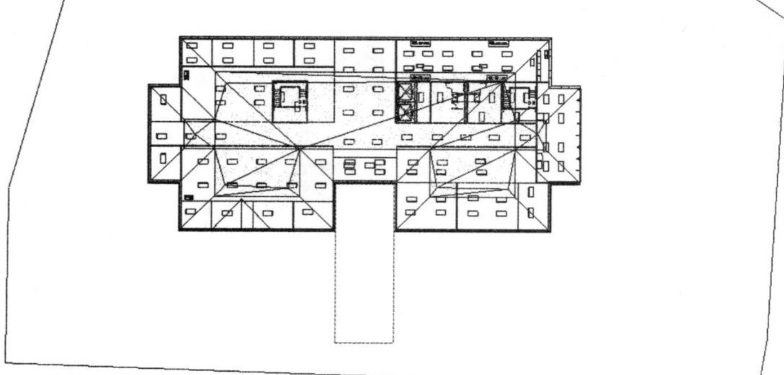

7. 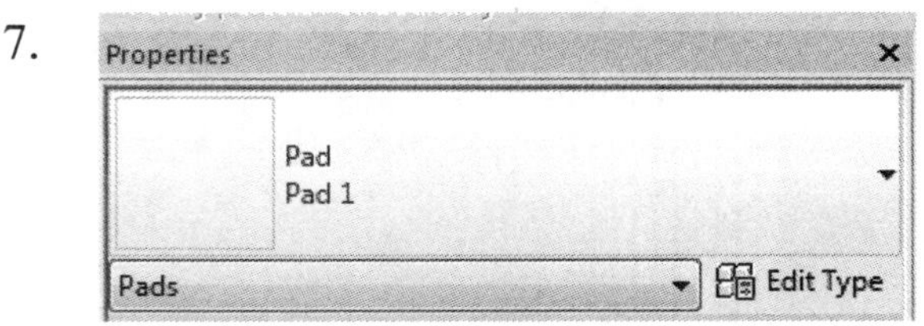

Select **Edit Type** on the Properties palette.

8. Select **Duplicate**.

9. Enter **Walkway** in the Name field.
Press **OK**.

10. 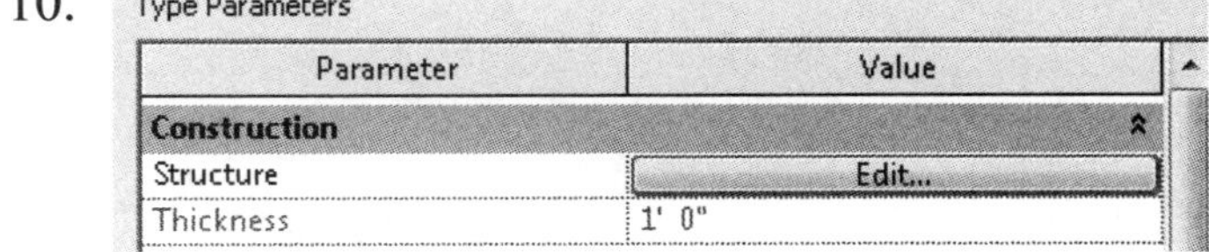

Select **Edit** under Structure.

11. Left click in the Material column to bring up the Material Library.

12. 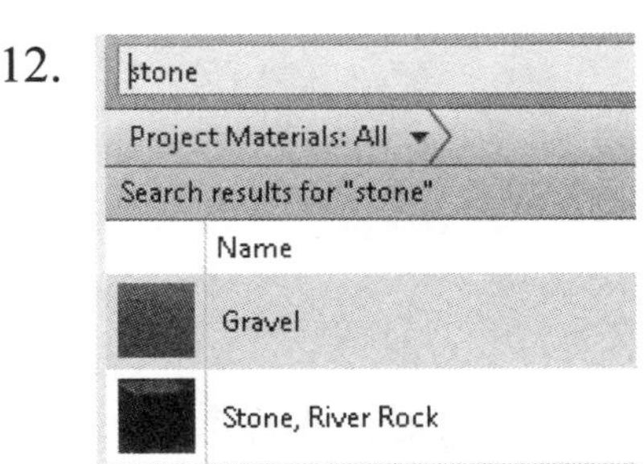

Locate the **Stone, River Rock** material.

Select and press **OK**.

13. 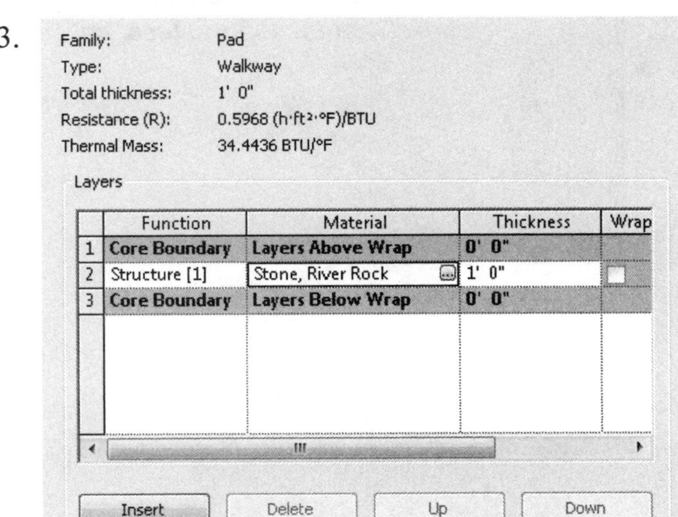

Verify that the **Stone, River Rock** material is assigned.

Press **OK**.

14. Type Parameters

Parameter	Value
Construction	
Structure	Edit...
Thickness	1' 0"
Graphics	
Coarse Scale Fill Pattern	
Coarse Scale Fill Color	Black

Left click in the Coarse Scale Fill Pattern field.

15. 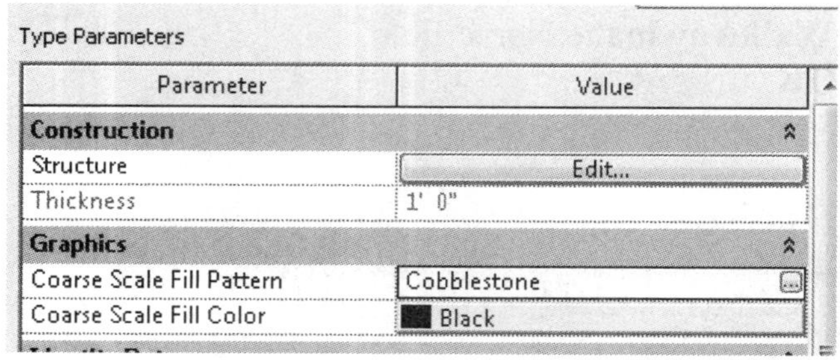

Assign the **Cobblestone** fill pattern.

Press **OK**.

16.

Pads	
Constraints	
Level	Level 1
Height Offset From L...	0' 2"
Room Bounding	☑
Dimensions	

Set the Height Offset from Level to **2″** on the Properties palette.

This allows the walkway to be slightly set above the grass and will make it more visible.

17. 

Select the **green check** on the Surface panel to **Finish Building Pad**.

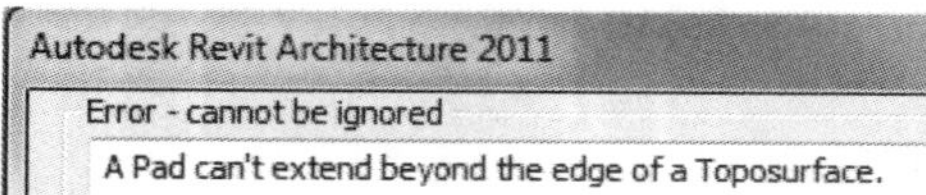

If you see this error, you need to adjust the rectangle sketch so it is entirely on the toposurface.

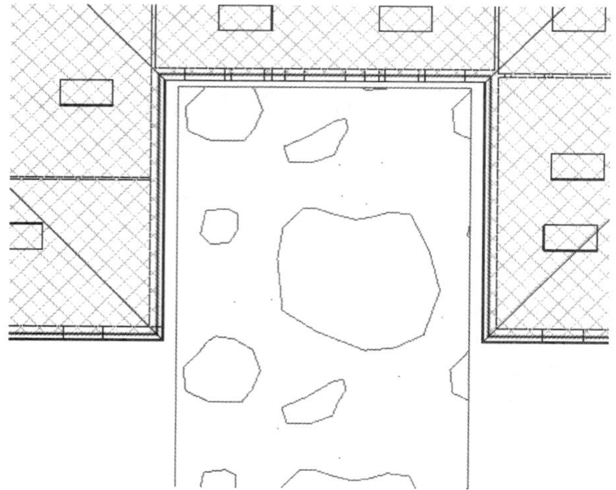

The rectangle is placed slightly away from the building, so that it is entirely on the toposurface, not the foundation.

18. 

Switch to a **3D** View.

19. Set the display to **Realistic**.

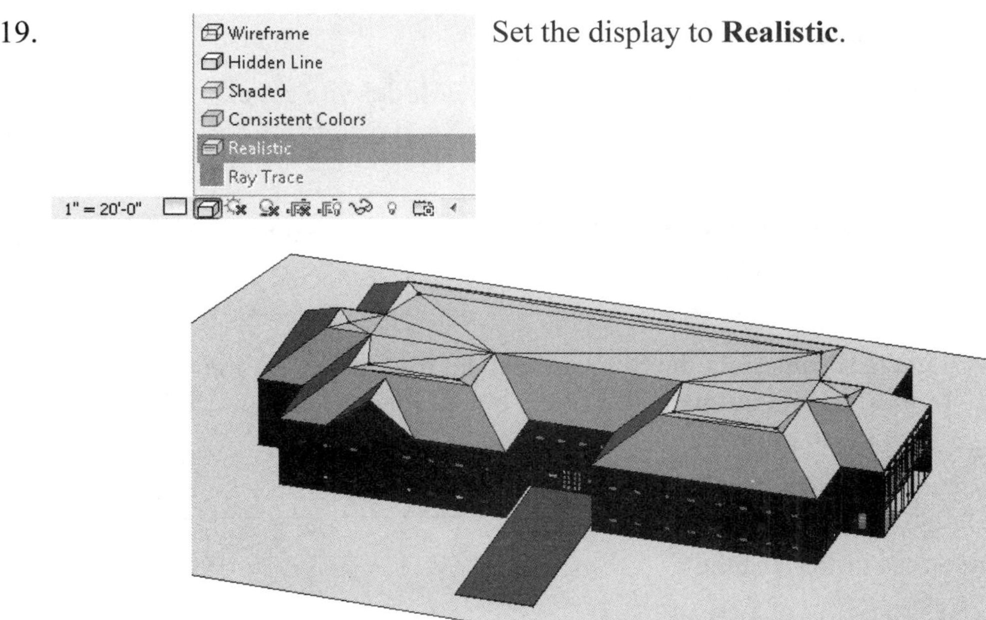

20. Save as *ex9-3.rvt.*

Exercise 9-4
Add Site Components

Drawing Name: 9-3.rvt
Estimated Time: 15 minutes

This exercise reinforces the following skills:

- Site
- Planting
- Entourage

1. Open *ex9-3.rvt.*
2. Activate the **Site** floor plan.
3. Switch to a **Wireframe** display.

4. Activate the **Massing & Site** ribbon.

5. 

Select the **Site Component** tool on the Model Site panel.

6. Select **Red Maple - 30′** [**Red Maple - 9 Meters**] from the Properties pane.

When you select the Site Component tool instead of the Component tool, Revit automatically filters out all loaded components except for Site Components.

7. Place some trees in front of the building.

To add plants not available in the Type Selector drop-down, load additional families from the Planting folder.

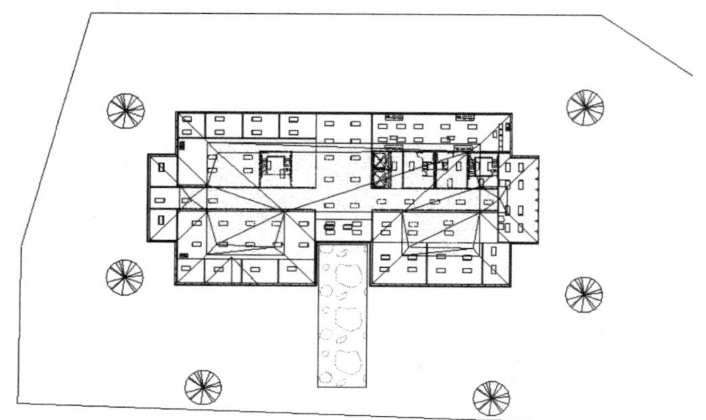

8. Select the **Site Component** tool on the Model Site panel.

9. Select **Load Family** from the Mode panel.

10. Browse to the *Entourage* folder.

11. Locate the **RPC Female** [**M_RPC Female.rfa**] file.

Press **Open**.

12. RPC Female Cathy Set the Female to **Cathy** on the Properties pane.

13. 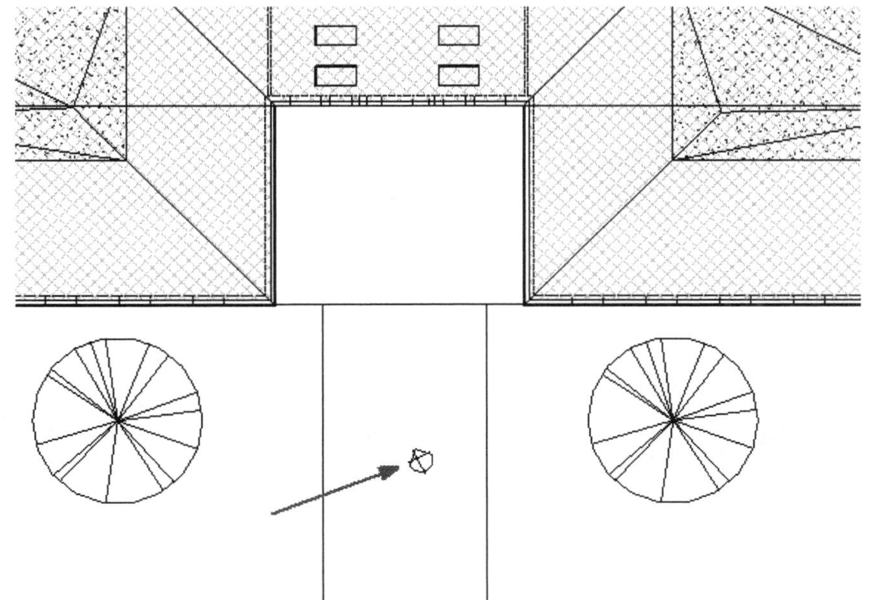

Place the person on the walkway.

14. If you zoom in on the person, you only see a symbol – you don't see the real person until you perform a Render. You may need to switch to Hidden Line view to see the symbol for the person.

The point indicates the direction the person is facing.

15. 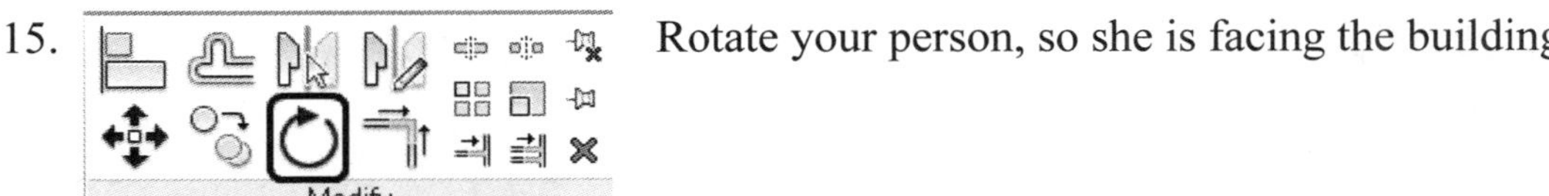

Rotate your person, so she is facing the building.

16. Save the file as *ex9-4.rvt.*

Make sure Level 1 or Site is active or your trees could be placed on Level 2 (and be elevated in the air). If you mistakenly placed your trees on the wrong level, you can pick the trees, right click, select Properties, and change the level.

Exercise 9-5

Defining Camera Views

Drawing Name: 9-4.rvt
Estimated Time: 15 minutes

This exercise reinforces the following skills:

- Camera
- Rename View
- View Properties

1. Open *ex9-4.rvt.*
2. Activate **Site** floor plan.
3. Activate the **View** ribbon.
4. Select the **3D View→Camera** tool from the Create panel on the View ribbon.
5. If you move your mouse in the graphics window, you will see a tool tip to pick the location for the camera.
6. Aim the camera towards the front entrance to the building.

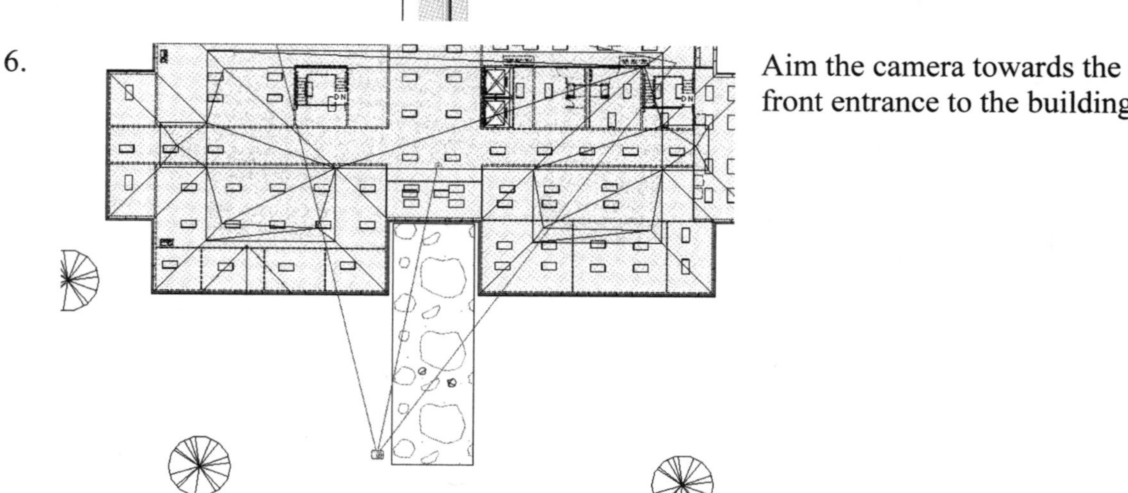

7. A window opens with the camera view of your model.

   The person and the tree appear as stick figures because the view is not rendered yet.

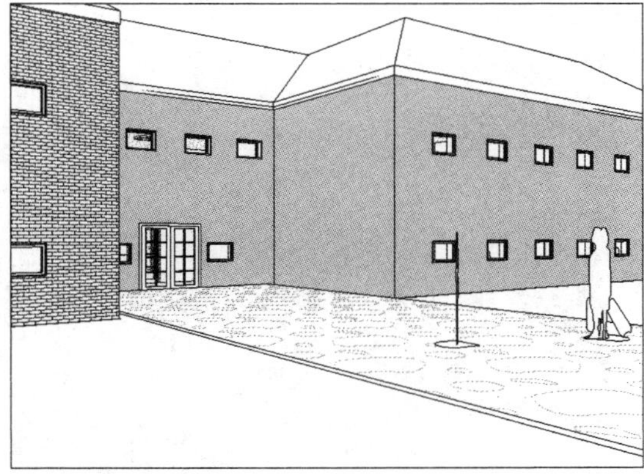

8. Change the Model Graphics Style to **Realistic**.

9. Turn ON Sun and Shadows.

10. If you are happy with the view orientation, select the 3D Lock tool on the bottom of the Display Bar and select **Save Orientation and Lock View**.

11. You should see the Locked Orientation enabled in the Properties pane.

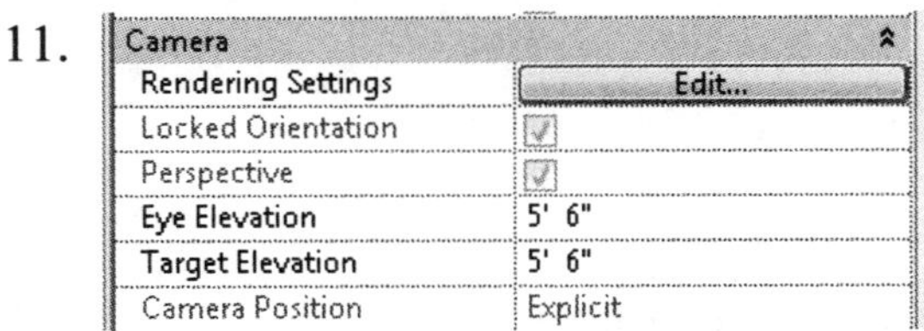

12. Our view changes to a realistic display.

13. If you look in the browser, you see that a view has been added to the 3D Views list.

14. Highlight the **3D View 1**.

    Right click and select **Rename**.

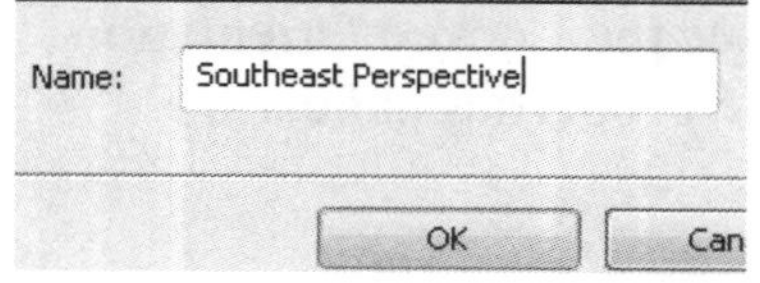

Rename to **Southeast Perspective**.

The view we have is a perspective view – not an isometric view.
Isometrics are true scale drawings. The Camera View is a perspective view with vanishing points. Isometric views have no vanishing points. Vanishing points are the points at which two parallel lines appear to meet in perspective.

15. Save the file as *ex9-5.rvt.*

Additional material libraries can be added to Revit. You may store your material libraries on a server to allow multiple users access to the same libraries. You must add a path under Settings→Options to point to the location of your material libraries. There are many online sources for photorealistic materials; www.accustudio.com is a good place to start.

Take a minute to add more plants or adjust your people before you proceed.

The same view with lighting, additional plants and people added.

Many school computers will not have the memory necessary to perform ray tracing. Be prepared to shut down Revit if it hangs up or freezes. Save your work before performing any rendering in case your computer hangs or freezes.

Exercise 9-6

Ray Trace

Drawing Name: 9-5.rvt
Estimated Time: Processing time depends on your workstation

This exercise reinforces the following skills:

- Ray Trace

1. Open *ex9-5.rvt.*
2. Activate the **Southeast Perspective** view.
3. Select Graphic Display Options.

4. 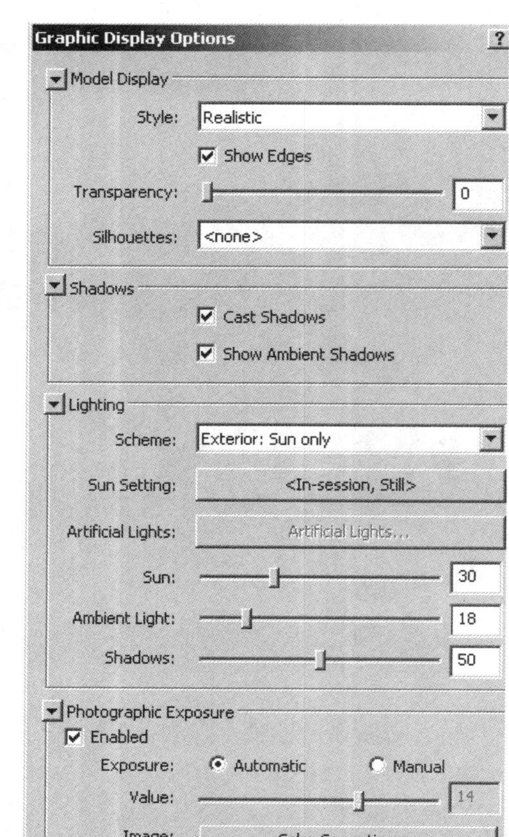

Enable Show Ambient Shadows.
Adjust the Lighting.
Enable Photographic Exposure.

5. Select Color Correction next to Image.

Adjust the sliders and observe all the image changes on the screen.

Press OK to close the dialogs.

6. Ray Trace creates a rendering.

The idea of ray trace is that you can adjust your view (zoom, pan, orbit) while rendering your model. In order for Ray Trace to work properly, you need a high-performance system.

Do not select this option if you do not want to wait for the processing.

7. Save as *ex9-6.rvt.*

Exercise 9-7

Rendering Settings

Drawing Name: 9-6.rvt
Estimated Time: 20 minutes

This exercise reinforces the following skills:

- Rendering
- Settings
- Save to Project

You can also assign a specific time, date, location, lighting, and environment to your model.

1. Open *ex9-6.rvt.*

2. Activate the **Southeast Perspective** view.

3. In the Properties palette:

   Under Camera:
   Select **Edit** for Render Settings.

4. 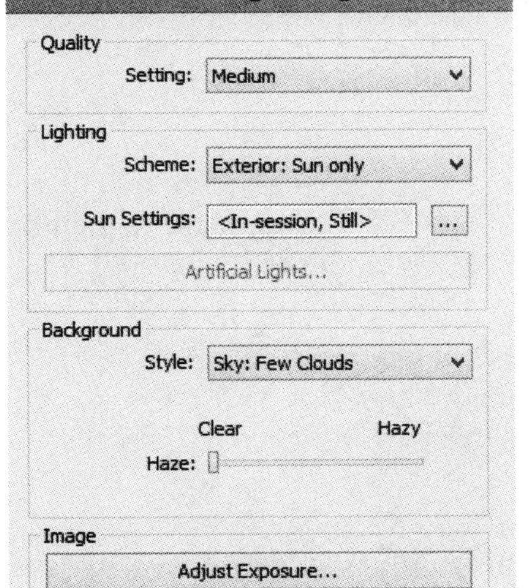

   Set the Quality Setting to **Medium**.

   Press **OK**.

5. 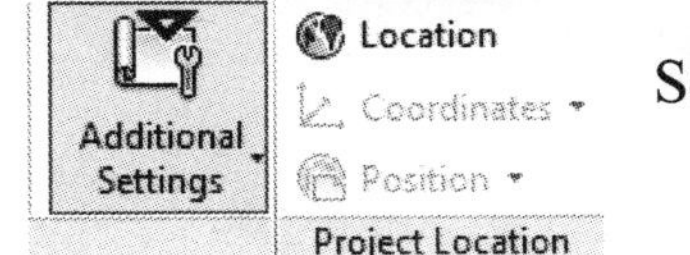

   Activate the **Manage** ribbon.

   Select **Location** on the Project Location panel.

6. 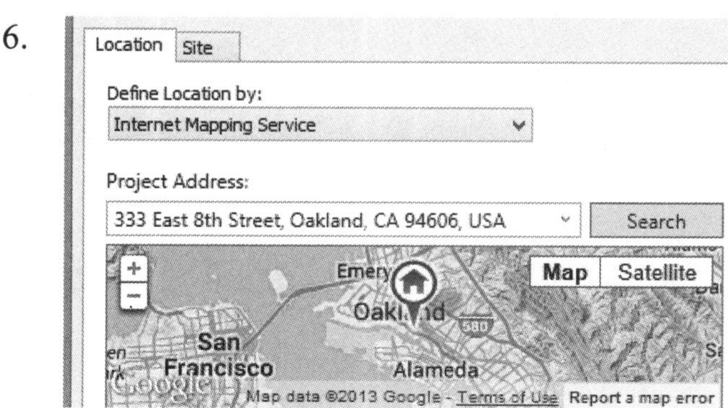

Set the Project Address to **333 E. 8th Street, Oakland, CA.**

The map will update to the location.

Press **OK**.

7. 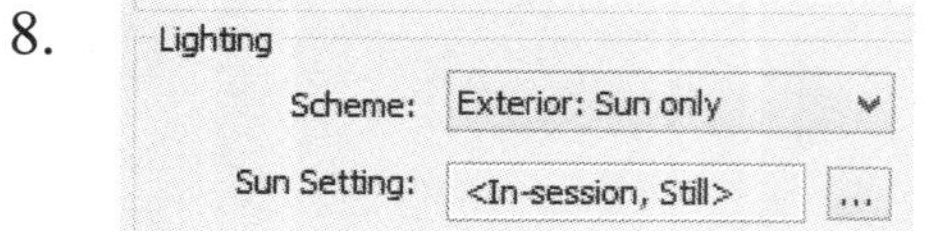

Select the **Rendering** tool located on the bottom of the screen.

8. Lighting
Scheme: Exterior: Sun only
Sun Setting: <In-session, Still> ...

Select the **…** browse button next to **Sun Setting**.

9. Solar Study
Still
Single Day
Multi-Day
Lighting

Set the Solar Study to **Still**.

10. Settings
Location : 333 East 8th Street, Oakland ...
Date : 6/ 1/2013
Time : 10:00 AM
Use shared settings

Set the Date and Time.

Press **OK**.

11. Render

Select the **Render** button.

12. 

Your window will be rendered.

13. Save to Project...

Select **Save to Project**.

14. 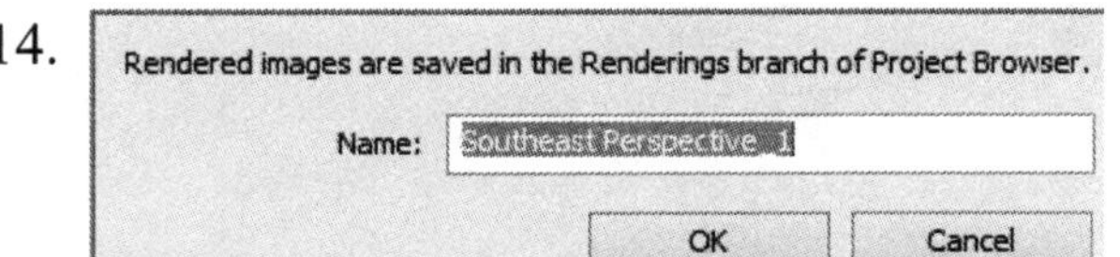

Press **OK** to accept the default name.

15. Renderings
Southeast Perspective_1

Under Renderings, we now have a view called **Southeast Perspective_1**.

You can then drag and drop the image onto a sheet.

16. Display
Show the model

Select the **Show the Model** button.

Close the Rendering dialog.

17. Our window changes to Realistic – not Rendered mode.

18. Save the file as *ex9-7.rvt.*

- The point in the person symbol indicates the front of the person. To position the person, rotate the symbol using the Rotate tool.
- Add lights to create shadow and effects in your rendering. By placing lights in strategic locations, you can create a better photorealistic image.

Exercise 9-8

Space Planning

Drawing Name: 9-7.rvt
Estimated Time: 20 minutes

This exercise reinforces the following skills:

- Components
- Duplicate View
- View Settings
- Load Family

1. Open *ex9-7.rvt*.

2. 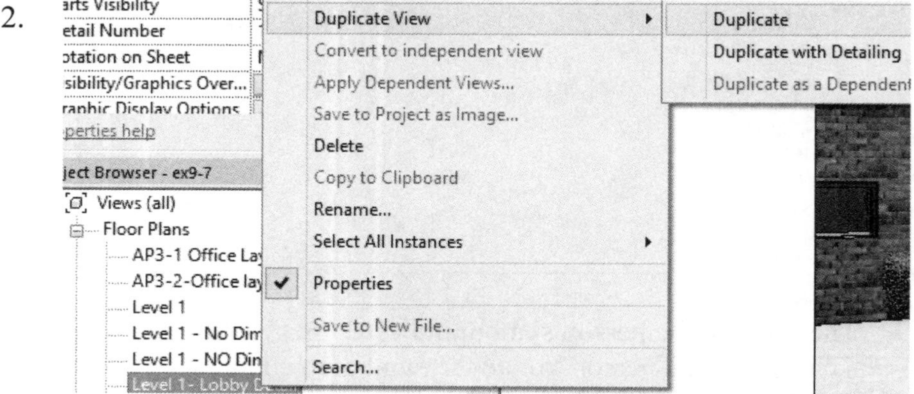

Select the **Level 1- Lobby Detail** Floor Plan.
Right click and select **Duplicate View → Duplicate.**

3. Rename the new view **Level 1 - Lobby Space Planning**.

4. Type **VV** to launch the Visibility/Graphics dialog.

Turn **off** the visibility of the elevation markers.

Press **OK** to close the dialog.

5. Select the **Component→Place a Component** tool on the Build Panel from the Architecture ribbon.

6. 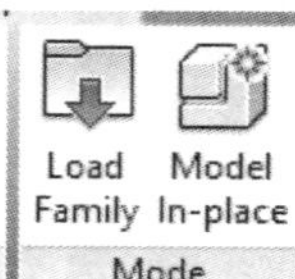

Select **Load** Family from the Mode panel.

7. Locate the *Television-Plasma, Chair-Corbu*, and *Table-Coffee* in the exercise files.

8. Hold down the **CTRL** key to select more than one file.

   Press **Open**.

9. Place the chair and table in the room.

   If you press the SPACE bar before you click to place you can rotate the object.

10. 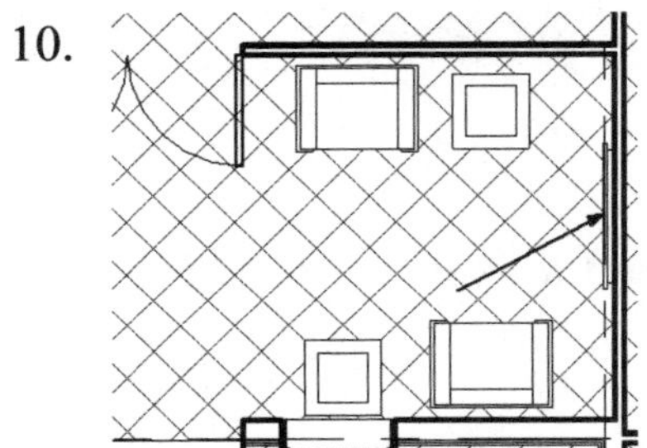

    Place the *Television-Plasma* on the East wall using the **Component** tool.

11. 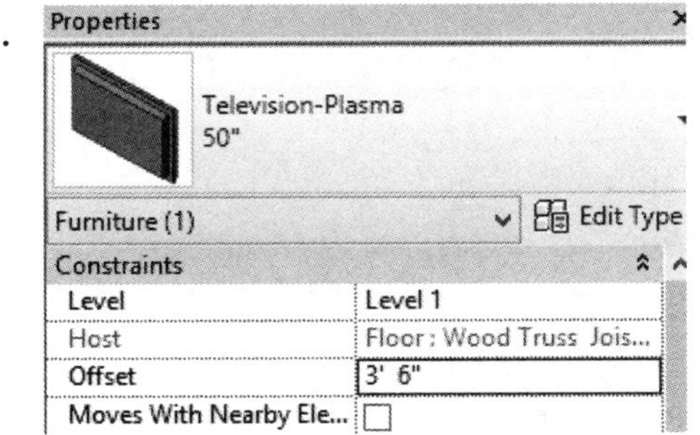

    In the Properties pane:
    Set the Offset to **3′ 6″**.

    This will locate the television 3′6″above Level 1.

12. Select the **Component→Place a Component** tool on the Build Panel from the Architecture ribbon.

13. Select **Load** Family from the Mode panel.

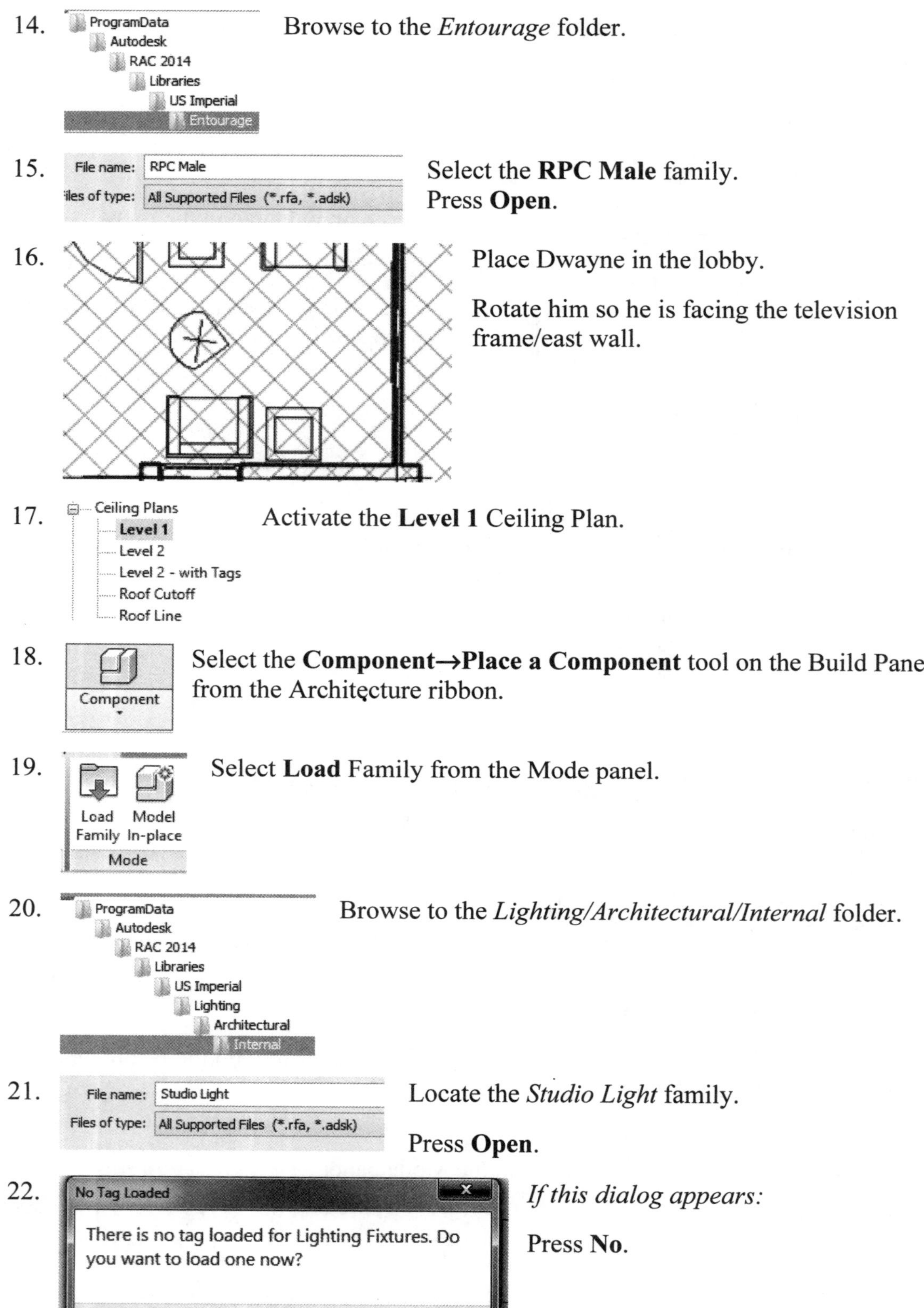

14. Browse to the *Entourage* folder.

15. Select the **RPC Male** family.
Press **Open**.

16. Place Dwayne in the lobby.

    Rotate him so he is facing the television frame/east wall.

17. Activate the **Level 1** Ceiling Plan.

18. Select the **Component→Place a Component** tool on the Build Panel from the Architecture ribbon.

19. Select **Load** Family from the Mode panel.

20. Browse to the *Lighting/Architectural/Internal* folder.

21. Locate the *Studio Light* family.

    Press **Open**.

22. *If this dialog appears:*

    Press **No**.

23. 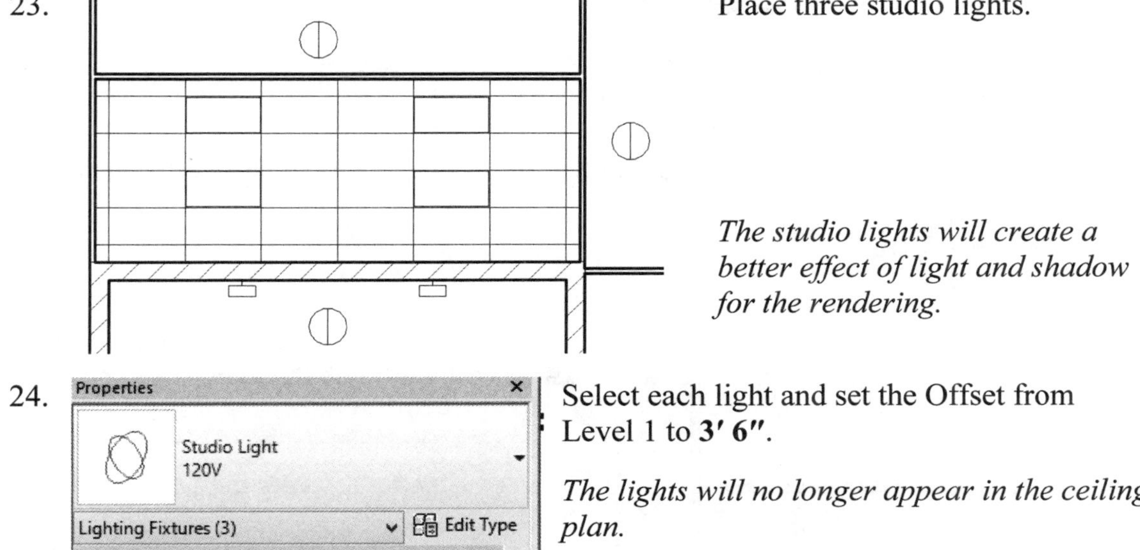

Place three studio lights.

The studio lights will create a better effect of light and shadow for the rendering.

24. Select each light and set the Offset from Level 1 to **3′ 6″**.

The lights will no longer appear in the ceiling plan.

25. Save as *ex9-8.rvt*.

Exercise 9-9
Building Sections

Drawing Name: 9-8.rvt
Estimated Time: 10 minutes

This exercise reinforces the following skills:

- Section Views
- Elevations
- Crop Regions

1. Open *ex9-8.rvt*.

2. 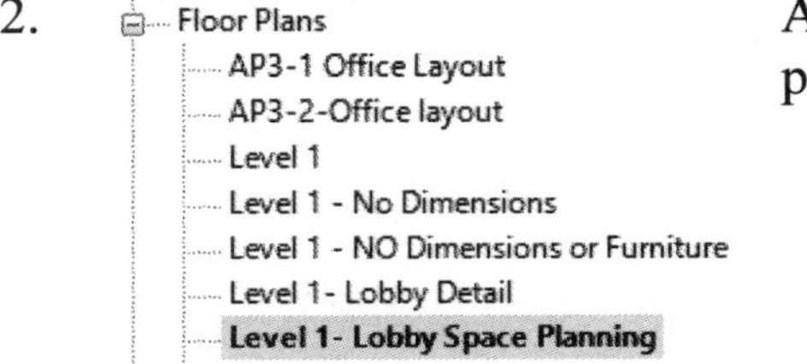

Activate the **Level 1 - Lobby Space Planning** floor plan.

3. 

Activate the **View** ribbon.

Select **Create→Section.**

4. 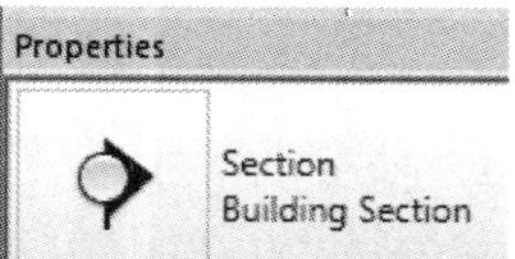

Verify **Building Section** is enabled on the Properties palette.

5. 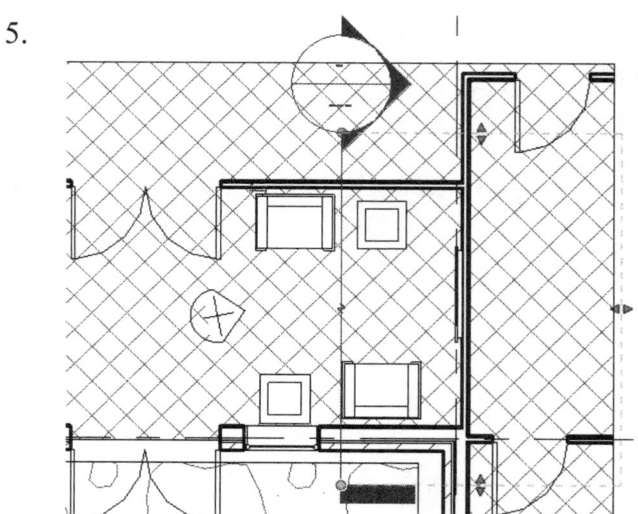
Place a section so it is looking at the east wall with the television.

6. Name: Lobby East Elevation | OK | Cancel

Rename the Section **Lobby East Elevation**.

7. Sections (Building Section) / Lobby East Elevation / Single Flush Door Elevation

Activate the **Lobby East Elevation** section.

8. 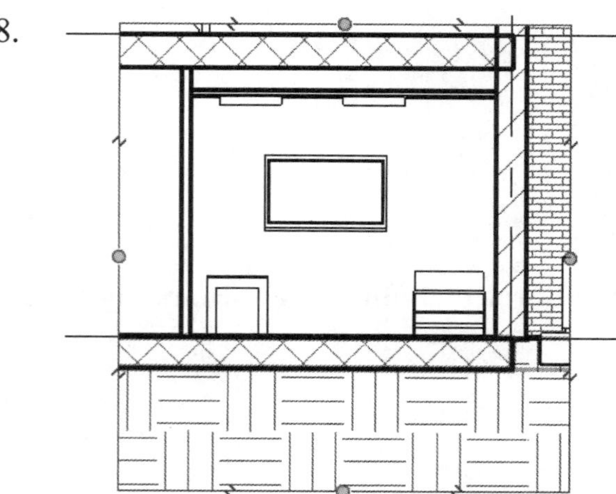
Adjust the crop region so only the lobby area is visible.

Note the position of the studio light. Adjust the elevation of the light so it is positioned on the frame. You can move it simply by selecting the light and moving it up or down.

9. Save as *ex9-9.rvt*.

Exercise 9-10
Decals

Drawing Name: 9-9.rvt
Estimated Time: 20 minutes

This exercise reinforces the following skills:

- Decal Types
- Decals
- Set Workplane

1. Open *ex9-9.rvt.*

2. Activate the **Lobby East Elevation** Section.

3. Activate the **Insert** ribbon.

4. 

Select **Decal→Decal Types** from the Link panel.

5. Select **Create New Decal** from the bottom left of the dialog box.

6. Type a name for your decal.

   The decal will be assigned an image. I have included several images that can be used for this exercise on the publisher's website.

   You can select the image of your choice or use your own image.

   Press **OK**.

7. Select the Browse button to select the image.

8. Browse to where your exercise files are located.

9. Select the image file of your choice.
Press **Open**.

10. 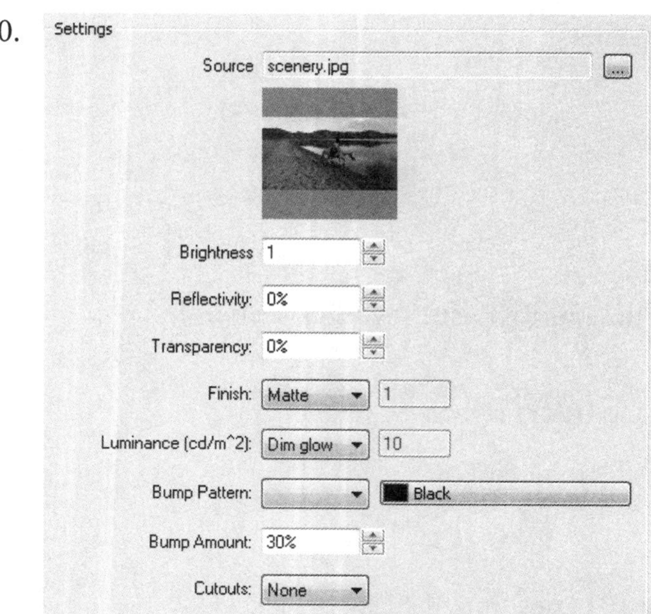

You will see a preview of the image.
Set the Finish to **Matte**.
Set the Luminance **to Dim glow**.

Press **OK**.

11. Activate the Insert ribbon.

Select **Decal→Place Decal** on the Link panel.

12. 

Place the decal on the television frame.

If you don't see the image, create a new decal with a different image file. I experienced inconsistent results – sometimes the decal appears and sometimes it doesn't. If you do not see the decal during the preview, do not assume it will render properly.

Display should be set to Realistic to preview the image decal.

13. On the Options bar:

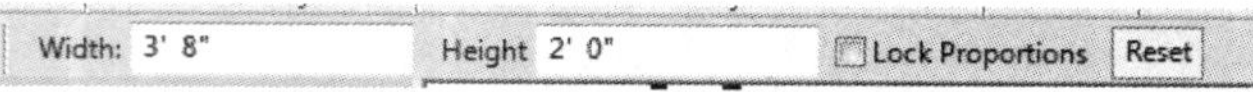

Disable **Lock Proportions**.
Set the Width to **3′ 8″**.
Set the Height to **2′ 0″**.

14. 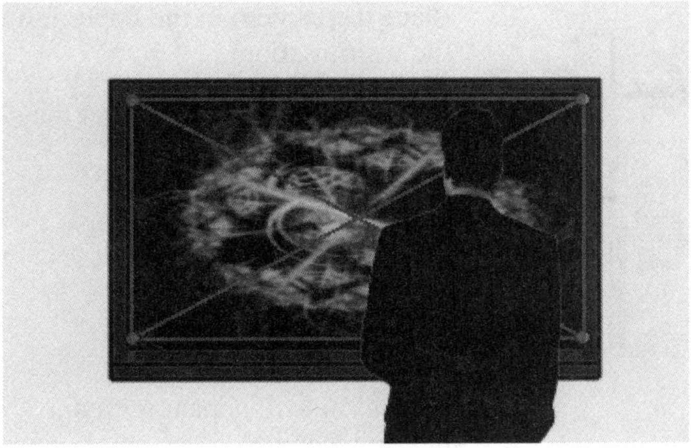 Position the decal so it is inside the frame.

15. Save as *ex9-10.rvt.*

Exercise 9-11
Creating a 3D Camera View (Reprised)

Drawing Name: 9-10.rvt
Estimated Time: 20 minutes

This exercise reinforces the following skills:

- 3D Camera
- Rename View
- Navigation Wheel
- Render

1.  Open *ex9-10.rvt.*

2. 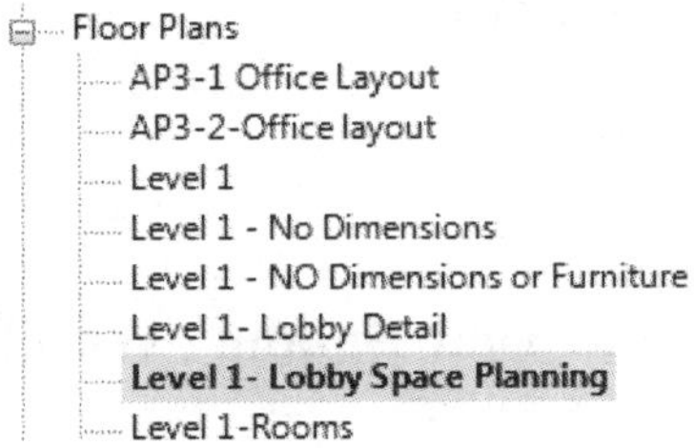 Activate the **Level 1 - Lobby Space Planning** floor plan.

Floor Plans
AP3-1 Office Layout
AP3-2-Office layout
Level 1
Level 1 - No Dimensions
Level 1 - NO Dimensions or Furniture
Level 1- Lobby Detail
Level 1- Lobby Space Planning
Level 1-Rooms

3.  View Activate the View ribbon.

4. 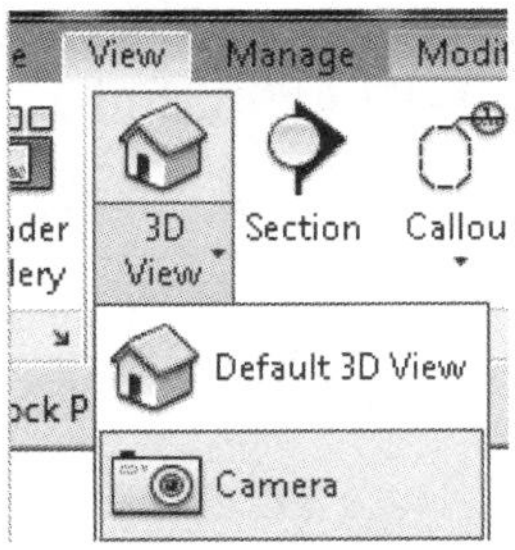 Select the **3D View→Camera** tool from the Create panel.

View Manage Modi
3D View Section Callou
Default 3D View
Camera

5. 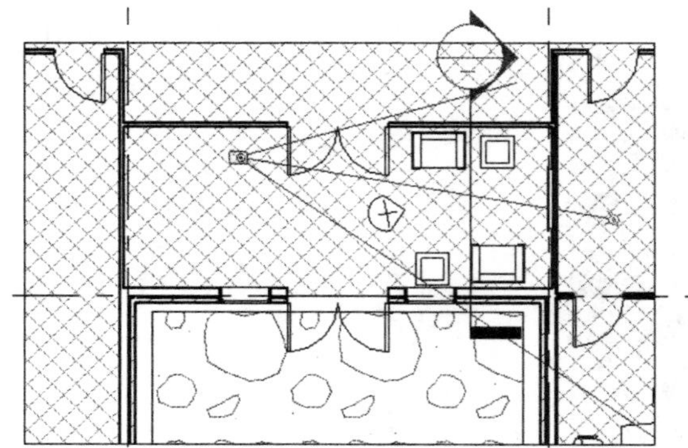

Place the camera in the upper left of the waiting room.

Rotate the camera and target the sitting area of the waiting room.

6. 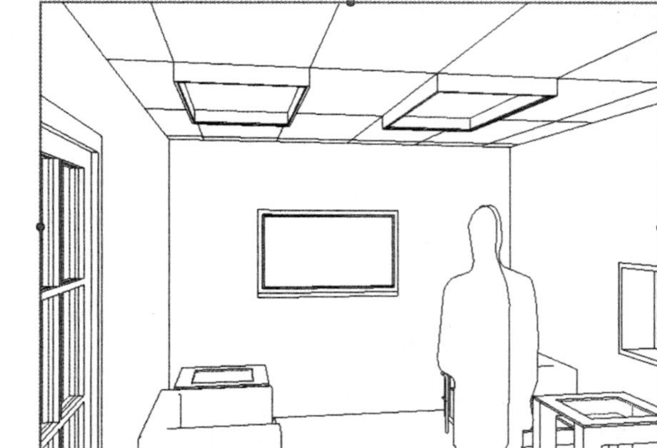

A window will appear with our interior scene.

7. 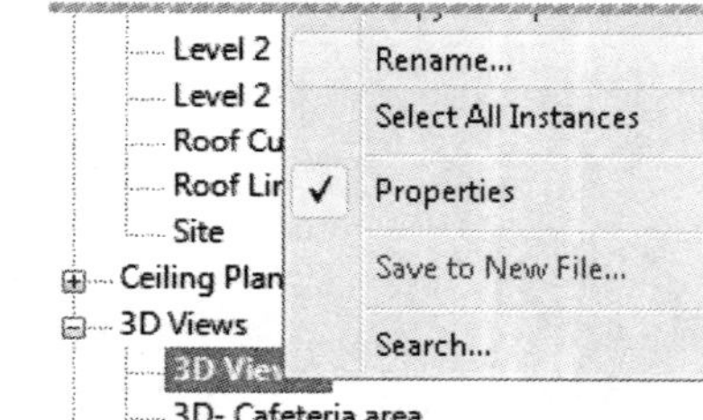

Highlight the 3D view in the Project Browser.

Right click and select **Rename**.

8. 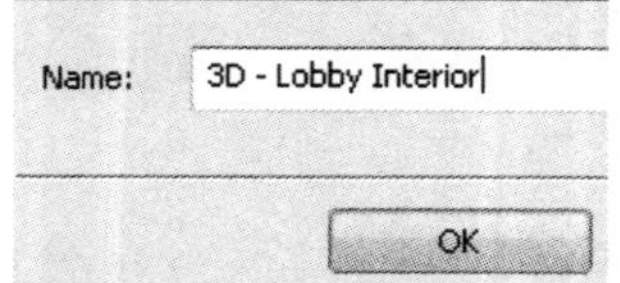

Rename the view **3D- Lobby Interior**.

9. 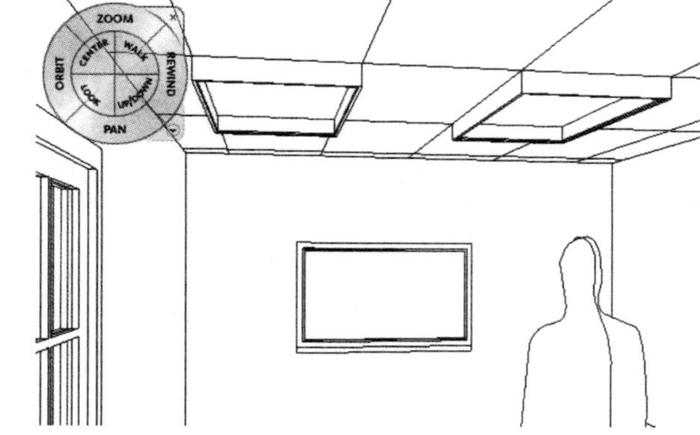

Select **Mini Tour Building Wheel** from View toolbar.

Use the Navigation Wheel to adjust your scene. Try the LOOK and WALK buttons.

10. 

Adjust the camera view.

You can also use this tool to 'walk through your model'.

11. 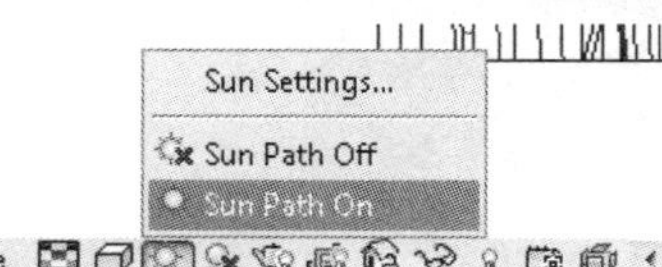

Click on the Sun on the Display toolbar. Turn **Sun Path ON**.

12. The sun will not display because Relative to View is selected in Sun Settings. What would you like to do?

Use the specified project location, date, and time instead.
Sun Settings change to <In-session, Still> which uses the specified project location, date, and time.

Continue with the current settings.
Sun Settings remain in Lighting mode with Relative to View selected. Sun will not display.

Select the **Use the specified project location date and time instead** option.

13. Perspective

Turn **Shadows On**.

14. Activate the **Rendering** dialog.

15. Render Region
Quality
Setting: Medium
Output Settings
Resolution: Screen
Printer
Width: 684 pixels
Height: 513 pixels
Uncompressed image size: 1.3 MB
Lighting
Scheme: Interior: Sun and Artificial
Sun Setting: <In-session, Still>
Artificial Lights...

Set the Quality Setting to **Medium**.

Set the Lighting Scheme to **Interior: Sun and Artificial Light**.

Press **Render**.

16. 

The interior scene is rendered.

A bright light coming from the south window and the door is from the studio light. Repositioning the light might make the rendering better.

17. Adjust Exposure... Select the **Adjust Exposure** button on the Rendering Dialog.

18. Reset to Default

Settings

Exposure Value:	12	Brighter	Darker
Highlights:	0.25	Darker	Brighter
Mid Tones:	1	Darker	Brighter
Shadows:	0.2	Lighter	Darker
White Point:	6500	Cooler	Warmer
Saturation:	1	Grey	Intense

If necessary:

Adjust the controls and select **Apply**.

Readjust and select **Apply**.

Press **OK**.

19. Save to Project... Press **Save to Project**.

20. Rendered images are saved in the Renderings branch of Project Browser.

Name: 3D Lobby Interior_1

OK Cancel

Press **OK**.

21. Close the Rendering Dialog.

22. Save the file as *ex9-11.rvt*.

Cameras do not stay visible in plan views. If you need to re-orient the camera location, you can do so by activating your plan view, then right clicking on the name of the 3D view you want to adjust and select the 'Show Camera' option.

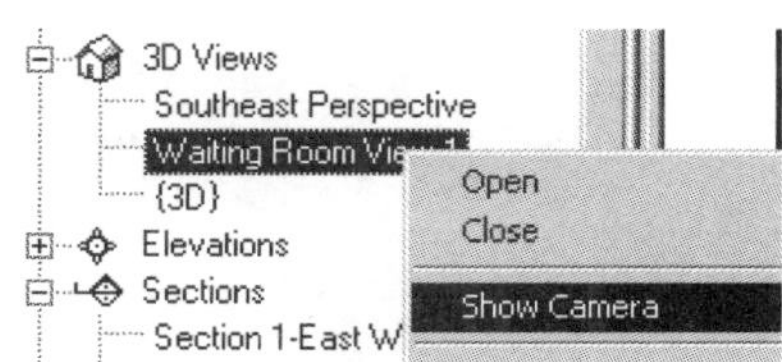

Exercise 9-12

Rendering using Autodesk 360

Drawing Name: 9-11.rvt
Estimated Time: 5 minutes

This exercise reinforces the following skills:

- Autodesk 360
- Rendering

If you have an Autodesk 360 account, you can render for free (if you are a student) or a limited number of renderings for free if you are a professional. By rendering using the Cloud, you can continue to work in Revit while the Rendering is being processed. Creating an Autodesk 360 account is free. An internet connection is required to use Autodesk 360 for rendering.

1. Open *ex9-11.rvt.*

2. Click the **Sign In** button next to Help.

   If you are already signed in, you can skip these steps.

3. Sign in using your name and password.

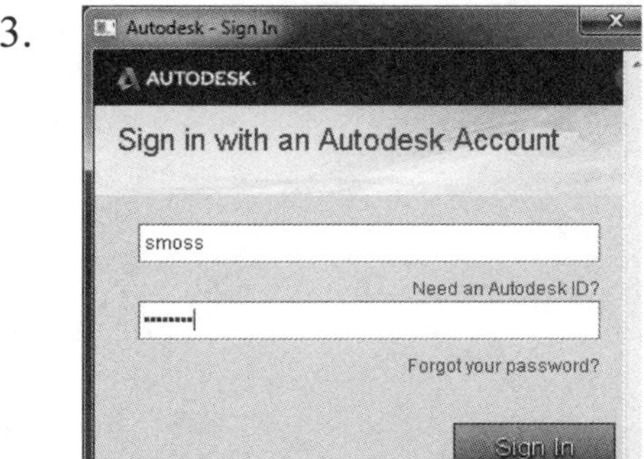

4. 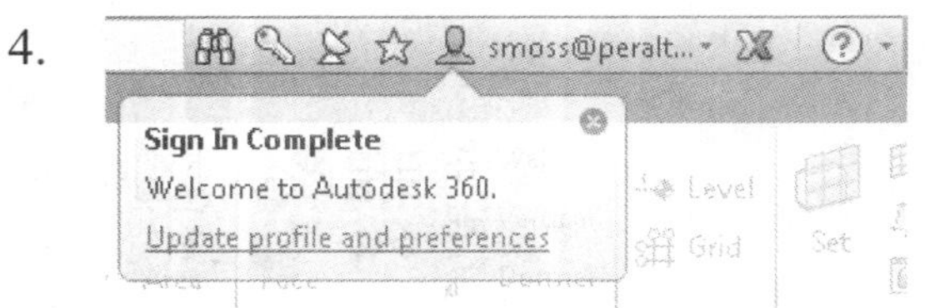

If sign-in is successful, you will see your log-in name in the dialog.

5. 3D Views
3D Lobby Interior
3D- Cafeteria area
3D- Lavatory
3D- Lobby
3D- No furniture
3D-Conference room
Southeast Perspective
{3D}

Activate the **3D Lobby Interior** view.

6. Massing & Site | Collaborate | View
Render | Render in Cloud | Render Gallery | 3D View

Activate the **View** ribbon.

Select **Render in Cloud**.

7. Render in Cloud
Autodesk® 360
Welcome to Rendering in the Cloud for Revit 2014
To begin rendering in the cloud:
Step 1
On the next screen, select 3D views and start rendering.
Step 2
The service will notify you when your images are ready.
Step 3
Select "View > Render Gallery" to view, download, or do more with your completed renderings online.
Don't show this message next time
Continue

Press **Continue.**

8. 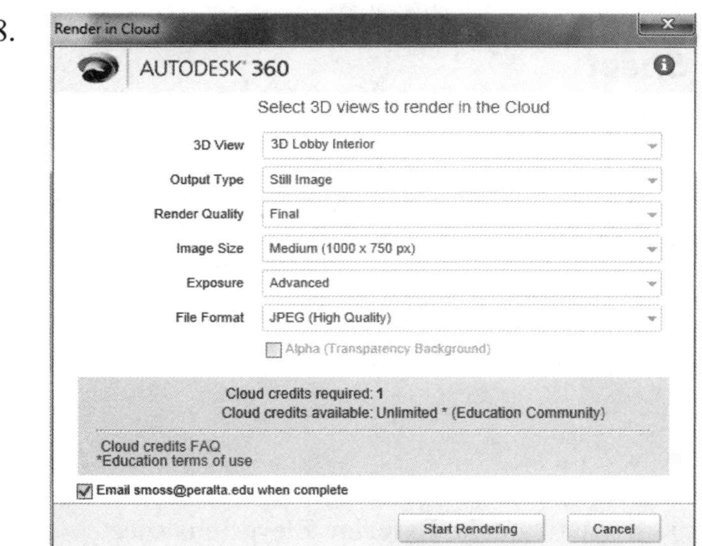

Set the Render Quality to **Final**.
Set the Image Size to **Medium**.
Set the Exposure to **Advanced**.
Set the File Format to **JPEG (High Quality)**.

Press **Start Rendering**.

Notice that you can enable email notification for when your rendering is completed.

9. 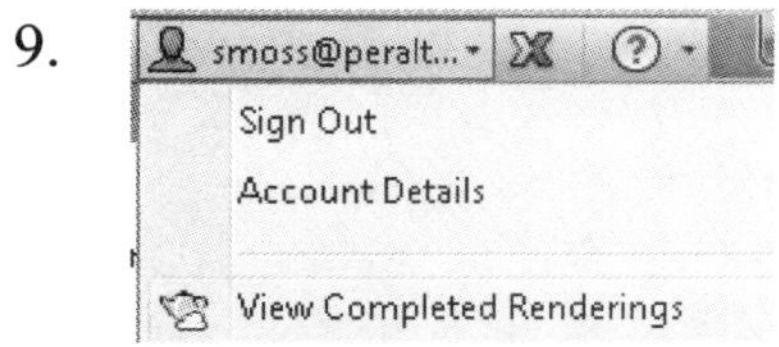

When the rendering is done, select **View Completed Renderings** in the drop-down under your sign-in name.

10. 

The rendering will be displayed.
To view a larger image, simply click on the thumbnail.

I have noticed that when I use the Autodesk 360 rendering only a small portion of the decal is used. However, rendering is faster using Autodesk 360.

11. Select **Download All** from the top right corner.

The file will be downloaded as a zipped file and you will have to extract it in order to use it.

12. Save as *ex9-12.rvt*.

Exercise 9-13

Placing a Rendering on a Sheet

Drawing Name: 9-12.rvt
Estimated Time: 5 minutes

This exercise reinforces the following skills:

- View Properties
- View Titles

1. Open *ex9-12.rvt.*

2. 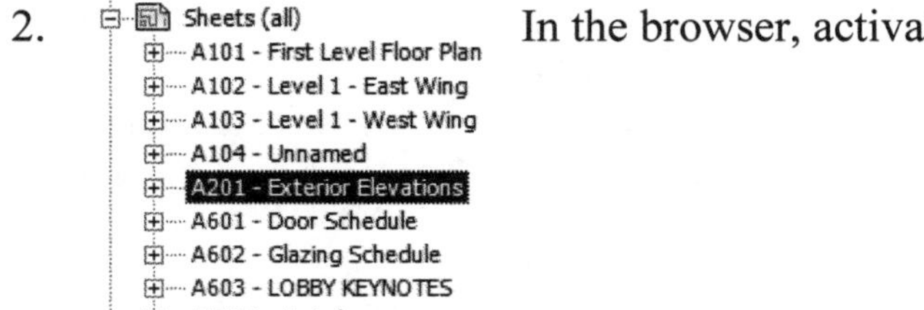

In the browser, activate the **Exterior Elevations** sheet.

3. Select the North Elevation.

   In the Properties pane:

   Set the View Scale to **1/16″ = 1′-0″** [**1:200**].

   Press **OK**.

   The scale on the South Elevation is set in the view template.

4. 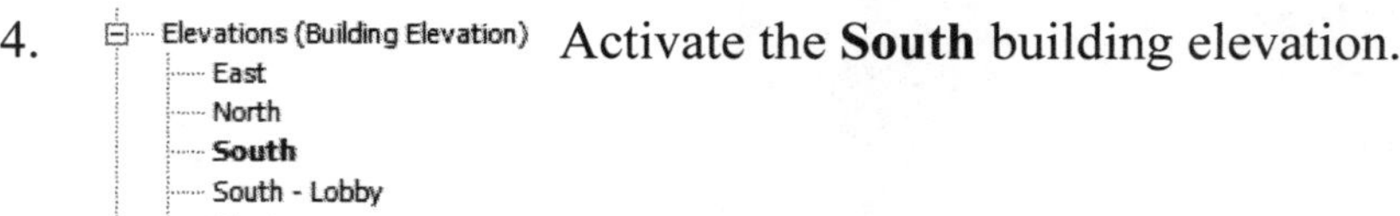

Activate the **South** building elevation.

5. 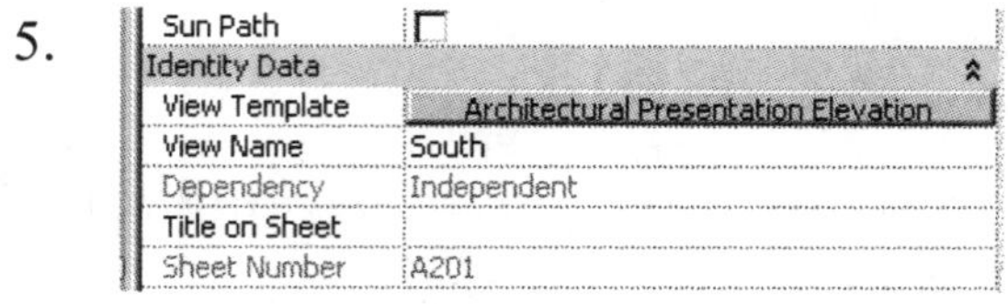

Select the **View Template** in the Properties panel.

6. 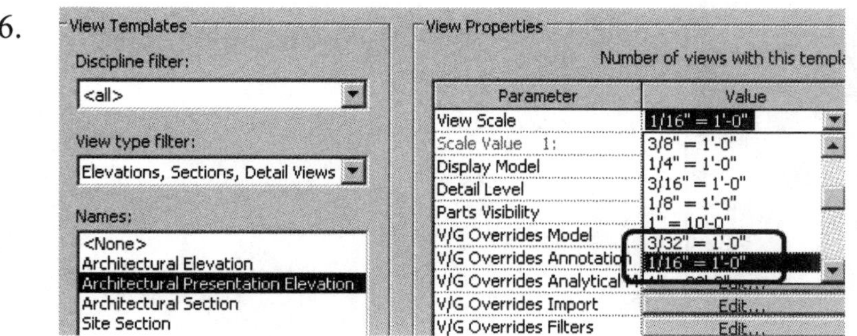

Change the View Scale to **1/16″ = 1′-0″**.

7. Sheets (all)
A101 - First Level Floor Plan
A102 - Level 1 - East Wing
A103 - Level 1 - West Wing
A201 - Exterior Elevations
Elevation: North
Elevation: South

Activate the **Exterior Elevations** sheet.

8. 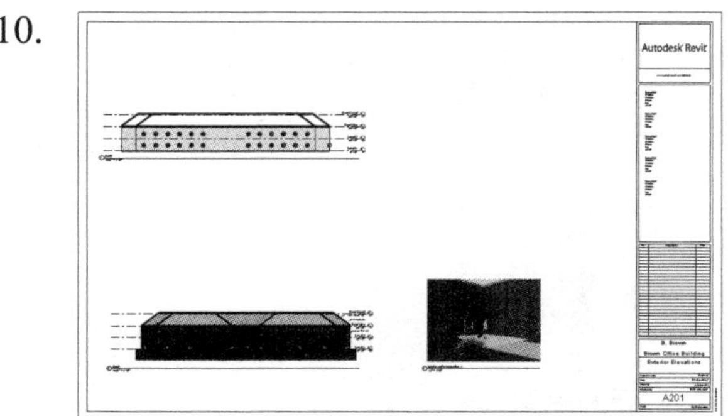

Zoom to Fit.

Shift the elevation views to the left to make room for an additional view.

Note you see a toposurface in the South elevation view because one was added for the exterior rendering.

9. 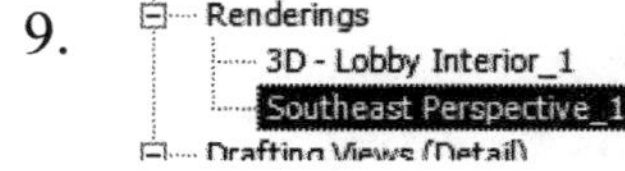

In the browser, locate the **Southeast Perspective** view under *Renderings*.

Drag and drop it onto the sheet.

10. You see how easy it is to add rendered views to your layouts.

11. 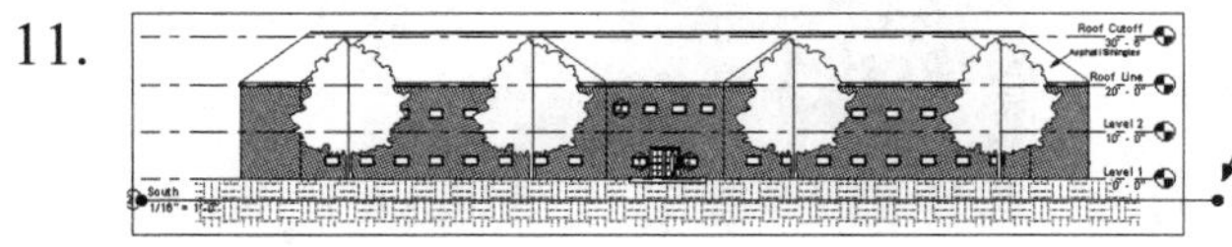

To adjust the length of the view title, click on the view. This will activate the grips and allow you to adjust the length and location of the title.

12. 

Select the rendering image that was just placed.

13. 

In the Properties pane:

Select **Edit Type**.

14. Type Properties

Family: System Family: Viewport — Load...

Type: Viewport 1 — Duplicate...

Rename...

Type Parameters

Parameter	Value
Graphics	
Title	View Title
Show Title	Yes
Show Extension Line	☑
Line Weight	1
Color	Black
Line Pattern	Solid

Note that the current type of Viewport shows the title.

Select **Duplicate**.

15. 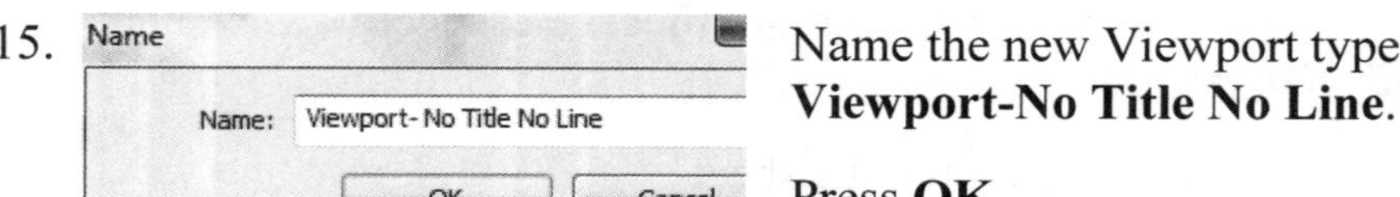

Name the new Viewport type: **Viewport-No Title No Line**.

Press **OK**.

16. Type Parameters

Parameter	
Graphics	
Title	View Title
Show Title	No
Show Extension Line	☐
Line Weight	1
Color	Black
Line Pattern	Solid

Uncheck **Show Extension Line**.

Set Show Title to **No**.

Press **OK**.

17. 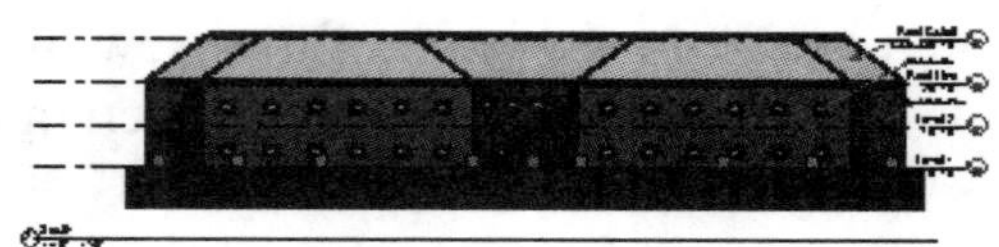

The rendering viewport has no title.

The elevation viewport has a title.

18. Sheets (all)
    - A101 - First Level Floor Plan
    - A102 - Level 2 Ceiling Plan
    - A201 - Exterior Elevations
    - A601 - Door Schedule
    - A602 - Glazing Schedule
    - **A603 - Lobby Keynotes**
    - AD501 - Details

    Activate the **Lobby Keynotes** sheet.

19. Image

    Activate the **Insert** ribbon.

    Select the **Image** tool.

20. 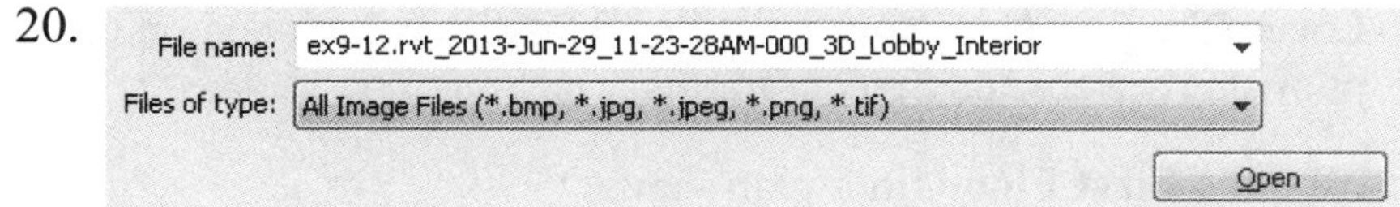

    Locate the rendering that was downloaded from the Autodesk 360 account.

    Press **Open**.

21. Place the image on the sheet and resize.

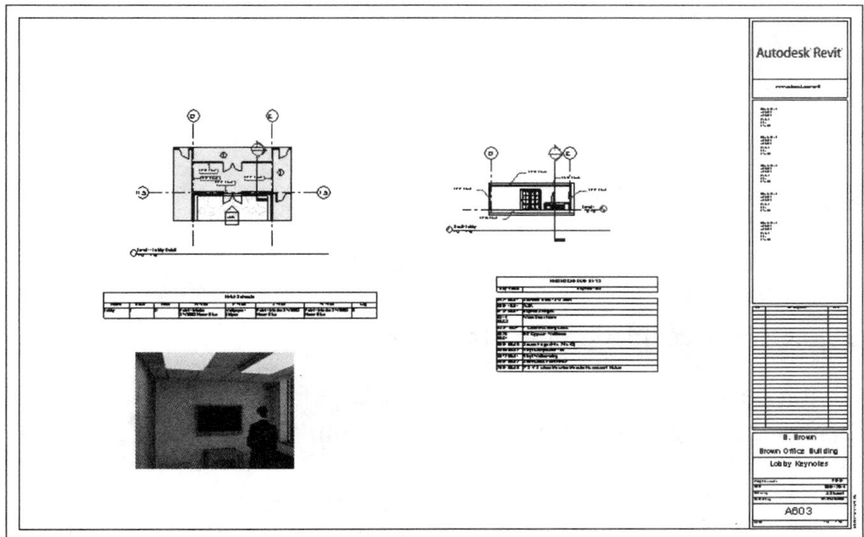

Note that it does not have a viewport associated with it because it is not a view. It is an image file.

22. Save the file as *ex9-13.rvt.*

You can free up memory resources for rendering by closing any windows you are not using. Windows with 3D or renderings take up a considerable amount of memory.

Exercise 9-14

Placing a Path for a Walkthrough

Drawing Name: i_Urban_House.rvt
Estimated Time: 10 minutes

This exercise reinforces the following skills:

- Creating a Walkthrough view

1. Locate the *i_Urban_House.rvt* file. This file is included on the publisher's website. Select **Open**.
2. Activate the **First Floor** floor plan view.
3. Activate the **View** ribbon.
4. Select the **Walkthrough** tool under the 3D View drop-down.
5. 

   Verify that **Perspective** is enabled in the Status Bar.

   This indicates that a perspective view will be created.
   The Offset indicates the height of the camera offset from the floor level.

6. 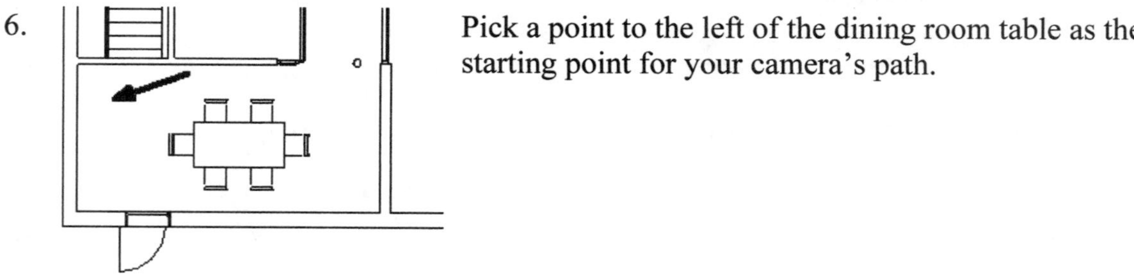
   Pick a point to the left of the dining room table as the starting point for your camera's path.

7. 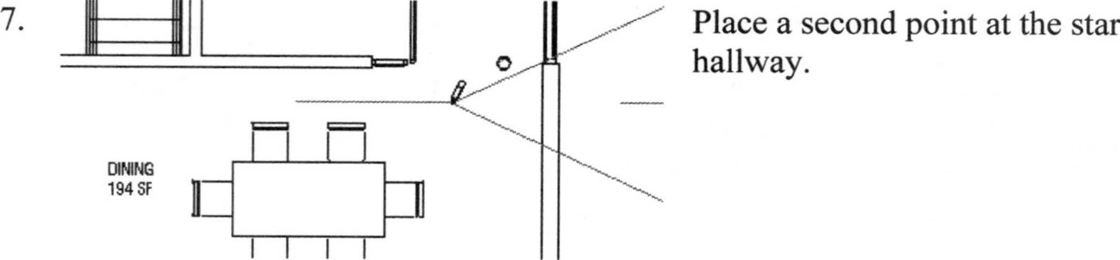

   Place a second point at the start of the hallway.

8. 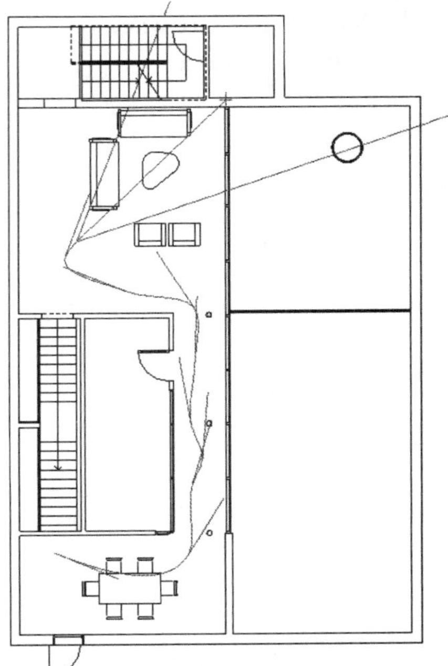

Place points at the locations indicated by the arrows to guide your walkthrough.

9. Select **Walkthrough→Finish Walkthrough** from the ribbon.

10. In the Project Browser, you will now see a Walkthrough listed under Walkthroughs.

11. Save as *ex9-14.rvt.*

Exercise 9-15

Playing the Walkthrough

Drawing Name: ex9-14.rvt
Estimated Time: 5 minutes

This exercise reinforces the following skills:

- Playing a Walkthrough

1. Open *ex9-14.rvt.*

2. Highlight the Walkthrough in the Browser. Right click and select **Open**.

3. 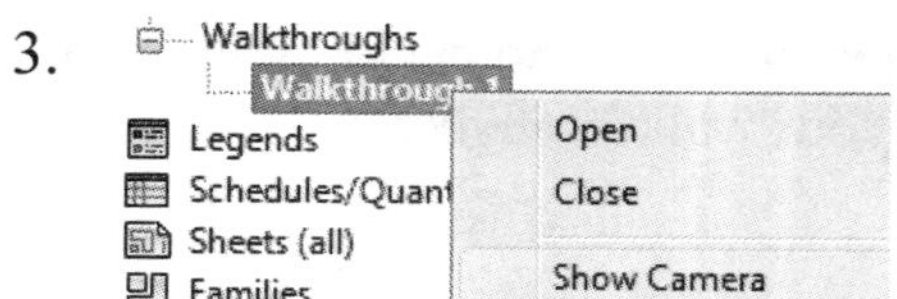

Highlight the Walkthrough in the Browser.
Right click and select **Show Camera**.

4. Select **Edit Walkthrough** on the ribbon.

5. Look at the Options bar.

Set the Frame number to **1.0**.

6. Activate the **Edit Walkthrough** ribbon.

7. 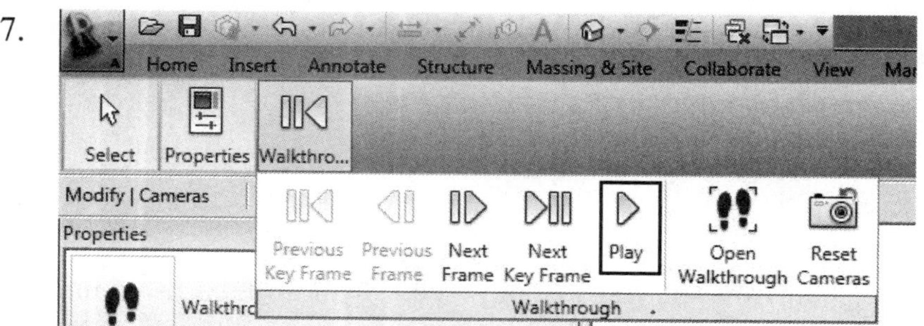

Press **Play** on the ribbon.

8. Press the button that displays the total frame number. Your frame number value may be different.

9. Change the Total Frames value to **50**.
Press **Apply** and **OK**.

10. Press **Play**.

11. Save as *ex9-15.rvt.*

Exercise 9-16

Editing the Walkthrough Path

Drawing Name: ex9-15.rvt
Estimated Time: 15 minutes

This exercise reinforces the following skills:

- Show Camera
- Editing a Walkthrough
- Modifying a Camera View

1. Open *ex9-15.rvt.*

2. Floor Plans / FIRST FLOOR — Activate the **First Floor** floor plan view.

3. 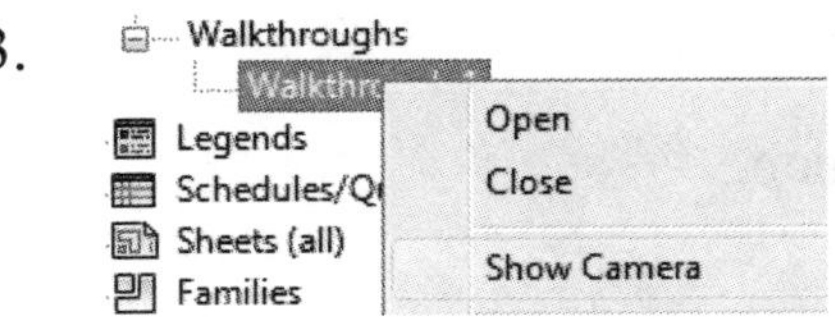

Highlight the Walkthrough 1 in the Project Browser.

Right click and select **Show Camera**.

4. 

Select **Edit Walkthrough** from the ribbon.

5. Disable **Far Clip Active**.

Extents	
Crop Region Visible	☑
Far Clip Active	☐

6. 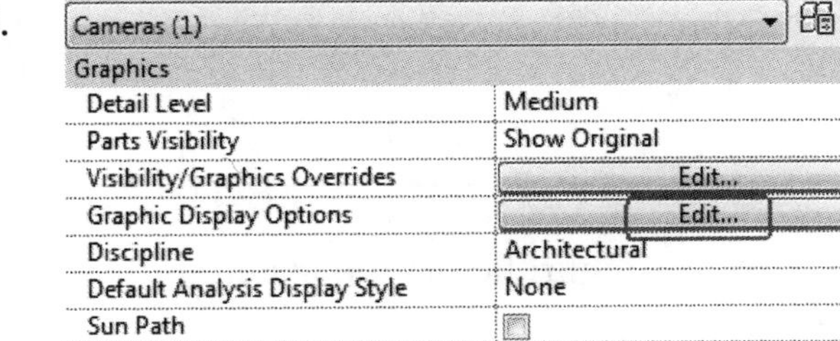

Select **Edit** next to Graphic Display Options.

7. 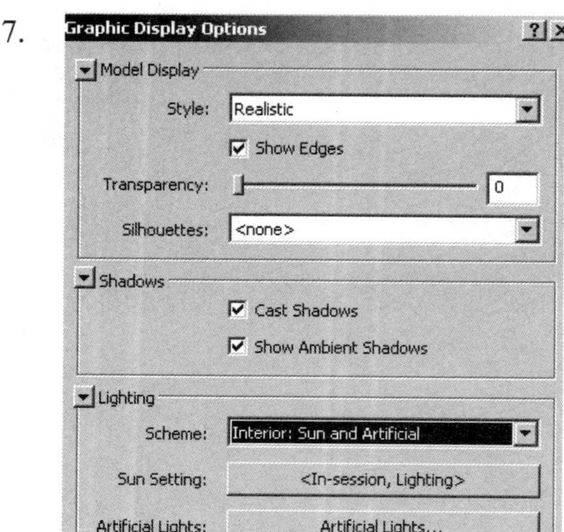

Set the Style to **Realistic**.
Enable **Show Edges**.

Enable **Cast Shadows**.
Enable **Show Ambient Shadows**.
Set the Lighting to Interior: Sun and Artifical.
Press **Apply** and **OK.**

8. Double left click on **Walkthrough 1** to open the view.

9. 

Select **Edit Walkthrough** from the ribbon.

10. Press **Play**.

11. Save as *ex9-16.rvt*.

The appearance of shaded objects is controlled in the material definition.
To stop playing the walkthrough, press **ESC** at any frame point.

Exercise 9-17
Creating an Animation

Drawing Name: ex9-16.rvt
Estimated Time: 15 minutes

This exercise reinforces the following skills:

- Show Camera
- Editing a Walkthrough
- Modifying a Camera View

1. Open *ex9-16.rvt.*

2. 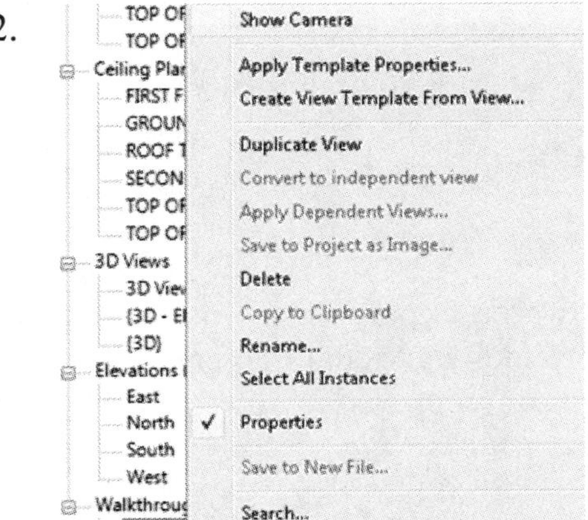

Highlight the Walkthrough 1 in the Project Browser.

Right click and select **Show Camera**.

3. 

Select **Edit Walkthrough** on the ribbon.

4. Frame 1.0 of 50

Set the Frame number to **1.0**.

5. 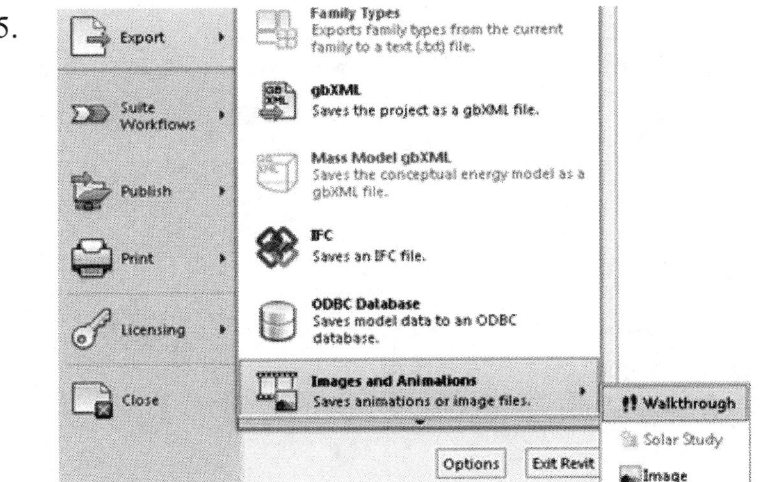

Go to **File→Export→ Images** and **Animations→ Walkthrough**.

6. 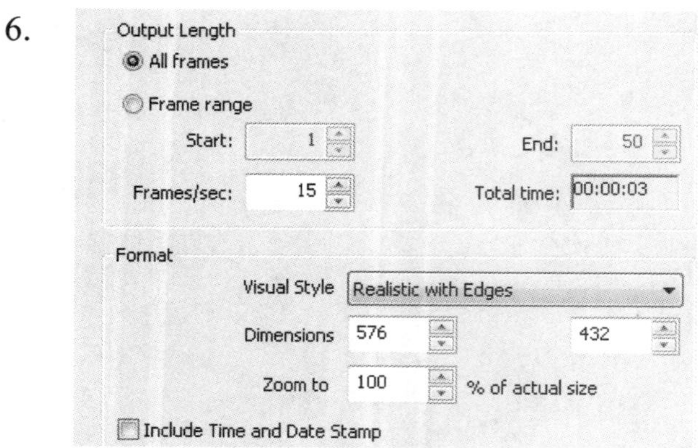

Set the Visual Style to **Realistic with Edges**.

Press **OK**.

You can create an animation using Rendering but it takes a long time to process.

7. File name: ex9-15 Walkthrough 1
Files of type: AVI Files (*.avi)

Locate where you want to store your avi file. You can use the Browse button (…) next to the Name field to locate your file.

8. Name your file *ex9-16 Walkthrough 1.avi.*

9. Press **Save**.

10. 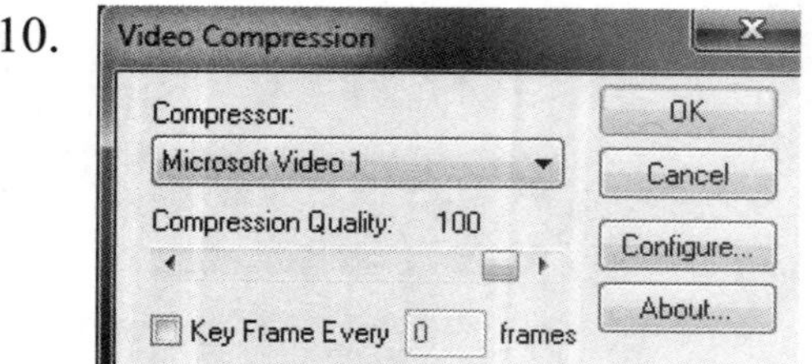

Select **Microsoft Video 1**.

This will allow you to play the avi on RealPlayer or Microsoft Windows Media Player.
If you select a different compressor, you may not be able to play your avi file.

Press **OK**.

11. 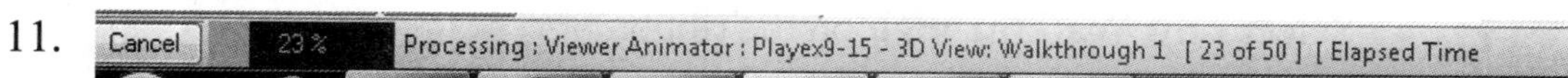

A progress bar will appear in the lower right of your screen to keep you apprised of how long it will take.

12. ex9-15 Walkthrough 1

Locate the file using Explorer.
Double click on the file to play it.

13. Save as *ex9-17.rvt.*

Additional Projects

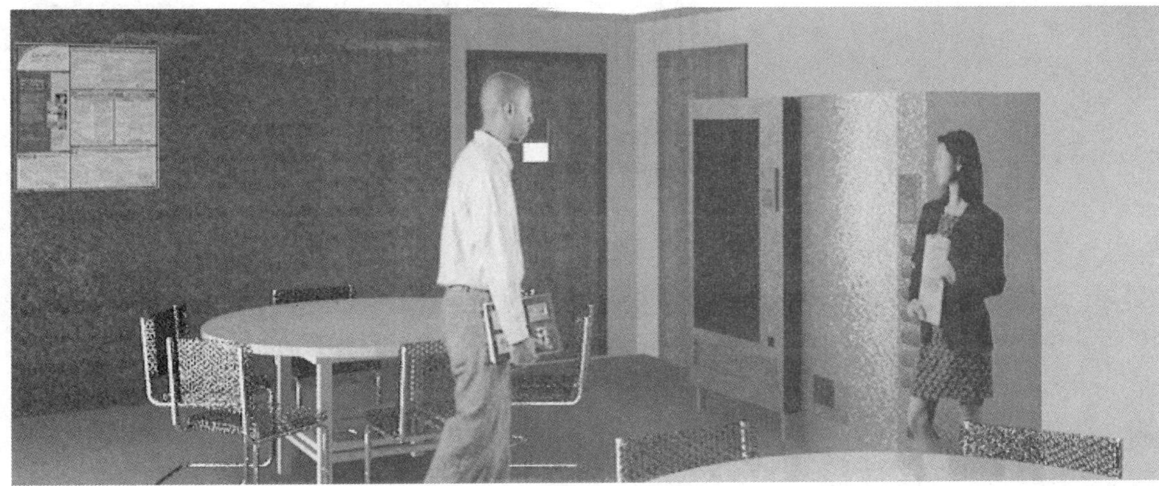

1) Create a rendering of the cafeteria area

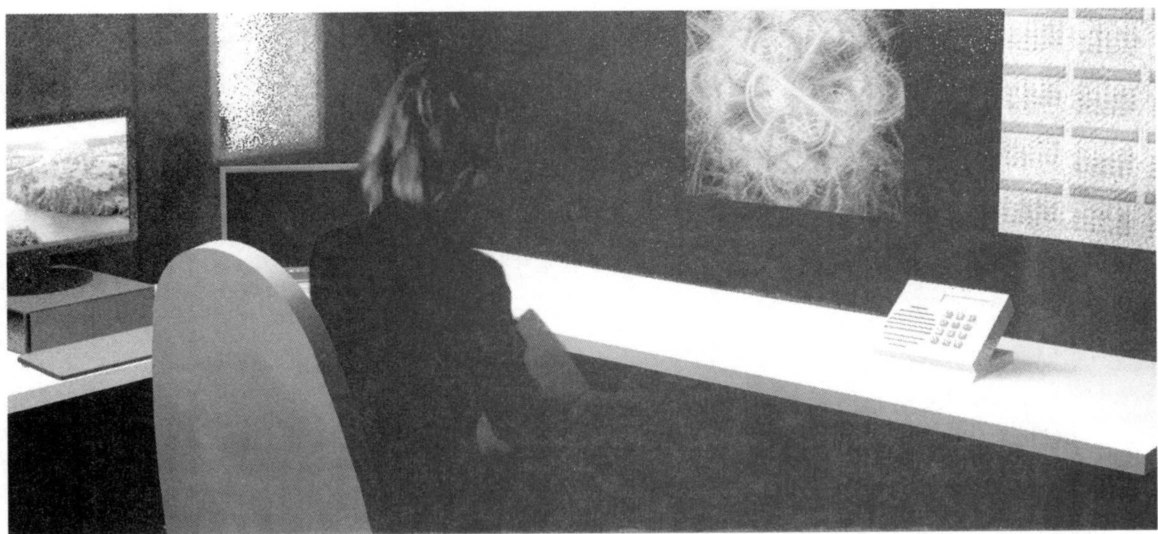

2) Create a rendering of one of the office cubicles
   The figure is the Female Entourage family - Cynthia. The publisher's website has the images and the families for the monitor, phone, keyboard, and CPU. Image files are also on the publisher's website which can be used in the rendering.

3) Add exterior lighting using the bollard lights in the Revit library to both sides of the walkway to the building.
Set the day to December 11 and the time at 7:30 pm.
Adjust the exposure after the rendering is done.

4) Create a walkthrough avi of one of your rendered scenes.

Lesson 9 Quiz

True or False

1. The Walkthrough tool on the View ribbon allows you to create an avi.
2. The Environment button on Render Settings dialog allows you to set the time of day.
3. The Sun button on Render Settings dialog allows you to set the time of day.
4. When you create a Rendering, you will be able to see how your people will appear.
5. Rendering is a relatively quick process.
6. Renderings can be added to sheets.
7. You can adjust the number of frames in a walkthrough.
8. You can not create walkthrough animations that go from one level to another.
9. Once a path is placed, it can not be edited.
10. You can not modify the view style of a walkthrough from wireframe to shaded.

Multiple Choice

11. The folder, which contains RPC People, is named:

    A. Site
    B. People
    C. Entourage
    D. Rendering

12. The Camera tool is located on the ____________________ ribbon.

    A. Rendering
    B. Site
    C. Home
    D. View

13. To see the camera in a view:

    A. Highlight the 3D view in the browser, right click and select Show Camera.
    B. Highlight the view in the browser, right click and select Show Camera.
    C. Go to View→Show Camera.
    D. Mouse over the view, right click and select Show Camera.

14. In order to save your rendering, use:

    A. File→Export
    B. Save to Project
    C. Capture Rendering
    D. Export Image

15. When editing a walkthrough, the user can modify the following:

    A. Camera
    B. Path
    C. Add Key Frame
    D. Remove Key Frame
    E. All of the above

16. Decals are visible in the display mode:

    A. Hidden
    B. Wireframe
    C. Realistic
    D. Raytrace

17. In order to render using the Cloud, the user needs:

    A. Internet access
    B. An umbrella
    C. A Revision Cloud
    D. A valid ID

18. When placing a building pad, the following elements are required:

    A. You must be in a site plan view
    B. There must be a toposurface
    C. There must be a building pad family defined
    D. There must be a building pad material defined

ANSWERS:
1) F; 2) F; 3) T; 4) T; 5) F; 6) T; 7) T; 8) F; 9) F; 10) F; 11) C; 12) D; 13) B; 14) B; 15) E; 16) C; 17) A; 18) B

Lesson 10
Customizing Revit

Exercise 10-1
Creating an Annotation Symbol

File: north arrow.dwg (located on the publisher's website)
Estimated Time: 30 minutes

This exercise reinforces the following skills:

- ❑ Import AutoCAD Drawing
- ❑ Full Explode
- ❑ Query
- ❑ Annotation Symbol

Many architects have accumulated hundreds of symbols that they use in their drawings. This exercise shows you how to take your existing AutoCAD symbols and use them in Revit.

1. Locate the north arrow.dwg on the publisher's website.

2. 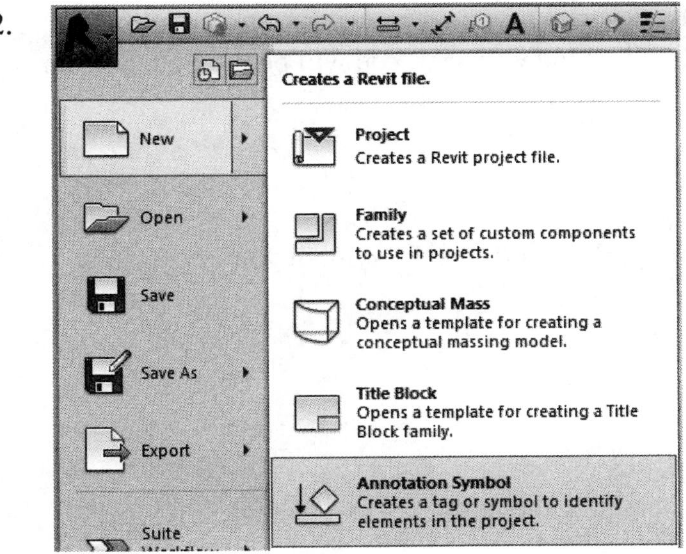

Go to **File→New→ Annotation Symbol**.

3. File name: Generic Annotation
Files of type: Family Template Files (*.rft)

Highlight the **Generic Annotation.rft** file under Annotations.

Press **Open**.

4. Activate the Insert ribbon.

Import CAD

Select **Import CAD**.

5. Locate the *north arrow.dwg* file on the publisher's website.

6. 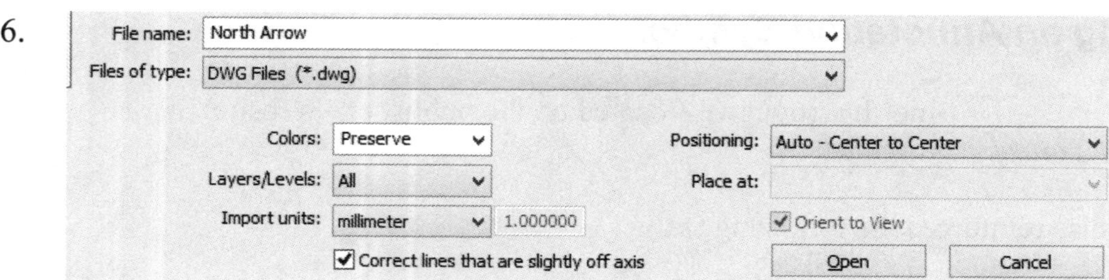

Under Colors:	Enable **Preserve**.
Under Layers:	Select **All**.
Under Import Units:	Select **millimeter**.
Under Positioning:	Select **Auto – Center to Center**.

This allows you to automatically scale your imported data.
Note that we can opt to manually place our imported data or automatically place using the center or origin.

Press **Open**.

7. The Import tool looks in Paper space and Model space. You will be prompted which data to import.
Press **Yes**.

8. **Zoom In Region** to see the symbol you imported.

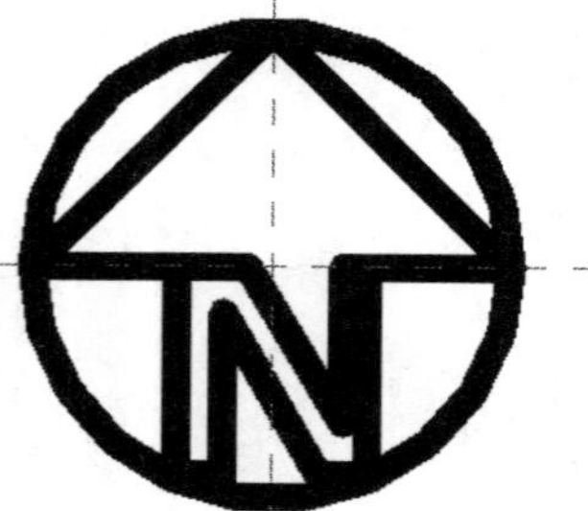

9. Pick the imported symbol.

Query

Select **Query** from the ribbon.

10. 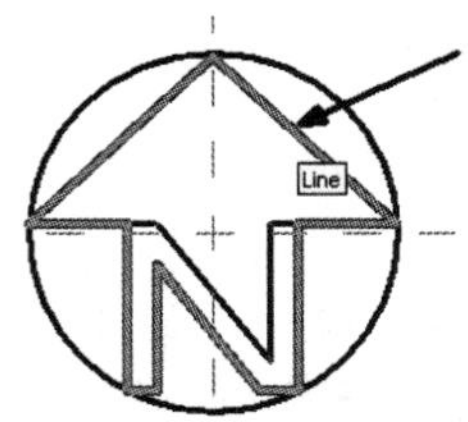

Pick on the line indicated.

11. **Import Instance Query**

Parameter	Value
Type	Arc
Block Name	N/A
Layer/Level	0
Style By	Layer/Level

A dialog appears that lists what the selected item is and the layer where it resides.

Press **OK**.

Right click and select **Cancel** to exit Query mode.

12. Pick the imported symbol.

Select **Full Explode**.

We can now edit our imported data.

13. Activate the Create ribbon.

Select the **Filled Region** tool on the Detail panel from the Architecture ribbon.

14. Enable **Chain** on the status bar.

15. Use the **Pick** tool on the Draw panel to select the existing lines to create a filled arrowhead.

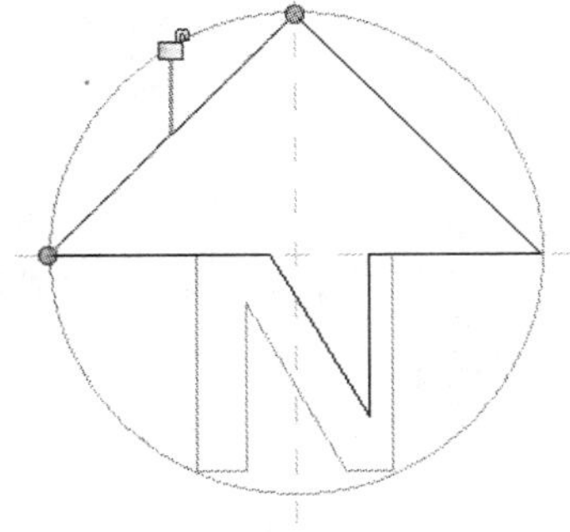

16. On the Properties palette:
Verify that the Region is set to a **Solid Black**.

17. 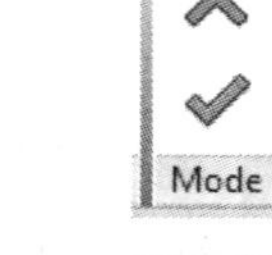

Select the **Green Check** under the Mode panel to **Finish Region**.

18. 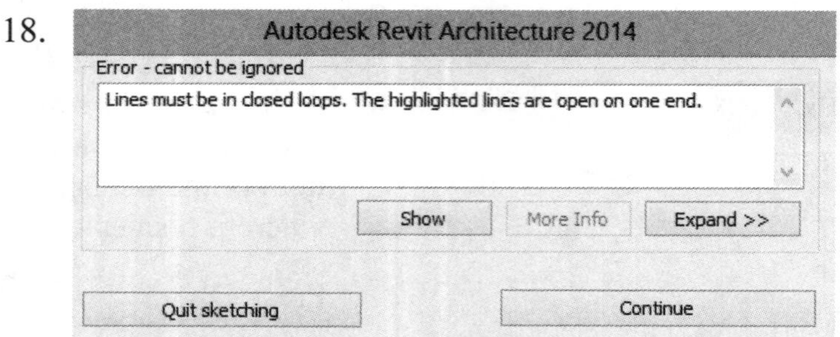

If you get an error message, check that you have a single closed loop.

19. 

Using grips, shorten the horizontal and vertical reference planes if needed.

You will need to unpin the reference planes before you can adjust the link.

Be sure to pin the reference planes after you have finished any adjustments. Pinning the reference planes ensures they do not move.

20. 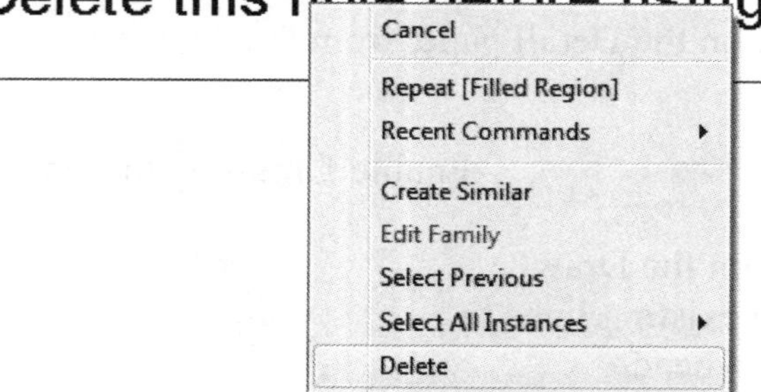

Select the note that is in the symbol. Right click and select **Delete**.

21. 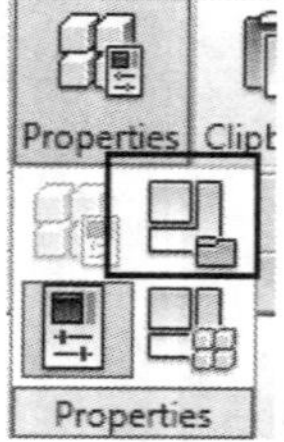

Select **Category and Parameters** under the Properties panel on the Modify ribbon.

22. 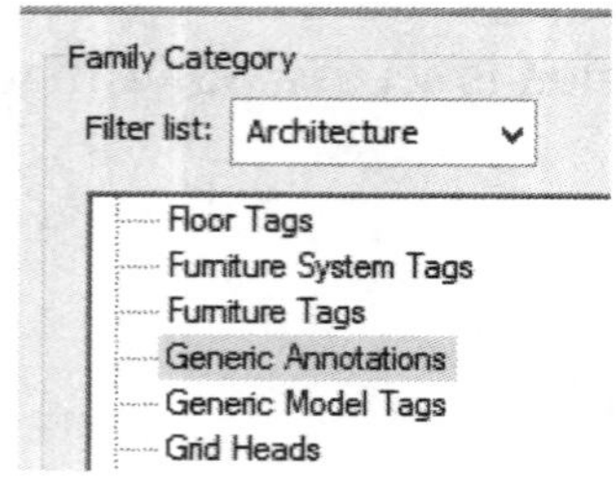

Note that **Generic Annotations** is highlighted. Press **OK**.

23. Save the file as a new family called **north arrow**.

24. Open *ex9-14.rvt.*

25. Activate the **First Level Floor Plan** sheet.

26. Activate the **Annotate** ribbon.

27. Select the **Symbol** tool.

28. Select **Load Family**.

29. Load the *north arrow.rfa* file that was saved to your student folder.

30. Place the North Arrow symbol in your drawing.

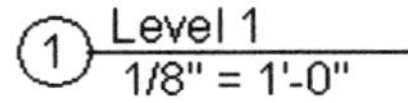

31. Save *ex9-14.rvt* as *ex10-1.rvt.*

Exercise 10-2

Creating a Custom Title Block

Estimated Time: 60 minutes

This exercise reinforces the following skills:

- Titleblock
- Import CAD
- Labels
- Text
- Family Properties

1.

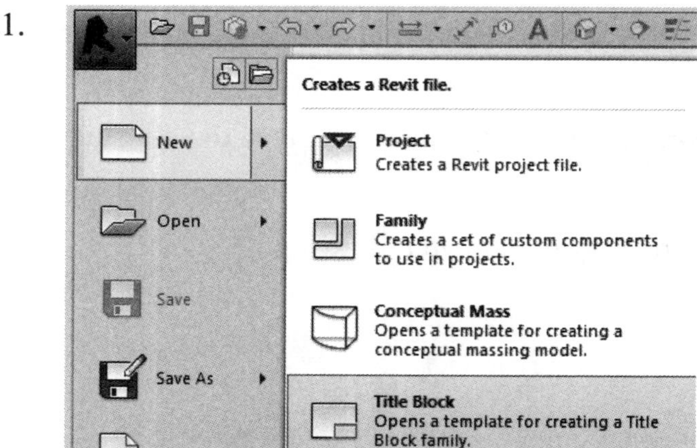

Go to **File→New→Titleblock**.

2. File name: New Size
Files of type: Family Template Files (*.rft)

Select **New Size**.

Press **Open**.

3.

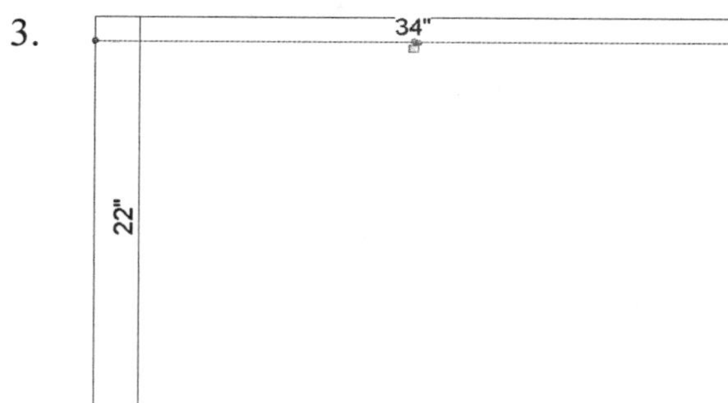

Pick the top horizontal line.
Select the dimension and change it to **22″**.

Pick the right vertical line.

Select the dimension and change it to **34″**.

I modified the dimension family to use a larger size font, but you don't have to do this.

The title block you define includes the sheet size. If you delete the title block, the sheet of paper is also deleted. This means your title block is linked to the paper size you define.

You need to define a title block for each paper size you use.

---

4. Right click in the graphics window and select **Zoom to Fit**.

5. Activate the Insert ribbon.
Select **Import→Import CAD**.

6. Locate the *Architectural Title Block* in the exercise files directory.

7.

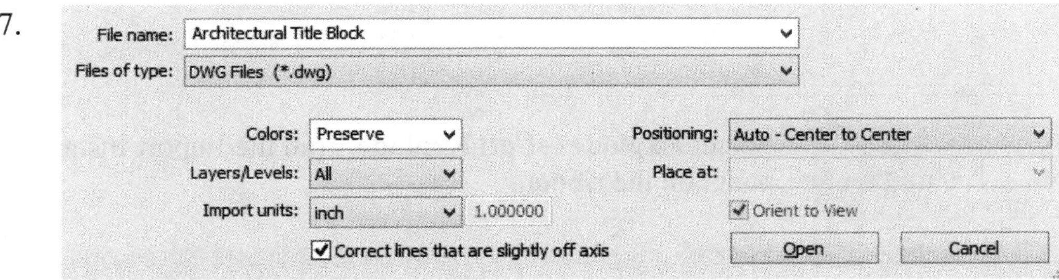

Set Colors to **Preserve**.
Set Layers to **All**.
Set Import Units to **Inch**.
Set Positioning to: **Auto - Center to Center**.

Press **Open**.

8.

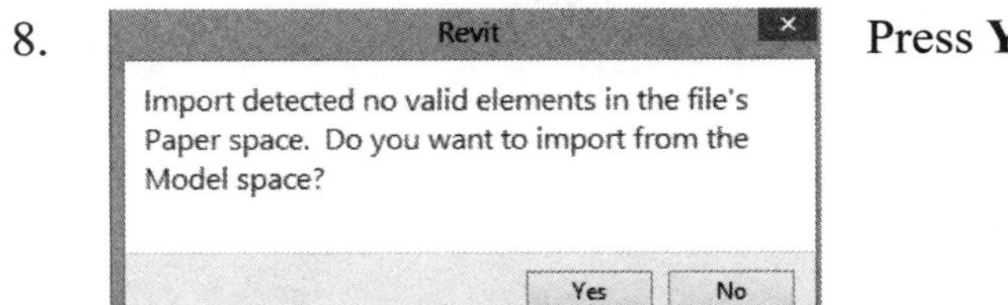

Press **Yes**.

9. Select the title block.

Use the **Move** tool on the Modify panel to reposition the titleblock so it is aligned with the existing Revit sheet.

10. 

Select the imported title block so it is highlighted.

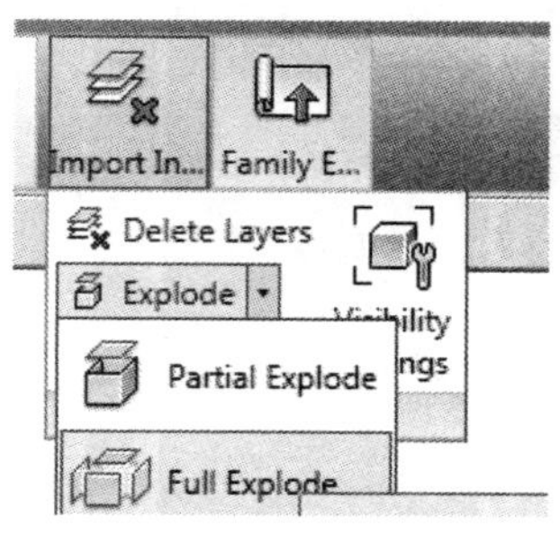

Select **Explode→Full Explode** from the Import Instance panel on the ribbon.

11. 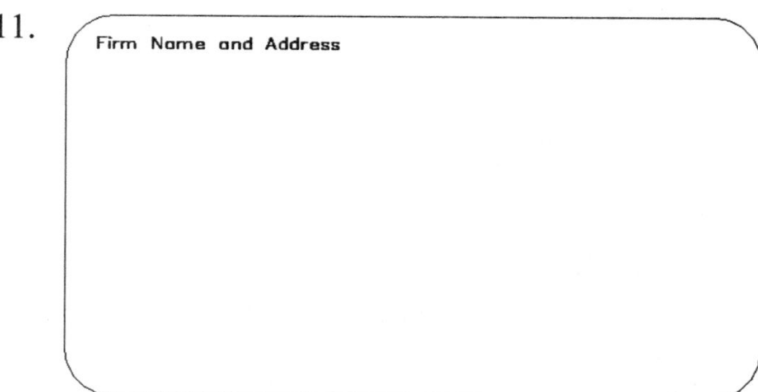

We will place an image in the rectangle labeled Firm Name and Address.

12. Activate the **Insert** ribbon.
Select the **Import→Image** tool.

13. 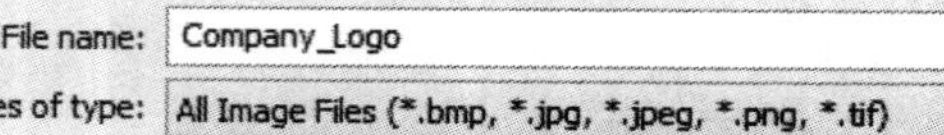

Open the *Company_Logo.jpg* file from the publisher's website.

14. 

Place the logo on the right side of the box.

Revit can import jpg, jpeg, or bmp files. Imported images can be resized, rotated, and flipped using activated grips.

15. A Text — Select the **Text** tool from the **Create** Ribbon.

16. Properties — Text, Text Note 1 — New Text — Edit Type

Select **Edit Type**.

17.

Text	
Text Font	Arial
Text Size	1/8"
Tab Size	1/2"

Change the Text Size to **1/8″**.

Press **OK**.

Revit can use any font that is available in your Windows font folder.

18. 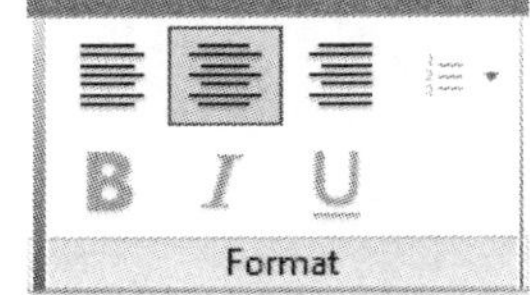

Select **CENTER** on the Format panel.

19. 

Type in the name of your school or company next to the logo.

The data entered in the Value field for labels will be the default value used in the title block. To save edit time, enter in the value that you will probably use.

20. A Text Select the **Label** tool from the Create ribbon.

Labels are similar to attributes. They are linked to file properties.

21. Project Name and Address

Left pick in the Project Name and Address box.

22. Press **OK**.
Left click to release the selection.
Pick to place when the dashed line appears.

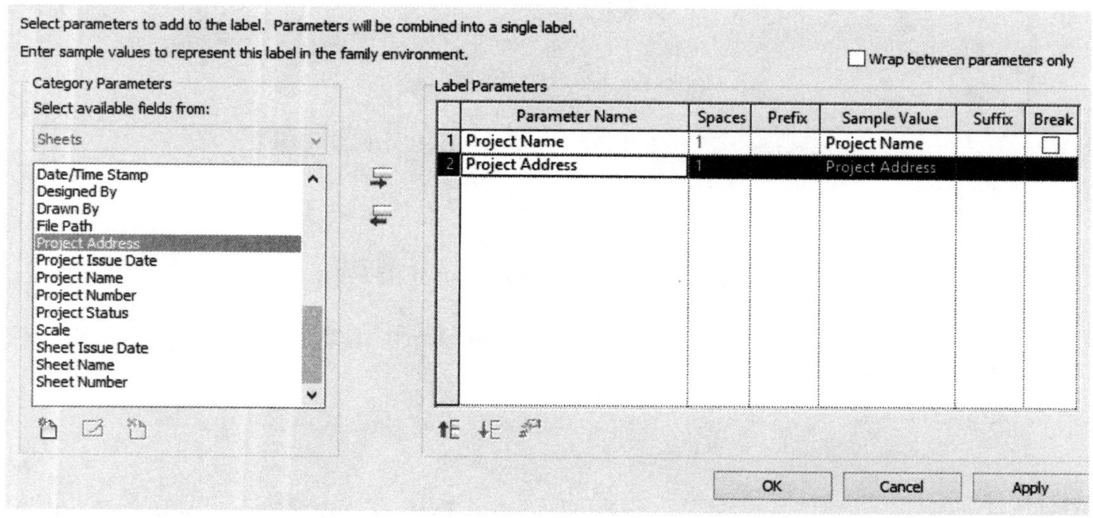

Select **Project Name**.
Use the **Add** button to move it into the Label Parameters list.
Add **Project Address**.

23. 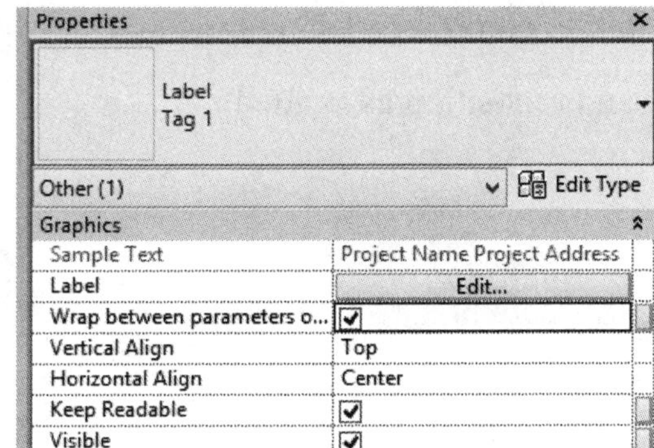

Select the label.

In the Properties panel:

Enable Wrap between parameters.

Verify that the Horizontal Align is set to Center.

24. 

Use Modify→Move to adjust the position of the project name and address label.

25. Select the **Label** tool.

Label

26. 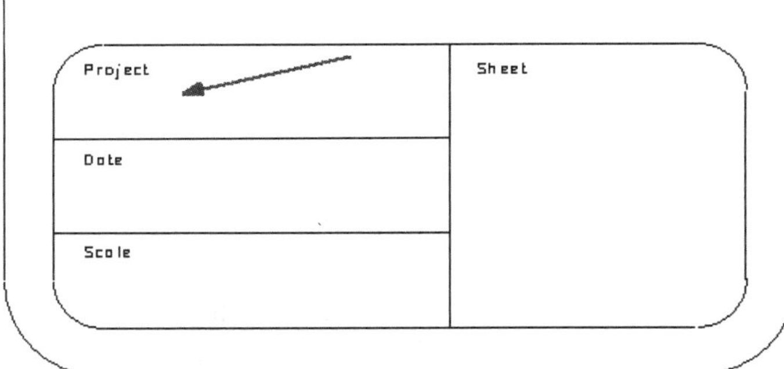

Left click in the Project box.

27. Locate **Project Number** in the Parameter list. Move it to the right pane.

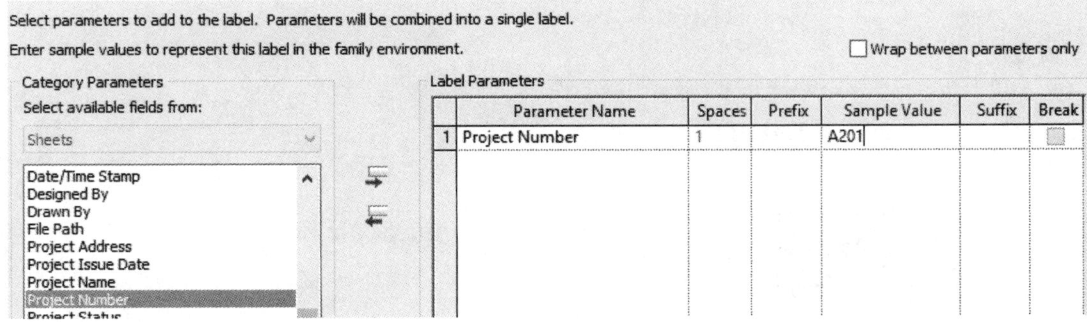

Add a sample value, if you like.

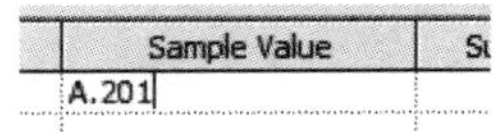

Press **OK**.

28. Left click to complete placing the label.

Select and reposition as needed.

29. Select the **Label** tool.

30. 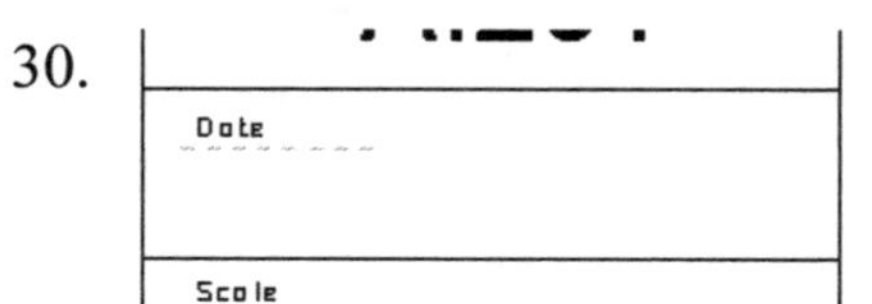

Left click in the Date box.

31. 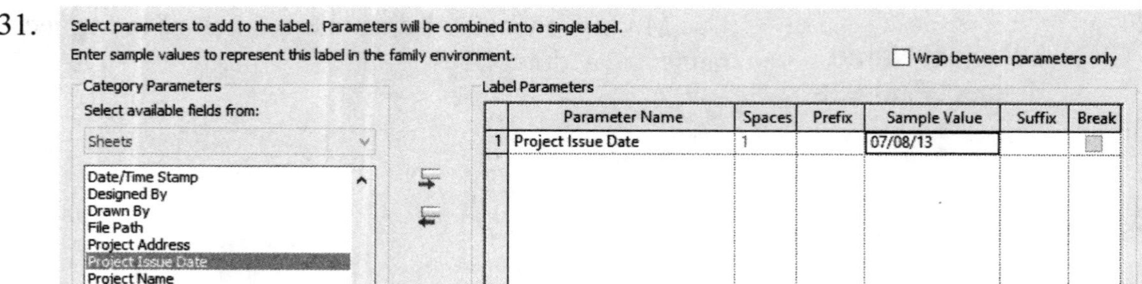

Highlight **Project Issue Date**.

Press the Add button.

In the Sample Value field, enter the default date to use.

Press **OK**.

32. 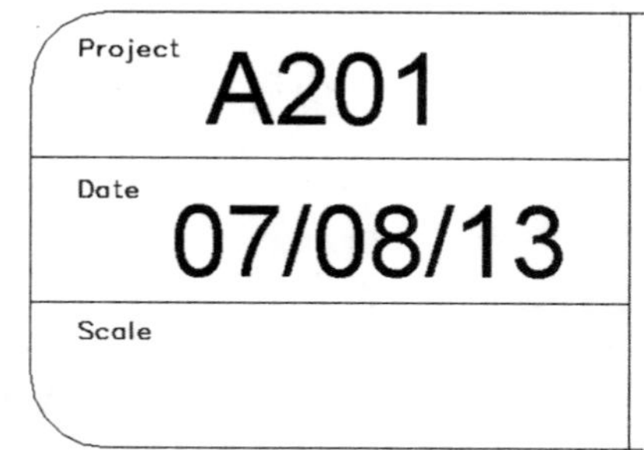

Position the date in the date field.

33. Select the **Label** tool.

34. 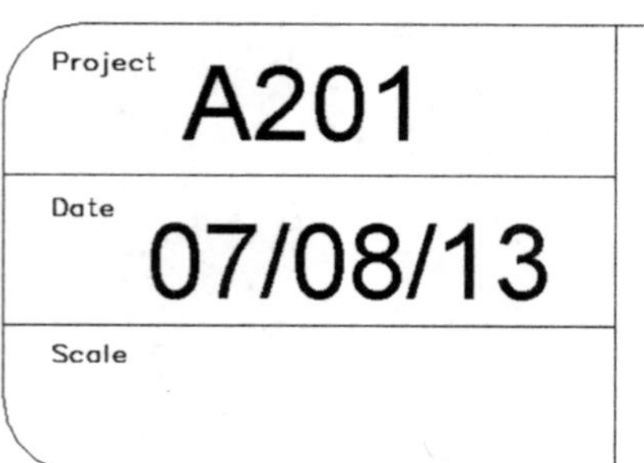

Left click in the Scale box.

35. 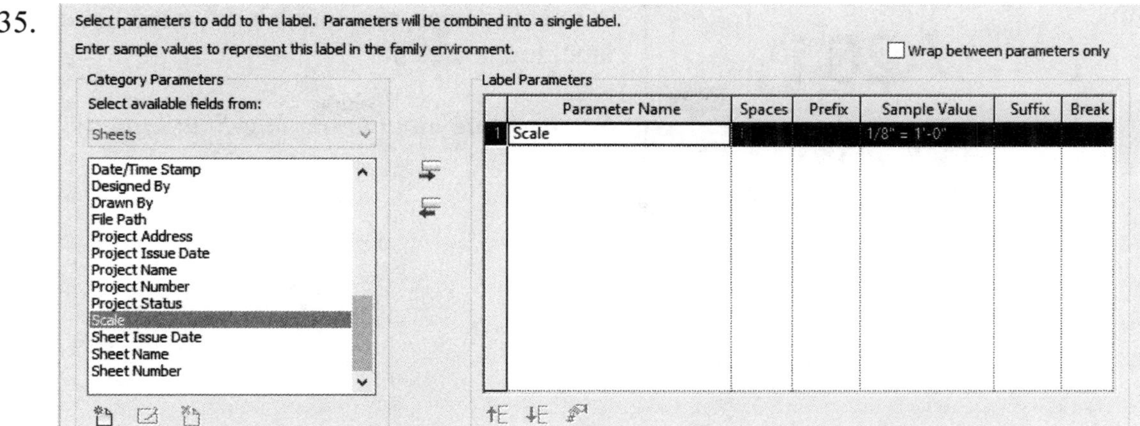

Highlight **Scale**.

Press the Add button.

Press **OK**.

36. Select **Edit Type** in the Properties pane.

37. Select **Duplicate**.

38. Rename **Tag - Small**.

Press **OK**.

39. 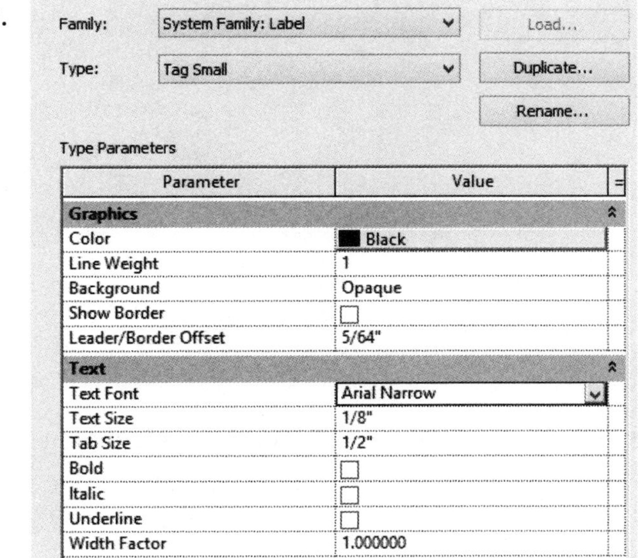

Set the Text Font to **Arial Narrow**.
Set the Text Size to **1/8″**.

Press **OK**.

40. 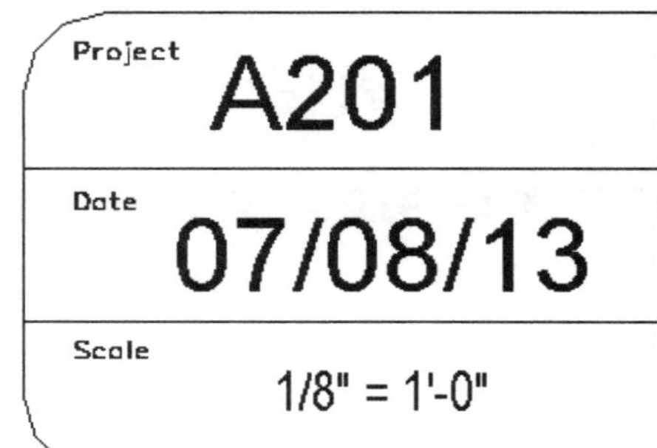

Adjust the lines, text and labels so the Sheet label looks clean.

Set the Scale label to the Tag-Small family.

41. Label Select the **Label** tool.

42. 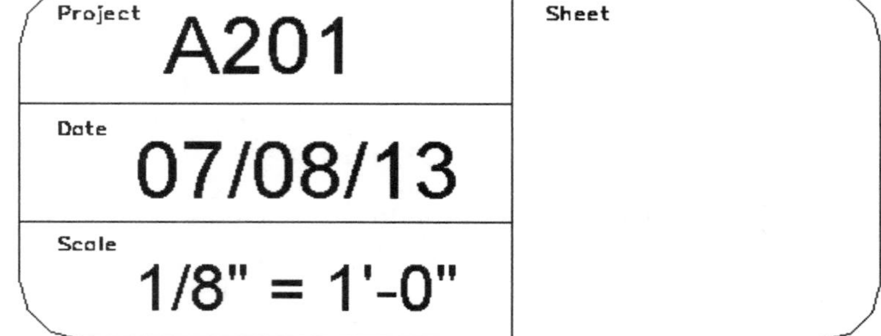

Left click in the Sheet box.

43. 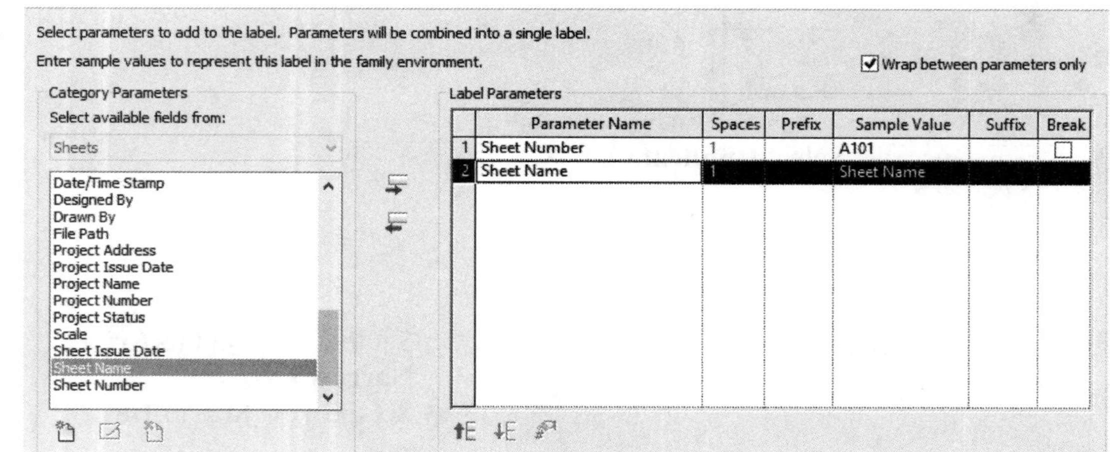

Highlight **Sheet Number**.

Press the Add button.

Highlight **Sheet Name**.

Press the Add button.

Enable **Wrap between parameters only** in the upper right corner of the dialog.

Press **OK**.

44. 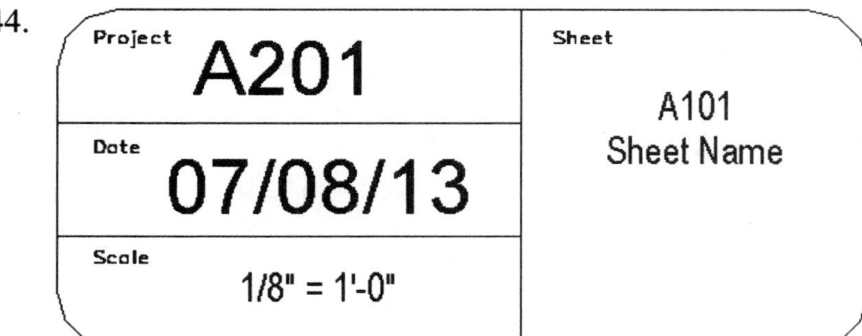

Position the Sheet label.

45. 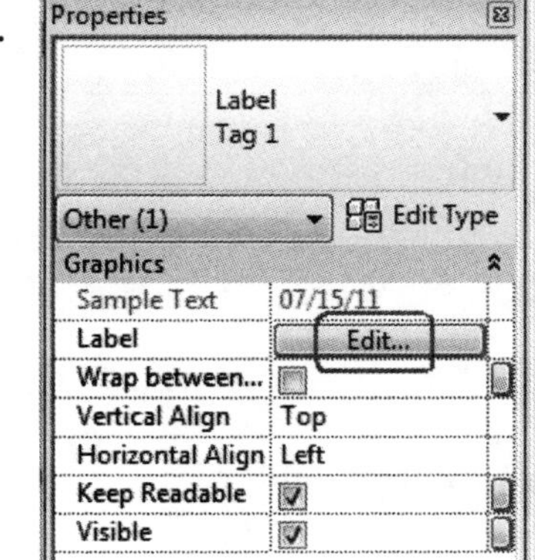

To modify a label, select the label.

On the Properties panel:
Select the **Edit** button next to Label.

This will allow you to select a different parameter, if desired.

46. Save the file as *Title block 22 x 34.rfa.*

You can select Shared Parameters for use in your title block.

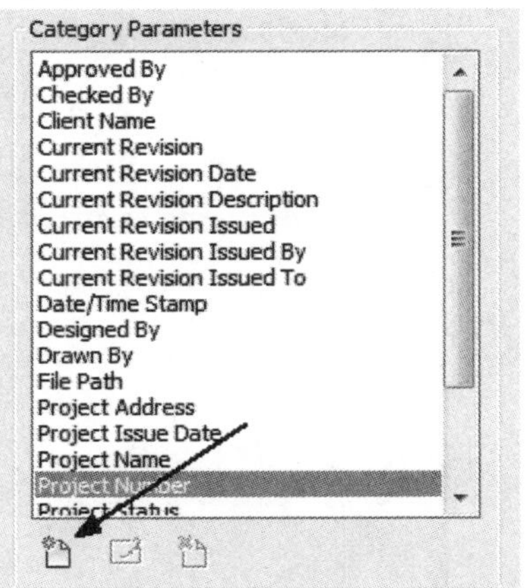

Exercise 10-3
Using a Custom Title Block

File: ex10-1.rvt
Estimated Time: 10 minutes

This exercise reinforces the following skills:

- Title block
- Import CAD
- Labels
- Text
- Family Properties

1. Open *ex10-1rvt*, if it is not already open.

2.  Load Family | Load as Group | Load from Library

   Activate the Insert ribbon.

   Select **Load Family** from the Load from Library panel.

3.  File name: Title block 22 x 34
   Files of type: All Supported Files (*.rfa, *.adsk)

   Browse to the folder where you saved the custom title block.

   Select it and press **Open**.

4. 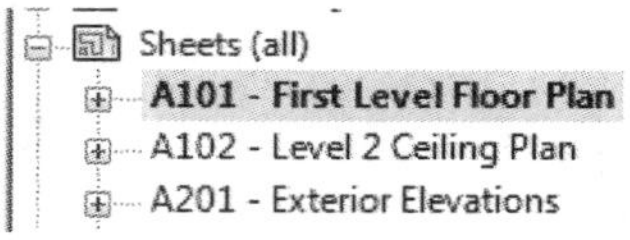 Sheets (all)
   A101 - First Level Floor Plan
   A102 - Level 2 Ceiling Plan
   A201 - Exterior Elevations

   Activate the **First Level Floor Plan** sheet.

5. 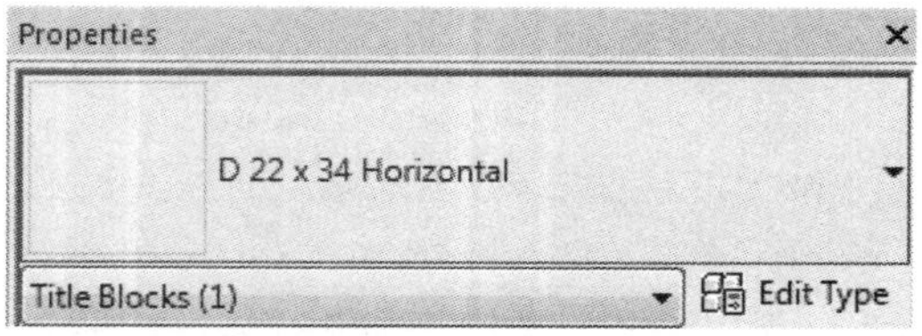 Properties
   D 22 x 34 Horizontal
   Title Blocks (1) | Edit Type

   Select the title block so it is highlighted.

   You will see the name of the title block in the Properties pane.

6. 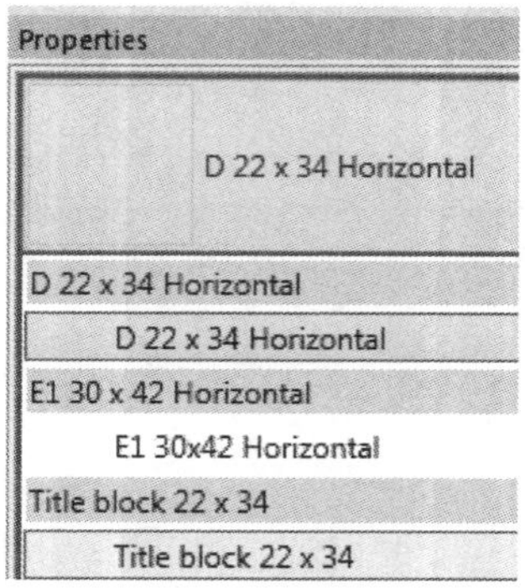 Properties
   D 22 x 34 Horizontal
   D 22 x 34 Horizontal
   D 22 x 34 Horizontal
   E1 30 x 42 Horizontal
   E1 30x42 Horizontal
   Title block 22 x 34
   Title block 22 x 34

   Select the **Title Block 22 x 34** using the Type Selector.

7. 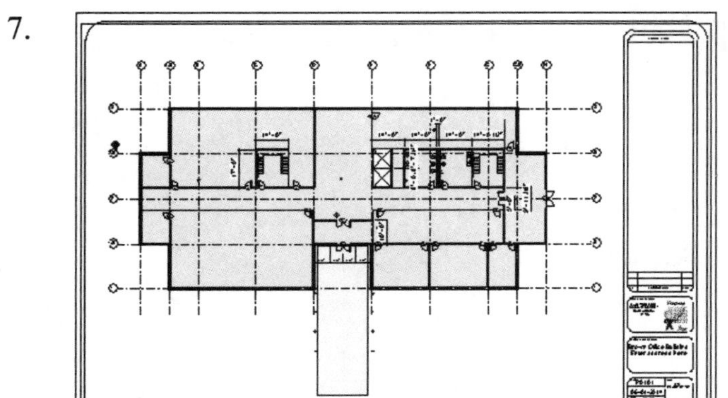

You may need to reposition the view on the title block.

8. 

Zoom into the title block.

Note that the parameter values have all copied over.

9. Save the file as *ex10-3.rvt.*

It is a good idea to save all your custom templates, families, and annotations to a directory on the server where everyone in your team can access them.

Exercise 10-4
Creating a Line Style

Drawing Name: 10-3.rvt
Estimated Time: 10 minutes

This exercise reinforces the following skills:

- Line Styles

1. Open *ex10-3.rvt.*

2. 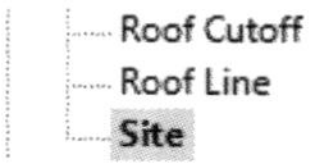 Activate the **Site** Floor plan.

3. 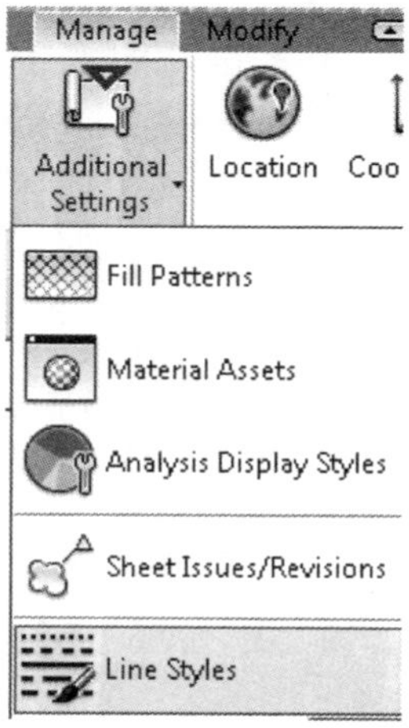 Activate the **Manage** ribbon.

   Go to **Settings→Additional Settings→Line Styles**.

4.  Select **New** under Modify Subcategories.

5. 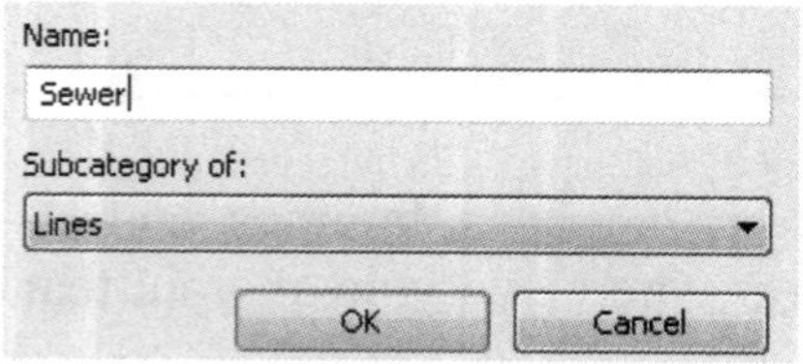 Enter **Sewer** in the Name field.

   Press **OK**.

6. 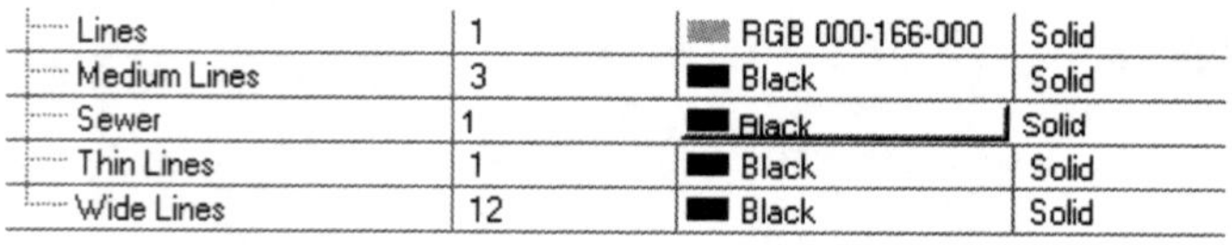 Sewer appears in the list.

Lines	1	RGB 000-166-000	Solid
Medium Lines	3	Black	Solid
Sewer	1	Black	Solid
Thin Lines	1	Black	Solid
Wide Lines	12	Black	Solid

Note Revit automatically alphabetizes any new line styles.

7. 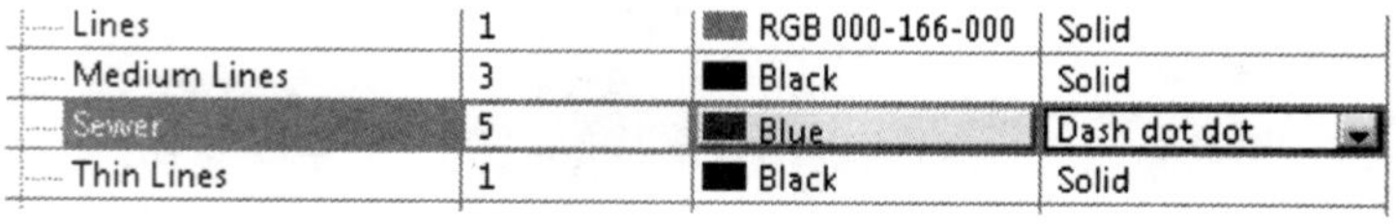 Set the Line Weight to **3**.
   Set the Color to **Blue**.
   Set the Line Pattern to **Dash Dot Dot**.

Lines	1	RGB 000-166-000	Solid
Medium Lines	3	Black	Solid
Sewer	5	Blue	Dash dot dot
Thin Lines	1	Black	Solid

Press **OK**.

8. Annotate Activate the **Annotate** ribbon.

9. Select the **Detail Line** tool under Detail.

   Detail Line

10. Line Style: Thin Lines

    <Beyond>
    <Centerline>
    <Demolished>
    <Hidden>
    <Overhead>
    Hidden Lines
    Lines
    Medium Lines
    Sewer
    Thin Lines
    Wide Lines

    Select **sewer** from the drop-down list in the Properties palette.

    You can also set the Line Style from the ribbon drop-down list.

11. 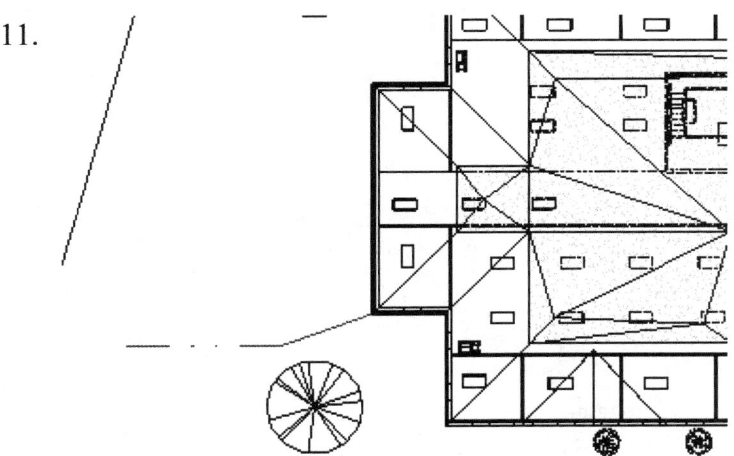

    Draw a line from the building to the toposurface edge.

12. Save the file as *ex10-4.rvt*.

Revit has three line tools: *Lines*, *Detail Lines*, and *Linework*. All of them use the same line styles, but for different applications. The *Lines* command draws model lines on a specified plane and can be seen in multiple views (i.e., score joints on an exterior elevation). The *Detail Lines* command draws lines that are view specific and will only appear on the view they were placed (i.e., details). The *Linework* tool is used to change the appearance of model-generated lines in a view.

Exercise 10-5

Defining Keyboard Shortcuts

Estimated Time: 5 minutes

This exercise reinforces the following skills:

- ❑ Keyboard Shortcuts

1. 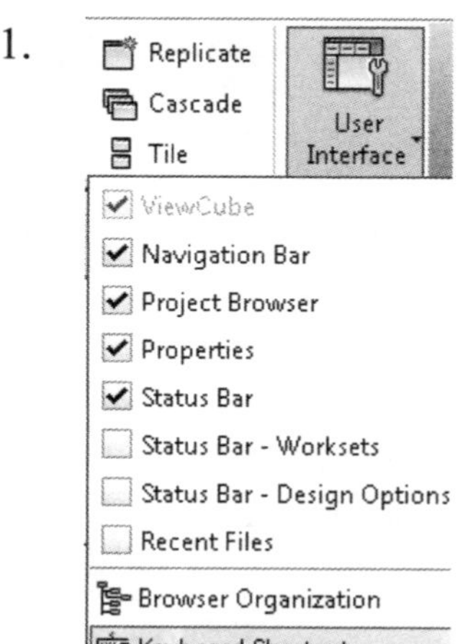

Activate the View ribbon.

Select **User Interface→Keyboard Shortcuts** from the Windows panel.

2. 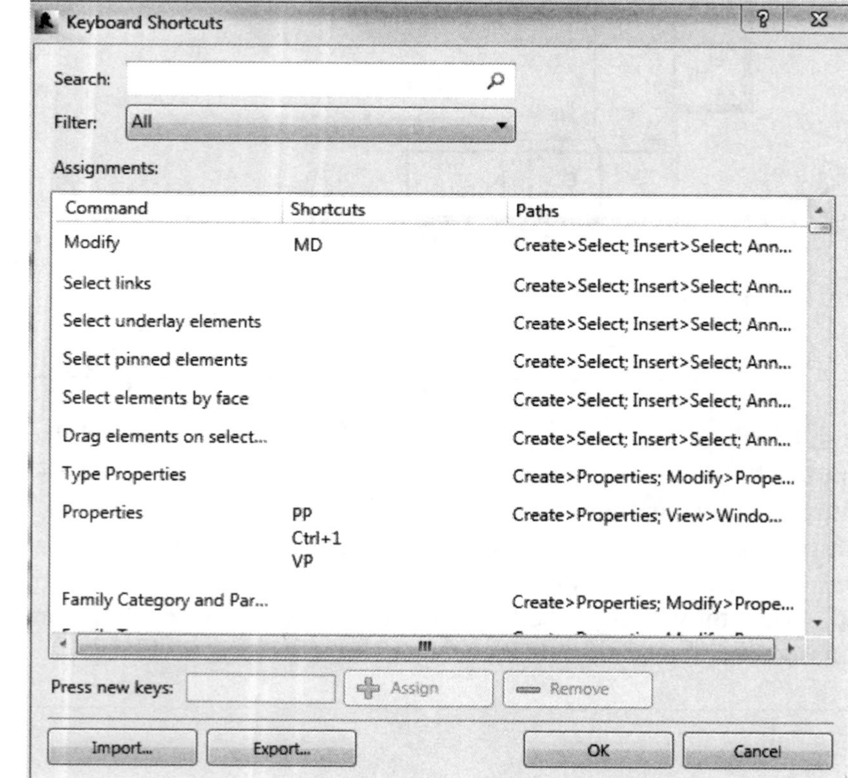

A dialog opens which allows you to assign shortcut keys to different Revit commands.

3. 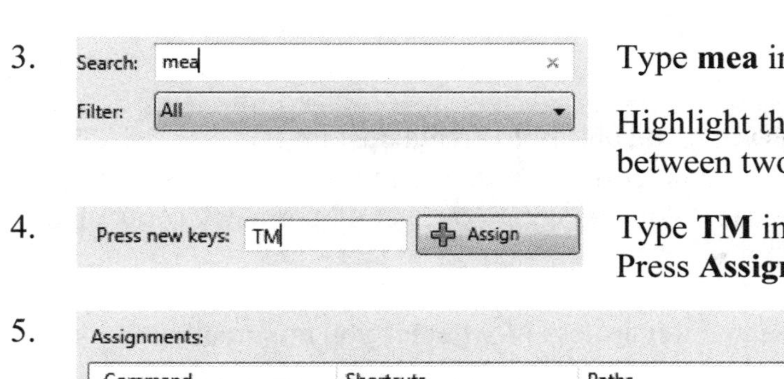

Type **mea** in the Search box.

Highlight the first command to Measure between two references.

4. Type **TM** in the Press new keys text box. Press **Assign**.

5. Assignments:

Command	Shortcuts	Paths
Measure:Measure Betwe...	TM	Modify>Measure; Quick Access T...
Measure:Measure Along...		Modify>Measure; Quick Access T...

The shortcut appears next to the command.

Press **OK** to close the dialog.

6. Type **TM**.

Total Length appears on the Options bar and your cursor is in Measure mode.

Creating Custom Families

One of the greatest tools inside of Revit is the ability to create custom families for common components, such as windows and doors. These are more powerful than blocks because they are completely parametric. You can create one set of geometry controlled by different sets of dimensions.

The steps to create a family are the same, regardless of whether you are creating a door, window, furniture, etc.

Step 1:
Select the appropriate family template to use.

Step 2:
Define sub-categories for the family
Sub-categories determine how the object will appear in different views

Step 3:
Lay out reference planes.

Step 4:
Dimension planes to control the parametric geometry.

Step 5:
Label dimensions to become type or instance parameters.
Step 6:
Create your types using the 'FamilyTypes' tool.

Step 7:
Activate different types and verify that the reference planes shift correctly with the dimensions assigned.

Step 8:
Label your reference planes.

Step 9:
Create your geometry and constrain to your reference planes using Lock and Align.

Step 10:
Activate the different family types to see if the geometry reacts correctly.

Step 11:
Save family and load into a project to see how it performs within the project environment.

Exercise 10-6
Creating a Furniture Family

Estimated Time: 120 minutes
File: generic model.rft

This exercise reinforces the following skills:

- Standard Component Families
- Templates
- Reference Planes
- Align
- Dimensions
- Parameters
- Sketch Tools
- Solid extrusion
- Materials
- Types

1. 

Start a **New** family.

2. Select the *Generic Model* template.

3. Select the **Reference Plane** tool from the Datum panel on the Architecture ribbon.

4. 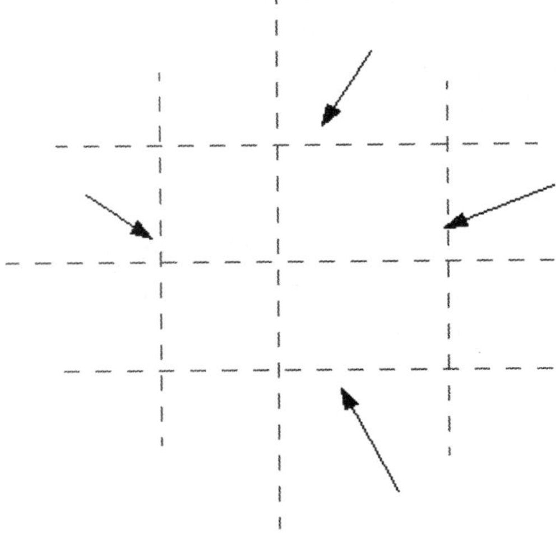
Draw four reference planes: two horizontal and two vertical on each side of the existing reference planes.

These will act as the outside edges of the table top.

5. Add a continuous aligned dimension horizontally and vertically so they can be set equal.

6.

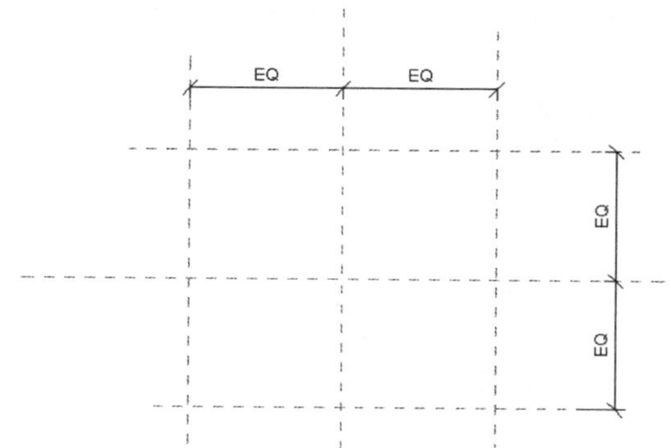

To place the dimension, select the reference planes by clicking in order without clicking to place until all three planes have been selected.

Then, left click on the EQ toggle to set equal.

7.

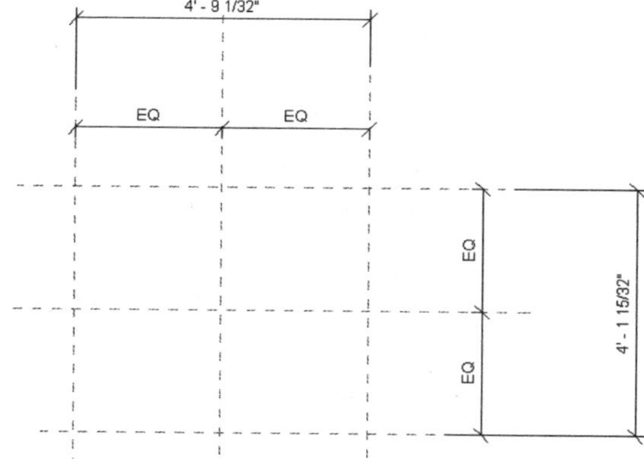

Place an overall horizontal dimension.

Place an overall vertical dimension.

8.

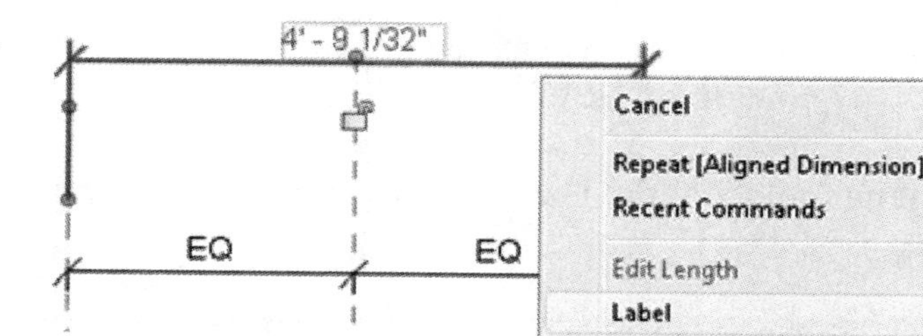

Select the overall horizontal dimension.

Right click and select **Label**.

Label: <None> Instance Parameter

You can also select Label from the Options bar.

9.

<None>
<None>
<Add parameter...>

Select **Add Parameter…**

10.

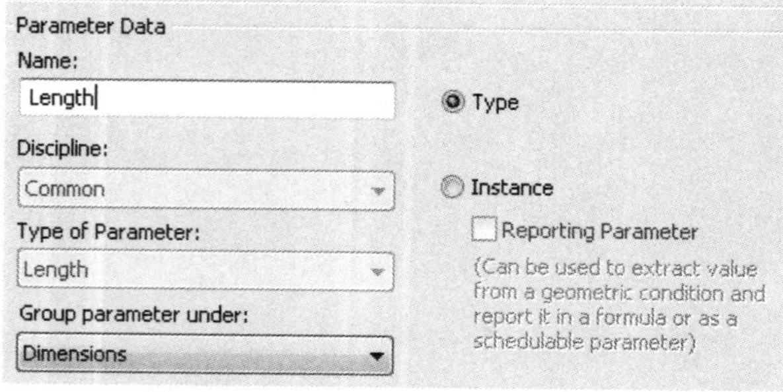

Under Name: type **Length**.
Set the group parameter to **Dimensions**.
Enable **Type**.
Press **OK**.

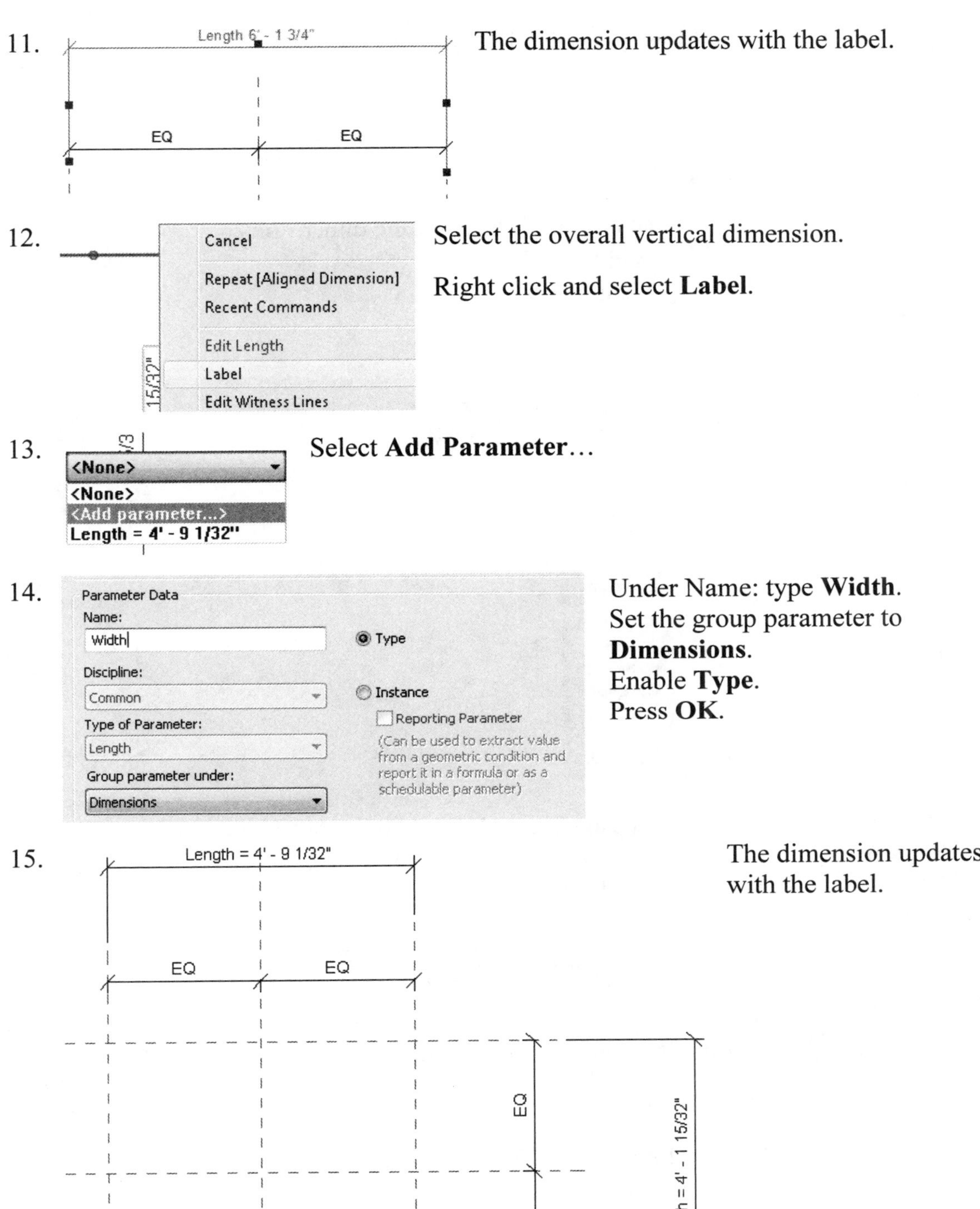

11. The dimension updates with the label.

12. Select the overall vertical dimension.

    Right click and select **Label**.

13. Select **Add Parameter…**

14. Under Name: type **Width**.
    Set the group parameter to **Dimensions**.
    Enable **Type**.
    Press **OK**.

15. The dimension updates with the label.

16. Select the **Family Types** tool on the Properties panel from the Modify ribbon.

17. Select **New** under Family Types.

18. Enter **Small** for the Name.

    Press **OK**.

19. Modify the values for the dimensions:
    Width: **2′6″**
    Length: **3′0″**

20. 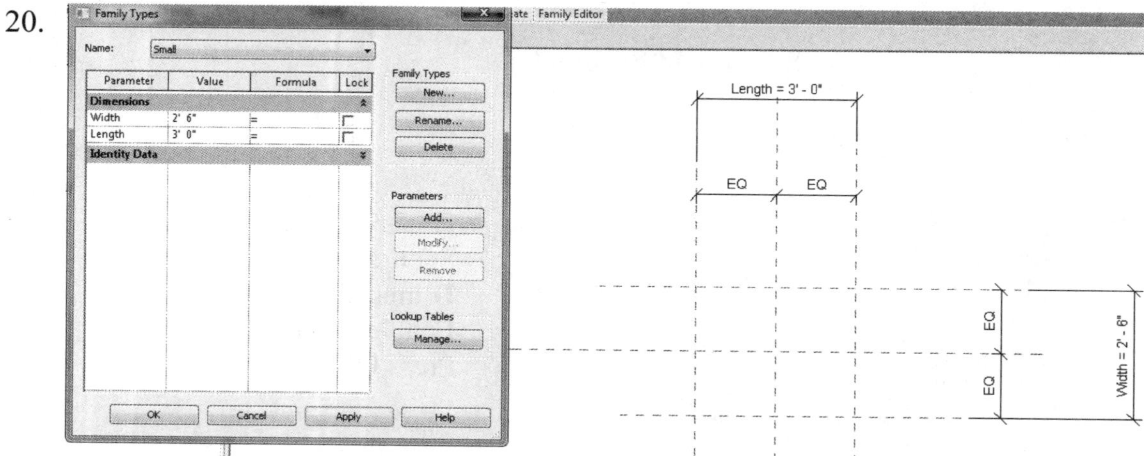

Move the dialog over so you can observe how the reference planes react.
Press **Apply**.
Note how the dimensions update.
This is called *flexing* the model.

21. Select **New** under Family Types.

22. Enter **Medium** for the Name.

    Press **OK**.

23. Modify the values for the dimensions:
    Width: **3′0″**
    Length: **4′0″**

24. Press **Apply**.
Note how the dimensions update.

25. Select **New** under Family Types.

26. Enter **Large** for the Name.

Press **OK**.

27. 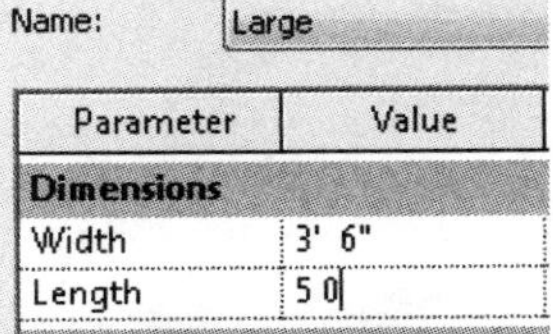

Name: Large

Parameter	Value
Dimensions	
Width	3' 6"
Length	5 0
Identity Data	

Modify the values for the dimensions:
Width: **3′ 6″**
Length: **5′ 0″**

28. 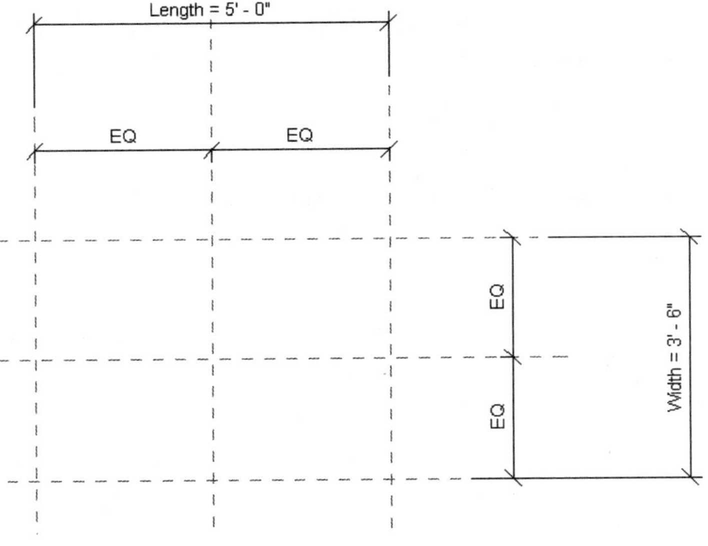

Press **Apply**.
Note how the dimensions update.

29. 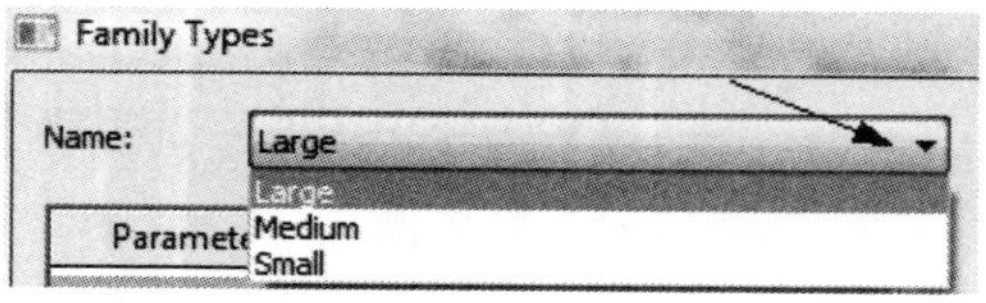 Left click on the drop-down arrow on the Name bar.
Switch between the different family names and press Apply to see the dimensions change.

Press **OK**.

30. 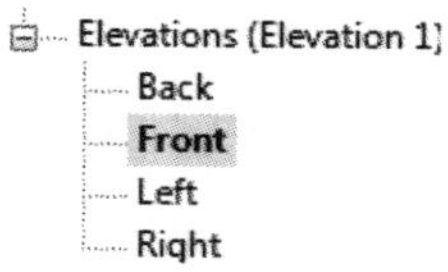 Activate the **Front** elevation.

31.  Select the **Reference Plane** tool on the Datum panel from the Create ribbon.

32. 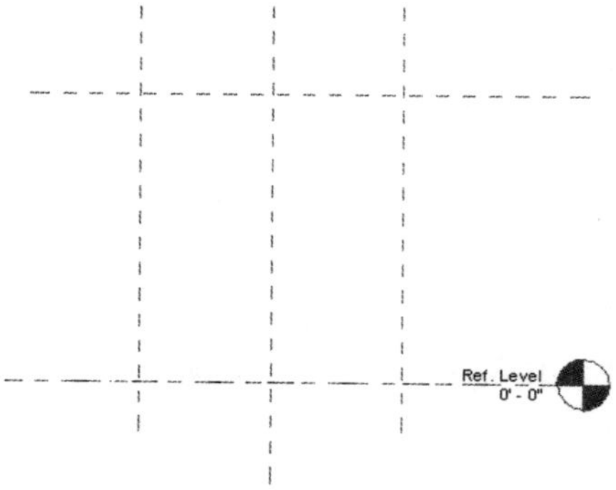 Draw a horizontal line above the Ref Level.

33.  In the Properties palette:

Rename the reference plane **Table Top**.

34. 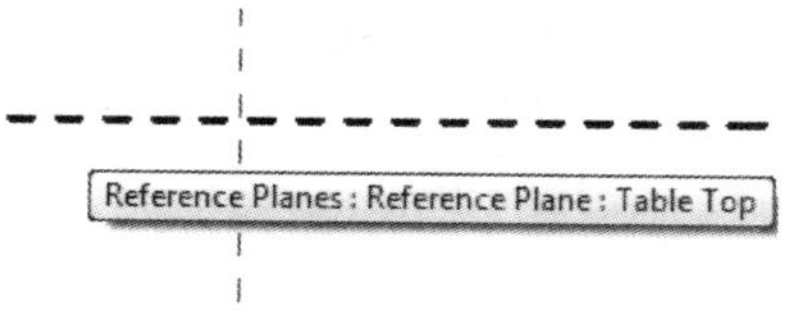 If you mouse over the reference plane, the name will appear.

35.  Select the **Reference Plane** tool on the Datum panel from the Architecture ribbon.

36. 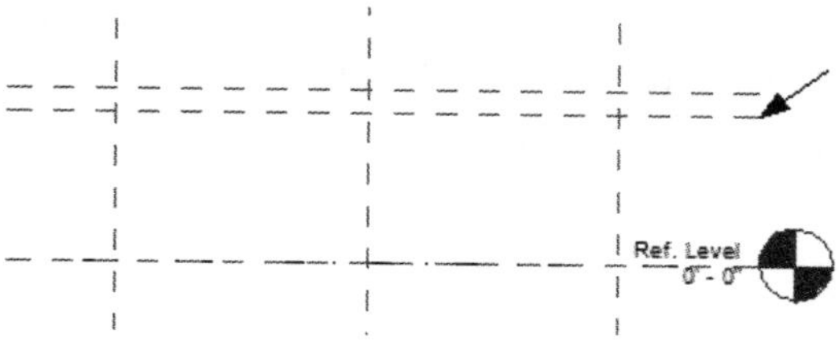 Draw a horizontal line below the Table Top Ref plane.

37.  In the Properties pane:

Rename the reference plane **Table Bottom**.

38. 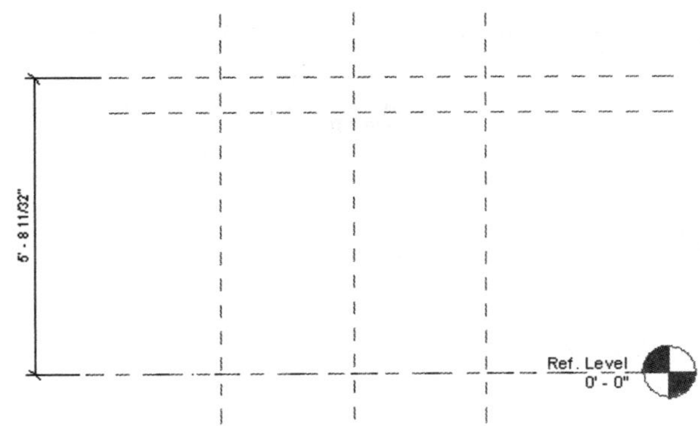

Place a dimension between the Ref. Level and Table Top ref. plane.

39. 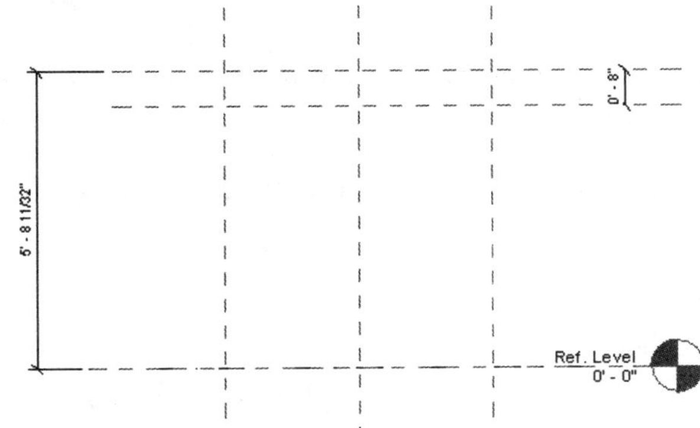

Place a dimension between the top ref. plane and the Table Bottom ref. plane.

40. Select the table height dimension, the dimension between the Ref. Level and Top ref. plane.

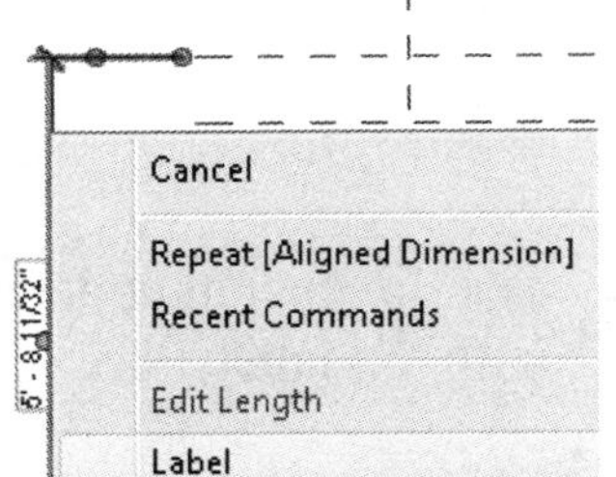

Right click and select **Label**.

<None>
<None>
<Add parameter...>
Length = 5' - 0"
Width = 3' - 6"

Select *Add Parameter* from the **Label** drop-down on the Option bar.

41. 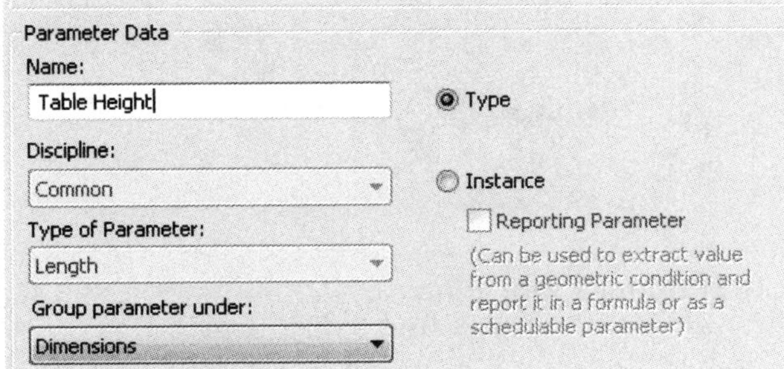

Under Name: type **Table Height**.
Set the group parameter to **Dimensions**.
Enable **Type**.
Press **OK**.

42. The dimension updates with the label.

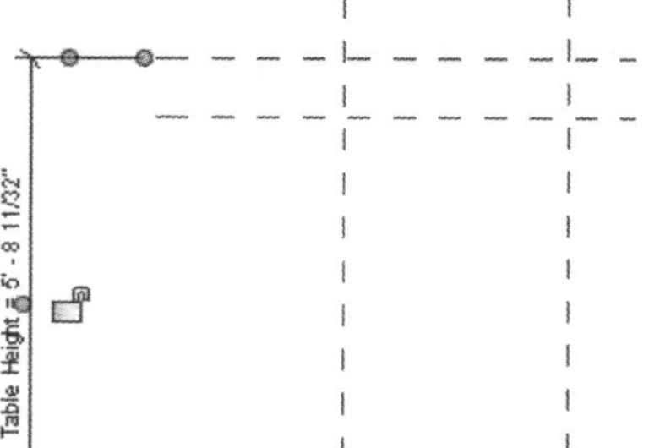

43. Select the table thickness dimension, the dimension between the Table Top ref. plane and the Table Bottom ref. plane below it.

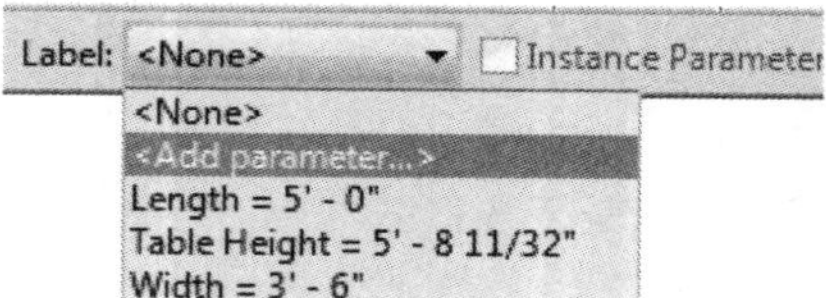

Select *Add Parameter* from the **Label** drop-down on the Option bar.

44.

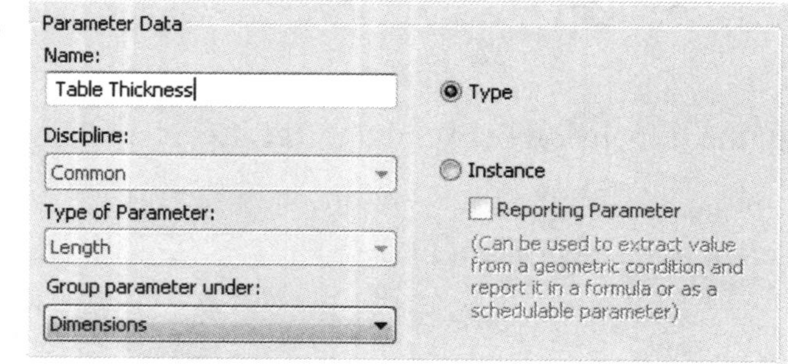

Under Name: type **Table Thickness**.
Set the group parameter to **Dimensions**.
Enable **Type**.
Press **OK**.

45.

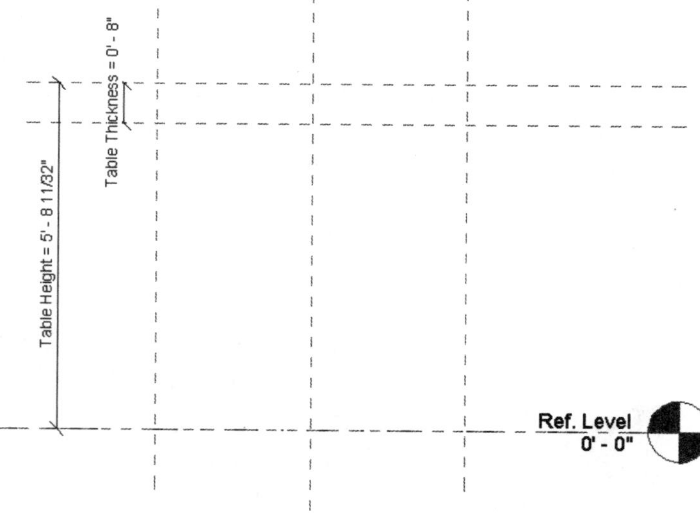

The dimension updates with the label.

46. Activate the **Ref. Level** under Floor Plans.

47. Select the **Extrusion** tool on the Forms panel from the Create ribbon.

Extrusion

48. Select **Work Plane→Set**.

Set

49. 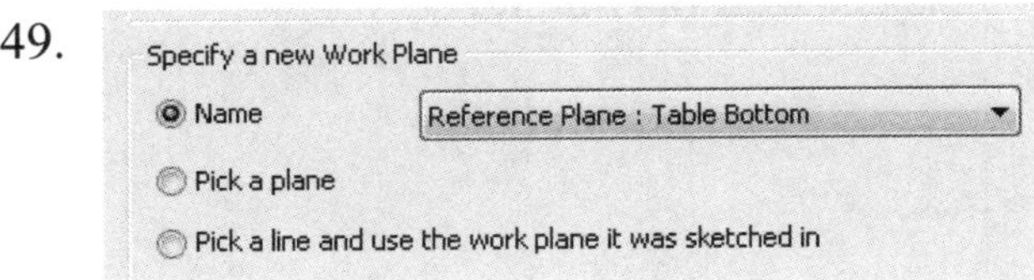

Enable **Name**.
Select the **Table Bottom** work plane from the drop-down list.
Press **OK**.

50. Select the **Rectangle** tool from the Draw panel.

Draw

51. 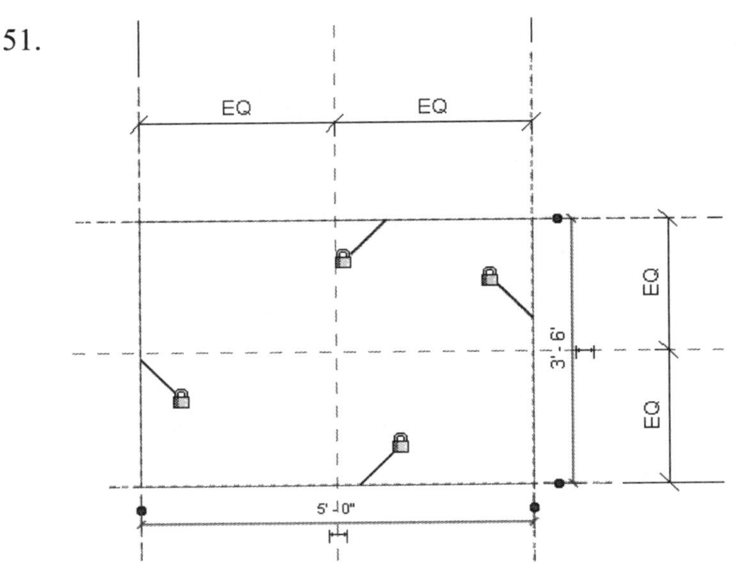

Place the rectangle so it is aligned to the outer reference planes.

Select each lock so it is closed.

This constrains the rectangle to the reference planes.

52. 

Select the **Family Types** tool from the Properties pane.

53. Select each type and press **Apply**.

Name: Large
Large
Medium
Small
Paramete

Verify that the rectangle flexes properly with each size.
If it does not flex properly, check that the side has been locked to the correct reference line using the Align tool.

Press **OK** to close the dialog.

54. Select the small button in the far right of the Material column.

This allows you to link the material to a parameter.

55. Select **Add parameter**.

56. 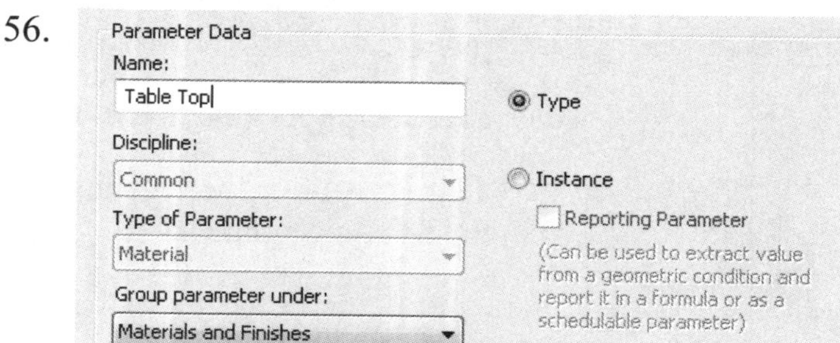

Type **Table Top** for the name.

Enable **Type**.

Press **OK**.

57. 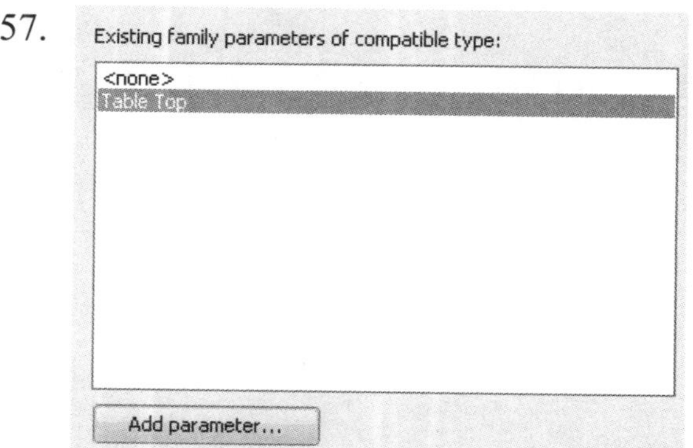

Table Top is now listed as a material parameter.

Press **OK**.

58. Select the **Family Types** tool.

59. Select the ... button next to Table Top to assign a material to the table top.

60. Type **wood** in the search field.

Locate the Walnut wood material in the AEC Materials library.

Copy it to the Document Materials by selecting the up arrow on the far right.

61. Highlight the **Walnut** material and press **OK**.

wood
Project Materials: All
Search results for "wood"
Name
Walnut

62. You now see the material listed in the Family Types dialog.

Parameter	Value	Formula
Materials and Finishes		
Table Top	Walnut	=
Dimensions		
Width	2' 6"	=
Table Thicknes	0' 8"	=
Table Height	5' 8 91/256"	=
Length	3' 0"	=
Identity Data		

63. If you switch to a different type, you will see that the material is unassigned.

Select the material column.

Name: Medium

Parameter	Value	Formula
Materials and Finishes		
Table Top	<By Category>	=
Dimensions		
Width	3' 0"	=
Table Thicknes	0' 8"	=
Table Height	5' 8 91/256"	=
Length	4' 0"	=
Identity Data		

64. 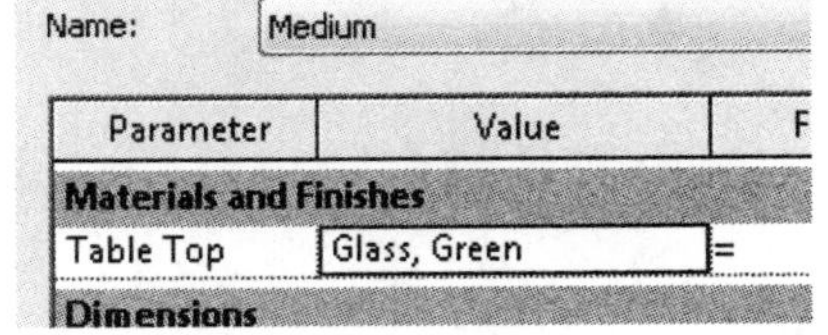

Assign each size table top a different material.

Press **OK**.

65. Click the button in the Extrusion End row.

Extrusion — Edit Type

Constraints	
Extrusion End	1' 0"
Extrusion Start	0' 0"
Work Plane	Reference Plane : Table Bottom

66. Select **Table Thickness** from the parameters list.

Press **OK**.

67. 

Select the **Family Types** tool from the Properties pane.

68. Table Thickness has now been added as a parameter to the Family Types.

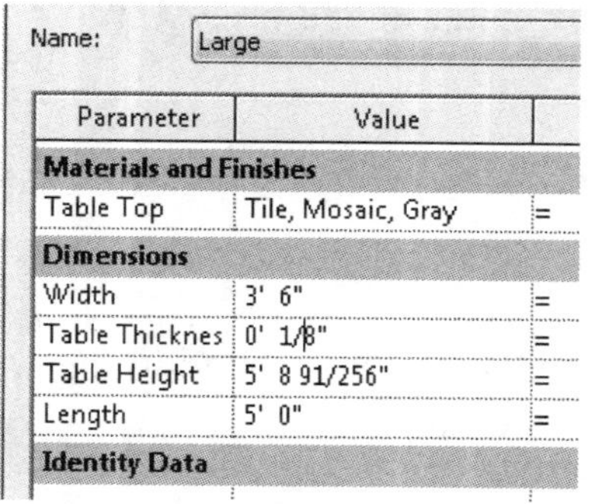

Name: Large

Parameter	Value	
Materials and Finishes		
Table Top	Tile, Mosaic, Gray	=
Dimensions		
Width	3' 6"	=
Table Thicknes	0' 1/8"	=
Table Height	5' 8 91/256"	=
Length	5' 0"	=
Identity Data		

Change the value of the Table Thickness to 1/8″ for each type.

Press **OK**.

69. 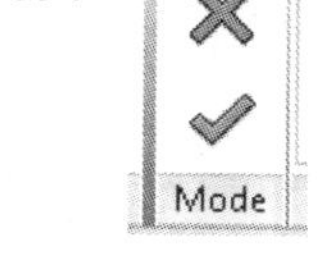

Select the **green check** under Mode to **Finish Extrusion**.

70. Activate the **Front** Elevation.

71. 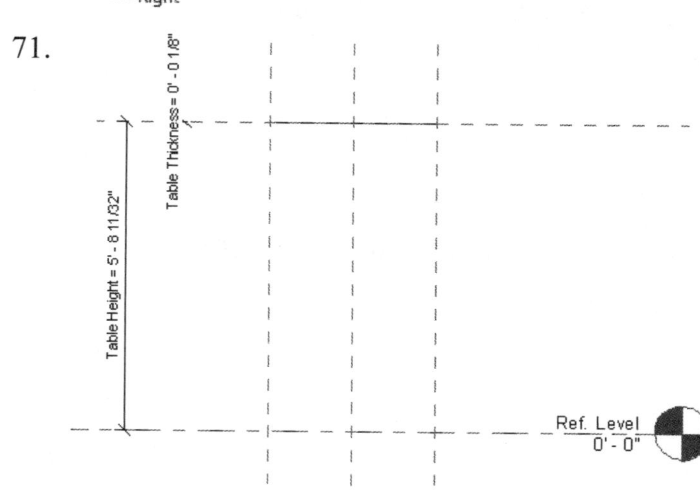

You see the table top which is equal to the table thickness.

72. Switch to a 3D view.

73. 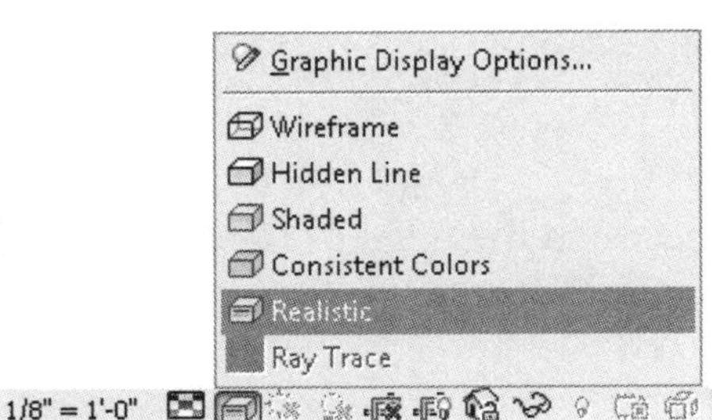

Set the Visual Style to **Realistic**.

74. 

Select the **Family Types** tool from the Properties pane.

75. 

Flex the model and see how the table top changes.

76. Views (all)
Floor Plans
Ref. Level
Ceiling Plans
Ref. Level

Activate the Ref. Level view.

77. Reference Plane

Activate the Create ribbon.

Select the **Reference Plane** tool from the Datum panel.

78. 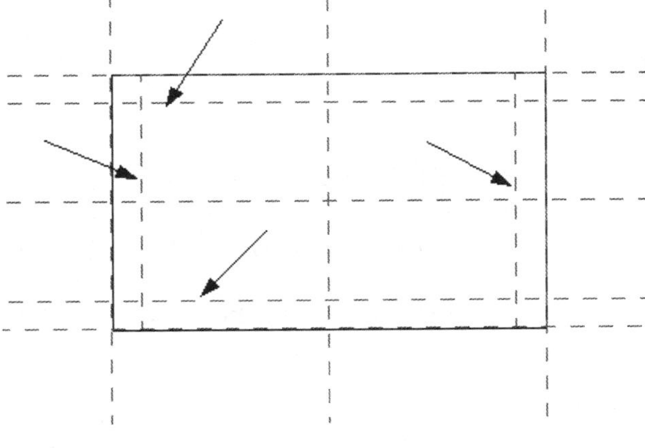

Place four reference planes 4″ offset inside the table.

These planes will be used to locate the table legs.

79. Measure — Select the **Aligned Dimension** tool.

80. 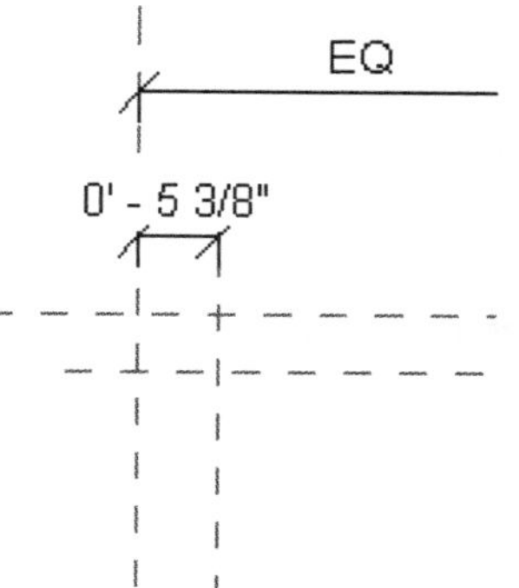

Place a dimension between the edge of the table and the inside reference plane.

81. 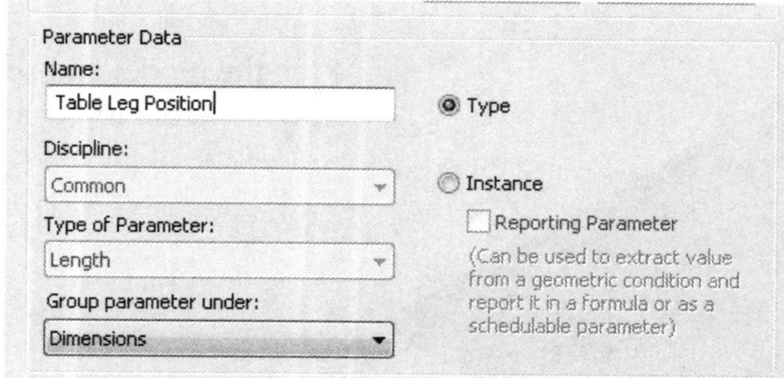

Add a parameter label to the dimension called **Table Leg Position**.

82. 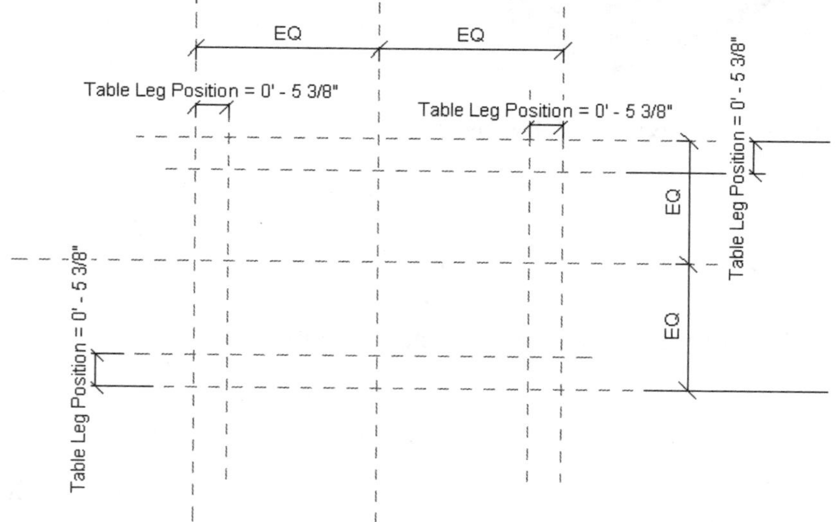

Add dimensions to constrain the reference planes to be offset four inches inside the table boundaries.

Make sure you place the dimensions between the reference planes and NOT between the table extrude edges and the reference planes. Do not lock any of the dimensions or reference planes or they won't shift when the table size changes.

83. Select each dimension and use the label pull-down on the Options bar to assign the Table Leg position parameter to the dimension.

84. Select **the Family and Types** tool.

85.

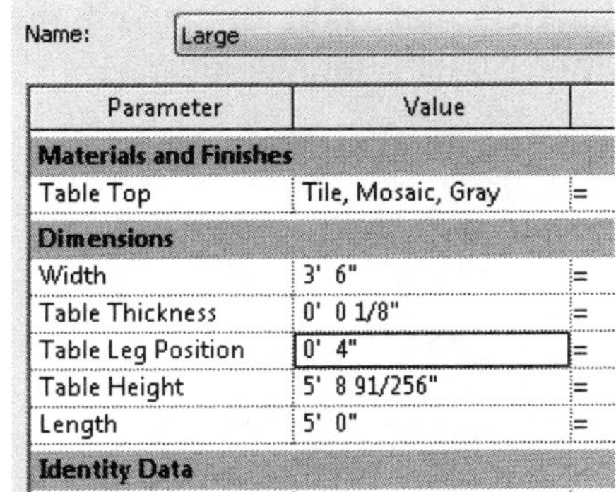

Name: Large

Parameter	Value
Materials and Finishes	
Table Top	Tile, Mosaic, Gray
Dimensions	
Width	3' 6"
Table Thickness	0' 0 1/8"
Table Leg Position	0' 4"
Table Height	5' 8 91/256"
Length	5' 0"
Identity Data	

Modify the Table Leg Position parameter to **4″**.

Press **Apply** and verify that the reference planes flex.

Repeat for each family name and flex the model to verify that the reference planes adjust.

Press **OK**.

86. 

Select **Blend** from the Create ribbon.

87. Select the **Set Work Plane** tool.

Set

88.

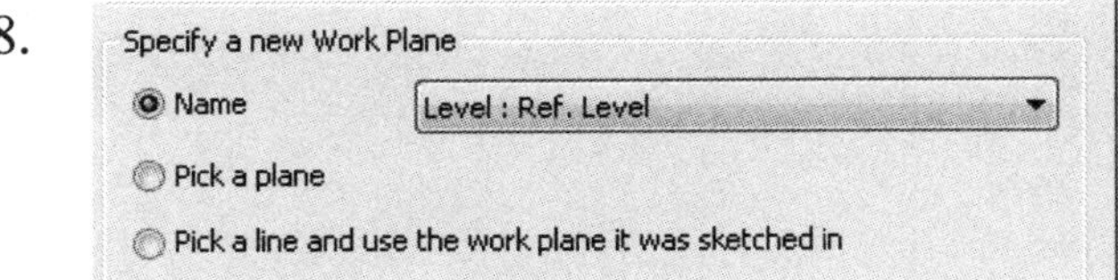

Select the **Ref. Level** for the sketch.

Press **OK**.

89.

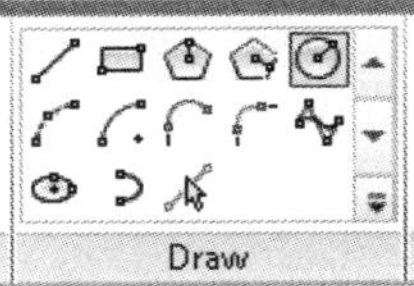

Select the **Circle** tool from the Draw panel.

90.

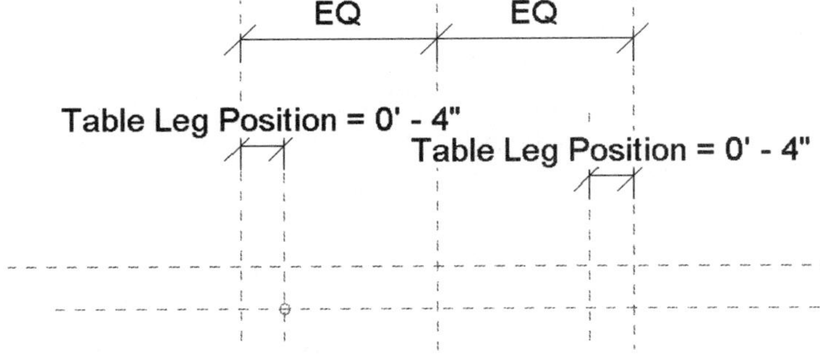

Draw a circle with a 1/2″ radius so the center is at the intersection of the two offset reference planes.

91.

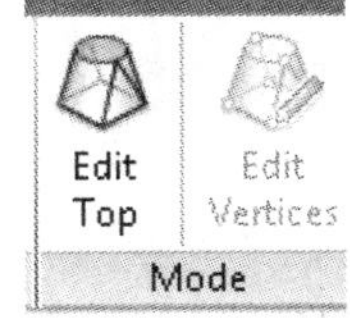

Select **Edit Top** from the Mode panel on the ribbon to switch to the top sketch plane.

92.

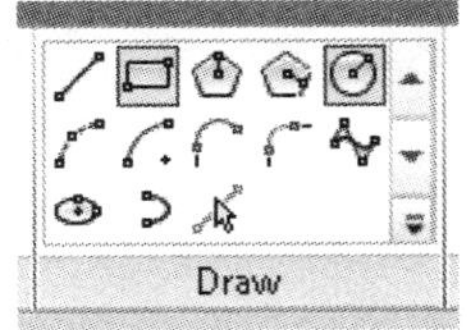

Select the **Circle** tool from the Draw panel.

93. 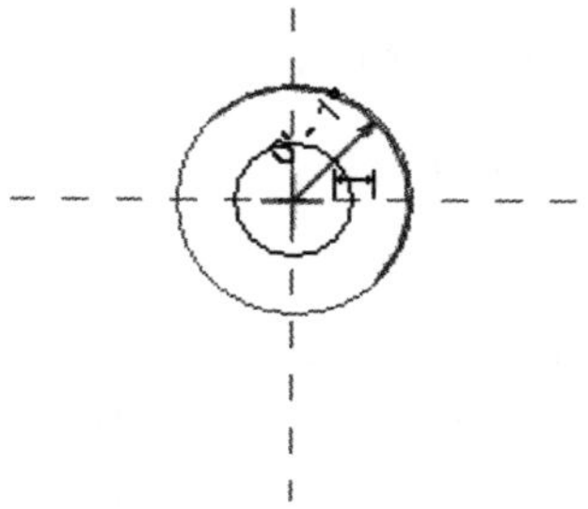 Place a circle with a 1″ radius so the center is at the intersection of the two offset reference planes.

94. 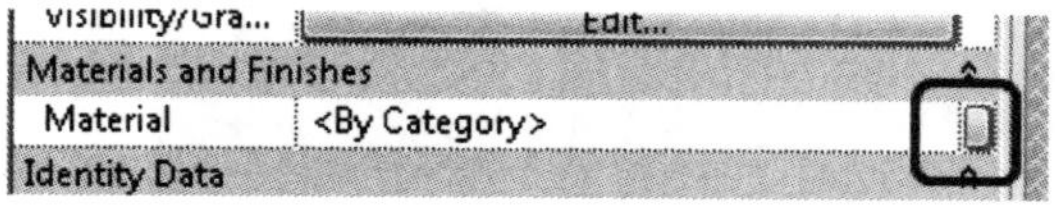 On the Properties palette:

Assign a parameter for the material.

95. 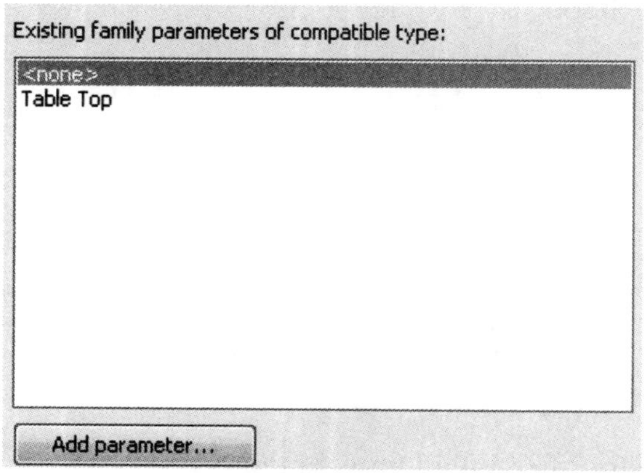 Select **Add parameter**.

96. 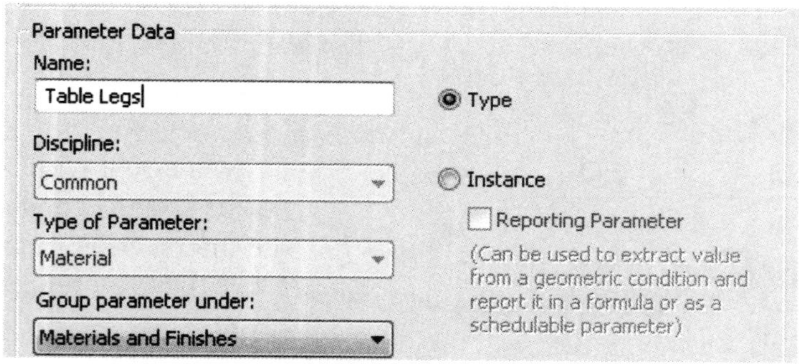 Type **Table Legs** for the name.

Press **OK**.

97. 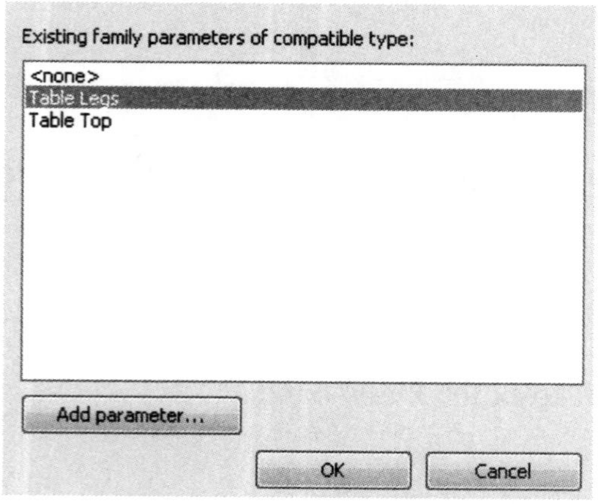 Highlight **Table Legs**.

Press **OK**.

98.  Select the **Family Types** tool.

99. Table Legs is now a material to be assigned for each type.

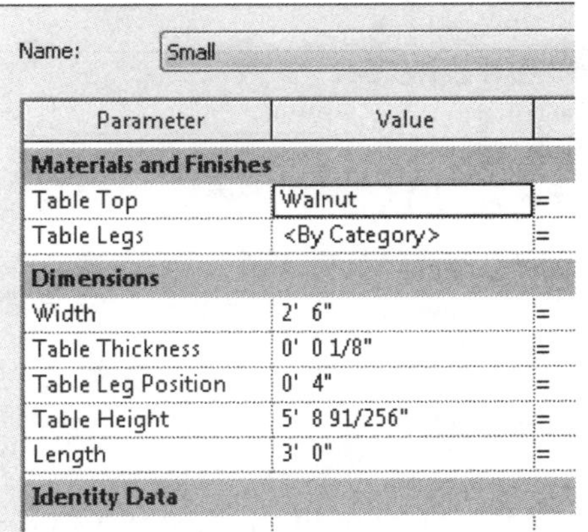

Select the **...** button in the Table Legs Value column.

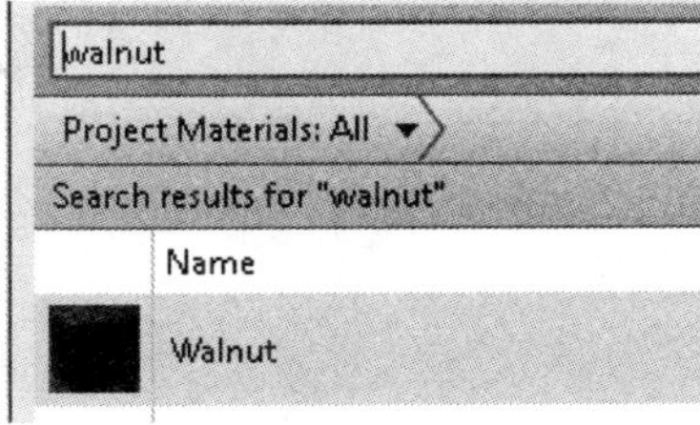

100. Type **concrete** in the search field.

101. 

Locate a concrete material.

Select **Add material to document**.

102. Type **pine** in the search field.

103. Locate the **pine** material.
Select **Add material to document.**
Close the dialog.

104. 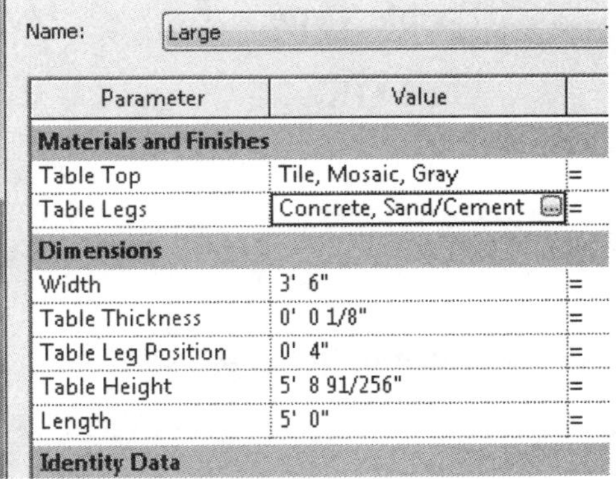

Each size of the table should be assigned a different material for the table top and the table legs.

Press **OK**.

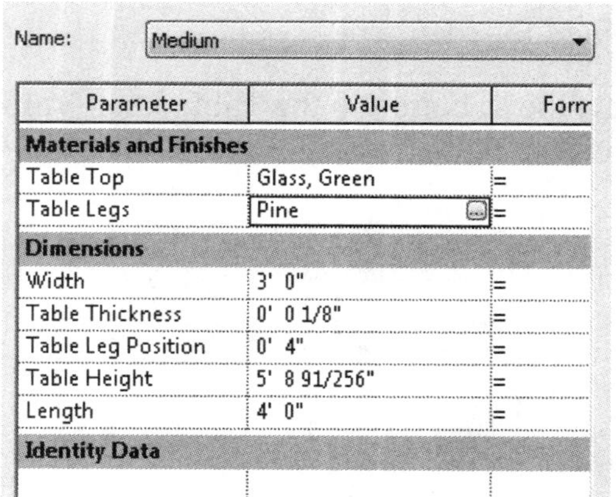

Name: Medium

Parameter	Value	Forr
Materials and Finishes		
Table Top	Glass, Green	=
Table Legs	Pine	=
Dimensions		
Width	3' 0"	=
Table Thickness	0' 0 1/8"	=
Table Leg Position	0' 4"	=
Table Height	5' 8 91/256"	=
Length	4' 0"	=
Identity Data		

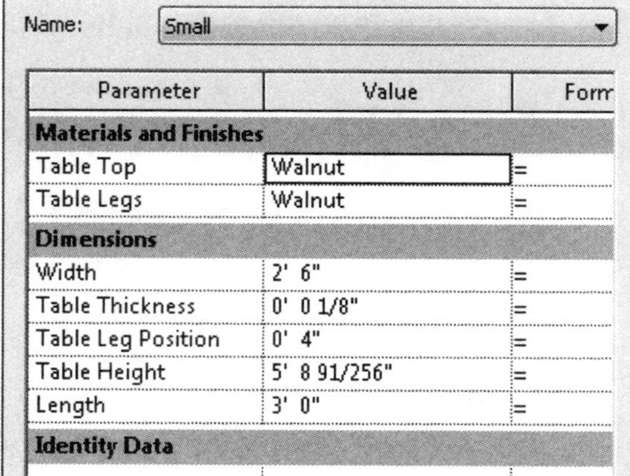

Name: Small

Parameter	Value	Forr
Materials and Finishes		
Table Top	Walnut	=
Table Legs	Walnut	=
Dimensions		
Width	2' 6"	=
Table Thickness	0' 0 1/8"	=
Table Leg Position	0' 4"	=
Table Height	5' 8 91/256"	=
Length	3' 0"	=
Identity Data		

105. Select the button on the Second End row to associate the table legs length with a parameter.

106. Select **Add parameter** at the bottom of the dialog.

107. Enter **Leg Length** for the Name.

Enable **Type**.

Press **OK**.

108. Highlight **Leg Length** in the parameter list.

Press **OK**.

109. Select **Family Types** from Properties pane on the Create ribbon.

110.

Parameter	Value	Formula	
Materials and Finishes			
Table Top	Tile, Mosaic,	=	
Table Legs	Concrete, Sa	=	
Dimensions			
Width	3' 6"	=	
Table Thickness	0' 0 1/8"	=	
Table Leg Position	0' 4"	=	
Table Height	5' 8 91/256"	=	
Length	5' 0"	=	
Leg Length	1' 0"	= Table Height - Table Thickness	
Identity Data			

In the Formula column, enter **Table Height – Table Thickness**.

Press **OK**.

111.

Constraints	
Second End	3' 9 73/128"
First End	0' 0"
Work Plane	Level : Ref. Level

The value for Second End will update.

112. 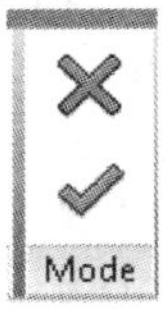 Mode

Select the **green check** on the Mode panel to finish the extrusion.

113. 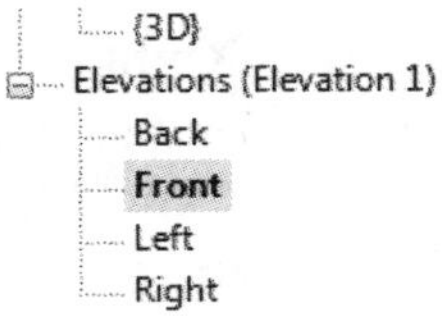 {3D}
Elevations (Elevation 1)
Back
Front
Left
Right

Activate the **Front** Elevation view.

114. 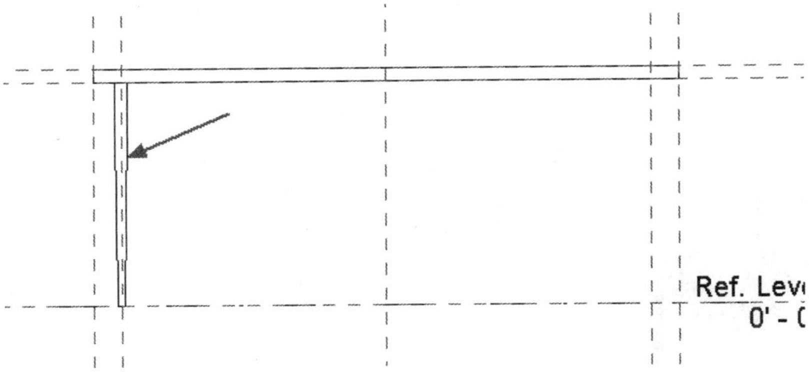 Ref. Level
0' - 0

You see a tapered leg.

115. 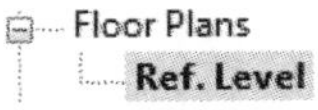 Floor Plans
Ref. Level

Activate the **Ref. Level**.

116. 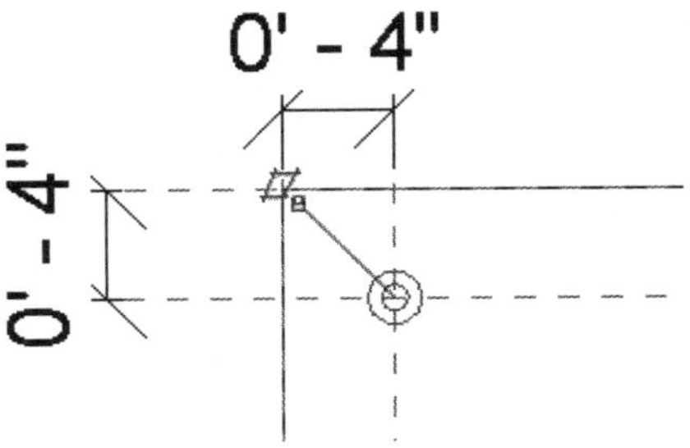 0' - 4"
0' - 4"

Select the leg so it highlights.

117.  Select the **Copy** tool from the Modify panel.

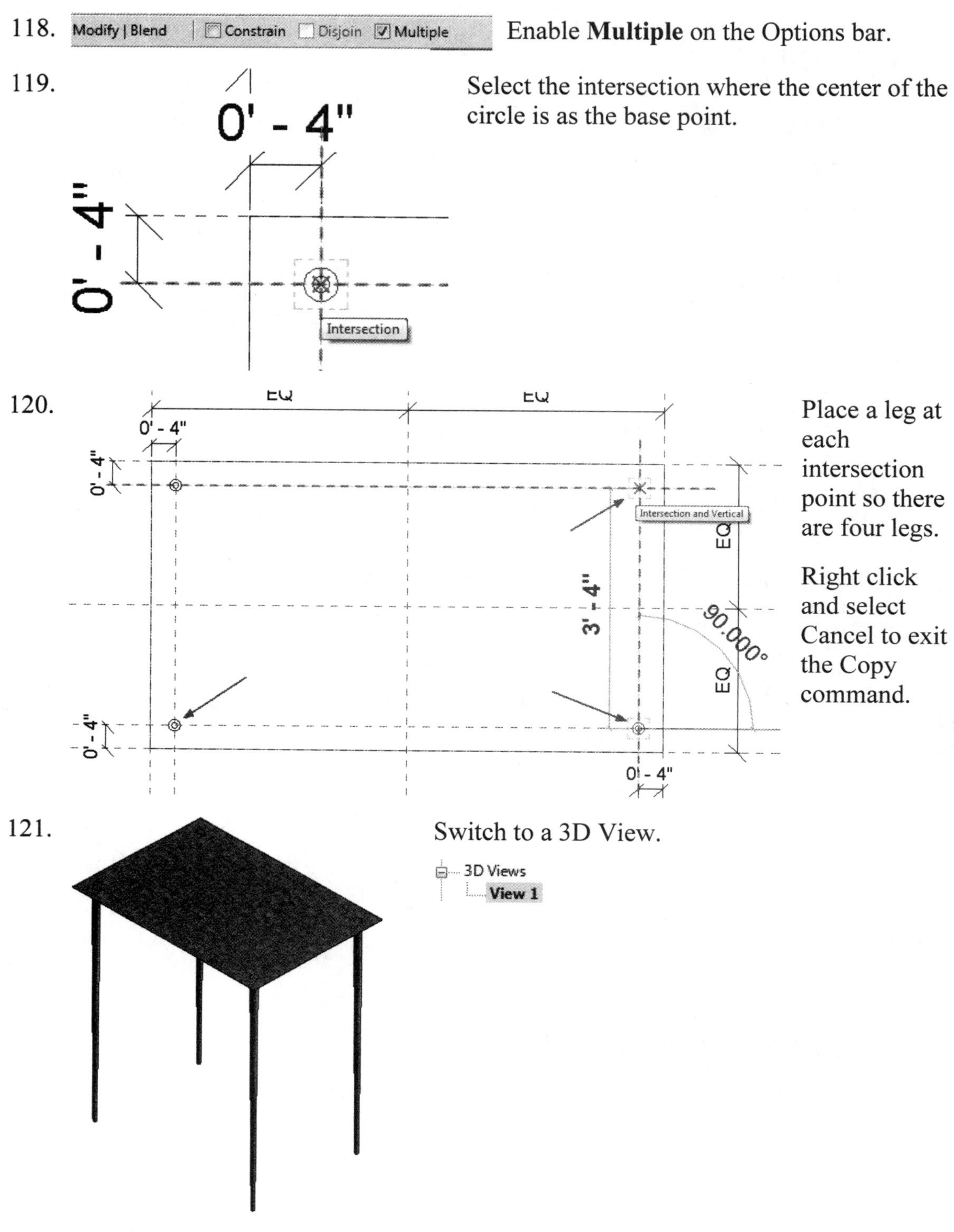

118. Enable **Multiple** on the Options bar.

119. Select the intersection where the center of the circle is as the base point.

120. Place a leg at each intersection point so there are four legs.

Right click and select Cancel to exit the Copy command.

121. Switch to a 3D View.

122. Select **Family Types** from Properties pane on the Architecture ribbon.

Flex the model to check if the legs adjust position properly.

123. Change the value for the Table Height and Table Thickness for each size to see what happens to the model.

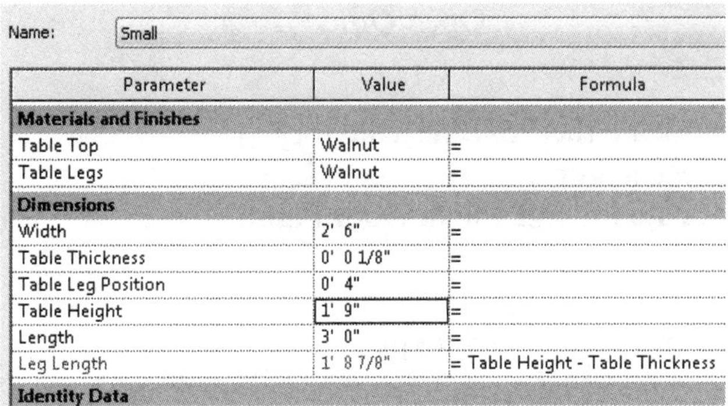

Name: Small

Parameter	Value	Formula
Materials and Finishes		
Table Top	Walnut	=
Table Legs	Walnut	=
Dimensions		
Width	2' 6"	=
Table Thickness	0' 0 1/8"	=
Table Leg Position	0' 4"	=
Table Height	1' 9"	=
Length	3' 0"	=
Leg Length	1' 8 7/8"	= Table Height - Table Thickness
Identity Data		

Name: Medium

Parameter	Value	Formula
Materials and Finishes		
Table Top	Glass, Green	=
Table Legs	Pine	=
Dimensions		
Width	3' 0"	=
Table Thickness	0' 0 1/8"	=
Table Leg Position	0' 4"	=
Table Height	2' 0"	=
Length	4' 0"	=
Leg Length	1' 11 7/8"	= Table Height - Table Thickness
Identity Data		

Name: Large

Parameter	Value	Formula
Materials and Finishes		
Table Top	Tile, Mosaic,	=
Table Legs	Concrete, Sa	=
Dimensions		
Width	3' 6"	=
Table Thickness	0' 0 1/8"	=
Table Leg Position	0' 4"	=
Table Height	2' 6"	=
Length	5' 0"	=
Leg Length	2' 5 7/8"	= Table Height - Table Thickness
Identity Data		

124. Save the family as *Coffee Table.rfa.*

125. Close the file.

Exercise 10-7
Modifying a Family

Estimated Time: 10 minutes
File: Office_2.rvt

This exercise reinforces the following skills:

- Standard Component Families
- Types

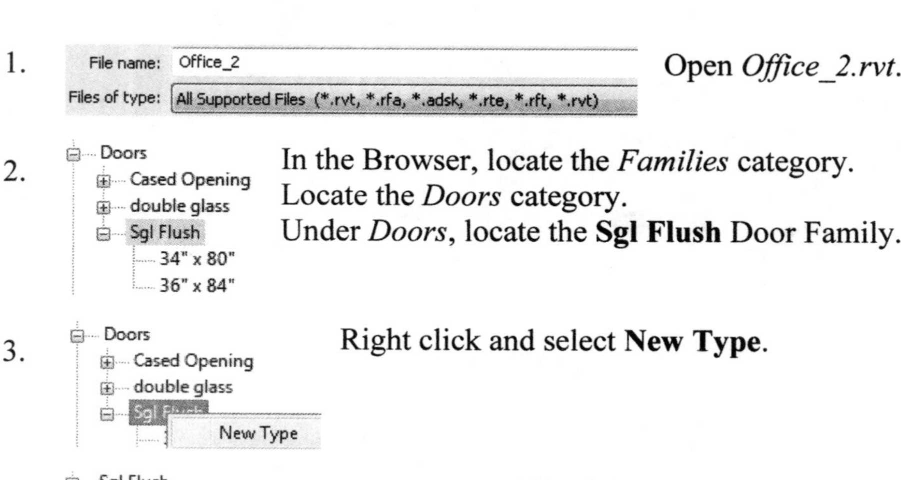

1. Open *Office_2.rvt.*

2. In the Browser, locate the *Families* category.
Locate the *Doors* category.
Under *Doors*, locate the **Sgl Flush** Door Family.

3. Right click and select **New Type**.

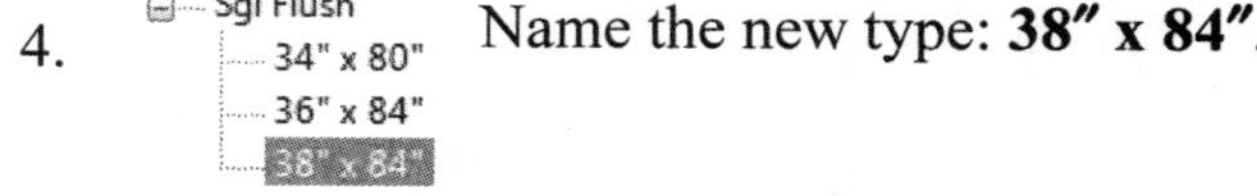

4. Name the new type: **38″ x 84″**.

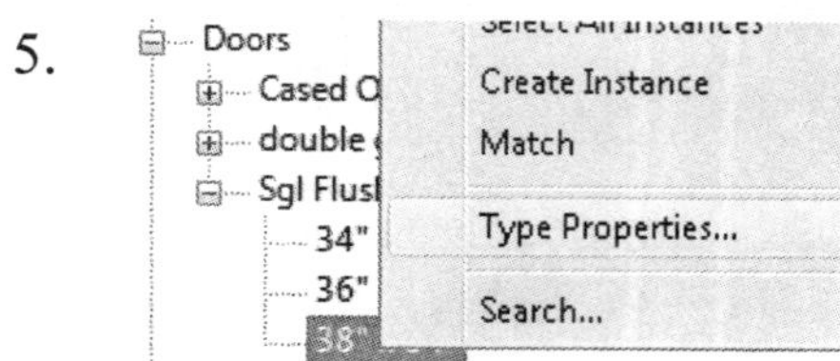

5. Highlight the **38″ x 84″** door type.
Right click and select **Type Properties**.

6. Change the Width to **3′ 2″**.
Press **OK**.

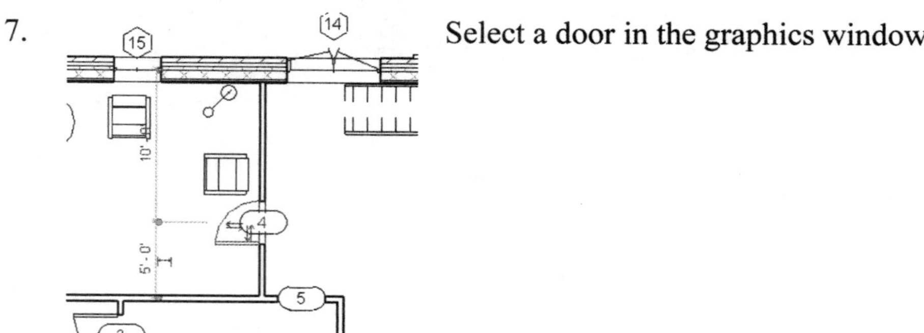

7. Select a door in the graphics window.

8. In the Properties palette:
Select **38″ x 84″** from the drop-down list.

Note that the door updates.

9. Close without saving.

Revit Hot Keys

3F	Fly Mode
3O	Object Mode
3W	Walk
AD	Attach Detail Group
AL	Align
AP	Add to Group
AR	Array
CC	Copy
CG	Cancel
CM	Component
CO	Copy
CS	Create Similar
DE	Delete
DI	Dimension
DL	Detail Lines
DM	Mirror - Draw Axis
DR	Door
EG	Edit Group
EH	Hide Element
EL	Spot Elevation
EOD	Override Graphics in View
EOG	Graphic Override by Element
EOH	Graphic Override by Element
EOT	Graphic Override by Element
ER	Editing Requests
EU	Unhide Element
EW	Edit Witness Lines
EX	Exclude
FG	Finish
FR	Find/Replace Text
GD	Graphic Display Options
GP	Group
GR	Grid
HC	Hide/Isolate Category
HH	Hide/Isolate Objects

HI	Hide/Isolate Objects
HL	Hidden Line
HR	Reset Temporary Hide/Isolate
IC	Isolate Category
KS	Keyboard Shortcuts
LC	Lose Changes
LG	Link
LI	Line
LL	Level
LO	Lock Objects
LW	Linework
MA	Match Properties
MD	Modify
MM	Mirror - Pick Axis
MP	Move to Project
MV	Move
OF	Offset
PC	Snap to Point Clouds
PN	Pin
PP or VP	Properties
PP	Pin Position
PR	Properties
PT	Paint
R3	Define a new center of rotation
RA	Restore All
RB	Restore Excluded Member
RC	Repeat Last Command
RE	Resize\Scale
RG	Remove from Group
RH	Reveal Hidden Elements
RM	Room
RO	Rotate
RL	Reload Latest Worksets
RP	Reference Plane
RR	Render
RT	Room Tag

RW	Reload Latest Worksets
RY	Ray Trace
S	Split Walls and Lines
SA	Select All Instances in Entire Project
SC	Snap to Center
SD	Shading with Edges On
SE	Snap to Endpoint
SF	Split Face
SH	Snap to horizontal/vertical
SI	Snap to Intersection
SL	Split Element
SM	Snap to Midpoint
SN	Snap to Nearest
SO	Snaps OFF
SP	Snap to Perpendicular
SQ	Snap to Quadrants
SR	Snap to Remote Objects
SS	Turn Snap Override Off
ST	Snap to Tangent
SU	Sun Settings
SW	Snap to Workplane Grid
SX	Snap to Points
SZ	Snap to Close
TG	Tag by Category
TL	Thin Lines
TR	Trim/Extend
TX	Text
UN	Project Units
UG	Ungroup
UP	Unpin
VH	Category Invisible
VI	View Invisible Categories
VG	Visibility/Graphics
VOG	Graphic Override by Category
VOH	Graphic Override by Category
VOT	Graphic Override by Category
VP	View Properties

VU	Unhide Category
VV	Visibility/Graphics
WA	Wall
WC	Window Cascade
WF	Wire Frame
WN	Window
WT	Window Tile
ZA	Zoom to Fit
ZC	Previous Zoom
ZE	Zoom to Fit
ZF	Zoom to Fit
ZN	Zoom Next
ZO	Zoom Out (2X)
ZP	Zoom Previous
ZR	Zoom in region (window)
ZS	Zoom to Sheet Size (limits)
ZV	Zoom Out (2X)
ZX	Zoom to fit
ZZ	Zoom in region (window)
//	Divide Surface
Alt+F4	Close Revit
Ctl+F4	Close Project file
Ctl+1	Properties
Ctl+	Activate Contextual Tab
Ctl+C	Copy to Clipboard
Ctl+O	Open a Project file
Ctl+P	Print
Ctl+S	Save a file
Ctl+X	Cut to Clipboard
Ctl-Y	Redo
Ctl-Z	Undo
Ctl+Shift+Z	Undo
F1	Revit Help
F5	Refresh Screen
F7	Spelling
F8	Dynamic View